**Gauteng and
Sun City**
Pages 310–329

**Limpopo,
Mpumalanga and
Kruger**
Pages 330–347

• Polokwane

GUATENG, LIMPOPO
AND MPUMALANGA

Nelspruit •

• Pretoria

Johannesburg •

Mbabane •

SWAZILAND

**Durban and
Zululand**
Pages 282–301

THE EAST COAST
AND INTERIOR

• Kimberley

Bloemfontein •

• Maseru

LESOTHO

Durban •

• Graaff-Reinet

Port
Elizabeth •

**South of
the Orange**
Pages 356–367

**The Garden
Route to
Grahamstown**
Pages 236–257

**The Wild Coast
Drakensberg
and Midlands**
Pages 266–281

EYEWITNESS TRAVEL

SOUTH AFRICA

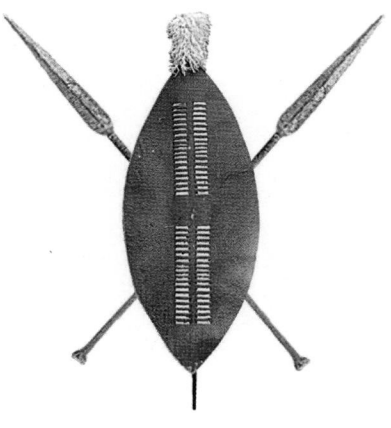

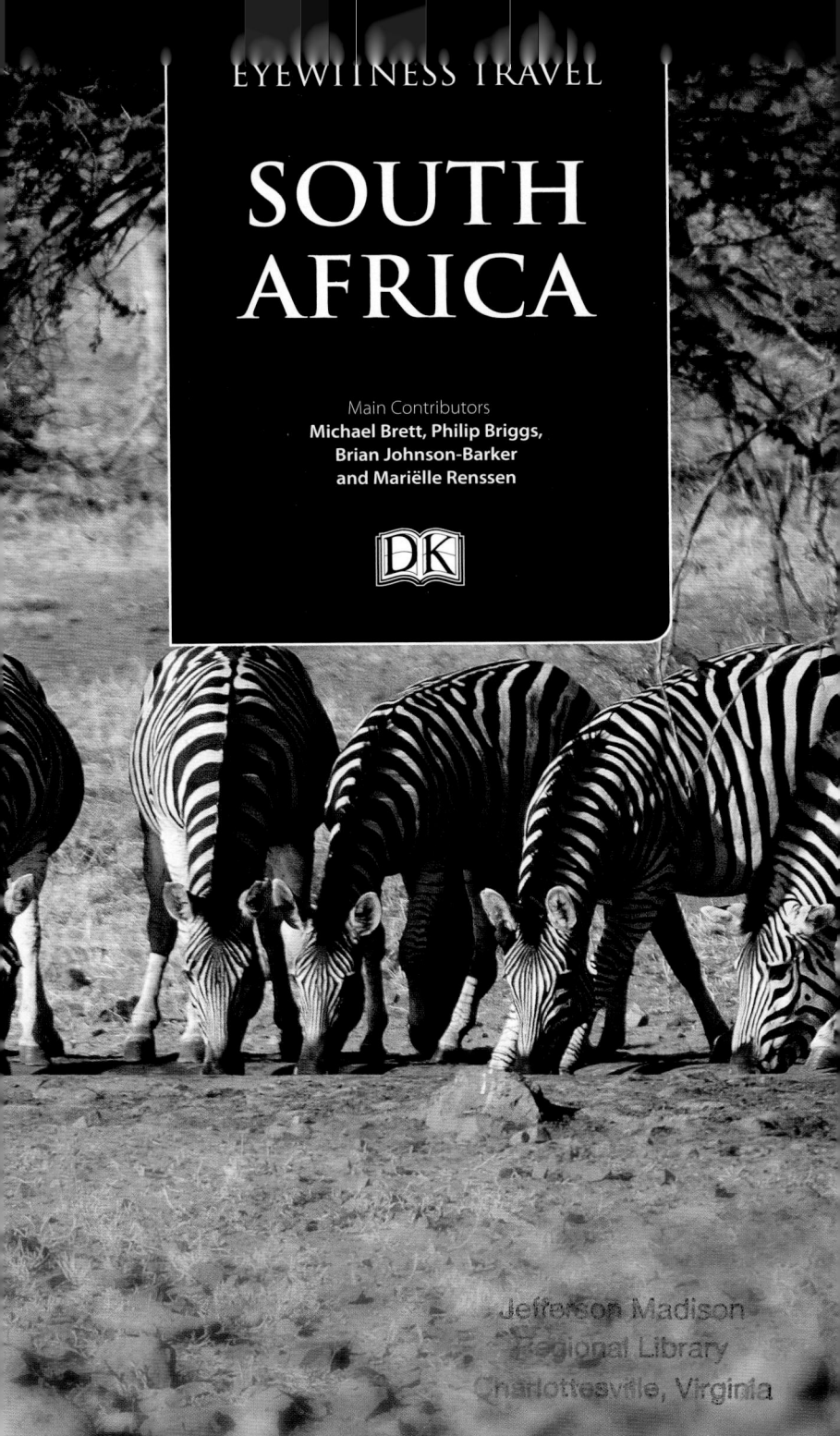

EYEWITNESS TRAVEL

SOUTH
AFRICA

Main Contributors
**Michael Brett, Philip Briggs,
Brian Johnson-Barker
and Mariëlle Renssen**

DK

30839 6272

N

DK

LONDON, NEW YORK,
MELBOURNE, MUNICH AND DELHI
www.dk.com

Produced by Struik New Holland Publishing (Pty) Ltd,
Cape Town, South Africa

Managing Editor Claudia Dos Santos
Managing Art Editors Peter Bosman, Trinity Loubser-Fry
Editors Gill Gordon, Gail Jennings
Designers Simon Lewis, Mark Seabrook
Map Co-ordinator John Loubser
Production Myrna Collins
Picture Researcher Carmen Watts
Researcher Jocelyn Convery

Dorling Kindersley Limited
Editorial Director Vivien Crump
Art Director Gillian Allan
Map Co-ordinator David Pugh

Main Contributors
Michael Brett, Philip Briggs, Brian Johnson-Barker, Mariëlle Renssen

Photographers
Shaen Adey, Roger de la Harpe, Walter Knirr

Illustrators
Bruce Beyer, Annette Busse, Bruno de Robillard,
Steven Felmore, Noel McCully, Dave Snook

Printed and bound in China

First American Edition, 1999

17 18 19 20 10 9 8 7 6 5 4 3 2 1

**Reprinted with revisions 2001, 2002, 2003, 2005, 2007,
2009, 2011, 2013, 2015, 2017**

Copyright © 1999, 2017 Dorling Kindersley Limited, London
A Penguin Random House Company

A catalog record for this book is available from the Library of Congress.

ISSN 1542-1554

ISBN 978 1 4654 6131 5

Floors are referred to throughout in
accordance with European usage; ie the "first floor"
is the floor above ground level.

MIX
Paper from
responsible sources
FSC
www.fsc.org **FSC™ C018179**

**The information in this
DK Eyewitness Travel Guide is checked regularly.**
Every effort has been made to ensure that this book is as up-to-date as possible
at the time of going to press. Some details, however, such as telephone numbers,
opening hours, prices, gallery hanging arrangements and travel information are
liable to change. The publishers cannot accept responsibility for any consequences
arising from the use of this book, nor for any material on third party websites, and
cannot guarantee that any website address in this book will be a suitable source of
travel information. We value the views and suggestions of our readers very highly.
Please write to: Publisher, DK Eyewitness Travel Guides, Dorling Kindersley,
80 Strand, London, WC2R 0RL, UK, or email: travelguides@dk.com.

Front cover main image: An African leopard relaxing in a tree

 Giraffe and plains zebras drinking from a water hole in Kruger National Park

Contents

Vasco da Gama

Introducing
South Africa

Wild South Africa

Crafts at Greenmarket Square, Cape Town

Erica flowering in the Harold Porter Garden

A male leopard patrols his territory at Londolozi Game Reserve

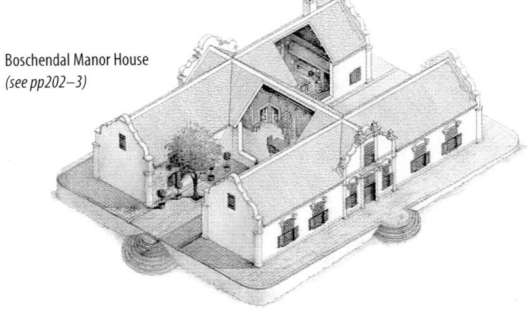

Boschendal Manor House
(see pp202–3)

HOW TO USE THIS GUIDE

This guide helps you to get the most from a visit to South Africa, providing expert recommendations and detailed practical information. *Introducing South Africa* maps the country and sets it in its historical and cultural context. *Wild South Africa* is a detailed guide to wildlife viewing and

safaris. The four regional sections, plus *Cape Town*, describe important sights, using photographs, maps and illustrations. Restaurant and hotel recommendations can be found in *Travellers' Needs*. The *Survival Guide* contains practical tips on everything from transport to personal safety.

Cape Town

The "mother city" has been divided into three sightseeing areas. Each has its own chapter opening with a list of the sights described. The *Further Afield* section covers many peripheral places of interest. All sights are numbered and plotted on an *Area Map*. Information on the sights is easy to locate as it follows the numerical order used on the map.

Sights at a Glance lists the chapter's sights by category: Museums and Galleries, Churches, Parks and Gardens, Historic Buildings, etc.

Each area has its own colour-coded thumb tabs.

A locator map shows clearly where the area is in relation to other areas of the city.

1 **Area Map** For easy reference, sights are numbered and located on a map. City centre sights are also marked on the Cape Town Street Finder maps (*see pp175–83*).

2 **Street-by-Street Map** This gives a bird's-eye view of the key areas in each sightseeing area.

Stars indicate the sights that no visitor should miss.

A suggested route for a walk covers the more interesting streets in the area.

3 **Detailed Information** All the sights in Cape Town are described individually. Addresses, telephone numbers and other practical information are also provided for each entry. The key to the symbols used in the information block is shown on the back flap.

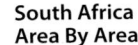

1 Introduction A general account of the landscape, history and character of each region is given here, explaining both how the area has developed over the centuries and what attractions it has to offer visitors today.

South Africa Area By Area

Apart from Cape Town, the rest of the country has been divided into ten regions, each of which has a separate chapter. The most interesting cities, towns and sights to visit are numbered on a *Regional Map* at the beginning of each chapter.

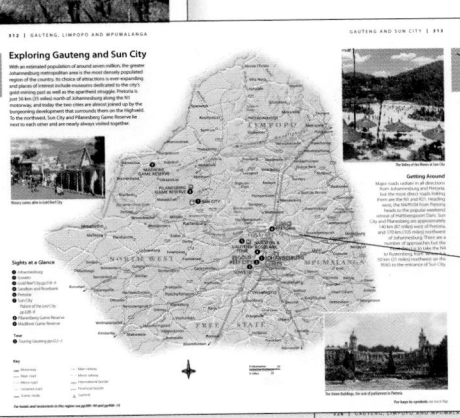

Each area of South Africa can be easily identified by its colour coding, shown on the inside front cover.

2 Regional Map This shows the main road network and gives an illustrated overview of the whole region. All interesting places to visit are numbered and there are also useful tips on getting to, and around, the region.

Story boxes explore specific subjects further.

3 Detailed Information All the important cities, towns and other places to visit are described individually. They are listed in order, following the numbering on the Regional Map. Within each entry, there is further detailed information on major buildings and other sights.

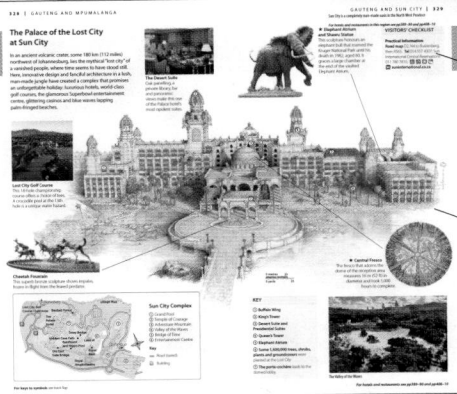

For all the top sights, a Visitors' Checklist provides the practical information you will need to plan your visit.

4 South Africa's Top Sights The historic buildings are dissected to reveal their interiors; national parks have maps showing facilities and trails. The most interesting towns or city centres have maps, with sights picked out and described.

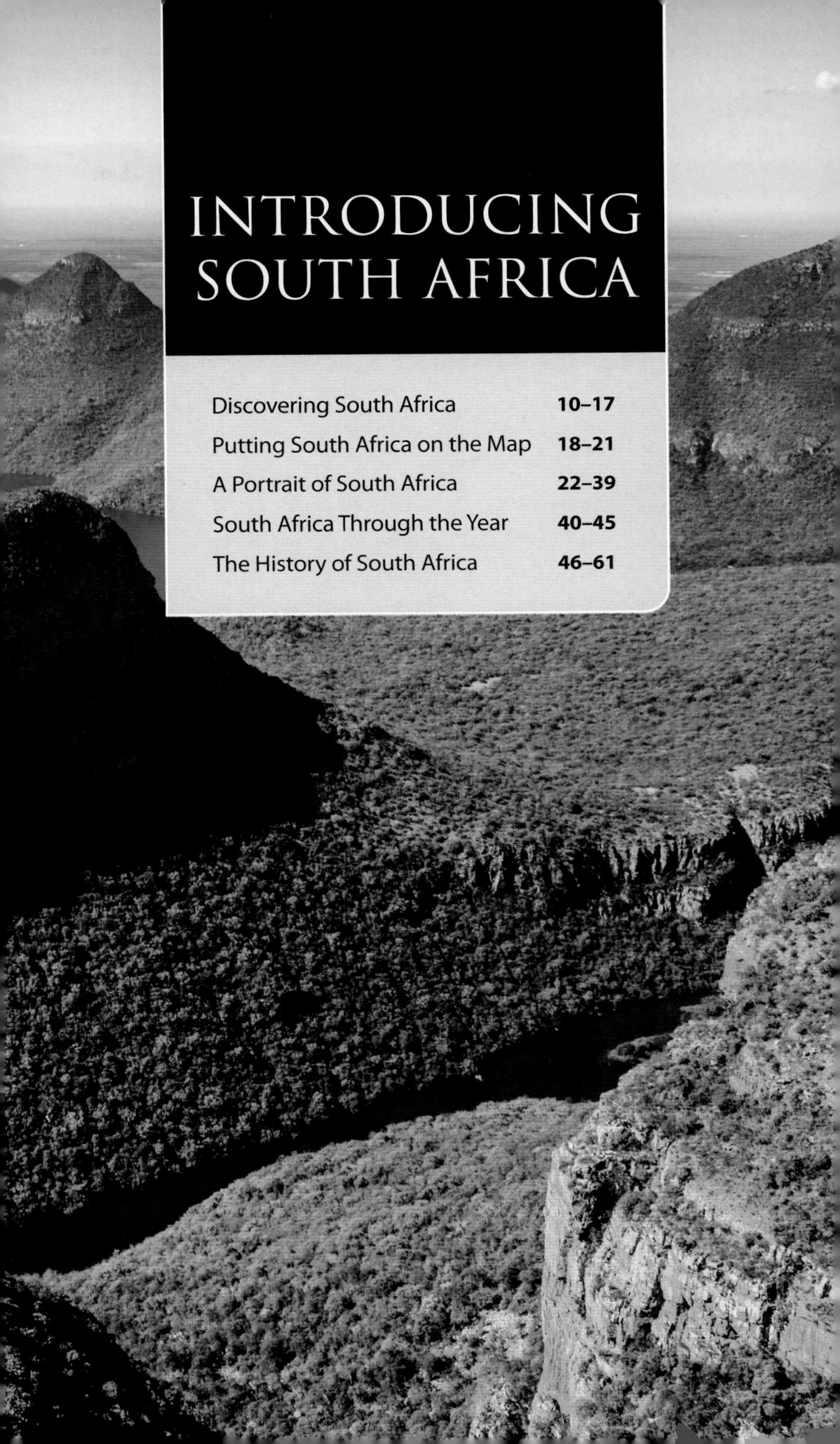

INTRODUCING
SOUTH AFRICA

DISCOVERING SOUTH AFRICA

South Africa is a vast country, with an unusually varied set of tourist attractions. These include some of Africa's finest game reserves, a coastline studded with idyllic beaches, the two world-class cities of Cape Town and Johannesburg, and a wealth of historic small towns, scenic mountain ranges and sumptuous wine estates. As such, it is advisable not to cram too much into your stay, or you risk spending most of it behind the wheel. Bearing this in mind, most of the tours described on the pages that follow are designed to explore one specific region of interest. To start is a 2-day tour of Cape Town and a 10-day exploration of the surrounding Western Cape. These are followed by a pair of week-long itineraries for the popular Garden Route and the Kruger National Park. Finally, a 2-day Johannesburg experience is followed by a 21-day "grand tour", from Cape Town to Johannesburg, taking in highlights of all of the above – and much more.

10 Days in the Western Cape

- Get close to sharks, penguins and other marine creatures in the **Two Oceans Aquarium**.
- Soak up the magnificent view from the **Rhodes Memorial** to the Hottentots Holland Mountains.
- Indulge in a tasting of succulent Sauvignon Blanc or plummy Pinotage at the historic **Boschendal Estate**.
- Climb to the top of Africa's most southerly lighthouse at **Cape Agulhas**.

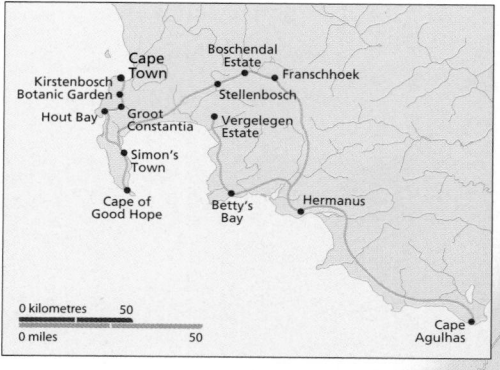

21-Day Grand Tour

- Drive out in search of rhinos, both black and white, among the rolling green hills of the **Hluhluwe-Imfolozi Game Reserve**.
- Get a taste of traditional Zulu culture, brought thrillingly to life at the **Shakaland** village.
- Spice up your life at the aromatic **Victoria Street Market** in Durban – Africa's most Indian-influenced city.
- Keep your shutter button busy with the photogenic pachyderms of **Addo Elephant National Park**.

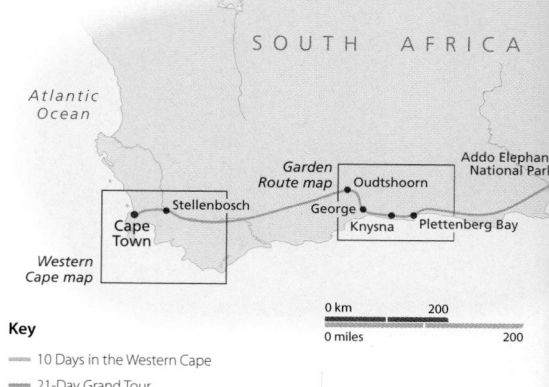

Key

— 10 Days in the Western Cape

— 21-Day Grand Tour

— 7 Days in Mpumalanga Escarpment and the Kruger National Park

— 7 Days on the Garden Route

One of the stars of the safari, a leopard resting on a tree branch

7 Days in Mpumalanga Escarpment and the Kruger National Park

- Travel back through time at **Pilgrim's Rest**, a restored gold-mining village dating to the 19th century.

- Gaze across the immense Blyde River Canyon to the iconic **Three Rondavels** rock formation.

- Get into the safari spirit spotting lions, leopards, rhinos and other wild animals in the **Kruger National Park**.

- Be charmed by elephants coming to drink at the river below **Olifants Camp**.

Mpumalanaga Escarpment and the Kruger National Park map

Blyde River Canyon
Pilgrim's Rest · Southern Kruger Tour
Dullstroom · Sabie
Johannesburg
Limpopo
SWAZILAND
Vaal
Hluhluwe-Imfolozi Game Reserve · Cape Vidal · St Lucia Estuary
Shakaland
LESOTHO
Caledon · Orange
Durban
Indian Ocean
Grahamstown

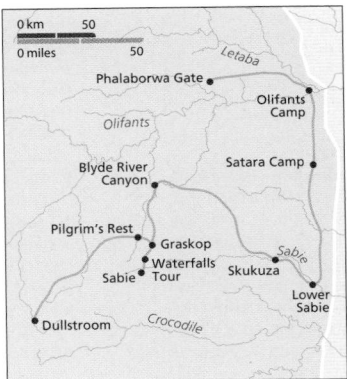

0 km 50
0 miles 50
Letaba
Phalaborwa Gate · Olifants Camp
Olifants
Blyde River Canyon · Satara Camp
Pilgrim's Rest · Graskop · Sabie
Sabie · Waterfalls Tour · Skukuza
Dullstroom · Crocodile · Lower Sabie

7 Days on the Garden Route

- Take a boat from Mossel Bay to **Seal Island** with its captivating Cape fur seals.

- Explore the limestone formations lurking in the depths of the **Cango Caves**

- Enjoy salty-fresh oysters with a sundowner on **Knysna's** pretty waterfront.

- Cross the spectacular suspension bridge that spans the cliff-enclosed **Storms River Mouth**.

0 kilometres 50
0 miles 50
Cango Caves
Olifants
Oudtshoorn
Kouga
Diepwalle Forest · Nature's Valley · Storms River Mouth
George · Knysna · Plettenberg Bay
Wilderness · Featherbed Nature Reserve · Robberg Nature Reserve
Mossel Bay

2 Days in Cape Town

One of the world's most beautiful cities, Cape Town has an inspirational harbourfront setting below majestic Table Mountain.

- **Arriving** All flights land at Cape Town International Airport, 20 km (12 miles) east of the city centre. Taxis are available to take you to the city centre, and there are also cheaper shuttles and buses.

- **Transport** A popular way of getting around is the tourist-oriented, hop-on-hop-off, open-top City Sightseer Cape Town bus, which connects the V&A Waterfront to most other sites of interest. There are also normal buses, and taxis readily available. Organized day tours are also easy to arrange.

Day 1

Morning The cableway to the top of **Table Mountain** (see p136) runs only in clear weather, so if dawn breaks brightly, it is advisable to start your exploration of the city there. Allow three to four hours for the round trip, so you have time to follow the well-marked trail system at the summit, which offers spectacular views across the City Bowl to Table Bay, and the opportunity to see wildlife such as rock hyrax, Chacma baboon and various *fynbos* birds. And while you're up there, it will be difficult to resist a late morning snack or light lunch at the scenically located cafe next to the upper cableway.

Afternoon It is easy to spend an afternoon in the vicinity of the **Company's Garden** (see p134), which was founded by Jan van Riebeeck in 1652, and is now the largest green area in the City Bowl. Bordering the garden, the **Iziko South African Museum** (see p135) is notable for its fine collection of prehistoric rock art and a marine section including a mounted whale skeleton. Other

The Table Mountain cableway, one of Cape Town's unmissable experiences

must-visit landmarks flanking the garden are the **Iziko South African National Gallery** (see p135), with its renowned collection of contemporary and classic artworks, and **Iziko Slave Lodge** (see p128), a poignant museum housed in Cape Town's second-oldest building.

Day 2

Morning The **Castle of Good Hope** (see p130), now a museum, is the oldest standing building in South Africa and requires at least 90 minutes to explore. A couple of blocks away, the superb **District Six Museum** (see p129) commemorates the mixed-race District Six suburb, which was razed in the name of apartheid in the 1970s.

Afternoon Following a harbourfront lunch at one of the dozens of eateries that line the **V&A Waterfront** (see p140), join a guided four-hour tour to **Robben Island** (see p146–7), the high security

prison where Nelson Mandela was detained for 18 years by the apartheid regime, which is now a UNESCO World Heritage Site. You will be back at the V&A Waterfront in time for a seafood dinner.

> **To extend your trip...**
> Pick as many of the day excursions included in the Western Cape tour (below) as you need to fill your time.

10 Days in the Western Cape

Using Cape Town as a base, explore the magnificent seascapes, winelands and other natural attractions of the Western Cape.

- **Arriving** Cape Town International Airport (see 2 Days in Cape Town, above).

- **Transport** Central Cape Town can be explored using public transport. Sites further afield are better suited to self-drive or to organized tours.

Days 1–3: Cape Town

Follow the 2 Days in Cape Town itinerary (above), then enjoy another day in the City Bowl, taking in the Victorian architecture of trendy Long Street (see p126), the hillside Malay enclave of **Bo-Kaap** (see p133) and the impressive and thoroughly enjoyable **Two Oceans Aquarium** (see p143).

The Company's Garden, a tranquil green space in the heart of Cape Town

Rose garden and vineyards on the Haute Cabrière Estate, which lies on the Franschhoek wine route

Day 4: Northern Cape Peninsula

Venture south of the City Bowl to loop around the northern half of the Cape Peninsula, allowing two hours to explore the tranquil **Kirstenbosch National Botanical Garden** (see p164–5) on the eastern slopes of Table Mountain, and two hours to explore the vineyards and venerable Cape Dutch architecture of the country's oldest wine estate, **Groot Constantia** (see p160–61). Worthwhile stops include the scenically located **Rhodes Memorial** (see p163) and the harbour at **Hout Bay** (see p152).

The Cape of Good Hope lighthouse, a legendary nautical landmark

Day 5: Southern Cape Peninsula

A full day is required to make the most of the southern peninsula, the highlights of which include the view rewarding the climb to the spectacular, continent-punctuating cliffs and light-house at the **Cape of Good Hope** (see p155), and a journey back in time at the historic naval village of **Simon's Town** (see p156), which is a great place to stop for lunch. A visit to the land-based penguin colony at nearby **Boulders Beach** (see p156), to enjoy the spectacle of these comical birds, is a must.

Day 6: Stellenbosch

Drive inland for an hour to **Stellenbosch** (see p196), South Africa's second-oldest town, and spend the rest of the day exploring its compact centre, lined with fine examples of stately Cape Dutch architecture, four of which comprise the **Stellenbosch Village Museum** (see p198).

Day 7: Franschhoek and the Cape Winelands

The scenic drive from Stellenbosch to **Franschhoek** (see pp204–5) passes through the heart of South Africa's oldest and finest centre of viniculture. Some might say it is an area best explored in a follow-your-nose spirit, but one essential stop midway between the two towns is **Boschendal Estate** (see p202–3), whose 200-year-old Manor House, set among shady lawns, now doubles as a museum and restaurant. In Franschhoek, do not miss the beautiful mountainside **Haute Cabrière Estate** (see p204) or the opportunity to dine at one of several award-winning restaurants.

Days 8–10: Hermanus and Agulhas

Continue south to the quaint harbour town of **Hermanus** (see pp226–7), which is famed for its clifftop location and peerless land-based whale-watching. The next day, take a day trip to **Cape Agulhas** (see p229), where a handsome lighthouse marks the treacherously rocky coastline of what is the most southerly spot in Africa. Return to Cape Town on Day 10, stopping en route to visit the penguin colony at scenic **Betty's Bay** (see p226), and the beautiful **Vergelegen Wine Estate** (see p201) on the slopes of the Helderberg outside Somerset West.

To extend your trip...
This is an action-packed 10 days. With two weeks to spare, you could slow down the pace with a relaxed afternoon or two on the beach at **Camps Bay** (see p151) or **Muizenberg** (see p157), or enjoy an extended session of retail therapy at Cape Town's trendy **Long Street** or the more **V&A Waterfront**. An additional day exploring the lush Winelands around Stellenbosch is also recommended, while more active visitors could make a loop eastwards from Hermanus to the hiker-friendly **De Hoop Nature Reserve** (see p230).

7 Days on the Garden Route

Tangled forests, characterful towns and idyllic beaches are among the many features that make the southern Cape's Garden Route so enduringly popular.

- **Arriving** The route below assumes you would fly in and out of George, a short hop from the international airports at Johannesburg and Cape Town. Alternatively, Mossel Bay and George are only half a day's drive from Cape Town or Hermanus in the Western Cape.

- **Transport** The Garden Route is best explored on a self-drive basis. You can pick up a rental car at George Airport. Organized tours are also possible, but public transport is limited.

Day 1: Mossel Bay

Although inland, George is the main point of entry and the largest town on the Garden Route, but nearby **Mossel Bay** *(see p241)* is a far more interesting prospect for the visitor. Here, the **Bartolomeu Dias Museum Complex** *(see pp240–41)* includes a full-scale replica of one of the boats used by its namesake in 1488, and a massive milkwood tree first used as a "post office" by Portuguese navigators in 1501. Boat trips to **Seal Island** *(see p241)* are also available.

Day 2: Oudtshoorn

A scenic hour's drive inland from Mossel Bay, **Oudtshoorn** *(see p232)* is best-known as the centre of the Karoo's century-old ostrich farming industry. Head to the out-of-town **Highgate** or **Safari Ostrich Show Farms** *(see p233)* to learn more about the world's largest bird, and visit the central **CP Nel Museum** *(see p233)* to explore the history of the booming Victorian ostrich-feather industry on which the town became rich. Afterwards, drive

to the 20-million-year-old **Cango Caves** *(see p235)* and take a guided tour through the series of subterranean chambers famed for their spectacular limestone formations.

Day 3: Wilderness

Back on the coast, east of George, chill out at beachfront **Wilderness** *(see p242-3)*, or explore the adjacent Wilderness sector of the Garden Route National Park, which protects a series of estuaries and lakes rich in birdlife, day hikes and kayaking opportunities.

Day 4: Knysna

The prettiest town on the Garden Route, **Knysna** *(see p244–5)* overlooks a beautiful, calm lagoon protected by a pair of cliffs called the Knysna Heads. For energetic walkers, a visit to **Diepwalle Forest** in the Knysna sector of the Garden Route National Park *(see p245)* beckons, while a more sedate alternative is an organized boat trip across the lagoon to the private **Featherbed Nature Reserve** *(see p244)*. Round off the day with fresh oysters and locally-brewed ale on the Knysna Quays.

Day 5: Plettenberg Bay

The most overtly resort-like town on the Garden Route, **Plettenberg Bay** *(see p246–7)* has a wide curving beach where weary travellers can pull up a deck chair for a well-earned break. More challengingly, the day hike through the nearby

Dare to make the crossing on a swaying suspension bridge at Storms River Mouth

Robberg Nature Reserve *(see p246)* incorporates some truly dramatic cliffs as well as good birding and a fair chance of spotting seals and other marine mammals.

Day 6: Storms River Mouth

Drive east via forested Nature's Valley to **Storms River Mouth** *(see p249)*, which lies in the Tsitsikamma sector of the Garden Route National Park. Another favourite with walkers, this park is famed for its sandy beaches, forest-covered cliffs and spectacular suspension bridge. On Day 7, return to George, a 2-hour drive, to catch your onward flight.

> **To extend your trip…**
> Continue east along the coast to spend two nights at **Addo Elephant National Park** *(see p254)* before flying out of **Port Elizabeth** *(see p250)*.

Extraordinary rock formations in the Cango Caves near Oudtshoorn

7 Days in Mpumalanga Escarpment and the Kruger National Park

Africa's finest do-it-yourself safari destination is twinned on this trip with the spectacularly scenic vistas and waterfalls of the mountainous escarpment rising to its west.

- **Arriving** Domestic flights connect Johannesburg with the towns of Nelspruit, Hoedspruit and Phalaborwa on the edge of the Kruger, as well as Skukuza and several more minor airstrips in the park environs. Alternatively, it's an easy 4–5 hour drive from Johannesburg to Pilgrim's Rest or the southern Kruger, but a more daunting 6–7 hours back from Phalaborwa and the northern reaches of the park.

- **Transport** Self-drive is ideal. Either drive across from Johannesburg, or book a rental car to pick up at one of the local airports. Many organized, guided tours to the Kruger are available but you will need to stick to the prescribed itinerary. There is no public transport in the park.

Day 1: Pilgrim's Rest
Drive east from Johannesburg, taking a lunch break at the sleepy highland village of **Dullstroom** *(see p334)*, famed for its fresh trout, then moving on to the restored 19th-century gold-mining village of **Pilgrim's Rest** *(see p336)*. The historic sites scattered around this hilly village provide a great opportunity to stretch your legs after the drive.

Day 2: Waterfalls Tour and Blyde River Canyon
Spend the morning exploring some of the pretty waterfalls that comprise the so-called **Waterfalls Tour** *(see p335)*, first driving south from Pilgrim's Rest to Sabie, then back north to the small town of Graskop for lunch.

Iron-rich rock creates stunning polychromatic effects at Blyde River Canyon

Continue north to the spectacular **Bourke's Luck Potholes** *(see p337)* and **Three Rondavels** *(see p337)*, the latter being the most spectacular of several viewpoints across the Blyde River Canyon, and best seen in the afternoon with the sun behind you.

Days 3–4: Southern Kruger
Allocate two nights to the part of the **Kruger National Park** *(see pp340–44)* south of the Sabie River, ideally using either the largest camp, **Skukuza** *(see p342)*, or **Lower Sabie** *(see p342–3)* (arguably the best, location-wise) as a base for game drives. These are always slightly hit-or-miss, but the **H4-1** *(see p343)* connecting Skukuza to Lower Sabie is the busiest in the park for good reason (lions, leopards and elephants are often seen here), while the main road

The African buffalo, often spotted in the Kruger National Park

running south from Lower Sabie is famed for its excellent rhino-spotting opportunities.

Days 5–6: Central Kruger
Less dense with tourist traffic than the south, the **Central Kruger** *(see p344)* still offers great game-viewing, typically in more open habitats than the north. Ideally spend your first night in **Satara Camp** *(see p343)*, which lies in an area of relatively open grassland where cheetahs and lions are often observed, along with large mixed herds of wildebeest and zebra.

The next day, continue north to **Olifants Camp** *(see p343)*, which has a superb clifftop setting overlooking the Olifants River, an area known for its plentiful tuskers and large herds of buffalo. On Day 7, be sure to allow at least 4 hours' driving time to exit the park at Phalaborwa Gate in order to fly out of Phalaborwa in the afternoon.

> **To extend your trip...**
> With a couple more days to spare, you could pad out your time in Kruger with an extra night at each of Satara and Olifants, or (budget permitting) treat yourself to an all-inclusive stay at a **private reserve** *(see p345)*. With at least five extra days, you could head all the way north to the genuinely off-the-beaten-track **Punda Maria Camp** *(see p344)*.

2 Days in Johannesburg

Explore the bustling city centre and suburbs of southern Africa's largest city and most important economic powerhouse.

- **Arriving** Johannesburg is served by OR Tambo International Airport, east of the city, within a 45-minute drive of the centre and most hotels, traffic permitting. Taxis are available at the airport, and the Gautrain is a high-speed rail service to the city centre, Sandton, Rosebank and Pretoria.

- **Transport** Soweto is best visited on an organized tour, and this would also be the safest option for the city centre of Johannesburg. Self-drive is a possibility for suburban attractions, and day tours can be arranged. Public transport is limited and not very tourist-friendly.

Day 1

Morning Most visitors regard a visit to **Soweto** (see p318–19), the most infamous of the black "townships" during the apartheid era and the former home of the late Nelson Mandela, as top on the list of Johannesburg's must-do activities. Though it is not as unsafe as it once was, Soweto is still best explored on a half-day guided tour, which will typically stop at several landmarks associated with the dark days of apartheid. Make sure your tour includes a lunch stop at one of the satellite city's famously welcoming shebeen bars or restaurants.

Afternoon After lunch, head north to **Johannesburg city centre** (see p314). A literal highlight of any visit to this bustling metropolis is the panoramic view of the city and suburbs offered from the Top of Africa observation deck at the summit of the 50-storey **Carlton Centre & Top of Africa** (see p316), Africa's tallest

building. A few blocks west of this, several worthwhile attractions are clustered in and around the historic Newtown Precinct, among them the **Market Theatre** and **Museum Africa** (both p314). Round off your exploration of the city centre by dropping in at the memorable **KwaZulu Muti** (see p315), a well-known vendor of traditional medicines.

Day 2

Morning Arguably the best museum in South Africa (but not suitable for under-11s), the **Apartheid Museum** (see p317), 8 km (5 miles) south of the city centre, documents the divisive and cruel effects that the apartheid policies pursued by the government of the time had on Johannesburg (and the rest of the country) between 1948 and 1994. Allow at least two hours to look around the museum, then cross the car park to **Gold Reef City** (see p321), a somewhat romanticized but nevertheless interesting (and fun) reconstruction of Johannesburg in its earliest gold boom days. Gold Reef City is also a good spot for lunch.

Afternoon Take the motorway northwest from Johannesburg to explore a cluster of attractions that lie within 40 km (25 miles) of the city. Make your first stop the **Sterkfontein Caves** (see p322), centrepiece of the Cradle of Humankind UNESCO World

Soweto, once the home of Nelson Mandela, attracts visitors from around the world

Heritage Site, which has yielded some of the world's most important human fossils. The cave tour is challenging – for families and the less mobile, the Maropeng visitor centre offers plenty of displays and interactive exhibits. Also in this area, if you prefer, is the **Lion Park** (see p323), which offers a soft introduction to wildlife that is often more elusive in larger game reserves.

Afterwards, head to **Lesedi Cultural Village** (see p323) for its spectacular late afternoon cultural show, which highlights a variety of different ethnic traditions, with the option of staying on to enjoy the menu of pan-African cuisine served at its restaurant.

While it is not one of South Africa's three capitals, Johannesburg is its largest city

21-Day Grand Tour

In three weeks, self-drivers with sufficient time can meander from Johannesburg to Cape Town via some of the country's finest game reserves and beaches.

- **Arriving** Fly into OR Tambo International Airport near Johannesburg and out of Cape Town International Airport, 20 km (12 miles) from Cape Town and 30 km (19 miles) from Stellenbosch.

- **Transport** This itinerary is aimed mainly at self-drivers, who can pick up a rental vehicle at one airport and drop it at another. Many organized tours offer variations on the same route, sometimes flying between Durban or Port Elizabeth and George or Cape Town to save time. Intercity public transport, where it is available, would not offer access to most small stops on the way.

Pachyderms on parade at Addo Elephant National Park

Days 1–2: Johannesburg
Follow the itinerary for 2 Days in Johannesburg (*see facing page*).

Days 3–6: Mpumalanga Escarpment and the Kruger National Park
As for Days 1–4 of the itinerary on page 15.

Days 7–9: iSimangaliso Wetland Park and Hluhluwe-Imfolozi
Leave the Kruger early for the long (9–10 hour) drive south to northern KwaZulu-Natal and the coastal village of St Lucia in the **iSimangaliso Wetland Park** (*see p300–301*). Using this lovely jungle-enclosed village as a base for three nights, spend your first morning on a boat cruising the **St Lucia Estuary** (*see p300*), with its plentiful hippos and birds, then head north to the stunning beach and forested dunes at **Cape Vidal** (*see p300*) for the afternoon. Spend the next day exploring the game-viewing roads of **Hluhluwe-Imfolozi**

Game Reserve (*see p298*), whose rolling green hills support the world's densest rhino population.

Days 10–11: Shakaland and Durban
A 3-hour drive from St Lucia leads south to Durban, with the option of diverting a short way inland for a daytime or overnight cultural programme at **Shakaland** (*see p297*), the original and best of several lodges dedicated to bringing traditional Zulu culture to life. Your itinerary in **Durban** (*see pp286–9*) will depend on whether you spend one or two nights there, but try to fit in a visit to the Indian-dominated **Victoria Street Market** (*see p288*) and world-class **uShaka Marine World** (*see p286*), and enjoy fresh seafood or tangy curry (a local speciality) at one of the restaurants on the beachfront **Golden Mile** (*see p286*).

The soaring cathedral of St Michael and St George, Grahamstown

Day 12: Grahamstown
Another long day behind the wheel leads from Durban to **Grahamstown** (*see p256–7*), a charming 200-year-old university town. Allow an hour or two to explore the excellent **Albany Museum Complex** (*see p256*).

Days 13–14: Addo Elephant National Park
Allow two nights and a full day to explore the short but very rewarding road network through **Addo Elephant National Park** (*see p254*), which now hosts all of the Big Five – lion, elephant, leopard, rhino and buffalo – but is famed for offering close-up encounters with some very relaxed elephants.

Days 15–16: Garden Route
Choose one or two of the stops on the Garden Route itinerary on page 14. The Tsitsikamma sector of the Garden Route National Park is noted for scenery and walking, Knysna for urban attractions in a lovely lagoonside setting, and Oudtshoorn for the quirkier combination of ostrich farms and limestone caverns.

Days 17–21: Cape Town and Stellenbosch
Drive or fly from George to Cape Town. With three to four full days, follow the 2-day itinerary on page 12, then days 5 and 6 of the itinerary on page 13, with the option of spending your last night in Stellenbosch or in one of the other Winelands towns.

Putting South Africa on the Map

The southernmost country on the African continent, South Africa is roughly five times the size of Britain. It covers an area of 1,223,201 sq km (472,156 sq miles), and has a population of around 55 million. The sovereign kingdom of Lesotho lies within its borders. The Atlantic, which washes its western shores, and the Indian Ocean, which laps the East Coast, meet at Cape Agulhas, Africa's most southerly tip. To the north of South Africa lie the neighbouring states of Namibia, Botswana, Zimbabwe, Swaziland and Mozambique.

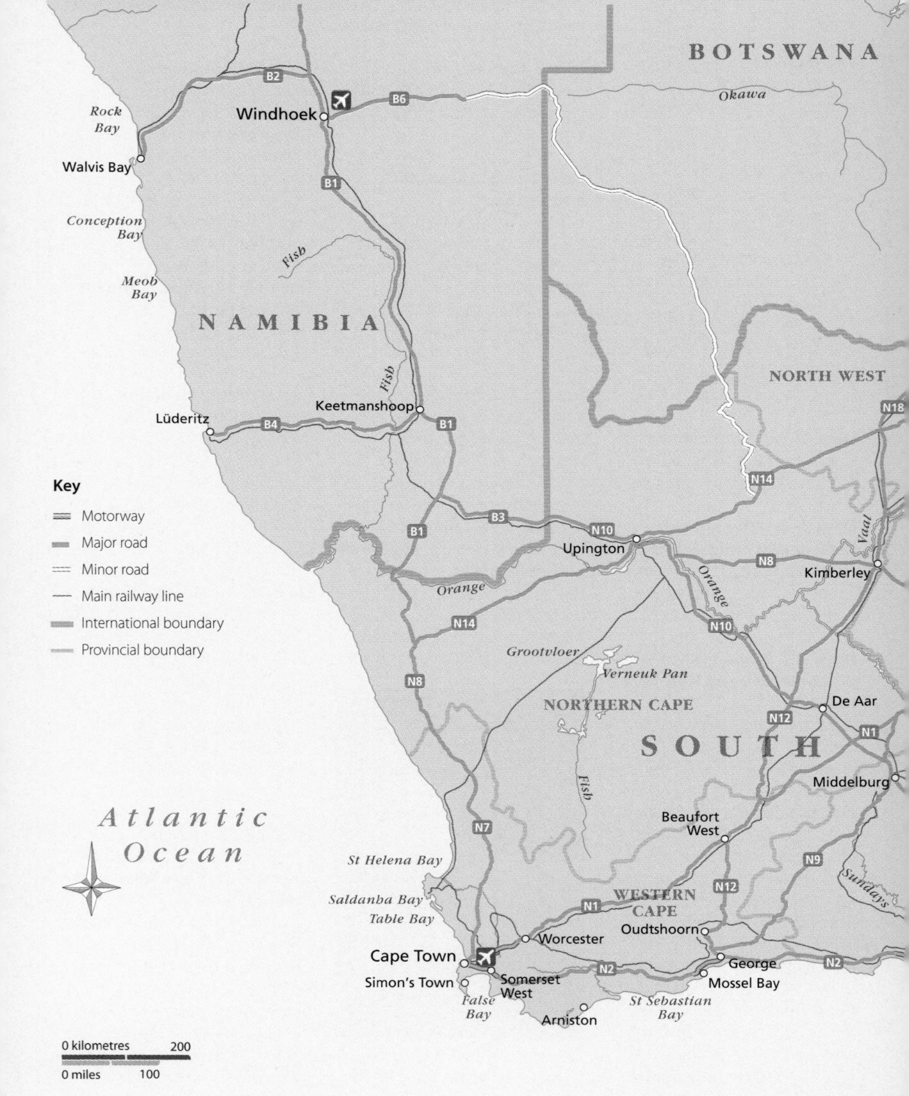

Key

≡ Motorway

▬ Major road

═ Minor road

— Main railway line

▬ International boundary

▬ Provincial boundary

Atlantic Ocean

0 kilometres 200

0 miles 100

For keys to symbols *see back flap*

Road Map of South Africa

International airports at Johannesburg, Cape Town and Durban link South Africa with the rest of the world, while domestic airports serve many of the smaller centres. International cruise liners dock at the ports of Cape Town, Durban and Port Elizabeth. An efficient road network spans the vast interior, linking cities and towns. This book divides the country into ten regions, with a separate chapter for Cape Town. Officially, South Africa has nine provinces.

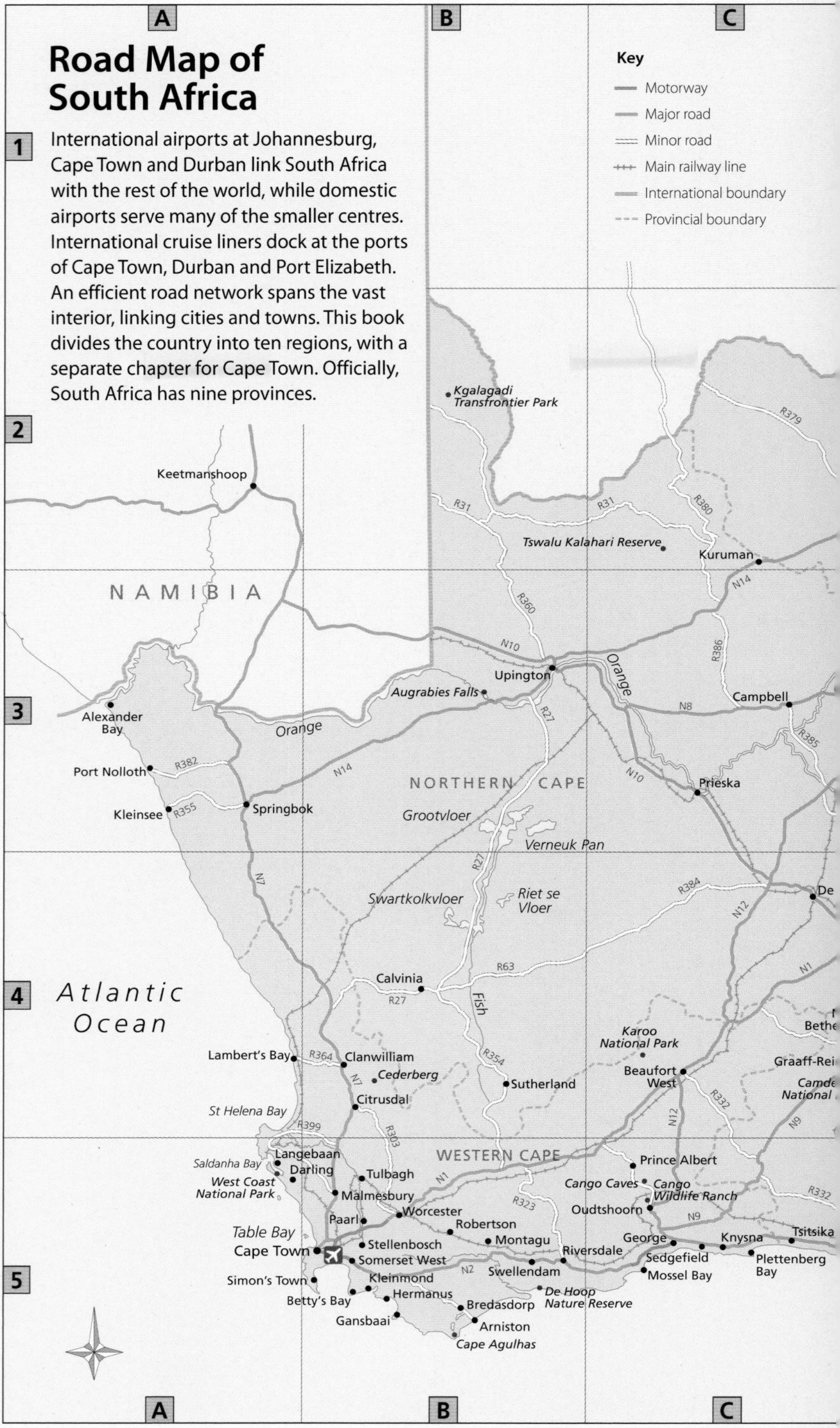

Key

—— Motorway
—— Major road
══ Minor road
+++ Main railway line
—— International boundary
--- Provincial boundary

Kgalagadi Transfrontier Park

Keetmanshoop

R379

R31

R31

R380

Tswalu Kalahari Reserve

Kuruman

NAMIBIA

N14

R360

Orange

N10

Upington

R386

Campbell

Augrabies Falls

R27

N8

Alexander Bay

Orange

N14

NORTHERN CAPE

N10

Prieska

Port Nolloth

R382

Grootvloer

De

Kleinsee

R355

Springbok

Verneuk Pan

R384

N12

N1

N7

Swartkolkvloer

Riet se Vloer

Bethe

Calvinia

R63

Fish

Karoo National Park

Graaff-Rei

Atlantic Ocean

Lambert's Bay

R364

Clanwilliam

R27

R354

Sutherland

Beaufort West

Camde National

Cederberg

N7

N12

R332

St Helena Bay

Citrusdal

R303

WESTERN CAPE

N9

R399

Saldanha Bay

Langebaan

Prince Albert

West Coast National Park

Darling

Tulbagh

N1

Cango Caves

Cango Wildlife Ranch

R332

Malmesbury

R323

Oudtshoorn

Paarl

Worcester

N9

Table Bay

Stellenbosch

Robertson

George

Knysna

Tsitsika

Cape Town

Somerset West

Montagu

Riversdale

Sedgefield

Plettenberg Bay

Simon's Town

Kleinmond

N2

Swellendam

Mossel Bay

Betty's Bay

Hermanus

De Hoop Nature Reserve

Gansbaai

Bredasdorp

Arniston

Cape Agulhas

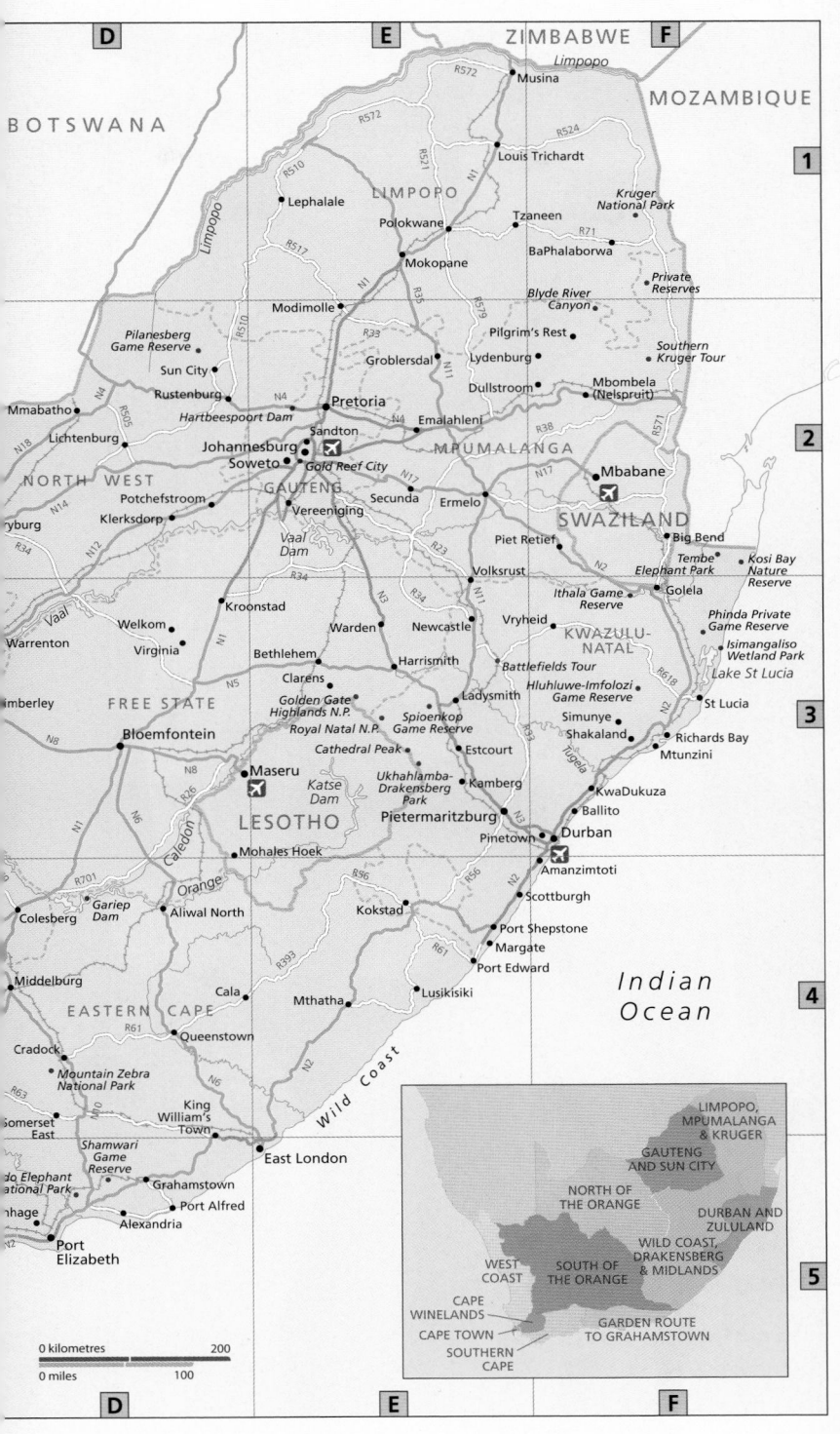

A PORTRAIT OF SOUTH AFRICA

Blue skies, fabulous beaches, game parks, wilderness areas, and the promise of a sun-drenched holiday are what attract most visitors to South Africa. Then there are its cosmopolitan and fast-paced cities, intriguing mix of friendly peoples and cultures, and its compelling museums and historic sites. In short, it is an inspiring and fascinating place to explore, and the choice of destinations, activities and itineraries is virtually inexhaustible.

South Africa, roughly the size of Spain and France combined, encompasses an astonishing diversity of environments: from the dramatic arid moonscapes of the northwest to the forest-fringed coastline of the Garden Route; from the flat, dry Karoo interior to the craggy Drakensberg in the east; and from the manicured vineyards of the Cape to the spring flower fields of Namaqualand.

South Africa is the only country in the world that can lay claim to an entire floral kingdom within its borders. Centred on a small area in the Western Cape, *fynbos* (literally "fine-leaved bush") comprises a unique mixture of proteas, ericas and grasses. The many wildlife parks further north are home to the "Big Five" –

buffalo, elephant, leopard, lion and rhinoceros – while the wetlands and marine reserves along the East Coast teem with sea creatures and colourful birds, great and small, that are often overlooked.

And then there are the beaches – favourite holiday destination of the locals and perfect for boardsailing, swimming, surfing, angling, or simply relaxing in the sun.

South Africa has no fewer than 11 official languages and numerous ethnicities and religions, but its people have experienced a great sense of reconciliation since the end of apartheid. Today, the South African nation is a conglomeration of beliefs, traditions, and heritages living within a country of breathtaking natural wonders.

Acacia trees survive along the parched fringes of the Kalahari Desert

◀ Carved wooden masks from the Western Cape

Groote Schuur Hospital, where the world's first successful heart transplant was carried out in 1967

The modern South African state began as a halfway station. Dutch traders of the 17th century, on long sea voyages to their colonies in the East, replenished their stores at the Cape. A fertile land, South Africa is still largely self-reliant today, compelled to become so as a result of the long period of international political isolation that resulted from its former policy of racial discrimination known as *apartheid* (apartness). South Africa became a world producer of gold and petroleum. Impressive advances were made in communication, weapons technology and mining, but apartheid stood in the way of harmony and economic growth. In the late 1960s, while the world's first human heart transplant was performed at Groote Schuur Hospital in Cape Town, the majority of South Africans struggled to fulfil their most basic needs: food, shelter and education.

Then, in the 1970s and 1980s, the nation went through a period of tense upheaval and protest from the majority non-white population, who demanded change. The struggle against apartheid began in earnest on 16 June 1976, when the youth of Soweto marched against being taught in the medium of Afrikaans. Police fired on them, precipitating a massive flood of violence that overwhelmed the country. Finally, in 1989, the log jam started to break up. Negotiations had been entered into with the imprisoned Nelson Mandela, and F W de Klerk became president. This led to democratic elections in 1994 and the final demise of the apartheid government.

People and Society

In the post-apartheid constitution that took effect in 1997, it was deemed that in a land of such differences, each group of people must be fairly recognized for their identity. English, Afrikaans and nine Bantu tongues were all made official languages. Afrikaans, derived from Dutch and altered through contact with other tongues, is spoken by 13 per cent of the population.

South Africa's cultural mix has its roots in a colonial past. The original hunter-

Farm labourers relaxing on a hay wagon, West Coast

gatherer inhabitants of the Cape were joined, about 1,000 years ago, by migrating Bantu-speakers from the north. In the 17th century, European settlers appeared – first the Dutch, then the British and French – with their slaves from Indonesia, Madagascar, and India. Later followed indentured labourers from India. Settlers and slaves alike brought with them their culinary traditions, and if there is a national cuisine it is Cape Malay: mild lamb and fish curries sweetened with spiced fruit. Although seafood is relished, South Africans are really a meat-loving nation. The outdoor *braai* (barbecue) is popular all around the globe, but no one does it quite like South Africans, with fiercely guarded secret recipes, and competitions for the best *boerewors* (a type of sausage) and *potjiekos* (a tasty stew prepared in a three-legged cast iron pot).

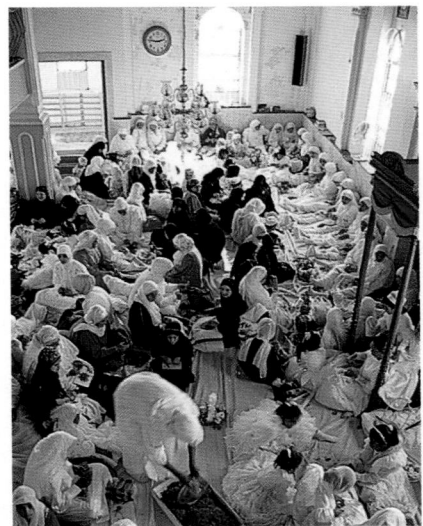
Feast day preparations in a Cape Town mosque

Religion crosses many of the cultural and social divides, and the post-apartheid constitution protects freedom of religion. Everyone is free to follow whatever faith they want to, or not to follow one at all. The African independent churches have a large following, while the Dutch Reformed, Roman Catholic, Presbyterian, and Anglican churches attract worshippers from all population groups. Islam is strongly represented in the Western Cape, while Buddhists and Hindus are mainly found in Durban. Traditional African religion is still practised in the rural areas, where the community is the most important part of someone's life. Ancestor-worship is part of every major event, such as weddings, births and deaths, and in some ethnic African cultures, such as the Zulu, there are spiritual leaders or *sangomas* who are responsible for healing and "divining".

Penny whistler

Culture and Sport

An awareness of African identity is the essence of cultural life, and music – always central to traditional ceremonies and celebrations – leads the way. Regular church choir festivals attest to the popularity of gospel and choral harmony. The distinctive sound of Zulu *mbube* (unaccompanied choral singing) has become one of South Africa's best-known exports.

African choir performing gospel and harmonies

Sindiwe Magona is the author of several books about her life as a black South African woman

In the cities, although the tunes are much influenced by popular North American music, jazz, soul, *kwela* (characterized by the piercing sound of the penny whistle), *kwaito* (transient pop), rock and reggae all have a strong local flavour.

The white Afrikaner's cultural heritage, accumulated over centuries of isolation from the European motherland, today embraces a powerful body of prose and poetry *(see pp32–3)*, and a distinctive musical tradition. Afrikaans songs tend to be nostalgic, often evoking gentler times. By contrast, the black African music is lively, distinguished by bouncy melodies and cheerful, racy lyrics that belie the sadness and indignities of the past.

During the dark years of apartheid, oppression and suffering offered ready-made source material for the arts, but contemporary writers have moved away from racial introspection towards more universal themes.

Most South Africans are passionate about sport. The Rugby World Cup, which was held in Johannesburg and other cities in 1995 and won by a jubilant South Africa, probably did more than anything else to unite the nation, and poignant images of then president Nelson Mandela and

Springbok captain Francois Pienaar holding up the trophy together were broadcast worldwide. South Africa won the tournament again in 2007, defeating England in the final.

Soccer, cricket, boxing, horse racing and athletics also draw enthusiastic crowds. The country hosted the 2010 FIFA World Cup.

Towards Democracy

The best point from which to chart the end of apartheid is President F W de Klerk's unbanning of the African National Congress (ANC), along with the Communist Party and Pan-Africanist Congress (PAC). On 11 February 1990, ANC leader Nelson Mandela was released from the Victor Verster Prison near Paarl. He had been imprisoned since 1963.

Amid escalating violence, negotiations began for a peaceful transition to democracy. Finally, on 27 April 1994, all South Africans voted. The ANC secured 63 per cent, and Nelson Mandela became the first black president of the "New South Africa". The new constitution, approved in May 1996, has arguably the most enlightened Bill of Rights in the world, outlawing discrimination on the grounds of ethnic

Cape minstrel

South Africa's rugby team celebrates its World Cup victory in 2007

Outdoor-loving South Africans on the popular Clifton beach in Cape Town

or social origin, religion, gender, sexual orientation and language. Yet, many citizens still live very close to poverty and, despite the country's wealth of natural resources, advanced technology and sophisticated infrastructure, the gap between South Africa's privileged and its poor is still noticeably wide. Nevertheless the government is implementing continuous programmes for improving housing, transport and other services, and overall, even poorer South Africans enjoy a far better standard of living than most people in African countries to the north.

South Africa's children had a special place in *"Madiba's"* heart

After Mandela

The ANC has remained in power since 1994. Nelson Mandela passed the mantle of power as president of the ANC over to his long-time deputy Thabo Mbeki in 1999. Mbeki was president of the country from the 1999 elections until his resignation in 2008 over allegations that he interfered in the corruption case against Jacob Zuma. He was replaced by "caretaker'" president Kgalema Motlanthe, who headed the state until the 2009 elections. A member of the ANC since 1959, Jacob Zuma was elected deputy president to Mbeki in 1999 and again in 2004, and once alleged corruption charges against him were dismissed, Zuma was able to stand as the country's president in the 2009 elections. He and the ruling ANC won again in general elections in 2014.

Nelson Mandela died in Johannesburg in December 2013 at the age of 95. Tributes flooded in from throughout the world, and South Africa held an emotional ten-day period of mourning in which memorial services took place in stadiums, and books of condolence were signed across the country. His funeral was held at his ancestral home of Qunu in the Eastern Cape. Thousands of mourners lined the streets as the military transported Mandela's casket on a gun carriage, and his peaceful burial was attended by family, friends and dignitaries.

A bold mural in Johannesburg portrays the multicultural nation

The Contrasting Coasts

Two ocean currents influence the coastal climate of South Africa: the tropical Agulhas Current, which flows south down the East Coast, and the cold, north-flowing Benguela Current along the western shores. The two merge somewhere off lonely Cape Agulhas, Africa's most southerly cape. Together with the winds and mountains, these ocean movements determine the region's coastal variance: the aridity of the west versus the luxuriant forest in the east. The coastal fauna and flora, both terrestrial and aquatic, display interesting variations. Here, too, the west differs notably from the east, as plants and animals have adapted to their specific environments.

Southern right whales, known for their massive heads and jaws, are one of the species of baleen whales that frequent South African coastal waters.

Drosanthemums are low-growing plants, well adapted to arid West Coast conditions. They store precious water in their small, thick leaves, and flower between August and October.

The black korhaan inhabits dry coastal scrubland. The males are strikingly coloured and protect their territory with raucous calls. Females are an inconspicuous mottled brown and avoid detection by standing perfectly still.

Atlantic Ocean

0 km   100
0 miles 50

Cape Basin

St Helena Bay

Saldanha Bay

Table Bay

Cape Town

False Bay

Cape Point

West Coast rock lobster, important to the region's economy, are harvested under special licence. They are not reared on a commercial basis.

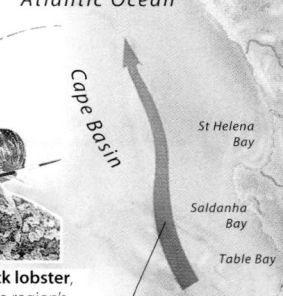

The Benguela Current flows north, carrying cold water from the Antarctic.

At Cape Agulhas, the waters of the two currents converge.

• **Cape Agulhas**

Agulhas Bank

The West Coast

Even in summer, water temperatures average only 14°C (57°F). This precludes the formation of rain-bearing clouds, and annual precipitation is below 250 mm (10 in). The lack of fresh water means that only tough succulents survive on dew from sea mists. The sea water, full of nutrients, sustains a rich and varied marine life.

Sea anemone

Memorial plaque at Cape Agulhas

Cape Agulhas

The southernmost point of the African continent is not Cape Point, but unassuming Cape Agulhas on the rocky east side of the windswept, shallow Danger Point headland. The Portuguese word *agulhas*, from which the Cape gets its name, means "needles". It was here that early navigators discovered that the compass needle was not affected by magnetic deviation, but pointed true north. A plaque is set into the rock, and markers give the distances to international cities.

Various dolphin species can be seen frolicking in the warm currents off towns such as Durban and Margate. They usually occur in groups of 10 to 15 individuals.

Kosi Bay●

iSimangaliso ●
Wetland Park

The genus *Crinum* (amaryllis family) is commonly seen in swampy grassland along the East Coast. It flowers in summer.

Umgeni River
Estuary

Durban ●

Aliwal Shoal

The knysna lourie (*Tauraco corythaix*) is found in the evergreen forests of southern and eastern South Africa. It is most likely to be spotted flying between trees or hopping along branches.

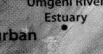

Natal Basin

Indian Ocean

The Port Elizabeth crayfish (or shoveller), one of many species of rock lobster found around the South African coast, has little commercial value.

Algoa Bay

Aguihas Basin

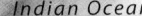

The warm Agulhas Current causes humid conditions along the East Coast.

The East Coast

The warm Agulhas Current that flows south through the Mozambique Channel creates hot, humid conditions along the East Coast. Vegetation is subtropical and mangrove forests flourish in the Umgeni River Estuary near Durban. The annual migration of big pilchard shoals is eagerly awaited by fish, birds and humans. Coral reefs, rare in South African waters, are found in the marine reserves of the iSimangaliso Wetland Park.

Nudibranch

The Landscapes and Flora of South Africa

South Africa's flora has charmed visitors and intrigued botanists for years. Many species are widely distributed within the country, but each region has produced distinct characteristics, the result of varying geographic, climatic and soil conditions. In the more arid western reaches of the country, plants tend to be small and low-growing, flowering briefly after the winter rains, while further east, open grassland and bushveld dominate. Lush subtropical coastal forests grow along the East Coast.

The Cape Floral Kingdom

Pelargonium

The Southwestern Cape, one of the world's six floral kingdoms, boasts almost 9,000 different plants in an area less than 4 per cent of the southern African land surface. This so-called *fynbos* (fine-leaved bush vegetation) includes some 350 species of protea, as well as pelargoniums, ericas, reeds and irises. Most are endemic to the area, and are well represented in the Kirstenbosch National Botanical Garden *(see pp164–5)*.

Semi-Desert

Succulent

In southern Africa, true desert is confined to the Namib. The semi-desert Great Karoo region covers about one-third of South Africa. Its flora has evolved to withstand aridity and extreme temperatures. Many succulents, including the aloes, mesembryanthemums, euphorbias and stapelias, store water in their thick leaves or roots. The seeds of daisy-like ephemeral plants may lie dormant for years, only to germinate and flower briefly when the conditions are favourable *(see pp220–21)*. Trees tend to grow along seasonal river courses.

Namaqualand *(see pp220–21)*

Many succulent plants in this region survive only through the condensation of nightly mists that roll in from the Atlantic Ocean. Adaptation has led to many bizarre species, such as the *kokerboom* (quiver tree), *half-mens* (half-human), and the insectivorous plants of the *Stapelia* genus. Dwarf shrubs and scraggy bushes are widely spaced over dusty land that is bare for most of the year, until even modest winter rains raise dense, multi-hued crops of daisy-like *vygie* blossoms.

Vygies

Temperate Forest

Dense evergreen forests thrive in the high-rainfall area around Knysna *(see pp244–5)*. They produce lovely rare hardwoods such as stinkwood and yellowwood, two types that also occur along the subtropical coastal belt of KwaZulu-Natal. Knysna's temperate forests have a characteristic undergrowth of shrubs, ferns, fungi, and creepers such as the wispy "old man's beard". Mature trees may reach a height of 60 m (195 ft), with a girth of 7 m (23 ft).

Forest fungus

Erica patersonia is one of over 625 erica species that occur in the Southwestern Cape. It is mainly found along streams.

Protea grandiceps is one of the most widely distributed of its genus. It grows at the higher altitudes of coastal mountains.

Pincushion proteas bloom from June to December in colours ranging from yellow to deep red. The flower heads last for up to three weeks and attract sunbirds and insects.

Ericas are found on Table Mountain, where *Erica dichrus* provides dense red splashes of colour.

Yellow pincushion proteas grow as a tall shrub that is found near the coast.

Bushveld

Large tracts of the interior are covered with tall grasses and low trees, most of them deciduous, fine-leaved and thorny. The Kruger National Park *(see pp340–45)* is an excellent example of several transitional types occurring between sparse shrub and savannah; here shrubs grow densely and larger tree types include marula, mopane and baobab. The many acacia species are characterized by pod-bearing trees and shrubs with clusters of small, golden-yellow flowers.

"Weeping boerbean" pod

High Mountain

Mountain flora, zoned according to altitude and increasing severity of the environment, rises from dense heath to mixed scrub and grasses. A relatively small subalpine belt, 2,800 m (9,000 ft) above sea level, is confined to the Drakensberg region *(see pp274–5)*. Characteristic flowering plants here are helichrysum ("everlastings"), sedges and ericas. In many areas, annuals make brief, colourful spring appearances. Among the proteas growing in this region is the rare snow protea on the high peaks of the Cederberg *(see pp218–19)*.

Watsonia

Subtropical Coastal Belt

Brackish swamps, saline estuaries and lush plant growth are characteristic of the KwaZulu-Natal coast. Mangroves anchor themselves to their unstable habitat with stilt-like roots, while higher up on the banks grow palms and the broad-leaved wild banana of the *Strelitzia* genus. A good example of typical East Coast vegetation can be seen at Kosi Bay *(see p301)*, where swamps surround lakes that are overgrown with water lilies and reeds. Dune forests and grasslands are dotted with wild palms.

Water lily

Literary South Africa

A rich literary tradition exists in all 11 national languages, which include nine Bantu tongues, mostly from the Nguni and Sotho branches. Most books were published in Afrikaans or English, while much of the African heritage was handed down orally. Books in African tongues are now beginning to enjoy a wider circulation, both locally and abroad, and are also appearing in foreign translation. Over the years, South Africa has inspired a number of outstanding authors and poets, among them Sir Percy FitzPatrick, Olive Schreiner, Sir Laurens van der Post, Nadine Gordimer and Mzwakhe Mbuli.

C J Langenhoven wrote *Die Stem*, one of the two national anthems

Painting by Credo Mutwa, taken from the book *African Proverbs*

Traditional African Stories

Many African communities have an oral tradition of stories, genealogies, proverbs and riddles that have been passed down from generation to generation.

Izibongo, simplistically translated as praise songs, are very complex oral presentations delivered by a skilled performer known as *mbongi*. This rhythmic form of poetry uses exalted language, rich in metaphor and parallelisms. At Nelson Mandela's inauguration, two *izibongo* were performed in isiXhosa.

Among the best written works are Samuel Mqhayi's historic *Ityala Lamawele* (Lawsuit of the Twins) (1914) and A Jordan's *Ingqumbo Yeminyanya* (The Wrath of the Ancestors) (1940), both in isiXhosa, and Thomas

Mofolo's *Chaka* (1925) in Sesotho, BW Vilakazi's *Noma Nini* (1935) in isiZulu, and Sol Plaatjie's *Mhudi* (1930) in Setswana.

English publications of traditional African tales, novels and poetry include *Indaba My Children* and *African Proverbs* by Credo Mutwa (1964).

Actor Patrick Mynhardt in a dramatization of Herman Charles Bosman's *A Cask of Jerepigo*

Afrikaans Literature

The Dutch spoken by the colonial authorities formed the basis of a local tongue that became known as Afrikaans, or simply *die taal* (the language). Efforts to translate the Bible into Afrikaans led to a vigorous campaign to have the language formally recognized. A direct result of these tireless efforts was the publication of almost 100 books before 1900.

The descriptive prose and lyrical poetry of literary greats such as Gustav Preller, C J Langenhoven, D F Malherbe and Totius (Jacob Daniël du Toit), who delighted in the use of their new language, helped to establish Afrikaans as the *lingua franca*. Later writers such as P G du Plessis and Etienne Le Roux placed Afrikaans literature in a wider context, while Adam Small and Breyten Breytenbach used it as a form of political and social protest against the white Afrikaner establishment.

"Afrikanerisms", deliberate use of Afrikaans words and sentence construction when writing in English, is a literary device used in Pauline Smith's *The Beadle*, and in Herman Charles Bosman's humorous short story *A Cask of Jerepigo* (1991). Both works describe the

Jock of the Bushveld statue in the Kruger National Park

life, joys and hardships of a rural Afrikaner community.

Afrikaans became a hated symbol of oppression during the apartheid years yet today, it is more widely spoken than any other local tongue.

English Poetry and Prose

Olive Schreiner's *The Story of an African Farm* (1883), first published under a male pseudonym, presented the rural Afrikaner to an international audience for the first time. The book was startling, also, for its advanced views on feminism – sentiments that the author expanded on in *Woman and Labour* (1911).

Percy FitzPatrick's *Jock of the Bushveld* (1907) became one of the best-known of all South African titles. A blend of romantic adventure and realism, it tells the story of a transport rider and his dog on the early gold fields.

Later popular authors who achieved international sales include Geoffrey Jenkins and Wilbur Smith, whose novels, such as *When the Lion Feeds* (1964), have made him one of the world's best-selling writers. A more thought-provoking book is Stuart Cloete's *The Abductors* (1966), once banned in South Africa, and Sir Laurens van der Post's touching description of a dying culture in *Testament to the Bushmen* (1984).

The works of André Brink and J M Coetzee deal mainly with social and political matters and were often viewed by the apartheid regime as attacks on the establishment. Brink's critical *Looking on Darkness* (1963) became the first Afrikaans novel to be banned in South Africa.

The 1924 publication of *The Flaming Terrapin* established Roy Campbell as a leading poet. Although the hardships of black South Africans had been highlighted in Herbert Dhlomo's short stories and Peter Abrahams' *Mine Boy* (1946), it was the subject matter of race relations in *Cry, the Beloved Country* (1948) by Alan Paton that attracted the world's attention.

As one of several superb female writers, Nadine Gordimer – *A Sport of Nature* (1988) and *July's People* (1981) among others – became the recipient of a Nobel Prize for Literature in 1991. The author contributed greatly to the standard of writing in South Africa, and her struggle against another of the apartheid era's crippling laws – censorship – paved the way for many others. Rose Zwi's *Another Year in Africa* (1980) is

Local edition of *A Sport of Nature*

an insight into the life of South Africa's Jewish immigrants, while the autobiographical *To My Children's Children* (2006) is Sindiwe Magona's account of a youth spent in the former homeland of Transkei, and of the daily struggle in Cape Town's townships.

Contemporary Literature

Autobiographies and travelogues, popular genres for modern local writers, offer insights into the lives of South Africans. Nelson Mandela's *Long Walk to Freedom* (1995) was a national bestseller. *Country of My Skull* (1998) is Antjie Krog's narrative of her two years spent reporting on the Truth and Reconciliation Commission, while *Beckett's Trek* and *Madibaland* (1998) by Denis Beckett, and Sarah Penny's *The Whiteness of Bones* (1997) are entertaining jaunts through South Africa and its neighbours. Zakes Mda's award-winning *Ways of Dying* (2002) gives the reader a glimpse of the professional mourner, while Ashraf Jamal's *Love Themes for the Wilderness* (1997) takes a life-affirming trip into contemporary urbanity.

Struggle Poetry

During the apartheid years, conflict and the repression of Africans provided recurring themes. Produced orally in various Bantu tongues and in written form in English, the new means of expression was termed "Struggle Poetry". Oswald Mtshali's *Sounds of a Cowhide Drum* (1971) signalled the shift in black poetry from lyrical themes to indirect political messages in free verse. Other creators of this form of protest were Mzwakhe Mbuli, known as "the people's poet", Mafika Gwala, James Matthews, Sipho Sepamla, Njabulo Ndebele and Mongane Wally Serote. Their verse expressed disapproval of the socio-political conditions in the country and was, at the same time, a conscious attempt to raise the level of awareness among their people.

Mongane Wally Serote, poet and politician

South African Architecture

Diverse factors have influenced building styles in South Africa: climate, social structure, and the state of the economy have all shaped the country's homes. In earlier days, when suitable raw materials were often unavailable, ingenious adaptations resulted. Variations include the *hartbeeshuisie* (hard-reed house), a pitched-roof shelter built directly on the ground, and the beehive-shaped "corbelled" huts, built of stone in areas where structural timber was unobtainable, as in the Northern Cape. Modern South African building and engineering skills have kept up-to-date with international trends, and many different styles can be seen throughout the country.

Weaving the reed fence surrounding a traditional Swazi village

Indigenous Architectural Styles

Most traditional rural dwellings, often called "rondavels", are circular in shape. The conical roofs are traditionally constructed of a tightly woven reed or grass thatch, while the walls may be made of mud blocks mixed with cow dung, or consist of a framework of woven branches, covered with animal hide. Most of these homes, except the *matjieshuise* of the arid Namaqualand nomads for whom rain was no threat, are well insulated and waterproof. In recent times, materials like corrugated iron, plastic sheeting and cardboard have become popular, especially in informal settlements on the outskirts of cities.

Zulu "beehives" are a community effort. The stick framework is erected by the men, and the women thatch it.

The *matjieshuise* (houses made of mats) of Khoina nomads consisted of portable hide or reed mats on a stick frame.

Xhosa huts are built of mud. The circular type shown here has largely been replaced by rectangular patterns.

A capping of clay covers the ridge of the roof to keep the thatch in place.

The thatch is made of sheaves of grass or reed.

Windows and decorations are symmetrically placed around the door.

Wall designs are hand-painted.

Low outside wall

Ndebele homes are, perhaps, the most eye-catching local style. The walls of the rectangular structures are traditionally painted by women, using bright primary colours. No stencils are used for the bold geometric motifs.

Ndebele wall detail

Basotho huts, originally circular, are built of blocks of turf, mud or stone, and plastered with mud. In rural areas, walls are still decorated with pebbles, but the use of paint is spreading.

Cape Dutch Architecture

The vernacular of the Western Cape, recognized by its symmetrical design and prominent gables, evolved around the mid-18th century from a simple row of thatched rooms whose sizes depended on the length of the available beams. The forms of the gables were derived from the Baroque architecture of Holland. End gables prevented the roof from being torn off by high winds, while the centre gable let light into the attic.

Gable of Franschhoek Town Hall

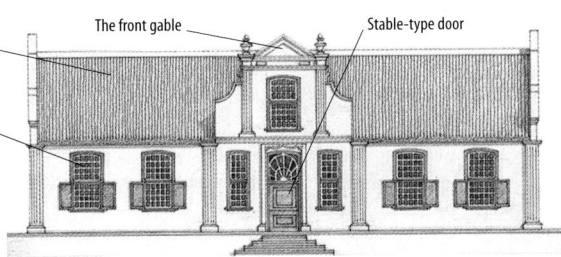

Thatching reed was widely available in the *vleis* (swamps).

The front gable

Sash windows had many small panes, and only the lower half could be opened.

Rhone, near Franschhoek, is a good example of an 18th-century homestead. The front gable dates back to 1795.

Stable-type door

Georgian Architecture

Modest examples of 18th-century Georgian-style architecture, with plain front pediments and flat roofs, survive along the narrow, cobbled streets of Cape Town's Bo-Kaap, or "Malay Quarter".

The neighbourhood of Artificers' Square in Grahamstown also has fine examples. Here, the houses display typical many-paned, sliding sash windows, plain parapets and a fanlight above the entrance.

Geometric brick detail

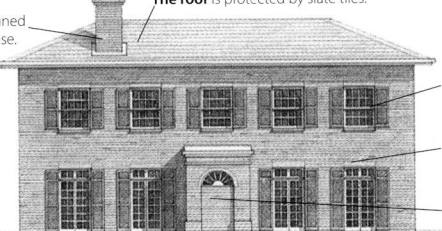

The chimney was designed to complement the house.

The roof is protected by slate tiles.

Bertram House, completed in 1839, is Cape Town's only surviving brick Georgian house.

Louvre shutters reduce the harsh glare of the sun.

Precise brick-laying adds attractive detail.

The wind lobby excludes draughts.

Victorian Architecture

The romantic Victorian style with its decorative cast-iron detail, brass fittings and stained-glass windows became extremely popular, especially in Cape Town, around the turn of the 19th century. Here, too, terrace housing, pioneered in 18th-century England by the Adam Brothers, provided affordable housing for a burgeoning middle class. Fine examples may be seen in suburbs such as Woodstock, Observatory, Mowbray and Wynberg.

Broekie lace detail, Prince Albert

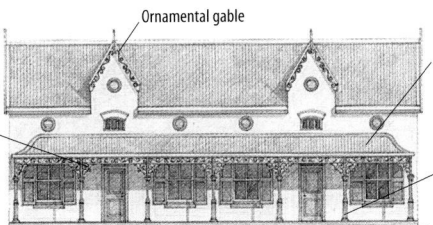

Cast-iron decorations were called *broekie* lace, because they resembled the lacy edging of ladies' undergarments.

Ornamental gable

A corrugated iron awning covers the verandah.

Oom Samie se Winkel (see p196), in Stellenbosch, displays a marked Cape Dutch influence. The porch encouraged the store's patrons to linger.

Cast-iron supports hold up the awning.

Multicultural South Africa

The South African nation is composed of a medley of different beliefs and cultures. Early influences, such as the languages and religions of slaves from India, Madagascar, Indonesia, West and East Africa and Malaysia, are preserved by their descendants. South Africa's mineral wealth attracted settlers from other parts of Africa, as well as Asia, America and Europe – heritages still reflected in today's faces. Most coloured people live in the former slave-owning Western Cape area, while many Indians live around Durban, where their ancestors worked on sugar plantations.

Weaving is an important skill, and many Sotho, Xhosa and Tswana wear patterned or sombre ochre blankets as over-garments. In the northerly parts of the Limpopo Province live the Venda, with a tradition, unusual in South Africa, of building in stone. The Venda is one of the few groups that traditionally used a drum as a musical instrument. Wood sculptures by leading Venda artists are treasured pieces.

Very few San still hunt and live in the traditional way

The Khoi

Khoi rock paintings, often found in caves overlooking the plains below, offer tantalizing evidence of the practical skills and the spiritual nature of the people who were almost certainly South Africa's original human inhabitants (see Drakensberg, pp274–5 and Kagga Kamma, p218.) Many were hunter-gatherers, living lightly on the natural bounty of the land.

Under pressure from more material cultures, some Khoi withdrew inland, where their descendants, the San (once widely called the Bushmen, a term not used today), are still found in the Northern Cape.

Other Khoi eventually threw in their lot with the Dutch settlers. Many of today's Cape Coloured people are descended from them.

The Bantu-Speakers

The Bantu languages are indigenous to Africa, although not related to those of the Khoi. Each group has its own complex system of cultures and relationships, although Westernized culture is replacing many of the older, traditional ways. Cattle and cattle pens (kraals) have an important place in Zulu, Xhosa and Ndebele cultures, and Zulu handicrafts include works in earthenware, iron and wood. Basket-making and weaving are other skills. The Xhosa, most of whom live in the Eastern Cape, are known for their beautifully designed and executed beadwork. The Ndebele of the Limpopo Province and Gauteng are renowned for their remarkably colourful and intricate beadwork, and their decorative painting applied to buildings is particularly eye-catching.

The Wartburger Hof Hotel in KwaZulu-Natal looks like an alpine lodge

The European Colonists

The first European settlers, in 1652, were Dutch and German. European politics further affected the composition of the Cape population, when French Huguenots were settled here from 1688, and French and German regiments were periodically brought in to boost the local defences against Britain. The British, however, took permanent possession of the Cape in 1806 and, during the depression

Xhosa women in the Eastern Cape

that followed the Napoleonic Wars, dispatched several thousand settlers to farm in the Eastern Cape. More (pro-British) German settlers arrived after the Crimean War, and many British ex-soldiers elected to stay in South Africa, or returned to it, after the South African War of 1899–1902 and the World Wars. The British custom of a hot Christmas dinner, for example, prevails in many quarters, despite its unsuitability in the local climate.

Franschhoek, near Cape Town, retains some of the atmosphere of a French wine-growing region, while Eastern Cape villages settled by Germans still carry the names of German cities, such as Berlin and Hamburg.

Women in traditional costume at an Afrikaner festival

Asian Origins

East Indian islanders who opposed Dutch colonization of their territory in the 17th and 18th centuries were banished to the Cape of Good Hope. Slaves imported from Indonesia and the Indian subcontinent swelled the size of the oppressed minority. Nearly all of them belonged to the Islamic faith, while many others converted.

During the 19th century, thousands of indentured Indians worked in the sugar cane fields of KwaZulu-Natal, and elected to stay on at the end of their contract. In Kwa-Zulu-Natal, Cape Town and Gauteng, the striking Eastern mosques and temples are a noteworthy architectural feature. Religious festivals are regularly observed, and the bustling oriental markets yield a treasure trove of spices, jewellery and handicrafts.

Afrikaners

The term "Afrikaner" was first recorded in 1706, and referred to a South African-born, Afrikaans- (or Dutch-) speaking white person. In more recent times, however, just the first-language use of Afrikaans has become the identifying factor. Afrikaner men are often associated with a love for outdoor sport (especially rugby) and a passion for the *braai* (barbecue).

The tunes delivered by a *Boere-orkes* (literally, a "farmers' band") are played on concertina, banjo, piano, accordion and fiddles, and bear great similarity to North American "country" music.

The Coloured People

The term "Cape Coloured" has been in use for almost two centuries to define members of what is sometimes called "the only truly indigenous population".

Many of these people are descended from relationships between settlers, slaves and local tribes, and many slave names survive in the form of surnames such as

Temple dancing is still being taught in Durban

Januarie, November, Titus, Appollis, Cupido and Adonis.

The most skilled fishermen, livery men and artisans were traditionally found in the Asian and Coloured communities, and many of the Cape's beautiful historic buildings were created by them.

A young Muslim girl prepares flower decorations for a festival

From All Quarters

Compared with countries such as the United States and Australia, South Africa offered little scope for unskilled or semi-skilled labour from Europe. However, small but steady numbers of immigrants did arrive, especially from Eastern European countries such as Bulgaria, Poland and the former Yugoslavia.

South Africa has citizens from Italy, Greece, Portugal and the Netherlands, as well as Jewish communities. Thanks to its climate and good standard of living, Cape Town in particular has seen a growth of European expatriates. The city is a popular place to live, particularly with British and German retirees.

Sport in South Africa

Given the country's favourable climate, sport plays a major role in the lives of many South Africans. In recent years, generous government funding and corporate sponsorship have resulted in the development of sporting facilities in the previously disadvantaged communities, encouraging much as yet unexplored talent. Sports events that are held in the major centres take place in world-class stadiums with superb facilities. Seats for the important matches are offered through Computicket *(see p415)*, while those for lesser events are obtainable directly at the respective venues.

Football attracts spectators from all sectors of South African society

Football

Football is played all over South Africa, in dusty township streets and in the elite professional clubs. Except for the hottest summer months (Dec–Feb), it is played year-round. The most popular clubs attract huge spectator and fan followings, and can easily fill 80,000-seat stadiums for top matches. The Premier Football League, made up of 16 clubs, is the top level football league in South Africa.

The national football team, known as Bafana Bafana, returned to the world stage in 1992 after years of being banned from FIFA during apartheid. Initially it did well in the African Cup of Nations, winning the contest in 1995 and reaching the finals in 1998. In 2010, South Africa became the first African nation to host the FIFA World Cup. However, despite the tournament being a great success for South Africa, Bafana Bafana failed to progress beyond the first round.

Rugby Union

Rugby is played at all levels – from school to regional club, and from provincial to national stage.

Teams from the 14 provincial unions contest the Currie Cup every season. These 14 unions supply players to the five regional teams that fight for victory in the Super 15, an international and regional tournament involving South Africa, as well as Australia and New Zealand.

South Africa's national team, the Springboks, rank as one of the world's best, and consistently do well in tournaments against the various rugby-playing nations.

In 1995 and 2007, South Africa won the Rugby World Cup (contested every four years). The local rugby season begins in early February, continuing through the winter months and ending in late October with the Currie Cup Finals *(see p40)*.

Cricket

South Africa has long been a major force in the world of cricket. Played during the summer months, cricket is a sport enjoyed by thousands of players and spectators at various levels, from club and provincial competitions to international test matches.

Development programmes have discovered great talent among the youth of once-disadvantaged communities.

Four-day provincial games and the more popular one-day matches are held, while five-day tests are contested between South Africa and visiting national teams. One-day and day/night limited-overs international and provincial matches are particularly popular, usually playing to packed stands.

The demand for tickets to these games is high, and advance booking is available through Computicket outlets countrywide, or from the cricket union hosting the match.

Rugby games attract crowds of up to 50,000 to the provincial stadiums

The Two Oceans Marathon takes place on Easter Saturday

Marathons and Ultra-Marathons

Long-distance running is both a popular pastime and a serious national sport. The strenuous 56-km (35-mile) Two Oceans Marathon, which takes place around the Cape Peninsula on Easter Saturday, and the energy-sapping 85-km (53-mile) long Comrades Marathon, run between the KwaZulu-Natal cities of Durban and Pieter-maritzburg in June, are two of the most difficult, yet popular, ultra-marathons in the country. Both events attract thousands of international and local entrants.

With its excellent training facilities and fine summer weather, South Africa is a popular place for European athletes to train during the winter months in Europe – especially at high-altitude venues in the country's interior.

Golf

South Africa boasts some of the finest golf courses in the world, and has also produced some of the world's finest golfers. The golfing prowess of Gary Player is legendary, while Ernie Els and Trevor Immelman rank among the top golfers in the world. Each December, Sun City hosts the Nedbank Golf Challenge (see p41), where 12 contestants compete for the largest prize in the world – 1.25 million dollars. The South African Golf Tour attracts professional golfers from around the globe.

Two popular local events are the South African Open, held in January, and the Alfred Dunhill PGA, held in December.

Cycling

Apart from various local professional events, the Cape Peninsula hosts the largest timed cycle race in the world, the annual Cape Argus Pick 'n Pay Cycle Tour. Over 35,000 enthusiasts, some costumed, race or trundle 105 km (65 miles) around the Peninsula on the second Sunday in March. About one-third of the contestants are from overseas. The Cape Town Cycle Tour MTB Challenge is run in the same week on a Stellenbosch wine estate. Other popular races include the Absa Cape Epic, an 8-day mountain bike stage race held in the Western Cape, usually in March. Covering more than 700 km (435 miles), it attracts amateurs and professionals, in teams of two, from around the world.

Equestrian Sports

Horse racing, until recently the only legal form of gambling in the country, has been an enormous industry for many years. The "Met" (Metropolitan Stakes), held in Cape Town in January, and the Durban July are major social events, with fashion and high stakes the order of the day. Show jumping and horse trials attract crowds every spring to venues such as Inanda near Johannesburg.

The Cape 2 Rio race leaves Table Bay with huge fanfare

Water Sports

Flanked by two oceans, South Africa enjoys a climate that allows for water sports all year. Surfing is very popular; the Mr Price Pro surfing event, held in Ballito in July, is a major draw. Cape Town is a popular port of call for round-the-world yacht races, and is also the starting point for the Cape 2 Rio event that takes place early in January every three years.

Sun City's Golf Course hosts the Nedbank Golf Challenge

SOUTH AFRICA THROUGH THE YEAR

There are many festivals and events in South Africa, which are generally well organized and attract enthusiastic crowds. South Africans love a good get-together, and while the long, sunny days of summer provide the perfect environment for outdoor celebrations, there is still plenty going on in the cooler months, both inside and out. Cities, towns and villages host festivals to mark a variety of occasions: the start of the oyster and wildflower seasons; the citrus, apple or grape harvest; even the arrival of the southern right whale from its Arctic breeding grounds – all are cause for celebration. The arts, music, religion, language and sport also take their places on the calendar of events.

Spring

All across the country, but especially noticeable in the semiarid Western and Northern Cape regions, the onset of warmer weather raises colourful fields of wildflowers. In wildlife reserves throughout South Africa, the newborn of various species will soon be seen.

September

Arts Alive *(Sep)*, Johannesburg *(see pp314–15)*. An exciting urban arts festival, with performers ranging from world-class musicians to children eager to show off the skills they have acquired at the workshops.
Wildflower Show *(late Sep)*, Darling *(see p215)*. The show displays the unique West Coast flora and cultivated orchids.

Whale Festival *(last week in Sep)*, Hermanus *(see p226–7)*. From early spring onwards, southern right whales and their calves can be seen close to shore in and around Walker Bay.
Prince Albert Agricultural Show *(Sep)*, Prince Albert *(see p231)*. The Southern Cape village proudly celebrates its agricultural heritage with a show featuring arts and crafts, horse displays, food stalls and entertainment.
Kalahari Kuierfees *(Sep)*, Upington *(see p372)*. Music, choir contests and fun on the Orange River.
Magoebaskloof Haenertsburg Spring Festival *(Sep–Oct)*, Magoebaskloof. A bustling arts, crafts and entertainment fair, held in a forest setting.

Orchids from Darling

October

Currie Cup Finals *(late Oct)*, Rugby match between the two best provincial teams. The location varies from year to year.
Macufe (Mangaung Cultural African Festival) *(Oct)*, Bloemfontein *(see pp376–7)*. Jazz, gospel, kwaito and classical music, plus drama, comedy and arts and crafts.
Bosman Weekend *(Oct)*, Groot Marico. A celebration of writer Herman Charles Bosman in the town where many of his stories are set.
Rocking the Daisies *(Oct)*, Darling *(see p215)*. A popular music festival showcasing top South African bands, as well as comedy, children's entertainment, wine tastings and a food and craft market.
Durban Diwali Festival *(Oct)*, Durban *(see pp286–9)*. The 3-day Hindu festival of lights, with classical Indian dancing, a float parade and fireworks.

November

Cherry Festival *(third week in Nov)*, Ficksburg. Celebrates South Africa's commercially-grown cherries and asparagus.
National Choir Festival *(Nov–Dec)*, Inkosi Albert Luthuli International Convention Centre, Durban *(see pp286–9)*. The culmination of a national competition.

The Oude Libertas open-air amphitheatre

Summer

Most tourists visit South Africa during the long summer months. The local long school holidays extend from December well into January. With many South African families traditionally heading for the seaside and wildlife reserves, this is when the roads are at their busiest. Summer is a season spent outdoors. Christmas lunch is more likely to be celebrated around an informal *braai* (barbecue) than at a dining table. Over much of the country, summer rain arrives in the form of short, noisy thunder showers.

The fiercely contested Dusi Canoe Marathon, Pietermaritzburg

Crowds at a concert in Cape Town

December
Carols by Candlelight
(pre-Christmas). Advent celebrations in the botanical gardens of the large cities.
Somerset West Festival of Lights *(Dec)*, Somerset West. Main Street display of festive lights combined with an evening Christmas market.
Kirstenbosch Summer Concerts, *(every Sun, Dec–Mar)* Kirstenbosch National Botanical Garden, Cape Town *(see pp164–5)*. Picnic on the lawns to music from rock and jazz to classical and opera.
Nedbank Golf Challenge, Sun City *(see p326)*. An internationally renowned golfing event with 12 of the world's best golfers.

January
Maynardville Open-Air Theatre *(Jan–Feb)*, Wynberg, Cape Town *(see p171)*. Shakespeare and ballet in a city park.
Oude Libertas Arts Programme *(Jan–Mar)*, Stellenbosch *(see pp196–7)*. Performances in an elegant amphitheatre.
Kaapse Klopse *(2 Jan)*, Cape Town. A colourful musical and minstrel procession that culminates in concerts at Cape Town Stadium.
J&B Metropolitan Handicap *(last Sat in Jan)*, Kenilworth Race Course, Cape Town. South Africa's major horse-racing meet is equally popular for its fashion and social activities.

February
FNB Dance Umbrella *(Feb–Mar)*, Braamfontein, Johannesburg *(see pp314–5)*. One of South Africa's most important dance events.

Dusi Canoe Marathon *(second week in Feb)*, Pietermaritzburg *(see pp280–81)*. This gruelling three-day canoe marathon to the mouth of the Umgeni River attracts more than 2,000 participants.
Up the Creek *(Feb)*, Breede River, near Swellendam *(see pp230–31)*. A four-day music festival with events on three stages set up on the banks of the Breede River.
Cape Town Pride *(last weekend in Feb)*, Cape Town. Colourful floats and a parade along Somerset Road in Green Point culminate in a street party in De Waterkant at this gay event.
Prickly Pear Festival *(Feb–Mar)*, Uitenhage, Port Elizabeth *(see pp250–53)*. A celebration of traditional South African food, such as *braais*, *potjiekos* (stews made in three-legged, cast-iron pots), ginger beer and bunny chow (curry served in a half-loaf of bread).

Cape Town's minstrels are a colourful sight in early January

Autumn

When deciduous trees and grapevines begin to shed their leaves, a new round of country fairs is ushered in. The harvest festivals of many small towns celebrate crops such as potatoes and olives – even sheep and gems are cause for cheerful get-togethers. A number of wine festivals are held, from Paarl in the fertile Western Cape to Kuruman in the arid Northern Cape.

March

Cape Town Carnival (second weekend in Mar), Cape Town. Rio-style carnival with parades of colourful floats, music and street parties.
Rand Show (Mar–Apr), Johannesburg (see pp314–15). What began as an agricultural show has become a blend of entertainment and consumerism.
Lambert's Bay Kreeffees (Mar), Lambert's Bay (see pp214–15). Kreef is Afrikaans for crayfish, and fees means both festival and feast. Stalls sell West Coast seafood, and there are also live bands.
Cape Town International Jazz Festival (late Mar), Cape Town (see pp124–47). A two-day affair featuring nearly 40 international and African acts performing on five stages. The musical extravaganza is accompanied by photographic and art shows.

More than a million followers of the Zionist Church gather at Easter

April

Zionist Church gathering (Easter), near Polokwane (formerly Pietersburg, see p338) in the Limpopo Province. More than a million followers of this African Christian church gather at Moria (also known as Zion City) over the Easter weekend; it is the largest Christian gathering in South Africa.
Fire-walking (Easter), Umbilo Hindu Temple, Durban. Devout Hindus, after careful spiritual preparation, walk uninjured across a bed of red-hot coals.

Devotee at a Hindu temple

Two Oceans Marathon (Easter), Cape Town. This 56-km (35-mile) marathon (see p39) around the Cape Peninsula is a qualifying race for the Comrades' Marathon.
Klein Karoo Arts Festival (Apr), Oudtshoorn (see p232). A mainly Afrikaans cultural festival.
Prince Albert Olive, Food & Wine Festival (Apr), Prince Albert (see p231). Live music, a cycle race, and an olive-stone spitting competition, plus plenty of food and wine tasting.
Splashy Fen Music Festival (last weekend in Apr), Splashy Fen Farm, Underberg, Kwa-Zulu-Natal. A popular festival with performances in main-stream, alternative, folk and traditional music styles.
Pink Loerie Mardi Gras (Apr–May), Knysna (see p244). A four-day gay festival, with charity-led events, exhibitions and food stalls.

May

Calitzdorp Port and Wine Festival (May), Karoo (see p234). A celebration of the region's famous port-style wine.
Franschhoek Literary Festival (third weekend in May), Franschhoek (see p204–5). A community library fund-raising showcase for the best local talent, as well as international authors.

Amusement park at the Rand Show in Johannesburg

Winter

This is the dry season for most of the country; only the winter rainfall area along the southwestern and Southern Cape coast is lush and green at this time. Inland, days are typically warm, although nightly frosts are common in high-lying areas. Snowfall occurs on the mountains of the Western and Eastern Cape and in the KwaZulu-Natal and Lesotho highlands. Late winter is particularly good for game-watching, as the thirsty wildlife gathers around waterholes.

Safari wildlife-viewing drive at Sabi Sabi, Mpumalanga

June

Comrades Marathon (mid-Jun), between Durban and Pietermaritzburg. This ultra-long-distance running event attracts top-class runners from all over the world (see p39).

July

Dullstroom Winter Festival (first weekend in Jul), Dullstroom (see p334). A delightful Christmas-in-winter themed event with restaurant evenings, chocolate, whisky and wine tasting, and a trout fly-fishing competition.

National Arts Festival (early to mid-Jul), Grahamstown (see pp256–7). An extremely popular two weeks of local and international drama, film, dance, visual arts and music.

July Handicap (first Sat in Jul), Greyville Race Course, Durban (see pp286–9). This is the glamour event of the Durban horse-racing fraternity.

Knysna Oyster Festival (early Jul), Knysna (see p244–5). The festival, centred on the commercial oyster beds in Knysna Lagoon, coincides with a forest marathon.

High fashion, July Handicap

Knysna oyster

Berg River Canoe Marathon (Jul), Paarl (see pp206–7). This strenuous four-day canoe race provides some high excitement. It is staged annually when the river is in full flood.

The Ballito Pro Presented by Billabong (see pp264–5) (mid-Jul), Ballito (see p296). This popular week-long surfing championship attracts the world's best surfers and hordes of spectators.

Mercedes-Benz Fashion Week (third weekend in Jul), Cape Town. Awash with glamour, this introduces the spring and summer collections of South Africa's top designers.

August

Standard Bank Joy of Jazz (Aug), Johannesburg (see pp314–15). Jazz festival with local and international acts.

Hantam Vleisfees, (last weekend in Aug), Calvinia. Located in the Northern Cape, Calvinia is sheep country. This festival is a celebration of lamb in all its forms: stewed, curried or grilled. The three-day event also offers music concerts, a vintage car rally, and the glittering Miss Vleisfees competition.

Oppikoppi Bushveld Festival (Aug), Northam/Limpopo, north of Sun City. Alternative rock festival.

Public Holidays

New Year's Day (1 Jan)
Human Rights Day (21 Mar)
Good Friday (Apr)
Family Day (Apr)
Freedom Day (27 Apr)
Workers' Day (1 May)
Youth Day (16 Jun)
National Women's Day (9 Aug)
Heritage Day (24 Sep)
Day of Reconciliation (16 Dec)
Christmas Day (25 Dec)
Day of Goodwill (26 Dec)

Performers at the National Arts Festival, Grahamstown

The Climate of South Africa

Situated halfway between the Equator and the Antarctic, South Africa has a temperate climate with short-term exceptions in certain locations. Day temperatures can soar to 50°C (122°F) over low-lying coastal plains in summer, and drop to -16°C (3°F) during a winter's night over the higher plateau areas. Rainfall increases from west to east. The most popular time of year to visit South Africa is during the summer months, from December to February, but winter days are sunny and cool and best for game-viewing.

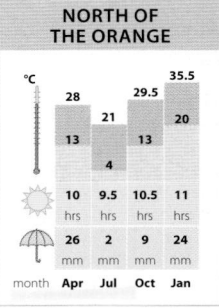

NORTH OF THE ORANGE

°C				
	28	21	29.5	35.5
	13	13		20
		4		
	10 hrs	9.5 hrs	10.5 hrs	11 hrs
	26 mm	2 mm	9 mm	24 mm
month	**Apr**	**Jul**	**Oct**	**Jan**

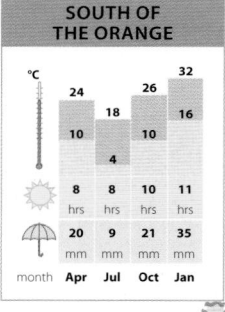

SOUTH OF THE ORANGE

°C				
	24	18	26	32
	10		10	16
		4		
	8 hrs	8 hrs	10 hrs	11 hrs
	20 mm	9 mm	21 mm	35 mm
month	**Apr**	**Jul**	**Oct**	**Jan**

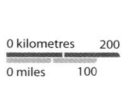

0 kilometres	200
0 miles	100

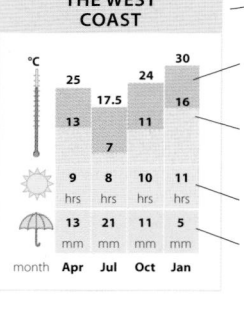

THE WEST COAST

°C				
	25	17.5	24	30
	13	11	11	16
		7		
	9 hrs	8 hrs	10 hrs	11 hrs
	13 mm	21 mm	11 mm	5 mm
month	**Apr**	**Jul**	**Oct**	**Jan**

Average monthly maximum temperature

Average monthly minimum temperature

Average daily hours of sunshine

Average monthly rainfall

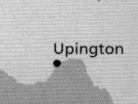

Upington

Springbok

Beaufort West

Langebaan

Worcester

Cape Town • Stellenbosch

Knysn

Riversdale

Moss

Bay

CAPE TOWN

°C				
	23	21		26
	12	17.5	10.5	16
		7		
	8 hrs	6 hrs	9 hrs	11 hrs
	41 mm	82 mm	30 mm	15 mm
month	**Apr**	**Jul**	**Oct**	**Jan**

THE CAPE WINELANDS

°C				
	25	18	24	31
	13	11	11	16.5
		7.5		
	7 hrs	6 hrs	9 hrs	11 hrs
	47 mm	90 mm	40 mm	18 mm
month	**Apr**	**Jul**	**Oct**	**Jan**

THE SOUTHERN CAPE

°C				
	25	19	23	28
	12	11	11	16
		6		
	6 hrs	6 hrs	6.5 hrs	8 hrs
	53 mm	34 mm	48 mm	27 mm
month	**Apr**	**Jul**	**Oct**	**Jan**

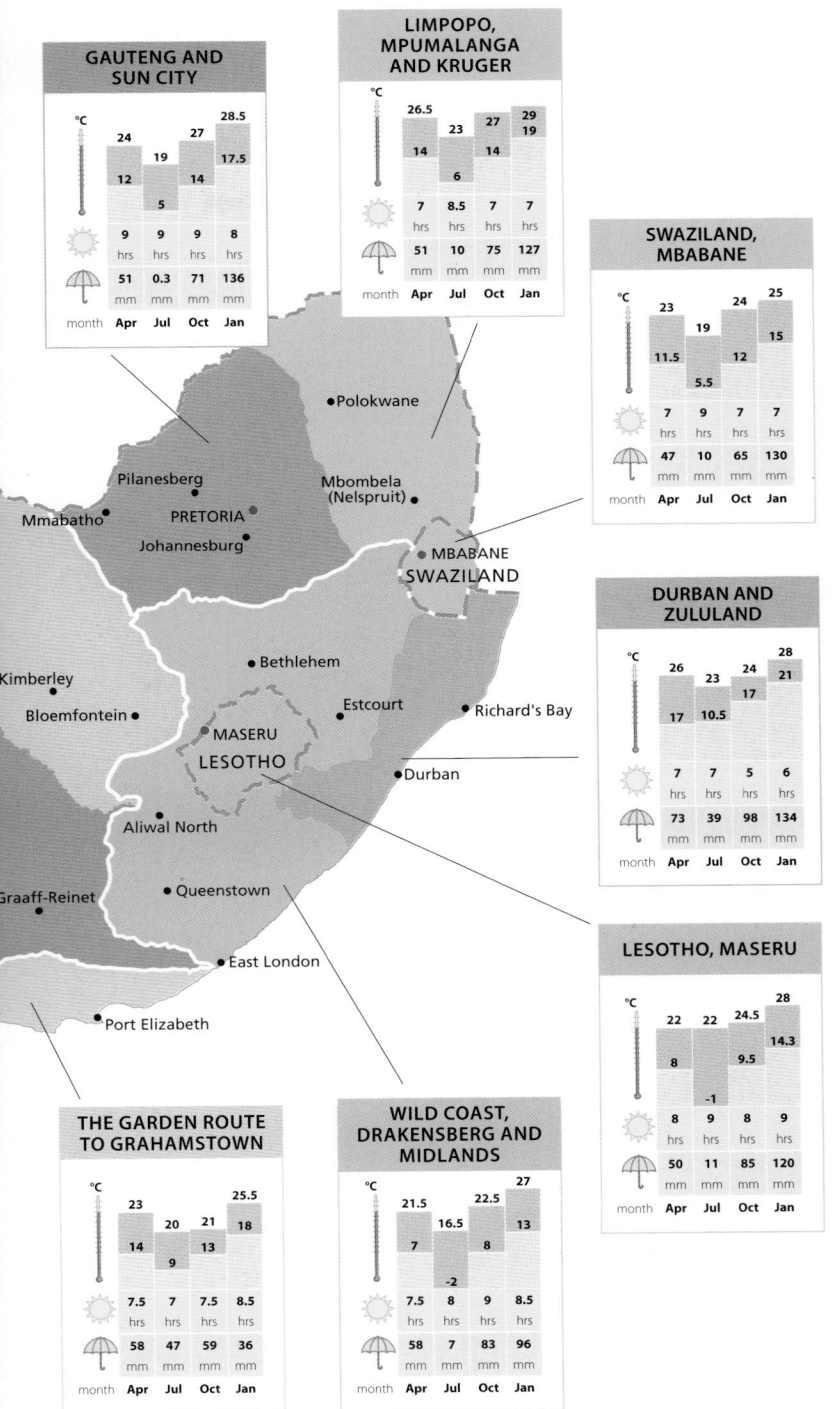

GAUTENG AND SUN CITY

°C				
	24	19	27	28.5
	12	5	14	17.5
☀	9 hrs	9 hrs	9 hrs	8 hrs
☂	51 mm	0.3 mm	71 mm	136 mm
month	Apr	Jul	Oct	Jan

LIMPOPO, MPUMALANGA AND KRUGER

°C				
	26.5	23	27	29
	14	6	14	19
☀	7 hrs	8.5 hrs	7 hrs	7 hrs
☂	51 mm	10 mm	75 mm	127 mm
month	Apr	Jul	Oct	Jan

SWAZILAND, MBABANE

°C				
	23	19	24	25
	11.5	5.5	12	15
☀	7 hrs	9 hrs	7 hrs	7 hrs
☂	47 mm	10 mm	65 mm	130 mm
month	Apr	Jul	Oct	Jan

DURBAN AND ZULULAND

°C				
	26	23	24	28
	17	10.5	17	21
☀	7 hrs	7 hrs	5 hrs	6 hrs
☂	73 mm	39 mm	98 mm	134 mm
month	Apr	Jul	Oct	Jan

LESOTHO, MASERU

°C				
	22	22	24.5	28
	8	-1	9.5	14.3
☀	8 hrs	9 hrs	8 hrs	9 hrs
☂	50 mm	11 mm	85 mm	120 mm
month	Apr	Jul	Oct	Jan

Polokwane
Pilanesberg
Mmabatho
PRETORIA
Johannesburg
Mbombela (Nelspruit)
MBABANE
SWAZILAND
Kimberley
Bethlehem
Estcourt
Richard's Bay
Bloemfontein
MASERU
LESOTHO
Durban
Aliwal North
Queenstown
Graaff-Reinet
East London
Port Elizabeth

THE GARDEN ROUTE TO GRAHAMSTOWN

°C				
	23	20	21	25.5
	14	9	13	18
☀	7.5 hrs	7 hrs	7.5 hrs	8.5 hrs
☂	58 mm	47 mm	59 mm	36 mm
month	Apr	Jul	Oct	Jan

WILD COAST, DRAKENSBERG AND MIDLANDS

°C				
	21.5	16.5	22.5	27
	7	-2	8	13
☀	7.5 hrs	8 hrs	9 hrs	8.5 hrs
☂	58 mm	7 mm	83 mm	96 mm
month	Apr	Jul	Oct	Jan

THE HISTORY OF SOUTH AFRICA

The ancient footprints discovered at Langebaan, casts of which are now in the South African Museum in Cape Town, were made 117,000 years ago. They are the world's oldest traces of anatomically modern man, *Homo sapiens sapiens*. Other early hominid remains found at the Sterkfontein caves in Gauteng and at Taung near Bloemfontein belong to the group known as *Australopithecus africanus*.

African and European civilizations drifted towards a cultural collision when the Dutch East India Company set up a refreshment station in Table Bay. The year was 1652, and the colonizers had come not just to visit, but to stay. On the whole, the Dutch sought to establish amicable relationships with the local Khoi, but the inability to understand one another doomed many attempts, and the pattern of relations over the subsequent centuries was set. Rivalry over water and grazing soon turned into open hostility, first around the bay and then further inland as Dutch "burghers" sought new land. Isolated clashes with indigenous groups escalated into the bitter frontier wars of the 18th and 19th centuries, a situation further aggravated by the arrival of the 1820 British settlers. Although outnumbered, the settlers' muskets, cannons and horses were an advantage that led to a prevailing sense of white supremacy, with both colonial and republican governments denying people of colour their rights.

Ironically, it was the exploitation of black labour in the mines of Kimberley and Johannesburg that ignited the spark of African nationalism, while the segregation and, later, apartheid laws of the mid-20th century focused world attention and pressure on South Africa. The release of Nelson Mandela in 1990 was the beginning of a transformation that set the country on a new course: the road to democracy.

This surprisingly accurate map was produced in 1570 by Abraham Ortelius from Antwerp

◀ Ancient San paintings adorn many rock walls like this one in the Cederberg, Western Cape

Prehistoric South Africa

Some 2–3 million years ago, long after the dinosaurs, *Australopithecus africanus* inhabited South Africa's plains. Australopithecines were the ancestors of anatomically modern people whose remains in South Africa date at least as far back as 110,000 years. Rock art created by San hunter-gatherers over the past 10,000 years is widely distributed. Some 2,000 years ago, pastoral Khoi migrated southwestward, while black farming communities settled the eastern side of the country. Their descendants were encountered by the 15th-century Portuguese explorers.

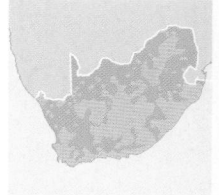

Early Man
Distribution in South Africa

0 km 100
0 miles 100

Australopithecus Africanus
In 1925, Professor Raymond Dart, then dean of the University of the Witwatersrand's medical faculty, first identified man's ancestor based on the evidence of a skull found near Taung, North West Province.

Langebaan Footprints
Homo sapiens tracks at Langebaan Lagoon are around 117,000 years old. They are the world's oldest fossilized trail of anatomically modern human beings.

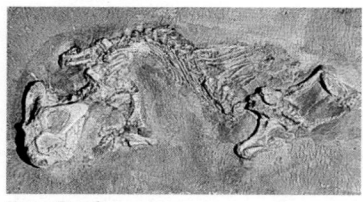

Karoo Fossils
Diictodon skeletons found in the Karoo *(see p360)* belonged to mammal-like reptiles that tunnelled into the mud along river banks some 255 million years ago.

Cradle of Humankind

Based on the evidence of fossilized remains from the Sterkfontein caves (see p322) and other sites in South and East Africa, palaeontologists believe that humans evolved in Africa. Stone tools and bone fragments indicate that modern humans lived and hunted in South Africa some 110,000 years ago.

c. 3,000,000 BC
Australopithecus africanus lives in central South Africa

c. 117,000 BC
Early modern man settlement at Langebaan

3,000,000 BC	2,000,000 BC	1,000,000 BC

c. 1,000,000 BC *Homo erectus* displaces earlier ape-like hominid species

Hand axe

c. 200,000 BC
Middle Stone Age

c. 35,000 BC
Start of Late Stone Age; man uses refined tools and weapons

Spear head

40,000 BC	30,000 BC	20,000

c. 38,000 BC
Iron ore is mined for its pigment at Ngwenya in Swaziland

c. 26,000 BC
Earliest known example of rock art (Namibia)

Early Goldsmiths
Gold ornaments, discovered in Mapungubwe grave sites in 1932, belonged to an Iron Age civilization that flourished until the end of the 12th century.

Sanga cattle were introduced into South Africa by Bantu-speaking tribes.

"Mrs Ples"
(2–3 million years). In 1947, the skull of an *Australopithecus africanus* found at the Sterkfontein Caves was first thought to belong to a species called *Plesianthropus transvaalensis*.

Lydenburg Heads
Seven clay heads found near Lydenburg (*see p334*) in Mpumalanga date back to AD 700. Experts believe they were used in rituals.

Rock Paintings
South Africa is a rich storehouse of prehistoric art. Some paintings are thought to date back 10,000 years, while others were painted as little as 200 years ago.

Where to See Prehistoric South Africa

The KwaZulu-Natal Museum in Pietermaritzburg (*p281*), the McGregor Museum in Kimberley (*p374*) and the National Museum of Natural History in Pretoria (*p324*) hold important collections of rock art, archaeological and palaeontological artifacts. Rock paintings can be seen in the Cederberg of the Western Cape (*p219*) and in the Drakensberg in Lesotho (*pp272–3*) and KwaZulu-Natal (*pp274–5*). Cape Town's Iziko South African Museum (*p134*) has dioramas of early people. Bloemfontein's National Museum (*p376*) and the museum in Lydenburg (*p334*) exhibit fossil finds. The Sterkfontein Caves (*p322*), where Mrs Ples was found, are near Krugersdorp. Many of these museums can assist visitors with information on outings to individual sites.

The Cave Museum is an open-air San rock art site in the Giant's Castle reserve (*see pp274–5*).

The Sudwala Caves (*see p334*) feature an interesting timeline display on the evolution of man.

c. 8,000 BC Microlithic [ston]e toolkit of [th]e San culture

| 10,000 BC | AD 1 | AD 350 | AD 700 | AD 1050 | AD 1400 |

c. AD 200 Black farmers and iron-workers settle south of the Limpopo River and plant sorghum crops

San bow and arrows

c. AD 1 Nomadic Khoi herders, originally from Botswana, move southwest into Cape coastal territory

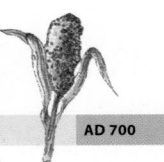

Sorghum

c. 1400 Stone settlements of Sotho people expand from the Highveld into present-day Free State

Explorers and Colonizers

Portuguese navigators pioneered the sea route to India, but it was the Dutch who set up a fortified settlement at the Cape in 1652. The indigenous Khoi, who initially welcomed the trade opportunities, were quickly marginalized. Some took service with the settlers, while others fled from the Dutch *trekboers* (migrant graziers). In 1688, the arrival of French Huguenot families swelled the numbers of the white settlers, driving even more Khoi away from their ancestral land.

Explorers' Routes

➡ Dias 1488   ➡ Da Gama 1498

▨ Cape Colony 1795

The Caravel of Dias
In 1988, a replica of the ship commanded by Bartolomeu Dias 500 years before retraced his voyage from Lisbon in Portugal to Mossel Bay. The ship is now housed in Mossel Bay's Bartolomeu Dias Museum Complex *(see pp240–41)*.

Unique Early Postal Systems
In the 15th and 16th centuries, Portuguese captains anchored in Mossel Bay and left messages for each other engraved on flat rocks. The stones soon became a type of post box, with letters stored beneath them.

Dutch flag

Jan van Riebeeck

Matchlock

Jan van Riebeeck's Arrival
On 6 April 1652, Jan van Riebeeck landed at the Cape to establish a permanent settlement for the Dutch East India Company. The first commander of the new outpost and his wife, Maria de la Quellerie, are commemorated by statues erected near the site of their historic landing.

1486 Portuguese sail as far as today's Namibia

c. 1500 Shipwrecked Portuguese sailors encounter Iron Age farmers along South Africa's south coast

1400	1450	1500	1550

Vasco da Gama

1498 Vasco da Gama discovers the route to India around the Cape of Good Hope

1510 Dom Francisco d'Almeida, viceroy of Portuguese India, and 57 of his men are killed by Khoi in Table Bay

The Vereenigde Oost-Indische Compagnie (VOC)
Several small trading companies joined in 1602 to form the Dutch East India Company (VOC). It was granted a charter to trade, draw up treaties and maintain an army and a fleet. The VOC was dissolved in 1798.

Where to See Explorers and Colonizers

Mossel Bay's museum complex houses a replica of Bartolomeu Dias's caravel (pp240–41), as well as the old milkwood tree in which passing sailors would leave messages for their fellow mariners. The Castle of Good Hope in Cape Town (pp130–31) is South Africa's oldest surviving structure. The Huguenot Memorial Museum in Franschhoek (p204) honours the French heritage of the town and contains antique furniture and paintings. Early colonial artifacts are on display at the Iziko Slave Lodge in Cape Town (p128–9).

Beads and trinkets were offered as gifts to the Khoi.

Autshumao, leader of the local *Strandlopers* (a people living near the sea who ate mainly fish and mussels) had been taken to Java, Indonesia, by the British in 1631. He had a basic knowledge of English and was able to negotiate with the Dutch.

Animal skins were worn by the native people of the Cape.

The De Kat Balcony, at the Castle of Good Hope in Cape Town, was designed by sculptor Anton Anreith.

Superior Weaponry
Matchlock rifles secured the settlers' advantage over the clubs and throwing spears of the Khoi, and the bows and poisoned arrows used by the San.

The French Huguenots
Fleeing from religious persecution in France, about 200 Huguenots arrived at the Cape of Good Hope in 1688. They were assigned farms around Franschhoek (see pp204–5), where they planted vineyards.

Almond Hedge
A remnant of the hedge that was planted to discourage unauthorized trading with the Khoi can be seen at Kirstenbosch National Botanical Garden (see pp164–5).

Maria de la Quellerie

1594 Portuguese barter with Khoi in Table Bay

1652 Jan van Riebeeck and his wife, Maria de la Quellerie, arrive in Table Bay

1693 Sheik Yusuf is exiled to the Cape after instigating a rebellion in Java. His *kramat* (shrine) near Faure (Western Cape) is revered by Muslims

1600	1650	1700	1750

1608 The Dutch barter with Khoi clans for food

1658 War against Khoi follows cattle raids and killing of settlers

1688 Huguenot refugees settle at the Cape

1713 Smallpox epidemic kills unknown hundreds of Khoi, as well as many white settlers

British Colonization

By 1778, settler expansion had reached the Eastern Cape and the Great Fish River was proclaimed the eastern boundary of the Cape Colony. As this was Xhosa territory, local herdsmen were deprived of their pastures and a century of bitter "frontier wars" ensued. In 1795, following the French Revolution, British forces were able to occupy the Cape. Having returned it to the Netherlands in 1802, they reclaimed it in 1806 and instituted a government-sponsored programme that assigned farms in the Zuurveld area to British settlers. To the east, Shaka Zulu was just beginning to build a powerful empire.

Settler Expansion

▢ 1814 — Cape today

Battle of Muizenberg (1795)
In this battle for possession of the Cape, British warships bombarded Dutch outposts at Muizenberg (see p157). Britain was victorious and thus acquired a halfway station en route to India.

Blockhouse ruins

Fort Frederick
In the 19th century, many private homes were fortified, and a succession of outposts and frontier forts were built in the Eastern Cape. Few were attacked; almost all are now in ruin. Fort Frederick in Port Elizabeth (see pp250–53) has been restored and is a superb example of what these frontier fortifications looked like.

Grave of Captain Francis Evatt, who oversaw the landing of the 1820 Settlers.

Rustenburg House
After the battle of Muizenberg, the Dutch surrendered the Cape to Britain. The treaty was signed in this house in Rondebosch, Cape Town. Its present Neo-Classical façade probably dates from around 1803.

1750 Worldwide, Dutch influence begins to wane	**1770** Gamtoos River made boundary of Cape Colony	**1778** Great Fish River made boundary of Cape Colony	**1789** Merino sheep are imported from Holland and thrive in South Africa
1750	**1760**	**1770**	**1780**
1751 Rijk Tulbagh appointed Governor of the Dutch Cape Colony (1751–71)		**1779** A year after it is made boundary of the Cape Colony, settlers and Xhosa clash at the Fish River – the first of nine frontier wars	*Merino sheep*

Battle of Blaauwberg (1806)
This battle between the Dutch and the British was fought at the foot of the Blouberg, out of range of British warships. Outnumbered and poorly disciplined, the Dutch defenders soon broke rank and fled.

Where to See British Colonization

The museums in Mthatha (the capital of the former Transkei) and the University of Fort Hare in Alice (in the former Ciskei) have interesting collections of colonial artifacts. Old weapons and ammunition, uniforms, maps, and even letters and medical supplies are displayed in the Military Museum at the Castle of Good Hope in Cape Town *(pp130–31)*. The museums in King William's Town, Queens-town and Grahamstown *(pp256–7)* exhibit collections of frontier-war memorabilia. The excellent Museum Africa in Johannes-burg *(p314)* has a superb collection of old prints and paintings.

The 1820 Settlers
About 4,000 Britons, mostly artisans with little or no farming experience, settled around Grahams-town *(see pp256–7)*.

The Powder Magazine
could hold some 900 kg (2,000 lb) of gunpowder.

Entrance

Museum Africa has three permanent exhibitions and various temporary displays.

The Xhosa
The Xhosa had farmed in the Zuurveld (present Eastern Cape) for cen-turies. The arrival of the 1820 Settlers caused friction and dispute.

Shaka Zulu
This gifted military strategist became Zulu chief after the death of Dingiswayo in 1817. Shaka introduced the *assegaai* (short spear) and united lesser clans into a Zulu empire.

1795 Battle of Muizen-berg and first British occupation	**1800** The *Cape Town Gazette* and *African Advertiser* are first published	**1806** Battle of Blaauwberg. Second British occupation of the Cape	**1818** Shaka's military conquests in Zululand begin	*Typical settler house* **1820** 4,000 British settlers arrive in Grahamstown	**1829** The Khoina are released from having to carry passes. The University of Cape Town is founded

1800	**1810**	**1820**	**1830**

1793 Lombard Bank, the first bank in the country, opens in Cape Town	**1802** Lady Anne Barnard, whose letters and diaries give an insight into colonial life, leaves the Cape	**1814** British occupation of the Cape is ratified by the Congress of Vienna	**1815** The Slagter's Nek rebellion, led by anti-British frontiersmen, ends with judicial executions near Cookhouse (Eastern Cape)	**1828** Shaka Zulu is murdered by his half-brothers, including Dingane

Colonial Expansion

The British colonial administration met with hostility from the Cape's Dutch-speaking community. Dissatisfied Voortrekkers (Boer pioneers) headed east and north in an exodus that became known as the Great Trek. In 1838, Zulu chief Dingane had one group of Voortrekkers killed, but in the subsequent Battle of Blood River his own warriors were beaten. A short-lived Boer republic, Natalia, was annexed by Britain in 1843. By 1857, two new Boer states, Transvaal and Orange Free State, landlocked and impoverished but independent, had been consolidated north of the Orange and Vaal rivers.

Voortrekker Movement

◻ 1836 Great Trek

◻ British territory by 1848

Emancipated Slaves
The freeing of 39,000 Cape Colony slaves in 1834 angered Boer farmers who relied on slave labour. The British decision was not due entirely to philanthropism; it was simply cheaper to employ free labour.

The Great Trek

Dissatisfied with the British administration, the Boers trekked inland in convoys of ox wagons to seek new territory. The pioneers, armed with cannons and muskets, were accompanied by their families, black and coloured retainers and livestock. Each wagon was "home" for the duration of the journey and contained all that the family owned. At night, or under attack, the convoy would form a laager – a circle of wagons lashed together with chains.

The Battle of Vegkop
In 1836 the Ndebele found themselves in the path of trekker expansion northwards. Traditional weapons were no match for blazing rifles. The 40 Voortrekkers beat off an attack by 6,000 Ndebele warriors at Vegkop, killing 430, but losing most of their own sheep, cattle and trek oxen.

Barrels were used to store food, water and gunpowder.

Wagon chest

The drive shaft was attached to the yoke, which was placed around the neck of the oxen.

1838 Battle of Blood River follows the murder of Voortrekker leader Piet Retief and his group

Dingane

1830	1835	1840

1834 Slaves freed, subject to a four-year "apprenticeship". Sixth Frontier War erupts; Voortrekkers travel to present-day Free State, KwaZulu-Natal, Northern Province and Namibia

1836 The Great Trek begins

1839 Boer Republic of Natalia is proclaimed

The Battle of Blood River
On 16 December 1838, the Ncome River ran red with blood as a 468-strong burgher commando defeated 12,500 Zulu warriors in retribution for the killing of trekker leader Piet Retief and his entourage.

Where to See the Colonial Expansion

British colonial history is well covered in cultural history and battle site museums nationwide. Museums at Grahamstown (pp256–7), Port Elizabeth (pp250–3), King William's Town and East London have displays of old weapons, maps and pioneer artifacts. Museum Africa (p314) in Johannesburg exhibits historic documents, war memorabilia and maps. The Worcester Museum (p208) is a living showcase of the lifestyles and farming processes of the Voortrekkers.

The Battle of Blood River Memorial, Dundee, shows a re-created, life-sized laager.

Tallow candles provided light.

A protective cover made of tanned hide sheltered the occupants inside.

Quilts were very often highly prized, complex pieces of craftsmanship.

Large wheels enabled the drivers to negotiate rough terrain without damaging the wagon.

Water barrel

Nongqawuse
In 1857, a Xhosa prophetess predicted that her people would regain their former power if they destroyed all their herds and crops, but the resulting famine further weakened their position.

The Kat River Rebellion
Khoina settlers on the Kat River in the Cape had fought for the government without compensation, but rebelled in the Eighth Frontier War of 1850. With their defeat, their land passed to white ownership.

1846 Seventh Frontier War (War of the Axe)

1850 Eighth Frontier War, in which the Kat River Khoina join the Xhosa

1854 Britain withdraws from the Orange River Sovereignty

1856 British and German settlers placed on Eastern Cape border; the Colony of Natal is granted a representative government

1845   1850   1855   1860

1852 The Cape is granted a representative government by Britain. Zuid-Afrikaansche Republiek (Transvaal) is formed

1853 Postage stamps available in the Cape Colony for the first time

1857 Thousands of Xhosa in the present-day Eastern Cape perish in a famine resulting from an ill-advised prophecy to kill their cattle and destroy crops as a sacrifice to ancestors who would rise up and drive out white settlers

First postage stamp

Clash for Gold and Diamonds

The discovery of diamonds in the Northern Cape laid the foundation for South Africa's economy and created a massive migrant labour system. Subsequent strikes of gold in the east of the country promised an untold source of wealth best exploited under a single British authority. African kingdoms and two Boer republics were coerced to join a British confederation. Resistance to the British masterplan led to a series of skirmishes that culminated in the South African (Boer) War of 1899–1902. The British crushed the Boer resistance, and on 31 May 1902, the Peace of Vereeniging was signed, ending hostilities.

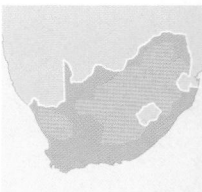

Areas of Conflict
Boer strongholds, war zones

Gold Fever
Finds of alluvial gold at Pilgrim's Rest *(see p336)* and Barberton preceded the 1886 discovery of Johannesburg's Main Reef.

Leander Jameson (1853–1917)
After the discovery of the Transvaal gold reefs, Jameson masterminded a failed revolt intended to topple President Paul Kruger of the Transvaal Republic.

Cecil John Rhodes (1853–1902)
This ruthless financier became involved in organizing the Jameson Raid into the Transvaal Republic in 1896, while he was prime minister of the Cape. The interference in the affairs of another state effectively ended his political career.

1867 A 21-carat diamond is found near Hopetown in the Northern Cape

1878 Walvis Bay (in today's Namibia) is proclaimed British territory

1860	1865	1870	1875

Cut diamond

1871 Diamonds found at Colesberg Kopje (Kimberley). Gold found in Pilgrim's Rest

1877 Britain annexes South African Republic

1879 Britain invades the Zulu kingdom of Cetshwayo, adjoining its colony of Natal

Jan Christiaan Smuts

General Smuts (1870–1950) played prominent roles in the South African War and in both World Wars. He also helped to draft the United Nations Charter, and was twice prime minister of South Africa (1919–24 and 1939–48).

Where to See the Clash for Gold and Diamonds

A number of coach tours include the major sites on the Battlefields Route *(p278)* in KwaZulu-Natal. Audiotapes for self-guided tours are available at the Talana Museum *(p278)*. Gold Reef City *(p321)* is an evocative re-creation of Johannesburg in the 1890s. The Big Hole: Kimberley Mine Museum *(pp374–5)* documents the history of diamond mining in Kimberley.

Isandhlwana Hill

Bayonets had to be used when the British ran out of ammunition.

Shields covered with cow hide were used to ward off the bayonets.

The *assegaai* (short stabbing spear) was useful in close combat.

British casualties were high; only a handful of men escaped alive.

Re-created saloon-style bar at the Big Hole: Kimberley Mine Museum.

Battle of Isandhlwana

In an effort to subjugate the fiercely independent Zulu, British officials provoked several incidents. In 1879, a 1,200-strong British and colonial force was annihilated by 20,000 Zulu warriors at Isandhlwana Hill.

Modern Warfare
The South African War (1899–1902) was the first war fought with high-velocity rifles and mechanical transport. Although the Boers were good shots and horsemen and could live off the land, limited manpower, as well as the loose and informal structure of their armies, counted against them.

1884 Lesotho becomes a British protectorate

1886 Discovery of the Main Reef on Witwatersrand (Gauteng)

1894 Kingdom of Swaziland becomes a British protectorate

1896 Jameson Raid into Transvaal fails. Rinderpest kills countless head of cattle as well as wild animals

1902 South African War ends

1885　　**1890**　　**1895**　　**1900**

1881 Boers defeat British army at Majuba

1883 Olive Schreiner publishes *The Story of an African Farm*

1885 Britain annexes part of Bechuanaland (Botswana)

Mahatma Gandhi

1893 Mohandas Karamchand Gandhi arrives in Durban to practise law

Winston Churchill as war correspondent in South Africa

1899 Start of the South African War. Sabie Game Reserve declared (forerunner of today's Kruger National Park)

The Apartheid Years

In 1910, the Union of South Africa became a self-governing colony within the British Commonwealth. The future of black South Africans was largely left undecided, leading to the founding of the South African Native National Congress (later known as the ANC) in 1912. The Great Trek centenary of 1938 renewed the white Afrikaners' hope for self-determination. In 1948, the Afrikaner-based National Party (NP) came to power and, by manipulating the composition of parliament, managed to enforce a series of harsh laws that stripped black South Africans of most of their basic human rights. In 1961, Prime Minister Verwoerd led the country out of the Commonwealth and into increasing political isolation.

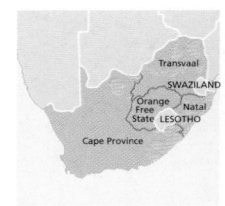

Apartheid South Africa
— Provincial boundaries (1994)
▨ Homelands up to 1984

Delville Wood
One of the most vicious battles of World War I was fought at Delville Wood, in France. For five days, 3,000 South African soldiers held out against the German line.

The Great Trek Centenary
The ox wagons rolled again in 1938, headed for a solemn celebration in Pretoria, where the first stone of the Voortrekker Monument (see p325) was laid. This re-enactment of the Great Trek was an impressive display of Afrikaner solidarity, patriotism and political strength.

Burning Pass Books
The 1952 Natives Act required all black men older than 16 to carry a pass book (permit to work in a "white" area) at all times, and show it to the police on demand. In 1956, the law was extended to women. In 1960, thousands burned their pass books at township police stations countrywide. The law was repealed in 1986.

1905 Cullinan Diamond found at Premier Diamond Mine

1907 Sir James Percy FitzPatrick writes *Jock of the Bushveld*

1912 South African Native National Congress founded (later becomes ANC)

1928 Kirstenbosch Botanical Gardens and University of South Africa founded

1936 First printing of the Bible in Afrikaar

1900 **1910** **1920** **1930**

1904 President Paul Kruger dies

President Paul Kruger

1910 Formation of the Union of South Africa

1914 South Africa declares war on Germany. Boer rebellion put down by Union government. The first National Party formed in Bloemfontein

1922 Miners' rebellion breaks out at coal mines in Witbank

1927 Compulsory racial segregation declared in many urban areas

Apartheid

Afrikaans for "separateness", this term was used as a slogan by the National Party, which brought it into force as a policy after winning the 1948 election. In keeping with racial classification laws, skin colour dictated where people were allowed to live, be educated, work and even be buried. Sex "across the colour bar" was punishable by imprisonment. Loss of land was among the system's most terrible inflictions.

Security police "house calls" enforced apartheid laws

Where to See the Apartheid Years

District Six Museum (p129), on the edge of this former Cape Town precinct, shows what life was like in this largely Muslim community before it was cleared under the Group Areas Act, a keystone of the apartheid regime, starting in 1966. Exhibits at Johannesburg's celebrated – if harrowing – Apartheid Museum (p317) and Liliesleaf Farm (p321), depict the struggle for democracy. The Iziko Slave Lodge (p128) in Cape Town and Museum Africa (p314) in Johannesburg also have interesting displays. The Voortrekker Museum and Monument (p325) in Pretoria offer an insight into Afrikaner Nationalism.

African Nationalism
Drum, first published in the 1950s, was important for black journalists. Not afraid to criticize the white regime, they rekindled African Nationalism.

Museum Africa in Johannesburg shows the living conditions in a township like Sophiatown.

District Six, "the life and soul of Cape Town", was declared a white area in 1966.

Apartheid's Architects
Dutch-born Hendrik Verwoerd (1901–66), prime minister from 1958 until his assassination, and Charles Robberts Swart (1894–1982), the minister of justice, implemented many apartheid measures.

First edition of Afrikaans Bible

1948 National Party elected as the country's government

1950 Communism is outlawed

1955 Petrol is made from coal for the first time in South Africa

1958 Hendrik Verwoerd becomes prime minister of South Africa

1940 | **1950** | **1960**

1939 South Africa declares war on Germany

1949 Prohibition of Mixed Marriages Act, the first of many apartheid laws, is passed by Parliament

1960 Police shoot 69 demonstrators at Sharpeville. Whites-only referendum opts for a republic

Age of Democracy

The laws imposed by the white Nationalist government outraged black African societies, and the decree that Afrikaans be the language of instruction at black schools sparked the revolt of 1976. States of emergency came and went, and violence increased. It became clear that the old system of administration was doomed. In 1990, State President Frederik Willem de Klerk undertook the first step towards reconciliation by unbanning the ANC, Communist Party and 34 other organizations, and announcing the release of Nelson Mandela.

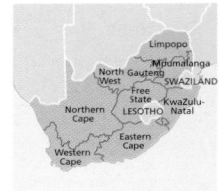

The New South Africa
— Provincial boundaries

A World First
Christiaan Barnard (pictured right) made medical history in 1967 when he transplanted a human heart.

Desmond Tutu won a Nobel Peace Prize (1984) and Martin Luther King Peace Prize (1986) for his dedicated anti-apartheid campaign.

The Soweto Uprising
On 16 June 1976, police fired on black students protesting against the use of Afrikaans in their schools. This picture of a fatally wounded boy became a world-famous symbol of this tragic struggle.

Arts Against Apartheid
The Black Christ by Ronald Harrison was inspired by the Sharpeville Massacre and banning of the then ANC president Chief Albert Luthuli (depicted as Christ). Banned for years, it now hangs in the Iziko South African National Gallery *(see p135).*

Democratic Election
On 27 April 1994, South Africans went to the polls – many for the first time. Five days later the result was announced: with 63 per cent of votes in its favour, the African National Congress (ANC) had achieved victory in all but two provinces, and Nelson Mandela was the new state president.

1961 South Africa becomes a republic outside the British Commonwealth

The Old flag

1971 International Court and UN Security Council recognize Namibia and revoke South Africa's mandate on the country

1980 ANC bombs Sasolburg Oil Refinery in the Free State

1990 Namib[ia] independe[nt] ANC unban[ned] Nelson Mand[ela] relea[sed]

| 1960 | 1965 | 1970 | 1975 | 1980 | 1985 |

1962 Nelson Mandela jailed. Start of UN-imposed sanctions

1963 Guerrilla war begins in South West Africa (Namibia)

1968 Swaziland gains independence

1966 Prime Minister Verwoerd assassinated. Lesotho gains independence

1976 Soweto riots erupt. Flight of foreign capital from South Africa

1984 New constitution for tricameral parliament

The new flag

Kwaito – Sound of a New Generation
Boom Shaka was a pioneering *kwaito* group that emerged in the 1990s. A uniquely South African sound, *kwaito* was born in the townships of Gauteng. The lyrics are influenced by *toyi-toyi* (protest) chants.

Free at Last
On 11 February 1990, after almost three decades in custody, Nelson Mandela emerged from the Victor Verster prison near Paarl. The high-profile event was watched by millions around the world.

Independent Electoral Commission monitor

Cricket World Cup 1992
Political change in South Africa saw the national cricket team included in a world event for the first time in over 20 years.

Ballot paper

Sealed ballot box

Freedom of Speech
The early 1980s saw the flamboyant Evita Bezuidenhout *(see p215)* on stage for the first time. Her outspoken, satirical views on internal politics made her famous in South Africa and abroad.

Sanctions Lifted
In 1993, trade sanctions (introduced in 1986) were lifted and global brands became available again.

The Truth and Reconciliation Commission (TRC)
Established in 1994 under the chairmanship of former Archbishop of Cape Town Desmond Tutu, this commission aimed to determine the motives behind political crimes committed during the apartheid years.

94 ANC wins the country's first ocratic election. Nelson Mandela omes president

1995 South Africa hosts and wins the Rugby World Cup

1998 Truth and Reconciliation Commission hearings begin

1999 Second democratic election

2004 The ruling party, ANC, wins a landslide election, taking 70 per cent of the votes

2010 South Africa hosts the Football World Cup

1995	2000	2005	2010	2015	2020	2025

1992 Referendum held regarding FW de Klerk's policy of change. South Africa participates in the Olympic Games, for the first time since 1960

2003 Walter Sisulu, a key member of the ANC, and Nelson Mandela's mentor, dies at the age of 91

2009 The ANC wins the national elections; Jacob Zuma becomes president

2013 Nelson Mandela dies aged 95; ten days of national mourning follow

Leopard reclining on a tree branch ▶

WILD
SOUTH AFRICA

THE SAFARI EXPERIENCE

There is something hugely satisfying about South Africa's wild places. Partly it's the liberating sense of space in the greatest reserves, many of them the size of small countries; but mostly it's the thrill of sighting a fascinating assortment of wildlife, so familiar from television, here made living flesh. Be it lions roaring on a moonlit night or jackal cubs at play, the safari offers limitless natural wonder.

A Swahili word that means journey, the term "safari" came into popular usage in the early 20th century to describe the trophy-hunting expeditions popularized by the likes of Theodore Roosevelt, Ernest Hemingway and Karen Blixen. By the late 1960s, these gun-toting safaris had largely become a thing of the past, as a combination of factors – dwindling wildlife numbers, increased conservation awareness and the greater international mobility offered by jet travel – ushered in the era of the photographic safari. Today, tourists arrive in Africa not with guns but with cameras, and the modern safari industry is able to accommodate them in a variety of ways, from simple camp sites and government rest camps to the exclusive, eco-friendly tented camps and lodges of the private reserves.

One surviving legacy of the colonial hunting era is the notion of the "Big Five" – lion, leopard, elephant, rhino and buffalo (see pp76–7). Ticking them off the list is considered a rite of passage. Certainly there are few experiences more thrilling than the sight of a herd of elephants marching peacefully across the savannah or of a leopard lying in a tree, but safari should never become limited to an obsessive quest for a quintet of select beasts. With more than 300 protected areas to choose from, South Africa has plenty to keep wildlife lovers occupied for months, if not years. Its many and diverse nature reserves range from the hippo- and crocodile-filled estuaries of iSimangaliso Wetland Park and the towering peaks of the uKhahlamba-Drakensberg, to the red dunes and dry riverbeds of the remote Kgalagadi Transfrontier Park, home to gemsbok and springbok. Further south, Table Mountain National Park protects a host of endemic species unique to South Africa, such as Cape mountain zebra and bontebok.

Three springboks grazing, Kgalagadi Transfrontier Park

◀ Safari-goers watching a herd of Cape buffalo, Sabi Sand Game Reserve

PRACTICAL INFORMATION

Arranging a safari is a fairly straightforward procedure. The biggest hurdles at the planning stage will be choosing between a self-drive adventure or an organized safari and deciding which reserves to visit – with the diversity of South Africa's national parks and wildlife reserves, visitors are spoiled for choice. If opting for the DIY approach, it is easy to book everything online – the South African National Parks (SANParks) website *(see p71)* is extremely user-friendly. For the less adventurous, there are plenty of reputable tour operators in South Africa and elsewhere to offer specialist guidance and to set transport and accommodation arrangements in place *(see p71).*

Elephants gather at a watering hole in Addo Elephant National Park

Best Time to Go

The best season for game-viewing is winter (July to September), when the dry weather forces animals to gather around rivers and waterholes. The disadvantages are that animals are not in optimal condition and the winter landscape is stark.

Summer (November to January) brings high rainfall, and the landscape becomes green and lush. This is the best time of year for viewing flora, though the wildlife will be more widespread and difficult to spot. The wide availability of water also leads to a higher threat of malaria in risk areas.

While many people visit for the "Big Five" *(see pp76–7)* and get a thrill from the pursuit of spotting them, it is also possible to relish the opportunity to spend quiet time in remote bush, take unbelievable hikes and view striking landscapes and lesser-known animal life. Each of the parks and reserves offers something exceptional, and the following pages will help visitors to decide where they want to go.

Organized and Independent Tours

Most of the safari companies operate out of Cape Town, Durban and Johannesburg, arranging accommodation and game-viewing trips as part of an organized tour. The cost of trips varies from budget excursions to more expensive holidays. Many of the safari companies offer package deals, which are often great value for money. It can be an easier option to let an organization take care of all the planning, but if so, it is best to choose a company that is recognized by the **Southern Africa Tourism Services Association** (SATSA).

A few companies are listed on p71. Going on your own can be cheaper, and it allows for greater flexibility to explore. Hiring a car, booking self-catering accommodation and obtaining maps and information are all easy to arrange.

Planning Your Trip

Most of the parks fall within three groups: **South African National Parks** (SANParks), **CapeNature** and **Ezemvelo KZN Wildlife**. Contacting these organizations is a good first step, along with checking their websites and those of safari companies. Seasonal and promotional specials are often found in the travel sections of leading newspapers.

The Wild Card provides unrestricted access to most of South Africa's conservation areas for a year, and is a sensible investment if your itinerary includes visits to more than one reserve.

Most parks can be visited by car, since roads and gravel paths are generally well kept. However, just after the rainy season (January to April), a 4x4 vehicle is a more suitable option. Also note that not all petrol stations accept credit cards.

Bontebok National Park, part of the SANParks group

A typically South African *braai* in the bush

Air-conditioning may seem a necessity when the weather is warm, but try to keep the car windows open to experience fully the sounds and smells of the bush. The best speed for game-viewing is 15 km/h (10 mph). To see which animals are in any particular area, check the sightings boards at the entrance of the camps. The wildlife identification books in camp shops are also useful, and it may be a good investment to buy a pair of binoculars.

Essential items to pack include: comfortable clothes to protect exposed body parts from insects (preferably in dull colours, so as not to disturb the wildlife), a hat, sunblock, sunglasses and a camera.

Accommodation

To avoid disappointment, it is best to book as far in advance as possible, especially during South African school and public holidays. Accommodation at parks and reserves ranges from camp sites, huts and safari tents to self-contained chalets and cottages. There is generally a choice of a private or shared bathroom and kitchen. In most parks, bedding, towels, a fridge and cooking utensils are included. All parks have electricity, but a few also have TVs, Internet and on-site medical services.

When booking self-catering accommodation, bear in mind that not all parks have well-stocked shops, and you may have to take some or all of your supplies with you. Once a

reservation has been made, the company sends details of the facilities at the camp.

The ultimate in accommodation are the luxurious lodges at private game reserves, mostly around the Kruger National Park. Prices are high, but they usually include accommodation, meals, and game activities, and sometimes drinks. This is a good option for visitors who have never experienced a safari, because there are well-informed rangers who lead game-viewing outings, which ensures a much greater chance of sighting some wildlife.

Choosing an Itinerary

The best times to view game are early morning and late afternoon. Be sure to return before the camp gates shut, just before dark.

Game drives, walks and night drives can be booked at the camp offices after arrival. They usually depart at dawn or in the afternoon. They last a few hours, and are often the best way to explore the area. Wilderness trails are longer and involve a stay at a remote base camp and walks with an armed ranger. These can be booked months in advance.

The private reserves generally plan the itinerary for their guests, although there is room for flexibility. Typical activities include drinks at dawn, followed by guided game-viewing, sundowners and night drives with dinner.

Safety Tips and Health Issues

It is recommended that you approach a sighting quietly, turn off the car engine and allow space for the vehicle in front to reverse, if necessary. Never feed animals, because once they are dependent on food from humans, they can become aggressive. Stay in your car at all times. If your car breaks down in

the park, wait until a park ranger comes to help. Other visitors will be able to pass on a message to the authorities or you can telephone the **KNP Emergency Hotline**, a dedicated call centre.

Water and other drinks are essential to prevent dehydration. Anti-malaria prophylactics may be recommended for those visiting seasonal risk areas, such as the Kruger. A doctor or travel clinic should be able to provide these. The highest-risk period is during the rainy season (December to April), when it is best to cover exposed skin with light clothing and insect repellent.

Most camps in the parks provide ramped access for disabled visitors and, often, accessible toilets and specially adapted accommodation.

A thrillingly close-up view of one of South Africa's "Big Five"

Children on Safari

Parks and reserves in South Africa are well equipped for families. There are excellent game reserves outside of malaria areas where you can see the "Big Five", and they are the best option for families with young children. It is also essential to find out the minimum age requirement of rest camps and lodges, and whether they are fenced in. Long drives can be dull, so it's worth considering hiring a guide to keep the children interested. It is also a good idea to bring a picnic and plan stops at waterholes.

Safaris, National Parks and Wildlife Reserves

South Africa has hundreds of parks and reserves, but most protect niche environments and cannot be considered true safari destinations. Even so, the first-time safari-goer faces a daunting array of possibilities, ranging from the vast Kruger National Park to the remote dunes of Kgalagadi and the lush subtropical landscapes of Hluhluwe-Imfolozi and iSimangaliso. Here, a brief region-by-region overview of the country's top reserves is provided to help narrow the options.

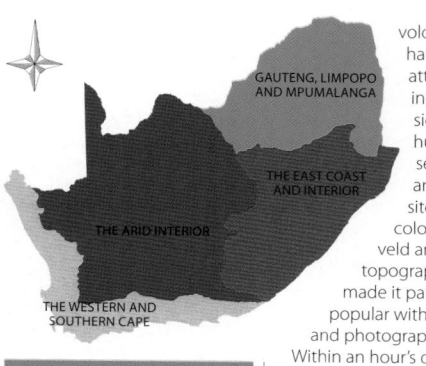

GAUTENG, LIMPOPO AND MPUMALANGA

THE EAST COAST AND INTERIOR

THE ARID INTERIOR

THE WESTERN AND SOUTHERN CAPE

Gauteng, Limpopo and Mpumalanga

The flagship of South Africa's game reserves and the ultimate destination for the wildlife fanatic is the **Kruger National Park**, with its 150 mammal and 500 bird species. There are also sites of historical and archaeological interest in the northern areas. Trails on offer include 4x4, wilderness and mountain-biking, while golfers will love the unfenced nine-hole course at Skukuza.

The **Madikwe Game Reserve** is situated in the corner of the Northwest Province bordering Botswana. A so-called "transition zone" on the edge of the Kalahari Desert, the region has a unique ecology with an enormous variety of flora and fauna, and several rare species occur here naturally. Madikwe is one of the few game reserves in the world that represents the most sustainable land use for the area. To visit it, you must stay at one of the lodges.

Pilanesberg Game Reserve is also based in the transition zone. Lying in an ancient volcano, it has many attractions, including signs of early humankind in several Stone and Iron Age sites. The park's colourful bushveld and varied topography have made it particularly popular with artists and photographers.

Within an hour's drive of Johannesburg is the **Suikerbosrand Nature Reserve**, named after the protea (suikerbos) plant found throughout the area. This reserve is an excellent choice for outdoor enthusiasts as the Suikerbosrand mountain range provides first-rate hiking and mountain-biking opportunities. There are several day and overnight trails, plus the 700-m (765-yd) Toktokkie trail, which has been designed with disabled visitors in mind – it has wide paved paths and there are several benches to stop at.

The East Coast and Interior

The **Golden Gate Highlands National Park** takes its name from the beautiful sandstone rock formations that change from purple to gold at sunset. The park provides many activities, including guided walks, hiking trails, abseiling, canoeing and horse riding. Accommodation ranges from luxury log cabins in the mountains to a rest camp that is reminiscent of an 18th-century Basotho village. Bird-watchers should look out for the rare bearded vulture and bald ibis.

iSimangaliso Wetland Park is South Africa's most significant wetland reserve and a World Heritage Site that incorporates bushveld, sand forest, grassland, wetland, coastal forest, swamp, beach, coral reef and sea. The best time to visit is during the turtle breeding season from October to April, or during the whale-watching season from June to December. Other animals to look out for are hippos, crocodiles, pelicans, Caspian terns and fish eagles.

Set in the heart of Zululand where tribal kings once hunted, **Hluhluwe-Imfolozi Game Reserve** is renowned for rhino conservation. The park also has several excellent wilderness trails and guided walks. Accommodation ranges from the well-located Hilltop Camp to more rustic bush camps.

Thirsty big cats at a watering hole in the Kruger National Park

Spectacular views of the Karoo National Park, Arid Interior region

Tembe Elephant Park was established in an isolated corner of KwaZulu-Natal to conserve the region's remaining elephants. which migrate over the border into Mozambique. Through a programme of reintroduction, Tembe now also has a healthy population of other mammal species, including the rare and elusive suni antelope. An area of sand forests, pans and wetlands, it is home to a large number of bird species.

A World Heritage Site, **uKhahlamba-Drakensberg Park** encompasses the highest range south of Kilimanjaro. The park is blessed with spectacular waterfalls and streams, rocky paths and sandstone cliffs, making it a great option for hikers, rock climbers and walkers. The mountains were home to the indigenous San people for 4,000 years, and the rock art here is the largest and most concentrated collection in Africa. Hikers can even stay in caves that were once inhabited by the San.

The Arid Interior

IAi-IAis/Richtersveld Transfrontier Park is truly extraordinary, but it is not for visitors who want to see large game. The park is a wild landscape that at first seems desolate, but on closer inspection reveals a treasury of the world's richest desert plants. Miniature rock gardens cling to cliff faces, and the strange stem succulents known as *halfmens* can appear almost human when viewed from a distance. The park is accessible only in 4x4 or high-clearance vehicles, and other cars are not allowed to enter.

The **Karoo National Park** is the largest ecosystem in South Africa, with an enormous diversity of plant and animal life. There are several species worth looking out for, such as the endemic black wildebeest, Cape mountain zebra, springbok, five species of tortoise and the rare black eagle. Activities include a scenic drive along the Klipspringer Pass, a guided night drive, and hiking along several trails. The Karoo Fossil Trail has been specifically designed for disabled visitors.

Called the "Place of the Great Noise" by the indigenous Khoi people, **Augrabies Falls National Park** is named after the magnificent 56-m (184-ft) high powerful waterfall formed by the Orange River.

Planning Your Trip This chart is designed to help you to choose your safari. The parks and reserves are listed alphabetically for each area on the map opposite.	Big Five	On-site restaurant	Swimming pool	On-site fuel	Seasonal malaria risk	Suitable for children	Suitable for disabled	Guided game drives	Picnic sites	Shops	Information Centre	Laundry	Hiking/walking trails	Whale-watching
Gauteng, Limpopo and Mpumalanga														
Kruger National Park	•	•	•	•	•	•	•	•	•	•	•	•	•	
Madikwe Game Reserve	•	•	•			•	•	•			•	•	•	
Pilanesberg Game Reserve	•	•	•			•	•	•	•		•	•		
Suikerbosrand Nature Reserve						•	•		•				•	
The East Coast and Interior														
Golden Gate Highlands National Park		•	•	•		•	•	•	•	•	•		•	
Hluhluwe-Imfolozi Game Reserve	•	•	•	•		•	•	•	•	•	•	•	•	
iSimangaliso Wetland Park			•		•	•	•	•	•	•	•	•		•
Tembe Elephant Park	•	•	•		•	•	•	•	•		•			
uKhahlamba-Drakensberg Park		•	•			•	•	•	•	•	•	•	•	
The Arid Interior														
IAi-IAis Richtersveld Transfrontier Park				•					•	•				
Augrabies Falls National Park		•	•			•	•	•	•	•	•		•	
Goegap Nature Reserve						•	•		•		•		•	
Karoo National Park		•	•			•	•	•	•	•	•	•	•	
Kgalagadi Transfrontier Park		•	•	•		•	•	•	•	•	•	•	•	
Namaqua National Park						•	•		•		•		•	
The Western and Southern Cape														
Addo Elephant National Park	•	•	•	•		•	•	•	•	•	•		•	
Bontebok National Park						•	•		•		•		•	
De Hoop Nature Reserve		•	•			•	•	•	•	•	•		•	•
Table Mountain National Park		•				•	•	•	•	•	•	•	•	•
Tsitsikamma		•	•			•	•		•	•	•	•	•	•
Wilderness		•				•	•		•		•	•	•	•

Visitors should be aware that the approach to the falls is very slippery and people have fallen in the past. The area is known for its traditional domed huts and excellent bird life. Sudden temperature changes are not unusual, so it is worth bringing extra layers of clothing.

Colourful flowers bloom in spring at **Goegap Nature Reserve**. The circular walks and challenging mountain-bike trails attract many visitors. Accommodation includes a self-catering guesthouse, bush huts and camping sites.

Kgalagadi Transfrontier Park is an "international peace park" comprising Kalahari Gemsbok National Park in South Africa and the much larger Gemsbok National Park in Botswana. This desert of glistening red sand dunes bisected by two dry rivers covers almost twice the area of the Kruger National Park (see p68). Accommodation is either in traditional rest camps or in unfenced wilderness camp sites, guarded by armed guides. Guests can experience the bush at close hand during their stay, so these sites are popular. The park is also famous for its gemsbok and birds of prey.

World-renowned for its spectacular displays of spring flowers, with butterflies and birds

darting among the blooms, **Namaqua National Park** is best visited during August and September. More than 1,000 of its estimated 3,500 plant species are unique to the park, which, though arid, is designated a biodiversity hotspot. Skilpad Rest Camp offers self-catering chalets, and a private luxury camp operates during the flower season.

The Western and Southern Cape

Addo Elephant National Park is home to more than 600 elephants, as well as the unique flightless dung beetle. The PPC Discovery Trail has a 500-m (547-yd) boardwalk, to accommodate people with mobility and sensory impairments. Overnight visitors can choose from safari tents, forest cabins, rondavels, and luxury guesthouses, as well as caravan and camping sites.

Named after the species of antelope it was established to conserve, **Bontebok National Park** is part of a World Heritage Site. The park has a wonderful view of the Langeberg mountains, and as part of the Cape Floral Kingdom it has particularly rich flora. This is an ideal spot in

Penguins waddling at Boulders Beach in the Table Mountain National Park

which to relax by the tranquil Breede River and to tour the Wine Routes and surrounding areas.

De Hoop Nature Reserve is a special reserve with an abundance of marine life such as dolphins, seals and whales. More than 260 species of resident and migratory birds are also found here. There are several hikes to choose from, including the Whale Trail, which has five overnight stops and provides an excellent opportunity to explore the area.

Table Mountain National Park is a unique mix of natural wonders within the bustling city life of Cape Town. Unusually, entrance to the park is free, except at three points: the Cape of Good Hope, Silvermine and Boulders Beach, which is worth

Young baboon, De Hoop Reserve

A floral feast for the eyes at Namaqua National Park, the Arid Interior region

visiting to see the delightful African penguins. The park is part of the Cape Floral Kingdom and has some of the most diverse wildlife in the world.

Garden Route National Park comprises three sections: Tsitsikamma, Wilderness and Knysna Lakes. Keen hikers can enjoy the superb Otter Trail in the Tsitsikamma section, which stretches for 41 km (25 miles) from Storms River Mouth in the east to Nature's Valley in the west. Visitors can frequently catch sight of dolphins and seals frolicking near the shoreline. During the migration season, southern right whales might be seen.

The Wilderness section of the park is popular with hikers and birdlovers alike. Bird-watchers should keep a look out for the Knysna lourie and half-collared kingfisher here. There are plenty of other activities on offer, including abseiling and paragliding.

In the Knysna Lakes section, private enterprises offer sailing, angling, boardsailing and power boating.

The Otter Trail in Tsitsikamma, Garden Route National Park

DIRECTORY

Tours

African Sky
Tel 27 12 809 1632.
🆆 africansky.com

Expert Africa (UK)
Tel (020) 8232-9777.
🆆 expertafrica.com

Intrepid Travel (Australia)
Tel (1300) 797-010.
🆆 intrepidtravel.com

Southern Africa Tourism Services Association (SATSA)
Tel 086 127 2872.
🆆 satsa.co.za

Planning Your Trip

CapeNature
Tel 021 483 0190.
🆆 capenature.co.za

Ezemvelo KZN Wildlife
Tel 033 845 1000.
🆆 kznwildlife.com

South African National Parks (SANParks)
Tel 012 428 9111.
🆆 sanparks.org

Health Issues

KNP Emergency Hotline
Tel 013 735 4325

Gauteng, Limpopo and Mpumalanga

Kruger National Park
N4, R538, R569, or R536.
Tel 012 428 9111.

🆆 sanparks.org

Madikwe Game Reserve
70 km (43 miles) N of Zeerust on R49.
Tel 071 687 2782.
🆆 madikwe-game-reserve.co.za

Pilanesberg Game Reserve
57 km (35 miles) N of Rustenburg on R510.
Tel 014 555 1600.
🆆 parksnorthwest.co.za/pilanesberg

Suikerbosrand Nature Reserve
Outside Heidelberg.
Tel 011 439 6300.

The East Coast and Interior

Golden Gate Highlands National Park
R711 or R712.
Tel 058 255 1000.
🆆 sanparks.org

Hluhluwe-Imfolozi Game Reserve
N2 to signposted turn-off at Mtubatuba.
Tel 033 845 1000.
🆆 kznwildlife.com

iSimangaliso Wetland Park
N2 from Mtubatuba.
Tel 033 845 1000.
🆆 kznwildlife.com

Tembe Elephant Park
N2 past Mkuze, Jozini turn-off. Tel 031 267 0144.
🆆 tembe.co.za

uKhahlamba-Drakensberg Park
N3 via Mooi River or Harrismith and Estcourt.
Tel 033 845 1000.
🆆 kznwildlife.com

The Arid Interior

IAi-IAis/Richtersveld Transfrontier Park
From Springbok, N7 to Steinkopf, Port Nolloth & Alexander Bay; gravel road to Sendelingsdrift.
Tel 027 831 1506.
🆆 sanparks.org

Augrabies Falls National Park
N14, 120 km (74 miles) W of Upington.
Tel 054 452 9200.
🆆 sanparks.org

Goegap Nature Reserve
E off N7; S of R14; 15 km (9 miles) SE of Springbok.
Tel 027 718 9906.
🆆 experience northerncape.com

Karoo National Park
N1 to Beaufort West.
Tel 023 415 2828.
🆆 sanparks.org

Kgalagadi Transfrontier Park
R360 from Upington.
Tel 054 561 2000.
🆆 sanparks.org

Namaqua National Park
Off N7 route to Namibia.
Tel 027 672 1948.
🆆 sanparks.org

The Western and Southern Cape

Addo Elephant National Park
N2 from Port Elizabeth, then R335.
Tel 042 233 8600.
🆆 sanparks.org

Bontebok National Park
Off N2.
Tel 028 514 2735.
🆆 sanparks.org

De Hoop Nature Reserve
56 km (35 miles) E of Bredasdorp on dirt road.
Tel 028 542 1114.
🆆 capenature.co.za

Garden Route National Park (Tsitsikamma; Wilderness; Knysna Lakes)
Tsitsikamma:
N2 from Plettenberg Bay;
Tel 042 281 1607.

Wilderness:
Close to N2,
15 km (9 miles)
from George;
Tel 044 877 0046.

Knysna Lakes:
N2 from Plettenberg Bay.
Tel 044 302 5600.
🆆 sanparks.org

Table Mountain National Park
Tel 021 712 0527.
🆆 sanparks.org

Habitats at a Glance

Habitat types are determined by a variety of factors, including climate, vegetation and geology. In South Africa, the most important of these factors are rainfall, soil type, altitude and latitude. Broadly speaking, rainfall is significantly higher in the east, while soil is sandiest in the west, altitude is highest in the central highveld area and temperatures tend to be highest at more northerly latitudes. Much of South Africa has rainfall in summer, with perhaps 90 per cent of precipitation occurring between November and April. By contrast, the Western Cape has a winter-rainfall climate, while much of the Eastern Cape falls between these extremes.

Key to Field Guide icons

- Diurnal
- Nocturnal
- Savannah woodland
- Semiarid
- Forest
- Highveld grassland
- Wetland
- Intertidal
- Fynbos

0 km   100
0 miles   100

Semiarid
The western part of South Africa mostly consists of thinly populated semi-arid plains and mountains, from the tall red dunes of the Kalahari to Namaqualand with its dazzling spring wildflower displays.

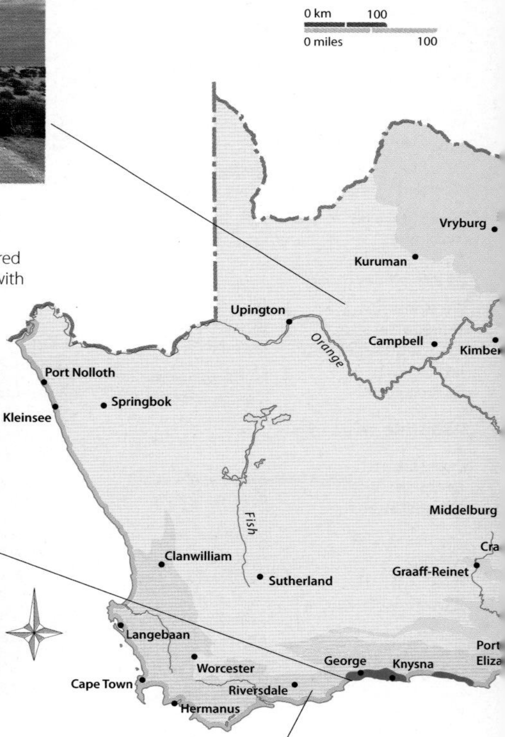

Forest
Closed-canopy forest, although scarce in South Africa, is highly biodiverse. It is particularly attractive to bird-watchers as it hosts many species of limited range.

Fynbos
The Cape Floral Kingdom supports a remarkably diverse cover known as fynbos (fine bush), comprising 9,600 plant species, most of which occur only here – probably the world's greatest repository of floral endemics. Much of the wildlife is unique to the region.

Vryburg
Kuruman
Upington
Campbell
Kimber
Port Nolloth
Springbok
Kleinsee
Orange
Fish
Middelburg
Cra
Clanwilliam
Sutherland
Graaff-Reinet
Langebaan
George
Knysna
Port Eliza
Cape Town
Worcester
Riversdale
Hermanus

Highveld Grassland
The largely high-lying central region of South Africa, rising to 3,480 m (11,420 ft) in the Drakensberg range, is dominated by open grassland. In the past century much of it has been lost to agriculture or urban development.

Termite hills provide an essential source of food for aardvarks

Niche Habitats

Within larger ecosystems exist many smaller microhabitats. For example, a termite hill not only supports its insect creators, but provides living space for small reptiles, food for aardvarks, and a vantage point for prowling cheetahs. Isolated *koppies,* or cliffs, support a unique set of creatures, from klipspringers to agama lizards, while puddles might provide a temporary home to terrapins.

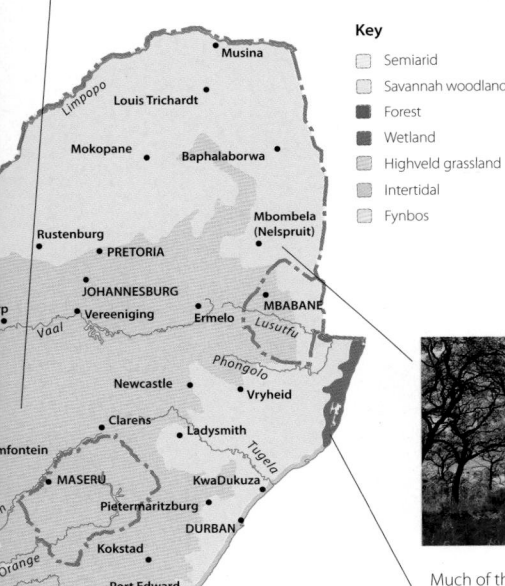

Key
- Semiarid
- Savannah woodland
- Forest
- Wetland
- Highveld grassland
- Intertidal
- Fynbos

Musina
Limpopo
Louis Trichardt
Mokopane
Baphalaborwa
Rustenburg
PRETORIA
Mbombela (Nelspruit)
JOHANNESBURG
Vereeniging
Ermelo
MBABANE
Vaal
Lusutfu
Phongolo
Newcastle
Vryheid
Clarens
Ladysmith
nfontein
MASERU
KwaDukuza
Pietermaritzburg
Tugela
Orange
DURBAN
Kokstad
Port Edward
Lusikisiki
East london
rahamstown

Savannah Woodland
Much of the north and east is covered in savannah woodland, mostly dominated by thorny acacia trees. In terms of viewing game, this is the most important habitat in South Africa.

Wetland
There are several natural lakes in the iSimangaliso Wetland Park, but South Africa is generally a dry country, and most other freshwater bodies are artificially dammed.

Intertidal
The intertidal zone is the stretch of coast dividing the permanent tree line from the open sea. The northeast coastal belt features lush mangrove swamps and offshore coral reefs teeming with fish.

FIELD GUIDE

South Africa's national parks and other protected areas are home to an astounding diversity of wildlife, from the charismatic "Big Five" *(see pp76–7)* to the lofty giraffe, greyhound-like cheetah, elegant impala and diminutive dwarf mongoose. Bird enthusiasts can look forward to sighting an enormous variety of birds. About 850 species have been recorded here, either typically African birds, migrants from Europe or endemics found only in South Africa. There are some 500 species of reptiles and amphibians, ranging from large crocodiles to tiny geckos.

The following pages introduce some of the many wild creatures that inhabit South Africa. Some, such as the gregarious impala and comical warthog, will be seen several times daily on safari. Others, like lions and elephants, can usually be sighted at least once over the course of a few days. On the other hand, creatures such as the nocturnal aardvark and pangolin are so secretive that you could spend a year in the bush without catching so much as a fleeting glimpse. While the main focus of this field guide is mammals, a more generic overview of South Africa's varied cast of reptiles and amphibians is also provided, along with a few dozen of the more conspicuous and memorable bird species.

The vast Kruger National Park, in particular, is one of the world's top destinations for the "Big Five" and host to many other popular favourites, including the giraffe, wildebeest and cheetah. These are just a fraction of what the country has to offer. However, despite the relative profligacy of wildlife in South Africa, much bio-diversity has been lost during the past three centuries of European settlement. The sable-like bluebuck and zebra-like quagga that once roamed the *fynbos*-strewn slopes of the Western Cape were hunted to extinction by the early settlers, while the protection of dwindling populations of fewer than 100 bonteboks, Cape Mountain zebras and white rhinos within national parks and game reserves saved these species from a similar fate. The conservation ethic that now prevails in South Africa is generally well-managed and forward-thinking, but the scourge of poaching and inevitable habitat loss caused by an expanding human population remain real concerns. For this reason, the descriptions that follow are accompanied by the International Union for Conservation of Nature (IUCN) Red List status of each species *(see p77)*.

Zebras mixing with an impala herd for protection against predators

◀ Cheetah in a tree in the Kruger National Park

South Africa's Wildlife Heritage

Before the arrival of the white colonists, the nomadic Khoisan hunted wild animals for food, while to the east, Zulu and Venda traded in ivory and organized ceremonial hunts – but their spears and pitfall traps had little impact. When Europeans arrived on the scene in the 17th century, South Africa's wildlife seemed inexhaustible. By the mid-19th century, with their deadly weapons, the settlers had seen to it that the vast herds had disappeared – many species were in danger of extinction. Conservation measures over the past century have brought about an amazing recovery, and South Africa's wildlife reserves are now among the finest in the world.

The klipspringer, agile and sure-footed, occurs in mountainous areas throughout the country.

White-fronted bee-eaters, one of around 850 bird species recorded in the country, gather in flocks along rivers in the Kruger National Park. They catch and consume flying insects.

Blue wildebeest

Zebra

Nyala bulls can be distinguished from the similar-looking kudu by the orange colour of their lower legs.

Warthog

The hunt is a brutal yet timeless African sequence. Cheetahs mainly prey on smaller antelopes, like springboks and impalas.

At the Waterhole

In the dry winter months (May to September), an ever-changing wildlife pageant unfolds as animals gather at waterholes to drink. Wooden hides have been erected at waterholes in KwaZulu-Natal's Hluhluwe-Imfolozi (see p298) and uMkhuze game reserves, while the rivers in the Kruger National Park offer the best vantage points.

Africa's Big Five

This term originated from hunting jargon for the most dangerous and sought-after trophy animals. Today, they are still an attraction, with the Kruger National Park *(see pp340–45)* the prime Big-Five viewing destination. Hluhluwe-Imfolozi, and the Pilanesberg and Madikwe reserves, too, are well-known sanctuaries.

Lions, the largest of the African cats, live in prides of varying size controlled by one or more dominant males.

The black rhinoceros is in serious danger of extinction. It is distinguished from the white rhino by its longer upper lip.

The First Wildlife Reserves

By the mid-19th century, hunters had decimated the big game. Subspecies like the quagga (a type of zebra) and Cape lion had become extinct. As towns expanded, people began to view wildlife as an asset, and in 1889, the Natal *Volksraad* (people's council) agreed to establish a wildlife reserve. In 1894, a strip of land between KwaZulu-Natal and Swaziland became the Pongola Game Reserve, Africa's first conservation area. In 1898, President Paul Kruger signed a proclamation establishing the forerunner of a sanctuary that was later named Kruger National Park in his honour.

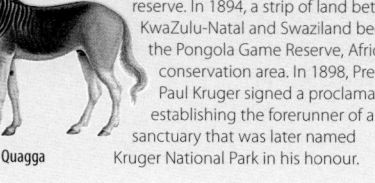

Quagga

Princeps demodocus demodocus, the attractive Christmas butterfly (also known as the citrus swallowtail), can be seen throughout South Africa from September to April. As one of its names suggests, the species often occurs in citrus groves.

Spotted hyenas are one of the most interesting of Africa's predators. Loose family groups are led by females who, due to high levels of male hormones, also have male genitalia.

Female impala

Nyala cows, usually accompanied by dominant bulls, are often spotted in the woodlands of northern KwaZulu-Natal.

Vervet monkeys usually avoid arid habitats.

Waterholes dry out rapidly in the summer heat, and the animals suffer much hardship.

Oxpeckers and kudu provide an example of the symbiosis that has evolved between different animals under the harsh African conditions. The birds free the antelopes of parasites, and also act as an alarm system at waterholes.

IUCN Red List

Established in 1963, the International Union for Conservation of Nature (IUCN) Red List of Threatened Species uses a set of criteria to evaluate the extinction risk of more than 40,000 species and subspecies of plants and animals globally. Each taxon evaluated is assigned to one of the following categories:
• Extinct (EX) – No individuals known to survive, e.g. bluebuck.
• Extinct in the Wild (EW) – Survives only in captivity or as an introduced population outside its natural range.
• Critically Endangered (CE) – Extremely high risk of extinction in the immediate future, e.g. black rhino.
• Endangered (EN) – Very high risk of extinction within the foreseeable future, e.g. African wild dog.
• Vulnerable (VU) – Significant medium-term risk of extinction, e.g. lion.
• Least Concern (LC) – No significant risk of extinction at present, e.g. impala.
• Data Deficient (DD) – Insufficient information available for assessment.

Buffaloes are the most abundant of the Big Five and occur in large herds. Old bulls become loners and may be extremely dangerous.

Leopards are shy cats that are largely nocturnal and often rest on tree branches.

Elephants live in tight-knit family groups led by a matriarch. The bulls remain solitary, or may band together to form bachelor herds.

Cats

Secretive and solitary, cats belong to the family Felidae and are the most stealthy and efficient killers among carnivores. Also the most strictly carnivorous, they feed exclusively on other warm-blooded creatures, from sparrows and mice to buffaloes and giraffes. Although they differ greatly in coloration and size, all cats have a similar body plan to their familiar domestic counterpart, with an elongated body, long tail, small head, sensitive whiskers, prominent canine teeth and keen, bifocal vision. Much wild felid behaviour will be familiar to the average cat owner.

Family

South Africa's seven felid species are traditionally split between three genera: *Felis*, with small- to medium-sized cats; *Panthera*, with big cats distinguished by a larynx modification that enables them to roar; and *Acinonyx*, with the cheetah – the only felid with non-retractable claws.

Cheetah

*Species: **Acinonyx jubatus*** • *Best Seen:* **Phinda, Kruger (central region), Sabi Sands**

VU

This large spotted felid is the greyhound of the African bush, with a streamlined build, small head and unique non-retractable claws tailored to its specialist pursuit of sprinting. The world's fastest runner, it is capable of accelerating from standstill to a speed of 115 kmph (72 mph) in 4 seconds. Where most feline predators combine hunting with scavenging, the cheetah feeds exclusively on fresh meat. It is also unusual in that it hunts by day as well as at dusk, creeping to within 15–30 m (50–100 ft) of its prey before opening chase and, if successful, knocking down and suffocating its victim. Less solitary than most cats, the cheetah is often seen in pairs or small groups – either male coalitions of up to three brothers, or a female with cubs. In common with other cats, a cheetah will purr when content and growl, hiss and yelp when threatened or annoyed. Unlike the true big cats, it cannot roar. Instead, its most common vocalization, often made by a mother looking for her cubs, is a high-pitched, bird-like twitter known as "yipping". The cheetah has a restless temperament, and is often seen trotting determinedly through the grass, breaking step only to climb on a tree trunk or termite mound that presents itself as a lookout post. Once widespread in Asia, Arabia and Africa, it has suffered a massive range-retraction in recent times, and is now practically restricted to sub-Saharan Africa.

IUCN status VU: Vulnerable; LC: Least Concern

The African wild cat, a versatile hunter

African Wild Cat

Species: Felis silvestris • Best Seen: Sabi Sands, Kgalagadi, Kruger

LC

This small, elusive felid is closely related to its much rarer European counterpart. DNA evidence suggests that it is the sole wild ancestor of the domestic cat – and indeed it looks much like a domestic tabby, but with longer legs. A versatile hunter of rodents, birds and insects, it is the most widely distributed of all African predators, absent only from rainforest interiors and deserts. Its genetic integrity is under increasing threat as a result of interbreeding with feral domestic cats.

Black-Footed Cat

Species: Felis nigripes • Best Seen: Kgalagadi, Pilanesberg

VU

Endemic to southern Africa, this tiny cat is associated with sandy, semiarid habitats, where it is very seldom seen. At a glance, it could be confused with the African wild cat, but it is much smaller, has shorter legs, and is heavily spotted as opposed to faintly striped. A nocturnal hunter, it preys mainly on small mammals such as gerbils, mice and elephant shrews.

The black-footed cat, nocturnal and seldom seen

The caracal, the cat most strongly associated with dry habitats

Caracal

Species: Felis caracal • Best Seen: Kgalagadi, Augrabies Falls

LC

The largest of Africa's "small cats", the caracal resembles the Eurasian lynx, although recent genetic studies suggest it has closer affinities to the serval. It has a fairly uniform tan coat, with light spotting sometimes distinguishable on the paler belly, and long tufted ears whose dark coloration is referred to in Turkish as *karakulak* (black ear), from which the cat gets its name. Because of this tufting, and some 20 muscles that control ear direction, it is exceptionally sharp of hearing, even by felid standards. Known to be active at night, this agile carnivore is a versatile hunter, and is particularly skilled at taking birds in flight.

Serval

Species: Felis serval • Best Seen: Kruger, uKhahlamba-Drakensberg, Ithala

LC

Superficially similar to the larger cheetah, the serval is a sleek spotted cat associated with rank grassland and other open, non-forested habitats. It typically has streaky (as opposed to circular) black-on-gold spots, although speckled and melanistic morphs also occur. It has the longest legs in relation to body size of any felid, and very large ears – adaptations that help it to locate prey in its preferred habitat of tall grassland. It feeds mainly on small mammals and birds, pouncing with a spectacular high spring, then delivering the fatal blow with one of its powerful claws. The serval is the most readily seen of the smaller felids, especially during the first 30 minutes after sunrise.

The serval, found in open habitats

Key to Field Guide icons *see p72*

Lion

The largest terrestrial predator in Africa, the lion is the most sociable and least secretive of the world's 36 cat species. Unusually among felids it seldom takes to the trees, and the adult male sports a regal blond or black mane. For most people, the charismatic "king of the jungle" is the ultimate African safari icon, so much so that it is often easy to forget that lions once ranged widely across Eurasia. Today, South Africa's lions are confined to a few protected areas. Elsewhere they have been hunted to extinction, and the continental population has plunged by an estimated 75 per cent since 1990.

Lions are remarkably indolent creatures, spending up to 20 hours a day at rest. Though seldom active in the heat of the day, they often cover long distances at night.

Family and Breeding

The most sociable of cats, the lion generally lives in prides of five to ten animals, including an adult male, a few adult females and their offspring. Larger prides also occur, often involving male coalitions; one such grouping, active in Sabi Sands in 2010, had five adult males, four of them siblings. Prides defend their territories, which cover anything from 20 to 200 sq km (8–77 sq miles). Takeover battles are often fought to the death and result in the usurper killing all existing cubs, thereby encouraging the females back into oestrus sooner. Lions undergo an extraordinary mating ritual. A male and female pair off, mating briefly but violently at gradually increasing intervals of 12–25 minutes for up to 3 days, after which they return to their pride.

Females in a pride give birth more or less simultaneously and rear their cubs cooperatively. Large prides consist of up to half a dozen lionesses and their offspring. Females usually stay with their birth pride, but young males are forced out by the dominant male when they reach sexual maturity.

What You Might See

The first lion sighting often results in disappointment, as the animals loll indifferently in the shade. Observe them for a while, however, and one is bound to see exciting interactions. It is always worth staying with an isolated female and male pair, as they may well start mating; and if a lioness is lying low in the grass, looking intently into the distance, odds are she is part of a hunt.

Rivalry between adult males can be intense and fights are often to the death.

Grooming and social licking are an important part of the daily ritual in any lion pride.

IUCN status VU: Vulnerable

Feeding

Hunting is normally a team effort undertaken by females, who rely on stealth more than speed. A common strategy is for one or two lionesses to herd their prey in the direction of other pride members lying hidden in tall grass. Males seldom take part in a hunt but are quick to exercise their feeding rights once a kill is made. Favoured prey includes antelope, and large prides can even bring down a giraffe or a buffalo.

A large male lion takes first pickings on a fresh giraffe kill

Communication and Voice

Adult lions are most active around dusk and dawn, but cubs interact throughout the day, playing and mock-fighting for hours on end. Subordinate individuals frequently stop to greet or groom dominant pride members, especially when they reunite after a period apart. The most common call, made by females as well as males, is a series of far-carrying moaning grunts that increase in volume, then fade away. As dominant males often move separately from the main pride (regrouping after a kill), this characteristic sound of the African night has the dual purpose of advertising the caller's presence to the pride and warning rivals off its territory.

A cub displays submissiveness to one of the adult males in the pride

KEY FACTS

Panthera leo

Local names: **Mbube (Zulu), Shumba (Shangaan), Leeu (Afrikaans)**

 Size Shoulder height: 100–130 cm (40–50 inches); Weight: up to 280 kg (617 lb).

Lifespan 12–15 years.
Population in South Africa 2,500–3,000.
Conservation Status VU.
Gestation Period 105–112 days.
Reproduction Females reach sexual maturity at 3 years and give birth to litters of two to six cubs every 18 months.

 Habitat Most often in savannah, but range into all except desert and rainforest.

Top Places to See Kruger, Sabi Sands, Kgalagadi, Madikwe, Pilanesberg.

Sighting Tips See resting prides in the day. Return at dawn or dusk to catch them in action.

Friends and Foes Lions are thought of as regal hunters and hyenas as scavengers, but lions are as likely to steal a carcass from hyenas as kill it themselves.

 Facts and Trivia A Setswana expression used in tough times translates as "I've still got the lion by the balls" – the implication being that if you lose your grip, you're in trouble!

The main diet of lions in South Africa comprises antelopes and other ungulates.

Cubs spend much time mock-fighting and playing with each other, and sometimes with adults.

A mating bout often lasts for less than a minute and is accompanied by growling and hissing.

Leopard

Paradoxically the most abundant yet most elusive of Africa's large predators, the leopard is distinguishable by its rosette-patterned coat, powerfully pugilistic physique and preference for dense cover. This determinedly nocturnal cat is the supreme solitary hunter, capable of creeping to within a metre of its prey before pouncing. Despite widespread persecution, the global leopard population stands at an estimated 500,000 individuals, ranging from Asia to South Africa. Sabi Sands *(see p345)* is the best place in the world for protracted sightings.

The melanistic leopard, popularly known as a panther, is found mostly in Asia. However, there have been a few South African records of so-called pseudo-melanistic leopards, which have much denser black spots than normal.

Family and Breeding

The leopard is among the most solitary and territorial of cats. Adults live alone in well-marked territories that are never shared with individuals of the same sex, although males and females frequently have partial territorial overlap. Even so, a chance meeting between two individuals is usually accompanied by real or feigned aggression. Far smaller than males, female leopards come into oestrus every 6–7 weeks. At this time, males from bordering or overlapping territories will often fight to the death for coupling rights. Mating itself is an ill-tempered and abruptly executed affair, and the male has no involvement in rearing the cubs. Females give birth to litters of two to three cubs in a sheltered cave or thicket, and keep a close watch over them for the next 10–14 days, when the cubs' eyes open. Infant mortality is high; it is unusual for more than one cub to survive to adulthood. Cubs can fend for themselves at around one year, but usually stay close to their mother for another 6–12 months before becoming fully independent.

Leopard cubs typically have greyer pelts than the adults. Leopards are famously solitary, and two individuals keeping peaceful company will almost certainly be a female and her cub.

What You Might See

For most safari-goers, the leopard is the most ardently sought of the Big Five. It is most likely to be seen resting up in a tree, in which case it is often worth waiting to see whether there is a kill secured nearby, or if it decides to descend to the ground. Even more thrilling is to catch a leopard on the move, showing off its sleek yet pugilistic build to the full.

A creature of shadow, cover and darkness, the leopard is most active after dark.

Sharpened claws are essential components in this cat's hunting and defensive arsenal.

IUCN status LC: Least Concern

Leopard dragging prey, often three times its weight, into the canopy

Feeding

The leopard is an adaptable and opportunistic hunter, feeding on anything from medium-sized antelopes to hares, birds, baboons, hyraxes and insects. It depends almost entirely on stealth, stalking silently through thick vegetation before emerging at the last possible moment to pounce and strangle its prey with its powerful jaws. In rainforests and other habitats where lions are absent, the leopard is typically the apex predator, and adults tend to be notably heavier than their savannah counterparts.

A leopard will frequently carry a large kill high into the canopy, where it is safely out of the reach of less arboreal scavengers such as lions, hyenas and jackals.

Communication and Voice

As might be expected of such a potentially fearsome creature known for its ability to survive in close, near-spectral proximity to humans, the leopard is not given to extensive vocalization. Males in particular advertise their presence with a repetitive rasping cough that sounds not unlike wood being sawed. Purring has also been recorded, probably indicating contentment during feeding. Territorial clashes between males are accompanied by snarling and hissing. However, the most remarkable feature of the leopard remains

Display of affection between leopards, seldom observed in unrelated adults

the capacity for furtiveness that ensures that the species still persists, although barely detected, in ranchland and many other unprotected areas throughout Africa.

The leopard is compulsively clean and spends much of the day grooming itself.

Although highly adaptable, leopards favour habitats that offer them plenty of cover and camouflage.

Leopards frequently spend their day lying quietly in the branches of the upper canopy.

Dogs and Hyenas

Cats aside, the two major families of large carnivore in South Africa, Canidae (dogs) and Hyaenidae (hyenas), are exciting to see in the wild. Indeed, spotted hyenas are probably the most socially complex of the region's carnivores, and it is riveting to watch clan members meet and greet at a den. Jackals, foxes and wild dogs are also at their boldest and most inquisitive while denning, offering plenty of opportunity to watch pups at play.

Family

Dogs and hyenas look similar, but their evolutionary lines split about 45 million years ago. The suborder Feliformia comprises cats, mongooses and hyenas. Caniformia includes seals, bears, otters, pandas and dogs.

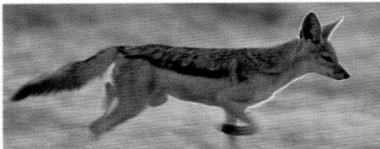

Young jackals often play in a puppy-like manner

Black-Backed Jackal

Species: **Canis mesomelas** • *Best Seen:* **Kruger, Kgalagadi, Madikwe**

LC

The more common of two closely related small dog species in South Africa, the black-backed jackal lives in pairs rather than in packs. It is most active at dusk and dawn, and its shrill yelping is a characteristic sound of the African night. It has a shoulder height of 40 cm (16 inches), and an ochre coat offset by a prominent silver-flecked black saddle. An opportunistic feeder, it subsists on small mammals, birds and carrion, and is often seen lurking near lion kills.

Side-Striped Jackal

Species: **Canis adustus** • *Best Seen:* **Kruger**

LC

Associated with brachystegia woodland, the side-striped jackal is more strictly nocturnal and less vocal than other jackals. It is similar in general coloration to the black-backed jackal, but with a pale stripe along the flanks. An adaptable omnivore seen singly or in pairs, it supplements a meat-based diet with fruit, grain and carrion. Its South African range is more or less restricted to the Kruger and adjacent private reserves.

The side-striped jackal also has a white-tipped tail

Bat-Eared Fox

Species: **Otocyon megalotis** • *Best Seen:* **Kgalagadi, Augrabies Falls**

LC

Easily distinguished from any jackal by its huge ears and black eye-mask, this small canid is not a true fox. A number of peculiarities – up to 50 sharp teeth, for instance – have led to it being placed in its own genus. Exclusively insectivorous, it tends to be nocturnal during the hot months and diurnal in the cooler ones. Pairs and small family groups can be seen throughout the year.

The small Cape fox, with its black-tipped tail

Cape Fox

Species: **Vulpes chama** • *Best Seen:* **Kgalagadi, Pilanesberg**

 LC

The only true fox occurring in sub-Saharan Africa, the Cape fox is a secretive nocturnal species whose range runs from southern Angola to the Western Cape. With a grizzled grey back and browner underparts, its general coloration is jackal-like, but its long bushy tail precludes confusion with any other canid in the region. A versatile feeder, it has an exclamatory yap, and is heard more often than it is seen – unsurprisingly so, given that it was officially persecuted as vermin for over a century.

The large ears help detect subterranean insect activity

IUCN status EN: Endangered; VU: Vulnerable; LC: Least Concern

The blotchy brown coat of the spotted hyena

Spotted Hyena

Species: **Crocuta crocuta** • *Best Seen:* **Kruger, Sabi Sands, Pilanesberg**

LC

Africa's second-largest predator after the lion stands 1 m (3 ft) high at the shoulder, and weighs about 70 kg (150 lb), with females being larger than males. The most common and conspicuous large predator in many reserves, it is most often seen at dusk and dawn. Though highly vocal at night, its famous "laugh" is less commonly heard than its haunted whoooo-whoop that ranks as perhaps the definitive sound of the African night. The hyena has a complex social structure, living in wide-ranging clans of five to 25 animals that follow a strict matriarchal hierarchy and perform an elaborate ritual when two members meet. Powerfully built, it has a characteristic sloping back, bone-crushingly powerful jaws and a dog-like face and snout. Routinely portrayed as a giggling coward whose livelihood depends on scavenging from the noble big cats, it is actually an adept hunter, capable of killing an animal as large as a wildebeest.

The aardwolf is jackal-sized but hyena-shaped

Aardwolf

Species: **Proteles cristatus** • *Best Seen:* **Pilanesberg, Madikwe, Kgalagadi**

LC

A lightly built and strictly nocturnal Hyaenid, the aardwolf (which literally means "earth wolf") weighs 10 kg (22 lb) and is often mistaken for a jackal, from which, however, it differs in appearance by having a soft creamy striped coat and prominent dorsal mane. It is exclusively insectivorous, feeding almost entirely on two specific termite genera, and its distribution, generally in drier areas, is linked strongly to the presence of suitable nests, into which it burrows nose-first to feed.

African Wild Dog

Species: **Lycaon pictus** • *Best Seen:* **Kruger, Hluhluwe-Imfolozi, Madikwe**

EN

Africa's largest canid, also known as the hunting or painted dog, is small compared with a Eurasian wolf, and is distinguished from similar species in the region by its black, brown and cream coat. It typically lives in packs of five to 50 animals that hunt cooperatively, literally tearing apart prey on the run. Once so common that it was treated as vermin, it has suffered enormous losses in recent decades, partly through direct persecution and partly through the packs' susceptibility to infectious diseases spread by domestic and feral dogs. It is now Africa's second-most endangered large carnivore, with a total wild population of around 5,000. Of these, around 10 per cent are found in South Africa, mostly in the vicinity of the Kruger National Park, and a small number are resident within Hluhluwe-Imfolozi. It is legendarily nomadic, however, and might turn up in absolutely any bush habitat.

African wild dog packs may include up to 50 animals

Brown Hyena

Species: **Hyaena hyaena** • *Best Seen:* **Pilanesberg, Kgalagadi, Madikwe**

VU

Endemic to the dry west of southern Africa, the brown hyena is a more solitary creature than its spotted counterpart, and a more dedicated scavenger, though it will hunt opportunistically. It is relatively lightly built, seldom weighing more than 50 kg (110 lb), and has a pale mane and shaggy dark brown coat offset by creamy vertical stripes on its side and flanks. It is the world's rarest hyena, and is likely to be seen only on night drives.

Brown hyena, more solitary than its spotted namesake

Key to Field Guide icons *see p72*

Small Carnivores

South Africa supports a wide diversity of small carnivorous mammals, some very conspicuous and easily observed, others highly secretive and elusive. Falling firmly into the first category are the mongooses of the family Herpestidae, several species of which are likely to be seen in the course of any safari. The nocturnal viverrids and mustelids are generally less likely to be seen, although genets often become very tame in lodges where they are regularly fed.

Family

Genets and civets belong to the most ancient of carnivore families, Viverridae, which is confined to Africa and Asia. Mustelidae, by contrast, is the most diverse carnivore family, represented by 55 species and 24 genera worldwide.

Cape Clawless Otter
Species: Aonyx capensis

LC

Arguably the largest of the "small" carnivores, weighing as much as 35 kg (77 lb) in some cases, the Cape clawless otter is a dark brown piscivore with a bold white collar. While seen in any suitable wetland habitat, it is most common in waters where it can evade crocodiles.

Honey-Badger
Species: Mellivora capensis

LC

The honey-badger, or ratel, has a fearless temperament and pugilistic build, with a black body bisected by an off-white stripe down its back, a deceptively puppyish face and heavy, bear-like claws. An opportunistic feeder, its diet includes snakes, scorpions and the soft parts of tortoises.

Striped Weasel
Species: Poecilogale albincha

LC

A widespread but uncommon resident of open grassland, the striped weasel is mostly black below and white on top, with an all-white tail. With its very short legs and almost cylindrical body shape, it could almost be mistaken for a snake at first glance. It preys almost exclusively on small rodents.

African Civet
Species: Civettictis civetta

LC

Larger and heftier-looking than the related genets, the African civet is a long-haired omnivore with a black, white and gold coat. It feeds on small animals, including certain snakes, but will also eat fruits and roots. It is seen on night drives, pacing deliberately with its nose to the ground as if following a scent.

Common Genet
Species: Genetta genetta

LC

Also known as the small-spotted genet, this is the most familiar member of a genus of cat-like predators represented by some eight species in sub-Saharan Africa. It regularly visits a few select lodges at night, and is quite often observed on night drives in Sabi Sands and other reserves.

Blotched Genet
Species: Genetta tigrina

LC

Similar-looking to the common genet but with a black-tipped instead of a white-tipped tail, the blotched or large-spotted genet has a slender, low-slung torso, a spotted black-on-gold coat and a long striped tail. It is most likely to be seen on a night drive or scavenging around lodges after dark.

IUCN status LC: Least Concern

Predator and Prey

Small carnivores are often undiscerning feeders, snaffling up anything from insects to small rodents and birds, as well as fruit and carrion. The honey-badger is famed for its symbiotic relationship with the greater honeyguide, a bird which leads it to beehives and feeds on the scraps as the hive is torn apart. The Herpestidae mongooses are known to prey on snakes, but this behaviour is more common in Asia than in Africa, where they prey on small animals that are less well-equipped to bite back.

Banded mongoose feasting on an egg

Banded Mongoose
Species: Mungos mungo

 LC

Among the most common and sociable of several mongoose species in South Africa, the banded mongoose is a slender, cat-sized carnivore whose dark brown coat bears a dozen or so faint black stripes along the back. Diurnally active, it is typically seen in family bands of 10 to 20 members.

Dwarf Mongoose
Species: Helogale parvula

 LC

The diminutive and highly social dwarf mongoose has a shoulder height of 7 cm (2¾ inches). It is a light brown predator often seen in the vicinity of the termite mounds and hollowed dead branches that it uses as a home. Family members can sometimes be seen interacting near the den.

Slender Mongoose
Species: Herpestes sanguineus

 LC

A widespread species, the slender mongoose divides its time between foraging terrestrially and arboreally. Though quite variable in shade, it is almost always uniform grey or brown in colour with an elongated body and tail – the latter with a prominent black tip.

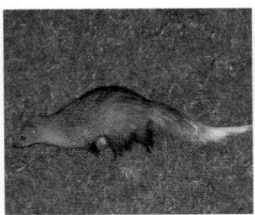

White-Tailed Mongoose
Species: Ichneumia albicauda

  LC

About the size of a badger, this is the largest African mongoose. One of the most strictly nocturnal and solitary species, it is often observed by spotlight on night drives, when the combination of size and a bushy white tail render it unmistakable.

Yellow Mongoose
Species: Cynictis pencillata

LC

Endemic to the dry western region of southern Africa, this distinctive mongoose with a bushy orange-yellow coat has a habit of standing alertly on its hind legs. It favours sandy environments, where it lives in sprawling burrows with dozens of entrance holes. It is common in Kgalagadi Transfrontier Park.

Meerkat
Species: Suricata suricata

 LC

A highly distinctive diurnal mongoose, the meerkat lives underground in closely knit gangs of 20 or so individuals. It has monkey-like fingers with long claws, with which it digs, grooms and forages. Alert, intelligent and playful, it often stands on its hind legs, particularly when disturbed.

Key to Field Guide icons *see p72*

Primates

Intelligent, hyperactive and graceful, monkeys are among the most entertaining of creatures. They are well represented in equatorial Africa, where certain individual forests contain up to a dozen species, but rather less so in South Africa, where only three species are present. This lack of diversity is attributable to the lack of suitably forested habitats. All of South Africa's monkeys are Cercopithecids (cheek-pouched monkeys), an adaptable family of omnivores that fills many ecological niches from swamp forests to semiarid plains, and is named for its inner cheek pouch, which can hold as much food as a full stomach.

Family

The three species of diurnal primate that inhabit South Africa are all classified as Old World Monkeys (family Cercopithecidae) and placed in the sub-family Cercopithecinae (cheek-pouched monkeys).

Bushbaby

Family: Galagonidae • Best Seen: Kruger, Sabi Sands, Pilanesberg

   Most Species: Variable

More closely related to the lemurs of Madagascar than to the diurnal monkeys of the African mainland, bushbabies (or galagos) are endearing creatures, with wide round eyes and agile bodies that enable them to leap between trees. Formerly, only two species were recognized – greater and lesser bushbaby – but a pioneering study used calls and genital patterns to identify around a dozen species in East Africa alone. Pending a similar study in South Africa, the taxonomy of bushbabies in the region remains indeterminate. Seldom seen in daylight, bushbabies become very active after dark, and are often seen on night drives in reserves with suitable wooded savannah habitats.

The wide-eyed bushbaby, rarely seen in daylight

Vervet Monkey

Species: Chlorocebus [Aethiops] pygerythrus • Best Seen: Kruger, Hluhluwe-Imfolozi, Durban

LC

Delightful or mischievous, depending on your point of view, the vervet monkey is one of the true characters of the African savannah. It lives in troops of 30–75 animals that are constantly engaged in interaction of one kind or another, whether fighting, grooming, carrying their young on their chest, clambering around branches in search of fruit, or raiding the nearest lodge's lunch buffet. Thought to be the world's most numerous primate species apart from humans, it is predominantly terrestrial, though it seldom strays too far from the trees in which it shelters when threatened. It is highly intelligent, boasting an array of different alarm calls that some scientists have likened to a rudimentary language. Smaller and lankier than any baboon, the vervet has a grizzled light olive or grey coat, a black face, white ruff and pale belly, though this rather dull coloration is offset in the male by a gaudy blue scrotum.

The highly intelligent vervet monkey

IUCN status LC: Least Concern

Chacma Baboon

*Species: **Papio ursinus** • Best Seen: **uKhahlamba-Drakensberg, Kruger, Cape Peninsula***

 LC

Weighing up to 45 kg (99 lb), the chacma baboon is the largest primate in South Africa and probably the most widespread. Dark grey-brown in coloration, it is distinguishable from all other South African monkeys by its pugilistic build, inverted U-shaped tail, dog-like head and long fangs. Like the vervet monkey, the baboon is behaviourally fascinating, living in large, quarrelsome matriarchal troops whose social structure allows for regular inter-troop movement of males seeking dominance. An adaptable omnivore, the baboon is at home in almost any habitat, from semi-desert to forest fringe, but is particularly fond of well-wooded savannah and mountains, where hikers are often alerted to its presence by a far-carrying barking call. Although mainly terrestrial, baboons feel safest when close to trees – their first path of retreat when predators (especially leopards) are in the vicinity. Baboons ordinarily steer clear of people, but they can become very aggressive in places where they have come to see humans as a source of food, as in some parts of the Cape Peninsula. If encountered, they should be treated with extreme caution, as they can inflict a nasty bite.

The chacma baboon, South Africa's largest primate

Blue Monkey

*Species: **Cercopithecus mitis** • Best Seen: **iSimangaliso, Hluhluwe-Imfolozi, Kruger (far north only)***

LC

The most widespread of African forest monkeys and the only one whose distribution extends south of the Limpopo River, the blue monkey is also known by a number of other names – diademed, white-throated, Sykes, and samango – in different parts of its range, reflecting its high level of regional variability. Associated mainly with forest margins, it lives in troops of up to 10 animals that willingly travel riparian corridors through savannah habitats. It has a very limited distribution in South Africa, where it is confined to the northeast corner of the country – the KwaZulu-Natal coast, the Mpumalanga escarpment forests, and the riparian forest along the Limpopo and its tributaries bordering Zimbabwe. The blue monkey can be distinguished from other South African monkeys by its more arboreal behaviour and retiring nature, and its cryptic but rather beautiful coat – dark grey-blue with flecks of orange-brown on the back, and a white belly and throat.

The shy blue monkey spends most of its time in trees

Key to Field Guide icons *see p72*

African Bush Elephant

The world's largest land animal, the African elephant is one of the most enduringly exciting creatures encountered on safari, not only for its imposing bulk, but also for its complex social behaviour. Elephants are notable for two unique adaptations – a long trunk that combines immense strength with the sensitivity to isolate and tear out a single blade of grass, and outsized tusks that grow throughout its life, sometimes reaching lengths in excess of 3 m (10 ft).

Bloody combat between male elephants is rare, since breeding rights are generally established within the community through mock fights which involve trunk-locking and tusk-clashing.

Family and Breeding

Elephants are intensely sociable creatures. Females and youngsters move around in close-knit matriarchal clans. Females typically come into oestrus between one and five years after giving birth. Once impregnated, they give birth about 22 months later. Unlike their female kin, males are generally booted out of their birth group in their early teens, after which they roam around singly or form bachelor herds, often tailing the larger breeding herds with which they share a territory. Males periodically come into musth, a sexually-related state characterized by a fifty-fold increase in testosterone levels. Such elephants are unpredictable and best treated with caution by other elephants and humans alike.

Adult females maintain a vigilant watch over their young until they are old enough to deter predator A female gives birth to a 100-kg (220-lb) calf every 5 to 10 ye Each calf thus represents a major genetic investment for the matriarchal herd, and is raised communally. Matriarchal herds comprise up to four generations of sisters, daughters and granc daughters, dominated by the oldest female.

What You Might See

Elephants are interactive, and great entertainers. Their tusks are versatile tools, used to dig for salt or water, to tear bark, and even for self-defence. The trunk is employed to place food in the mouth and suck up water, and may be wielded threateningly in displays of dominance. When an elephant raises its trunk in your direction, trumpeting and stamping its feet, it is best to retreat.

Ears flap continuously in hot weather to cool circulating blood below the thin skin.

Faced with a potential threat, a herd "periscopes" – moves its trunks around to investigate.

The trunk is used to reach high branches or to dislodge ripe fruit

Feeding

A versatile feeder, the African elephant is a mixed grazer-browser that spends up to 15 hours daily chomping 200 kg (440 lb) of vegetable matter. It drinks up to 200 litres (44 gallons) daily, arriving at a waterhole a few hours after sunrise and often lingering on until late afternoon to play in the water or spray itself. Herds range widely in search of food, but concentrated populations in protected areas often cause serious environmental degradation by uprooting trees.

Communication and Voice

It was long thought that aural communication between elephants was limited to bouts of trumpeting. In 1987, researchers discovered that the elephant's main means of communication are subsonic rumblings, below or at the edge of human perception, that can travel through the earth for several miles. These are picked up by the skin on the trunk and feet, allowing dispersed herds to coordinate their movements over a vast area. Elephants also have an exceptional sense of smell and good eyesight.

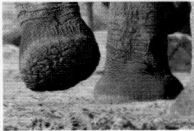

Elephants use their feet to sense the distant subsonic rumblings of a peer

KEY FACTS

Loxodonta africana

Local names: **Ndlovu (Zulu), Tlou (Tswana), Olifant (Afrikaans)**

 Size Shoulder height: 2.5–4 m (8–13 ft); Weight: up to 6,300 kg (13,890 lb).

Lifespan 65 years.
Population in South Africa 25,000.
Conservation status VU.
Gestation Period 22 months.
Reproduction Typically, females first conceive in their early teens and give birth at 5-yearly intervals until their late 50s.

 Habitat All except desert.

 Top Places to See Addo Elephant, Tembe Elephant, Madikwe, Pilanesberg, Kruger.

Sighting Tips
A trail of football-sized dung and mangled vegetation are sure signs that elephants have passed by.

Friends and Foes
Elephant droppings are a treat for dung beetles, which feed almost exclusively on fecal matter.

 Facts and Trivia
The legend of elephant graveyards has a factual basis. Old elephants whose last set of teeth has worn down gather in marshes to feed on waterlogged vegetation, until even that becomes difficult and they starve to death.

Tusks and trunk are both used to dig for subterranean water in riverbeds during the dry season.

The trunk is regularly used to tear juicy branches from the canopy and manoeuvre them into the mouth.

Elephants spray themselves with water or dust to help cool down under the hot tropical sun.

Rhinoceros

With their armoured hide, massive bulk and fearsome horns, the world's five surviving rhino species represent one of the most ancient and impressive branches of the ungulate line. Sadly, all three Asian species are on the danger list, while their African counterparts are still in tentative recovery from the critical population declines that occurred during the 20th century. It is no exaggeration to say that South Africa stands at the forefront of rhino conservation – some 75 per cent of the world's surviving rhinos are protected within its borders.

The rhino and oxpecker were long thought to have had a symbiotic relationship, with the birds cleansing the rhino's skin of ticks and other pests. It is now known that oxpeckers also suck blood from cuts and wounds in their host's hide.

The bond between mother and calf is generally strong and lasts for 3–4 years. During the first 12 months, the calf is vulnerable to predation from lions and hyenas, and is protected aggressively by its mother. The female will eventually terminate the relationship once another birth is imminent.

Family and Breeding

Adult rhinos are essentially solitary creatures, though not especially territorial. Both sexes are aggressive towards unfamiliar individuals but equable towards rhinos with neighbouring or over-lapping territories, sometimes even pairing off temporarily. The bond between mother and calf, however, is more enduring. Courtship between rhino is a protracted affair. In the case of the black rhino, the female scrapes her territorial dung piles vigorously, an the first male to pick up the scent trails behind her, try to cover it up with his own faeces. Prior to mating, the pair often indulge in noisy mock-sparring. Once the m is accepted, the two stay together for days or even weeks. A single calf weighing up to 50 kg (110 lb) is bo 15–16 months later, and is fully mobile within days.

What You Might See

Black rhinos are reclusive animals that feed in thick bush. Most safari-goers consider themselves lucky to see one in the wild. White rhinos are more numerous, and easier to spot in the grasslands where they feed. Visitors may occasionally locate a mother and calf, or a few adults assembled at a wallow. Black rhinos tend to charge when disturbed; white rhinos are more passive.

An adult male defecates at a communal dung post, signalling his passing to other rhinos.

Rhinos enjoy wallowing in mud, the colour of which often alters their own appearance.

IUCN status CE: Critically Endangered; VU: Vulnerable

Feeding

The black rhino is a dedicated browser, utilizing the leaves, branches and fruits of at least 200 plant species, while the white rhino subsists mainly as a grazer. This dietary distinction is also accountable for the misleading names of black and white rhinos, both of which are a similar shade of grey in colour. The original Dutch name *weit* (wide) was an allusion to the square grass-cropping mouth of the white rhino, but was later mistranslated to "white", leaving the black rhino to be named by default. Rhinos feed mostly in the early morning and late afternoon, ideally retiring to a wallow or waterhole at midday, though the black rhino can go almost a week without drinking water if need be.

Black rhino plucking twigs with its prehensile upper lip

Communication and Voice

Vocalizations, though complex and varied, are seldom observed during a casual rhino encounter. When two individuals meet, they may growl or trumpet to signal aggression, but will more likely snort in amicable greeting. Rhinos give a high-pitched alarm call when moderately threatened, and emit a loud, pig-like squeal when seriously alarmed. Indirect communication between neighbours includes the sharing of common dung heaps at waterholes and feeding places, which allows every individual to know which other rhinos have passed by recently. In contrast to its acute sense of smell, it has poor sight: black rhinos have a focal range of less than 10 m (33 ft).

The awesome sight of two adult males locking horns in combat

KEY FACTS

Diceros bicornis (black); *Caratotherium Simum* (white)

Local names: Tshukudu (Sotho), Ubhejane (Zulu), Renoster (Afrikaans)

Size Shoulder height: 1.4–1.8 m (4½–6 ft) (black), 1.7–1.85 m (5½–6 ft) (white). Weight: up to 1,400 kg (3,086 lb) (black); up to 3,600 kg (7,937 lb) (white).

Lifespan 40–45 years.
Population in South Africa 2,000 (black), 16,500 (white).
Conservation status CE (black), VU (white).
Gestation Period 16 months.
Reproduction Females mature sexually at 5 years and give birth to a calf every 3–4 years.

Habitat Dense woodland, thicket (black); open woodland, grassland (white).

Top Places to See Hluhluwe-Imfolozi, Kruger, Pilanesberg, Ithala.

Sighting Tips Mud wallows are good places to spot these elusive animals.

Friends and Foes A fully-grown rhino has little to fear from predators, but can be chased away by elephants.

Facts and Trivia The decline in Africa's rhinos is mainly due to the mistaken belief that the horn has aphrodisiacal qualities.

Rhinos are solitary creatures and seldom interact with each other or with different species.

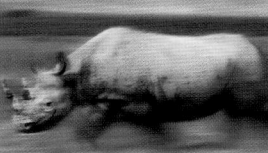
A black rhino might charge at the slightest provocation, and can quickly reach an alarming 55 kmph (34 mph).

Individual rhinos return daily to favoured rubbing posts, gradually polishing the top smooth.

African Buffalo

Africa's only wild ox, the African buffalo, is similar in appearance to the Indian water buffalo and closely related to domestic cattle. Powerfully built, with a bulk of up to 800 kg (1,764 lb) and heavy, splayed horns, it is famed for its unpredictable temperament. Indeed, the "great white hunters" who coined the term Big Five regarded this ox as the most dangerous of foes. Buffaloes are the most numerous of the Big Five, with a continent-wide population estimated at almost a million, and are highly conspicuous in several South African reserves.

Affectionately known as Daga Boys after an African word meaning mud, elderly male buffaloes tend to live singly or in small bachelor herds, and have a reputation for grumpiness, as well as for being quicker to charge than individuals in breeding herds.

Family and Breeding

The African buffalo is highly gregarious and non-territorial, generally moving in mixed-sex herds of 10 to 50 animals, with one dominant male and a hierarchical structure binding the adult females and non-dominant males. Females come into oestrus at the start of the rainy season and give birth to a single calf, or more infrequently twins, almost exactly a year later. Tensions between males run high during the mating season, with dominant bulls trying to pull rank, and subordinate males fighting to challenge their breeding rights. The imposing bulk of an adult buffalo ensures that it has few natural enemies, and a strongly bonded herd will cooperate to chase away predators. Nevertheless, buffaloes are sometimes preyed upon by lions, with the predator occasionally coming off second best in the confrontation.

Seasonal aggregations of more than 1,000 buffaloes can still be seen in some parts of South Africa, most notably in the central and northern Kruger National Park (see p344).

What You Might See

Buffaloes are less visibly interactive than certain other sociable animals. When a vehicle approaches a buffalo herd, the mass response will often be to stare down the vehicle or even to close in on it. While this can be quite intimidating, it signals curiosity – and chronic myopia – more than anything sinister. Buffaloes often support hitchhiking birds – cattle egrets, oxpeckers and starlings.

Rival males often lock horns during the mating season, but serious injuries are rare.

Buffaloes take to a wallow during the day, more so than even rhinos and elephants.

IUCN status LC: Least Concern

Feeding

Primarily a grazer, the African buffalo requires a significant proportion of grass in its diet, although it can supplement this by feeding on low trees and shrubs. Large herds are common in most grassland habitats, while forests support smaller herds. The buffalo feeds throughout the day, but will readily adopt a nocturnal feeding pattern in areas where it is repeatedly disturbed. It must drink at least once every 24 hours, and also enjoys wallowing. Herds rarely stray more than 10–15 km (6–9 miles) away from a reliable water source.

Buffalo herd gathering at a waterhole to drink and wallow

Communication and Voice

The African buffalo is generally far quieter than its mooing domestic counterpart when it comes to day-to-day communication. However, upon sighting a predator it makes an explosive snorting alarm call that swiftly mobilizes the rest of the herd into defensive mode. A threatened animal may also grunt aggressively. The buffalo has an acute sense of smell and exceptional hearing, but poor eyesight, which may cause a herd to stand and stare myopically at a perceived intruder.

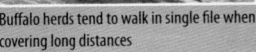
Buffalo herds tend to walk in single file when covering long distances

KEY FACTS

Syncerus caffer

Local names: **Inyathi (Zulu), Nare (Tswana), Buffel (Afrikaans)**

 Size Shoulder height: 1.2–1.7 m (4–6 ft); Weight: 500–800 kg (1,102–1,764 lb).

Lifespan 20–25 years.
Population in South Africa 30–60,000.
Conservation status LC.
Gestation Period 11–12 months.
Reproduction Females mature at the age of 4–5 years and give birth to a single calf at the start of the rainy season.

 Habitat Mostly non-arid environments.

 Top Places to See Kruger, Hluhluwe-Imfolozi, Pilanesberg.

Sighting Tips
The buffalo is still present in some places where unguided walking is permitted, such as the iSimangaliso Wetland Park.

Friends and Foes
Cattle egrets flock around herds of buffalo to feed on insects that are disturbed as the mammals move through the grass.

 Facts and Trivia
The Zulu military formation "Impondo Zekomo" – Buffalo Horn – consisted of a strong body of troops with two flanking "horns" to cut off escape routes.

A courting male buffalo will rest his head on the female's rump as a prelude to mating.

Female calves stay with their birth herd, but males may be forced out upon reaching sexual maturity.

Large prides of lions sometimes attempt to prey on buffaloes, with mixed success.

Giraffes, the world's tallest land mammal

Southern Giraffe

Species: **Giraffa camelopardalis** • *Best Seen:*
Kruger, Hluhluwe-Imfolozi, Pilanesberg

                                        LC

As the world's heaviest ruminant and the
tallest land mammal, the giraffe is a
specialized canopy-feeder, browsing on
high-grade leaf foliage at heights of up
to 6 m (20 ft), though it will occasionally
eat grass too. Giraffes typically move
in impermanent groups of up to
15 animals, with individuals often
leaving or joining at will; a herd may
be all-male, all-female or mixed in
composition. Males are significantly
larger in size than females, and often
engage in a form of behaviour called
necking – intertwining their necks and
heads and occasionally dealing out
heavy blows. This has various functions,
ranging from combat to a prelude to
homosexual mounting, which is
more frequent among giraffes than
heterosexual coupling. Females normally
have one calf, and give birth standing,
with the newborn dropping up to
2 m (7 ft) to the ground, then standing
up and suckling within 30 minutes.

Common Hippopotamus

Species: **Hippopotamus amphibius** • *Best Seen:*
iSimangaliso, Kruger, Pilanesberg

VU

The most characteristic resident of
Africa's rivers and freshwater lakes is the
common hippo, whose purple-grey
hairless hide, pink undersides and cheeks,
barrel-like torso and stumpy legs render
it unmistakable. Ears, eyes and nostrils
are placed high on the skull, allowing it
to spend most of its time submerged in
the shallows. It feeds terrestrially,
however, emerging between dusk and
dawn to crop grass with its wide mouth,
often ranging far from water in the
process. The hippo is highly gregarious,
living in pods of up to 30 members,
and very territorial, with fights for
dominance between males often
resulting in serious injury or death.
Contrary to appearance, the hippo
is highly mobile on land and can
easily attain a speed of above
32 kmph (20 mph). It can be very
dangerous to humans, as it typically
heads straight to the safety of the
water when disturbed, mowing down
anything in its path. The communal
grunting of the hippo, a characteristic
sound at waterside lodges, can be
heard by day as well as after dark.

Hippos are poor swimmers, tending to stick to shallow water

IUCN status EN: Endangered; VU: Vulnerable; LC: Least Concern

The Cape mountain zebra has no shadow stripes

Mountain Zebra

Species: **Equus zebra** • *Best Seen:* **Goegap, Table Mountain**

                     EN

The mountain zebra is a vulnerable southern African endemic associated with dryish mountainous habitats up to 2,000 m (6,562 ft) above sea level. Two races are recognized, and regarded by some authorities as distinct species. The Cape mountain zebra is a fynbos endemic which was hunted close to extinction in the early 20th century, when the population bottlenecked at below 100 individuals, but has since bred up to an estimated population of 2,700. Hartmann's mountain zebra is near-endemic to Namibia, though a small South African population is protected within the Goegap Nature Reserve outside Springbok. In most respects, the mountain zebra is very similar to the South African race of plains zebra, from which it can be distinguished by the absence of shadow stripes, but it lives in smaller core herds which never form larger temporary aggregations.

The striping on a plains zebra reaches right under the belly

Plains Zebra

Species: **Equus quagga** • *Best Seen:* **Kruger, Hluhluwe-Imfolozi, Sabi Sands**

                    LC

More common than the mountain zebra, the plains zebra, or Burchell's zebra, is a grazer whose natural distribution ranges from Ethiopia to the Cape. The plains zebra is often seen in large ephemeral herds, but its core social unit is an aggressively defended non-territorial herd comprising one stallion, up to five mares and their respective foals. The purpose of the zebra's stripes is often cited as camouflage, breaking up the animal's outline in long grass, but this fails to explain their benefit in arid habitats. It is more likely that the striping is visually confusing to predators when the herd scatters. The quagga, a partially-striped Western Cape endemic that was hunted to extinction in the early years of colonialism, is thought to have been a race of plains zebra (hence the Latin name *Equus quagga*).

Key to Field Guide icons *see p72*

Small Mammals

South Africa is best-known for its rich megafauna, but the country also supports a fascinating variety of smaller and more obscure mammals. These range from diverse and highly conspicuous orders such as the rodents and bats, which keen observers are likely to encounter on a daily basis, to the more quirky and elusive aardvark and pangolin, both of which come close to topping the wish list of seasoned safari-goers.

Family

Many of these animals are evolutionary one-offs. For instance, the aardvark is the only living member of the order Tubulidentata. By contrast, pigs belong to the same order as giraffes, camels and antelopes.

A pangolin, with its thick armour-plated scaling

Ground Pangolin

Family: *Manidae* • Best Seen: *Kgalagadi*

Most Species: LC

Also known as scaly anteaters, pangolins are unobtrusive nocturnal insectivores whose name derives from the Malay *penguling*, a reference to their habit of curling into a tight ball when disturbed. The savannah-dwelling ground pangolin is the only species found in South Africa, where it is more or less confined to the northern border regions. Weighing up to 18 kg (40 lb), it is exceptionally unlikely to be seen in the wild.

Hyrax

Order: *Hyracoidea* • Best Seen: *Table Mountain, Mapungubwe, uKhahlamba-Drakensberg*

All Species: LC

Endemic to Africa, hyraxes are dwarfish relicts of a once-prolific near-ungulate order more closely related to elephants than to any other living creature. The Cape rock hyrax (or dassie) *Procavia capensis* is a conspicuous resident of rocky slopes, where it lives in territorial family groups of up to 20 individuals. Confined to the forests of the eastern coastal belt, the seldom-seen southern tree hyrax *Dendrohyrax arboreus* is best-known for its terrifying, banshee-like call.

Hyraxes spend long periods basking in the sun

Aardvarks use clawed feet to dig into termite mounds

Aardvark

Species: *Orycteropus afer* • Best Seen: *Sabi Sands, Kruger, Pilanesberg*

LC

One of the most peculiar of African mammals, the aardvark – a Dutch name meaning earth pig – weighs up to 80 kg (176 lb). It is a shy, strictly nocturnal insectivore with a stout body, an arched back, pinkish skin, a heavy tail not unlike a kangaroo's and long, upright ears. It uses its elongated snout and a long, retractable sticky tongue to snaffle up as many as 50,000 termites in one night.

Cape Porcupine

Species: *Hystrix africaeaustralis* • Best Seen: *Sabi Sands*

LC

Porcupines are the largest of African rodents, though the species found in South Africa is not quite so bulky as its 27-kg (60-lb) East African counterpart. It is coated in long black-and-white quills, which occasionally betray its presence by rattling as it walks.

The long quills of the porcupine are modified hair

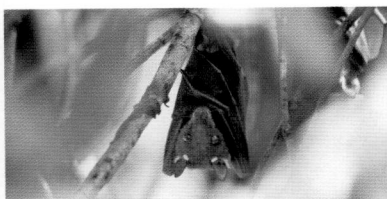
Fruitbats generally roost in colonies in trees

Bats

Order: **Chiroptera** • *Best Seen:* **Common in most non-urban environments**

 Most Species: Variable

Chiroptera (bats) is the second-most successful mammalian order, with 1,000-plus species globally. Although widely feared, no African bat sucks blood, and they play a vital ecological role in controlling flying insect populations. Small, insect-eating bats are often seen hawking at dusk throughout South Africa, most commonly in game reserves and other relatively unspoiled habitats. The larger fruitbats tend to prefer forest and other wooded habitats, and are seldom seen in South Africa.

Springhare

Species: **Pedetes capensis** • *Best Seen:* **Kgalagadi, Augrabies Falls, Mapungubwe**

LC

This peculiar and unmistakable rodent most resembles a miniature kangaroo, with powerful hind legs that enable it to cover up to 2 m (6 ft) in one bound. Sandy brown with a long, black-tipped tail, the springhare weighs up to 4 kg (9 lb) and is most likely to be seen after dark – initially as a pair of eyes bouncing around in the spotlight. By day, the springhare rests up in deep burrows in sandy soils, and is particularly common in the semiarid savannah of the Kalahari region.

The springhare, with its long black-tipped tail

Common Warthog

Species: **Phacochoerus africanus** • *Best Seen:* **Kruger, Hluhluwe-Imfolozi, Pilanesberg**

 LC

The most common and conspicuous of Africa's wild pigs, the warthog is a long-legged, slender-bodied swine that stands 80 cm (32 inches) high at the shoulder and weighs up to 150 kg (331 lb) in exceptional cases. It has an almost hairless grey coat, a long dorsal mane, upward-curving tusks and a trio of callus-like "warts" on its face. Family groups, a regular sight in many savannah reserves, are often seen trotting briskly away with long, thin tails stiffly erect. The warthog is an unfussy omnivore whose favoured food consists of roots and bulbs. It defends itself against predators by reversing into a burrow with tusks facing out aggressively. The common warthog's South African range is now confined to the north and east, but a similar-looking race of desert warthog, *Phacochoerus aethiopicus*, also known from the Horn of Africa, inhabited the Cape until it was hunted out in the 1860s.

The bushpig lives in dense forest and along rivers

Bushpig

Species: **Potamochoerus larvatus** • *Best Seen:* **Sabi Sands, Kruger, Hluhluwe-Imfolozi**

 LC

Larger, more hirsute and shorter-legged than the warthog, the bushpig is also fairly widespread in South Africa. It is less conspicuous as a result of its strictly nocturnal habits, its secretive nature and a preference for dense riverine and forested vegetation. The bushpig can be recognized by its small eyes, blunt snout, pointed, tufted ears and buckled toes. It has small tusks, and can be quite aggressive when cornered. It displays a high degree of colour variation, ranging from grey-brown to chestnut. Bushpigs are quite often seen after dark at the rest camp in Hluhluwe-Imfolozi Game Reserve, and you might well see traces of their foraging for roots on forest trails elsewhere in the country.

The tusks of the warthog are the largest of any swine

Key to Field Guide icons *see p72*

Antelopes

A constant of South Africa's wild places, antelopes thrive in every habitat from rainforest to desert. They range from the tiny blue duiker, which weighs about the same as a domestic cat, to the cattle-sized eland. Otherwise similar in appearance to deer, antelopes sport permanent horns rather than seasonal antlers. The family has its very own photogenic "Big Five": eland, kudu, gemsbok, sable antelope and roan antelope.

Common Eland

*Species: **Taurotragus oryx** • Best Seen: **uKhahlamba-Drakensberg, Pilanesberg, Kgalagadi***

 LC

Also known as the Cape eland, Africa's largest antelope has a maximum shoulder height of 1.8 m (6 ft) and can weigh almost 950 kg (2,094 lb). The most overtly cow-like of the spiral-horned antelope, it is light tan in colour, with faint white vertical stripes, small unisex horns and a hefty dewlap. It moves in groups of about 10 animals, but larger parties are also seen. The eland was revered by the San – hunter-gatherers who once inhabited South Africa – and is the animal most commonly depicted in their rock paintings.

The common eland – both sexes have spiral horns

The male greater kudu is unique in having horns that go into a full double spiral.

An adult male kudu sporting well-developed horns

Greater Kudu

*Species: **Tragelaphus strepsiceros** • Best Seen: **Kruger, Pilanesberg, Mapungubwe***

 LC

The most magnificent of African antelopes, the greater kudu is second in stature only to the eland. It stands up to 1.5 m (5 ft) high and has a greyish coat with up to 10 vertical white stripes on each side. Males have massive double-spiralled horns. Small family parties are seen in dense woodland along dry-country watercourses. An accomplished jumper, the greater kudu can clear fences twice its shoulder height. It is the most common large antelope in unprotected parts of South Africa.

Gemsbok (Common Oryx)

*Species: **Oryx gazella** • Best Seen: **Kgalagadi, Augrabies Falls, Pilanesberg***

LC

This handsome dry-country antelope has a shoulder height of 1.2 m (4 ft), a cleanly marked grey, black and white coat, a long black tail and long straight horns that sweep back from the skull at the same angle as the forehead and muzzle. Seen in nomadic herds of up to 10 animals, it can survive without water for almost as long as a camel, obtaining all its needs from the plants it eats. It is naturally restricted to the more arid northwest of South Africa, but has also been introduced to the Pilanesberg National Park and other reserves outside that range.

The gemsbok, with its long straight horns

IUCN status VU: Vulnerable; LC: Least Concern

A lone sable antelope in woodland

Sable Antelope

Species: **Hippotragus niger** • *Best Seen:* **Pilanesberg, Sabi Sands, Kruger (Around Pretoriuskop and Letaba)**

 LC

Among the largest and most handsome of antelopes, the male sable stands up to 1.4 m (4 ft 7 inches) at the shoulder and weighs up to 270 kg (595 lb). It has a jet-black coat offset by a white face, underbelly and rump, and its splendid decurved horns reach up to 1.4 m (4 ft 7 inches) in length. The female is less striking, with a chestnut-brown coat and shorter horns. Common elsewhere on the African continent, the sable is confined to the far northeast of South Africa, where it is very localized. Sightings are uncommon in the Kruger National Park, but quite frequent in Pilanesberg.

Roan Antelope

Species: **Hippotragus equinus** • *Best Seen:* **Kruger (Letaba area), Pilanesberg**

 LC

Similar in proportions to the sable antelope, the roan has short, decurved horns and a fawn-grey coat with a pale belly and light mane. Its South African distribution is comparable to that of the sable, but it is probably less common, with the Pilanesberg National Park offering perhaps the best opportunity of a sighting in the wild. Captive populations of roan are also held on some private ranches in the north of the country. Roan form groups of five to fifteen animals, with a dominant male. Fighting among males for control of the herd is not uncommon. The closely related bluebuck is a *fynbos* endemic that was hunted to extinction in the 19th century and now survives only in the form of a few mounted specimens found in museums.

The roan antelope, less common than the sable

A pair of common waterbucks

Common Waterbuck

Species: **Kobus ellipsiprymnus** • *Best Seen:* **Kruger, iSimangaliso, Hluhluwe-Imfolozi**

VU

The largest and most distinctive member of the kob family, the common waterbuck stands up to 1.3 m (4 ft 3 inches) at the shoulder, and weighs up to 240 kg (529 lb). It is recognized by its shaggy grey-brown to chestnut coat (which darkens with age), the male's large, lyre-shaped horns, and the bold white inverted U-mark on its rump. Waterbuck are usually found in open grassland or woodland – almost always, as the name suggests, in the vicinity of standing water, although they spend relatively little time actually in the water. Herds comprise up to 10 individuals lorded over by a dominant male, who will defend his territory and mating rights with vigorous aggression. In his prime, a male will control a territory of around 120 hectares (297 acres).

Key to Field Guide icons *see p72*

The impala, a fast runner and prodigious jumper

Impala

Species: Aepyceros melampus • Best Seen: Kruger, Hluhluwe-Imfolozi, Madikwe

 LC

A relative of the wildebeest, this elegantly proportioned, medium-sized antelope has a chestnut coat with black-and-white stripes on the rump and tail. Males have magnificent black-ringed horns. Impalas are usually seen in herds of over 100, dominated numerically by females and young. They are agile jumpers, and herds often leap in all directions to confuse predators. They are by far the commonest antelope in the Kruger National Park, whose impala population exceeds 100,000, and they are also prolific in bush habitats elsewhere in the northeast, although they don't occur naturally in the rest of the country. The much rarer black impala owes its coloration to a recessive gene.

Red Hartebeest

Species: Alcelaphus buselaphus • Best Seen: Kgalagadi, Madikwe, Pilanesberg

 LC

One of the more conspicuous large antelopes in the tropical grasslands of Africa, the hartebeest is similar in height to the related wildebeests, with large shoulders, a backward-sloping back, slender torso, pale yellow-brown coat, and smallish unisex horns whose somewhat heart-shaped appearance may be alluded to in its name (which is Dutch in origin). Males frequently climb on termite hills to scan, as a display of territorial dominance. Half a dozen races are recognized, the one present in South Africa being the red hartebeest. It occurs naturally only in the north, on the border with Botswana, but is farmed in many other parts of the country.

Red hartebeest, with its distinctive narrow face

Tsessebe

Tsessebe, mainly found in open grassland

Species: Damaliscus lunatus • Best Seen: Kruger (north only)

 LC

Known as the topi or tiang elsewhere in its range, the tsessebe comes across as a darker and glossier variation of the red hartebeest, with which it shares similar habits and a habitat preference for open grassland. It is dark brown in general coloration, with some black on the flanks and snout, and striking yellow lower legs. It is very rare in South Africa, with a natural range more or less confined to the Kruger National Park, where it is most likely to be seen on the eastern basaltic plains, north of the Olifants River.

Blesbok/Bontebok

Species: Damaliscus pygargus • Best Seen: Bontebok, Table Mountain, Golden Gate

 LC

Endemic to South Africa, the blesbok and bontebok are smaller and more boldly marked relatives of the tsessebe that freely interbreed where their ranges overlap and are thus regarded as races of the same species. The bontebok is a *fynbos* endemic that was hunted to within 100 individuals of extinction prior to the creation of the eponymous national park in the 1930s, but since then the population has recovered to the thousands. The blesbok is a more numerous resident of highveld grassland in the centre of the country. Both are dark brown with white faces and legs.

Bontebok, found only in South Africa

IUCN status LC: Least Concern

Blue wildebeest

Blue Wildebeest

*Species: **Connochaetes taurinus** • Best Seen: **Kruger, Hluhluwe-Imfolozi, Sabi Sands***

LC

Although common in southern-hemisphere grassland habitats from the Serengeti-Mara to KwaZulu-Natal, the blue wildebeest is totally absent north of the equator. It is a highly gregarious creature, particularly in areas where it follows an annual migration, often assembling in groups of several hundred. Its dark grey-brown coat precludes confusion with other antelopes, but at a distance it could be mistaken for a buffalo, although its slighter build and shaggy beard are distinguishing features.

Black Wildebeest

*Species: **Connochaetes gnou** • Best Seen: **Golden Gate***

LC

Another South African endemic hunted close to extinction by early European settlers, the black wildebeest or white-tailed gnu is rather more handsome than the more widespread blue wildebeest, from which it is most easily distinguished by its off-white mane and tail. Some authorities regard it as extinct in the wild, since the only surviving herds are farmed or semi-captive, but the population of several thousand is high enough for it to be IUCN-listed in the "Least Concern" category. It might be seen from the roadside on farmland anywhere in the central highveld northwest of Lesotho.

Black wildebeest bull

A lone bushbuck grazing in a forest clearing

Bushbuck

*Species: **Tragelaphus scriptus** • Best Seen: **Kruger, Hluhluwe-Imfolozi, uKhahlamba-Drakensberg***

LC

The closest thing in Africa to a Bambi lookalike, the bushbuck is a widespread medium-sized antelope of forest and riparian woodland. The male is usually dark brown or chestnut in colour, while the more petite female is generally pale red-brown. Both sexes have white throat patches, and a variable combination of white spots, and sometimes stripes on the coat. The bushbuck usually moves singly or in pairs and, although common, tends to be rather furtive in its behaviour.

Nyala

*Species: **Tragelaphus angasii** • Best Seen: **Hluhluwe-Imfolozi, Kruger, iSimangaliso***

LC

Intermediate in size between the related greater kudu *(see p100)* and bushbuck, the nyala typically occurs in small family groups in thicketed habitats close to water. The male is truly spectacular – dark chestnut-grey in general coloration, but with a grey-black leonine mane, light white stripes along the sides, yellow leg stockings and handsome lyre-shaped horns that can grow to a length of 80 cm (2 ft 8 inches). Hunted to near-extinction in most of its former range, the nyala would probably be listed as endangered were it not for the population of 25,000 animals (70 per cent of the global total) in northern KwaZulu-Natal.

The spectacular-looking male nyala

Key to Field Guide icons *see p72*

Springbok

Species: **Antidorcas marsupialis**
• Best Seen: **Kgalagadi, Augrabies
Falls, Goegap**

LC

South Africa's national animal,
the springbok is the only gazelle
(that is, antelope of the genus
Gazella or related genera) that is
found south of the Zambezi. It
strongly resembles the East
African "Tommy" (Thomson's
gazelle), with fawn upperparts
and creamy belly separated by
a black side-stripe. Despite its
iconic status, it is far rarer than
it was in the 18th century;
today it is largely confined to
the extreme northwest of
the country.

Suni

Species: **Neotragus moschatus** *• Best
Seen:* **Phinda, iSimangaliso, Ndumo**

LC

The suni is a small antelope that
lives in coastal forests and
thickets whose posture,
coloration and habits make it
easy to confuse with a duiker. It
has a more freckled coat than
any duiker, however, and on
close inspection it can also be
distinguished by its backward-
sweeping horns (only the rams
grow horns), large, rounded
and almost rabbit-like ears,
pronounced facial glands, and
its habit of flicking its black-and-
white tail from side to side,
rather than up and down.

Common Duiker

Species: **Sylvicapra grimmia**
• Best Seen: **Kruger, Pilanesberg,
uKhahlamba-Drakensberg**

LC

The least typical but most
widespread and conspicuous
of Africa's 18 duiker species, the
common or grey duiker is a
variably coloured resident
of wooded savannah habitats
that may be seen almost
anywhere in South Africa,
apart from in forest interiors.
Most often seen in pairs, it could
be confused with steenbok, but
it is generally greyer. The duiker
has a unique identifier in the
form of a black tuft of hair that
divides its horns.

Blue Duiker

Species: **Philantomba
monticola** *• Best Seen:* **Eshowe,
Phinda, iSimangaliso**

LC

A widespread but shy resident
of coastal forests, the blue
duiker is the smallest South
African antelope, with a height
of about 35 cm (14 inches) and
a weight of 5 kg (11 lb). It is one
of a group of hunchbacked
forest-dwellers that rank as
perhaps the most elusive and
least well understood of East
African antelope. Seldom seen,
it can be distinguished by its
white under-tail, which it flicks
regularly. Both sexes have
short sharp horns.

Natal Red Duiker

Species: **Cephalophus natalensis**
• Best Seen: **Hluhluwe-Imfolozi,
Phinda, iSimangaliso**

VU

The 46-cm (18-inch) tall
Natal red duiker is among the
South African representatives
of a cluster of red duiker
species, most of which are
deep chestnut in colour with
a white tail and black snout
patch. A specialized forest-
dweller confined to the eastern
coastal littoral, it is liable to be
confused only with the blue
duiker or the suni, but it is more
widespread than either and,
when seen clearly, its rich
coloration distinguishes it.

Klipspringer

Species: **Oreotragus oreotragus** *• Best
Seen:* **Mapungubwe, uKhahlamba-
Drakensberg, Augrabies Falls**

LC

A relict of an ancient antelope
lineage, the klipspringer
(Africaans for "rock jumper")
boasts several unusual
adaptations to its mountainous
habitat. Binocular vision
enables it to gauge jumping
distances accurately, it has a
unique ability to walk on its
hoof tips, and its hollow fur
insulates at high altitude. Pairs
bond for life, and both sexes
have a grizzled grey-brown
coat, short, forward-curving
horns and an arched back.

IUCN status VU: Vulnerable; LC: Least Concern

Reedbuck

Species: Redunca spp. • Best Seen: iSimangaliso, Kruger, uKhahlamba-Drakensberg

 LC

Two species of reedbuck occur in South Africa – the common and the mountain. Both are pale, skittish and lightly built grassland-dwellers with white underbellies and small horns. The common reedbuck, a lowland and mid-altitude species with short, forward-curving horns, is exceptionally common in iSimangaliso, along the road to Cape Vidal. The chunkier and greyer mountain reedbuck is commonest in uKhahlamba-Drakensberg.

Oribi

Species: Ourebia ourebi • Best Seen: uKhahlamba-Drakensberg, Kwazulu-Natal (Midlands)

 LC

A patchily distributed small-to-medium-sized antelope, the oribi has a shoulder height of around 50 cm (20 inches) and small, straight unisex horns. It has a sandy coat with a white belly and can be recognized by the round black glandular patch below its ears. Typically seen in pairs or small herds in tall open grass, the oribi tends to draw attention to itself with a trademark sneezing alarm call before rapidly fleeing.

Steenbok

Species: Raphicerus campestris • Best Seen: Kruger, Pilanesberg, Hluhluwe-Imfolizi

 LC

Somewhat resembling a scaled-down version of the oribi, the steenbok is a small antelope with tan upperparts, white underbelly and short straight horns. However, it tends to prefer thicker vegetation than the oribi, and its smaller size means it is more likely to be mistaken for a duiker. The name steenbok is Afrikaans for stone buck, and refers not to the animal's habitat, but to its habit of "freezing" when disturbed.

Cape Grysbok

Species: Raphicerus malanotus • Best Seen: Table Mountain, De Hoop, Cedarberg Mountains

 LC

Endemic to fynbos and other thicket habitats in the Western and Eastern Cape, the Cape grysbok can be distinguished from other small antelope in its geographic range by its larger size, chunky build, tailless appearance and the combination of a flecked russet coat and white circles around the eyes. Despite being somewhat localized, it remains reasonably common in suitable habitats in the Western and Eastern Cape.

Sharpe's Grysbok

Species: Raphicerus sharpei • Best Seen: Kruger (Central and Northern Regions), Mapungubwe

 LC

The core range of Sharpe's grysbok, the tropical counter-part to the Cape grysbok, lies north of the Limpopo, but it is sparsely distributed in suitable habitats – thickets and rocky slopes – in parts of the Kruger National Park. The reddish, white-flecked coat and unusual grazing posture, with white rump tilted skywards, preclude confusion with other antelope in its range. Very timid, it sometimes retreats into aardvark burrows when threatened.

Grey Rhebok

Species: Pelea capreolus • Best Seen: uKhahlamba-Drakensberg, Mountain Zebra, Bontebok

 LC

This South African endemic is superficially similar to the mountain reedbuck, but has a woollier grey coat, a longer neck and snout, and distinctive elongated hare-like ears. Because it has several goat-like adaptations, it is something of a taxonomic enigma. Around 20 per cent of the global population lives in the uKhahlamba-Drakensberg, and it is commonly depicted in that park's ancient rock art.

Key to Field Guide icons *see p72*

Amphibians and Reptiles

Amphibians and reptiles tend to get plenty of bad press, and not entirely without reason, considering that the Nile crocodile kills dozens of villagers annually, and several snake species can inflict lethal bites. However, most reptiles are harmless to people and are of great ecological value. These cold-blooded creatures maintain their body heat using external sources, for instance by basking in the sun. They are therefore prolific in warm climates and tend to be poorly represented at high altitudes.

Family

DNA and fossil evidence indicate that crocodiles are more closely related to birds than to lizards or snakes. As such, the class Reptilia is an artificial construct, one that would only gain scientific validity were it to include birds.

African Bullfrog
Species: Pyxicephalus adspersus

LC

South Africa's largest frog species is an aggressive carnivore that weighs up to 2 kg (4 lb) and takes prey as large as rats. During the rains, it emits a memorable medley of lusty bellows and grunts. In the dry season it estivates, burying itself in a subterranean cocoon for months on end.

Tree Frog
Family: Hyperoliidae

Variable

Africa's most diverse frog family, found in moist woodland habitats, tree frogs are small and brightly coloured, with long broad-tipped toes used to climb trees and reeds. A common species is the bubbling kassina, whose popping chorus is among the most wondrous of African sounds.

Skink
Family: Scincidae

Variable

Represented in South Africa by over a dozen species, skinks are small, fleet-footed lizards with slender bodies, long tails and dark scaling. Among the more visible species are the variable, striped and rainbow skinks of the genus *Mabuya*, most of which are associated with rocks.

Gecko
Family: Gekkonidae

NE

The most diverse African lizard family, geckoes have lidless bug-eyes for nocturnal hunting and adhesive toes that allow them to run upside-down on smooth surfaces. Most familiar is the common house gecko, a translucent white lizard that can be seen in safari lodges in the Kruger area.

Chameleon
Family: Chamaeleonidae

NE

These charismatic lizards are known for their colour changes (caused by mood rather than background), independently swivelling eyes and long sticky tongues that uncoil to lunge at insects. Most common is the flap-necked chameleon, but there are also several endemic dwarf chameleons.

Agama
Family: Agamidae

NE

Agamas are medium to large lizards with bright plastic-looking scales – blue, purple, red or orange, depending on the species. The flattened head is generally differently coloured from the torso. Often observed basking on rocks, the male red-headed agama is particularly spectacular.

IUCN status LC: Least Concern; NE: Not Evaluated

Harmless Snakes

Of the 120 snake species recorded in South Africa, only eight are classed as highly venomous. Most of the others are entirely harmless. Among the more common of these benign slitherers, snakes of the genus *Philothamnus* are generally bright green with large dark eyes, and are often seen near water. The widespread rhombic egg-eater, sometimes mistaken for a puff adder, can dislocate its jaws to swallow an egg whole, regurgitating the crushed shell in a neat package.

Rhombic egg-eater, a non-venomous snake

African Rock Python
Species: Python sebae
NE

As Africa's largest snake, this python can reach lengths of 6 m (20 ft), and is very likely to be seen on safari. It is non-venomous, wrapping its body around its prey, swallowing it whole and slumbering for weeks or months while the digestive juices do their work.

Mamba
Genus: Dendroaspis spp
NE

Mambas are fast-moving and widely feared snakes that generally attack only when cornered. The 4-m (12-ft) black mamba, Africa's largest venomous snake, has a distinctive coffin-shaped head. The green mamba is smaller and shyer. Bites are rare but the venom is fatal.

Cobra
Genus: Naja spp
NE

Cobras are long snakes – up to 3 m (10 ft) – whose trademark hoods open in warning when they raise their head to strike or spit venom into the target's eye. Bites are fatal, but spitting, though it can result in temporary blindness, causes little long-term damage if the venom is diluted with water.

Boomslang
Species: Dispholidus typus
NE

As its Afrikaans name suggests, the boomslang (tree snake) is almost exclusively arboreal. It is generally green in colour, but may also be brown or olive. Theoretically the most toxic of African snakes, it is back-fanged and passive, and, except on snake handlers, it has never inflicted a fatal bite.

Adder and Viper
Family: Viperidae
Variable

The puff adder's notoriously sluggish disposition means that it is more frequently disturbed than any other venomous snake – and is thus responsible for more bites than other species. Thickset and cryptically marked, it is most common in rocky areas, but also occurs in most bush habitats.

Monitor
Family: Varanidae
NE

Africa's largest lizard, the Nile monitor can grow to be 3 m (10 ft) long, and is often seen along river margins. The closely related savannah monitor is a little smaller in size. Both species feed on meat and carrion and, though not normally dangerous, can inflict a nasty bite if cornered.

Key to Field Guide icons *see p72*

Nile Crocodile

Species: **Crocodylus niloticus** • *Best Seen:* **Kruger, iSimangaliso, Ndumo**

 LC

Crocodiles have lurked in the lakes and rivers of Africa for at least 150 million years, and are the nearest thing alive to a relict of the Jurassic Era, as they are more closely related to dinosaurs than to any living creature. South Africa is home to the Nile crocodile, Africa's bulkiest and longest-lived predator, which grows to a maximum recorded length of 8 m (26 ft), weighs up to 1,000 kg (2,205 lb) and boasts a lifespan similar to that of humans. It occurs naturally in freshwater habitats, basking open-mouthed on the sandbanks before it slips, silent and sinister, into the water on the approach of a boat. The St Lucia Estuary in iSimangaliso Wetland Park harbours the country's densest population of Nile crocodiles, but they are also common in the rivers of the Kruger National Park.

A female lays up to 100 hard-shelled eggs in a small hole, covers them to protect them from predators, then returns three months later to carry the hatchlings to the water, where she leaves them to fend for themselves. The Nile crocodile feeds mainly on fish, but occasionally drags a mammal as large as a lion into the water. Several crocodile farms in South Africa breed these reptiles for their valuable hide, the best-known farm being located on the outskirts of St Lucia town.

The hide of dark, heavy scales is valued by commercial poachers to make handbags, shoes and other leather goods.

A crocodile can stay submerged in water without drawing breath for 45–60 minutes.

A Nile crocodile has about 8 teeth, which are shed and replaced twice annually.

Crocodiles make for a primeval sight as they bask on a bank

Like other reptiles, the leopard tortoise has scaled skin

Tortoise

Family: **Testudinidae** • *Best Seen:* **Kruger, Addo Elephant, Pilanesberg**

 Most Species: Variable

The term tortoise is used to describe any terrestrial chelonian, an order of shelled reptiles that also includes freshwater terrapins and marine turtles. The most visible species on safari is the leopard tortoise, which is South Africa's largest terrestrial chelonian, occasionally weighing as much as 40 kg (88 lb). It can be recognized by the tall, domed, gold-and-black-mottled shell after which it is named. Often seen inching along game-reserve roads, the leopard tortoise has a lifespan of over 50 years and few natural enemies, but its lack of mobility makes it susceptible to fast-spreading bush fires. It is also frequently hunted by local people. Another dozen species are recognized in South Africa, all but one of them endemic to the country. At up to 9 cm (3½ inches) long, the speckled padloper (literally, "roadwalker"), a Karoo endemic, is the world's smallest chelonian.

IUCN status CE: Critically Endangered; EN: Endangered; LC: Least Concern

The long muscular tail is used to propel and steer through the water.

Terrapin

Family: **Pelomedusidae** • *Best Seen:* **iSimangaliso, Kruger, Ndumo**

 Most Species: LC

South Africa is home to four freshwater terrapin species, most of which are flatter and a plainer brown than any of the region's tortoises. They are usually seen in or close to water, sunning on partially submerged rocks or dead logs, or peering out from roadside puddles. Far and away the most common and widespread species is the marsh terrapin, which inhabits waterholes, puddles and other stagnant water bodies in savannah habitats, but often wanders considerable distances on land in rainy weather. It estivates during the dry season, burying itself deep in mud to re-emerge only after the first rains – hence the local legend that terrapins drop from the sky during storms.

Marsh terrapin basking in the sun

Marine Turtle

Family: **Chelonioidea** • *Best Seen:* **iSimangaliso**

 Most Species: CE or EN

Five of the world's seven marine turtle species occur along the South African coast, and all are much larger than any indigenous tortoises or terrapins. Two species, the leatherback and loggerhead, breed on the beaches of northern KwaZulu-Natal, while the other three (olive ridley, hawksbill and green turtle, the latter named for the colour of its fat) are visitors that breed further to the north. An individual turtle lays several hundred eggs in the sand every season. After two months of incubation, the hatchlings make their way towards the sea, whose temperature will affect their sex – the cooler it is, the higher the proportion of males. In the late 19th century, marine turtles were common to abundant throughout their natural habitat, with some populations numbering well into the millions. Today, as a result of poaching and pollution, all but one species is classed as either endangered or critically endangered.

Hawksbill turtle swimming gracefully through a reef

Key to Field Guide icons *see p72*

Birds

With a national checklist of about 850 species, South Africa supports an exceptionally varied avifauna. The most prolific areas for birding are in the northeast (especially the Kruger National Park, Ndumo Game Reserve and iSimangaliso Wetland Park), where enthusiasts may easily see up to 100 species in a day. Avian diversity is greatest from September to April, when migrants arrive and residents shed their drab plumage to emerge in brilliant breeding colours.

Family

A growing body of genetic and fossil evidence suggests that birds are most properly placed with crocodiles as the only living members of the Archosauria, a group that also includes the extinct dinosaurs.

The marabou, with a unique fleshy neck pouch

Marabou Stork

Species: **Leptoptilos crumeniferus** • *Relatives:* **Saddle-Billed Stork, Yellow-Billed Stork, Open-Billed Stork**

 LC

A fabulously ungainly omnivore that stands 1.5 m (5 ft) tall, the marabou is identified by its scabrous bald head and inflatable flesh-coloured neck pouch. The most habitat-tolerant of South Africa's eight stork species, it may be seen near water, alongside vultures at a kill, or in urban environments. Its South African range is largely confined to the Kruger National Park and surrounds.

Hadeda Ibis

Species: **Bostrychia hagedash** • *Relatives:* **Sacred Ibis, Glossy Ibis, Southern Bald Ibis**

 LC

A characteristic bird of suburban lawns, hotel gardens and grassy wetlands, the hadeda is best-known for its harsh onomatopoeic cackle, most often emitted on take off or in flight. Like other ibises, it is a robustly built bird that uses its long, decurved bill to probe for snails and other invertebrates. Also common is the sacred ibis, which was revered and frequently mummified in ancient Egypt. The endemic southern bald ibis is scarcer.

Hadeda ibis, known for its raucous "ha-ha-hadeda" call

Egyptian goose, seen in large lakes and open water

Egyptian Goose

Species: **Alopochen aegyptiacus** • *Relatives:* **Spur-Winged Goose, Yellow-Billed Duck, White-Faced Whistling Duck**

 LC

South Africa supports 19 species of resident and migrant waterfowl, of which the largest is the spur-winged goose, but the most conspicuous is the ubiquitous Egyptian goose – a large reddish-brown bird that is very assertive and perpetually honking. Waterfowl populations tend to be densest during the European winter, when the Palaearctic migrants arrive.

African Darter

Species: **Anhinga rufa** • *Relatives:* **White-Breasted Cormorant, Long-Tailed Cormorant, African Finfoot**

LC

Frequently seen perching on bare branches overhanging rivers and lakes, the African darter or snakebird looks like a distended cormorant, with a kinked serpentine neck almost as long as its torso, and striking russet patches that glow off-gold in the right light. The gregarious, boldly marked white-breasted cormorant and the more solitary long-tailed cormorant are also common.

The African darter has a distinctive snake-like neck

IUCN status VU: Vulnerable; LC: Least Concern

Pelicans often roost communally on lakeshores

Great White Pelican

Species: Pelecanus onocrotalus • Relatives: Pink-Backed Pelican

 LC

Easily recognized by their bulk, enormous wingspan and larder-like bills, South Africa's two pelican species are its largest water-associated birds. Most common is the great white pelican, an almost all-white bird with a large yellow pouch hanging from its long bill, and black underwings that are clearly visible in flight. The smaller and more sparsely distributed pink-backed pelican has a pink-grey back and dark grey flight feathers. Both species are rather localized in South Africa, but might be seen on any large lake in synchronized flotillas of around six to 12 individuals.

Goliaths have the largest wingspan of any African heron

Goliath Heron

Species: Ardea goliath • Relatives: Grey Heron, Black-Headed Heron, Great White Egret, Cattle Egret

 LC

The herons and egrets of the Ardeidae family are among South Africa's most distinctive waterbirds. Most are tall and long-necked, and use their sharp, elongated bills to spear fish, frogs and other prey. The star of the group is the goliath heron, which stands up to 1.5 m (5 ft) tall and is commonest in the north and east. More prevalent, however, are the familiar Eurasian grey heron, black-headed heron and cattle egret.

Greater Flamingo

Species: Phoenicopterus roseus • Relatives: Lesser Flamingo

 LC

Represented by two species in South Africa, both of which are associated with flat, shallow pans, flamingoes are pink-tinged birds that feed on algae and microscopic fauna, which are sifted through filters in their unique down-turned bills. They are very sensitive to water levels and chemical composition, and will easily relocate. The greater flamingo is the larger of the two species found in South Africa, but it is outnumbered by the lesser flamingo, which is much pinker, especially on the bill.

Flamingoes, the most gregarious of waterbirds

Blue Crane

Species: Anthropoides paradisea • Relatives: Grey Crowned Crane, Wattled Crane

 VU

South Africa's national bird stands up to 1.2 m (4 ft) tall and has a uniform silvery-blue plumage, broken only by its white bulbous forehead and long black tail plumes. This handsome near-endemic has a declining population currently estimated at around 20,000. The blue crane is most often seen in grasslands and swampy habitats in the uKhahlamba-Drakensberg foothills, alongside the grey-crowned and wattled cranes.

The blue crane, once revered by Zulu and Xhosa royalty

Key to Field Guide icons *see p72*

The lappet-faced vulture is usually seen singly or in pairs

Lappet-Faced Vulture

Species: Torgos tracheliotos • Relatives: White-Backed Vulture, Hooded Vulture, Cape Vulture

VU

Africa's largest raptor is a truly impressive bird, with a bald pink head, a massive blue-and-ivory bill and heavy black wings that spread open like a cape, reinforcing its menacing demeanour. It often shares kills with the region's five other carrion-eating vulture species, squabbling and squawking over the spoils. Capable of soaring on thermals for hours on end, this vulture ranks among the world's most powerful fliers, and its vision is practically unmatched in the animal kingdom. It is also unexpectedly fastidious, and will spend hours preening itself after feeding.

The broad-winged jackal buzzard in flight

Jackal Buzzard

Species: Buteo rufofuscus • Relatives: Yellow-Billed Kite, Chanting Goshawk, Harrier Hawk

LC

Named for its jackal-like call, this handsome, medium to large raptor has a black back and head, a striking chestnut breast (though some individuals are blotched black and white), a white throat band and a distinctive bright orange-red tail. Like other buzzards, it has long, broad wings, a relatively short tail and a stocky build. Probably the commonest large resident raptor in and around the uKhahlamba-Drakensberg, it is outnumbered by the duller migrant steppe buzzard in the northern winter.

African Fish Eagle

Species: Hakliaeetus vocifer • Relatives: Martial Eagle, Bateleur, Verreaux's Eagle

LC

Among the most evocative sounds of the bush is the far-carrying call of two African fish eagles, a high, piercing banshee wail delivered in duet, with both birds throwing back their heads dramatically. This strongly monogamous eagle is visually striking and distinctive, with a hooked yellow bill and black-and-white feathering against a rich chestnut belly. It is a conspicuous resident of rivers and lakes, perching high in the branches of tall fringing trees, or soaring above the water for long periods, sweeping down occasionally to scoop a fish into its talons. It might be easily confused with another water-associated raptor, the osprey.

African fish eagles perch openly in the vicinity of water

Verreaux's Eagle-Owl

Species: Bubo lacteus • Relatives: Barn Owl, Spotted Eagle-Owl, Scops Owl

LC

Also known as the giant eagle-owl, Africa's largest nocturnal bird is most often seen near the large acacia trees in which it likes to breed. It is identified by its black eyes with pinkish eyelids that it closes during diurnal rest, and it is distinguished from the similarly proportioned Pel's fishing owl by its grey-brown feathering, crested ears and bold black facial disk marks. Usually unobtrusive, it is sometimes heard hooting at night. As with other owls, it is feared as a harbinger of death in many South African cultures.

Verreaux's eagle-owls stand more than 60 cm (2 ft) tall

IUCN status VU: Vulnerable; LC: Least Concern

The secretary bird, the world's most atypical raptor

Secretary Bird

Species: Sagittarius serpentarius • Relatives: No close relatives, affinities uncertain

 LC

A bizarre grassland bird with long skinny legs, a slender grey torso, long black tail and bare red face-mask, the 1.5-m- (5-ft-) tall secretary bird may have been named for its flaccid black crest, which recalls the quills used by Victorian secretaries. It is also claimed that "secretary" is a corruption of the Arabic *saqr-et-tair* (hunting bird). The family to which it belongs is thought to be ancestral to all modern eagles, buzzards and vultures. A terrestrial hunter, it feeds on snakes and lizards, which it stamps to death in a flailing dance ritual. It roosts in trees, but otherwise flies only when disturbed.

The flightless ostrich is associated with open landscapes

Common Ostrich

Species: Struthio camelus • Relatives: No close relatives in South Africa

LC

At a height of 2 m (7 ft 6 inches) and weighing more than 100 kg (220 lb), ostriches are the world's largest birds. Two very similar species are recognized, but the common ostrich (which has pink legs, as opposed to the Somali ostrich's blue legs) is the only one to occur in South Africa. A familiar resident of protected grassland areas, the larger male has a handsome black-and-white plumage, while the female is smaller and duller. Ostriches are farmed in the Oudtshoorn area (and elsewhere) for their feathers, eggs and low-cholesterol meat.

Southern Ground Hornbill

Species: Bucorvus cafer • Relatives: Trumpeter Hornbill, Silvery-Cheeked Hornbill, Crowned Hornbill

 LC

Ground hornbills are rather fantastic turkey lookalikes, with black feathers, white under-wings, large casqued bills, conspicuous red throat and eye wattles, and long fluttering eyelashes. They are typically seen marching along in small family parties in open habitats, probing the ground for insects. Despite their terrestrial habits, they are strong fliers. Their low, booming call is most often heard shortly after dusk. The southern ground hornbill is confined to the eastern part of the country, where it is most common in protected savannah and woodland habitats, in particular the Kruger National Park and Sabi Sands.

The southern ground hornbill, with large red wattles

Kori Bustard

Species: Ardeotis kori • Relatives: Stanley's Bustard, Black-Bellied Korhaan, Black Korhaan

LC

Loosely related to cranes but more sturdily built, bustards and korhaans are medium to large ground birds associated with open habitats. The most conspicuous species is the kori bustard, the world's heaviest flying bird, weighing up to 12.5 kg (28 lb) and standing about 1.3 m (4 ft 3 inches) tall. Usually rather measured and stately in demeanour, it performs a manic courtship dance, raising and fanning its tail and flapping its wings up and down in apparent agitation.

The kori bustard, the world's heaviest flying bird

Key to Field Guide icons *see p72*

Helmeted Guineafowl

Species: Numida meleagris • Relatives: Crested Guineafowl, Swainson's Francolin, Coqui Francolin

 LC

Guineafowl are large, gregarious ground birds with spotted white-on-grey feathers and blue heads. The distinctive helmeted guineafowl is commonly seen everywhere from Kirstenbosch Botanical Garden to the Kruger National Park. The striking crested guineafowl, with its "bad hair day" head-plumes, is restricted to forest and riparian woodland in the northeast of the country.

Hamerkop

Species: Scopus umbretta • Relatives: No close relatives, affinities uncertain

 LC

The sole member of its family, the hamerkop is a rusty brown, rook-sized bird whose long, flattened bill and angular crest combine to create its hammer-headed appearance. This bird's proverbially massive and amorphous nest is normally constructed untidily over several months in a tree fork close to the water, and is made of litter, branches, mud and other natural and artificial objects.

African Jacana

Species: Actophilornis africanus • Relatives: Blacksmith Plover, Pied Avocet, Crowned Plover

 LC

Also known as the lily-trotter, the African jacana is one of South Africa's most characteristic waterbirds, usually associated with lily pads and other floating vegetation, on which it is able to walk, thanks to its exceptionally far-spreading toes. An unmistakable and very attractive bird, it has a rich chestnut torso and wings, white neck, black cap and blue bill and frontal shield.

Yellow-Billed Hornbill

Species: Tockus flavirostris • Relatives: African Grey Hornbill, Red-Billed Hornbill

 LC

Often seen in rest camps and picnic sites in the Kruger National Park, typical savannah hornbills of the genus *Tockus* are clownish birds with heavy, decurved bills. One of the more common species is the yellow-billed hornbill. Most nest in holes in tree trunks. During the incubation period, the female plasters the entrance to seal herself in and the male feeds her through a slit until the eggs hatch.

Cape Sugarbird

Species: Promerops cafer • Relatives: Gurney's Sugarbird

 LC

The larger of two species in the family Promeropidae, the Cape sugarbird is a striking nectar-eater (especially partial to flowering proteas) with a sunbird-like bill, orange chest, yellow vent and graduated tail that can be almost three times longer than the torso in the male. The similar but shorter-tailed Gurney's sugarbird inhabits the uKhahlamba-Drakensberg and escarpment region, with a range that extends into Zimbabwe.

African Hoopoe

Species: Upapa africana • Relatives: Green Woodhoopoe, Common Scimitar-Bill

 LC

The African hoopoe is a handsome bird with orange, black and white coloration and a crest that is very striking when held erect. Seen singly or in pairs, it is most common in park-like habitats and hotel gardens, where it feeds on the lawn, poking around for insects with its long, curved bill. Its closest relatives are wood hoopoes – glossy-black birds with long tails and decurved bills.

Grey Go-Away Bird

Species: Corythaixoides concolor • Relatives: Knysna Loerie, Purple-Crested Loerie

 LC

Endemic to Africa, go-away birds and loeries are vocal frugivores with elongated bodies, long tails and prominent crests. The grey go-away bird is named for its explosive onomatopoeic call. Far more beautiful are the green-and-red knysna and purple-crested loeries. The former inhabits eastern coastal and montane forests; the latter is associated more with riparian woodland.

Lilac-Breasted Roller

Species: Coracius caudata • Relatives: Broad-Billed Roller, Eurasian Roller, Racket-Tailed Roller

 LC

One of the most popular and recognizable safari birds, the lilac-breasted roller is a robust, jay-like bird with a lilac chest, sky-blue underparts and gold back. It is often seen perching on an acacia branch, then swooping down to hawk on its prey. Four similar-looking roller species occur in bush habitats in South Africa, all indulging in the agile aerial displays to which their name refers.

Long-Tailed Widow

Species: Euplectes progne • Relatives: White-Winged Widow, Red Bishop, Golden Bishop

 LC

Related to the smaller weavers, this black bird with red-and-white shoulder markings has an extraordinary long, droopy tail that gives it a total length of up to 80 cm (32 inches) during the breeding season. It is often seen from the roadside, flying low over reedy marshes and highveld grassland, where it occurs alongside several other attractive but less dramatic widows and bishops.

White-Fronted Bee-Eater

Species: Merops bullockoides • Relatives: Little Bee-Eater, Southern Carmine Bee-Eater, Eurasian Bee-eater

LC

A common resident of the Kruger National Park and other bushveld reserves, this stunning bird has a bright green back, red neck and chest, cobalt vent and white head with black eye-stripe. Like other bee-eaters, it is a dashing insectivore whose sleek profile is determined by an upright stance, long wings and tail, and long, decurved bill.

Fork-Tailed Drongo

Species: Discrurus adsimilis • Relatives: Square-Tailed Drongo

LC

A characteristic savannah and woodland passerine, the fork-tailed drongo is an all-black insectivore that tends to hawk its prey from an open perch below the canopy. It is a bold and assertive bird, and emits a wide array of indignant nasal calls. It is sometimes confused with black cuckoos, male black cuckoo-shrikes and black flycatchers, but none of these have the drongo's comparably deep fork in their tail.

White-Browed Coucal

Species: Centropus superciliosus • Relatives: Red-Chested Cuckoo, Yellowbill, Diederick's Cuckoo

LC

The white-browed coucal is a large, clumsy bird seen in rank grassland, marsh and lake margins. It has a white eye-stripe and streaked underparts. It is most visible before rainstorms, which it tends to predict with a dove-like bubbling that gives it the name of rainbird. The coucal is related to cuckoos, which are common but secretive in African habitats.

Key to Field Guide icons *see p72*

African Firefinch

Species: Lagonosticta rubricata
• *Relatives: Common Waxbill, Pin-Tailed Wydah, Blue Waxbill*

   LC

Bright red with light spotting on the flanks, this ubiquitous but unobtrusive gem frequents gardens and lodge grounds. It is one of several small, colourful seedeaters in the family Estrildidae, most of which have conical bills whose waxen sheen gives them the common name of waxbill. They are parasitized by the related colourful wydahs.

Black-Eyed Bulbul

Species: Pycnonotus barbatus
• *Relatives: Cape Bulbul, Red-Eyed Bulbul, Spotted Nicator*

   LC

The black-eyed bulbul is one of the commonest birds in the northeast. Its counterparts in the southwest and northwest respectively are the very similar Cape and red-eyed bulbuls. All three are cheerful, habitat-tolerant garden birds with a bright tuneful song, slight crest and yellow vent. The main difference between them is eye colour (the Cape bulbul's eyes are white).

Malachite Sunbird

Species: Nectarinia famosa
• *Relatives: Collared Sunbird, Scarlet-Chested Sunbird, Orange-Breasted Sunbird*

LC

Sunbirds are small, restless nectar-eaters with long, decurved bills. In most species, the rather dowdy females are smaller and less conspicuous than the iridescent males. The widespread malachite sunbird, long-tailed and dazzling metal-lic green in colour, is arguably the most beautiful of these, and is associated with aloes and other flowering shrubs.

Masked Weaver

Species: Ploceus intermedius
• *Relatives: Red-Billed Quelea, Spotted-Backed Weaver, White-Browed Sparrow-Weaver*

   LC

The *Ploceus* weavers are surely the most characteristic of African bird genera, and the masked weaver is probably the commonest species in South Africa. The dexterous male builds intricate, ball-shaped nests at the end of a thin hang-ing branch, which is stripped of leaves as protection against snakes. Once completed, the nest is inspected by the female, who deconstructs it ruthlessly if she deems it unsatisfactory.

Cape Wagtail

Species: Motacilla capensis
• *Relatives: African Pied Wagtail, Long-Tailed Wagtail, Orange-Throated Longclaw*

LC

Frequently seen walking along the edge of rivers, lakes and swimming pools, the boldly marked grey-and-white Cape wagtail is easily identified by its incessantly bobbing tail. The most common and widespread wagtail in South Africa, it is outnumbered in the northeast by the African pied wagtail, and seasonally in some areas by the migrant yellow wagtail. The colourful longclaws and duller pipits are closely related.

Speckled Mousebird

Species: Colius striatus • *Relatives: White-Backed Mousebird, Red-Faced Mousebird*

LC

This scruffy frugivore is the most widespread member of the order Coliidae, which is endemic to Africa and consists of half-a-dozen long-tailed and prominently crested species. It is generally seen in flocks of around five to eight birds. The name mousebird refers to its habit of shuffling nimbly along branches, though it might equally apply to its grey-brown coloration. Three species occur in South Africa.

Olive Thrush

Species: **Turdus olivaceous**
• *Relatives:* **Cape Robin-Chat,
Common Rock Thrush, Stonechat**

 LC

The Turdidae is a diverse family of medium to small insectivores, represented by about 40 species and 15 genera in South Africa. Among the most recognizable is the olive thrush, which is often seen hopping around hotel lawns. The family also includes robin-chats, a group of orange, blue, black and white birds that are also common in gardens, but tend to prefer thicker cover.

African Paradise Flycatcher

Species: **Terpsiphone viridis**
• *Relatives:* **Vanga Flycatcher, Chin Spot Batis, Common Wattle-Eye**

 LC

This hyperactive, leaf-gleaning flycatcher tolerates most habitats apart from true desert. It might be seen anywhere, although local abundance is affected by complex seasonal intra-African movements. Usually bluish with an orange tail, it also has black-and-white and intermediate morphs. The male's tail can be up to three times the body length.

Pied Kingfisher

Species: **Ceryle rudis** • *Relatives:*
Malachite Kingfisher, Giant Kingfisher

LC

Probably the most numerous and visible of South Africa's water-associated kingfishers, this black-and-white bird has a unique hunting method that involves hovering above open water then diving down sharply to spear a fish with its dagger-like bill. Other water-associated species range from the gem-like, finch-sized malachite kingfisher to the crow-sized giant kingfisher.

Crested Barbet

Species: **Trachyphonus vaillantii**
• *Relatives:* **Black-Collared Barbet,
Red-Fronted Tinker-Barbet, Cardinal Woodpecker**

 LC

The repetitive trilling of the crested barbet – rather like a muted alarm clock – is one of the most distinctive sounds of the Kruger National Park. The bird is mainly yellow, but with a black-and-white back and bib, and red streaking on the face and belly. An equally conspicuous garden bird is the black-collared barbet, which has a red head and performs a haunting whirring duet.

Cape Glossy Starling

Species: **Lamprotornis nitens**
• *Relatives:* **Red-Winged Starling,
Plum-Coloured Starling, Red-Billed Oxpecker**

 LC

Common and colourful, with cryptic but glossy green-blue feathering, red eyes and a faint black eye-stripe, this is the most widespread and visible of several beautiful South African starlings. Even more stunning is the plum-coloured starling, which occurs in riverine woodland and acacia bush, while the bulkier cliff-dwelling red-winged starling is often seen on Table Mountain.

Fiscal Shrike

Species: **Lanius collaris** • *Relatives:*
Long-Tailed Shrike, Crimson-Breasted Shrike, Southern Boubou

LC

This handsome resident of the South African highveld, usually seen perching openly on acacia trees or fences, is sometimes referred to as the butcher-bird, for its habit of impaling and storing its prey on thorns or barbs to eat later. The related southern boubou and spectacular crimson-breasted shrike are more furtive bush-shrikes that tend to betray their presence with antiphonal duets between male and female.

Key to Field Guide icons *see p72*

CAPE TOWN

Cape Town at a Glance

Cape Town lies on a small peninsula at the southern tip of Africa which juts into the Atlantic Ocean. It is South Africa's premier tourist destination and its fourth largest urban centre. Enriched by Dutch, British and Cape Malay influences, its cosmopolitan atmosphere is a unique blend of cultures. Lying at the foot of its most famous landmark, Table Mountain, Cape Town has a host of well-preserved historic buildings. Many, such as the Old Town House on Greenmarket Square, now house museums. Outside the city, attractions include Chapman's Peak Drive, along a winding coastline where sheer cliffs drop to the swirling sea below, and a tour of the vineyards around Franschhoek and Stellenbosch.

Locator Map

Lion's Head separates the Atlantic suburbs of Sea Point and Camps Bay from the city centre. On Signal Hill an old cannon, the Noon Gun, is fired daily at noon.

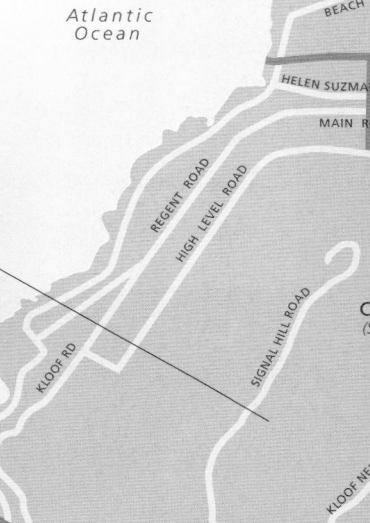

Atlantic Ocean

BEACH ROAD

HELEN SUZMAN BLVD

MAIN ROAD

REGENT ROAD

HIGH LEVEL ROAD

SIGNAL HILL ROAD

KLOOF RD

KLOOF NEK RD

KLOOF ST

CITY B●
(See pp12

0 metres 500
0 yards 500

◀ Signal Hill, with the Cape Town Stadium, as seen from Table Bay

Table Mountain looms over Cape Town's city centre. Several hiking trails lead to the summit, while for the less adventurous there is a leisurely cable car ride. The restaurant on top serves refreshments.

Victoria Wharf Shopping Centre, an upmarket complex at the V&A Waterfront (see pp140–41), is a veritable shopper's delight. The modern structures have been designed to fit in with renovated older buildings.

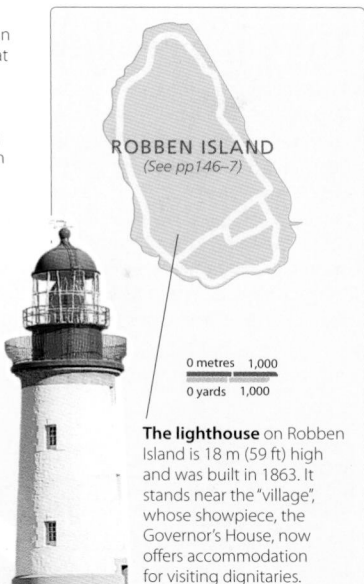

ROBBEN ISLAND
(See pp146–7)

0 metres 1,000
0 yards 1,000

The lighthouse on Robben Island is 18 m (59 ft) high and was built in 1863. It stands near the "village", whose showpiece, the Governor's House, now offers accommodation for visiting dignitaries.

Table Bay

V&A WATERFRONT
(See pp138–45)

TABLE BAY BLVD

LONG ST
HERTZOG ST
ADDERLEY ST
PLEIN ST
DARLING ST
BUITENKANT ST
NELSON MANDELA BLVD
MILL ST
DE WAAL DRIVE

The Grand Parade is the main public square in the city centre. It is flanked by the City Hall, the Castle of Good Hope and the railway station. On weekday mornings it hosts a lively flea market.

The Castle of Good Hope re-creates the days of Jan van Riebeeck and the early settlers.

Greater Cape Town Area

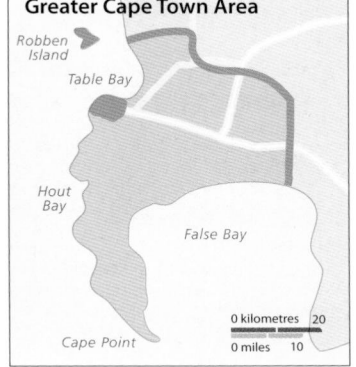

Robben Island
Table Bay
Hout Bay
False Bay
Cape Point

0 kilometres 20
0 miles 10

The Cape Peninsula

For four centuries, the Cape Peninsula's most prominent feature, Table Mountain, has been a welcome landmark for travellers. This rugged mountain chain that stretches from Table Bay to Cape Point soars out of the sea to a height of 1,087 m (3,566 ft) above sea level, dwarfing the high-rise buildings of Cape Town and its surrounding suburbs. The impressive front wall of Table Mountain and its surrounding buttresses and ravines are a spectacular natural wonder. The rock formations and twisted strata indicate turbulent geological processes that span a 1,000-million-year period.

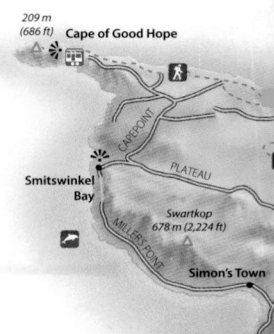

Cape Point juts into the southern Atlantic Ocean and forms the tip of the peninsula's mountain chain. A scenic drive leads to the Cape of Good Hope *(see p155)*, which offers hiking and mountain biking trails. The less energetic can ride the funicular to a lighthouse with superb views.

The Constantia Winelands *(see pp160–61)* nestle on the southeast slopes of the peninsula's mountain range, within easy reach of the city. The fertile slopes, combined with a mild Mediterranean climate, create perfect conditions for choice grape cultivars.

Table Mountain's Tablecloth

The tablecloth

An old local legend tells of a Dutchman, Jan van Hunks, who engaged in a smoking contest with a stranger on the slopes of Devil's Peak. After several days, the disgruntled stranger had to admit defeat and revealed himself as the Devil. Vanishing in a puff of smoke, he carried van Hunks off with him, leaving wreaths of smoke curling around Devil's Peak (which is where the cloud begins pouring over the mountain, forming the famous "tablecloth").

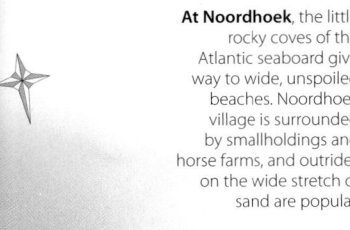

At Noordhoek, the little rocky coves of the Atlantic seaboard give way to wide, unspoiled beaches. Noordhoek village is surrounded by smallholdings and horse farms, and outrides on the wide stretch of sand are popular.

Llandudno displays good examples of Cape granite, formed by rock melting under the earth's crust some 550 million years ago.

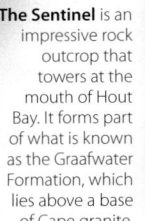

The Sentinel is an impressive rock outcrop that towers at the mouth of Hout Bay. It forms part of what is known as the Graafwater Formation, which lies above a base of Cape granite.

Sea Point, below Signal Hill, is built on metamorphic rock. This is the oldest of the peninsula's rock formations and weathers easily. Several road cuttings and old quarries in the area exhibit the red clayey soils that typify these strata.

Map labels:
gh
Kommetjie
KOMMETJIE MAIN
un Valley
Kommetjie Beach
Noordhoek
Chapman's Peak 593 m (1,945 ft)
CHAPMAN'S PEAK
Constantiaberg 928 m (3,044 ft)
The Sentinel 653 m (2,142 ft)
rest rack
Hout Bay
HOUT BAY MAIN
antia Nek
Llandudno
VICTORIA
Twelve Apostles
ountain 3,566 ft)
280 ft)
TAFELBERG
Camps Bay
Clifton
KLOOF NEK
Lion's Head 669 m (2,195 ft)
Signal Hill
BEACH
E TOWN
SOMERSET
Sea Point

0 kilometres   5
0 miles   3

THE CITY BOWL

Cape Town's Central Business District is cradled at the foot of Table Mountain. The city is bounded by Devil's Peak to the east and Lion's Head to the west. Table Bay harbour and the V&A Waterfront separate the city centre from the Atlantic Ocean. Visitors are often surprised by Cape Town's sophistication: it offers a plethora of culturally varied, exciting restaurants, and vibrant nightlife in the clubs and bars around Kloof and Long streets.

The many open-air markets and informal stalls with an ethnic African flavour are attractions in their own right, and nature lovers are enthralled by the city's scenic beauty. Early Cape Dutch and 19th-century Victorian architecture may be admired on a stroll through the town. Particularly interesting buildings are Heritage Square on the corner of Shortmarket and Buitengracht streets, as well as the Blue Lodge on Long Street.

Sights at a Glance

Museums and Galleries
- ❷ Iziko Slave Lodge
- ❹ District Six Museum
- ❽ Iziko Bo-Kaap Museum
- ❿ Iziko South African National Gallery
- ⓫ South African Jewish Museum
- ⓬ Iziko South African Museum and Planetarium

Churches
- ❻ Lutheran Church

Parks and Gardens
- ❾ Table Mountain pp136–7

Historic Buildings
- ❶ Iziko Michaelis Collection
- ❸ Grand Parade and City Hall
- ❺ Castle of Good Hope pp130–31
- ❼ Iziko Koopmans-De Wet House

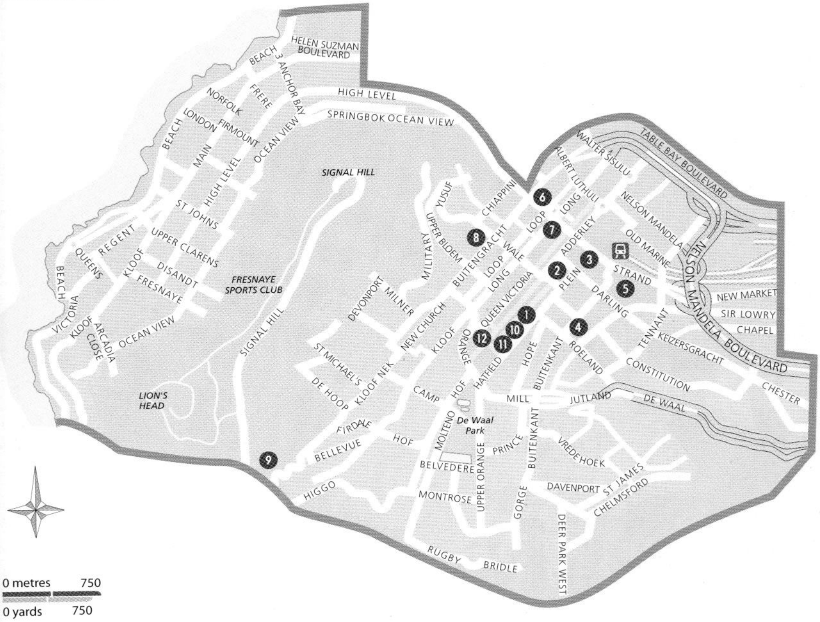

<Cape Town's City Hall, home to the Cape Philharmonic Orchestra

For keys to symbols *see back flap*

Street-by-Street: City Centre

The compact city centre lends itself to walking, because most of its major sights are easily accessible. Cape Town is dissected by a number of thoroughfares, one of which is Adderley Street. The parallel St George's Mall is a lively pedestrian zone where street musicians and dancers entertain the crowds. Greenmarket Square, the focal point of the city, is lined with many historically significant buildings. One block west of here, towards Signal Hill, is Long Street. Some beautiful examples of elaborate Victorian buildings with balconies and intricate ironwork – now housing shops, bars and hostels – can be seen along this street.

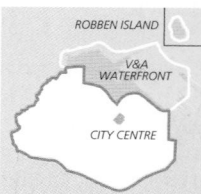

Locator Map
See Street Finder, map 5

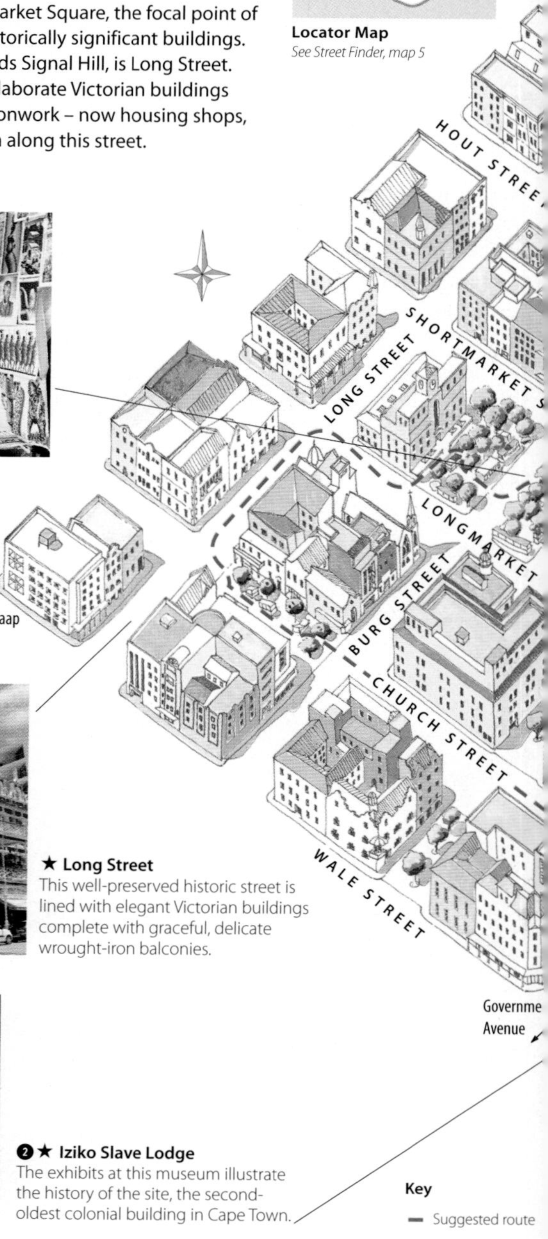

★ Greenmarket Square
A produce market since 1806, and now a national monument, this cobbled square supports a colourful, daily open-air craft market. Among the historic buildings surrounding it is the Old Town House.

← Bo-Kaap

★ Long Street
This well-preserved historic street is lined with elegant Victorian buildings complete with graceful, delicate wrought-iron balconies.

❷ ★ Iziko Slave Lodge
The exhibits at this museum illustrate the history of the site, the second-oldest colonial building in Cape Town.

Governme
Avenue ↙

Key
— Suggested route

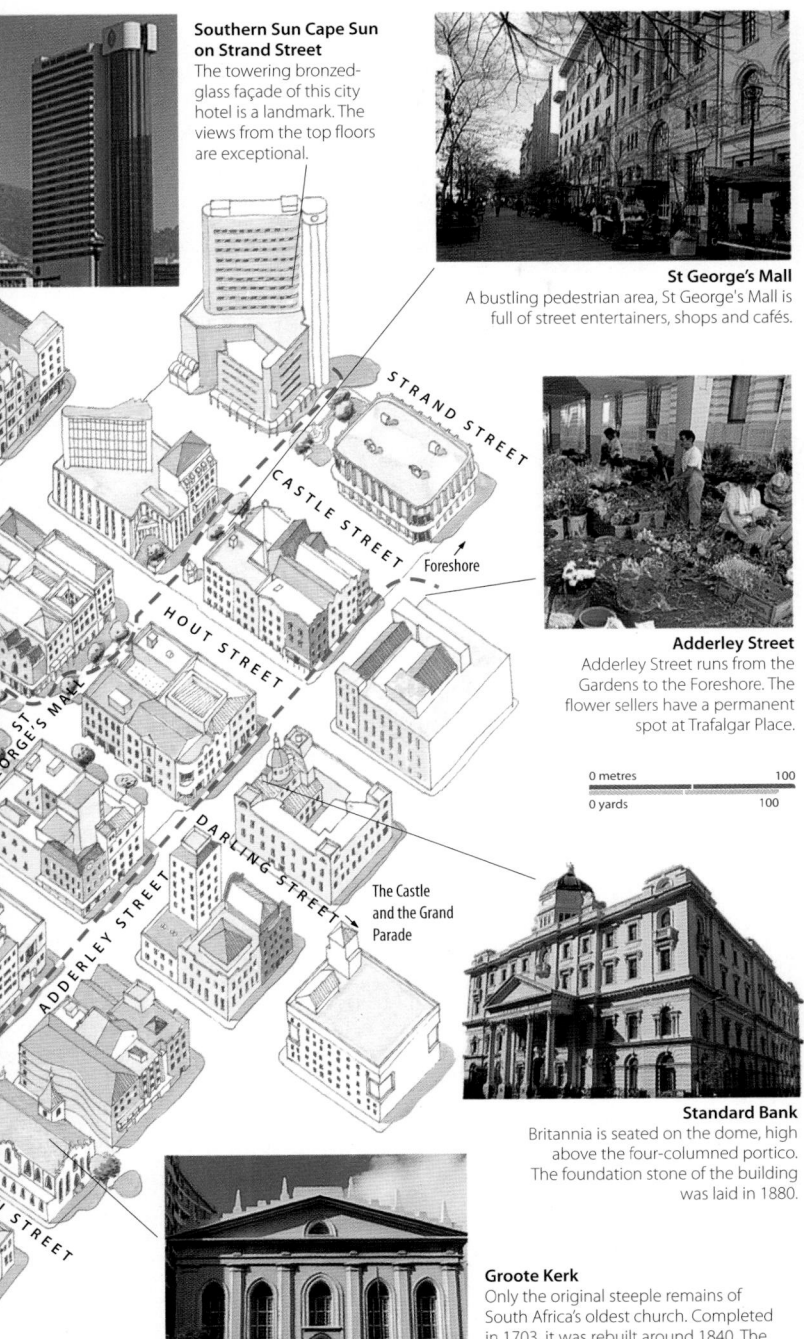

Southern Sun Cape Sun on Strand Street
The towering bronzed-glass façade of this city hotel is a landmark. The views from the top floors are exceptional.

St George's Mall
A bustling pedestrian area, St George's Mall is full of street entertainers, shops and cafés.

Adderley Street
Adderley Street runs from the Gardens to the Foreshore. The flower sellers have a permanent spot at Trafalgar Place.

Foreshore

The Castle and the Grand Parade

0 metres 100
0 yards 100

Standard Bank
Britannia is seated on the dome, high above the four-columned portico. The foundation stone of the building was laid in 1880.

Groote Kerk
Only the original steeple remains of South Africa's oldest church. Completed in 1703, it was rebuilt around 1840. The carved pulpit, dating to 1789, is the work of sculptor Anton Anreith and carpenter Jan Jacob Graaff.

The Old Town House, where the Iziko Michaelis Collection is kept

❶ Iziko Michaelis Collection

Greenmarket Square. **Map** 5 B1.
Tel 021 481 3933. **Open** 10am–5pm
Mon–Sat. **Closed** 1 May, 25 Dec. 🗑
🅦 iziko.org.za

Located in the Old Town House, this national monument was built in 1755 in the Cape Rococo style. It initially served as the "Burgherwacht Huys" (house of the night patrol) and the magistrate's court. In 1839, it was claimed as a town hall by the newly formed municipality. After renovations in 1915, the building was handed over to the Union Government for use as an art gallery.

The original collection was donated to the city by the wealthy financier Sir Max Michaelis in 1914. It was added to by Lady Michaelis after the death of her husband in 1932. The collection consists of a world-renowned selection of Dutch and Flemish art from the 17th-century Golden Age. The portraits are particularly interesting, offering an insight into Dutch society at the time.

In addition to the permanent collection, the gallery has a series of temporary exhibitions that have been designed to appeal to both locals and visitors alike.

After hours, the gallery becomes a cultural centre, hosting chamber-music concerts and lectures.

❷ Iziko Slave Lodge

Cnr Wale & Adderley sts.
Map 5 B2. **Tel** 021 467
7229. **Open** 10am–5pm
Mon–Sat. **Closed** 1 May,
25 Dec. 🗑 🅖
🅦 iziko.org.za

The first building on this site was a lodge that housed the slaves who worked in the Company's Garden (see pp134–5). One of the oldest buildings in Cape Town, it was built around 1679 on land that originally formed part of the garden.

By 1807, new premises from which to administer the Cape Colony were needed, and the Slave Lodge suited most requirements. Many slave inhabitants of the lodge were sold, while others were moved to the west wing of the building. The vacated area was turned into offices. In 1811, the west wing was also converted.

The people responsible for the conversion were the builder Herman Schutte, the sculptor Anton Anreith and the architect Louis Michel Thibault. As well as government offices, the lodge also housed the Supreme Court, the post office and the public library. The present building once extended into Adderley Street, but this portion had to be demolished when the road was widened. However, the original façade, designed by Thibault, has been restored to its former splendour.

Iziko Museums of Cape Town have transformed the Slave Lodge into a major site that increases public awareness of slavery, cultural diversity and the struggle for human rights in South Africa. The history of slavery at the Cape is illustrated with three-dimensional and audiovisual displays along with text, images and maps. A section that focuses on life at the lodge is based on archaeological and archival sources, as well as the memories of people who trace their roots to the time of slavery in the Cape.

Plaque on the Iziko Slave Lodge

The Michaelis Collection

This important art collection was established in 1914, when Sir Max Michaelis donated 68 paintings collected by Lady Phillips and Sir Hugh Lane. The gallery formally opened three years later, and today houses some 104 paintings and 312 etchings. It includes works by Frans Hals, Rembrandt, van Dyck, David Teniers the Younger, Jan Steen and Willem van Aelst. Although the collection is rather small compared with collections in international galleries, it presents a valuable source of reference of the evolution of Dutch and Flemish art over two centuries. One of the most famous paintings in the collection is the *Portrait of a Lady* by Frans Hals.

Portrait of a Lady, Frans Hals (1640)

For hotels and restaurants in this area see p384 and pp398–9

Many Cape Muslims have greengrocer stalls on the Grand Parade

Across the road from the Slave Lodge is the **Groote Kerk** (big church). Soon after their arrival at the Cape, the Dutch held religious services on board Jan van Riebeeck's ship, *Drommedaris*. Later, they used a small room at Castle Good Hope. However, they soon realized the need for a permanent site. A first, temporary structure at the northeast end of the Company's Garden was replaced by a thatched church on the same site in 1700, at the order of Governor Willem Adriaan van der Stel.

The church was completely rebuilt in the 19th century, and the new building was dedicated in 1841. All that remains of the original church today is the Baroque belfry, which, unfortunately, is now almost obscured by tall modern buildings.

Of interest in the church is the splendid original pulpit supported by carved lions. It is believed that sculptor Anton Anreith's original concept including the symbolic images of Hope, Faith and Charity was rejected as being too papist.

The façade of the church has high Gothic windows divided by bold pilasters. In front of the building is a statue of Andrew Murray, minister of the

Andrew Murray (1828–1917)

Dutch Reformed Church in Cape Town from 1864–71.

🏛 **Groote Kerk**
43 Adderley St. **Map** 5 B2. **Tel** 021 422 0569. **Open** 10am–2pm Mon–Fri. Ring ahead for a free guided tour.

❸ Grand Parade and City Hall

Darling St. **Map** 5 C2.

The Grand Parade was the site van Riebeeck selected for his first fort in 1652. The structure was levelled in 1674 when the Castle of Good Hope *(see pp130–31)* was completed – until 1821 the area was used as a parade and exercise ground for the troops. As buildings went up around the perimeter, greengrocers established fruit stalls, precursors of today's flea market, which operates from Monday to Friday. The site is now used both as a car park and as a venue for popular events.

Overlooking the Grand Parade is Cape Town's imposing City Hall. Built in 1905 in the elaborate Italian Renaissance style, it presents its elegant façades on four different streets. A 39-bell carillon tower was added in 1923, which is an impressive half-sized replica of London's Big Ben. It was from the balcony of the City Hall that Nelson Mandela addressed the world after spending 27 years in prison.

On that day in 1990, 250,000 people streamed to the Grand Parade to celebrate the release of the country's future president. Today, the City Hall is home to the Cape Philharmonic Orchestra, which regularly performs here.

❹ District Six Museum

25a Buitenkant St. **Map** 5 B2. **Tel** 021 466 7200. **Open** 9am–4pm Mon–Sat. 🅿 📷 📧
🌐 **districtsix.co.za**

Up until the 1970s, the Sixth Municipal District of Cape Town was home to almost a tenth of the city's population. In 1965, the apartheid government declared the area "white", under the Group Areas Act of 1950. Removals began in 1968, and by 1982, more than 60,000 people had been forcibly uprooted from their homes and relocated 25 km (16 miles) away onto the barren plains of the Cape Flats *(see pp158–9)*.

The District Six Museum was launched in 1994 to commemorate the events of the apartheid era and to preserve the memory of District Six as it was before the removals. It does this through a fascinating collection that includes historical documents, photographs, audio-visual recordings and physical remains of the area such as street signs. Visitors can explore the museum alone, or take a guided tour with a former resident of the destroyed District Six.

Cape Town's City Hall, opposite the Grand Parade

❺ Castle of Good Hope

Cape Town's Castle of Good Hope is South Africa's oldest structure. Built between 1666 and 1679, it replaced an earlier clay-and-timber fort erected by Commander Jan van Riebeeck *(see p50)* in 1652. The castle overlooks the Grand Parade and is now a museum that also houses traditional Cape regiments and units of the National Defence Force.

Dolphin Pool
Descriptions and sketches made by Lady Anne Barnard *(see p162)* in the 1790s enabled the reconstruction of the dolphin pool more than 200 years later.

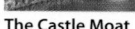

The Castle Moat
Parts of the original moat have been restored after it was filled in in 1896 to make way for a railway line.

The Archway
Slate taken from a quarry on Robben Island *(see pp146–7)* in the 17th century was used for the paving stones inside the castle.

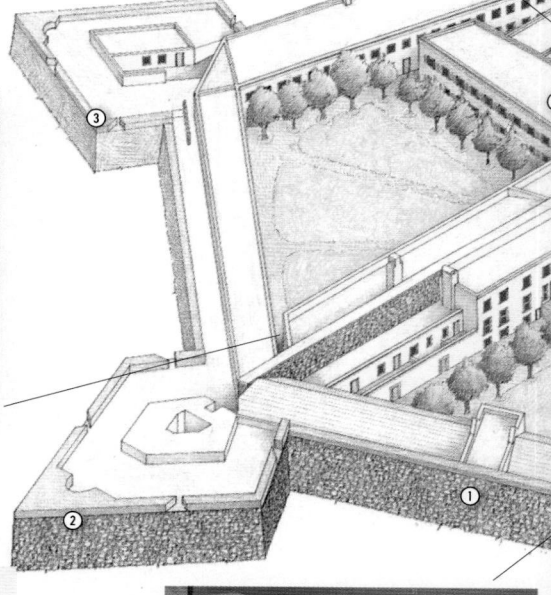

KEY

① **The original entrance** (1679–82) to the castle faced the sea, but has since been closed.

② **Catzenellenbogen Bastion**

③ **Nassau Bastion**

④ **The inner wall**

⑤ **Het Bakhuys**

⑥ **Oranje Bastion**

⑦ **Moat**

⑧ **Colonnaded verandah**

⑨ **Buuren Bastion**

★ **The Castle Military Museum**
On display is an array of military artifacts, as well as weapons and uniforms from the VOC and British periods of occupation of the Cape.

★ William Fehr Collection
Exhibits include paintings by old masters such as Thomas Baines, as well as period furniture, glass, ceramics and metalware.

Entrance Gable
A teak copy of the original VOC gable reflects martial symbols: a banner, flags, drums and cannon balls.

Leerdam Bastion
Leerdam, Oranje, Nassau, Catzenellenbogen and Buuren were titles held by Prince William of Orange.

The Castle Entrance
The original bell, cast in Amsterdam in 1697, still hangs in the belfry. The coat of arms of the United Netherlands can be seen on the pediment above the gate.

★ De Kat Balcony
The original staircase, built in 1695 as part of a defensive crosswall, divided the square into an inner and outer court, and was remodelled between 1786 and 1790.

❻ Lutheran Church

99 Strand St. **Map** 5 B1. **Tel** 021 421 5854. **Open** 10am–2pm Mon–Fri and for Sun services.
🌐 **lutheranchurch.org.za**

Since the ruling authority was intolerant of any religion other than that of the Dutch Reformed Church, the Lutheran Church began its life as a hall that had to be officially described as a "warehouse". Wealthy Lutheran businessman Martin Melck built it with the intention of modifying it into a place of worship once the religious laws were relaxed, and the first service was held there in 1776. A few years later, the sexton's house was added.

From 1787 to 1792, the German-born sculptor Anton Anreith embellished the church, designing a more fitting front elevation and adding a tower. Today, both the church and the sexton's house are national monuments.

Next door to the church is the Martin Melck House, which was built in 1781 and declared a national monument in 1936. It is a fine example of an 18th-century Cape townhouse.

The dining room in Iziko Koopmans-De Wet House

❼ Iziko Koopmans-De Wet House

35 Strand St. **Map** 5 B1. Tel 021 481-3935. **Open** 10am–5pm Mon–Fri. **Closed** 1 May, 25 Dec. 🌐
🌐 **iziko.org.za**

This Neo-Classical home was built in 1701 when Strand Street, then close to the shore, was the most fashionable part of Cape Town. The building was enlarged in subsequent centuries; a second storey was added, and renowned French architect Louis Michel Thibault remodelled the façade around 1795 in Louis XVI-style. The De Wet family was the last to own the house. After the death of her husband in 1880, Maria De Wet lived here with her sister until her death in 1906.

Over the years, the sisters assembled the fine antiques that can still be seen in the museum today. Maria De Wet, apart from being a renowned society hostess, was also responsible for taking the first steps to protect Cape Town's historic buildings. It was due to her intervention that the destruction of part of the castle was prevented when the new railway lines were being planned.

❽ Iziko Bo-Kaap Museum

71 Wale St. **Map** 5 A1. **Tel** 021 481 3938. **Open** 10am–5pm Mon–Sat. **Closed** Eid-ul-Fitr, Eid-ul-Adha, Good Fri, 25 Dec, 2 Jan. 🌐 🌐 **iziko.org.za**

The Iziko Bo-Kaap Museum is housed in the oldest house in the area (1763) still in its original form. The characteristic features are a *voorstoep* (front terrace) and a courtyard, both emphasizing the social aspect of Cape Muslim culture. The museum focuses on the history of Islam in the Cape of Good Hope, highlighting its local cultural expressions.

The Bo-Kaap area has traditionally been associated with the Muslim community of South Africa, and the Auwal Mosque, the oldest mosque in the country, is located on Dorp Street, just behind the museum.

❾ Table Mountain

See pp136–7.

The Lutheran Church on Strand Street

Malay Culture in Cape Town

The original Malays were brought to the Cape from 1658 onwards by the Dutch East India Company. Most of them were Muslims from Sri Lanka, the Indonesian islands and India. A large proportion of them were slaves, while others were political exiles of considerable stature. After the abolition of slavery in the early 1830s, the Cape Malays (or Cape Muslims as they now prefer to be called) settled on the slope of Signal Hill in an area called Bo-Kaap ("above Cape Town") to be near the mosques that had been built there (Auwal Mosque dates from 1794). The Malays had a significant influence on the Afrikaans tongue, and many of their culinary traditions *(see pp394–5)* were absorbed by other cultures. Today, the Muslim community is very much a part of Cape Town: the muezzins' haunting calls, ringing out from minarets to summon the faithful, are an integral part of the city.

Streets of the Bo-Kaap

Just above modern Cape Town, and within easy walking distance of the city centre, lies the traditional home of the Cape Muslims. Here, narrow-fronted houses in bright colours open onto the streets.

Houses were painted in bright colours from the 1990s after the end of apartheid.

Muslim tradition dictates that formal attire be worn on festive occasions. This includes the traditional fez for men, while women don the characteristic chador (full-length veil or shawl).

The fez, of Turkish origin, is still worn occasionally, but knitted or cloth caps are more common nowadays.

Signal Hill is the traditional home of the Cape Muslim community. Many of the quaint Bo-Kaap cottages have been replaced by modern apartment blocks higher up.

The mosque in Longmarket Street, like many of the Bo-Kaap's mosques, stands wedged in-between the homes of residents. Religion is a fundamental part of every devout Muslim's life.

Street-by-Street: Gardens

Jan van Riebeeck's famous vegetable garden, established in 1652 to provide ships rounding the Cape of Good Hope with fresh supplies, is still today known as the "Company's Garden". It is a leafy, tranquil area that contains an array of exotic shrubs and trees, an aviary (records show that a "menagerie" existed here during the time of governor Simon van der Stel), a conservatory and a sundial dating back to 1787. There is also an open-air restaurant. Nearby stands a Saffren pear tree, planted soon after the arrival of Jan van Riebeeck, which makes it the oldest cultivated tree in South Africa. Look out for the disused old well, and the tap that protrudes from the gnarled tree nearby.

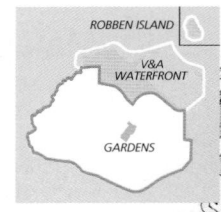

Locator Map
See Street Finder, map 5

The garden is a tranquil haven in the city with water features, lawns and benches under tall, old trees.

⑫ ★ **Iziko South African Museum and Planetarium**
The museum concentrates on natural history, archaeology, entomology and palaeontology. The sophisticated equipment in the planetarium reconstructs the southern night skies.

⑪ **South African Jewish Museum**
The entrance to this museum is situated in the Old Synagogue, which was the first synagogue built in South Africa, in 1863.

Key

— Suggested route

⑩ ★ **Iziko South African National Gallery**
Temporary exhibitions of the work of contemporary local artists augment the permanent collection of 6,500 paintings.

Table Aerial

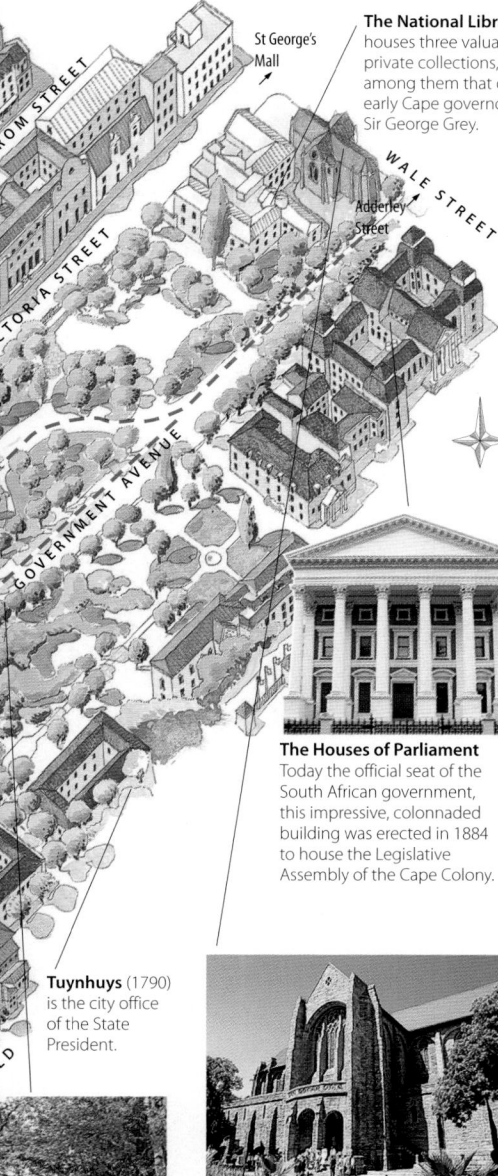

St George's Mall

The National Library houses three valuable private collections, among them that of early Cape governor, Sir George Grey.

WALE STREET

Adderley Street

FROM STREET

VICTORIA STREET

GOVERNMENT AVENUE

The Houses of Parliament
Today the official seat of the South African government, this impressive, colonnaded building was erected in 1884 to house the Legislative Assembly of the Cape Colony.

Tuynhuys (1790) is the city office of the State President.

St George's Cathedral
This Anglican cathedral (1901) features stained glass by Gabriel Loire of Chartres and a rose window by F Spear.

★ **Government Avenue**
he original lemon tree ane has been replaced y tall, shady oak trees.

| 0 metres | 100 |
| 0 yards | 100 |

❿ Iziko South African National Gallery

Government Ave, Company's Garden. **Map** 5 B2. **Tel** 021 481 3970. **Open** 10am–5pm daily. **Closed** 1 May, 25 Dec. 🖼 🅿 ♿ 📷
W **iziko.org.za**

South Africa's premier gallery houses outstanding collections of British, French, Dutch, Flemish and South African paintings. Selections from the permanent collection change regularly to allow for a full programme of temporary exhibitions of contemporary photography, sculpture, beadwork and textiles. They provide a great insight into the range of artworks produced in this country, the African continent and further afield.

⓫ South African Jewish Museum

88 Hatfield St. **Map** 5 A2. **Tel** 021 465 1546. **Open** 10am–5pm Mon–Thu, Sun; 10am–2pm Fri. **Closed** Jewish hols. 🅿 ♿ 🖼 🚫
W **sajewishmuseum.co.za**

This museum, housed in a building opened in 2000 by Nelson Mandela, narrates the story of South African Jewry from its beginnings, setting it against the backdrop of the country's history. The interactive exhibits celebrate the pioneering spirit of the early Jewish immigrants and their descendants.

⓬ Iziko South African Museum and Planetarium

25 Queen Victoria St. **Map** 5 A2. **Tel** 021 481 3800. **Open** 10am–5pm daily. **Closed** 1 May, 25 Dec. 🅿 ♿ 📷 W **iziko.org.za**

Of special interest here are the coelacanth, reptile fossils from the Karoo, and the Shark World exhibition. There are also exceptional examples of rock art, including whole sections from caves.

The planetarium presents a diverse programme on the wonders of the universe.

❾ Table Mountain

The Cape Peninsula mountain chain is a mass of sedimentary sandstone lying above ancient shales deposited some 700 million years ago, and large areas of granite dating back some 540 million years. The sandstone sediment which forms the main block of the mountain was deposited about 450 million years ago when the peninsula, then a part of the ancient supercontinent Gondwana, lay below sea level. After the subsidence of the primeval ocean, the effects of wind, rain, ice and extreme temperatures caused erosion of the softer layers, leaving behind the characteristic mesa of Table Mountain.

Royal Visitors
In 1947, Britain's King George VI and the future Queen Mother accompanied Prime Minister Smuts on a hike.

Kirstenbosch National Botanical Garden
The garden (see pp164–5) nestles at the foot of the peninsula range. Three major trails and numerous paths lead up the mountain slopes.

Kirstenbosch National Botanical Garden

Southern Suburbs

Contour Path

Window

● Forest Station

Maclear's, 1,087 m (3

Newlands

Newlands Reservoir

T A

Devil's Peak 1,000 m (3,280 ft) △

● University of Cape Town

● Rhodes Memorial

King's Blockhouse

Woodstock Cave

Plumpudding Hill 291 m (955 ft) △

Queen's Blockhouse

Prince of Wales Blockhouse ●

Key

0 kilometres — 1
0 miles — 0.5

━━ Major road
═══ Road
- - Hiking trail

KEY

① **Platteklip Gorge** is one of the popular hiking routes that lead up the face of the mountain.

② **A circular route** leads up to Lion's Head.

Table Mountain Fauna and Flora

More than 1,500 plant species of the 2,285 that make up the Cape Floral Kingdom of the peninsula can be found in the protected natural habitat of Table Mountain. They include *Disa uniflora* (also called Pride of Table Mountain), which mostly grows near streams and waterfalls, and several members of the regal protea family. Wildlife, consisting mostly of small mammals, reptiles and birds, includes the rare and secretive ghost frog, which is found in a few perennial streams on the plateau.

Disa orchid

Ghost frog

City Centre and Foreshore

King's Blockhouse
This is the best preserved of the three 18th-century stone forts that were built during the first British occupation of the Cape (see pp52–3).

The Plateau
The high plateau affords superb views of the Hely-Hutchinson reservoir and the Back Table, and southwards to False Bay and Cape Point.

Viewing Platform
The Table Mountain Aerial Cableway has been operating since 1929, and today near the upper station there are special reinforced viewing platforms at strategic vantage points.

Tafelberg Road
The spectacular views of the city make this one of Cape Town's most popular walking routes.

De Villiers Dam

Original Disa

Victoria Reservoir

Alexandra Reservoir

Reserve Peak 844 m (2,769 ft)

Disa Stream

Hely-Hutchinson Reservoir

Woodhead Reservoir

Kasteelpoort

Junction Peak 919 m (3,015 ft)

Orion's Cave

Pipe Track

M O U N T A I N

Plotteklip Gorge

①

Upper Cableway Station

Camps Bay

P

Platteklip

Upper Contour Path

Lower Cableway Station

Mocke Reservoir

P

↓ *Sea Point and Clifton*

City Centre

② Lion's Head 669 m (2,195 ft)

P

P

L I O N ' S   R U M P

P

Signal Hill 350 m (1,148 ft)

Kramat
The burial place of Goolam Muhamed Soofi is one of six Muslim shrines that form a holy circle around the Cape Peninsula.

Tips for Walkers

Several well-marked trails, graded according to their degree of difficulty, lead to the summit. Hikers are advised to check with the Lower Cableway Station before setting out, since weather conditions may deteriorate without warning. Hiking on windy or misty days is not recommended. For safety reasons, do not hike alone.

Hikers on the plateau

For additional keys to symbols *see back flap*

V&A WATERFRONT

Cape Town's successful Waterfront project was named after the son of Queen Victoria. In 1860, a young Prince Alfred initiated the construction of the first breakwater in stormy Table Bay, by toppling a load of rocks that had been excavated from the sea floor into the water. The Alfred Basin, which was subsequently created, successfully protected visiting ships from the powerful gales howling around the Cape in winter that had previously caused an alarming number of vessels to founder.

Increased shipping volumes led to the building of the Victoria Basin in order to ease the pressure on Alfred. From the 1960s, the basins and surrounding harbour buildings gradually fell into disrepair. Then, in 1988, the Waterfront Company set out to modernize,

upgrade and develop the site. Today, visitors can stroll through the shopping areas and enjoy a meal in one of the many eateries, while watching the daily workings of the harbour.

In Table Bay, some 11 km (7 miles) north of the Waterfront, lies Robben Island, the political enclave that gained international fame for the high-profile exiles incarcerated there. For most of its recorded history, the island has served as a place of confinement – for early slaves, convicts, lepers and the mentally unstable. In 1961, however, it became a maximum security prison for leading political activists, among them Nelson Mandela. Today, the island is a protected area, and the prison is now a museum.

Sights at a Glance

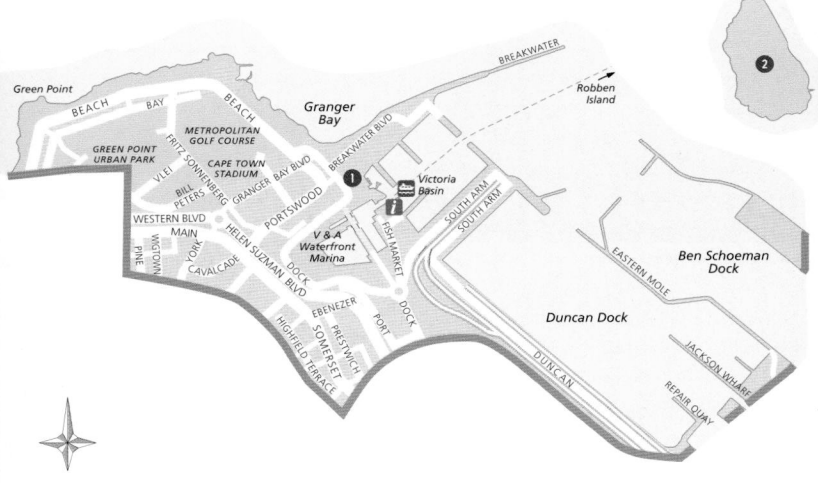

◀ The Cape Wheel, which provides panoramic views of Cape Town from its cabins

For keys to symbols see back flap

❶ The V&A Waterfront

The V&A Waterfront is a shopper's paradise, offering designer boutiques, outlets selling quirky, hand-painted clothing, health and beauty stores and shops selling homeware and speciality gifts. It also has more than 80 ethnically diverse food outlets. Most eating places have harbour views, and alfresco dining on the wharfs and waterside platforms is extremely popular. Many bars and bistros offer live music, while regular outdoor concerts are staged at the Waterfront Amphitheatre. Excursions of all kinds start at the Waterfront, from boat tours around the harbour and to Robben Island, to helicopter rides over the peninsula and sunset champagne cruises off Clifton Beach. The Waterfront, which also boasts luxurious hotel accommodation, is a port of call for visiting cruise ships.

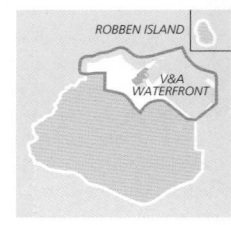

Locator Map
See Street Finder maps 1 & 2

The Scratch Patch affords visitors the opportunity to "dig" for their own selection of polished semi-precious stones, such as amethyst and tiger's eye.

★ Two Oceans Aquarium
Glass tanks and tunnels are filled with shoaling fish such as yellowtail, *steenbras* and musselcracker, as well as penguins, turtles and short-tailed stingray.

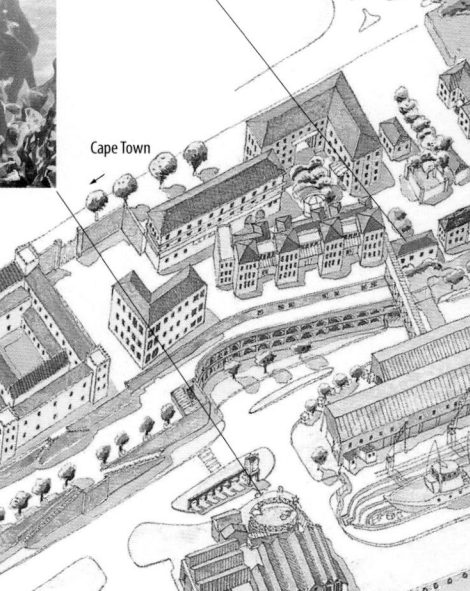

Granger Bay and Sea Point

BREAKW

Sea Point

BEACH

Cape Town

Foreshore

VISITORS' CHECKLIST

Practical Information
Cape Town harbour. **Map** 2 D3–4, E3–4. ℹ V&A Waterfront Information Kiosk, Victoria Wharf, 021 408 7791. **Open** Shops: most 9am–9pm; restaurants: most open until midnight. 🚾 waterfront.co.za

Transport
🚌 MyCiTi buses from Civic Centre, Adderley St in the city centre, Sea Point and Green Point. 🚢 to Robben Island; N Mandela Gateway (*see p147*).

0 metres 50
0 yards 50

Table Bay Hotel
One of the best-appointed establishments at the V&A Waterfront, the glamorous Table Bay Hotel, offers the ultimate in comfort and luxury. Each room has wonderful views of Table Mountain and the busy harbour.

★ Victoria Wharf Shopping Centre
Exclusive shops, cosy eateries and informal "barrow" stalls give this shopping centre a festive, market-day feel.

The V&A Waterfront Amphitheatre
This venue offers a vast array of musical and other events. Jazz, rock, classical concerts and the rhythms of traditional drumming take place here.

Quay Four

Cape Wheel

Nelson Mandela Gateway to Robben Island

To Clock Tower Centre and Diamond Museum

The Springbok Experience Rugby Museum is a celebration of South Africa's most adored sport; visitors can try interactive skills tests to determine whether they would make the national squad.

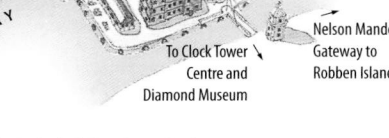

Cape Grace Hotel
Another of the V&A Waterfront's fine accommodation offerings, the Cape Grace Hotel on West Quay has wonderful views.

Exploring the Waterfront

The V&A Waterfront is one of Cape Town's most visited attractions. The multibillion-rand redevelopment scheme incorporates ideas from other ventures, such as San Francisco's harbour project. Easily accessible, with frequent bus services running to and from the city centre, it also provides ample covered and open-air parking for vehicles. There are many shops, more than 80 restaurants and some of the city's most luxurious hotels are here.

Volvo Ocean round-the-world racers moor at the Waterfront

🚢 Two Oceans Aquarium

Dock Rd. **Map** 2 D4. **Tel** 021 418 3823. **Open** 9:30am–6pm daily. 🅿 🅱 ✔ 🅒 🅦 **aquarium.co.za**

One of the top attractions in Cape Town, this complex aims to introduce visitors to the incredible diversity of sealife that occurs in the ocean around the Cape coast. A world first is the interesting exhibit of a complete river eco-system that traces the course of a stream from its mountain source down to the open sea. One of the most fascinating features is the kelp forest, one of only three in the world. It is housed in a ceiling-high glass tank that holds various shoals of line fish swimming among the waving fronds. Apart from waterbirds such as oystercatchers, there is a resident colony of African penguins and a touch pool, which has children exploring delicate underwater creatures such as crabs, starfish and sea urchins.

Victorian clock tower

Alfred Basin (West Quay)

Off Dock Rd. **Map** 2 E4. 🅱

Alfred Basin forms a crucial part of the working harbour, as fishing boats chug to the Robinson Graving Dock for repair and maintenance. Alongside the dry dock is the Watershed craft market, one of South Africa's largest indoor markets, which sells handcrafted gifts, toys, furniture and art. The **Iziko Maritime Centre** holds a model ship collection and includes the John H Marsh Maritime Research Centre, an important archive of photos of ships from the 1920s to the 1960s. The SAS *Somerset*, a former naval defence vessel, is also part of the centre.

🏛 Iziko Maritime Centre

Union Castle Building, Dock Rd. **Tel** 021 405 2880. **Open** 10am–5pm daily. **Closed** 1 May, 25 Dec. 🅿

Victoria Basin

Map 2 E3.

Located in Quay Four, at the edge of the basin, the Quay Four Tavern offers superb views of the harbour and its constant boat traffic. Nearby, the Amphitheatre regularly stages free recitals and concerts, from the Cape Town Philharmonic Orchestra to African musicians. Also in this area is the **Cape Wheel**, a 40-m (131-ft) high Ferris wheel with 30 air-conditioned cabins. There are great views across the Waterfront and Table Mountain from the top. In the **Red Shed Craft Workshop**, visitors can observe glass-blowers at work and buy handmade pottery and ceramics, leathercraft, hand-painted fabrics, jewellery and gifts.

Cape Wheel

V&A Waterfront. **Tel** 021 418 2502 . **Open** 11am–10pm Mon, Tue & Thu–Sun. 🅿 🅱 🅦 **capewheel. co.za**

🏪 Red Shed Craft Workshop

Victoria Wharf. **Tel** 021 408 7600. **Open** 9am–9pm Mon–Sat, 10am–9pm Sun & public hols. 🅱

The Cape Town Diamond Museum

Cape Town Diamond Museum

1st Floor, Clock Tower Centre. **Map** 2 E4. **Tel** 021 421 2488. **Open** 9am–9pm daily. 🅿 🅒 🅦 **capetowndiamondmuseum.org**

Run by Shimansky, one of South Africa's leading diamond jewellers, this museum traces the evolution of diamonds from their underground formation to a sparkling gem. Exhibits document the Orange River diamond rush that started in 1867, and there are replicas of famous South African diamonds, such as the Cullinan and the Taylor-Burton. Visitors can also watch stones being cut and polished in the workshop.

Exhibits at the Two Oceans Aquarium

An innovative approach to education has assured the popularity and success of this venture. The complex is constantly upgraded to accommodate new exhibits, such as a fun gallery dedicated to frogs. All the exhibits introduce the public to unfamiliar aspects of the fragile marine environment and the need for its preservation. Young visitors, in particular, enjoy the hands-on experience. The wholesome Children's Play Centre offers an interesting programme, including daily puppet shows and supervised arts and crafts. Novel "sleep-overs" in front of the Predator Tank are a hit with children between the ages of six and 12. Adventurous visitors in possession of a valid scuba licence may book dives during the day, although not during feeding sessions in the Predator and Kelp tanks.

The Displays

The aquarium's displays are well planned and create an interesting, stimulating environment. Quite a few of them are interactive, offering visitors the opportunity to experience sealife at first hand. The latest technology is used to reveal the secrets of even the tiniest of sea creatures.

The interior of the aquarium has been carefully designed to re-create various ocean and riverine habitats.

The Touch Pool invites children to handle and examine sea dwellers such as anemones and kelp.

The I & J Predator Tank is a two-million-litre (440,000-gallon) exhibit protected by shatterproof glass. The semi-tunnel surrounding the tank allows close encounters with turtles, yellowtails and ragged-tooth sharks.

African penguins have a small colony in the complex. There are also rockhopper penguins.

The Intertidal Pool contains mussels, barnacles, starfish, sea anemones and various sponges.

Short-tailed stingray, like this one, can be seen in the Predator Tank.

❷ Robben Island

Named "Robben Eiland" – seal island – by the Dutch in the mid-17th century, Robben Island has seen much human suffering. As early as 1636 it served as a penal settlement, and it was taken over by the South African Prisons Service in 1960. Its most famous inmate was Nelson Mandela, who spent 18 years here. When the last political prisoners were released in 1991, the South African Natural Heritage Programme nominated the island for its significance as a seabird breeding colony – it hosts more than 130 bird species. In 1997 the island was designated a museum, and in 1999 it was declared a UNESCO World Heritage Site.

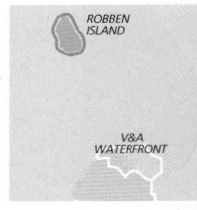

★ Governor's House
This splendid Victorian building dates from 1895 and was originally the home of the Island Commissioner. Today it serves a conference centre and provides upmarket accommodation for visiting dignitaries and VIPs.

KEY

① **Van Riebeeck's Quarry**

② **The kramat** was constructed in 1969 over the grave of an Indonesian prince. It is a place of pilgrimage for devout Muslims.

③ **Murray's Bay Harbour**

④ **Faure Jetty**

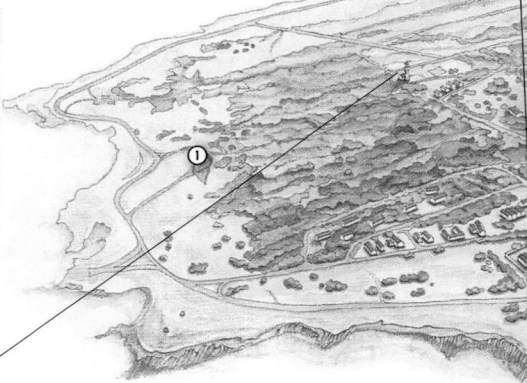

The Lighthouse
This lighthouse was built in 1863 to replace the fire beacons in use until then. It is 18 m (59 ft) high, and its beam can be seen from a distance of 25 km (16 miles).

Political Prisoners

In the 18th century, high-ranking princes and sheikhs from India, Malaysia and Indonesia were sent to Robben Island by the Dutch East India Company for inciting resistance against their European overlords. The British banished rebellious Xhosa rulers to the island in the early 1800s. In 1963, Nelson Mandela and seven other political activists were charged with conspiracy against the state for their political beliefs and were condemned to life imprisonment here.

Former inmate Nelson Mandela

Offshore Island
This flat, rocky island lies 11 km (7 miles) north of Cape Town in the icy Atlantic Ocean. Composed mainly of blue slate, it is only 30 m (98 ft) above sea level at its highest point. None of the trees on the island are indigenous.

VISITORS' CHECKLIST

Practical Information
Road map B5. **Tel** 021 413 4200.
Closed rough seas.
obligatory; book 2 days ahead
(2 wks in high season). give
ticket office advance notice.
robben-island.org.za

Transport
Apr–Sep: 9 & 11am, 1pm daily;
Oct–Mar: 9 & 11am, 1 & 3pm daily
(N Mandela Gateway, Clock Tower
Precinct, V&A Waterfront).

Caspian Tern
This endangered migrant bird species breeds on the northern part of the island.

★ The Prison
Robben Island served as a place of banishment from 1658, when Jan van Riebeeck sent his interpreter here. The maximum security prison was completed in 1964.

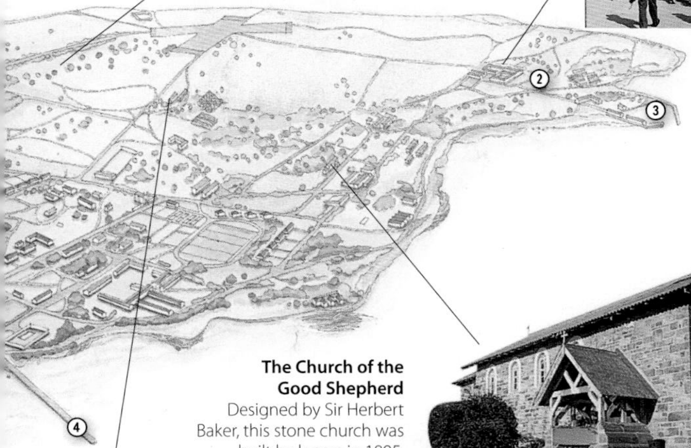

0 metres 150
0 yards 150

The Church of the Good Shepherd
Designed by Sir Herbert Baker, this stone church was built by lepers in 1895, for use by men only. Worshippers had to stand or lie down because there were no pews.

★ Lime Quarry
Political prisoners, required to work in this quarry for at least six hours a day, suffered damage to their eyesight due to the constant dust and the glare of the sunlight on the stark white lime cliffs.

FURTHER AFIELD

In summer, the compact City Bowl bakes at the foot of Table Mountain's northern slopes, initiating a migration to the superb beaches of the Atlantic Seaboard: Clifton, Camps Bay and Llandudno. Parking space is at a premium as sunseekers move on to the coastal villages of Hout Bay, Kommetjie and Scarborough, as well as Cape Point, with its dramatic ocean views. The wooded southern slopes of Table Mountain are cooler – it is known to rain in Newlands – while the beaches of the Atlantic Seaboard bask under clear skies. Also on the cool southern incline is Kirstenbosch National Botanical Garden, with its 7,000 plant species, and the world-famous wine estate, Groot Constantia. On the popular False Bay coast, the water at Fish Hoek and Muizenberg is up to 5°C (10°F) warmer than the water along the western side of the Cape Peninsula.

Sights at a Glance

Historic Buildings
- ⓮ Groot Constantia pp160–61
- ⓱ Mostert's Mill
- ⓲ Rhodes Memorial
- ⓳ South African Astronomical Observatory

Parks and Gardens
- ⓯ Kirstenbosch National Botanical Garden pp164–5
- ⓴ Ratanga Junction

Suburbs
- ❶ Green Point and Sea Point
- ❷ Atlantic Seaboard
- ❸ Hout Bay
- ❺ Noordhoek
- ❼ Simon's Town
- ❽ Fish Hoek
- ❾ Muizenberg
- ⓫ Khayelitsha
- ⓬ Gugulethu
- ⓭ Langa
- ⓰ Newlands

Nature Reserves
- ❻ Cape of Good Hope, Table Mountain National Park
- ❿ False Bay Nature Reserve

Driving Tours
- ❹ Touring the Cape Peninsula

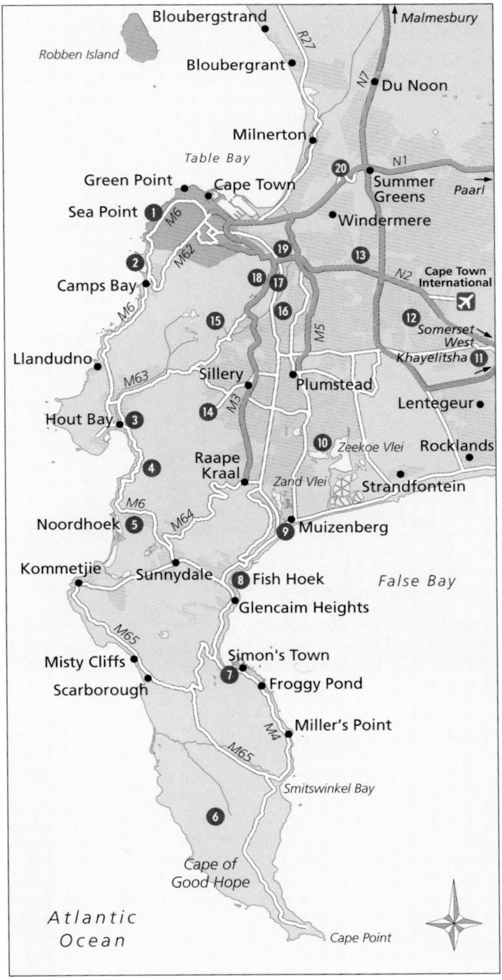

0 kilometres   10

0 miles   10

Key

- Main sightseeing area
- Motorway
- Major road
- Minor road

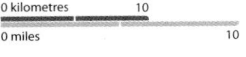

◄ The Lion's Head peak dominates the Green Point and Sea Point suburbs of Cape Town

For keys to symbols see back flap

An aerial view of Sea Point on the slopes of Signal Hill

❶ Green Point and Sea Point

Main or Beach rds. **Map** 1 B4, 3 C1.

Since the development of the V&A Waterfront began in 1995, the real estate value in neighbouring seaside suburbs such as Green Point and Mouille Point has soared. Beach Road, only a stone's throw from the sea, is today lined with expensive high-rise apartments, as well as trendy restaurants and upmarket office blocks.

Green Point Common backs the residential strip. It started in 1657 as a farm granted to Jan van Riebeeck, but the soil proved unfit for cultivation. The sports complexes and clubs on the common have athletics, rugby and cricket fields, bowling greens, and tennis and squash courts. Cape Town Stadium, built for the 2010 FIFA World Cup, borders the Metropolitan Golf Course and the Green Point Urban Park. Green Point's red and white candy-striped lighthouse, built in 1824, is still functional. Its resonant foghorn is notorious for keeping Mouille Point's residents awake when mist rolls in from the sea.

Further along Beach Road lies the suburb of Sea Point. It, too, has undergone intensive development over the years and today sports towering apartment blocks, hotels and offices. Sea Point is one of Cape Town's most popular entertainment districts after the V&A Waterfront, and Main Road teems with restaurants, bars and night spots. New shopping malls also add to the suburb's attractions.

In the afternoon, the 3-km (2-mile) Sea Point promenade is abuzz with joggers, roller-bladers, children, tanned people-watchers and older residents strolling along with their lap dogs.

The promenade ends with a large parking area and the open-air **Sea Point Swimming Pool**, which is filled with filtered seawater and has an impressive diving pool.

Small sandy coves that are packed with sunbathers in summer dot the rocky shoreline. The tidal pools among the rocks are always a source of amazement, particularly for children, who enjoy scrambling around looking for sea anemones, tiny starfish, shells and the occasional octopus. Other amenities along the promenade include a mini-golf course, a small maze, outdoor gyms and children's playgrounds.

Sea Point Swimming Pool
Beach Rd. **Tel** (021) 434-3341.
Open Oct–Apr: 7am–7pm daily;
May–Sep: 9am–5pm daily.
Closed only in bad weather.

The distinctive striped Green Point Lighthouse

Lion's Head and Signal Hill

A fairly easy climb to the top of Lion's Head, 670 m (2,198 ft) high, affords views of the City Bowl and Atlantic coastline. Climbers can leave their cars at a parking area along Signal Hill Road (take the right-hand fork at the top of Kloof Nek Road), which opens to the contour path that encircles Lion's Head. At the end of Signal Hill Road is a viewpoint and another parking area. This spot is popular for its night views of the city, but be aware of safety issues, and climb only when there is a full moon. Signal Hill is the site of Cape Town's noon gun, a battery originally built by the British in 1890 to defend the harbour. The cannon is fired daily at precisely noon.

The view from Lion's Head is spectacular

❷ Atlantic Seaboard

Victoria Rd. **Map** 3 B2–5.

Shortly after the Sea Point Swimming Pool, Beach Road runs via Queens into Victoria Road, which winds southward along Cape Town's Atlantic Seaboard. Bantry Bay, Clifton, Camps Bay and Llandudno are the desirable addresses along this steep stretch of coast, which is flanked by million-dollar homes with spacious terraces and glittering swimming pools. With incomparable views and beautiful beaches right on their doorsteps, this is the haunt of the wealthy.

The coastal route extends all the way to idyllic Hout Bay, which lies over the saddle that separates the Twelve Apostles mountain range from the peak of Little Lion's Head. The 12 impressive sandstone buttresses, named after the biblical apostles by Sir Rufane Donkin, one-time governor of the British Cape Colony, flank the Riviera's suburbs. First is **Bantry Bay**, whose luxury apartments, many supported on concrete stilts, are built into the steep mountain slope.

Trendy **Clifton** follows, with its four famous small beaches separated by granite boulders. Fourth Beach is especially popular among families, as it has a car park nearby, while

A good meal and sweeping sea views at a Camps Bay restaurant

the other three are accessible only from the road via steep flights of stairs. The Atlantic's waters are icy, but the beaches are sheltered from the strong southeasterly gales by Lion's Head, so during the summer months all of the four beaches are tremendously popular with sunseekers, and the resulting traffic congestion is enormous.

Victoria Road continues along the shore past **Maiden's Cove**, which has a tidal pool and good public facilities, and **Glen Beach**, which has no amenities but is frequented nonetheless by surfers and sunbathers. At **Camps Bay**, the broad sweep of beach lined with tall, stately palms is another very popular spot, although the southeaster tends to bluster through here quite strongly, especially during the

summer months. Backed by Lion's Head and the Twelve Apostles, Camps Bay's lovely setting has been the inspiration for the establishment of a number of luxurious hotels and a string of good restaurants.

Llandudno arguably has the city's most beautiful little beach, about 10 km (6 miles) east of Camps Bay. The small elite residential area, settled on a rocky promontory at the foot of the mountain known as Little Lion's Head, is first spotted from the cliff top. Its curve of pristine white beach and distilled turquoise sea is a favourite spot from which to toast the sunset. A 20-minute walk to the west over the rocky shore leads to secluded and sheltered **Sandy Bay**, Cape Town's nudist beach.

Camps Bay Beach with the Twelve Apostles in the background

❸ Hout Bay

Since the 1940s, Hout Bay has been an important fishing centre. It is also a pretty residential area and a popular weekend resort. Its name derives from a diary entry made by Jan van Riebeeck in July 1653, in which he refers to "t'houtbaaijen", the wooded bays in the area. Hout Bay's fisheries centre on snoek and rock lobster, and include canning factories, a fishmeal plant and a fresh fish market. The 1 km-long (half mile) beach is backed by low, scrub-covered dunes and flanked by tall mountains. To the west, the Karbonkelberg mountain range culminates in the towering 331-m (1,086-ft) Sentinel Peak. To the east rises the Chapman's Peak range, along the slopes of which snakes a world-famous scenic drive.

A colourful fishing trawler in the Hout Bay harbour

Exploring Hout Bay

Road Map B5. 20 km (12 miles) S of Cape Town on M6 or M63. ▥ MyCiTi bus from Civic Centre or Adderley St.

The green valleys of Hout Bay are threaded with oak-lined roads. Horse paddocks and stables abound; many local riding centres offer instruction and recreational horse riding. Residents walk their dogs on Hout Bay beach in the early mornings. The beach is also frequented by swimmers, paddlesurfers and, at its west end, by windsurfers and Hobie Cat sailors. From the harbour, tour operators launch regular cruises that take visitors out to watch seabirds and see the Cape fur seal colony on Duiker Island. Boat trips last for about 45 minutes. The vessels have large portholes or glass bottoms so seals can be viewed frolicking

underwater among giant wavy kelp forests. Sunset cruises are always popular and local game-fishing companies organize expeditions to catch a variety of gamefish such as yellowfin and longfin tuna, broadbill sword-fish and marlin.

At the eastern edge of the bay, a 1.4-m (4.5-ft) high bronze statue of a leopard is perched on a rock pinnacle.

Bronze leopard, a reminder of the wildlife that once roamed the area

It was cast in 1963 by the late Ivan Mitford-Barberton, a local artist.

The suburb of Hout Bay itself offers a great variety of small coffee shops, restaurants, clothing and curio shops. Closer to the harbour there are pubs,

such as the popular Dunes, which has a verandah over-looking the beach and harbour. At the start of the scenic coastal drive, Chapmans Peak Hotel is very well-positioned, with beautiful views across the bay. Its terrace is popular in summer for seafood lunches and relaxed sundowners.

Mariner's Wharf

Harbour Road. **Tel** 021 790 1100. **Open** daily. ⬤ ⬤ ⬤ ⬤ ⬤ **marinerswharf.com**

Mariner's Wharf was built by a local family, the Dormans, whose predecessors farmed in the Hout Bay valley during the 1900s. It lies sandwiched between Hout Bay's beach and the busy little fishing harbour, and offers an open-air bistro, a seafood restaurant and a shop that sells marine-related curios. Visitors can also enjoy a stroll along the pier flanked by moored fishing boats.

Bay Harbour Market

31 Harbour Road. **Tel** 083 275 5586. **Open** 5pm–9pm Fri, 9:30am–4pm Sat & Sun. ⬤ ⬤ ⬤ ⬤ **bayharbour.co.za**

At weekends, the Bay Harbour Market is held in one of the old fishing factories. It features more than 100 craft and food stalls and is popular for brunch and

A hiker's view of Hout Bay, seen from Chapman's Peak

Mariner's Wharf, known for its fresh fish and chips

lunch, which is enjoyed at communal tables and accompanied by live music. Traders are mostly small local producers, organic farmers and artisans supporting a green and sustainable lifestyle.

Hout Bay Museum

4 Andrews Rd. **Tel** 021 790 3270.
Open 8am–4:30pm Mon–Thu, 8am–4pm Fri. **Closed** public hols.

This museum has interesting displays on the history of the Hout Bay valley and its people, focusing on forestry, mining and the fishing industry. The museum also organizes weekly guided nature walks into the surrounding mountains.

Environs

Just north of Hout Bay, **World of Birds** has high, landscaped, walk-through aviaries that are home to 400 bird species. Around 3,000 individual birds are kept in the sanctuary for rehabilitation purposes, many of them brought in injured. Others are endangered species here for captive breeding. Wherever possible, birds are released into their natural habitat as soon as they are fit to survive.

Visitors can watch them feed, build nests and incubate their eggs. Among the endangered bird species that have benefited from special breeding projects are the blue crane, the citron-crested cockatoo and the Egyptian vulture, extinct in South Africa.

Rare primates can also be seen at the sanctuary, such as the endangered pygmy marmoset and Geoffrey's tufted-ear marmoset. There are also terrapins, skinks and iguanas. The Robin's Nest café offers drinks and light meals and there is a picnic spot next to the flamingo enclosure.

World of Birds
Valley Rd. **Tel** 021 790 2730.
Open 9am–5pm daily.
W worldofbirds.org.za

Black-shouldered kite

Linefish of the Western Cape

The cold, nutrient-bearing water along the West Coast results in a greater number of fish than off the East Coast, but not as great a variety. The biggest catches are of red roman, kabeljou and white stumpnose. The uniquely South African national fish, the galjoen, has now become very rare. The deep gulleys along the rocky shores of the Western Cape, with their characteristic kelp beds, are perfect fishing spots for anglers.

Red Roman Particularly tasty when stuffed and baked, this fish is found in great numbers off the Cape reefs.

Snoek Winter and early spring see the "snoek run", when this predatory fish migrates south in search of its prey – pilchards. Its rich, rather oily flesh is either canned, smoked or dried.

Kabeljou (kob) One of the most common food fishes, this is invariably served as the "linefish catch of the day".

Yellowtail This is one of the finest seasonal gamefish available in South African waters. The flesh is very firm and tasty, but can be coarse, especially in older and larger fish.

White stumpnose A delicious sport fish, which is eagerly sought by ski-boat anglers.

Cape salmon Its flesh is similar to that of its cousin, the kob, but more flavourful.

❹ Touring the Cape Peninsula

Tours of the Cape Peninsula should start on the Atlantic Seaboard and include Chapman's Peak Drive, a scenic route that took seven years to build. The drive, cut into the cliff face, has splendid lookout points with picnic sites. A highlight of the tour is the panorama at Cape Point, where the peninsula juts into the sea. The views encompass False Bay, the Hottentots Holland mountains and Cape Hangklip, 80 km (50 miles) away. The return journey passes the penguin colony at Boulders and goes through charming Simon's Town.

① Chapman's Peak
The highest point rises to 592 m (1,942 ft). An observation platform is set on sheer cliffs which drop 160 m (525 ft) to the swirling seas below.

```
0 kilometres        5
0 miles        2
```

② Kommetjie
Flashes from the powerful beams of Slangkop Lighthouse can be seen from Hout Bay at night.

Key
▬ Tour route
═ Other roads
--- Park or reserve boundary

Tips for Drivers

Tour length: 160 km (99 miles). From De Waal Drive via Camps Bay and Chapman's Peak Drive to Cape Point, returning through Simon's Town and Muizenberg, then back to the city via the M3. Chapman's Peak Drive may close in bad weather. Check first by calling 021 791 8222 or at www.chapmanspeakdrive.co.za.
Duration: A full day, including a stop for a leisurely lunch.

⑥ Muizenberg
Muizenberg beach has flat, warm water and is safe for swimming.

⑤ Boulders
This accessible African penguin colony attracts many visitors each year.

④ Funicular
The Flying Dutchman funicular rail provides easy access to the lookout atop Cape Point.

③ Cape of Good Hope
There is a variety of wildlife here, including ostriches, bontebok, eland and zebras.

Horse riding on Noordhoek Beach is a popular pastime

❺ Noordhoek

Road Map: B5. Via Chapman's Peak Drive or Ou Kaapse Weg.

The best feature of this little coastal settlement is its 6-km (4-mile) stretch of pristine white beach. Strong currents make the water unsafe for swimming but it is popular with surfers and paddleskiers. The shore is good for horse riding and long walks (tourists are advised to walk in groups, while along its length lies the wreck of the *Kakapo*, a steamer that was beached during a storm in 1900. Part of the Hollywood movie *Ryan's Daughter* (1970) was filmed here.

Environs

Another coastal hamlet, **Kommetjie**, adjoins a tidal lagoon situated inland from Noordhoek Beach. Long Beach, which stretches north as far as Klein Slangkop Point, is a venue for surfing championships and is very popular with board-sailors. **Scarborough**, at the mouth of the Schuster's River, is a sought-after residential area. In summer, the seasonal lagoon is very popular.

❻ Cape of Good Hope, Table Mountain National Park

Road Map: B5. M4 via Simon's Town. **Tel** 021 780 9010. **Open** Main gate: Oct–Mar: 6am–6pm (spring/summer) daily; Apr–Sep: 7am–5pm (autumn/winter) daily; funicular: 9am–5:30pm daily. 🚗 🍴 🅿️ ♿ 📷 ♿ 🌐 sanparks.org 🌐 capepoint.co.za

Strictly speaking, the Cape of Good Hope is the rocky headland that marks the most southwesterly point of the Cape Peninsula. Originally named Cape of Storms by Bartolomeu Dias in 1488, it was given its more optimistic title by King John of Portugal, who saw it as a positive omen for a new route to India.

Cape of Good Hope is also the name given to the southernmost sector (formerly referred to as the Cape of Good Hope Nature Reserve) of Table Mountain National Park, which encompasses the whole of the Table Mountain chain from the southernmost point of the peninsula to Signal Hill in the north. Most of the park is open access, with only three points at which conservation fees are payable: Boulders (see p156), Silvermine and Cape of Good Hope.

Not surprisingly, this part of the park is exposed to gale-force winds, so the vegetation is limited to hardy milkwood trees and *fynbos*. Small antelopes live here, as do Cape mountain zebras. Visitors may also encounter troops of chacma baboons, which can sometimes be aggressive.

For stunning views from Cape Point, take the Flying Dutchman funicular up to the old lighthouse, 238 m (781 ft) above the crashing ocean waves. From here, a path leads down to the new lighthouse at Dias Point.

Along the park's east coast, the tidal pools at Venus Pool, Bordjiesrif and Buffels Bay attract hordes of tourists. A number of scenic walking trails along the west coast include the Thomas T Tucker shipwreck trail and the path to Sirkelsvlei – maps are available at the park's entrance gate.

Bontebok, Cape of Good Hope

The Flying Dutchman

The Flying Dutchman

This legend originated in 1641, when the Dutch sea captain Hendrick van der Decken was battling wild seas off Cape Point while sailing home. No match against the storm, his battered ship started sinking, but van der Decken swore that he would round the Cape, even if it took him until Judgement Day. Since then, many sightings of a phantom ship, its masts smashed and sails in shreds, have been reported in bad weather. The most significant was recorded in July 1881 in the diary of a certain midshipman sailing on HMS *Bacchante*. He was crowned King George V of England in 1910.

Victorian architecture along the main road in Simon's Town

❼ Simon's Town

Road map B5. ⛰ 6,600. 🚊 from Cape Town station, Adderley St. ℹ Simon's Town Museum, Court Rd, 021 786 3046. **Open** 10am–4pm Mon–Fri, 10am–1pm Sat. 🆆 simonstown.com

Picturesque Simon's Town in False Bay has been the base of the South African navy since 1957. It was named after Simon van der Stel *(see p160)*, who visited this sheltered little spot around 1687. In 1743, the Dutch East India Company decided to make Simon's Bay its fleet's winter anchorage, safe from the storms of Table Bay. From 1814 until handover to South Africa, it served as the British Royal Navy's base in the South Atlantic. The town's characterful hotels and bars have been frequented by generations of seamen.

Simon's Town's naval history is best absorbed by walking the "historical mile" that begins near the railway station and ends at the Martello Tower on the East Dockyard, taking in the **Simon's Town Museum**, the South African Naval Toy Museum, and the Warrior Toy Museum along the way. The Simon's Town Museum is housed in The Residency, believed to be the town's oldest building. It was built in 1777 as a weekend retreat for Governor Joachim van Plettenberg. Later, it also served

African penguin

as a naval hospital. Among the exhibits is a replica of a World War II royal naval pub and the cramped quarters of the original slave lodge. Martello Tower, the walk's endpoint, was built in 1796 as a defence against the French. Guided walks can be arranged at the museum on request.

🏛 **Simon's Town Museum**
Court Rd. **Tel** 021 786 3046. **Open** 10am–4pm Mon–Fri, 10am–1pm Sat. **Closed** Sun & public hols. 📷 📸
🆆 simonstown.com/museum

Environs
Between Simon's Town and the Cape of Good Hope sector of Table Mountain National Park, the M4 passes through charming settlements that offer safe

swimming and snorkelling in protected bays such as Froggy Pond, Boulders and Seaforth. The big granite rocks after which Boulders is named provide shelter when the southeaster blows. A major attraction is the **Boulders Penguin Colony**, a land-based colony of more than 2,100 African penguins. A wheelchair-friendly boardwalk allows visitors to see their nesting sites in the dunes and to watch them waddle along the beach.

Further south, Miller's Point has picnic areas and tidal rock pools. The Black Marlin Restaurant here is popular for its fresh seafood. At Smitswinkel Bay, a lovely cove lies at the foot of a steep path.

🐧 **Boulders Penguin Colony**
Kleintuin Rd. **Tel** 021 786 2329. **Open** Feb–Mar & Oct–Nov: 8am–6:30pm; Apr–Sep: 8am–5pm; Dec–Jan: 7am–7:30pm. 📷 ♿ 🆆 sanparks.org

Able Seaman Just Nuisance

In Jubilee Square, overlooking Simon's Town's naval harbour, stands the statue of a Great Dane called Just Nuisance. During World War II this dog was the much-loved mascot of British sailors based in Simon's Town. The animal, formally enrolled in the Royal Navy, was given the title Able Seaman. When he died in a Simon's Town naval hospital, he was honoured with a full military funeral, which was attended by 200 members of the British Royal Navy. One room at the Simon's Town Museum is filled with memorabilia of the unusual cadet.

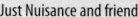

Just Nuisance and friend

❽ Fish Hoek

Road map B5. M4, False Bay.
11,900. 🚉 from Cape Town station, Adderley St.

Only recently was liquor allowed to be sold in Fish Hoek; until then it was a "dry" municipality. This condition had been written into a property grant made by Governor Lord Charles Somerset in 1818, and was repealed only in the 1990s.

The broad stretch of Fish Hoek beach is lined with changing rooms, cafés and a yacht club, and is popular with families and the sailing fraternity. Regattas are held regularly, and catamarans and Hobie Cats often line the beach. Jager's Walk, a pleasant pathway overlooking the sea and the beach, runs along the edge of the bay.

Environs
The M4 continues northwards, staying close to the shore. It passes through the seaside suburb of St James, which has a small, safe family beach and is characterized by a row of wooden bathing huts that have all been painted in bright primary colours.

At the picturesque little fishing harbour of Kalk Bay, the daily catches of fresh fish, particularly snoek, are sold directly from the boats. The height of the snoek season varies, but usually extends from June to July. The Brass Bell restaurant, sandwiched between the railway station and the rocky shore, has a popular pub, good seafood and, at high

Muizenberg's beachfront seen from Boyes Drive

tide, waves crash against the breakwater between the restaurant and the sea. Kalk Bay is also popular for the many antique and art shops that line Main Road.

❾ Muizenberg

Road map B5. M4, False Bay.  36,900. 🚉 from Cape Town station, Adderley St.

The name Muizenberg comes from the Dutch phrase *Muijs zijn berg*, meaning "Muijs's mountain". Wynand Willem Muijs was a sergeant who, from 1743, commanded a military post on the mountain overlooking the beach.

Muizenberg's white sands, which curve for 40 km (25 miles) around False Bay as far as the town of Strand, rightly earned the town its status as the country's premier holiday retreat in the 19th century. Traces of this early popularity are still visible in the now-shabby façades of once-grand beach mansions. Today, a fast-food pavilion, seawater pool and wide lawns

attract young and old alike. The railway station perches on a rocky section of shoreline, where the curve of the bay is known as Surfer's Corner, due to its popularity among surfers. There are several surf shops here that offer lessons for beginners.

Rhodes Cottage

Environs
Cecil John Rhodes, prime minister of the Cape Colony from 1890–95, started a trend when he bought Barkly Cottage in Muizenberg in 1899. Soon, holiday mansions began to mushroom at the seaside resort, although most were in stark contrast to his simple, stone-walled, thatched cottage. The cottage is today a museum in Main Road and has been renamed **Rhodes Cottage**.

The museum contains photographs and personal memorabilia of the powerful empire builder and statesman, including his diamond-weighing scale and the chest in which he carried his personal belongings.

🏛 **Rhodes Cottage**
246 Main Rd. **Tel** 021 788 1816.
Open 10am–2pm Mon–Sat.
Closed 25 Dec. 🖼 by donation.

Fish Hoek beach offers safe bathing

Beautiful coastline of the beach at False Bay Nature Reserve

⑩ False Bay Nature Reserve

Road Map B5. Entrances on Perth and Zeekooivlei Road. **Tel** 021 706 2404. **Open** 7:30am–5pm daily (Dec–Feb: to 7pm Sat & Sun).
w capetown.gov.za/naturereserves

The largest remaining swathe of green on the Cape Flats, False Bay Nature Reserve, protects a rich biodiversity of fragile habitats including several perennial lakes and marshes, and relict patches of Cape Flats Dune Strandveld and Sand Fynbos (both critically endangered types of vegetation). Extending over 2,300 ha (5,684 acres) northeast of Muizenberg, the reserve was recognised as a Ramsar wetland in 2015, and it is also listed as an IBA (Important Bird Area), with more than 240 bird species recorded. The reserve has existed only in its present form since 2011, but the Rondevlei (literally "Round Pan") Sector – the oldest of its six parts and the best developed for tourists – was designated as a bird sanctuary in 1952.

The finest aquatic bird-watching site in the vicinity of Cape Town, Rondevlei is serviced by a short walking trail and six hides, from where species including great crested grebe, purple swamp-hen, great white pelican, greater flamingo, African spoonbill and a profusion of water-fowl and waders can be observed. Look out, too, for the hippos that were introduced in 1982 to help to prevent the wetland from

being choked by vegetation, and the herd of eland – Africa's largest antelope – that joined them in 2015. Other wildlife ranges from small predators such as the Cape clawless otter and large-spotted genet to endangered endemics such as the Cape dwarf chameleon and western leopard toad. Rondevlei aside, the most frequently visited of the other five sectors are Strandfontein, whose sewerage works might lack the aesthetic appeal of Rondevlei but often offers even better birding, and Zeekooivlei ("Hippo Pan"), a large lake primarily used for local recreation activities.

Black statue of Jesus in a church at Khayelitsha

⑪ Khayelitsha

Road Map B5. 👥 400,000.

Created in 1983, Khayelitsha – an isiXhosa name meaning "new home" – was one of the apartheid regime's final bids to enforce the Group Areas Act.

As South Africa's second-largest township (after Soweto), it is also the country's fastest-growing settlement, with a predominantly Xhosa population that has soared from 30,000 in the late 1980s to an estimated 400,000 today.

Khayelitsha is conspicuously poorer than Langa, it's neighbouring township. Unemployment stands at more than 50 percent, and more than half of the township's residents live in makeshift shacks, despite the construction of 25,000 government houses since the turn of the millennium.

An overview of Khayelitsha can be obtained from a viewing platform on **Lookout Hill**, the Cape Flats' tallest sand dune. Heading into the township, **Khayelitsha Craft Market**, housed at St Michael's Church, was established in 1997 as a place where local craftspeople and artists can create and sell their work, much of which makes imaginative use of recycled household objects to create beadwork, handbags, sculptures and other artifacts with a funky contemporary feel.

Just outside Khayelitsha stands the grim **Lwandle Migrant Labour Museum**: a former single-sex hostel where migrant labourers at a nearby canning factory were crammed six-in-a-room into a concrete block with rudimentary bathroom facilities.

⚜ Lookout Hill
Cnr Mew Way & Spine Rd. **Tel** 021 361 7098. **Open** 8am–4:30pm Mon–Fri.

Khayelitsha Craft Market
Open 8am–4:30pm Mon–Fri.
W stmichaels.org.za

Lwandle Migrant Labour Museum
N2. **Tel** 021 845 6119. **Open** 8:30am–4:30pm Mon–Thu, 8:30am–4pm Fri.
W lwandle.com

⓬ Gugulethu

Road Map B5. 100,000.

A contraction of an isiXhosa phrase meaning "Our Pride", Gugulethu, established in the late 1950s, became a focus of anti-apartheid activity in the 1980s. It retains a reputation as a crime hotspot, though this is no obstacle to visiting by day in the company of a guide. The township's most poignant landmark is the Gugulethu Seven Monument, a line of seven tombstone-like slabs, with human outlines carved out of their centres, marking the place where seven young men from Gugulethu were shot dead by police in 1986. The nearby Amy Biehl Memorial commemorates a 26-year-old American anti-apartheid activist who was stoned by an angry mob in 1993.

⓭ Langa

Road Map B5. 55,000.

Cape Town's first planned township, Langa was established in 1927 for migrant labourers from the Eastern Cape, and it remains relatively homogenous in cultural terms, with a predominantly Xhosa population. The township's name – which means "Sun" in isiXhosa and several other Nguni languages – is a contraction of Kwa-Langa-libalele (Place of Langalibalele), a reference to the eponymous Hlubi chief, who in 1874 became one of the first Black African dissidents to be incarcerated on Robben Island, and was subsequently held under house arrest at a farm on the site of present-day Langa for 13 years.

Langa's main sites of interest line Washington Street. The modernist Langa-Sharpeville Massacre Memorial was unveiled on 21 March 2010 to commemorate the fiftieth anniversary of the police opening fire on protesters in Langa (at least two were killed, but some accounts suggest the death toll was higher) on the same day as the Sharpeville Massacre near Johannesburg. These 1960 protests were a reaction to the Pass Law, which required Black South Africans to carry a passbook when they travelled outside designated areas. The *Dompas* (literally "stupid pass") is also the focal point of the **Langa Township Heritage Museum**, which is set in a former Pass Office. A more forward-looking landmark, the **Guga S'Thebe Cultural Centre**, decorated with a riot of colourful ceramic murals, is a com-munity centre offering arts-based activities from dance

Intricate tile painting at the cultural centre in Langa

classes to craft workshops. The complex, which has long welcomed tourists, was expanded in 2015 following the completion of the Guga S'Thebe Theatre, an innovative construction built with recycled shipping containers, wooden fruit crates and local materials such as straw and clay.

Langa Township Heritage Museum
Washington St. **Tel** 021 694 8320.
Open 9am–4pm Mon–Sat.

Guga S'Thebe Cultural Centre
Washington St.
Tel. 021 695 3493 **Open** 8:30am–4:30pm Mon–Fri, 8:30am–2pm Sat & Sun.

Amy Biehl Memorial at Gugulethu

The Cape Flats

The sandy and agriculturally unyielding flatlands to the east of Cape Town saw little permanent settlement until the 1920s, when an influx of migrant labour led to the establishment of the area's first "township" (a residential suburb reserved for individuals classified as Black, Coloured or Indian by the government of the time). Following this, the implementation of the Group Areas Act in 1950 led to the creation of an easterly sprawl of townships, many designed to house non-white Capetonians relocated from the city's established suburbs. The townships were more crowded than the residential areas designated for Whites, and basic amenities were often lacking. They later became a hotbed of anti-apartheid activism. While living conditions are vastly improved today, poverty remains rife in this part of Cape Town.

The townships of the Cape Flats are best visited on an organized tour or with a local guide. Tours usually incorporate most of the townships' best-known sights, but they should also offer the opportunity to experience local culture, with scheduled stops at markets, shops and homesteads. False Bay Nature Reserve (the Cape Flats' one substantial green area) is close to Muizenberg and easily visited independently.

Shanty homes in Khayelitsha

⓮ Groot Constantia

The oldest wine estate in South Africa, Groot Constantia was built on land granted in 1685 to Simon van der Stel, newly appointed Commander of the Cape. On his death in 1712, the farm was subdivided into three parts and sold. After several changes of ownership, the portion with the manor house was bought in 1778 by Hendrik Cloete, whose family owned it for three generations thereafter and was responsible for the present appearance of the buildings. Today, as well as being a fully operational farm, Groot Constantia is also a popular tourist attraction, incorporating a museum belonging to the Iziko Museums group – its exhibits include furniture, paintings, textiles and ceramics.

Display of Carriages
A collection of carts and other implements tells the story of transport in the Cape's early colonial days.

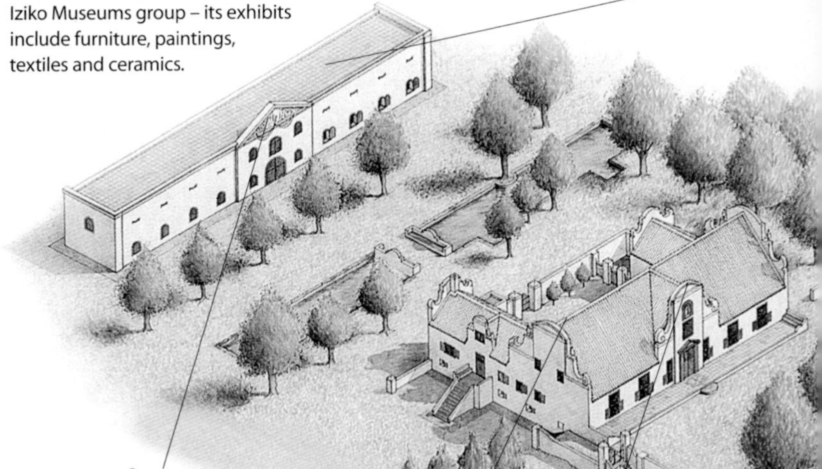

★ Cloete Wine Cellar
This façade, commissioned by Hendrik Cloete and built in 1791, is attributed to Louis Thibault. The Rococo pediment was sculpted by Anton Anreith.

★ Manor House
This museum contains an authentic representation of a wealthy 19th-century farming household. Most of the antiques were donated by Alfred A de Pass, member of a Dutch family.

Cape Gable
The very tall gable of the manor house was added between 1799 and 1803. The sculpted figure of Abundance that decorates its lofty niche is the work of respected sculptor, Anton Anreith.

Groot Constantia
The Mediterranean climate of temperate summers and cool, rainy winters has ensured the success of the vines planted on this estate.

Vin de Constance
This naturally sweet Muscat de Frontignan by Klein Constantia, part of the Groot Constantia estate until 1712, is made in the style of the early 18th-century wines.

★ Jonkershuis
Once the abode of the estate owner's bachelor sons, the quaint Jonkershuis is now a restaurant that serves traditional Cape dishes.

Trees in the front garden
included oak, chestnut, olive and banana. By 1695, some 8,401 had been planted.

The Development of Gable Design

Government House (1756) is an example of the concave, or lobed, gable style.

Libertas (1771) has a convex-concave gable style, also called the Cape Baroque.

Klein Constantia (1799) has a classical gable, inspired by the Italian Renaissance.

Nederburg (1800) has a convex-concave out-line, broken pediment and low pilasters.

Newlands Forest, a popular destination for weekend excursions

⑮ Kirstenbosch National Botanical Garden

See pp164–5.

⑯ Newlands

Road map B5. 🚆 from Cape Town station, Adderley St. 🚌 Terminus in Strand St to Mowbray station.

An exclusive suburb nestled at the foot of Table Mountain's southern slopes, Newlands is the headquarters for the Western Province rugby and cricket unions. The big Newlands sports grounds have served as the venue for many international matches. The rugby stadium can hold up to 50,000 spectators, and hosted the opening game of the 1995 Rugby World Cup *(see p38)*.

Newlands Forest runs along the edge of the M3, a major route that links Muizenberg with the southern suburbs and the city centre. Local residents love to take long walks and exercise their dogs through the forest's tall blue gums, pines and silver trees, which are watered by the Newlands stream.

A little further on stands a beautifully restored national monument, **Josephine Mill**. This mill, with its cast-iron wheel, was built in 1840 by a Swede, Jacob Letterstedt, on the bank of the Liesbeeck River, to grind wheat. It was named after the Swedish Crown Princess, Josephine. Today, this fine example of 19th-century architecture is managed by Cape Town's Historical Society, and is Cape Town's only surviving operational mill. Demonstrations take place from Monday to Friday (at 11am and 3pm), and fresh biscuits and flour are for sale. A pleasant restaurant in the grounds has outside tables next to the river.

🏠 Josephine Mill
13 Boundary Rd. **Tel** (021) 686-4939.
Open summer: 10am–7pm Mon–Fri, 10am–2pm Sat; winter: 10am–4pm Mon–Fri, 10am–2pm Sat. Milling demonstrations: 11am & 3pm. 🅿️ 🅲
🚭 🆆 **josephinemill.co.za**

Josephine Mill, Cape Town's only surviving water mill

⑰ Mostert's Mill

Road map B5. Rhodes Drive.
🚌 Terminus in Strand St to Mowbray station. **Tel** 021 782 1305.
Open phone to book. 🅿️
🆆 **mostertsmill.co.za**

This old-fashioned windmill dates to 1796 and stands on part of the Groote Schuur estate bequeathed to the country's people by financier Cecil John Rhodes *(see p56)*. Rhodes bought the estate in 1891, donating a portion to the University of Cape Town, which today sprawls across the lower slopes of the mountain, its red-tiled roofs and ivy-covered walls an unmistakable landmark above Rhodes Drive (M3). The mill is the only working windmill in South Africa and is operated from 10am to 2:30pm once a month on a Saturday, subject to weather and volunteers.

Environs
Directly east of Mostert's Mill, in the suburb of Rosebank, is the **Irma Stern Museum**, dedicated to one of South Africa's most talented and prolific modern painters, who died in 1966. Her magnificent home, The Firs, features 200 paintings and her collection of antiques.

Travelling northwest from Mostert's Mill along the busy M3, the road curves around Devil's Peak to become De Waal Drive, which heads into the city centre. On the right is the famous Groote Schuur Hospital, where, in 1967, the world's first heart transplant was performed by Professor Christiaan Barnard. The story is told in the **Heart of Cape Town Museum**, inside the hospital, using life-sized models in a

Lady Anne Barnard (1750–1825)

A gracious Cape Georgian homestead in Newlands, now the Vineyard Hotel, was once the country home of political hostess Lady Anne Barnard, who lived here from 1797 to 1802 with her husband Andrew, the colonial secretary. A gifted writer, she is remembered for her witty accounts of life in the new colony. She was also a talented artist: dainty sketches often accompanied her letters and the entries in her journal.

Lady Anne Barnard

Mostert's Mill, a prominent landmark near the University of Cape Town

re-created operating theatre. Tribute is paid to both the heart donor, Denise Darvall, who had lost her life in a car accident, and the recipient, Louis Washkansky.

🏛 **Irma Stern Museum**
Cecil Rd, Rosebank. **Tel** (021) 685-5686. **Open** 10am–5pm Tue–Fri, 10am–2pm Sat. **Closed** public hols.
📷 🌐 **irmastern.co.za**

🏛 **Heart of Cape Town Museum**
Groote Schuur Hospital, Main Rd, Observatory. **Tel** (021) 404-1967. 📷 9am, 11am, 1pm & 3pm daily; book in advance. **Closed** Good Fri, 25 Dec. 📷
🌐 **heartofcapetown.co.za**

🔟 Rhodes Memorial

Road map B5. Groote Schuur Estate. Exit off M3. 🛈 (021) 687-0000.
Open May–Sep: 8am–6pm daily; Oct–Apr: 7:30am–7pm daily. Restaurant: 9am–5pm daily.
🌐 **rhodesmemorial.co.za**

Directly opposite Groote Schuur homestead – the state president's official Cape Town residence – the Rhodes Memorial overlooks the busy M3, and affords sweeping views of the southern suburbs.

The white granite, Doric-style temple on the slopes of Devil's Peak was designed by Sir Herbert Baker as a tribute to Cecil John Rhodes, and was unveiled in 1912. It contains a bust of Rhodes by J M Swan, who also sculpted the eight bronze lions which guard the stairs. Beneath the bust is an inscription from "The Burial", written by one of Rhodes'

good friends, Rudyard Kipling. The focus of the memorial, however, is the bronze equestrian statue, titled "Physical Energy", which was executed by George Frederic Watts.

The sweeping views from the monument across the southern suburbs and out to the distant Hottentots Holland mountains are superb. Mixed oak and pine woodlands cover the mountain slopes around the memorial, and there are hiking trails from the car park. The Rhodes Memorial Restaurant is a lovely spot for lunch or afternoon tea at outdoor tables.

🔟 South African Astronomical Observatory

Road map B5. Off Liesbeeck Pkway, Observatory Rd. **Tel** (021) 447-0025.
Open 8pm on 2nd and 4th Sat of every month. 📷 groups of 10 or more must book. 🌐 **saao.ac.za**

The site for the Royal Observatory was selected in 1821 by the first Astronomer Royal stationed at the Cape, Reverend Fearon Fellows. Today, as the national headquarters for astronomy in South Africa, it controls the Sutherland laboratory in the Great Karoo and is responsible for transmitting

the electronic impulse that triggers the daily Noon Day Gun on Signal Hill *(see p120)*, thus setting standard time for the entire country.

🔟 Ratanga Junction

Road map B5. Off N1, 10 km (6 miles) N of Cape Town. **Tel** (021) 550-8504.
Open phone for information. **Closed** 25 Dec. 📷 🚉 🌐 **ratanga.co.za**

Ratanga Junction theme park logo

Ratanga Junction is the country's first full-scale theme park. This imaginative venue is situated north of the city centre on the N1, at the Century City shopping, hotel and office complex.

Ratanga Junction provides entertainment for the entire family. Chief among its many attractions are the thrilling tube ride through Crocodile Gorge, the spine-chilling Cobra roller coaster and a breathtaking 18.5-m (60-ft) log-flume drop on Monkey Falls.

Also on offer is a nine-hole crazy-golf course and various shows, "jungle cruises" and fun rides specifically designed for younger children. There are also family-friendly games that allow players to test their strength or their aim in a fun way. The Food Court, situated in The Walled City on Ratanga Island, offers a variety of food outlets.

The Rhodes Memorial, designed by Sir Herbert Baker

⑮ Kirstenbosch National Botanical Garden

In July 1913, the South African government handed over the running of Kirstenbosch estate (which had been bequeathed to the state by Cecil John Rhodes in 1902) to a board of trustees. The board established a botanical garden that preserves and propagates rare indigenous plant species. Today, the world-renowned garden covers an area of 5.3 sq km (2 sq miles), of which 7 per cent is cultivated and 90 per cent is covered by natural *fynbos* and forest. Kirstenbosch is spectacular from August to October when the garden is ablaze with spring daisies and gazanias.

Birds
Proteas here attract the endemic Cape sugarbirds.

★ Colonel Bird's Bath
Tree ferns and Cape Holly trees surround this pool, named after Colonel Bird, deputy colonial secretary in the early 1800s.

KEY

① **Jan van Riebeeck's Wild Almond Hedge** – in the 1660s a hedge was planted to keep the Khoi out of the settlement and discourage illegal trading.

② **Harold Pearson**, first director of the garden, is buried above Colonel Bird's Bath.

③ **The Centenary Tree Canopy Walkway**, also known as "The Boomslang" (tree snake), is a curved steel and timber raised boardwalk through and over the trees of the Arboretum. It was added to the garden to celebrate its centenary in 2013.

Main entrance

★ Conservatory
This glasshouse, with a baobab at its centre, displays the flora from the country's arid areas: coastal *fynbos*, bulbs, ferns and alpines.

Braille Trail
A guide rope leads visually impaired visitors along this interesting 470-m (1,542-ft) long walk through a wooded area. Signs in large print and braille describe the plant species that grow along the trail.

0 metres   100
0 yards   100

Floral Splendour
After the winter rains, carpets of indigenous Namaqualand daisies and gazanias echo the flower display found along the West Coast *(see p220)*.

Two Shops
The shop located at the upper entrance to the garden sells indigenous plants and seeds, while the lower shop offers a variety of natural history books, gifts and novelty items.

Parking

★ Camphor Avenue
This avenue of camphor trees was
anted by Cecil John Rhodes in 1898
along his favourite ride – from his
home at Groote Schuur to
Constantia Nek.

SHOPPING IN CAPE TOWN

Cape Town is known as the international gateway to Africa, and the vast array of appealing shopping options supports its reputation. The bustling V&A Waterfront *(see pp140–45)*, in convenient proximity to the city centre, is just one of several large, sophisticated shopping complexes that offer everything under one roof – from fresh produce to high fashion and gourmet dining. Old and new contend with one another in the city centre – antique jewellery and modern art are both worth searching for. The lively Long and Kloof streets, pedestrianized St George's Mall and the informal Greenmarket Square houses shops with a strong local flavour. The streetside art displays, buskers and stalls offering African masks, beadwork and carvings add much to the vibrant atmosphere. Surrounding suburbs such as Hout Bay regularly host outdoor craft stalls and noisy fish markets.

Opening Hours

Most shops in the city centre and in the suburbs are open from 9am–5pm on weekdays, and from 9am–1pm on Saturdays. Major malls open at 9am and close between 7pm–9pm throughout the week and on most public holidays. Fridays are usually the busiest time of the week and many shops stay open until 9pm, although Muslim-owned businesses are closed between noon and 2pm. Supermarkets and many delis are open on Sundays.

A relaxing corner of the busy Cape Quarter shopping mall

Shopping Malls

Cape Town's malls offer one-stop dining, entertainment, banking and shopping, with convenient parking facilities.

Canal Walk, the largest mall, has more than 400 upmarket shops open until 9pm every day, and is a 20-minute drive from the city centre. With its children's entertainment options and

Greenmarket Square in central Cape Town, a good destination for souvenirs

massive food court, it is an excellent choice for families.

The 185 shops in elegant **Cavendish Square** stock a range of high fashion clothing, homeware and gourmet fare. The **V&A Waterfront**, a unique centre in the heart of the old harbour, is an attractive modern shopping venue offering outstanding jewellery, curios, make-up stores, restaurants and supermarkets.

Fashionable Capetonians prefer to browse at **Cape Quarter** in Green Point, which houses home decor, art, fashion, beauty, health and lifestyle-related shops in a unique Cape Malay-style building which has two outdoor piazzas with restaurants.

Markets

The cobblestoned **Greenmarket Square**, in the centre of Cape Town, is a vibrant crafts market held Monday to Saturday, weather permitting. Here one can buy African carvings, masks, drums, beadwork, jewellery, leatherwork, ceramics and handmade clothing.

The **Red Shed Craft Workshop** and **The Watershed** crafts market, both at the V&A Waterfront, are indoor venues open all week. Clothing, jewellery, mosaics and an array of textiles and artwork are available here.

On Saturday and Sunday mornings the **Milnerton Flea Market** is great for bargain hunters, who rummage through the junk in search of precious finds. Everything from arts and crafts to plants and car parts is up for sale.

For African baskets, ceramics and shell art, visit the weekend **Bay Harbour Market**, which has more than 100 trendy crafts and decor stalls and a vintage clothes bazaar in a former fish factory. The **Kirstenbosch**

Canal Walk mall, containing hundreds of shops

Craft and Food Market is held on Sundays (Sep–May) opposite the world-famous botanical gardens with Table Mountain as a backdrop. More than 200 craftspeople sell their products here, from unique woodcarvings to beautifully fashioned jewellery. Remember to take cash with you: many markets don't accept credit cards.

The entrance to African Image

African Crafts

African Image and the **Pan African Market** stock choice fabrics, ethnic furniture, beads, utensils and sculptures. **Africa Nova** specializes in locally-produced handmade art, beautiful textiles from all over Africa and a range of unusual ceramic designs. **Heartworks** offers colourful beads, bags and glass, as well as innovative wood, wire and ceramic items.

In Newlands, the **Montebello Design Centre** is home to several artisan studios producing jewellery, textiles and pottery. The items made on-site are sold in the shop. There is also a pleasant restaurant situated in the shade of several oak trees.

Another working artists' studio is **Streetwires**, which boasts more than 80 wire and bead artists under one roof, all creating enchanting items. The studio is open to visitors, and the artists chat to their clients while they work. **Monkeybiz**, with its distinctive yellow building painted with red monkeys, sells one-off beaded products made by township women in their homes rather than in factories. Profits from the beadwork support the Monkeybiz Wellness Clinic for HIV-affected women.

Township tour itineraries often include a visit to the Khayelitsha Craft Market *(see pp158–9)* and the Sivuyile Craft Centre in Gugulethu.

Books and Music

Found in all the larger shopping malls, the **Exclusive Books** chain stocks newspapers, maps, guides, novels, CDs and a wide range of magazines. Some branches also have an in-store coffee shop. Long Street is renowned for its bookshops. **Select Books** and **Clarke's Bookshop** both sell new, second-hand and collector's editions of southern African books. Clarke's also specializes in books on southern African art. **Wordsworth Books** offers a wide range of fiction, biographies, coffee table volumes and other books. It has a particularly strong selection of South African interest and cookery titles. The bookshop at the **Kirstenbosch National Botanical Garden** sells travel, plant and wildlife guides specific to South Africa, as well as a range of titles for children. Fans of comic books, graphic novels and action figures will adore **Reader's Den** in Claremont.

There are a number of music megastores offering a range of commercial and more alternative CDs. **Musica**, open until late, is the largest in Cape Town. At the small, centrally-located **African Music Store**, visitors are introduced to the exciting sounds of Africa.

Food and Wine

Giovanni's in Green Point is Cape Town's best and busiest deli for imported cheese, cold meats and olives, fresh bread and pastries, and it has a popular coffee bar. Head to **Melissa's The Food Shop** for an extensive range of attractive handmade products – the cafe offers a "farm table" at lunchtime.

Many supermarkets stock wine, but specialist shops can offer advice and freight facilities, and they are able to suggest Wine Route itineraries. **Vaughn Johnson's Wine & Cigar Shop** stocks a number of unusual Cape wines, such as Meerlust, Cordoba and Welgemeend. **Caroline's Fine Wine Cellar** stocks more than a thousand bottles, including classic wines from France, Italy, Spain and Australia, and holds regular wine-tasting evenings.

Vaughn Johnson's Wine & Cigar Shop

Entrance to Naartjie, a popular children's clothes shop

Homeware and Gifts

Imaginative homeware is readily available in Cape Town and shoppers will be spoiled for choice. In recent years, the city has witnessed a steady rise in lifestyle shops selling everything from kitsch china to stylish teapots.

Carrol Boyes, a perfect stop for gift shopping, sells designer cutlery, tableware and household items in silver, pewter, aluminium and steel. Situated in an elevated loft space on Cape Town's trendy Bree Street, **SAM** (South African Market) specializes in decor, homeware and jewellery made by a host of hip local designers. **Clementina Ceramics** stocks contemporary South African ceramics that are sure to cheer up any kitchen.

Two household names in South Africa are the chains **@ Home**, ideal for trendy homeware and creative pieces for the bathroom, bedroom and kitchen, and **Mr Price Home**, which is equally popular. Its wide range of fashionable household goods are sold at very reasonable prices.

Antiques and Jewellery

Quality antiques do not come cheap in Cape Town, but there is no shortage of wonderful items to buy.

In the city centre, both casual shoppers and serious collectors will enjoy browsing **Church Street Antique Market**, as well as the **Long Street Antique Arcade**, with its 12 antique shops. Both stock brassware, jewellery, old coins, china, vintage clothing and other interesting bric-a-brac. **Kay's Antiques** specializes in period jewellery from the Victorian to the Art Deco era.

Private Collections, in De Waterkant, has a fascinating stock of colonial Indian artifacts. Nearby, **Burr & Muir** offers Art Deco and late 19th- and early 20th-century ceramics and furniture of museum quality. Both are worth visiting just to browse through their interesting pieces.

The Shipwreck Shop in Hout Bay is a very unusual shop specializing in maritime memorabilia, nautical antiques and fascinating shipwreck finds. Cape Town is renowned for its gold and jewellery, and the V&A Waterfront is a particularly good place to browse – **Shimansky** and **Uwe Koetter** are popular choices.

Both **The Diamond Works** and **Prins & Prins**, among others, offer tourists the chance to witness the art of diamond cutting, from the design stage to the finished product. At the end of the tour visitors can view a special collection of diamonds, with no obligation to buy.

Clothes and Accessories

Cape Town has an eclectic collection of clothing shops. The **Young Designers Emporium (YDE)** showcases South Africa's younger design talent and offers the latest fashions at reasonable prices. **KLûK CGDT** is known for its exquisite couture and bridal wear by designer Malcolm Klûk apprenticed under John Galliano. Classic, well-cut garments can be found at **Hilton Weiner** and **The Space**, and quality menswear shops can also be found in the major shopping malls.

Families may want to take some time to explore the children's clothes shops, which are excellent in Cape Town. **Naartjie** is one of the most popular – its 100 per cent cotton items come in bright colours and cute designs.

Before venturing into the great outdoors, head to **Cape Union Mart** for good-quality hiking and climbing gear, as well as camping equipment.

Shoppers who wish to pick up quality clothes and accessories such as shoes, bags, hats and scarves at good prices should copy the locals and head to **Woolworths** – South Africa's favourite department store. It also sells food, wine and homeware, and branches can be found in almost all the shopping malls, although Cape Town's flagship store is at the V&A Waterfront.

The streamlined interior of Carrol Boyes at the V&A Waterfront

DIRECTORY

Shopping Malls

Canal Walk
Century Boulevard,
Century City, Milnerton.
Tel 021 529 9699.

Cape Quarter
27 Somerset Rd, De
Waterkant. **Map** 2 D5.
Tel 021 421 1111.

Cavendish Square
Dreyer St, Claremont.
Tel 021 657 5620.

V&A Waterfront
Map 2 D3.
Tel 021 408 7600.

Markets

Bay Harbour Market
31 Harbour Rd, Hout Bay.
Tel 083 275 5586.

Greenmarket Square
Between Shortmarket &
Longmarket sts.
Map 5 B1.

**Kirstenbosch Craft
and Food Market**
Cnr Kirstenbosch Dr and
Rhodes Ave, Newlands.
Tel 071 480 5836.

**Milnerton Flea
Market**
Marine Drive, Milnerton.
Tel 021 551 7879.

**Red Shed Craft
Workshop**
V&A Waterfront.
Map 2 D3.
Tel 021 408 7600.

The Watershed
V&A Waterfront.
Map 2 D3.
Tel 021 408 7600.

African Crafts

African Image
Cnr Church & Burg sts.
Map 5 B1.
Tel 021 423 8385.

Africa Nova
Cape Quarter, Green
Point. **Map** 2 D5.
Tel 021 425 5123.

Heartworks
Shop 51B, Gardens
Centre, Gardens.
Map 4 F3.
Tel 021 465 3289.

Monkeybiz
61 Wale St, Bo-Kaap.
Map 5 B1.
Tel 021 426 0145.

**Montebello Design
Centre**
Newlands Ave, Newlands.
Tel 021 685 6445.

Pan African Market
76 Long St. **Map** 5 A2.
Tel 021 426 4478.

Streetwires
77 Shortmarket St,
Bo-Kaap. **Map** 5 B1.
Tel 021 426 2475.

Books and Music

African Music Store
134 Long St. **Map** 5 B1.
Tel 021 426 0857.

Clarke's Bookshop
199 Long St. **Map** 5 B1.
Tel 021 423 5739.

Exclusive Books
Tel 011 798 0111.

**Kirstenbosch
National Botanical
Garden**
Rhodes Drive, Newlands.
Tel 021 799 8783.

Musica
Cavendish Sq,
Dreyer St, Claremont.
Tel 021 683 0665.

Reader's Den
Main Rd, Claremont.
Tel 021 671 9551.

Select Books
232 Long St. **Map** 5 B1.
Tel 021 424 6955.

Wordsworth Books
Gardens Centre, Gardens.
Map 5 B3.
Tel 021 461 8464.

Food and Wine

**Caroline's Fine Wine
Cellar**
62 Strand St.. **Map** 5 B1.
Tel 021 419 8984.

Giovanni's
103 Main Rd, Green Point.
Map 1 C4.
Tel 021 434 6893.

**Melissa's The Food
Shop**
94 Kloof St, Gardens.
Map 5 A2. **Tel** 021 424
5540.

**Vaughn Johnson's
Wine & Cigar Shop**
Pierhead, Dock Rd, V&A
Waterfront. **Map** 2 E3.
Tel 021 419 2121.

Homeware
and Gifts

@ Home
Breakwater Centre , Break-
water Boulevard, V&A
Waterfront. **Map** 1 B1.
Tel 021 418 4210.

Carrol Boyes
Victoria Wharf, V&A
Waterfront. **Map** 2 E3.
Tel 021 418 0595.

Clementina Ceramics
The Old Biscuit Mill, 375
Albert Rd, Woodstock.
Tel 021 447 1398.

Mr Price Home
Dreyer St, Claremont.
Tel 021 671 0810.

SAM
67–69 Shortmarket St.
Tel 083 690 6476.

Antiques and
Jewellery

Burr & Muir
Cnr Strand and Hudson
sts, De Waterkant. **Map** 2
D5. **Tel** 021 418 1269.

**Church Street
Antique Market**
Church St Mall. **Map** 5 B1.
Tel 021 438 8566.

The Diamond Works
7 Walter Sisulu Ave.
Map 2 E5. **Tel** 021 425
1970.

Kay's Antiques
Cavendish Sq, Dreyer St,
Claremont.
Tel 021 671 8998.

**Long Street Antique
Arcade**
127 Long St. **Map** 5 A2.
Tel 021 423 2504.

Prins & Prins
66 Loop St.
Map 5 B1.
Tel 021 422 1091.

Private Collections
22 Hudson St,
De Waterkant.
Map 2 D5.
Tel 021 421 0298.

Shimansky
Clock Tower Centre,
V&A Waterfront.
Map 2 E3.
Tel 021 421 2788.

The Shipwreck Shop
Mariner's Wharf,
Hout Bay Harbour.
Tel 021 790 1100.

Uwe Koetter
Alfred Mall, V&A
Waterfront.
Map 2 E4.
Tel 021 421 1039.

Clothes and
Accessories

Cape Union Mart
Quay 4, V&A Waterfront.
Map 2 E3.
Tel 021 425 4559.

Hilton Weiner
Cavendish Sq,
Dreyer St, Claremont.
Tel 021 683 3069.

KLûK CGDT
43–45 Bree St.
Map 5 A1.
Tel 083 377 7780.

Naartjie
Victoria Wharf,
V&A Waterfront.
Map 1 B1.
Tel 021 421 5819.

The Space
Cavendish Sq,
Dreyer St, Claremont.
Tel 021 674 6643.

Woolworths
Victoria Wharf, V&A
Waterfront.
Map 1 B1.
Tel 021 415 3411.

**Young Designers
Emporium (YDE)**
Cavendish Sq,
Dreyer St, Claremont.
Tel 021 683 6177.

ENTERTAINMENT IN CAPE TOWN

Much of Cape Town's leisure activity centres on the beaches and mountains, but the city is developing a fine reputation for its nightlife and vibrant cultural events. Some of the best entertainment is found alfresco, with buskers and local beat dancers fighting it out on the streets of the city. The grand flagship venue is the Artscape Theatre Centre, which attracts audiences to local and international music performances, dance, cabaret, theatre and comedy. Cape Town has its own original form of jazz, which can be heard in many of the restaurants, bars and clubs in and around Long Street. Capetonians are known to be laid-back, and enjoy dinner followed by a visit to the cinema, but the city also caters for serious clubbers. Much of the action is concentrated on the trendy clubs and bars in the city centre and at the V&A Waterfront.

Information

For details of entertainment in the city, check the daily and weekend newspapers. They review and list events in the cinema, arts and theatre. Good choices include the *Cape Times*, *Cape Argus* on Tuesdays, *Mail & Guardian* on Fridays and the *Weekend Argus*. The Cape radio station Good Hope FM mentions events from time to time, and the websites **Cape Town Magazine** and **What's On in Cape Town** are great resources for listings, reviews and ideas of what to do and see.

For details of nightlife events, flyers are the best bet and are found all over the city. Try www.capetownlive.com for more information. Many venues have leaflets about forthcoming attractions, and the major venues have information telephone lines and websites. For information on all live performances, check Computicket *(see Booking Tickets, right)*, and for any other specific questions, **Cape Town Tourism** is also very helpful.

Computicket booking office, V&A Waterfront

Booking Tickets

Computicket is South Africa's nationwide booking agency for all concerts, theatre performances and live performances, plus events and sports fixtures. It has a comprehensive website for online booking, or you can phone its call centre. In addition, tickets can be purchased via mobile phone using the Computicket mobisite, or by visiting one of the branches in the major shopping malls, or any branch of Shoprite and Checkers supermarkets. Tickets can be collected from these outlets or can be printed at home. A credit or debit card is required, which also means you can book tickets prior to your arrival in South Africa, but cash is also accepted at the outlets. Alternatively, tickets can be purchased directly at the venues.

Disabled Visitors

In general, most public buildings, museums and top visitor attractions cater for wheelchair-users. Many of the theatres, including Artscape and the Baxter, as well as some Ster-Kinekor and Nu Metro cinemas, have spaces at the back or sides of the auditoriums that can comfortably accommodate wheelchairs. Most also have dedicated parking, adapted toilets and a lift from the entrance. For rock and pop concerts, Cape Town Stadium (and South Africa's other large stadiums built for the 2010 FIFA World Cup) has special areas for wheelchair-users and their

The Baxter Theatre in Rondebosch

companions. At any venue it is important to tell Computicket at the time of booking if a space is required. For smaller venues, phone direct and the staff will be able to advise.

Free Entertainment

The **St George's Cathedral Choir** gives performances free of charge – contact them for details or check with Computicket. From time to time, there are free lunchtime concerts at the Baxter Theatre *(see p172)*, showcasing the work of students from Cape Town University's **South African College of Music**.

During the summer months, the **V&A Waterfront Amphitheatre** is an excellent spot for free live entertainment, from concerts and recitals to puppet shows and important sports matches on the big screen. Performances usually start from 4pm and a calendar can be found on the website. Also around the V&A Waterfront, visitors are entertained by a number of professional busker groups including marimba bands and acrobats.

Open-Air Entertainment

From December to March, Kirstenbosch National Botanical Garden *(see pp164–5)* hosts the Summer Sunset Concert series where a wide variety of music is presented, from pop and rock to the Cape Town Philharmonic and Carols by Candlelight. This is

Summer concert, Kirstenbosch National Botanical Garden

a great event for families, and spectators will enjoy the fresh air and attractive surroundings. Warm clothing is an essential precaution as the weather can change suddenly.

In January and February, performances under the stars are held at **Maynardville Open-Air Theatre** in the park of the same name in the Southern Suburbs. Artscape holds its annual Shakespeare-in-the-Park here, and there are some wonderful ballet performances by the Cape Town City Ballet.

Concerts in the Park is a popular free summer programme by local bands. They are held in De Waal Park in Oranjezicht on Sunday afternoons from November to March.

All these open-air events are very special and many theatre- and concert-goers take along a

pre-performance picnic and perhaps a bottle of wine to enjoy on the lawns.

Cinema

Mainstream Hollywood movies are shown at Cape Town's multi-screen **Ster-Kinekor** and **Nu Metro** cinema complexes in the larger shopping malls. There are screenings throughout the day, and a food court for popcorn and soft drinks. More intimate, though more expensive, **Cine Prestige** at Cavendish Square, also operated by Ster-Kinekor, has reclining seats, side tables with refrigerated cup holders and waiter service for refreshments. Nu Metro offers **SCENE**, a similar luxury cinema at the V&A Waterfront.

Art-house cinemas in Cape Town specialize in thought-provoking independent films along with international art releases. **Cinema Nouveau** at the V&A Waterfront and Cavendish Square offer refreshing alternatives to the usual Hollywood fare. The charming **Labia Theatre**, originally an Italian embassy ballroom, has operated as an art-house cinema since the 1970s and caters for the more discerning viewer.

For an exclusive experience, consider dinner followed by a private movie screening while enjoying dessert at the 16-seater cinema at **The Twelve Apostles Hotel** in Camps Bay.

Open-air concert at the Amphitheatre, the V&A Waterfront

Cape Town Philharmonic Orchestra and choir at the City Hall

Classical Music and Opera

Cape Town City Hall offers classical music and opera performances in majestic surroundings. The **Artscape Theatre Centre** is the home of the **Cape Town Philharmonic Orchestra**, which usually gives performances on Thursday evenings. Occasionally, rather different concert venues are chosen, such as the Two Oceans Aquarium or the South African Museum. The Artscape stages opera and musicals, as well as popular lunchtime and Sunday afternoon concerts. There are 1,500 seats in the Opera House and the view is exceptional from every angle.

The Baxter Theatre Centre is where the South African College of Music performs its repertoire of chamber music, string ensembles, organ recitals and orchestral productions. It is also the venue for recitals by visiting soloists and chamber ensembles, and it hosts occasional lunchtime concerts. **Cape Town Opera**, with its impressive soloists and chorus, creates an inspiring listening experience. They perform at the Artscape and Baxter and give additional performances at the V&A Waterfront in February.

Theatre and Dance

The **Artscape Theatre Centre** hosts world-class drama, ballet and satire, as well as experimental theatre and community and children's productions. It is one of the few venues in southern Africa with the facilities to stage internationally-known musicals

such as *War Horse, Cats* and *The Sound of Music,* as well as big touring shows. A calendar of events is available from the box office.

Another theatre and dance venue is the **Baxter Theatre Centre** in Rondebosch. The Main Theatre shows mainstream productions, whereas the intimate Studio Theatre hosts more challenging works. The **Theatre on the Bay** in Camps Bay offers a good mix of popular musicals, revues, cabaret and light comedy. The **Fugard Theatre,** named after one of South Africa's best-known playwrights, is located in a historical District Six warehouse. It offers a broad spectrum of performances from serious plays to comical satire. In the Southern Suburbs, the old Kalk Bay Dutch Reformed Church has been converted into the **Kalk Bay Theatre** and restaurant. With only 77 seats, it hosts intimate performances of music, drama and comedy.

In addition to the impressive **Cape Town City Ballet**, Cape Town has a great variety of jazz, contemporary dance and hip

hop companies performing styles such as African dancing, gumboots and Pantsula.

Comedy

At **Evita se Perron** in the town of Darling *(see p215),* a short drive from Cape Town, the cutting wit of Pieter-Dirk Uys launches amusing attacks on current political issues. Set in a restored pump house at the V&A Waterfront, the **Cape Town Comedy Club** is the brainchild of South African comedian Kurt Schoonraad. Entertainment includes established comedians, and open-mike sessions and patrons can dine here, too.

Dinner show at the Crypt Jazz Restaurant

Jazz, African and Rock Music

Cape Town's unique, indigenous style of jazz is heavily influenced by traditional African sounds. A fashionable spot is the **Winchester Mansions Hotel**, which has Sunday brunch with live jazz. **The Crypt Jazz Restaurant** is in the historic stone crypt below St George's Cathedral (hence the name), and the circular stage plays host to performances by local and

Cape Town City Ballet production of *Giselle*

Virtuoso sax playing at the Cape Town jazz festival

international musicians. The annual Cape Town International Jazz Festival at Cape Town International Convention Centre (CTICC) at the end of March is the greatest jazz event on the continent. It showcases dozens of local and international greats, and attracts an audience of more than 35,000 over a long, performance-packed weekend.

Mama Africa is popular with visitors, who come for its traditional percussion groups, hearty African menu, jungle-inspired decor and relaxed, fun atmosphere.

International live acts often perform at the **Cape Town Stadium**, while local rock bands favour the **Mercury Live and Lounge**, which is the leading live rock venue.

Other popular live music venues include **Dizzy's Pub, Cigar Bar and Lounge**, in Camps Bay, which features local cover bands and karaoke, and **The Piano Bar** in De Waterkant, a moody musical joint that has live music most nights, ranging from African-infused jazz to classical piano recitals on its own baby grand.

Children's Entertainment

There is no need to worry that children will be bored in Cape Town. In addition to the endless outdoor activities that the city has to offer, there are plenty of family-friendly attractions, too. For many children, the thrilling amusement park Ratanga Junction (see p163) is top of the list, but the Two Oceans Aquarium (see pp142–3) is also a big hit. **The Ice Station** skating rink at the Grandwest Casino keeps childrens occupied while the adults gamble.

In Observatory, the **Cape Town Science Centre** is a great complex with about 300 interactive displays. Another educational option is the **Planetarium**, where shows are held seven days a week.

The V&A Waterfront often stages concerts and events during the holidays and the Zip Zap Circus at Easter is very popular.

Scratch Patch at the V&A Waterfront and **Mineral World** in Simon's Town offer a fantastic activity: it involves digging for semi-precious gems – and children get to keep what they find.

Clubs, Bars and Cafés

It is not always easy to distinguish between the clubs and bars of Cape Town, as drinking and dancing usually take place in the same venue. Trendy bars along the Camps Bay strip offer cocktails and sundowners – try **Café Caprice** if you're up for a showy summer scene and people-watching, or the **Grand Café**, a stylish pavement café. Long Street in the city centre provides an eclectic mix of places. Try **Fiction**, a DJ bar and lounge with electro, drum and bass and indie music, or the **Fireman's Arms** – a fun 1906 vintage-style bar that is also a popular place for watching sports on TV.

For sophisticated cocktails, champagne, caviar and oysters in an upmarket ambience, head straight to **Planet Champagne & Cocktail Bar** at Mount Nelson Hotel, or **Asoka** in arty Kloof Street.

There are dozens of clubs in Cape Town, varying from standard disco-playing dance venues to profoundly alternative clubs, and the scene continues to grow. With a cigar bar, whisky lounge and regular events and DJs, one of the most fashionable is **Chrome**, located off trendy Long Street.

The gay and lesbian scene in Cape Town is big and there is a wealth of clubs to choose from on the outskirts of the city centre, on the "Green Mile" strip in Green Point. A fun place to start an evening is **Beefcakes**, a gay-oriented restaurant with an amusing 1950s diner theme that is famous for its cheekily named burgers, late cocktail bar and regular drag shows.

Long Street has some of the best bars and clubs in Cape Town

DIRECTORY

Information

Cape Town Magazine
W capetownmagazine.com

Cape Town Tourism
W capetown.travel

What's On in Cape Town
W whatsonincapetown.com

Booking Tickets

Computicket
Tel 0861 915 8000.
W online.computicket.com

Free Entertainment

St George's Cathedral Choir
St George's Cathedral, 5 Wale St. Map 5 A2.
Tel 021 424 7360.
W sgcathedral.co.za

South African College of Music
Tel 021 650 2626.
W sacm.uct.ac.za

V&A Waterfront Amphitheatre
Victoria Wharf. Map 2 D3.
Tel 021 408 7600.
W waterfront.co.za

Open-Air Entertainment

Concerts in the Park
De Waal Park, Oranjezicht.
Map 5 A4. Tel 021 423 4526. W concertsinthepark.co.za

Maynardville Open-Air Theatre
Maynardville Park, cnr of Wolfe Rd & Piers St, Wynberg.
Tel 021 761-0593.
W maynardville.co.za

Cinema

Cine Prestige
Cavendish Square, Dreyer St, Claremont.
Tel 082 16789.

Cinema Nouveau
V&A Waterfront.
Map 2 E3. Tel 082 16789.

Labia Theatre
68 Orange St, Gardens.
Map 5 A2. Tel 021 424 5927. W labia.co.za

Nu Metro
W numetro.co.za

SCENE
V&A Waterfront. Map 2 E3.
Tel 021 419 9700.

Ster-Kinekor
W sterkinekor.com

The Twelve Apostles Hotel
Victoria Rd, Camps Bay.
Map 3 B5. Tel 021 437 9000.
W 12apostleshotel.com

Classical Music and Opera

Artscape Theatre Centre
DF Malan St, Foreshore.
Map 5 C1.
Tel 021 410 9800.
W artscape.co.za

Cape Town Opera
Tel 021 410 9807.
W capetownopera.co.za

Cape Town Philharmonic Orchestra
Tel 021 410 9809.
W cpo.org.za

Theatre & Dance

Artscape Theatre Centre
See Classical Music & Opera.

Baxter Theatre Centre
Main Rd, Rondebosch.
Tel 021 685 7880.
W baxter.co.za

Cape Town City Ballet
Tel 021 650 2400.
W capetowncityballet.org.za

Fugard Theatre
Cnr Caledon and Lower Buitenkant Sts. Map 5 C2.
Tel 021 461 4554.
W thefugard.com

Kalk Bay Theatre
52 Main Rd, Kalk Bay.
Tel 021 788 7257.
W kalkbaytheatre.co.za

Theatre on the Bay
Link St, Camps Bay. Tel 021 438 3301. W theatre-onthebay.co.za

Comedy

Cape Town Comedy Club
4 The Pumphouse, Dock Rd, V&A Waterfront. Map 1 B2. Tel 021 418 8880.
W capetowncomedy.com

Evita se Perron
Darling Station, Darling.
Tel 022 492 3930.
W evita.co.za

Jazz, African and Rock Music

Cape Town Stadium
Fritz Sonnenberg Rd, Green Point. Map 1 C3.
Tel 021 417 0120.

The Crypt Jazz Restaurant
1 Wale St. Map 5 B2.
Tel 079 683 4658.
W thecryptjazz.com

Dizzy's Pub, Cigar Bar and Lounge
41 The Drive, Camps Bay.
Tel 021 438 2686.
W dizzys.co.za

Mama Africa Restaurant & Bar
178 Long St. Map 5 B2.
Tel 021 426 1017.
W mamaafricarestaurant.co.za

Mercury Live and Lounge
De Villiers St, Zonnebloem. Map 5 C3.
Tel 021 465 2106.

The Piano Bar
47 Napier St, De Waterkant. Map 2 D5.
Tel 021 418 1096.
W thepianobar.co.za

Winchester Mansions Hotel
221 Beach Rd. Map 1 B3.
Tel 021 434 2351.
W winchester.co.za

Children's Entertainment

Cape Town Science Centre
370b Main Road, Observatory. Tel 021 300

3200. W ctsc.org.za

The Ice Station
Grandwest Casino, 1 Vanguard Dr, Goodwood
Tel 021 535 2260.
W icerink.co.za

Mineral World
Dido Valley Rd, Simon's Town. Tel 021 786 2020.
W scratchpatch.co.za

Planetarium
25 Queen Victoria St.
Map 5 B2. Tel 021 481 3900. W iziko.org.za

Scratch Patch
1 Dock Rd, V&A Waterfront.
Tel 021 419 9429.
W scratchpatch.co.za

Clubs, Bars and Cafés

Asoka
68 Kloof St. Map 4 F3.
Tel 021 422 0909.
W asokabar.co.za

Beefcakes
34 Somerset Road. Map 2 D5. Tel 021 425 9019.
W beefcakes.co.za

Café Caprice
37 Victoria Rd, Camps Bay.
Map 3 B5.
Tel 021 438-8315.
W cafecaprice.co.za

Café Manhattan
74 Waterkant St.
Map 2 D5.
Tel 021 421 6666.
W manhattan.co.za

Fiction
226 Long St. Map 5 B2.
Tel 021 422 0400.

Fireman's Arms
Mechau St. Map 5 A1.
Tel 021 419 1513.
W firemansarms.co.za

Grand Café
35 Victoria Rd, Camps Bay.
Map 3 B5.
Tel 021 419 1513.
W grandafrica.com

Planet Bar
78 Orange St.
Map 5 A2.
Tel 021 483 1948.
W mountnelson.co.za

CAPE TOWN STREET FINDER

The map references appearing with the sights, shops and entertainment venues that are mentioned in the Cape Town chapter refer to the maps in this section. The key map below shows the areas covered, including: the City Bowl, the City Centre, the trendy Gardens area, Green point, Mouille Point and Sea Point, and the V&A Waterfront. All the principal sights

mentioned in the text are marked, as well as useful facilities like tourist information offices, police stations, post offices and public parking areas, always at a premium in the inner city. A full list of symbols appears in the key. Map references for Cape Town's hotels *(see pp384–5)* and restaurants *(see pp398–401)* have been included in the Travellers' Needs section.

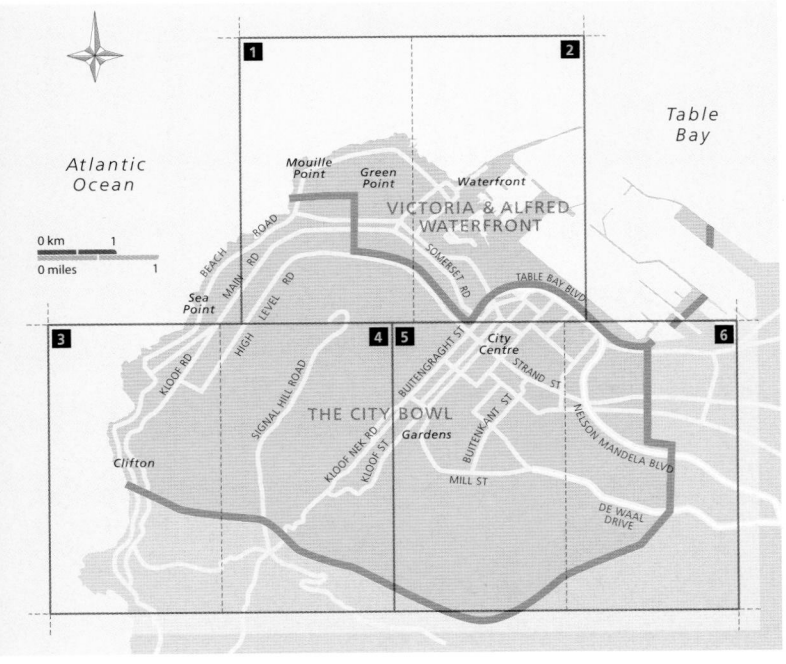

Key

	Major sight		Mosque
	Place of interest		Synagogue
	Other building	✹	Viewpoint
	Railway station	═	Railway line
	Bus terminus		Pedestrianized street
	Ferry boarding point		Motorway
i	Tourist information		
	Hospital with casualty unit		
	Police station		
	Bathing beach		
	Church		

Scale for Street Finder Pages

0 metres   400

0 yards   400

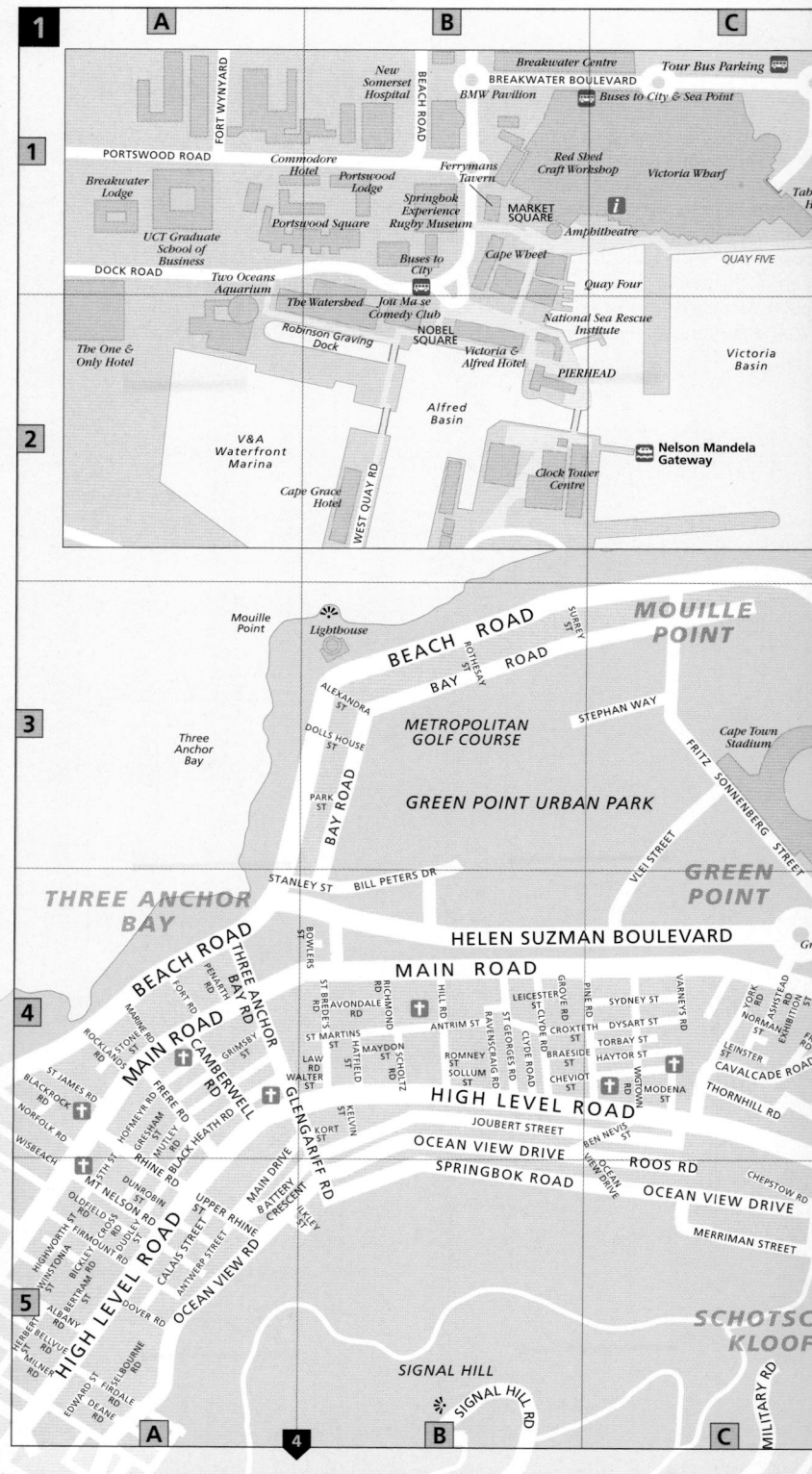

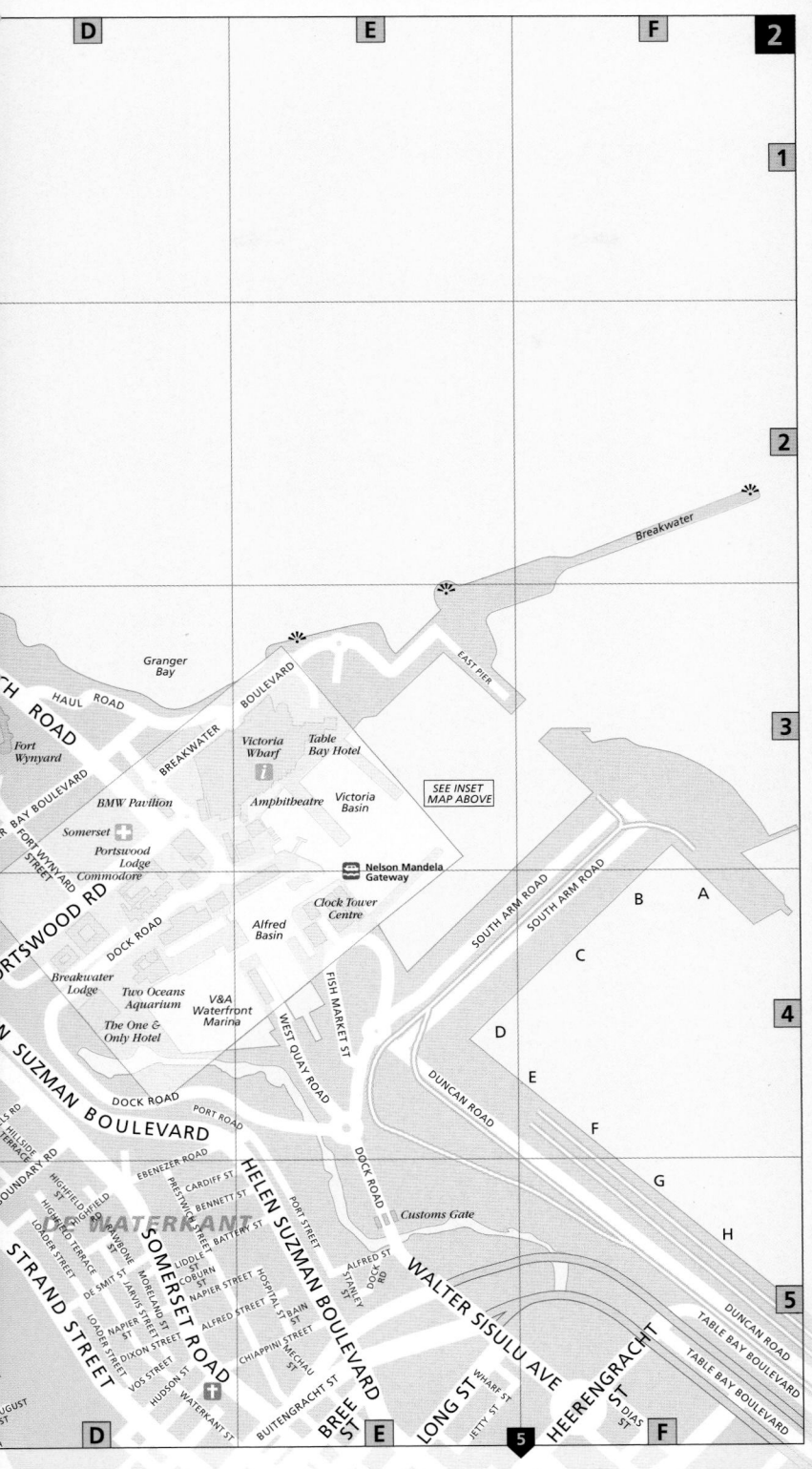

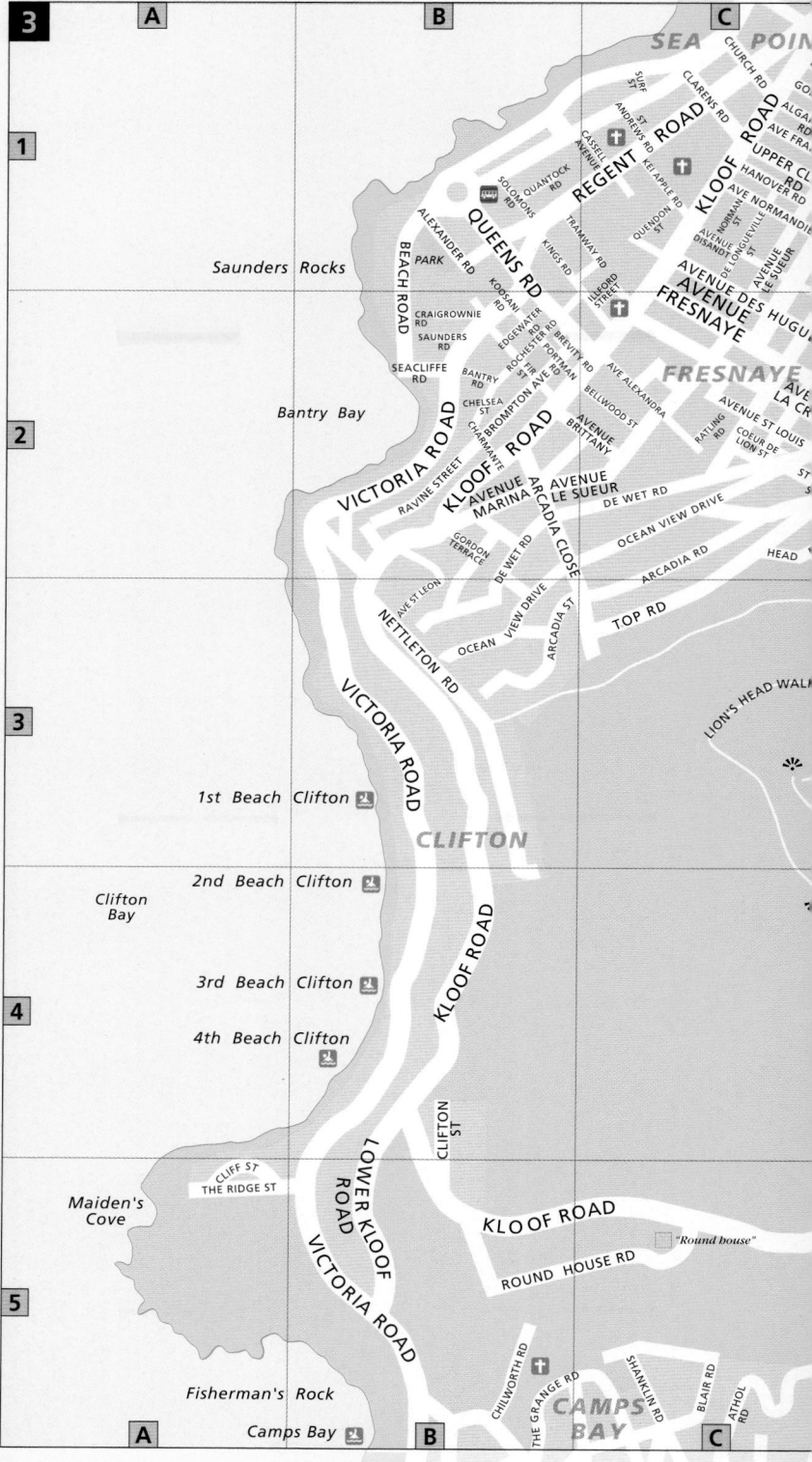

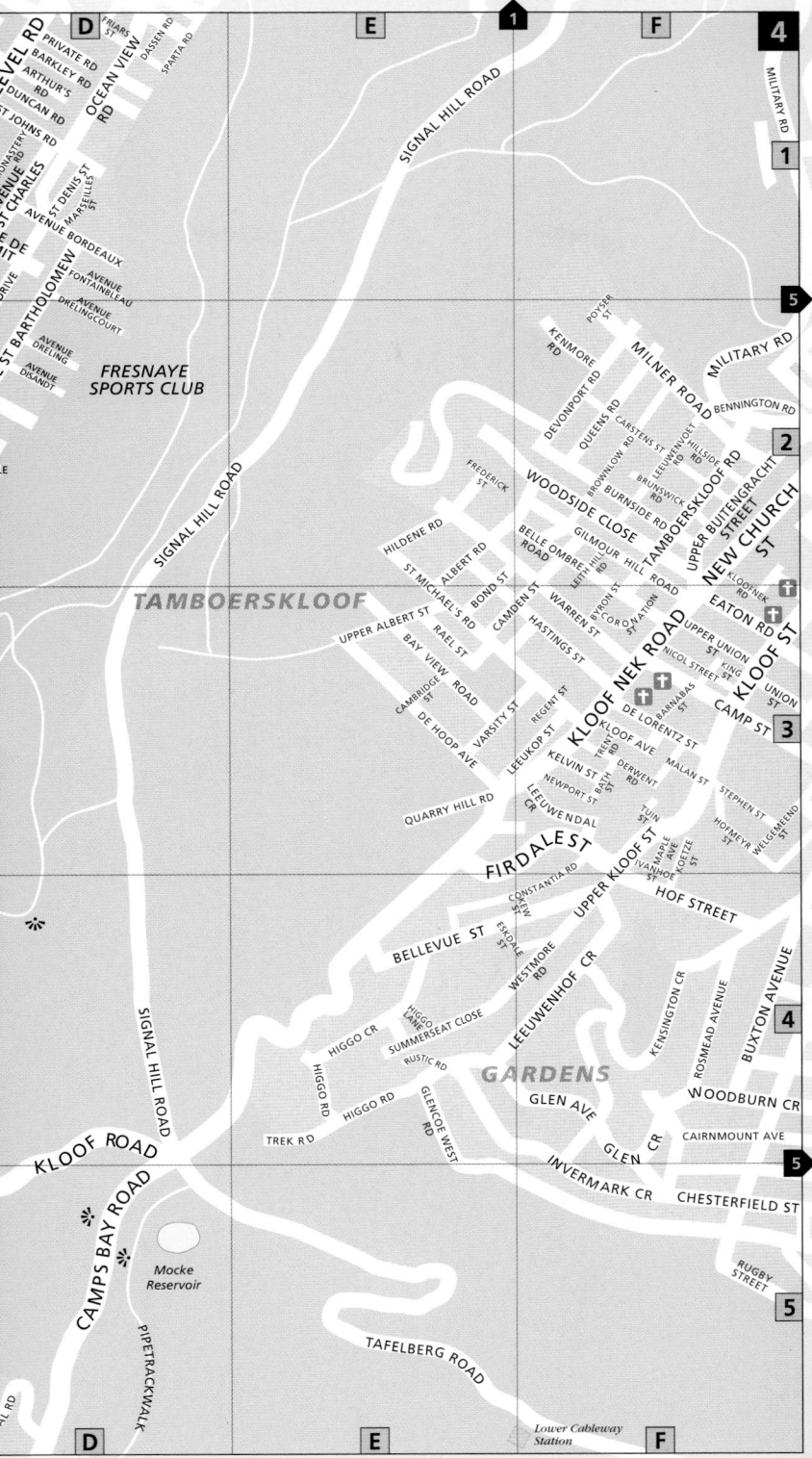

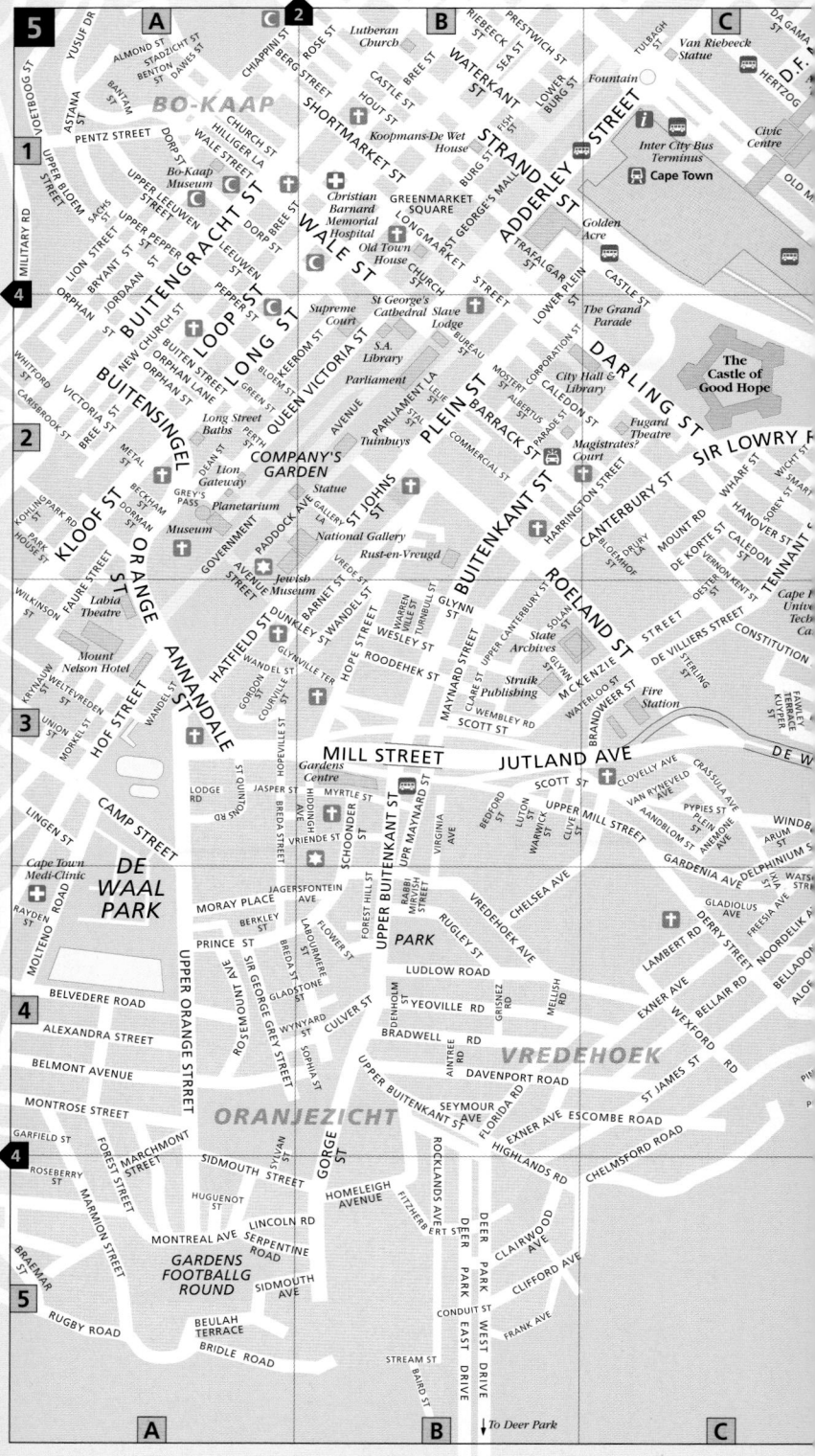

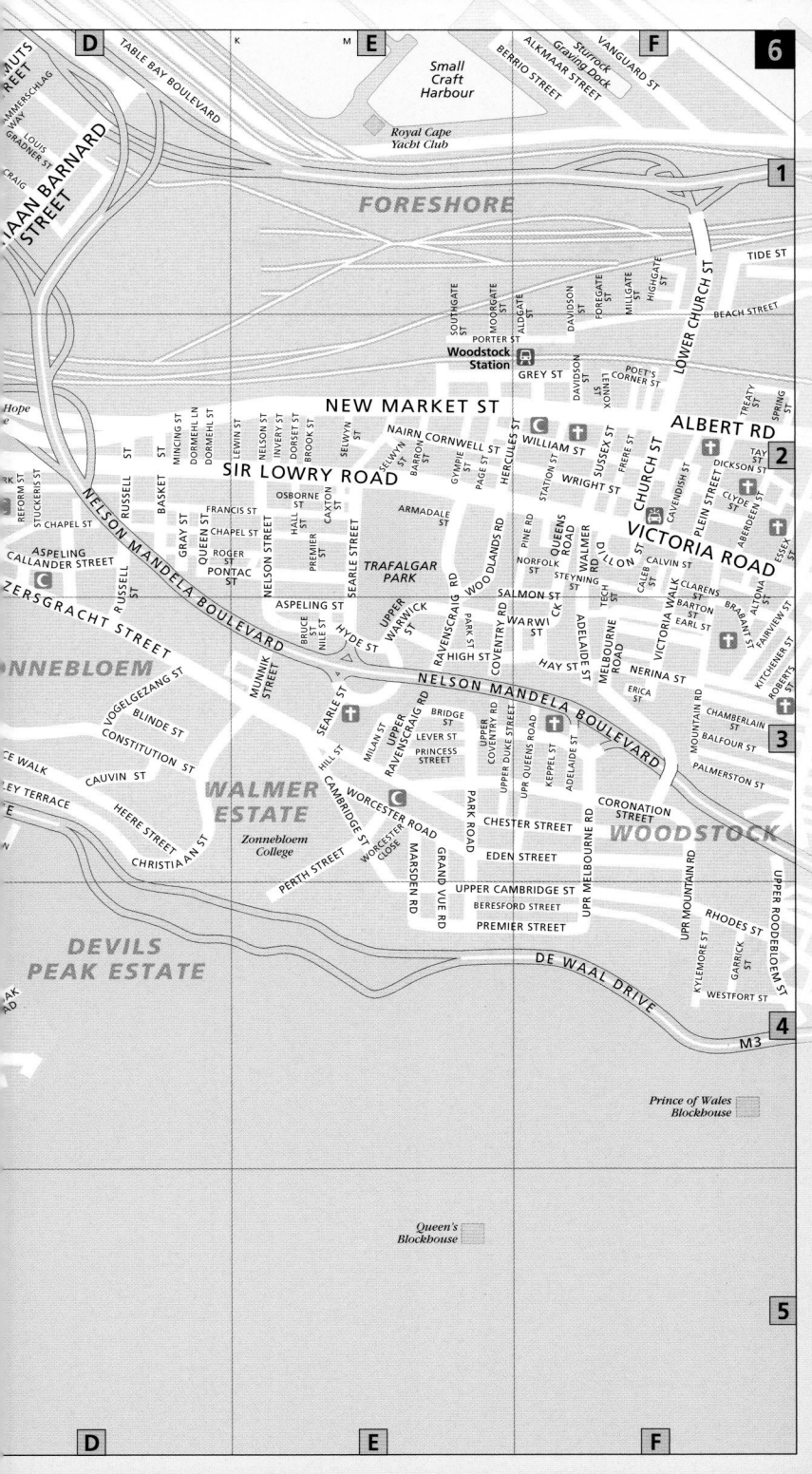

Cape Town Street Finder Index

THE WESTERN & SOUTHERN CAPE

Introducing the Western and Southern Cape

This region is dominated by a rugged mountain chain, comprising what is geologically known as the Cape folded mountains. The landscapes found in this territory are diverse. The arid and rather barren West Coast gives way to fertile winelands, cradled by jagged mountains. Beyond the terraced valleys, the dramatic passes that traverse the massive mountain ranges of the Southern Cape are a testament to the efforts of early road builders. The spectacular Cango Caves lie here and, on the other side of the mountains, the magnificent Garden Route. All along the rocky coastline, which is one of the most dangerous in the world and where swells can reach up to 30 m (98 ft) in height, fishermen reap the harvest of the sea.

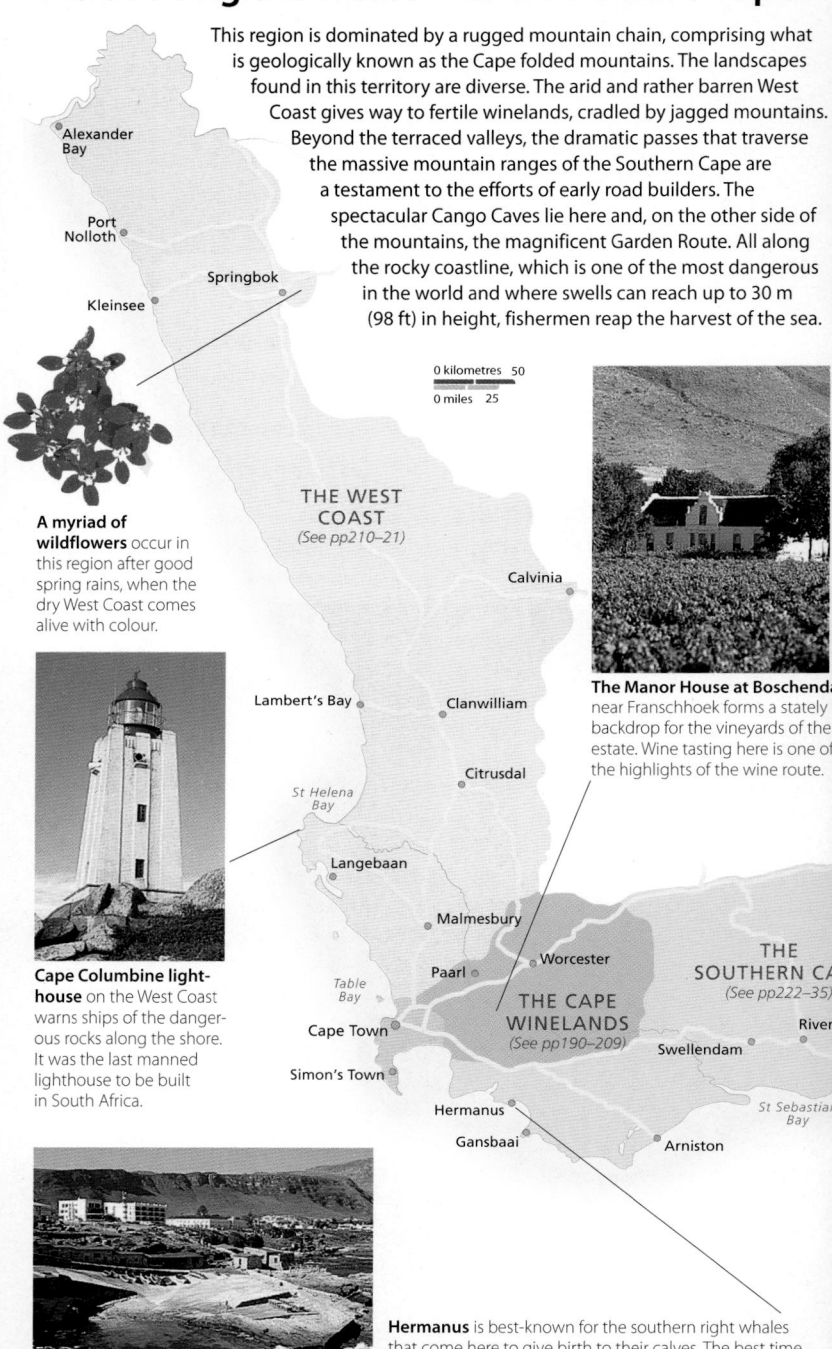

0 kilometres 50

0 miles 25

A myriad of wildflowers occur in this region after good spring rains, when the dry West Coast comes alive with colour.

The Manor House at Boschendal near Franschhoek forms a stately backdrop for the vineyards of the estate. Wine tasting here is one of the highlights of the wine route.

Cape Columbine light-house on the West Coast warns ships of the danger-ous rocks along the shore. It was the last manned lighthouse to be built in South Africa.

Hermanus is best-known for the southern right whales that come here to give birth to their calves. The best time of year for whale-watching is around September.

◀ Brilliant aloes in flower in the Tsitsikamma sector of the Garden Route National Park

THE WEST COAST
(See pp210–21)

Alexander Bay

Port Nolloth

Kleinsee

Springbok

Calvinia

Lambert's Bay

Clanwilliam

Citrusdal

St Helena Bay

Langebaan

Malmesbury

Worcester

Table Bay

Paarl

THE CAPE WINELANDS
(See pp190–209)

Cape Town

Simon's Town

THE SOUTHERN CA
(See pp222–35)

Rivers

Swellendam

St Sebastian Bay

Hermanus

Gansbaai

Arniston

Knysna Forest is known for its tall stinkwood trees and ancient yellowwoods, some of which are 650 years old. The dense canopy is alive with birds, such as the elusive, emerald-green lourie.

Locator Map

Addo Elephant National Park in the Eastern Cape is a major tourist attraction. It is home to more than 450 elephants.

Port Elizabeth's attractions include Bayworld, on the beachfront, where the highlight is the breeding colony of African penguins. In the city, a number of historic buildings date back to British colonial times.

Albert

THE GARDEN ROUTE TO GRAHAMSTOWN
(See pp236–57)

Grahamstown

hoorn

Uitenhage

Port Alfred

Alexandria

Tsitsikamma

Algoa Bay

Port Elizabeth

Plettenberg Bay

sel

The Cango Caves near Oudtshoorn contain many fascinating dripstone formations, caused by the constant percolation of water through limestone.

Pinotage Wine-Making

Pinotage is a unique South African cultivar developed in 1925 by Stellenbosch University professor Abraham Perold, from a cross of Pinot Noir and Cinsaut (then called Hermitage). The world's first commercially bottled Pinotage was released in 1961 under the Lanzerac label. The fruity, purple-red wine has since then achieved international acclaim. Pinotage comprises only a small percentage of South Africa's total grape plantings, with most of the crop grown around Stellenbosch. There are small Pinotage plantings outside South Africa, notably in California and New Zealand.

Old grape press in the Stellenryck Museum, Stellenbosch

Pinot Noir

Cinsaut

Pinotage

The Pinotage Cultivars

Pinot Noir, the noble cultivar from France's famous Burgundy district, contributed complexity, flavour and colour, while Cinsaut improved the yield. Today, Pinotage is an early-ripening cultivar that results in a light- to medium-bodied wine with unique flavour characteristics.

The large oak barrels used for maturation and storage of red wines are often decorated with hand-carved designs, like this beautiful example from the Delheim cellar in Stellenbosch.

Stellenbosch *(see pp196–200)* i surrounded by gentle hills that are ideal for growing Pinotage

Pinotage International Awards

1987:	Kanonkop (1985) – Beyers Truter voted Diners' Club "Winemaker of the Year"
1991:	Kanonkop (1989 Reserve) – Robert Mondavi Trophy (USA)
1996:	Kanonkop (1992) – Perold Trophy (International Wine and Spirit Competition)
1997:	L'Avenir (1994) – Perold Trophy
1997:	Jacobsdal (1994) – gold medal at Vin Expo Competition (France)

Two of South Africa's well-known Pinotage labels

Lanzerac, in Stellenbosch, combines a luxury country hotel *(see p386)* with a working winery. Pinotage is one of a range of wines made by the estate.

The Red Wine-Making Process

Wine is a natural product, and winemakers take great care during harvesting, production and maturation to ensure that their wines are of a high quality and meet the requirements of the consumer. Modern trends call for minimal interference in the vineyard and cellar in order to allow the wines to "speak" for themselves.

Grapes are cut from the vine with sharp shears to minimize damage to the mature berries

Harvesting is carefully timed to achieve the best flavours and characters from the grape. Red grapes are traditionally harvested later than white grapes, to allow the development of riper and more concentrated fruit.

Destalking removes the stems, whose high tannin content influences the wine's flavour. The grapes are then lightly crushed before being put into a vat for fermentation to begin.

Destalker and crusher

Fermentation tank

Fermentation occurs over three to five days. The juice is periodically pumped over the "cap" formed by the skins to extract the desired amount of colour and tannin. After fermentation, the juice is separated from the skins, and matured before blending and bottling.

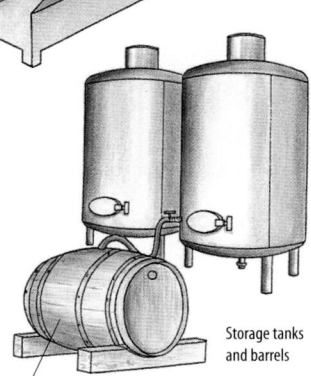

Storage tanks and barrels

Racking is the transfer of fermented wine from one tank or cask to another to remove the "lees", sediments that would cause the end product to appear cloudy. Filtration and fining, often using egg whites, removes impurities.

Maturation of pinotage takes 12–15 months. Traditionally, big vats were used, but the modern trend is to use small barrels made of French or American oak. The size of the barrel, type of wood and maturation time combine to shape the character of the wine. Once matured, the red wines are ready for bottling.

Wooden maturation barrels

The Pinotage Association, formed in November 1995, strives to maintain a consistently high standard for South African Pinotage. It holds an annual competition to judge the year's 10 best wines.

More than 130 Pinotages are made in South Africa

Whale-Watching

Some 37 whale and dolphin species and around 100 different types of shark occur in southern African waters. Only a small number come in close to the coast, however. Of the dolphins, bottlenose, common and Heaviside's are the most prolific, while common predatory sharks include the great white, tiger, ragged-tooth, oceanic white tip, bull (Zambezi) and mako. A large portion of the world's 4,000–6,000 southern right whales migrates north annually, with numbers increasing by seven per cent every year. They leave their subantarctic feeding grounds from June onwards to mate and calve in the warmer waters of the protected rocky bays and inlets that occur along the South African coastline.

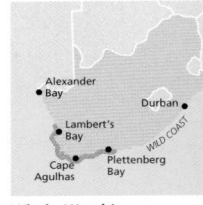

Whale-Watching

▨ Best vantage points

An albino calf was born in Hermanus in 1997.

Callosities are tough, wart-like growths on the whale's skin, not barnacles as is often thought. Scientists use these unique markings to distinguish between individuals.

The Southern Right Whale

Early whalers named this species "southern right" (Eubalaena australis) *because it occurred south of the Equator and was the perfect species to hunt. Its blubber was rich in oil, the baleen plates (filter-feeders made of keratin) supplied whalebone for corsets, shoe horns and brushes, and when dead the whale floated, unlike other types of whale which sank. A protected species, it can migrate up to 2,600 km (1,615 miles) annually.*

A characteristic V-shaped "blow" can be seen when the southern right exhales. The vapour is produced by condensation, as warm breath comes into contact with cooler air.

The "Whale Crier" patrols the streets of Hermanus, blowing a kelp horn to inform passers-by of the best sightings of the day.

Whale Antics

The reasons for some types of whale behaviour are, as yet, unclear. Breaching, for example, may either indicate aggression or joyfulness – it may also simply help the animal to get rid of lice.

Breaching: the whale lifts its upper body out of the water and falls back into the sea with a massive splash.

ern right whales their calves for at six months.

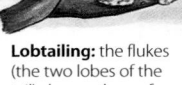

Blowhole   Callosities

Lobtailing: the flukes (the two lobes of the tail) slap on the surface to produce a loud clap.

Spyhopping: the whale lifts its head vertically from the sea to observe what is happening on the surface.

Shore-based whale-watching is superb at Hermanus.

Humpback whales are well-known for their spectacular breaching behaviour, lifting their bodies well above the water. A striking feature of this species is its extremely long flippers.

Whale Exploitation

In the years from 1785 to around 1805, some 12,000 southern right whales were killed off the southern African coast, but the northern right whale was the most ruthlessly hunted and is virtually extinct today. After the introduction of cannon-fired harpoons, humpbacks were the first large whale to be exploited. Some 25,000 were killed between 1908 and 1925. By 1935, when the League of Nations' Convention for the Regulation of Whaling came into effect, fewer than 200 southern right whales remained in southern African waters. Although numbers are increasing steadily, today's total population is only a fraction of what it once was.

Early whalers in False Bay

THE CAPE WINELANDS

The Cape's Winelands are a scenically enchanting region of lofty mountains and fertile valleys and slopes planted with orchards and vines. Nestled in the valleys are graceful Cape Dutch manor houses, of which stately Nederburg in Paarl (which hosts a famous wine auction), elegant Boschendal near Franschhoek and the charming Lanzerac Hotel in Stellenbosch are the best-known.

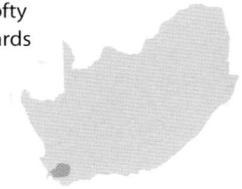

Stellenbosch was the first of the wineland towns to be established by Simon van der Stel, who had succeeded Jan van Riebeeck as governor in 1679. After van der Stel visited the area in November of that year and proclaimed it to be well watered and fertile, the first free burghers (early Dutch settlers who were granted tracts of land, together with implements and oxen to help them establish farms) were sent to this valley to start a new life. Settlement in the Franschhoek valley followed with the arrival of the French Huguenots (Protestant refugees from Europe), and later, Dutch as well as French pioneers who established themselves in the Paarl area. The temperate Mediterranean climate of the Cape has ensured the survival of the early wine-making traditions. The cool mountain and sea breezes create diverse conditions, and variable soil types – from the acidic and sandy alluvial soils of Stellenbosch to the lime-rich soils of Robertson – ensure a wide range of superb wines, both red and white, making South Africa the world's ninth-largest producer.

Most of the historic wine estates have been lovingly restored, and almost all offer tastings – their wines may be enjoyed on the sunny lawns of a beautiful Cape Dutch manor house or in the cool cellars among the vats. Many estates also offer gourmet restaurants, and others have accommodation that varies from luxury hotels in sublime Winelands settings to simple country cottages next to the vines.

Typical Cape Dutch gabling and thatched roof on a wine estate manor house

◀ Vines flourishing in the shelter of the mountains at Stellenbosch, the heart of the Cape Winelands

Exploring the Cape Winelands

After Table Mountain, the V&A Waterfront and Cape Point, the Winelands are the Western Cape's most popular attraction. The towns of Stellenbosch and Paarl are famous for their elegant, gabled architecture. Viewed from majestic mountain passes, the vineyards of Worcester and Robertson fit together like puzzle pieces, and Franschhoek has an exquisite valley setting, beautiful Cape Dutch architecture and some of the best restaurants in the country.

Delheim's vineyards, Stellenbosch

Eight Restaurant at Spier Wine Estate offers farm-style outdoor eating

Sights at a Glance

| 0 kilometres | | 25 |
| 0 miles | | 15 |

Getting Around

The Winelands are served by two major national routes, the N1 and N2. All of the connecting principal roads are clearly signposted. Franschhoek, Paarl and Worcester are accessed from the N1, Stellenbosch from either the N1 or N2 national route. Robertson is reached from Worcester via the R60. The scenic mountain passes are well worth an excursion and your own transport is essential if you wish to tour these areas. Alternatively, visitors can join one of the coach tours organized by major tour operators in Cape Town. Cape Town International is the closest airport.

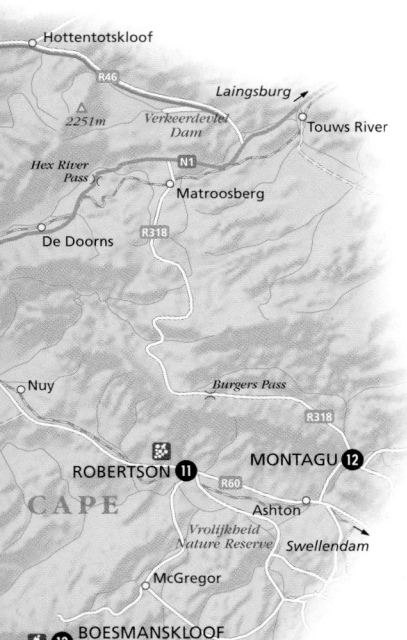

Hottentotskloof

R46

Laingsburg

2251m Verkeerdevlei Dam

Touws River

Hex River Pass

N1

Matroosberg

R318

De Doorns

Nuy

Burgers Pass

R318

ROBERTSON **11**

MONTAGU **12**

CAPE

R60

Ashton

Vrolijkheid Nature Reserve Swellendam

McGregor

13 BOESMANSKLOOF HIKING TRAIL

Greyton

Swellendam

Montagu is renowned for its hot springs

Rhebokskloof wine estate in Paarl has converted a cellar into a cosy wine tasting venue

Key

▬▬ Motorway

▬ Major road

═══ Minor road

══ Untarred road

▬ Scenic route

⌐ Main railway

─ Minor railway

╳ Pass

For additional keys to symbols *see back flap*

❶ Street-by-Street: Stellenbosch

A centre of viticulture and learning, the historic university town of Stellenbosch is shaded by avenues of ancient oaks. The streets are lined with homes in the Cape Dutch, Cape Georgian, Regency and Victorian styles. Through the centuries, Stellenbosch has been ravaged by three fires, and several homes have had to be restored. Walking is the best way to explore the town and to see the historic buildings and other attractions. A "Stellenbosch on Foot" brochure for a self-guided walk is available from the tourist information centre on Market Street.

The Burgher House was built in 1797. Its gable is an early example of the Neo-Classical style. The house is the headquarters of the Historical Homes of South Africa foundation.

ALEXAND

VOC Kruithuis
The powder magazine of the VOC (Dutch East India Company) was built in 1777 to defend the early settlement. It now houses a small military museum.

MARK STREET

Tourist information

Slave Houses, built around 1834 for the settlers' servants, are no longer thatched but still retain their original character.

HERTE STREET

OOM SAMIE SE WINKEL

★ Oom Samie se Winkel
In this "olde-worlde" village store (see p198) shoppers can step back in time and buy antiques, collectables, sticky toffee and biltong (see p394).

DORP STREET

KRIGE STREET

VISITORS' CHECKLIST

Practical Information
Road map B5. N2, 46 km (28 miles) E of Cape Town. 🅼 156,000. 🚹 36 Market St, 021 883 3584. 🎏 Wine Festival (Feb/Mar). 🆆 stellenbosch.travel

Transport
✈ Cape Town. 🚆 & 🚌 Adam Tas Rd.

Libertas
Parva and N2

KEY
— Suggested route

0 metres   250
0 yards   250

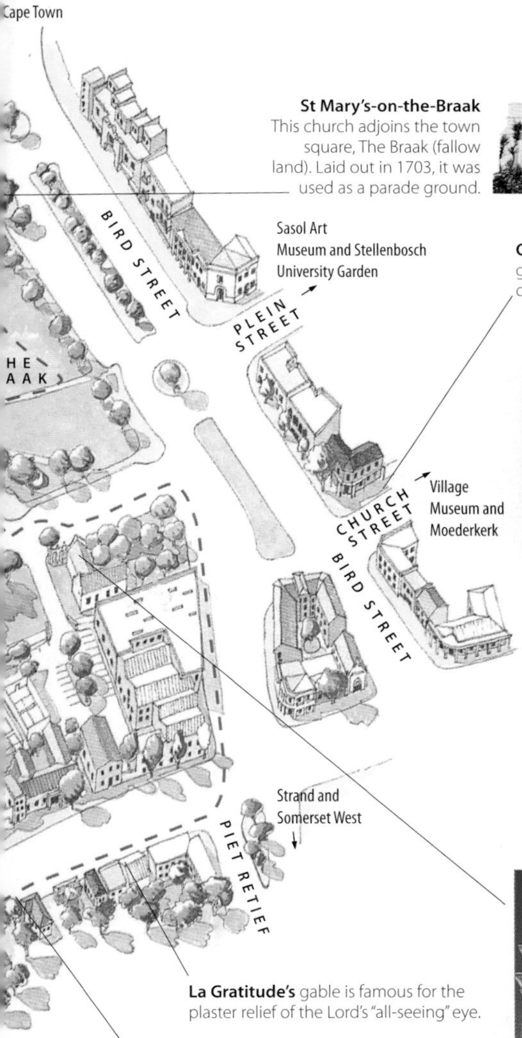

Cape Town

BIRD STREET

HE
AAK

PLEIN STREET

CHURCH STREET

BIRD STREET

PIET RETIEF

St Mary's-on-the-Braak
This church adjoins the town square, The Braak (fallow land). Laid out in 1703, it was used as a parade ground.

Sasol Art Museum and Stellenbosch University Garden

Village Museum and Moederkerk

Strand and Somerset West

La Gratitude's gable is famous for the plaster relief of the Lord's "all-seeing" eye.

Church Street is the site of various art galleries, as well as D'Ouwe Werf, one of South Africa's oldest inns

The Village Museum
The historic houses that comprise the Village Museum on Ryneveld Street *(see pp198–9)* are decorated in different period styles and are regarded as one of South Africa's best restoration projects.

The Rhenish Church
The church was built in 1823 as a school for slaves' children and "coloured" people.

★ **Dorp Street**
Some of the best-preserved historic façades in Stellenbosch are found on this oak-lined street.

Exploring Stellenbosch

The heart of the Winelands, this beautiful university town was founded in 1679 and is the cradle of Afrikaans culture. Its proud educational heritage began in 1863 with the establishment of the Dutch Reformed Theological Seminary. The Stellenbosch College, completed in 1886, was the forerunner of the university, which was established in 1918. Today, the university buildings are beautifully integrated with the surrounding historic monuments, reinforcing the town's dignified atmosphere of culture and learning.

🎴 Rhenish Complex
Herte St.

This lovely group of old buildings, which is flanked by two modern educational centres – the Rhenish Primary School and the Rhenish Girls' High School – is representative of most of the architectural styles that have appeared in Stellenbosch over the centuries.

Parts of the Cape Dutch-style Rhenish Parsonage are much older than the date of 1815 that is marked on the building's gable.

Leipoldt House, which was built around 1832, is an interesting combination of Cape Dutch and English Georgian architectural styles, while the Rhenish Church, on the south side of The Braak (the town's main square), was erected in 1823 by the Missionary Society of Stellenbosch as a training centre and school for slaves and "coloured" people.

Also overlooking the Braak is St Mary's-on-the-Braak (see p197), an Anglican church completed in 1852.

Old-world interior, Oom Samie se Winkel

🎴 Oom Samie se Winkel
84 Dorp St. **Tel** 021 887 0797.
Open 8:30am–5:30pm (to 6pm summer) Mon–Fri, 9am–5pm (to 5:30pm summer) Sat, Sun.
Closed 1 Jan, Good Fri, 25 Dec.

This charming, restored Victorian shop, whose name means "Uncle Samie's Store", has been operating as a general store since 1904. Its original proprietor, bachelor Samie Volsteedt lived in the house next door. The store, a Stellenbosch institution and a national monument,

has an eclectic stock ranging from bottled preserves, *biltong* and other South African delicacies, basketry, candles and curios to 19th-century butter churns, plates and kitchen utensils, clothing and straw hats. Visitors may also browse in Samie's Victorian Wine Shop for a special vintage.

🏛 Toy and Miniature Museum
Market St (next to tourist information office). **Tel** 079 981 7067.
Open 9am–4:30pm Mon–Fri, 9am–2pm Sat & Sun. **Closed** Sun (May–Aug). 🚆 🅿 🅆 **stelmus.co.za**

The Toy and Miniature Museum offers a world of enchantment for both young and old and is well worth a visit. Housed in the Rhenish Parsonage of 1815, the museum is the first of its kind in Africa. On display is an amazing collection of old toys, including antique dolls and Dinky Toy motor cars, as well as a model railway layout and miniature houses. The museum also boasts a number of finely detailed and exquisite 1:12 scale miniature rooms, each with delicate filigree work.

On sale in the small museum shop are furniture and accessories for dolls' houses, as well as mementos of the museum's unique treasures.

🏛 The Stellenbosch Village Museum
37 Ryneveld St. **Tel** 021 887 2937.
Open 9am–4:30pm Mon–Sat, 10am–4pm Sun. **Closed** Good Fri, 25 Dec.
🚆 🅗 🅿 🅆 **stelmus.co.za**

This complex features houses dating from Stellenbosch's early settlement years to the 1920s, although the Edwardian and other early 20th-century houses are not open to the public.

The museum features four buildings. Schreuder House was built in 1709 by Sebastian Schreuder. It is the oldest of the homes and shows the spartan, simple lifestyle of the early settlers. Bletterman House, erected in 1789, belonged to

The Rhenish Complex, a splendid example of Cape Dutch architecture

The 18th-century Schreuder House at the Village Museum, Stellenbosch

Hendrik Bletterman, a wealthy *landdrost* (magistrate). Parts of Grosvenor House, the most elegant of the four, date back to 1782, but later additions represent the Classicism of the 1800s. The house has furnishings from that era.

Constructed in 19th-century Victorian style, the interiors of Bergh House, occupied by Deputy Sheriff of Stellenbosch Olof Marthinus Bergh from 1837 to 1866, accurately reflect the comfortable lifestyle of a wealthy burgher of the 1850s.

🏛 Sasol Art Museum
52 Ryneveld St. **Tel** 021 808 3695.
Open 10am–4:30pm Mon, 9am–4pm Tue–Sat. **Closed** Good Fri, 25 Dec.
🅿 ♿ ⬡

Part of the Stellenbosch University, the interesting exhibition at the Sasol Art Museum focuses on anthropology, cultural history and art. Of particular interest to many visitors are the prehistoric artifacts, reproductions of San rock art and crafted utensils and ritual objects from South, West and Central Africa.

🌿 Stellenbosch University Botanical Garden
Neethling St. **Tel** 021 808 3054.
Open Open 8am–5pm daily. 🖥 📷
⬡ sun.ac.za

These gardens were established in the 1920s and have a fine collection of ferns, orchids and bonsai trees. The tropical and succulent plants are housed in four glasshouses. There is a pleasant tearoom under the shade of a red-flowering gum tree *(Corymbia ficifolia)*, and university students can be seen revising on the lawns.

Environs
The **Jonkershoek Nature Reserve** lies in a valley 10 km (6 miles) southeast of Stellenbosch that is flanked by *fynbos*, which in spring and summer includes tiny pink and white ericas, blushing bride *(Serruria florida)* and the king protea. The waterfalls and streams of the Eerste River provide abundant water for hikers, mountain bikers and horse riders. For the less energetic, there is a 12-km (7-mile) scenic drive into the mountains. Baboons and dassies may be sighted, and sometimes the elusive klipspringer. Of the many bird species in the reserve, the Cape sugarbird and malachite and orange-breasted sunbirds are most likely to be seen.

The rich history of **Van Ryn's Brandy Cellar** in the heart of the Vlottenburg Valley just southwest of Stellenbosch dates back to 1845 when the Dutch immigrant Jan van Ryn arrived at the Cape. Today, well-known local brands Van Ryn and Viceroy are made here, and guided tours introduce the visitor to the intricate art of brandy production. The traditional copper potstills and maturation cellar can be seen, and a tasting is included in which brandy is paired with handmade Belgian chocolate and Brazilian coffee. A highlight is to watch the skilled coopers make the barrels in the cooperage – the staves of wood are sealed with bulrushes collected from the nearby Eerste River.

Van Ryn's Brandy Cellar

🏞 Jonkershoek Nature Reserve
Jonkershoek Rd. **Tel** 021 866 1560.
Open 8am–6pm daily. **Closed** heavy rains (Jun–Aug). 🅿 🚶
⬡ capenature.co.za

🥃 Van Ryn's Brandy Cellar
R310 from Stellenbosch, exit 33.
Tel 021 881 3875. **Open** 8am–5pm Mon–Fri, 9am–2pm Sat, 11am–4pm Sun (Nov–Apr only but no cellar tours). **Closed** public hols.
🅿 ♿ ⬡ 📷 ⬡ vanryn.co.za

The sandstone mountains of the Jonkershoek Nature Reserve

❷ Stellenbosch Winelands

The Stellenbosch wine route was launched in April 1971 by the vintners of three prominent estates: Spier, Simonsig and Delheim. Today, the route comprises a great number of estates and cooperatives. Tasting, generally for a small fee, and cellar tours are offered throughout the week at most of the vineyards. A few of the estates can be visited by appointment only and many are closed on Sundays, so phoning ahead is advisable.

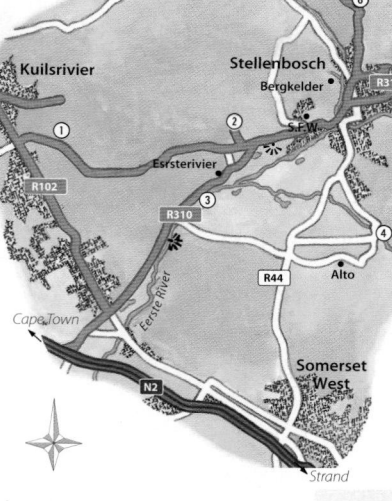

⑦ Delheim
Particularly atmospheric is Delheim's wine cellar, with its brick arches, wooden benches and mellow light.
Tel 021 888 4600.

① Saxenburg
First established as a farm in 1693, today the *terroir* at Saxenburg is perfectly suited to Shiraz and it wins many accolades for its wines.
Tel 021 903 6113.

⑥ Morgenhof
Established in 1692, this historic farm is owned by the Cointreau family of Cognac, in France.
Tel 021 889 2007.

⑤ Thelema
A family-run estate, Thelema is in a particularly scenic location at the top of the Helshoogte Pass.
Tel 021 885 1924.

② Neethlingshof
A famous avenue of pines leads to the gabled home-stead (1705), the central motif on the estate's wine labels.
Tel 021 883 8988.

Key

▬ Motorway
═ Tour route
═ Other roads

0 kilometres ———— 5
0 miles ———— 3

④ Ernie Els Wines
Established by golfer Ernie Els, the estate has a room displaying his golfing trophies.
Tel 021 881 3588.

③ Spier Estate
This complex *(see facing page)* includes a riverside pub, farm stall, two restaurants, wine centre, a dam and an open-air amphitheatre.

Tips for Drivers

Tour length: Due to the great number of wine estates, most visitors tour three or four cellars, stopping for lunch at one of the superb estate restaurants.
Getting there: Visitors need a car, unless they join an organized tour from Cape Town.

❸ Spier Wine Estate

Road map B5. Stellenbosch. N2, then R310. **Tel** 021 809 1100. **Open** tastings: 9am–5pm daily. 🏞️ ♿ ✏️ 📷 🍴 Ⓤ Ⓦ **spier.co.za**

Bounded by the Eerste River, the Spier Wine Estate is one of the oldest in the country. It produced its first wine in 1712 and has buildings dating back to 1767. The estate has undergone major renovations since the early 1990s, when businessman Dick Enthoven purchased it from the Joubert family.

Spier grows all the major South African red grape varietals – Merlot, Cabernet, Shiraz and Pinotage – and produces a good range of everyday reds and whites, along with some award-winning winemaker's specials aimed at connoisseurs.

There is plenty to do at this family-friendly estate besides wine tasting. Dining is at the gourmet Eight Restaurant, which uses produce from its own estates, grown using biodynamic practices. At the Eight to Go deli visitors can assemble (or pre-book) a picnic to enjoy on the rolling lawns beside the lake. You can walk around the Protea Garden, visit Eagle Encounters – a bird of prey rehabilitation centre – and explore the farm on horseback. The well-stocked crafts market offers locally-produced items. The estate is also home to a luxury hotel with a swimming pool, and a spa that is open to day visitors.

The vineyards surrounding the Tokara estate

❹ Tokara

Road map B5. Stellenbosch. Off R310, on Helshoogte Pass. **Tel** 021 808 5900. **Open** tastings: 9am–5pm Mon–Fri, 10am–3pm Sat & Sun. Restaurant and deli: Tue–Sun to 5pm. 🏞️ ♿ Ⓦ **tokara.co.za**

Located up on the Helshoogte Pass, Tokara has sweeping views across False Bay and all the way to Table Mountain. The first bottling, in 2000, was under the Zondernaam ("without name") label: it was an immediate success, winning a string of medals.

As well as excellent wines, the estate produces brandy and olive oil. The restaurant is housed in a striking elevated glass-and-steel cube with wonderful mountain views. The delicatessen has a child-friendly, sunny deck for breakfast and light meals, and sells Tokara's own olive oil and kalamata olives, as well as handmade Belgian chocolates and South African cheeses. The public buildings are also a showcase for the work of some of the region's modern artists.

❺ Vergelegen

Road map B5. Somerset West. Lourensford Rd from R44. **Tel** 021 847 2122. **Open** 9:30am– 4:30pm daily. **Closed** Good Fri, 1 May, 25 Dec. 🍷 Cellar tours: 11:30am & 3pm. Garden tours: 10am. 🏞️ 📷 ♿ 🅿️ Ⓦ **vergelegen. co.za**

Choice white wine of the area

The vines and the five old camphor trees in front of this estate's magnificent manor house were planted in 1700, when the property belonged to Willem Adriaan van der Stel. Lady Florence Phillips, an art patron, lived here from 1917 to 1940. The extensive renovations undertaken by the Phillips family revealed the foundations of an octagonal garden, built by Willem van der Stel and now restored.

The manor house is filled with period furniture and fine paintings, a tasting room, shop, displays on the history of the estate, and two restaurants: Camphors at Vergelegen is the formal à la carte restaurant and Stables at Vergelegen is a café/bistro open for breakfast, lunch and teas. From November to April, picnics complete with white tablecloths can be arranged under the shade of van der Stel's camphor trees.

Visitors enjoying an outdoor meal at the Spier estate

For hotels and restaurants in this region see pp385–6 and pp402–3

❻ Boschendal Manor House

In 1685, Simon van der Stel granted the land on which the manor house stands to the French Huguenot, Jean le Long. Originally named "Bossendaal" (which literally means "forest and valley"), the property was transferred in 1715, together with adjacent fertile farmland, to another Huguenot settler, Abraham de Villiers. It remained in the wine-farming de Villiers family for 100 years. Jan de Villiers built the wine cellar and coach house in 1796. His youngest son, Paul, was responsible for Boschendal Manor House in its present H-shaped form, which he built in 1812. Today, this historic estate is open to the public and offers a museum, a wine tasting facility and restaurants.

The Back Entrance
Visitors to Boschendal enter the elegant Manor House via the gabled back door.

Crafted Room Dividers
Screens divided the front and back rooms in elegant Cape Dutch homes. Boschendal's original teak-and-yellowwood screen is decorated with geometric designs in dark ebony.

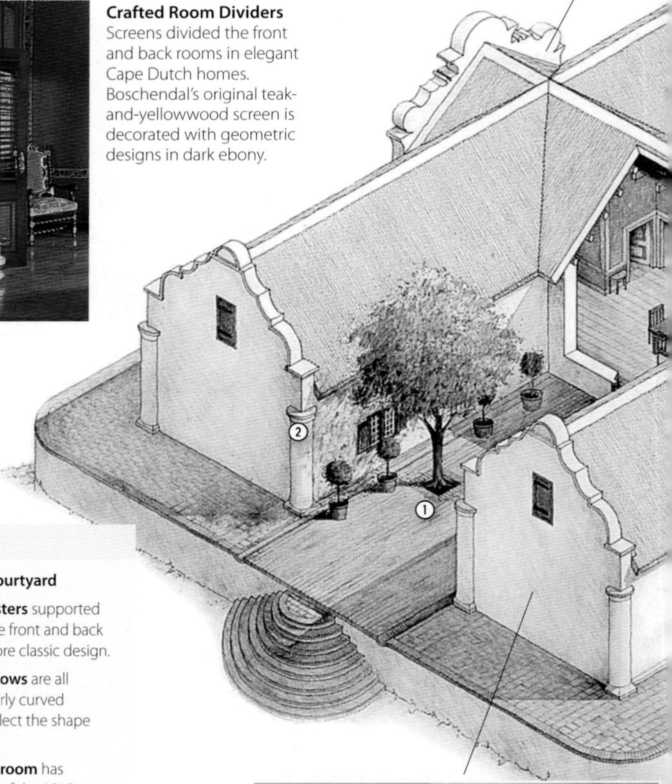

KEY

① **Brick-paved courtyard**

② **Rounded pilasters** supported the end gables. The front and back pilasters have a more classic design.

③ **The sash windows** are all mounted by similarly curved mouldings that reflect the shape of the gables.

④ **The reception room** has an original section of the 1812 wall frieze.

⑤ **The drop-fanlight** had to be raised to allow visitors to enter.

★ **Master Bedroom**
This antique stinkwood four-poster bed was crafted in 1810 by local artisans. It is decorated with a hand-crocheted lace hanging and a light, embroidered cotton bedspread, both of which date from around 1820.

★ Kitchen
The original clay floor was washed with a mixture of water and cow dung to keep it cool and vermin-free. Walls were painted dark brown or red to hide the dirt.

VISITORS' CHECKLIST

Practical Information
Road map B5. On R45 from Stellenbosch. **Tel** 021 870 4200.
Open 9:30am–5pm daily; wine tastings: 10am–4:30pm daily.
Vineyard tours: 11:30am daily (Nov–Apr); cellar tours: 10:30am, noon, 1:30pm & 3pm daily.
W boschendal.com

Long-Case Clock
This Dutch long-case clock was made by Carol Willem Bakker of Groningen, in the Netherlands, in the late 18th century.

★ Sitting Room
A gabled beefwood and stinkwood cabinet-on-stand is the focal point of the sitting room, which is resplendent with Cape, Dutch and East Indian furniture.

Friezes

Painted wall decoration using oil-based pigments is a craft believed to derive from Europe. Pilasters and swags would feature in reception and dining rooms, entwined roses in drawing rooms and, in less important rooms, a dado of a single colour on a plain background would suffice. The original 1812 wall frieze (in the reception rooms) of black acorns and green leaves was discovered during restoration of Boschendal in 1975.

The Gift and Wine Shop
Boschendal wines, as well as preserves, souvenirs and gifts, are sold at this shop.

❼ Franschhoek

Farms in this beautiful valley encircled by the Franschhoek and Groot Drakenstein mountains were granted to several French Huguenot families *(see p51)* by the Dutch East India Company (VOC) in 1694. The new settlers brought with them considerable skill as farmers, crafters and viticulturists, leaving a marked influence on the area, which the Dutch named *De Fransche Hoek* (French Corner).

VISITORS' CHECKLIST

Practical Information
Road map B5. N1, exit 47, R45.
🏛 17,600. ℹ️ 62 Huguenot St,
021 876 2861.. 🎭 Bastille Day
(14 Jul). 🅦 franschhoek.org.za

Transport
✈ Cape Town 79 km
(49 miles) E.

A collection of period furniture in the Franschhoek Huguenot Museum

Exploring Franschhoek

Upon arrival, the town's French heritage is immediately evident in lilting names such as L'Ormarins and Haute Cabrière. The main attraction, besides an exquisite setting, is its gourmet cuisine, accompanied by the area's excellent wines. Around 30 restaurants *(see p402)* offer superb Malay, country and Provençale dishes.

Franschhoek's wine route was established in 1980 by Michael Trull, a former advertising executive. He formed the Vignerons de Franschhoek, with five founder cellars – today there are 20 estates.

A unique experience is a visit to the **Haute Cabrière** estate.

After an interesting cellar tour, a sommelier cleanly shears the neck off a bottle of Pierre Jourdan sparkling wine with a sabre, an old technique known as *sabrage*, before serving the wine.

Visible at the top end of the main street is the **Huguenot Monument**, unveiled in 1948 to commemorate the arrival of the French settlers. A wide, semi-circular colonnade frames three tall arches representing the Holy Trinity. Before them is the figure of a woman standing on a globe, with her feet on France.

On a tall spire that surmounts the central arch is the "Sun of Righteousness".

🍷 Haute Cabrière

Lambrechts Rd. **Tel** 021 876 2630.
Open 9am–5pm Mon–Fri, 10am–4pm Sat, 11am– 4pm Sun. 🍷 Cellar tours: 11am Mon–Sat 🚻 ♿
🅦 cabriere.co.za

🏛 Franschhoek Motor Museum

L'Ormarins Wine Estate, on the R45 outside Franschhoek. **Tel** 021 874 9000. **Open** 10am–5pm daily (to 4pm Sat–Sun). 🚻 🅦 fmm.co.za

The museum charts the evolution of the automobile with a collection of some 220 vehicles, more than 80 of which will be on show at any one time.

🏛 Huguenot Memorial Museum

Lambrecht St. **Tel** 021 876 2532.
Open 9am–5pm Mon–Sat, 2–5pm Sun. **Closed** Good Fri, 25 Dec.
🚻 ♿ 🏛 🅦 museum.co.za

This museum celebrates the history and genealogy of the Cape's Huguenot families and their descendants. Of special note is a copy of the Edict of Nantes (1598), which permitted freedom of worship to Protestants in France, and a fine collection of old Bibles, including one printed in 1636.

The Huguenot Monument in Franschhoek was built in 1943

Franschhoek's French Heritage

Franschhoek is a charming little country town with a distinctly French character. Wine-making traditions introduced by the early French Huguenot settlers are still pursued by viticulturists with surnames such as Malherbe, Joubert and du Toit. Restaurants such as Le Quartier Français and La Petite Ferme offer Provençale cuisine in light-filled, airy interiors, while Chez Michel serves delicacies including escargots, and Camembert marinated in Calvados brandy. Architecturally, the influence of French Classicism is evident in the graceful lines of the historic buildings. A good example is the Huguenot Memorial Museum, which was based on a design by the 18th-century French architect Louis Michel Thibault.

Freedom of religion is symbolized by the dramatic central figure at the Huguenot Monument, which depicts a woman holding a Bible in her right hand and a broken chain in her left.

Refined classic gables like that of the Huguenot Memorial Museum replaced the Baroque exuberance of earlier gables.

Powdered wig

The tricorn was worn by gentlemen.

Mother-of-pearl buttons on garments were very fashionable.

The French Huguenots

After King Louis XIV of France revoked the Edict of Nantes in 1685, countless French Huguenots were forced to flee to Protestant countries. The Dutch East India Company's offer of a new life at the Cape of Good Hope was eagerly accepted by some 270 individuals.

Many Khoi were employed as slaves.

Hoop skirts were reinforced by stiff petticoats made from whalebone.

Grape presses like this one, which stands outside the Huguenot Memorial Museum, were used by the French settlers to produce the first wines of the region.

Restaurants in Franschhoek exude typical French *joie de vivre* and ambience.

Rocco Catoggio (1788–1858), a settler from Italy, who is depicted here with his grandson Rocco Cartozia de Villiers, married into a prominent Huguenot family.

❽ Paarl

In 1687, farms were allocated to early Dutch colonists in the pretty Berg River Valley, which is flanked to the north by Paarl Mountain. The name Paarl comes from the Dutch *peerlbergh* (pearl mountain), given to the outcrops by early Dutch explorer Abraham Gabbema when he spotted the three smooth domes after a rain shower. Mica chips embedded in the granite glistened in the sun, giving it the appearance of a shiny pearl. The town of Paarl was established in 1690.

The three granite domes on the outskirts of Paarl

Exploring Paarl

Large agricultural, financial and manufacturing companies are based in Paarl, making it a major player in the industry of the Western Cape. Its many tree-lined streets and graceful gabled homes, however, lend it a certain country charm. Paarl's 11-km (7-mile) Main Street, which runs along the Berg River, is shaded by oak trees and makes a very good starting point from which to explore the town. A number of well-preserved 18th- and 19th-century Cape Dutch and Georgian houses are found along both sides of Main Street, some of the later ones displaying marked Victorian architectural influences.

La Concorde, a stately structure in the Neo-Classical style built in 1956, is the head-quarters of the *Kooperatiewe Wijnbouwers Vereeniging* (KWV), the Cooperative Wine Farmers Association. The KWV was a controlling body which aimed to administer wine production, check the quality and develop export markets. It has since been privatized. Further along Main Street, the **Paarl Museum** presents historical aspects of the town. Exhibits include a collection

Antique cupboard, Paarl Museum

of stinkwood chairs, a Dutch linen press and yellowwood armoires. An excellent porcelain collection features Imari, Kang Hsi, VOC and Canton pieces, and the kitchen is crammed with authentic utensils and furniture. Temporary displays on a wide field of related themes, such as the Khoi *(see pp50–51)*, are arranged regularly.

Just off Paarl's Main Road lies **Laborie Estate**, first granted to a Huguenot settler in 1688. In 1774 it was acquired by Hendrick Louw, who subsequently built the Cape Dutch homestead on it. Today, Laborie is best-known for producing Méthode Cap Classique sparkling wines.

🏛 Paarl Museum
303 Main Rd. **Tel** 021 872 2651.
Open 9am–4pm Mon–Fri, 9am–1pm Sat. **Closed** Good Fri, 25 Dec. 🅿

🍷 Laborie Estate
Taillefer St, off Main Rd. **Tel** 021 807 3390. **Open** wine tastings: 9am–5pm daily. **Closed** 1 Jan, 25 Dec. 📷 book in advance. 🅿 ♿ ✎
🌐 laboriewines.co.za

Environs

Just off Main Street, opposite La Concorde, is Jan Phillips Drive, an 11-km (7-mile) route to Paarl Mountain. The 500 million-year-old massif is the world's second-largest granite outcrop, after Uluru in Australia, and can be climbed with the aid of handholds.

The entrance to the Paarl Mountain Nature Reserve also lies on Jan Phillips Drive. From here, visitors can gain access to the **Afrikaans Language Monument** *(Afrikaanse Taalmonument)*. Designed by the architect Jan van Wyk, it was constructed around 1975, and is a tribute to the official recognition of the Afrikaans language 100 years earlier. The imposing monument is composed of three domes and three small pillars, all of varying height and size, as well as a tall obelisk and a soaring column. Each of the elements acknowledges the linguistic influence and contribution of a different culture.

Afrikaans Language Monument
Signposted from Main St. **Tel** 021 863 0543. **Open** Apr–Nov: 8am–5pm daily; Dec–Mar: 8am–8pm daily. 🅿 ♿ ▢
🌐 taalmuseum.co.za

The Afrikaans Language Monument, Paarl

❾ Paarl Winelands Tour

Picturesque wine farms spread out to either side of the imposing Paarl Mountain, with its three rounded domes. Estates dotted along its eastern slopes face the Klein Drakenstein and the Du Toitskloof mountains, while those on the west face look towards Table Mountain and False Bay. The vineyards around Paarl produce about one-fifth of South Africa's total wine crop. All of the estates on this route, which include well-known names such as Nederburg and Laborie, offer wine tasting and sales most days. Certain farms arrange cellar tours by appointment only.

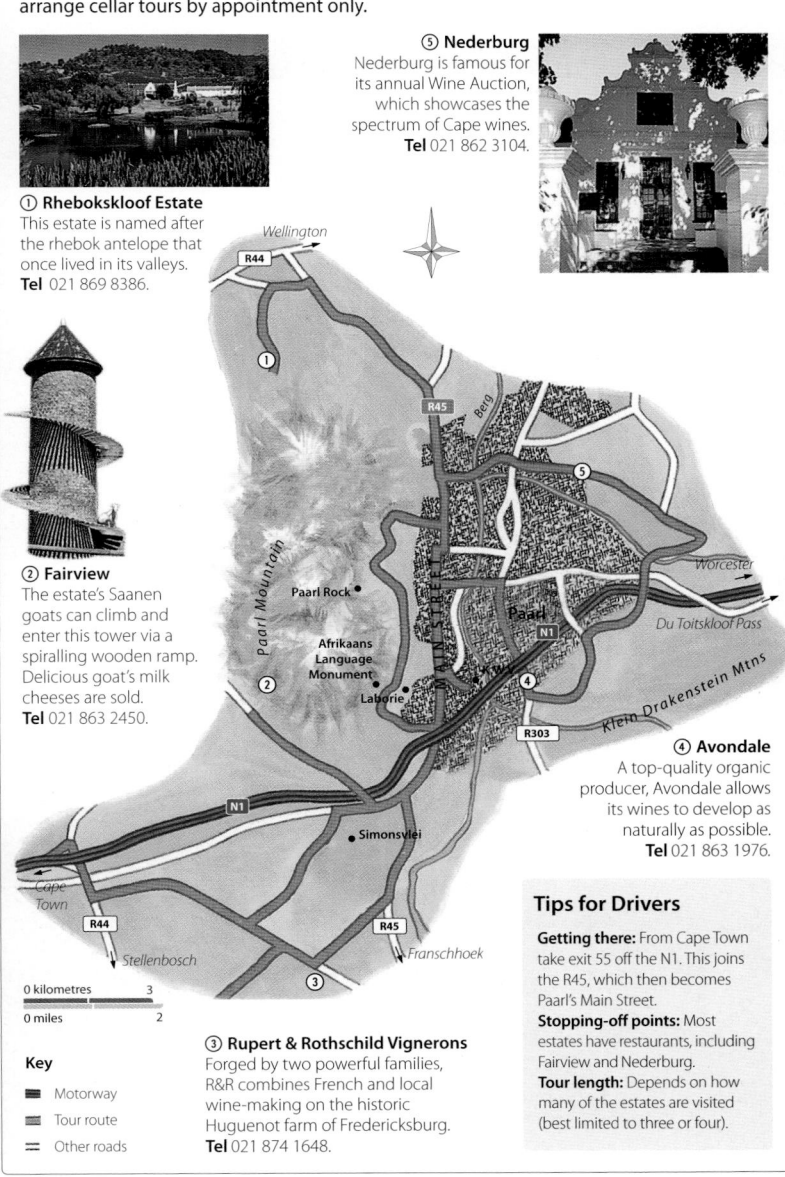

⑤ Nederburg
Nederburg is famous for its annual Wine Auction, which showcases the spectrum of Cape wines.
Tel 021 862 3104.

① Rhebokskloof Estate
This estate is named after the rhebok antelope that once lived in its valleys.
Tel 021 869 8386.

② Fairview
The estate's Saanen goats can climb and enter this tower via a spiralling wooden ramp. Delicious goat's milk cheeses are sold.
Tel 021 863 2450.

④ Avondale
A top-quality organic producer, Avondale allows its wines to develop as naturally as possible.
Tel 021 863 1976.

③ Rupert & Rothschild Vignerons
Forged by two powerful families, R&R combines French and local wine-making on the historic Huguenot farm of Fredericksburg.
Tel 021 874 1648.

Wellington
R44
R45
Berg
Worcester
Paarl Mountain
Paarl Rock
Paarl
Du Toitskloof Pass
Afrikaans Language Monument
Laborie
N1
Klein Drakenstein Mtns
R303
Simonsvlei
Cape Town
R44
Stellenbosch
R45
Franschhoek

0 kilometres 3
0 miles 2

Tips for Drivers

Getting there: From Cape Town take exit 55 off the N1. This joins the R45, which then becomes Paarl's Main Street.

Stopping-off points: Most estates have restaurants, including Fairview and Nederburg.

Tour length: Depends on how many of the estates are visited (best limited to three or four).

Key

▬ Motorway
▬ Tour route
═ Other roads

The road to Worcester goes through the scenic Du Toitskloof Pass

❿ Worcester

Road map B5. N1 from Cape Town via Dutoitskloof Pass. 🗺 97,000. 🚉 Worcester Station. 🛈 25 Baring St, 023 348 2795. **Open** Mon–Sat.

This city, named after the Marquis of Worcester, the brother of one-time Cape governor Lord Charles Somerset, lies some 110 km (68 miles) east of Cape Town. It is the biggest centre in the Breede River Valley and the largest producer of table grapes in South Africa. Its wineries produce a substantial amount of wine too, and Worcester is known for everyday affordable reds, whites and fortified wines. Eleven estates on the Worcester Wine and Olive Route are open for tastings and cellar tours, most in the Breede River Valley.

Old water pump in Worcester

The attraction of a trip to Worcester is the drive through the Du Toitskloof Pass, which climbs to a height of 823 m (2,700 ft). Construction of the Huguenot Tunnel in 1988 shortened the pass by 11 km (7 miles), but the route still affords scenic views of Paarl and the Berg River Valley. At Church Square in Worcester, there is a Garden of Remembrance designed by Hugo Naude, the World War I Memorial and a stone cairn erected at the time of the symbolic *Ossewa* (ox wagon) Trek of 1938 (*see p58*), undertaken to commemorate the Great Trek (*see pp54–5*).

Worcester's Dutch Reformed Church was built in 1832. The imposing Gothic-style steeple was added in 1927 after the original was blown away in gales.

The open-air **Worcester Museum**, 2km (1.25 miles) southeast of High Street, is a recreation of an early Cape farm, complete with a shepherd's hut, horse mill, labourer's cottage and harness room. Visitors can watch bread being baked outdoors, a traditional blacksmith at work and seasonal activities such as brandy distillation.

🏛 **Worcester Museum**
Road map B5. N1, signposted from Worcester. **Tel** 023 342 2225. **Open** 8am–4:30pm Mon–Fri, 8am–1pm Sat. **Closed** Good Fri, 25 Dec, 1 Jan. **W** worcestermuseum.org.za

Environs
The **Karoo Desert National Botanical Garden**, a short drive north of Worcester, contains plants that thrive in a semi-desert environment. Jewel-bright mesembryanthemums are lovely in spring, while the unusual year-round species include the prehistoric welwitschias, and the *halfmens* (half-humans) and quiver trees.

One area features plants grouped by regional and climatic zones. The succulent plant collection, the largest in Africa, is ranked by the Organization for Succulent Plant Study as one of the most authentic of its kind in the world. There is also a trail with Braille text signs.

🌿 **Karoo Desert National Botanical Garden**
Roux Rd, Worcester. **Tel** 023 347 0785. **Open** 7am–7pm daily. 🎫 📷 (Aug–Oct only.) ♿ 🚻 🍴 **W** sanbi.org

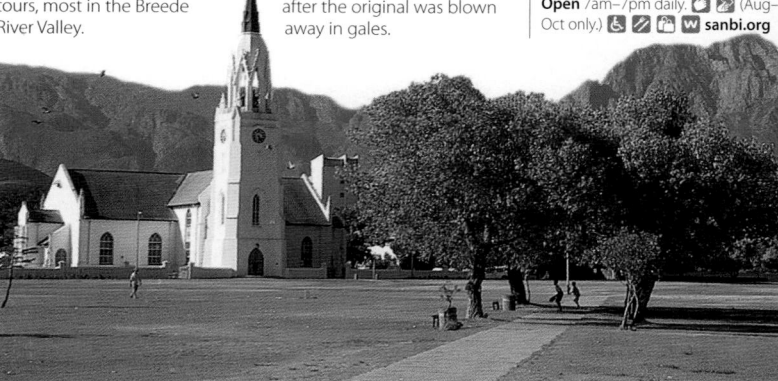

The Dutch Reformed Church in Worcester

Blacksmith at work, Worcester Museum

⑪ Robertson

Road map B5. R60 from Worcester or Swellendam. ⊠ 27,800. ℹ️ 17 Voortrekker Rd, 023 626 3059. **Open** daily. 🎪 Wacky Wine Weekend (Jun), Robertson Slow (Aug). 🔲 robertson62.com

Robertson lies in the Breede River Valley where sunny slopes create perfect conditions for vineyards and orchards. As well as wine and grapes, dried fruit is a major industry. The Robertson Wine Route comprises more than 50 cellars, many of which are acclaimed for their choice Chardonnays. The **Robertson Klipdrift Distillery** is a popular stop at which to taste this iconic South African brandy and tour the distillery. The restaurant serves breakfast and lunch.

🏰 Robertson Klipdrift Distillery
4 Voortrekker Rd. **Tel** 081 896 7695. **Open** daily. 🍽️ 📞 10am, noon & 2:30pm Mon–Fri, 10am, noon & 2pm Sat & public hols; Oct–Apr: 11am & 1pm Sun. ⏱️ 🅿️ 🔲 klipdrift.co.za

⑫ Montagu

Road map B5. N15 fm Robertson. ⊠ 15,200. ℹ️ 24 Bath St, 023 614 2471. **Open** daily. 🔲 montagu-ashton.info

The charm of Montagu lies in its many houses dating back to the early 1850s. In Long Street alone there are 14 national monuments. The best-known feature is the thermal springs (at a constant 43°C/109°F), 2 km (1 mile) from town.

The scenery of the northern edge of the Langeberg range has led to the establishment of trails for hikers, mountain bikers and 4WD enthusiasts.

The route to Montagu from Robertson passes through a 16-m (52-ft) long tunnel, above which stands the ruined Sidney Fort built by the British during the South African War.

Avalon hot springs in Montagu

⑬ Boesmanskloof Hiking Trail

This popular 5-hour walking trail follows a gap through the Riviersonderend mountains. It runs between the rustic hamlets of Greyton and McGregor and can be tackled from either village. Hikers will need to be reasonably fit as the trail ascends and descends the mountainside. The views here are impressive, and the stream running along the scenic McGregor section of the trail ensures an abundant water supply. The Oakes Falls, 9 km (6 miles) from Greyton, a series of waterfalls and pools, are ideal for swimming. There are no overnight huts.

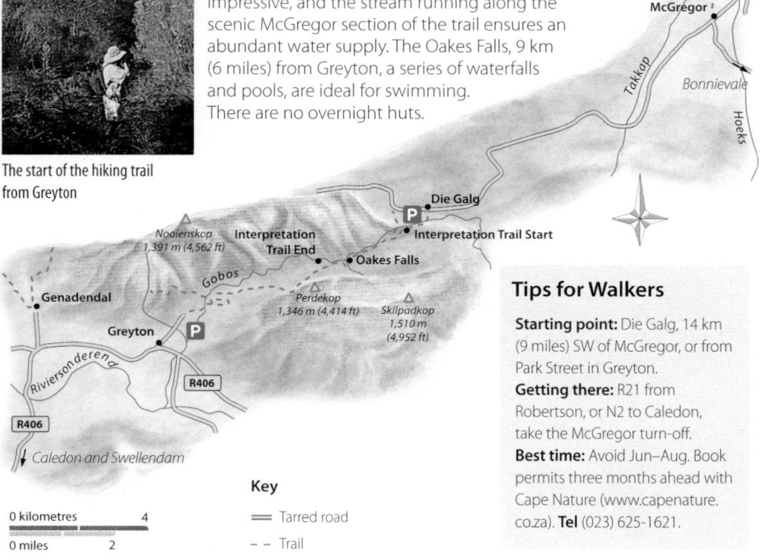

The start of the hiking trail from Greyton

Robertson

McGregor

Bonnievale

Takkap

Hoeks

Die Galg

Noalenskop 1,391 m (4,562 ft)

Interpretation Trail End

Interpretation Trail Start

Gobos

Oakes Falls

Perdekop 1,346 m (4,414 ft)

Skilpadkop 1,510 m (4,952 ft)

Genadendal

Greyton

Riviersonderend

R406

R406

↓ Caledon and Swellendam

Tips for Walkers

Starting point: Die Galg, 14 km (9 miles) SW of McGregor, or from Park Street in Greyton.
Getting there: R21 from Robertson, or N2 to Caledon, take the McGregor turn-off.
Best time: Avoid Jun–Aug. Book permits three months ahead with Cape Nature (www.capenature. co.za). **Tel** (023) 625-1621.

Key

━━ Tarred road

- - Trail

| 0 kilometres | 4 |
| 0 miles | 2 |

THE WEST COAST

The dry, sunbaked landscape of South Africa's west coast is bounded to the east by the rugged Cederberg mountain range and to the west by the rocky, wind-blown Atlantic coastline. Attractions in the region are manyfold: charming fishing villages, bleached-white beaches, delectable seafood, whale-watching and hiking. An unexpected surprise in this forbidding terrain is the appearance every spring of colourful fields of exquisite wildflowers.

The West Coast extends north of Cape Town to the Namibian border, where the fringes of the Namib desert epitomize the extremes of this vast, rain-deprived area. The arid, bleak and infertile vegetation zones support only hardy, drought-resistant succulents and geophytes (plants whose bulbs, corms or tubers store water and nutrients). The *fynbos* area south of Nieuwoudtville possesses a stark beauty, embodied in the weird forms of the Cederberg's outcrops that were eroded over millennia by wind and rain.

Further inland the country's wheatbelt centres on Malmesbury, and is an area of undulating golden corn whose texture changes constantly with the play of light on the rippling fields. Also in the interior are the West Coast wine farms around the Swartland and Sandveld. Here, the good soils, combined with a low level of rain and warm summers, create rich and earthy flavours in the wines.

The upwelling of the Atlantic Ocean's cold Benguela Current along the coast brings rich phytoplanktonic nutrients to the surface, attracting vast shoals of pelagic fish. This harvest from the sea supports an important fishing industry in the Western Cape. Saldanha Bay, a rather unappealing industrial town, is the fishing and seafood processing hub. It is also a major centre for the export of iron ore, which is mined at Sishen, further inland in the Northern Cape Province. Sishen is the site of the largest iron ore deposits in the world.

The Namaqualand is an arid belt stretching north of the Cederberg almost to the Namibian border, which is marked by the mighty Orange River. This belt only receives about 140 mm (6 inches) of rainfall during March and April, but the brief downpours provide sufficient moisture to blanket the landscape with colourful blooms from August to October every year.

Fishing nets with bright yellow floats on the beach at St Helena Bay

◀ Boats drawn up on Langebaan beach in the West Coast National Park

Exploring the West Coast

Although first appearances seem to indicate that the West Coast is a hot, barren wilderness, the region is a magnet to visitors during the spring months (August to mid-October), when flowering daisies and gazanias paint the landscape with bold colour splashes. It is also known for its spectacular walking and hiking trails in the Cederberg Mountains, which are famous for their contorted rock formations and breathtaking views. Along the coastline, the cold waters of the Atlantic yield a vast array of delicious seafood, from rock lobster and black mussels to fresh linefish, which can be sampled at a number of *skerms* (open-air restaurants) on the beaches.

Orange

Sendelingsdr
/Ai-/Ais/
Richtersvelt
Transfronti
Park
Kuboes

Alexander Bay

Eksteenfontein

Lekker

Port Nolloth   *Aninaus*

NORTH
CAPI

Grootmis   B

Koma

Koingnaa

Hondeklip B

Fishing trawlers at anchor in Lambert's Bay harbour

The Wolfberg Arch in the Cederberg

Sights at a Glance

Getting Around

A car is essential for touring this region as no regular public transport service exists. Private coach companies do operate along this section of coast, however. During the flower season, a large number of organized coach tours are available from operators based in Cape Town. The N7, a major national route, runs straight up the West Coast from Cape Town to the Namibian border, with main roads leading off to the coast and interior. Between Cape Town and St Helena Bay, the R27 offers a more scenic route with intermittent views of the coastline. The closest international airport is in Cape Town.

For hotels and restaurants in this region see pp386–7 and pp403–4

White Namaqualand daisies *(Dimorphotheia pluvialis)*, tall yellow bulbinellas *(Bulbinella floribunda)* and magenta *Senecio* open their petals to the sun

0 kilometres 50
0 miles 25

rif

kopf

rap

Upington
N14 →

Springbok

Burke's Pass

Kamieskroon

NAMAQUALAND TOUR

ies

Kliprand
△ 1024 m

en

tterfontein

Nuwerus

Landplaas

Lutzville

Doring Bay

Loeriesfontein

Klein Doring

Brandkop

Upington →
Nieuwoudtville
Grootdrif R27 Calvinia

Vanrhynsdorp

Vredendal
Klawer *Botterkloof Pass*

Olifants R364
Doringbos
Uitspankraal

WESTERN
CAPE

N7

BERT'S BAY **3**

Leipoldtville

Elands bay

Paleisheuwel

Noordkuil

elena Bay

er

burg

nha

EST COAST
ONAL PARK

Yzerfontein

8 CLANWILLIAM
Wuppertal

Sandberg

CEDERBERG

9

7 CITRUSDAL

Eendekuil

R27

Velddrif
Sauer

De Hoek
Porterville

Hopefield R44

Moorreesburg *Gydopas*

Riebeek
Wes

6 TULBAGH

4 DARLING

1

5 MALMESBURY

WEST
COAST R27

Philadelphia
→ *Worcester*

Melkbosstrand

Bloubergstrand
Milnerton
Cape Town ↓

Langebaan

2

Pikeberg

Groot Berg river

Klein Doring

Sauer-doring

Bokkeveldberge

Wellington

Key

— Major road

‧‧‧‧‧ Minor road

▪ ▪ ▪ Untarred road

— Scenic route

━━━ Main railway

─── Minor railway

▬▬▬ International border

▬▬▬ Provincial border

△ Summit

✕ Pass

Lookout, West Coast National Park

For keys to symbols *see back flap*

Fishermen drag their boat to the water at Paternoster

❶ The West Coast

Road map A4, A5.

From Cape Town, the R27 leads up the West Coast to the Olifants River, linking Cape Town's coastal suburbs of Milnerton, Blouberg-strand and Melkbosstrand, and is a scenic road with wonderful views of the dunes and sea. Bloubergstrand, today a sought-after residential area, is famous for its unsurpassed views of Table Mountain seen across the 16-km (10-mile) wide expanse of Table Bay, and lies at the foot of the Blouberg (blue mountain). The broad beaches and bays are popular for watersports, though southeasterly summer gales can create windy conditions.

Heading north along the R27, silver domes come into view. They belong to Koeberg Nuclear Power Station, the only nuclear facility in Africa. A left turn from the R27 onto the R315 leads to Yzerfontein, whose claim to fame is its prolific crayfish (rock lobster) reserves. These are a sought-after local delicacy and

during the crayfishing season (Dec–Apr), the local camp site attracts countless divers and their families. Permits, allowing daily catches of four crayfish per person, are obtainable at any post office.

Continuing north on the R27, past the industrial fishing hub and harbour of Saldanha, is Vredenburg. From here, a 16-km (10-mile) drive leads to Pater-noster, a typical little wind-blown fishing village with whitewashed cottages. Legend recounts that the Portuguese sailors wrecked here recited the Paternoster (Our Father) to give thanks for their survival. The village is a popular weekend retreat for Capetonians. Local regulations stipulate that new holiday cottages must be built in the traditional West Coast style. Just to the south of the village the small **Cape Columbine Nature Reserve** covers a rocky stretch of coastline with inlets and coves. It is the furthest westerly point in the Western Cape, and in it stands the Cape Columbine

Lighthouse, the first to be seen by ships coming from Europe. Built in 1936, it is 80 m (263 ft) tall and casts a beam visible for about 50 km (31 miles). For a small fee you can climb to the top. Around a rocky headland from Paternoster, the village of **St Helena** perches at the edge of a sheltered bay. Just before the village a signed turnoff leads to the monument commemorating navigator Vasco da Gama's landing here on St Helena's Day, 7 November, in 1497.

The fishing industry here benefits from the cold, north-flowing Benguela Current. It ensures a ready supply of rich nutrients that sustain the vast populations of pelagic fish.

⊠ Cape Columbine Nature Reserve
St Augustine Rd, Tietiesbaai. **Tel** 022 752 2718. **Open** 7am–7pm daily. Lighthouse: 10am–3pm. 🏕 ⛰

❷ West Coast National Park

See pp216–17.

A seal pup relaxes on the rocks of Bird Island, Lambert's Bay

❸ Lambert's Bay

Road map A4. 🏘 6,200. 🛈 Hoof St, 027 432 1000. **Open** Mon–Sat; also Sun during flower season. 🦐 Kreeffees (Crayfish Festival) (Apr). 🌐 lambertsbay.co.za

This little fishing town, an hour's drive west of Clanwilliam on the R364, was named after Rear Admiral Sir Robert Lambert, a senior Royal Navy officer who monitored the marine survey of this section of coastline.

Open-Air Seafood Feasts

Along the West Coast, there are a wide variety of open-air eating places known as *skerms* (Afrikaans for "shelters") with names like Die Strandloper *(see p404)*, in Langebaan, and Muis-bosskerm *(see p403)*,

in Lambert's Bay. Reed roofs provide shade and mussel shells are used as utensils, but the major appeal is the abundance of fresh seafood on offer: smoked angelfish, *snoek* (a large gamefish that tastes best when barbecued), spicy mussel stews, thin slices of *perlemoen* (abalone), and calamari.

Lunch at Die Strandloper

For visitors, the main attraction is **Bird Island**, about 100 m (328 ft) offshore. It is accessible via a breakwater-cum-harbour wall. The island is a breeding ground for thousands of African penguins, Cape cormorants and the striking Cape gannet with its yellow-painted face. There is a small museum, and a viewing tower allows visitors to remain unobtrusive while observing the birds' behaviour.

Bird Island
Tel 071 657 5651. **Open** Apr–Sep: 7:30am–6pm daily; Oct–Mar: 7am–7pm daily. **capenature.co.za**

❹ Darling

Road map B5. R307. 10,450. Pastorie St, 022 492 3361. Wildflower Show (Sep), Rocking the Daisies (Oct). **darlingtourism.co.za**

Darling is surrounded by a farming region of wheatfields, vineyards, sheep and dairy cattle, but is best-known for its spring flower show *(see p40)*.

Darling also lays claim to satirist Pieter-Dirk Uys *(see p172)*, who has gained fame for the portrayal of his female alter ego, Evita Bezuidenhout, fictitious ambassadress of the equally fictitious homeland called Baphetikosweti. His bar, **Evita se Perron** (Evita's platform), is situated on a defunct railway platform and attracts crowds to hear hilarious, razor-sharp analyses of local politics.

A National Monument on historic Church Street in Tulbagh

Evita se Perron
8 Arcadia St. **Tel** 022 492 2831. **evita.co.za**

❺ Malmesbury

Road map B5. N7. 35,900. Bokomo Rd. 1 Church St, 022 487 1133. **Open** Mon–Fri. **malmesburytourism.co.za**

Malmesbury, the heart of South Africa's wheatland, lies in the *Swartland* (black country), a term that has, at times, been attributed to the region's soil, and at other times to its renosterbush, a local shrub that turns a dark hue in winter. The wheatfields, with their velvety shoots rippling in the breeze, or cropped furrows with bales piled high, are a lovely sight. Wine is also produced in the region. The Swartland Wine and Olive Route includes 20 estates and coops that are open for tastings and sales around the Riebeek Valley, Malmesbury, Piketberg and Porterville.

Swartland Wine and Olive Route
Cnr Church and Voortrekker sts. **Tel** 022 487 1133. **Open** Mon–Sat. **swartlandwineandolives.co.za**.

❻ Tulbagh

Road map B5. R44. 9,000. 4 Church St, 023 230 1375. **Open** daily. **tulbaghtourism.co.za**

In 1700, Governor Willem Adriaan van der Stel initiated a new settlement in the Breede River Valley, naming it Tulbagh, after his predecessor.

Encircled by the Witzenberg and Winterhoek mountains, in 1969 the town was hit by an earthquake measuring 6.3 on the Richter scale. Eight people died and many historic buildings were badly damaged. The disaster resulted in a five-year restoration project undertaken along Church Street, lined with no less than 32 18th- and 19th-century Victorian and Cape Dutch homes. The oldest building, Oude Kerk (old church) Volksmuseum, dates back to 1743 and contains the original pulpit, pews and Bible. De Oude Herberg, Tulbagh's first boarding house (1885), is now a guest-house and restaurant *(see p386)*.

Cape gannets populate Bird Island in their thousands

❷ West Coast National Park

The West Coast National Park encompasses Langebaan Lagoon, the islands Schaapen, Jutten, Marcus and Malgas, and the Postberg Nature Reserve, which is opened to the public each spring (Aug–Sep), when it is carpeted with colourful wild flowers such as daisies and gazanias. The park is one of South Africa's most important wetlands, harbouring some 250 species of waterbird including plovers, herons, ibis, and black oyster-catchers. Antelope species such as elands and kudus can also be seen, along with zebras. The park can be explored by car or on hiking trails; accommodation consists of chalets and houseboats on the lagoon.

Cape Cormorants
Abundant on the coast, they feed on pelagic shoaling fish, but have been affected by overfishing.

Seabirds

Langebaan Lagoon, 15 km (9 miles) long, and with an average depth of 1 m (3 ft), offers a sheltered haven for a great number of seabirds, including waders, gulls, flamingoes and pelicans. Resident and migrant species take advantage of the Atlantic's nutrient-rich water to rear their chicks.

The curlew sandpiper's curved bill enables it to probe for small crustaceans.

Hartlaub's gulls are endemic to the West Coast and forage for food along the shore in the early morning hours.

Lesser flamingoes, distinguished from greater flamingoes by their smaller size and red bill, often congregate in large flocks.

White Pelicans
Langebaan Lagoon is home to one of only a handful of white pelican breeding colonies in southern Africa. The species feeds on fish, which it scoops up in the large pouch under its beak.

★ **Geelbek Homestead**
The visitor centre has information on the fauna, flora and ecology of the park. Bird-watchers can observe many different species from the nearby hide, and there is also a restaurant specializing in traditional Cape cooking.

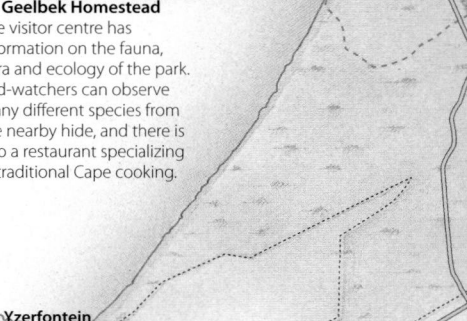

Plank...
Stoney Head
Kreeftebaai
Vondeling Island
Sixteen Mile Beach
Churchhave...
Atlantic Viewpoint
Bird Hide
Yzerfontein
Capetown
West Ce...
Gat...

0 kilometres 5
0 miles 2.5

For hotels and restaurants in this region see pp386–7 and pp403–4

Saldanha

Malgas Island

*tic
n*

en Island

Marcus Island

en Bay

*d
rea*

*Saldanha
Bay*

Salamander Bay

Club Mykonos

*Schaapen
Island*

Langebaan

*Langebaan
Gate*

*Bird
hide*

*Coast
al Park*

VISITORS' CHECKLIST

Practical Information
Road map A5. Gates on the R27
and Langebaan. *i* (022) 772-
2144. **Open** Sep–Mar: 7am–7pm
daily; Apr–Aug: 7am–6pm daily.
Postberg Nature Reserve:
Open only during flower season
(usually Aug–Sep).
w sanparks.org

Club Mykonos
Located at the water's edge north of the
lagoon is this attractive Mediterranean-style
hotel and timeshare resort. The complex offers
self-contained units with balconies.

Postberg Nature Reserve
In spring, bonteboks graze on a
dense carpet of wild flowers,
such as yellow *gousblomme*
(gazanias) and white *wit-
botterblomme* (rain daisies).

Langebaan Beach
This beach is very popular with
anglers, who use mainly sand
prawns to catch white stumpnose,
kob, elf and skate.

Catamaran on the beach

Watersports at Langebaan

Almost year-round sunshine, safe waters and reliable
winds make Langebaan Lagoon ideal for watersports,
particularly kite- and wind-suring, kayaking, water-
skiing and sailing. Watersports centres in the town
rent out equipment and offer lessons. In order to
protect the natural environment without curtailing
the activities of other interest groups, the lagoon has
been zoned into three recreational areas: in the north
all watersports are allowed; the central part is out of
bounds for motorboats and fishing; and no activities
are permitted in the southern wilderness area.

ey
= Tarred road
= Untarred road
-- Trail
= Major Road

Houses along Church Street in Clanwilliam

❼ Citrusdal

Road map B4. R303. 🏔 7,200.
ℹ 39 Voortrekker St, 022 921 3210.
Open Mon–Fri. 🖥 citrusdal.info

Frost-free winters and the Olifants River Irrigation Scheme have made Citrusdal South Africa's third-largest citrus district. The first orchard was planted with seedlings from Van Riebeeck's garden at the foot of Table Mountain *(see pp136–7)*. One tree, after bearing fruit for some 250 years, is now a national monument.

The Goede Hoop Citrus Co-operative has initiated scenic mountain bike trails around Citrusdal, such as the old Ceres and Piekenierskloof passes.

❽ Clanwilliam

Road map B4. N7. 🏔 7,700. ℹ Main Rd, 027 482 2024. **Open** Mon–Sat.
🖥 clanwilliam.info

Clanwilliam is the headquarters of the *rooibos* (red bush) tea industry. The shoots of the wild shrub are used to make a caffeine-free tea that is low in tannin and also considered to have medicinal properties *(see p395)*.

Clanwilliam Dam, encircled by the Cederberg Mountains, stretches for 18 km (11 miles) and is popular with water-skiers. Wooden holiday cabins line the banks, and an attractive camp site has been established right at the water's edge.

❾ Cederberg

Road map: B4. Cape Nature office, Algeria: turnoff N7 between Citrusdal and Clanwilliam. ℹ 027 482 2403. Anyone wishing to hike or stay in the Cederberg area will require a permit.
🏔 🚶 🎣 🏕 🖥 capenature.co.za

From the north, the Cederberg range is reached via Pakhuis Pass and the Biedouw Valley, 50 km (31 miles) from Clanwilliam. Travelling from the south, take the N7 from Citrusdal. The Cederberg range is a surreal wilderness of sandstone peaks that have been eroded into jagged formations. It is part of the Cederberg Wilderness Area which was proclaimed in 1973 and covers 710 sq km (274 sq miles). The attraction of the range is its recreational appeal – walks, hikes, camping and wonderful views. The southern part, in particular, is popular for its dramatic rock formations: the Maltese Cross, a 20-m (66-ft) high pillar, and the Wolfberg Arch with its sweeping views of the area. At the Wolfberg Cracks, the main fissure measures more than 30 m (98 ft). The snow protea *(Protea cryophila)*, endemic to the upper reaches of the range, occurs on the Sneeuberg which, at 2,028 m (6,654 ft), is the highest peak. The Clanwilliam cedar, after which the area was named, is a species that is protected in the Cederberg Wilderness Area.

Road marker at Kagga Kamma

At the southern end of the Cederberg is the **Kagga Kamma Private Game Reserve**, where visitors can go on game drives, view San rock art and take part in activities such as bird-watching, stargazing or hiking. Accommodation is in thatched chalets, unique cave rooms and a camp site. Pre-booked day visitors are welcome.

🎋 **Kagga Kamma Private Game Reserve**
Southern Cederberg. **Tel** Reservations: 021 872 4343. **Open** daily. 🚗 🏊 🏕
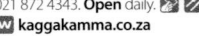 🖥 kaggakamma.co.za

Scenic view over Clanwilliam Dam to the Cederberg Mountains

Rock Formations of the Cederberg

During the Palaeozoic pre-Karoo period several hundred million years ago, the formations that over time became the Cape Folded Mountains were under water. Of the sandstones, shales and quartzites of these Cape formations, Table Mountain sandstone was the most resilient. In the Karoo Period, tectonic forces produced the crumpled folds of the Cape mountains. Subsequent erosion wore away the soft rock, leaving the harder layer. The resulting formations can be seen today in the Cederberg's twisted landscape. The original grey-coloured sandstone of the bizarre terrain has frequently been stained a rich red by iron oxides.

The Maltese Cross

This unusual rock formation, a day's hike from Dwarsrivier Farm (Sanddrif), consists partly of Table Mountain sandstone. More resistant to erosion, it forms the upper portion of the cross.

Hiking
Paths made by woodcutters some 100 years ago now provide access for hikers.

Softer layers erode faster, causing a thinner base.

Cederberg Cedar
Some 8,000 trees are planted annually to ensure the survival of this endemic species. The cedars were once widely used to make telephone poles.

The scree slope is composed of fallen debris from above.

Wolfberg Cracks
Lovely views greet hikers at the Wolfberg Cracks, a 75-minute walk from the Wolfberg Arch.

Wolfberg Arch
The majestic Wolfberg Arch is the Cederberg's most unique formation. A favourite with photographers, it provides a natural frame for memorable images.

Bizarre rock sculptures supported on brittle pillars.

Cracks are caused by the expansion and contraction of the rock.

The arch, 30 m (98 ft) high, overlooks a region known as the Tankwa Karoo.

Erosion
Over aeons, wind and water have carved the Cederberg into a fairytale landscape. Pinnacles, arches and fissures resemble the strange castles of another world, while the rock outcrops seem alive with gargoyles and goblins.

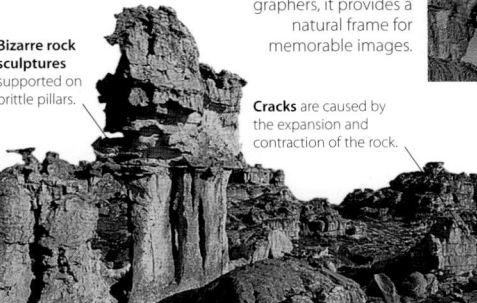

❿ Namaqualand Tour

Namaqualand, an area of about 48,000 sq km (18,500 sq miles), from the Orange River in the north to the mouth of the Olifants River in the south, is a region of sharp contrasts. In spring, this scrub-covered, arid land blazes with colour – from fuchsia pinks to neon yellows and oranges – as a myriad daisies and flowering succulents open their petals to the sun. The seeds of the drought-resistant plants lie dormant in the soil during the dry months, but if the first rains (usually around March and April) are good, they burst into bloom from August to October.

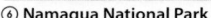

⑥ Namaqua National Park
Lying 17 km (11 miles) west of Kamieskroon, this park has a circular drive with viewpoints, several short nature trails, picnic sites, and a SANParks visitor information centre during the spring flowering season. The higher rainfall resulting from the park's proximity to the West Coast guarantees excellent displays. Bright orange daisies (Ursinia sp) and gazanias are at their most spectacular here.

① Tienie Versfeld Wildflower Reserve
After attending the Darling wild flower and orchid shows, visitors can drive to this nearby reserve and view expanses of wild flowers in their natural habitat. Namaqualand's best displays vary from season to season, depending on the rainfall patterns.

② Postberg Nature Reserve
Located in the West Coast National Park, this popular flower-viewing spot is an easy day-trip from Cape Town, and visitors are rarely disappointed by its multicoloured bands of annuals stretching as far as the eye can see.

Key

━━ Tour route
═══ Other roads
--- Park boundary

⑦ Goegap Nature Reserve
Situated 15 km (9 miles) east of Springbok, the "capital" of Namaqualand, the Goegap Nature Reserve's flat plains and granite koppies support hundreds of succulents. Over the years, the reserve has recorded 580 plant species within its boundaries.

⑤ Nieuwoudtville Wildflower Reserve
This reserve contains the world's largest concentration of geophytes (plants with bulbs, corms or tubers). Of the 300 plant species, the more prominent ones are the irises and lily family.

④ Vanrhynsdorp
This town is situated in the stony *Knersvlakte* (a name that literally translates as "gnashing plains"). Spring ushers in dramatic displays of succulents such as *vygies*, and annuals such as *botterblom* and *gousblom* (*Ursinia sp*).

Key map locations: N7, Nieuwoudtville ⑤, Calvinia, R27, R27, ④, ng Bay, R364, ③, Clanwilliam, Clanwilliam Dam, Cederberg Mountains, Doring, Citrusdal, R303, Ceres, R399, Piketberg, Berg, West Coast National Park, Darling, R315, R27, Malmesbury, Paarl, Cape Town

0 kilometres 50
0 miles 25

③ Biedouw Valley
This valley is famous for its mesembryanthemums, a succulent species more commonly known by its Afrikaans name, *vygie*. Daisies and mesembryanthemums form the major group of Namaqualand's 4,000 floral species.

Tips for Drivers

Tour length: Due to the extent of the area, trips can vary from one to three days. Contact Cape Town Tourism for details of tour operators.

When to go: Flowers bloom Aug–Oct. Call Namaqualand Tourism for the best viewing areas. Flowers open only on sunny days, and are best between 11am and 4pm; drive with the sun behind you and the flowers facing you.

Where to stay and eat: Each town has its own hotel, as well as guesthouses and a camp site.

ℹ️ Cape Town Tourism:
ⓦ capetown.travel.com
Namaqualand Tourism:
027 712-2820;
ⓦ namaqualand.com

THE SOUTHERN CAPE

The Southern Cape's interior is characterized by its towering mountains, whose high-walled passes offer visitors a number of awe-inspiring scenic drives. The region's largest town, Oudtshoorn, upholds its reputation as the ostrich-farming capital, while on the coast, tourists are drawn to Hermanus every year to watch southern right whales from excellent vantage points along the coast.

The quaint seaside towns of the Southern Cape lie in a region known as the Overberg, which extends east of the Hottentots Holland Mountains, and is defined to the north by the Riviersonderend Mountains and the Langeberg and Outeniqua ranges. Along the coast, the Overberg stretches to the mouth of the Breede River, just north of the De Hoop Nature Reserve. Sir Lowry's Pass, a circuitous road that winds high above Gordon's Bay and offers splendid views across the False Bay coastline, is the gateway to the Overberg.

Early European settlers were prevented from crossing this formidable mountain barrier until Sir Lowry's Pass was constructed by Major Charles Michell in 1828. Before this, the Overberg was populated by the nomadic Khoi (see pp50–51), who were attracted by abundant mountain water and grazing for their herds. Elephant and other wildlife also roamed the area – in fact, the pass follows an ancient migratory trail, named *gantouw* (eland's path) by the indigenous peoples. As the settlers penetrated further into unexplored territory they faced another mountain barrier: north over the Langeberg and Outeniqua lay the Little Karoo, protected by the Swartberg Mountains. It was in this territory that two of South Africa's greatest road builders, Andrew Geddes Bain and his son, Thomas Bain, made their fame. The spectacular Four Passes Tour *(see pp234–5)* is a worthwhile excursion. Visitors can detour to the exquisite dripstone formations of the nearby Cango Caves or ride a giant bird at Oudtshoorn's ostrich farms.

At the coast, windswept Cape Agulhas marks the meeting point of the cold Atlantic and warm Indian oceans.

Thatched fishermen's cottages at Arniston (Waenhuiskrans)

◀ Whale breaching the surface at Hermanus, famed for its whale-watching opportunities

Exploring the Southern Cape

An alternative route to the N2 over Sir Lowry's Pass, which drops down into wheatfields and farmland dotted with cattle and woolly merino sheep, is the R44, a scenic road that hugs the coastline from Gordon's Bay to Hermanus. Further south, coastal hamlets such as Cape Agulhas – official meeting point of two oceans – offer a calm contrast to the majestic passes that lead through the mountains. Oudtshoorn is where the mansions of former "ostrich barons" can be seen, and nearby lies the underground splendour of the Cango Caves.

Wind-blown sand dunes at De Hoop Nature Reserve

Rocky beach near Arniston's cave

Getting Around

Once over Sir Lowry's Pass, the N2 cuts across the Southern Cape. The most scenic route to Oudtshoorn is to take the N2 to beyond Swellendam and turn onto the R324 after Buffelsjags, which goes via the Tradouws Pass to Barrydale. Here it joins the R62, which heads east to Oudtshoorn, the Cango Caves and the country's most dramatic passes, which are linked by the R328. All of the coastal towns are accessed via main routes feeding off the N2. The De Hoop Nature Reserve can be reached from both Bredasdorp and the N2. Tour operators offer day-trips, otherwise public transport is severely limited, so a car is essential for touring this region.

For hotels and restaurants in this region see pp386–7 and pp403–4

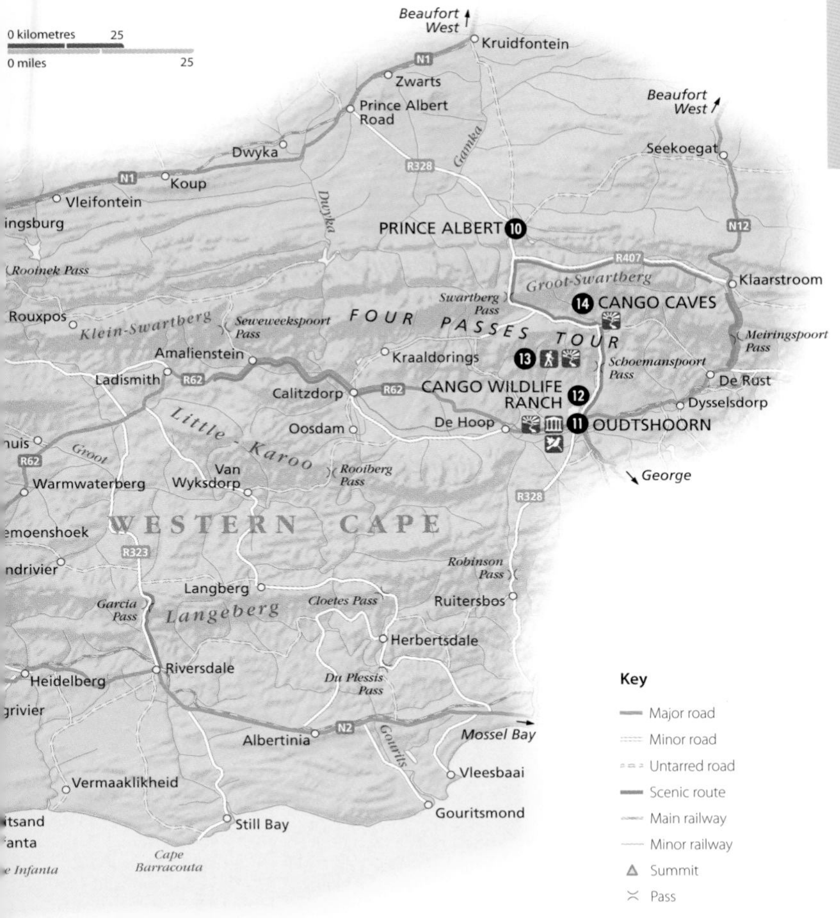

Map

0 kilometres 25
0 miles 25

Beaufort West

Kruidfontein

Zwarts

Prince Albert Road

Beaufort West

Dwyka

Seekoegat

Koup

N1

Vleifontein

ingsburg

Rooinek Pass

PRINCE ALBERT ⑩

Groot-Swartberg

Klaarstroom

N12

Rouxpos

Klein-Swartberg

Seweweekspoort Pass

Swartberg Pass

FOUR PASSES TOUR

⑭ CANGO CAVES

Meiringspoort Pass

Amalienstein

Kraaldorings

⑬

Schoemanspoort Pass

De Rust

Ladismith

R62

Calitzdorp

R62

CANGO WILDLIFE RANCH ⑫

Dysselsdorp

Oosdam

De Hoop

⑪ OUDTSHOORN

Little-Karoo

huis

R62

Groot

Van Wyksdorp

Rooiberg Pass

George

R328

Warmwaterberg

WESTERN CAPE

emoenshoek

R323

Robinson Pass

ndrivier

Langberg

Cloetes Pass

Ruitersbos

Garcia Pass

Langeberg

Herbertsdale

Heidelberg

Riversdale

Du Plessis Pass

grivier

N2

Mossel Bay

Vermaaklikheid

Albertinia

Gourits

Vleesbaai

tsand
anta

Still Bay

Gouritsmond

e Infanta

Cape Barracouta

Key

— Major road
···· Minor road
·-·- Untarred road
— Scenic route
—·— Main railway
— Minor railway
△ Summit
✕ Pass

Sights at a Glance

❶ Betty's Bay
❷ Kleinmond
❸ Hermanus
❹ Gansbaai
❺ Bredasdorp
❻ Cape Agulhas
❼ Arniston
❽ De Hoop Nature Reserve
❾ Swellendam
❿ Prince Albert
⓫ Oudtshoorn
⓬ Cango Wildlife Ranch
⓮ Cango Caves

Driving Tour
⓭ *Four Passes Tour pp234–5*

A group of residents at Highgate Ostrich Show Farm, near Oudtshoorn

For keys to symbols *see back flap*

● Betty's Bay

Road map B5. R44 SE of Gordon's Bay. 🗺 1,400. ℹ️ Protea Centre, Main Rd, Kleinmond, 028 271 5657.
Ⓦ ecoscape.org.za

This seaside village, named after Betty Youlden, the daughter of a property developer who lived here in the 1900s, is a popular weekend retreat. Hundreds of timber holiday cottages are scattered throughout the dunes, while the beach offers tremendous views across False Bay to the Cape Peninsula.

Of significance is the **Harold Porter National Botanical Garden** on the slopes of the Kogelberg, which rises behind Betty's Bay. Harold Porter, a partner in a property agents' business in the village, bought this tract of land in 1938 to preserve the rich mountain and coastal *fynbos* vegetation. More than 1,600 species of ericas, proteas and watsonias – one of the densest concentrations in the Southern Cape – attract sugarbirds and sunbirds. The Leopard Kloof Trail runs through dense riverine forest to a picturesque waterfall. The penguin reserve at Stoney Point (open daily) protects a small breeding colony of African penguins.

Wide lagoon mouth and beach at Kleinmond

Erica, Harold Porter Garden

🌐 **Harold Porter National Botanical Garden**
Cnr Clarence Dr and Broadwith rds.
Tel 028 272 9311. **Open** 8am–4:30pm Mon–Fri, 8am–5pm Sat & Sun. 🚶 📷 Ⓦ sanbi.org

● Kleinmond

Road map B5. R44 E of Betty's Bay. 🗺 2,900. ℹ️ Protea Centre, Main Rd, 028 271 5657. Ⓦ ecoscape.org.za

Surrounding Kleinmond, the stony hills with their thin green veneer of *fynbos* scrub once harboured small bands of Khoi and runaway slaves. In the 1920s, Kleinmond, at the foot of the Palmietberg, was a fishing settlement; today it is a holiday spot where rock angling for *kabeljou* (kob), and fishing for yellowtail and tunny are popular pastimes. Kleinmond Lagoon, where the Palmiet River reaches the sea, offers safe swimming and canoeing. Visitors can enjoy beautiful sea and mountain views from a well-planned network of hiking trails in the **Kogelberg Nature Reserve**, and maybe even glimpse some of the dainty, shy gazelles such as klipspringers, as well as the grysbok and steenbok that occur in the coastal fynbos and on the lower slopes of the mountain.

🌐 **Kogelberg Nature Reserve**
Off R44, 8 km (5 miles) W of Kleinmond. **Tel** 028 271 5138. **Open** 7:30am–4pm daily. 📷 🚶
Ⓦ capenature.co.za

● Hermanus

Road map B5. 🗺 32,800. 🚌 Bot River 30 km (19 miles) N on N2. ℹ️ Old Station Building, Mitchell Street, 028 312 2629. 🎭 Wine & Food Festival (Aug), Whale Festival (Oct).
Ⓦ hermanustourism.info

Originally established as a farming community by Hermanus Pieters, the town became a fashionable holiday and retirement destination due to the sunny climate and attractive location. Fishermen and sailors also found a relatively easy life, while visitors frequented the Windsor, Astoria and other august hotels. Today the town's grandeur is a little faded, but it still has plenty to offer most tourists.

The focal point is the **Old Harbour Open-Air Museum**, which traces the history of the town's whaling days, and contains a whale skull and old weapons. Fishermen's boats dating from 1850 to the mid-1900s lie restored and hull-up. There are also *bokkom* stands, racks on which fish are hung to dry in the sun, and reconstructed fishing shacks.

The tranquil Harold Porter Botanical Garden at Betty's Bay

For hotels and restaurants in this region see pp386–7 and pp403–4

Today, Hermanus is famous for its superb whale-watching sites. Every year, southern right whales *(see pp190–91)* migrate from the sub-Antarctic to calve in the shelter of Walker Bay. They arrive in June and leave again by December, but the peak whale-watching season is from September to October, when visitors are more than likely to sight the large mammals frolicking offshore. The town's official whale crier blows his kelp horn as he walks along Main Street, bearing a signboard that shows the best daily sighting places.

Hermanus has a beautiful coastline. Unspoiled beaches such as Die Plaat, a 12-km (7-mile) stretch from Klein River Lagoon to De Kelders, are perfect for walks and horse riding. A clifftop route extends from New Harbour to Grotto Beach – the regularly placed benches allow walkers to rest and to enjoy the superb views. Swimming is generally safe, and there is a tidal pool below the Marine Hotel, to the east of the old harbour.

Activities nearby include the Rotay Way, a 10-km (6-mile) scenic drive, and the Hermanus Wine Route, which features four vineyards in the pretty Hemel en Arde Valley.

The popular Marine Hotel in Hermanus

Approximately 20 km (12 miles) east of Hermanus lies **Stanford**, a rustic crafts centre. The heart of this little village contains many historic homes built in the late 1800s and early 1900s, and has been proclaimed a national conservation area. The early school building and Anglican Church both date back to 1880, while the reputedly haunted Spookhuis (ghost house) is dated about 1885.

Fernkloof Nature Reserve boasts 40 km (25 miles) of waymarked footpaths, a 5-km (3-mile) circular nature trail and more than a thousand species of fynbos.

🏛 Old Harbour Open-Air Museum
Marine Drive. **Tel** 028 312 1475.
Open 9am–4:30pm Mon–Sat, noon–4pm Sun. **Closed** Good Fri, 25 Dec.
📷 **W** old-harbour-museum.co.za

Whale-Watching in Hermanus

The World Wide Fund for Nature (WWF) has recognized Hermanus as one of the best land-based whale-watching spots on earth. October sees a peak in whale numbers (between 40 and 70 have been recorded). The mammals can be seen as close as 10 m (11 yd) away. Particularly special is the Old Harbour Museum's sonar link-up. A hydrophone buried in the seabed transmits the whale calls to an audio room on shore.

Cape Whale Coast logo

The rocky coastline around Hermanus offers good vantage points for whale-watchers

Coming face to face with a great white on a shark-diving expedition

❹ Gansbaai

Road map B5. R43 SE of Hermanus.
🗺 11,600. 𝒊 Kapokblom St,
028 384 1439. **Open** daily. 🏖
🆆 gansbaaiinfo.com

The name Gansbaai (Bay of Geese) originates from the flocks of Egyptian geese that used to breed here.

Gansbaai is renowned for the tragedy of HMS *Birkenhead*. In February 1852, this ship hit a rock off Danger Point, 9 km (6 miles) away, and sank with 445 men – all the women and children were saved. To this day, the phrase "Birkenhead Drill" describes the custom of favouring women and children in crisis situations.

From Gansbaai there are several boat trips to Dyer Island, where you can watch great white sharks feed on the seals that breed on nearby Geyser Island. This area is also home to large numbers of African penguins, another food source for the great whites that congregate here. Nicknamed "Shark Alley", the channel between the islands and the mainland is a popular destination for shark-diving.

❺ Bredasdorp

Road map B5. 🗺 15,500.

Bredasdorp lies in a region of undulating barley fields and sheep pasture. The town is a centre for the wool industry, but serves mainly as an access route to Cape Agulhas (via the R319) and Arniston (via the R316). The town's most interesting

feature is the **Shipwreck Museum**, which pays tribute to the southern coast's tragic history. This treacherous length of coastline has been labelled the "graveyard of ships" as its rocky reefs, gale-force winds and powerful currents make it one of the most dangerous in the world. Since 1552, more than 130 ships have foundered here, an average of one wreck per kilometre of coast.

The best time to visit Bredasdorp's Heuningberg Nature Reserve is from mid-September to mid-October, when the countryside becomes bathed in colour from hundreds of blooms bursting into flower. It is home to a number of South African endemic plants and of these, the Bredasdorp lily *(Cyrtanthus guthriea)* is found only on the Heuningberg Mountain.

🏛 Shipwreck Museum

Independent St. **Tel** 028 424 1240.
Open 9am–4:45pm Mon–Fri, 9am–2:45pm Sat, 10:30am–12:30pm Sun.
Closed Good Fri, 25 Dec, 1 Jan. 🈂

This museum was officially opened in April 1975 and is housed in an old rectory and church hall, both of which have been declared national monuments. The rectory, built in 1845, is furnished in the style of a 19th-century townhouse typical of South Africa's southern coast. The interiors and furnishings contain artifacts from the many shipwrecks that occurred along this capricious stretch of coastline. The salvaged wood, as well as ships' decor, frequently appear in door and window frames and in the ceiling rafters.

The museum is full of shipwrecked figureheads, porcelain, cannons, anchors, old bottles and coins. The beautiful marble-topped washstand in the bedroom was salvaged from the *Queen of the Thames*, which sank in 1871, while the medicine chest came from the *Clan MacGregor*, which was shipwrecked in 1902.

The church hall, dating back to 1864, is now called the Shipwreck Hall. Its rather gloomy interior is a suitable environment for the interesting and diverse relics displayed in glass cases, all of which were recovered from major shipwrecks in the area.

Figurehead, Shipwreck Museum

A 19th-century kitchen in the Shipwreck Museum at Bredasdorp

Arniston's fishermen live in Kassiesbaai

❻ Cape Agulhas

Road map B5. R319, 45 km (28 miles) S of Bredasdorp. Agulhas National Park: **Tel** 028 435 6078. **Open** daily. 🅿 🆆 sanparks.org

Cape Agulhas was named by early Portuguese navigators – the first to round Africa in the 15th century. At the southernmost point of their journey, the sailors noticed that their compass needles were unaffected by magnetic deviation, pointing true north instead. They called this point the "Cape of Needles".

At this promontory, where the tip of the African continental shelf disappears undramatically into the sea to form what is known as the Agulhas Bank *(see p28),* the Atlantic and Indian oceans merge. The only physical evidence of this convergence is a simple stone cairn.

This is one of the world's most treacherous stretches of coast. The often-turbulent waters are shallow, rock-strewn and subject to heavy swells and currents.

This is the graveyard of more than 250 once-proud vessels, including the Japanese trawler *Meisho Maru 38,* whose rusting wreck can be seen 2 km (1 mile) west of the Agulhas Lighthouse.

The area around the southernmost tip of Africa is now part of the Agulhas National Park.

🏛 Lighthouse and Museum
Tel 028 435 7185. **Open** 9am– 5pm daily. 🅿

Agulhas Lighthouse, whose design is based on the ancient Pharos Lighthouse of Alexandria in Egypt, was built in 1848. After the Green Point lighthouse in Cape Town, it is the oldest working lighthouse in southern Africa. It fell into disuse, but was restored and reopened in 1988.

Today, its lamp is visible for 30 nautical miles. There are 71 steps to the top of the tower, which affords superb views of the coast and seascape.

A plaque at Cape Agulhas

❼ Arniston

Road map B5. 🅼 1,500.

Arniston's name originates from the British vessel *Arniston,* which was wrecked east of the settlement in May 1815. Tragically, of the 378 soldiers on board, who were homebound from Ceylon (now Sri Lanka), only six survived. The little fishing settlement is located some 24 km (15 miles) southeast of Bredasdorp, off the R316, and is characterized by its turquoise waters.

The locals call the village Waenhuiskrans (wagonhouse cliff), after a cave situated 2 km (1 mile) south of the modern Arniston Hotel that is large enough to accommodate serveral fully spanned ox wagons. The cave is accessible only at low tide, however, and visitors should beware of freak waves washing over the slippery rocks.

Kassiesbaai is a cluster of rough-plastered and thatched fishermen's cottages with traditional tiny windows to keep out the midday heat. This little village lies to the north of Arniston, very close to undulating white sand dunes. Further to the south lies Roman Beach, which is especially good for youngsters, with its gently sloping seabed, rock pools and caves. Continuing further from here is a windy, wild rocky point that attracts many hopeful anglers.

Agulhas Lighthouse is at the southernmost point of Africa

Mountain biking in the De Hoop Nature Reserve

❽ De Hoop Nature Reserve

Road map B5. R319, 56 km (35 miles) W of Bredasdorp. **Tel** 028 542 1114. **Open** 7am–7pm daily (to 6pm May–Sep). Permits required for hiking and mountain-biking. 🏞
🌐 capenature.co.za

This reserve encompasses a 50-km (31-mile) stretch of coastline, weathered limestone cliffs and spectacular sand dunes, some of which tower as high as 90 m (295 ft). De Hoop's main attraction is a 14-km (9-mile) wetland that is home to 12 of South Africa's 16 waterfowl species.

Eland at De Hoop Nature Reserve

Thousands of red-knobbed coot, yellow-billed duck and Cape shoveller, as well as Egyptian geese, can be seen here, although populations do fluctuate with the water level of the marshland. The bird-watching is best between the months of September and April, when migrant flocks of Palaearctic waders arrive. Of the 13 species that have been recorded, visitors may expect to see ringed plover, wood and curlew sandpiper, greenshank and little stint.

The rich variety of *fynbos* species includes the endemic Bredasdorp sugarbush (*Protea obtusfolia*), stinkleaf sugarbush (*Protea susannae*) and pincushion protea (*Leucospermum oliefolium*).

Wildlife can also be seen in the reserve, and there is a short circular drive from the rest camp to Tierhoek. Species to look out for are the rare Cape mountain zebra and bontebok, eland, grey rhebok, baboons and the yellow mongoose.

A mountain bike trail traverses the Potberg section of the reserve, which contains a breeding colony of the rare Cape vulture. Comfortable camp sites and self-catering cottages are available and overnight visitors can experience the spectacular southern night sky almost free of light pollution. De Hoop is also the start of the popular 5-day Whale Trail hike along the coast, which must be booked well in advance.

❾ Swellendam

Road map B5. 🏛 17,550. 🚉 22 Swellengrebel Street, 028 514 2770. **Open** 9am–5pm Mon–Fri, 9am–2pm Sat & Sun.
🌐 swellendamtourism.co.za

Nestling in the shadow of the Langeberg Mountains, Swellendam is one of South Africa's most picturesque small towns. The country's third-oldest town, after Cape Town and Stellenbosch, Swellendam was founded by the Dutch in 1742 and named after the governor and his wife.

The thatched-roofed and whitewashed **Drostdy** was built by the Dutch East India Company in 1747 as the seat of the *landdrost*, or magistrate. It now serves as a museum of Dutch colonial life. Built shortly afterwards, the Old Gaol is situated at the rear of the Drostdy. Originally it was a simple, single-storey building with lean-to cells, but it was subsequently enlarged to include an enclosed courtyard created by linking the two cell blocks with high walls.

Near the museum is the *Ambagswerf* (trade yard), which features a smithy and wagonmaker's shop, a mill and bakery, a tannery, a cooperage and a coppersmith. Crafts demonstrations are held here regularly. Also on site is the pretty Mayville Cottage. Built between 1853 and 1855, it represents a transition of architectural styles, using both Cape Dutch and Cape Georgian influences. Its rose garden features heritage species.

Swellendam is renowned for its many fine old buildings. The **Oefeningshuis** was built in 1838 as a school for freed slaves. An interesting feature of the building is the clock designed for the illiterate: when the time painted on the sculpted clock face matches that on the real clock below, then it is time for worship.

Also noteworthy are the imposing Dutch Reformed Church, the wrought-iron balconies of the Buirski & Co shop, which opened for trade in 1880, and the elegant Auld House on the same street.

The whitewashed Dutch Reformed Church in Swellendam

Scenic view of the Swartberg Pass from the village of Prince Albert

🏛 Drostdy

18 Swellengrebel Street. **Tel** 028 514 1138. **Open** 9am–4:45pm Mon–Fri, 10am–3pm Sat & Sun. **Closed** 1 Jan, Easter, 25 Dec. 🎫 🎫 🖥

W drostdymuseum.com

Environs

Bontebok National Park is 6 km (4 miles) outside Swellendam. This scenic wilderness was set up to protect the endangered species of antelope after which it was named. The bontebok has since recovered enough to share the habitat with several other introduced animals. Most of the park is accessible by car, and there are excellent self-guided walking trails.

The more challenging 74-km (46-mile) Swellendam Trail takes in the Marloth Nature Reserve, along the southern slopes of the Langenberg Mountains. Continuing along the N2, the **Garden Route Game Lodge** is 129 km (80 miles) beyond Swellendam. It has been stocked with a number of species including giraffes, lions, elephants, white

rhinos, kudu, zebra, wildebeest and buffalo, and there is a reptile centre. A popular excursion from Cape Town, it is one of the nearest places to the city for wildlife viewing.

🛡 Bontebok National Park

Tel 028 514 2735. **Open** 7am–7pm daily (to 6pm May–Sep). 🏕 🏠

W sanparks.org

🛡 Garden Route Game Lodge

Off the N2, 7 km (4 miles) east of Albertinia. **Tel** 028 735 1200. **Open** daily. 🎫 🎫 🎫

W grgamelodge.co.za

❿ Prince Albert

Road map C5. 🏔 7,100. 🛈 Fransie Pienaar Museum, Church Street, 023 541 1366. **Open** daily. 🎫 Olive Festival (Apr). **W** princealbert.org.za

This pretty village, which is part of the Four Passes Tour *(see pp234–5)*, has several attractions. The **Fransie Pienaar Museum**, which hosts one of the world's largest fossil collections, also houses the tourist information centre,

where guided walking tours of Prince Albert can be booked.

The **Prince Albert Gallery**, opposite the museum, was set up by local artists who wanted to find a venue to show their work. There are regular exhibitions of paintings, sculpture and photographs. The Gallery Café is open for dinner. On Saturday mornings, in the square opposite the museum, there is a food and crafts market, and each April, Prince Albert holds a popular olive, food and wine festival *(see p42)*, with live entertainment and stalls selling local produce.

Environs

The spectacular Swartberg Pass, key to the Karoo Desert, starts just 2 km (1 mile) from Prince Albert. The slopes of the pass provide the irrigation that makes the village an oasis in this arid area. The pass was built by the road engineer Thomas Bain after heavy floods in 1875 swept away the previous road, depriving local farmers of their link with the nearest seaports.

🏛 Fransie Pienaar Museum

42 Church St. **Tel** 023 541 1172. **Open** 9:30am–4:30pm Mon–Fri, 9:30am–noon Sat, 10:30am–11:30am Sun. **Closed** public hols. 🎫

🏛 Prince Albert Gallery

57 Church St. **Tel** 023 541 1057. **Open** 9am–4pm Mon–Fri, 9:30am–2pm Sat. 🎫 from 6:30pm.

W princealbertgallery.co.za

Beautiful proteas blooming on the Swartberg Pass

⓫ Oudtshoorn

Road map C5. N12 from George.
🏚 95,900. 🛈 80 Voortrekker St,
044 279 2532. **Open** Mon–Sat.
🌐 oudtshoorn.com

The town of Oudtshoorn was established in 1847 at the foot of the Swartberg Mountains, to cater for the needs of the Little Karoo's growing farming population. It gained prosperity when the demand for ostrich feathers – to support Victorian, and later Edwardian fashion trends – created a sharp rise in the industry in 1870–80.

The Karoo's hot, dry climate proved suitable for big-scale ostrich farming – the loamy soils yielded extensive crops of lucerne, which forms a major part of the birds' diet, and the ground was strewn with the small pebbles that are a vital aid to their somewhat unusual digestive processes (see box on opposite page).

Oudtshoorn's importance as an ostrich-farming centre continued for more than 40 years, and the town became renowned for its sandstone mansions, built by wealthy ostrich barons. However, World War I and changes in fashion resulted in the industry's decline, and many farmers went bankrupt. Ostrich farming eventually recovered in the 1940s with the establishment of the tanning industry. Today, ostrich products include eggs, leather, meat and bonemeal. The town also produces crops of tobacco, wheat and grapes.

Visitors to Cango Wildlife Ranch can stroke tame cheetahs

⓬ Cango Wildlife Ranch

Road map C5. R328 to Cango Caves.
Tel 044 272 5593. **Open** 8am–5pm
daily. 🚻 ♿ 🅿 🌐 cango.co.za

Part wildlife sanctuary, part theme park, the ranch lies 3 km (2 miles) north of Oudtshoorn. Since the establishment of the Cheetah Conservation Foundation in 1993, the ranch has ranked among the leading cheetah breeders in Africa and is one of the world's top five protection institutions. The breeding enclosure is not accessible, but visitors may enter a fenced area to interact with tame cheetahs.

Walkways elevated over a natural bushveld environment

Nile crocodile at the Cango Wildlife Ranch

allow the visitor close-up views of other powerful hunters, including lions, tigers and jaguars. The Valley of the Ancients is a well-forested string of lakes that are home to Nile crocodiles, pygmy hippos, monitor lizards and otters, while birds include flamingos and storks. You can watch the crocodiles being fed by hand, and other thrills include crocodile cage-diving. Lemur Falls is the newest exhibit: built to replicate a Madagascan forest, it is home to three species of Madagascan lemur – brown, ring-tail and white ruff. Exotic snakes in the Snake Park include a black mamba, a king cobra, a 4-m (13-ft) boa constrictor and a copperhead viper.

The ranch has a well-regarded programme of tours and special events, a fast-food outlet and a restaurant that serves, among other things, crocodile and ostrich meat.

A sandstone "feather palace" on the outskirts of Oudtshoorn

The early 20th-century sandstone façade of the C P Nel Museum

The Ostrich's Unusual Eating Habits

Ostriches have neither teeth nor a crop, so have developed the habit of eating stones, which help to grind and digest their food. Perhaps by extension of this habit, or perhaps because they are naturally curious, there is little that an ostrich won't eat. A few years ago, an Oudtshoorn farmer was mystified by the theft of his washing – shirts, socks and trousers vanished every washday – until the death of one of his ostriches revealed the culprit. The birds have also been seen to eat babies' shoes, combs, sunglasses, buttons and earrings (ripped from the shirts and the ears of tourists).

Spark plugs and bullet cases – ostriches eat almost anything

🏛 C P Nel Museum

3 Baron van Reede St. **Tel** 044 272 7306. **Open** 8am–5pm Mon–Fri, 9am–1pm Sat. **Closed** public hols. 📷
🌐 cpnelmuseum.co.za

This building, formerly a boys' school, was designed in 1906 by the local architect Charles Bullock. Its green-domed sandstone façade is considered to be one of the best examples of stone masonry found anywhere in South Africa. The school hall was designed in 1913 by J E Vixseboxse.

The museum was named in honour of its founder, Colonel C P Nel. A series of dioramas traces the history of ostrich farming in the town and its community. Displays also depict the cultural history and lifestyle of the people of the Klein Karoo region, and the museum prides itself on its excellent replica of an early 20th-century pharmacy. There is a section devoted to the vital role played by the Jewish community in the development of Oudtshoorn's feather industry.

A carved ostrich egg lamp

🏛 Le Roux Townhouse

146 High St. **Tel** 044 272 3676. **Open** 9am–1pm and 2–5pm Mon–Fri, Sat & Sun by app. **Closed** public hols. 📷

Built in 1909, this is an outstanding example of the feather palaces of the time. As an annexe of the C P Nel Museum, it has exhibits of authentic European furniture from the period 1900–20 and a collection of porcelain, glassware and pieces made from Cape silver.

🦤 Highgate Ostrich Show Farm

Off R328 to Mossel Bay. **Tel** 044 272 7115. **Open** 8am–5pm daily. 📷 🎫
🏨 🅿 🌐 highgate.co.za

Located 10 km (6 miles) south of Oudtshoorn, this large farm offers a tour of its ostrich-breeding facilities where visitors can learn more about the various stages of the bird's development, and have an opportunity to cuddle the chicks, handle the eggs and visit an ostrich pen. The adventurous can even ride an ostrich. Those who don't have the nerve can watch jockeys take part in an ostrich derby. The tour length is 1.5 to 2 hours and the fee includes refreshments.

The curio shop offers ostrich-feather products, handbags, wallets, belts and shoes.

Coloured ostrich plumes are available in shops in Oudtshoorn

🦤 Safari Ostrich Show Farm

Off R328 to Mossel Bay. **Tel** 044 272 7311/2. **Open** 8am–4pm daily. 📷 🎫
🏨 🅿 🌐 safariostrich.co.za

Situated 5 km (3 miles) from Oudtshoorn, this show farm has more than 2,500 ostriches. The conducted tours leave every half-hour and include an ostrich race and visits to the breeding camp and museum.

Ostriches at Highgate Ostrich Show Farm in Oudtshoorn

⓭ Four Passes Tour

The Little Karoo is a region sharply defined by mountain ranges. Sandwiched between the Swartberg to the north and the Langeberg and Outeniqua mountains to the south, it is surrounded by spectacular peaks which severely tested the genius of South Africa's famous road engineer, Thomas Bain. The most majestic of the four passes is the one that winds its way through the Swartberg.

① Seweweekspoort

The pass is a 15-km (9-mile) gravel route through sheer walls of rough-hewn rock, criss-crossing a rivercourse that meanders through the Klein Swartberg mountains. Towering over the northern extent is the 2,325-m (7,628-ft) Seweweekspoort ("seven weeks pass") Peak. Local legend claims that this name refers to the time it used to take brandy smugglers to cross this route.

② Calitzdorp

The streets of this Karoo village are lined with Victorian houses. Nearby is a natural hot-spring spa, and some of the best port wines in the country are produced at Boplaas, Die Krans Estate and the Calitzdorp Wine Cellar.

Key

━━ Tour route

═══ Other roads

--- Park boundary

0 kilometres 10

0 miles   10

③ Oudtshoorn

The grand Victorian and Edwardian sandstone mansions in Oudtshoorn *(see p232)* were built on the riches reaped during the ostrich-feather boom of the 1880s. Lucerne (or alfafa), the favourite food of ostriches, flourished in the Karoo climate, enabling farmers to raise these flightless birds commercially.

⑤ Swartberg Pass
This spectacular 24-km (15-mile) gravel route took Bain's convict labour gang seven years to complete (see p231).

Tips for Drivers

Tour length: From Laingsburg on the N1: 337 km (209 miles); from Oudtshoorn: 175 km (109 miles).
Getting there: On the R323 from Laingsburg turn left after 19 km (12 miles). After 50 km (31 miles) turn right for Seweweekspoort. Take the R62 at Amalienstein, then head north on the R328. Before Prince Albert turn onto the R407 via Meiringspoort. To return to Oudtshoorn take the N12.
When to go: In spring–autumn. Passes may close during Jun–Aug due to snowfalls.

⑥ Prince Albert
Traditional architecture (see pp34–35) and a perennial spring that waters fruit and olive trees make this isolated village an old-fashioned delight.

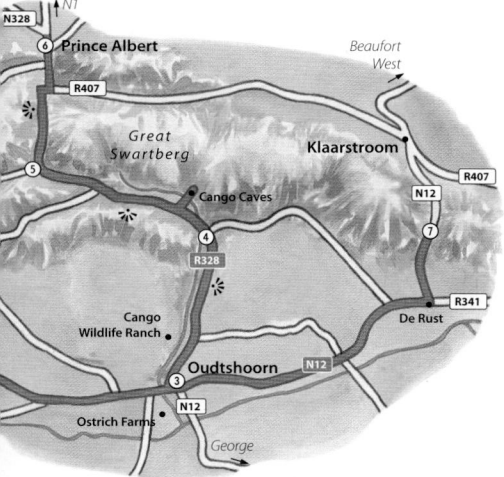

④ Schoemanspoort
This pass leads 10 km (6 miles) through a narrow chasm. It was built by Thomas Bain in 1862 along an existing bridle path near a mountain stream. Washed away in 1869, it took 11 years to rebuild the route above the flood level.

⑦ Meiringspoort
A 23-km (14-mile) long tarred route runs along the valley of the majestic Groot River gorge. The sandstone cliffs, coloured deep red and burned orange, loom above the pass in contorted folds, evidence of geological upheaval within the earth aeons ago.

⑭ Cango Caves

Road map C5. R328 from Oudtshoorn. **Tel** 044 272 7410. **Open** 9am–5pm daily. **Closed** 25 Dec. every hour. **w** cango-caves.co.za

Deep in the foothills of the Swartberg Mountains lies an underground network of chambers and passages, where dissolved minerals have crystallized to form stalactite and stalagmite dripstone formations that resemble fluted columns and delicate, ruffled drapes.

The complex was first explored by Jacobus van Zyl after his herdsman stumbled upon the cave opening in 1780, but rock paintings and stone implements discovered near the entrance indicate that the site was occupied as early as 80,000 years ago.

Only Cango 1 is open to the public. Access to Cango 2 and 3, discovered in 1972 and 1975 respectively, is prohibited in order to preserve the crystals. Some of the dramatic dripstone formations in Cango 1, which is 762 m (2,500 ft) in length, are the 9-m (30-ft) high Cleopatra's Needle, which is believed to be some 150,000 years old, a dainty Ballerina and a Frozen Waterfall. The largest chamber is Van Zyl's Hall, 107 m (350 ft) long and 16 m (52 ft) high.

An hour-long standard tour takes in the first six chambers, while the full tour is a 1.5-hour hike with 416 stairs that is best attempted only by the fit. The temperature inside is a constant 18°C (64°F), but humidity can reach an uncomfortable 99.9 per cent.

Stalagmite and stalactite dripstone formations in the Cango Caves

THE GARDEN ROUTE TO GRAHAMSTOWN

This magnificent stretch of coastline encompasses mountains, rivers, lagoons, lakes, beaches and the indigenous forests and wetlands of the Garden Route National Park, which comprises the Tsitsikamma, Wilderness and Knysna regions.

The Garden Route, backed by the Outeniqua, Tsitsikamma and Langkloof mountain ranges, extends all the way from Mossel Bay in the west to the Storms River Mouth in the east.

In 1780, French naturalist Francois Le Vaillant wrote of the area: "Nature has made an enchanted abode of this beautiful place." In the 1800s, however, furniture makers began to value the indigenous hardwoods, and large tracts of Outeniqua yellowwood (*Podocarpus falcatus*), ironwood (*Olea capensis*), and the smaller stinkwood (*Ocotea bullata*) were felled by the European settlers. Of the original forest, only 650 sq km (251 sq miles) has survived, of which 430 sq km (166 sq miles) is on state land. Nowadays, plantations of exotic pines and bluegum supply the paper mills, as well as the furniture-making and building industries.

Tourists are drawn to the Garden Route for its scenic drives, forested walks and trails and pristine coastline, as well as the tranquil inland lakes and lagoons. The birdlife is spectacular. Knysna alone has recorded more than 230 different species, among them the African spoonbill, osprey and avocet. Of special interest among forest birds are the Knysna lourie and Narina's trogon.

Plettenberg Bay is an upmarket coastal retreat. Balmy weather attracts visitors even in the winter months.

Beyond the Garden Route, Port Elizabeth, the centre of South Africa's car-manufacturing industry, has lovely golden beaches and is famous for its Bayworld Complex.

A group of ostriches along the Garden Route

◀ Sandstone cliffs surrounding the beautiful Knysna lagoon

Exploring the Garden Route to Grahamstown

The Garden Route, from Wilderness to the end of Tsitsikamma, where the N2 heads inland for the last stretch to Port Elizabeth, is a scenic treat. Upon leaving the town of Wilderness, vehicles can park at Dolphin's Point for an uninterrupted view of the coastline with its long white rollers. After Wilderness, the N2 hugs the coast almost all the way to Knysna. From here it passes through indigenous forest as far as Storms River. Between Nature's Valley and Storms River, detours can be made off the N2 to cross the spectacular old pass routes of Grootrivier and Bloukrans. Lush vegetation, mountains, lagoons, rivers and the sea combine to make this route a visual feast.

The beach at Nature's Valley

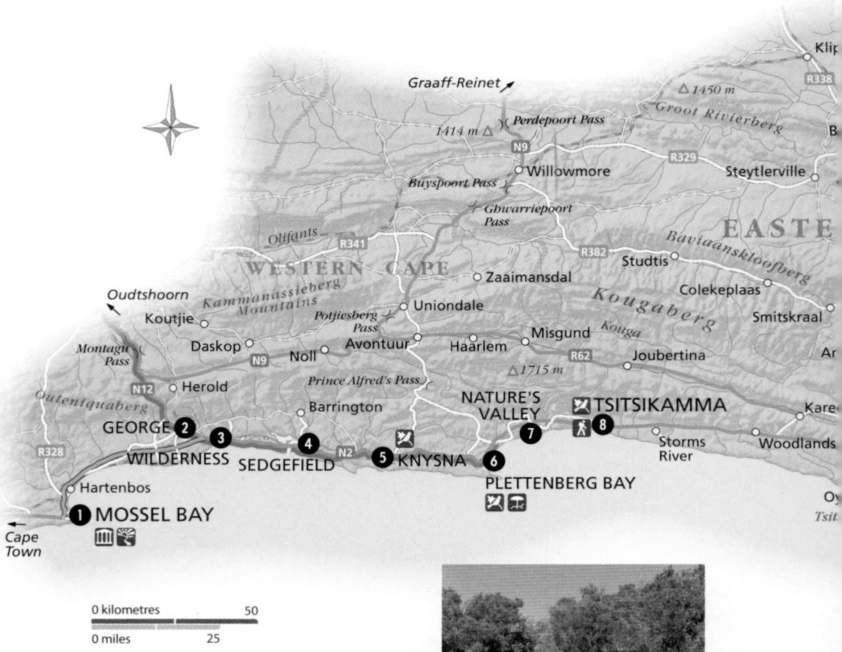

Visitors on a nature walk at the picturesque Knsyna Lagoon

Key

▬▬ Motorway

── Major road

▭▭▭ Minor road

▪▪▪ Untarred road

── Scenic route

▬▬▬ Main railway

▭▭▭ Minor railway

▬▬ Provincial border

△ Summit

✕ Pass

ting Around

N2 traverses the entire length
e Garden Route, from Mossel
o Port Elizabeth and beyond,
s way up the east coast.
ough coach tours to the area
vailable, travel by car is ideal as
ows the visitor to explore the
y coastal towns along the way
sure. The seven- and five-day
g trails of Tsitsikamma, as well
orter forest walks, may also
e visitors to linger. There are
estic airports at Port Elizabeth
George.

At a waterhole in the Addo Elephant National Park

Knysna Lagoon as seen from the Heads

Sights at a Glance

1. *Bartolomeu Dias Museum Complex (Mossel Bay) pp240–41*
2. George
3. Wilderness
4. Sedgefield
5. Knysna
6. Plettenberg Bay
7. Nature's Valley
8. *Tsitsikamma pp248–9*
9. St Francis Bay
10. Jeffreys Bay
11. *Port Elizabeth pp250–53*
12. Addo Elephant National Park
13. Shamwari Game Reserve
14. Alexandria
15. Port Alfred
16. *Grahamstown pp256–7*

For keys to symbols *see back flap*

❶ Bartolomeu Dias Museum Complex (Mossel Bay)

The Bartolomeu Dias Museum Complex, established in 1988, celebrates the 500th anniversary of Dias's historic landfall. A full-sized replica of his ship was built in Portugal in 1987 and set sail for Mossel Bay, arriving on 3 February 1988. Here, the 130-ton vessel was lifted from the water and lowered into the specially altered museum with its high, angled roof, clerestory windows and sunken floor for the keel.

★ The Caravel
The intrepid Spanish and Portuguese seafarers of the 15th and 16th centuries sailed into the unknown in small two- or three-masted ships like this.

Letter Box
Mail posted in this unusual post box in the museum complex is marked with a special postmark.

Post Office Tree
The 16th-century seafarers left messages for each other in a shoe suspended from a milkwood tree, like this one next to the museum building.

KEY

① **Barrels** filled with fresh water were stored in the hold.

② **Rudder**

③ **Portuguese flag**

④ **Lateen sails** are characteristic of Mediterranean ships.

⑤ **The pennant** flown at the top of the main mast bore the Portuguese royal coat of arms (the House of Braganza).

⑥ **The red cross** of the Order of Christ was emblazoned on the sails of Portuguese sailing vessels.

⑦ **Pulleys and ropes** enabled sailors to furl and unfurl the sails at great speed.

⑧ **Anchor**

⑨ **Rope ladder**

Crew Cabin
Cramped confines in the crew's quarters left little room for privacy on sea voyages that often lasted many months.

VISITORS' CHECKLIST

Practical Information
Road map C5. Mossel Bay.
Cnr Church and Market sts,
044 691 2202. Museum: 1 Market
St. **Tel** 044 691 1067.
W diasmuseum.co.za

★ **Stained-Glass Windows**
Three beautiful windows by Ria
Kriek commemorate the early
voyages of discovery. Shown here
are the sails of the Dias caravel.

The Epic Voyage of Dias

*A small fleet left Portugal around August 1487
under the command of Bartolomeu Dias
(see p50). The explorer made several
landfalls on the West African coast, erecting*
padrões *(stone crosses) along the way. In
February 1488, he dropped anchor off the
South African coast. The inlet he named
after São Bras (St Blaize) is today
called Mossel Bay.*

Exploring Mossel Bay and the Bartolomeu Dias Museum Complex

One of the main attractions
in the seaside town of Mossel
Bay, situated 397 km (246 miles)
east of Cape Town, is the
interesting museum complex
and the historic centre, both
overlooking the harbour.

Seafaring history is the subject
at the Bartolomeu Dias Museum
Complex. Apart from the
outstanding reconstruction of
Dias's caravel, there are old maps,
photographs and documents
detailing the first explorations
around the tip of Africa. The
complex also includes the Protea
Hotel Mossel Bay, which dates
back to 1846 and is thought to
be the oldest building in town.

The town is probably best-
known for its controversial and
costly Mossgas development,
initiated by the discovery of
natural offshore gas fields.

The real charm of the settlement lies in its natural beauty,
fine beaches and walks. The
15-km (9-mile) St Blaize Hiking
Trail winds along an unspoiled
stretch of coastline from Bat's
Cave to Dana Bay. Santos Beach,
the only north-facing beach in
South Africa, guarantees sunny
afternoons and safe swimming.

Regular cruises take visitors
out to **Seal Island**, while **White
Shark Africa** offers shark cage
dives or snorkelling and certi-
fication diving courses.

Romonza–Seal Island Trips
Mossel Bay Harbour. **Tel** 044 690 3101.
W mosselbay.co.za/romonza

White Shark Africa
7 Church St. **Tel** 044 691 3796.
W whitesharkafrica.com

Bartolomeu Dias Museum Complex

Protea Hotel
Mossel Bay

Maritime
Museum

MARKET ST

The
Granary

P

CHURCH ST

SANTOS RD

Post Office
Tree

GRAVE ST

FOOTPATH

Fountain

FOOTPATH

Malay
Graves

Munrohoek
Cottages

Ethno-Botanical
Garden

Shell Museum

FOOTPATH

0 metres   100

0 yards   100

Cape fur seals on Seal Island, Mossel Bay

For keys to symbols *see back flap*

❷ George

Road map C5. 🅜 193,700.
✈ 10 km (6 miles) NW of town.
🚌 St Mark's Sq. ℹ 124 York St, 044
801 9299. **Open** Mon–Sat.
Ⓦ georgetourism.org.za

The wide streets of George were
laid out in 1811 during the British
occupation of the Cape. Named
after King George III, the town is
today the Garden Route's largest
centre, primarily serving the
farming community. Victoria Bay,
9 km (6 miles) from George
off the N2, is the closest beach,
nestled in a pretty narrow cove.

The **Outeniqua Transport
Museum** provides an insight into
the history of steamtrain travel
in South Africa. The **Outeniqua
Nature Reserve** is the starting
point for 12-day walks in the
indigenous forest of the
Outeniqua Mountains. At least
125 tree species grow here, and
more than 30 forest birds have
been recorded. The Tierkop Trail
is a circular overnight route that
covers 30 km (19 miles). The
difficult Outeniqua Trail between
here and Knysna covers 108 km
(67 miles) in seven days.

🏛 **Outeniqua Transport Museum**
2 Mission St. **Tel** 044 801 8288.
Open Sep–Apr: 8am–5pm Mon–
Sat; May–Aug: 8am–4:30pm
Mon–Fri, 8am–2pm Sat. ♿
Ⓦ outeniquachootjoe.co.za

🦅 **Outeniqua Nature Reserve**
Witfontein. On R28 NW of George.
Tel 044 870 8323. **Open** 7:30am–4pm
Mon–Fri. Ⓦ capenature.co.za

Beach houses at Victoria Bay, a pretty beach
with a tidal pool, ideal for children

❸ Wilderness

Road map C5. N2 12 km (7 miles)
SE of George. 🅜 6,200.
ℹ Leila's Lane, 044 877
0045. **Open** Mon–Sat.
Ⓦ wildernessinfo.org

Ten kilometres
(6 miles) east of the
city of George is South
Africa's lake district. This
chain of salt- and fresh-
water lakes at the foot
of forested mountain
slopes forms part of
the Wilderness sector
of the **Garden Route National
Park**. Protecting some 30 km
(19 miles) of unspoiled coastline, the park features two long
white beaches – Wilderness
and Leentjiesklip. However,
note that swimming is
not safe here due to the
strong undercurrents.

Of the five lakes in this
region, the three westernmost

ones – Island Lake, Langvlei
and Rondevlei – are all linked
and fed by the Touws River
via a natural water channel
called the Serpentine.
Swartvlei is the largest and
deepest lake, and it is
connected to the sea by
an estuary, although its
mouth silts up for six months
of the year. Groenvlei, which
is the only lake not located
within the park, is not fed by
any river and has no link to the
sea. Instead, it receives its
water through springs and
rainfall; as a result, it is
the least brackish.

Birdlife viewing in the park
is excellent, with as many as
79 of the country's waterbird
species having been
recorded here. Five
species of kingfisher
can be spotted –
pied, giant, half-
collared, brown-
hooded and
malachite. The
area is also popular
for angling and a
variety of water-
sports, and a sceni[c]

A malachite kingfisher

drive starting at Wilderness
runs along Lakes Road, which
skirts the lake chain and meet[s]
up with the N2 at Swartvlei.

There are many hiking trails
in and around Wilderness. Wit[h]
the magnificent Outeniqua
range stretched along the
northern perimeter of the area[,]
visitors can ramble through
natural forests on such trails a[s]
the Brown-Hooded Kingfisher
Trail, the Pied Kingfisher Trail,
the five-day Biking & Hiking
Trail or the three-day Canoe &
Hiking Trail.

Horse trails can be followed,
and more extreme activities
such as paragliding and
abseiling can be enjoyed. At
Wilderness Heights, the Map o[f]
Africa can be found, a foreste[d]
area shaped like the African
continent. Splendid views
of the river valley can be
admired from here.

Wilderness is worth
exploring, particularly if you
enjoy water or adventure
sports. For the most daring
visitors, one-day paragliding

Steam locomotive at the Outeniqua Transport Museum

For hotels and restaurants in this region see pp387–8 and pp404–5

Paragliding over the beautiful coastline near Sedgefield

courses with a full-time instructor are available at **Cloudbase Paragliding**.

Off the N2, between Wilderness and Sedgefield, is **Timberlake Farm Village**, a collection of charming wooden cabins with a café, a country deli and a wine shop. Activities here include a quad-bike course, a mountain bike trail, a delightful fairy-themed garden, an adventure playground for children and a zipline cable ride between aerial platforms in the trees.

The **Goukamma Nature Reserve** borders on the Garden Route National Park and supports grysbok and blue duiker. Resident Cape clawless otters are also present, though they are seldom seen. Of the several hiking trails, the circular Bush Pig Trail starts from the reserve office and takes about 2–3 hours. It runs along a fynbos-covered ridge of dunes with fine views of the ocean, and returns via a milkwood forest. Kayak and pedalo hire and guided horse riding along the beach are also on offer.

Garden Route National Park (Wilderness)
044 877 1197. **Open** 7am–8pm daily.
sanparks.org

Cloudbase Paragliding
Tel 044 877 1414. cloudbase-paragliding.co.za

Timberlake Farm Village
N2 between Wilderness and Sedgefield. **Tel** 044 882 1211.
Open 8am–5pm daily.
timberlakeorganic.co.za

Goukamma Nature Reserve
8 km (5 miles) from the N2 on the Buffalo Bay road. **Tel** 044 383 0042.
Open 8am–6pm daily.
capenature.co.za

❹ Sedgefield

Road map C5. N2 21 km (13 miles) E of Wilderness.
8,500. Shell Garage, Main Street. 30 Main Street, 044 343 2007. **Open** Mon–Sat.
visitknysna.co.za

Between Wilderness and Knysna, the small coastal town of Sedgefield can be a useful base for visitors planning a visit to the Goukamma Nature Reserve (see left). Sedgefield also boasts a variety of its own attractions, and this has resulted in some resort-type developments being built along the previously unspoiled beach front.

Sedgefield Beach offers safe swimming (perfect for families), or you may fish for bass at Cola Beach, Myoli Beach, Swartvlei Beach or Gerike's Point. In addition to the several lakes and beaches, there are pretty forest and lakeside walking trails.

Fairy Knowe, a popular hotel near Wilderness

❺ Knysna

Road map C5. 🔼 69,000. 🚉 Old railway station near the Knysna Quays. 🛈 40 Main Rd, 044 382 5510. 🎭 Pink Loerie Mardi Gras (Apr–May), Oyster Festival (Jul). 🆆 **visitknysna.co.za**

A significant figure in Knysna's history was George Rex, who, according to local legend, was the son of Britain's King George III and his first wife Hannah Lightfoot, a Quaker (she never gained royal approval and was exiled after the birth of her son). The claim, made as a result of Rex's opulent lifestyle, was never proved. He played a leading role in developing the lagoon harbour, and his ship, the *Knysna*, regularly traded along the coast. At the time of his death, in 1839, he was the most prominent landowner in the area.

Furniture, boat building and oysters cultivated in the lagoon are Knysna's major industries. Today it is one of the Garden Route's most popular tourist destinations. The Knysna Quays is a modern complex developed around the old harbour, complete with restaurants, boutiques and souvenir shops. An extensive marina has been built on Thesen Island, linked to the town by a causeway, and has apartments, hotels, a man-made beach, and a pleasant park with bird hides overlooking the lagoon.

Paddle cruiser on the Knysna Lagoon

Environs

One of Knysna's most attractive features is the 17-km (11-mile) long Knysna Lagoon, which is protected from the sea by two sandstone cliffs, the Knysna Heads. George Rex Drive provides access to the Eastern Head, from where there are superb views. On the Western Head, accessible via a ferry run by the **Featherbed Co.**, is the private Featherbed Nature Reserve. The four-hour excursion includes the boat trip, a 2.5-km (2-mile) guided nature walk called the Bushbuck Trail, a short four-wheel-drive ride to the top of the Western Knysna Head, and a buffet lunch. In fine weather this is served outside, under a grove of milkwood trees.

Knysna loerie

The Featherbed Co. operates boats for sightseeing trips on the lagoon. The most popular is the *John Benn*, a double-storey pontoon and floating restaurant that departs twice daily on 90-minute cruises.

South Africa's largest commercial oyster-farming centre is based at Knysna Lagoon. Delicious Pacific oysters can be sampled on tasting tours organized by **Knysna Charters**, or at one of the restaurants on Thesen Island. Another popular culinary activity is a guided tour of Mitchell's Brewery, South Africa's oldest microbrewery, which prides itself on producing natural beers with no artificial preservatives or chemicals.

Only 200 m (656 ft) from Knysna's main road, the **Pledge Nature Reserve** is an urban reclamation project comprising a former brickfield located on the slopes north of the town centre. Created in 1991, the reserve has been restored to near pristine condition due to the the planting of indigenous trees and the creation of dams to purify streams. Criss-crossed by a network of wheelchair-friendly footpaths offering lovely views to the lagoon and Knysna Heads, the reserve contains more than 250 plant species, while a checklist of 80 bird species includes forest specialists such as Knysna loerie, olive bush shrike and African paradise flycatcher.

About 6 km (4 miles) east of Knysna, a turnoff to Noetzie ends at a clifftop parking area. From here visitors can descend a path to a secluded bay with a pristine beach and a quiet estuary guarded by five castles, all of which are now private homes.

Knysna Head promontories surrounding the lagoon entrance

For hotels and restaurants in this region see pp387–8 and pp404–5

Young wild African elephants playing in Knysna Elephant Park

🏠 **Featherbed Co.**
Knysna Quays, Waterfront Drive.
Tel 044 382 1693. 🚐
🌐 **knysnafeatherbed.com**

🏠 **Knysna Charters**
Long St, Thesen Island. **Tel** 082 892
0469. 🌐 **knysnacharters.com**

Mitchell's Brewery
New St. **Tel** 044 382 4685.
⏰ 12:30pm & 2.30pm Mon–Fri.
🌐 **mitchellsbrewery.com**

🏛 **Pledge Nature Reserve**
Bond St. **Tel** 044 382 3712.
Open summer: 7am–6pm daily;
winter: 8am–5pm daily.
🌐 **pledgenaturereserve.org**

🏕 **Knysna's Forests**
Knysna is surrounded by
some of South Africa's
most magnificent
indigenous forests. These
were protected in a patch-
work of state forest reserves,
including Diepwalle and
Harkerville, prior to 2009,
when 600 km (373 miles) of
forest around Knysna was
amalgamated into the newly
created Garden Route National
Park. This can be explored along
many walking trails, scenic drives,
cycling routes and picnic sites.

Despite past logging, the cool
evergreen forests around Knysna
support many impressively old
Outeniqua yellowwood, ironwood and stinkwood trees, while
the lichen-draped bark, lush ferns
and twisted lianas create a fairytale atmosphere. Plenty of wildlife inhabits the forest. The
famously elusive Knysna
elephants represent the last free-
ranging population in South
Africa, with only half a dozen
individuals surviving. More likely
to be seen are blue duiker, bushbuck, vervet monkey, bushpig

and a wealth of forest birds such
as the green-and-scarlet Knysna
turaco, Knysna wood-pecker and
Knysna scrub warbler.

Northwest of town, Goldfields
Drive leads to a picnic site at
Jubilee Creek lined with gold-
panning relics, then on to the old
mineshafts and machinery of
Millwood, a former gold-mining
settlement. A scenic drive north
of Knysna leads to the **Diepwalle Forest Station**, the start
point of a cycling route and the
circular Elephant Walk. The
Diepwalle Forest is also
home to the King
Edward Tree, a
gigantic Outeniqua
yellowwood that
stands 39 m (128 ft)
tall, has a circum-
ference of 7 m (23 ft), and
is around 650 years old.
On the north side of the N2, east
of Knysna, the "Garden of
Eden" is a patch of forest
that can be explored along
a few short circular trails
where many trees are labelled.
On the opposite side of the N2,
Harkerville Forest is traversed
by a set of mountain-biking trails

**Watsonia
flower**

that range from 12 km (7 miles)
to 23 km (14 miles), and emerge
from the forest to reveal some
dramatic coastal scenery.
Although walking is permitted
along these trails, the nearby
Kranshoek Trail, is surely a
contender for South Africa's
loveliest coastal day hike. Only 9
km (6 miles) long, this circular trail
passes through an exceptional
variety of habitats, including
indigenous forest, rocky seashore
and patches of Protea-studded
coastal fynbos. On the north side
of the N2, shortly after it exits
Harkerville Forest, lies **Knysna
Elephant Park**; a refuge and
rehabilitation centre for
unwanted elephants – orphans,
individuals rescued from culls,
former circus animals. Several of
the 40-plus elephants that have
passed through the facility since
it started in 1994 have been
relocated to other reserves, while
others remain as part of a small
permanent herd. The park is a hit
with children, who take delight in
touching, feeding or walking
with these relaxed animals.

🏞 **Diepwalle Forest Station**
R339, 20 km (12 miles) N of Knysna.
Tel 044 382 9762. **Open** 6am–6pm
daily. 🌐 **sanparks.org**

🏞 **Harkerville Forestry Station**
N2, 15 km (9 miles) east of Knysna.
Tel 044 532 7770. **Open** 6am–6pm
daily. 🌐 **sanparks.org**

🏞 **Knysna Elephant Park**
N2, 20 km (12 miles) east of Knysna.
Tel 044 532 7732. **Open** 8:30am–
4pm daily. 🌐 **knysnaelephant
park.co.za**

Hiker backpacking along the scenic Harkerville Coast

Steps leading down to one of the idyllic bays in Robberg Nature Reserve

❻ Plettenberg Bay

Road map C5. 🚗 31,200.
🚏 Shell Ultra City, Marine Way.
ℹ️ Melville's Corner, Main St.
Tel 044 533 4065. **Open** Mon–Sat.
🌐 plett-tourism.co.za

Upmarket Plettenberg Bay, 30 km (19 miles) east of Knysna, is the holiday playground of the wealthy. A coast of rivers, lagoons and white beaches, "Plett", as it is called by the locals, earned the name Bahia Formosa ("beautiful bay") from early Portuguese sailors.

The town is perched on red sandstone cliffs that rise above the coastline; its most recognized feature is a large luxury hotel complex on Beacon Island. South of the town, the **Robberg Nature Reserve** juts out into the sea, its cliffs rising to 148 m (486 ft) in places. The three trails on offer range from a 30-minute stroll to a four-hour hike, all offering fantastic views of the dramatically churning seas and pristine secluded bays. The reserve also extends 1.8 km (1.2 miles) offshore, protecting a range of vulnerable fish species, and dolphins are often seen, as are whales, in spring.

On the east side of the Keurbooms River Bridge on the N2, 7 km (4 miles) east of Plettenberg Bay, **Keurbooms River Nature Reserve** encompasses the headwaters

The pansy shell is Plettenberg Bay's emblem

of the Keurbooms River, which flows down from the Langkloof Mountains. Its forested gorge is well worth a voyage upstream by canoe, to enjoy the unspoiled beauty and birdlife – canoes can be hired from the reserve office. Look out for the Knysna loerie, malachite, giant kingfisher and sunbird.

🏞️ Robberg Nature Reserve
Robberg Rd. **Tel** 044 533 2125.
Open 7am–5pm daily (Dec–Jan: to 8pm). 🚗 🚶 🌐 **capenature. co.za**

🏞️ Keurbooms River Nature Reserve
On the N2. **Tel** 044 533 2125. **Open** 7am–5pm daily (Dec–Jan: to 8pm). 🚗 🚶 🚣
🌐 **capenature.co.za**

Environs

Situated south of the N2 about 10 km (6 miles) east of Plettenberg Bay, **Jukani Wildlife Sanctuary** is a refuge for carnivores rescued from breeding facilities and other non-viable circumstances. Indigenous carnivores such as lion, leopard, cheetah, honey-badger and spotted hyena are all present, along with a few exotic creatures such as a white tiger and a jaguar. Guided tours with experts take around 90 minutes.

Jukani Wildlife Sanctuary forms part of the award-winning South African Animal Sanctuary Alliance (SAASA), which also includes two other facilities. Just 10 km (6 miles) further east is the popular **Monkeyland Primate**

Sanctuary, the world's first only multi-species free-roaming primate sanctuary. It is home to more than a dozen different primate species, including baboons from South Africa, lemurs from Madagascar and athletic squirrel monkeys from South America, all of them rescued from domestic captivity.

Birds of Eden, situated right alongside Monkeyland, is the world's largest free-flight aviary. Its enormous dome spans a gorge lined with indigenous forest, and is divided by a walkway and suspension bridge. It is inhabited by more than 3,500 individual birds, comprising 200-plus indigenous and exotic species, ranging from colourful forest-loving macaws, toucans and turacos to majestic blue cranes (the national bird of South Africa) and 30 types of waterfowl.

Athletic squirrel monkeys can be found at Monkeyland Primate Sanctuary

Jukani Wildlife Sanctuary
Tel 044 5348409. **Open** 9am–4pm daily. Every 15–20 minutes. **w** jukani.co.za

Monkeyland
Tel. 044 534 8906. **Open** 8am–5pm daily. Hourly tours. **w** monkeyland.co.za

Birds of Eden
Tel 044 534 8906. **Open** 8am–5pm daily. **w** birdsofeden.co.za

❼ Nature's Valley

Tucked away in a forested gorge about 10 km (6 m) south of the N2, Nature's Valley is one of the prettiest but least-visited villages on the Garden Route. The village runs down to a magnificent sandy beach separated from the eastern border of the Garden Route's Tsitsikamma Sector by a wide, shallow and dramatically beautiful lagoon whose surface is usually as calm as the forested surrounds. The village lies at the centre of a 50 km (31 miles) network of day trails that lead deep into an ancient forest of towering yellowwoods, as well as traversing slopes lined with the country's most easterly tracts of fynbos. The cool forest is inhabited by a wealth of colourful birds, along with several types of antelope.

Non-hikers who want to explore the forest and enjoy the views can cruise slowly along a looping pair of backroads that connect Nature's Valley to the N2 at Kurland 22 km (14 m) east of Plettenberg Bay, and at Tsitsikamma, a further 13 km (8 miles) east. About 3.5 km (2 miles) east of the second junction, the Bloukrans River Bridge not only marks the provincial boundary between the Western Cape and Eastern Cape, but it is also the platform used for what is reputedly the world's highest commercial bungee jump at 216 m (709 ft).

Bloukrans River Bungee Jump
Tel 044 697 7001. **Open** 9am–5pm daily. **w** faceadrenalin.com

❽ Tsitsikamma

See pp248–9.

The beautiful sandy beach at St Francis Bay

❾ St Francis Bay

🏠 5,000. 🚌 Village Centre. **Tel** 042 294 0076. **w** stfrancistourism.co.za

Running along a wide sandy beach 30 km (19 miles) south of Jeffreys Bay, this picturesque seaside town of thatched and white-washed houses is known for its superb surfing, though it lacks the trendy scene associated with its northern neighbour, Jeffreys Bay. It is also very popular with hikers and nature-lovers thanks to the five nature reserves and abundant walking trails in the immediate vicinity. The pick among these is the **Cape St Francis Nature Reserve**, which protects a rocky headland and unspoiled coastline immediately south of town. Bottlenose dolphins and, from August–December, southern right whales, are often spotted off-shore, while terrestrial wildlife includes Cape grysbok, yellow mongoose, African black oyster-catcher and African penguin.

Since 1878, the Cape has been guarded by the 28 m (92 ft) tall Seal Point Lighthouse, which houses a small museum and offers fantastic views of the bay.

Cape St Francis Nature Reserve
Tel 042 298 0073. **w** capestfrancis.co.za

❿ Jeffreys Bay

🏠 27,000. 🚌 Da Gama Rd. **Tel** 042 293 2923. **w** jeffreysbaytourism.org

This once sleepy seaside town, reputedly named after the whaler Captain Jeffreys and referred to as "J-Bay" by locals, is now the centre of South Africa's surfer scene. It is often ranked among the world's top 10 surfing spots, with a tubing right-hand break that offers a ride more than 1 km (half a mile) long in the right conditions. The town is busiest in early July, when the World Surf League (WSL) holds its only African championship tour event there.

Jeffreys Bay's blue flag beach is perfect for sunbathing and swimming, while the **Jeffreys Bay Shell Museum**, established in 1945 by Charlotte Kritzinger, is the finest collection of its sort in the country, showcasing 600 plus shells from all around the world.

Jeffreys Bay Shell Museum
Da Gama Rd. **Tel** 042 293 2923. **Open** 9am–4pm Mon–Sat.

A surfer catching a wave at Jeffreys Bay, one of the area's best surfing spots

❽ Tsitsikamma

Tsitsikamma is a San word meaning "place of abundant waters". It is part of the Garden Route National Park and extends for 68 km (42 miles) from Nature's Valley to Oubosstrand, and stretches seawards for some 5.5 km (3 miles), offering licensed snorkellers and divers a unique "underwater trail". Within the park's boundaries lie two of South Africa's most popular hikes, the Tsitsikamma and Otter trails. Primeval forest, rugged mountain scenery and panoramic views contribute to their popularity with hikers.

★ **Yellowwood trees**
The yellowwood is protected as South Africa's national tree; its hard timber is highly valued.

Fynbos
The typical vegetation of this area is coastal fynbos, which consists of low-growing species of ericas and proteas.

Bloukrans River gorge is the site of an overnight trail hut.

Common dolphins
Hikers on the Otter Trail are sure to see dolphins frolicking in the waves.

★ **Otter Trail**
This five-day coastal hike was the country's first official trail and stretch⋯ from the mouth of the Storms River t⋯ the superb beach at Nature's Valley. Hikers may spot whales, dolphins, se⋯ and Cape clawless otters along the w⋯

★ Tsitsikamma Trail

The relatively easy inland walking route leads 60 km (37 miles) through fynbos and indigenous forest in the Tsitsikamma mountains and takes five days to complete.

VISITORS' CHECKLIST

Practical Information
Road map C5. 68 km (42 miles)
E of Plettenberg Bay on N2.
🛈 Garden Route National Park:
042 281 1607; 012 428 9111
(reservations and permits for
hiking trails). **Open** 6:30am–7pm.
Otter Trail: 41 km (25 miles).
Tsitsikamma Trail: 60 km (37
miles). 🅿 🍴 🏕 🚶 🏊 🏠
w sanparks.org

The Storms River Bridge,
built in 1956, is a 120-m
(394-ft) high bridge spanning
the Storms River Gorge. There is
a viewing platform, curio stalls
and a restaurant.

Tsitsikamma Mountains

🚶 Tsitsikamma Trail

Heuningbos

Sleepkloof

Big Tree

N2

Storms River
Bridge

*Port
Elizabeth*
→

Storms River

...tering
...est Station

Kleinbos

Kleinbos River

Elandsbos River

🏕 **Scott**

🚶 Otter Trail

Ngubu

*Lourie, Blue Duiker
& Waterfall Walks* 🚶

🚶 Mouth Trail

Storms River
Mouth

Storms River

Storms River Mouth Rest Camp
Cosy wooden chalets line a narrow
strip of grass between the crashing
ocean and forested hills.

0 kilometres   3

0 miles   3

Key

━━ Motorway

━━ Major road

━━ Tarred road

--- Trail

Tips for Walkers

**En route to Storms
River Mouth**

Visitors should be fit, and sturdy walking shoes
are essential. For the longer hikes, all provisions
as well as cooking gear and sleeping bags
must be carried, as the overnight huts are
equipped only with mattresses. The Bloukrans
River along the Otter Trail can be forded only
by swimming or wading, so waterproof
backpacks are advisable.

⑪ Street-by-Street: Port Elizabeth

The third-largest port and fifth-largest city in the country, Port Elizabeth, part of the Nelson Mandela Bay Municipality, faces east across the 60-km (37-mile) wide sweep of Algoa Bay. Modern Port Elizabeth has spread inland and northwards along the coast from the original settlement. It is often referred to as the "Friendly City" and its wide open beaches are popular with visitors. Among the many attractions in this sedate industrial city are a host of well-preserved historic buildings, splendid architecture, Bayworld, Donkin Reserve and the SA Marine Rehabilitation and Education Centre.

Donkin Lighthouse
Built in 1861, the lighthouse is home to the Nelson Mandela Bay Tourism office.

★ Donkin Street
The row of quaint, double-storey Victorian houses lining this street was built between 1860–80. The entire street was declared a national monument in 1967.

| 0 metres | 100 |
| 0 yards | 100 |

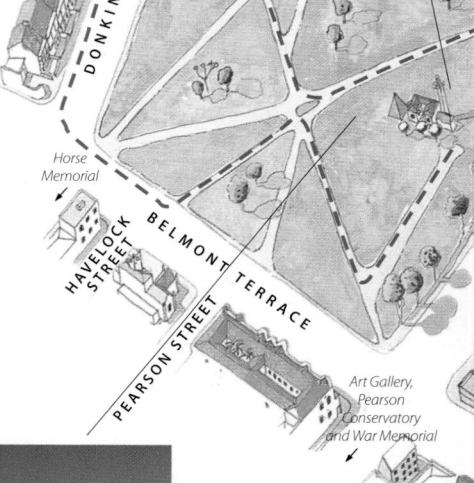

CHAPEL STREET

DONKIN STREET

Horse Memorial

HAVELOCK STREET

BELMONT TERRACE

PEARSON STREET

Art Gallery, Pearson Conservatory and War Memorial

Donkin Reserve
Overlooking the city and harbour, Donkin Reserve features the Opera House, a lighthouse, a flagpole and the touching memorial to Sir Rufane Donkin's wife Elizabeth, after whom the city was named.

Key
— Suggested route

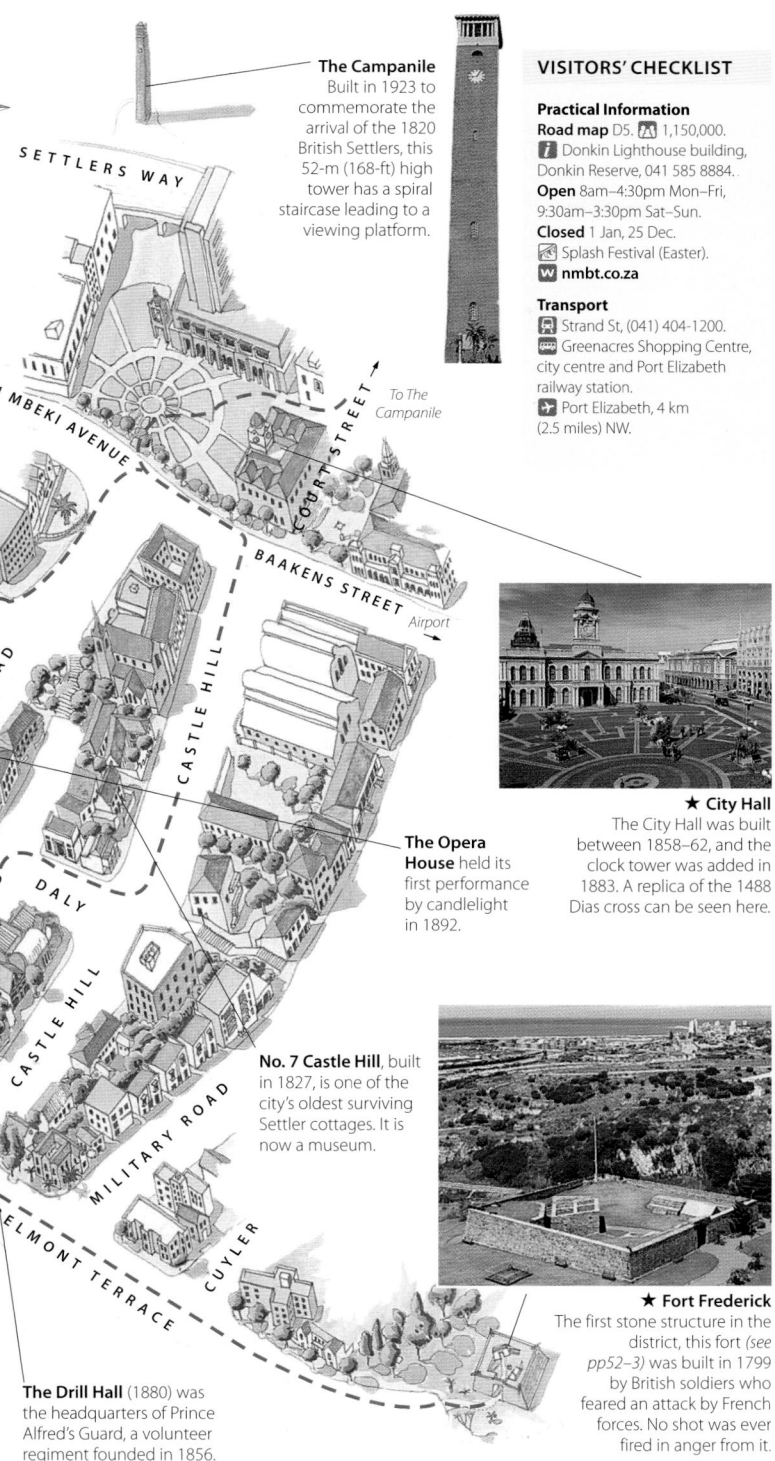

The Campanile
Built in 1923 to commemorate the arrival of the 1820 British Settlers, this 52-m (168-ft) high tower has a spiral staircase leading to a viewing platform.

To The Campanile

SETTLERS WAY

N MBEKI AVENUE

COURT STREET

BAAKENS STREET

Airport

CASTLE HILL

DALY

CASTLE HILL

MILITARY ROAD

BELMONT TERRACE

CUYLER

The Opera House held its first performance by candlelight in 1892.

No. 7 Castle Hill, built in 1827, is one of the city's oldest surviving Settler cottages. It is now a museum.

The Drill Hall (1880) was the headquarters of Prince Alfred's Guard, a volunteer regiment founded in 1856.

★ **City Hall**
The City Hall was built between 1858–62, and the clock tower was added in 1883. A replica of the 1488 Dias cross can be seen here.

★ **Fort Frederick**
The first stone structure in the district, this fort *(see pp52–3)* was built in 1799 by British soldiers who feared an attack by French forces. No shot was ever fired in anger from it.

Exploring Port Elizabeth

Port Elizabeth sprawls inland and northwards on the windy shores of Algoa Bay. Many of the city's most popular attractions are situated along Humewood Beach. The city is proud of its settler heritage, and a wealth of historic buildings and museums, as well as memorials and statues, await exploration further inland. Port Elizabeth, along with the neighbouring towns of Uitenhage and Despatch, is part of the Nelson Mandela Bay Metropolitan Municipality.

🏛 Donkin Reserve

Belmont Terrace. ℹ Donkin Lighthouse *(see p250).* 🏛

This park-like reserve, a national monument since 1938, includes the Donkin Lighthouse (site of the tourist office), and the tallest flagpole in the country, with a South African flag about the size of a tennis court. Its most unusual attraction is the pyramid-shaped memorial which the acting governor of the Cape, Sir Rufane Donkin, dedicated to his late wife in 1820. The settlement was named Port Elizabeth in her honour.

The Horse Memorial

🎭 Port Elizabeth Opera House

Whites Rd. **Tel** 041 586 2256.
🌐 peoperahouse.co.za

On the southern edge of the reserve, the Opera House was established in 1892 on a gallows site where public hangings once took place. It is not only the oldest opera house in the southern hemisphere, but the last Victorian theatre in Africa. The two stages are not large by modern standards, but host many plays, musicals and ballets.

🏛 Horse Memorial

Cape Road.

During the South African War, Port Elizabeth was the port of entry for the horses of British soldiers. After the war, local resident Harriet Meyer raised money to honour the estimated

Donkin Memorial

347,000 horses that had died. The statue by sculptor Joseph Whitehead, unveiled in 1905, was relocated to its present site in 1957. The inscription reads: "The greatness of a nation consists not so much in the number of its people or the extent of its territory as in the extent and justice of its compassion."

🌳 St George's Park

Park Drive.

As the setting of the well-known play, *Master Harold and the Boys,* by Athol Fugard, this lovely park is home to the oldest cricket ground and bowling green in South Africa. It also contains tennis courts, a swimming pool, a botanic garden and several historic monuments, such as the War Memorial in the north-east corner of the park.

The Pearson Conservatory, named after Henry Pearson who served as mayor of the city for 16 terms, was completed in 1882 and houses a collection of exotic plants. Always hire a tour guide to visit St George's Park, since it is not safe to walk there alone.

🏛 The Boardwalk

Beach Rd, Summerstrand.
Tel 041 507 7777. 🛝 💻 ✏ 🎱
🌐 suninternational.com

Situated right on the seafront and centred around a man-made lake, this is a slick entertainment complex from Sun International of Sun City fame. It features a shopping mall, numerous restaurants, fast-food outlets and bars, a grassed open-air theatre, a Nu Metro cinema, a 24-hour casino and a hotel. An impressive attraction is the musical fountain in the lake, and children can be entertained on the Victorian-style carousel.

🏰 Fort Frederick

Belmont Terrace. **Tel** 041 582 2575.
Open sunrise–sunset daily.

In 1799, a British garrison was sent to Algoa Bay to prevent an invasion by French troops supporting the rebel republic of Graaff-Reinet *(see pp362–3).* Small, square Fort Frederick *(see pp52–3)* was built on a low hill overlooking the mouth of the Baakens River, and named after the Duke of York, who was commander-in-chief of the British army at the time. Although it was defended by eight cannons, no salvoes were ever fired from them in an act of war. The arrival of the English settlers in 1820 was supervised by the commander of the garrison, Captain Francis Evatt, whose grave can be seen at the fort.

The gateway to The Boardwalk, an entertainment complex on Port Elizabeth's seafront

The all-important "19th hole" at Humewood Golf Club

🏖 Humewood Beach

2 km (1 mile) S of the city centre.
The recreation hub of
Port Elizabeth, Humewood
Beach is bordered by Marine
Drive, which provides quick
access to all the attractions that
line the shore. An attractive
covered promenade provides
welcome shelter from the
wind, and hosts a flea market at
weekends. There is also an
inviting freshwater and tidal
pool complex nearby.
Lifeguards are stationed at
all the main beaches. Sailing
and scuba diving are
particularly popular here, and
the windy expanse of Algoa
Bay is often punctuated by the
white sails of yachts.

Many hotels and holiday
apartments line Marine Drive,
and there are also numerous
little restaurants and eateries.

Bayworld is an unusual
combination of a natural and
cultural history museum
with an aquarium and a snake
park. At a different location, in
the city centre, the Bayworld
complex also includes No 7
Castle Hill, a Victorian house
museum depicting the early
Settler way of life.

The entrance to the main
museum is lined with several
open enclosures containing
waterbirds. The fascinating
exhibits inside include a marine
gallery containing salvaged
items and fully rigged models
of early sailing ships, and the
skeleton of the last southern
right whale to be harpooned
in Algoa Bay.

An exhibition entitled
"The First People of the Bay"
features original artifacts
of the Khoi people. The
Khoi arrived in Algoa Bay more
than two millennia ago – long
before any other population

group. Items on display here
include medicinal herbs,
musical instruments, examples
of rock art and clothing.

On view at the snake park are
snakes from around the world,
including South African species
such as the puffadder and the
green mamba, as well as lizards,
tortoises and crocodiles.

The green mamba, a venomous
resident of Bayworld

The penguin pool at the
aquarium has underground
observation windows allowing
visitors to view the sea birds
swimming underwater, where
their grace and speed are in
marked contrast with their
comical gait on shore.

🐠 Bayworld

Beach Rd. **Tel** 041 584 0650. **Open**
9am–4:30pm daily. **Closed** 25 Dec.
🅿 ♿ ⌖ 🏠 **W** **bayworld.co.za**

Environs

The championship **Humewood
Golf Club**, some 3 km (2 miles)
south along the coast from
Humewood, is considered one
of the best in South Africa. At
the clubhouse, golfers can enjoy
a well-earned drink and
splendid views across the bay.

About 3 km (2 miles) south
of Humewood lies the
cape that marks the entrance
to Algoa Bay. **Cape Recife** and
its surrounding nature reserve
is an ideal destination for
bird-spotting and exploring
the unspoiled rocky shore.
A 9-km (6-mile) hiking
trail explores the reserve, and
traverses several different
coastal habitats that include
redbuds and dune vegetation.

The route passes the Cape
Recife lighthouse, a spot that
is a favourite with divers. Near
the lighthouse is the **SA Marine
Rehabilitation & Education
Centre (SAMREC)**, which
rescues and rehabilitates
marine birds – in particular,
African penguins. Visitors can
tour the premises and watch
the penguins being fed
(2:30pm daily). The Flying
Penguin Café is a good place
to take a break.

⛳ Humewood Golf Club

Marine Drive. **Tel** 041 583 2137.
W **humewoodgolf.co.za**

🏖 Cape Recife

Tel 041 583 4004. **Open** sunrise–
sunset daily. **W** **caperecife.co.za**

🐧 SA Marine Rehabilitation &
Education Centre (SAMREC)

Tel 041 583 1830. **Open** 9am–4pm
daily. **Closed** 1 Jan, 25 Dec. ♿ 🅿
W **samrec.org.za**

The jetty at Humewood Beach

⓬ Addo Elephant National Park

Road map D5. 72 km (45 miles) NE of Port Elizabeth. **Tel** 042 233 8600. Reservations: 012 428 9111. **Open** 7am–7pm daily. 🏞 📷 🚗 🏕 ☑ **sanparks.org**

In the past, elephants lived throughout the Cape Colony, but as the land was settled they were hunted to extinction. In 1919 Major Philip Pretorius was appointed to exterminate the last survivors and he shot 120 over 11 months. Only 15 terrified elephants survived in the densest thickets.

When public opinion turned in the elephants' favour, a 68-sq-km (26-sq-mile) tract of surplus land was declared national park territory in 1931. However, the animals raided nearby farms at night and a suitable fence was needed to prevent escapes.

After numerous experiments, warden Graham Armstrong constructed a guard from railway tracks and elevator cables. By 1954, some 23 sq km (9 sq miles) had been fenced in this way, and the elephants were safely contained.

For many years, Addo resembled a large zoo. Oranges were placed below the rest camps at night to lure the shy beasts, while the stout fences separated visitors and animals. The herd responded well to protection – increasing to 265 by 1998 – making it necessary to enlarge their territory.

A herd of elephants at a waterhole in Addo Elephant National Park

Today, there are more than 450 elephants. The park, which includes the Zuurberg mountains to the north and a belt of coastal dunes to the south, covers 2,920 sq km (1,127 sq miles) and is the third-largest in the country.

Addo's rest camp has a shop, restaurant, pool, caravan park and 61 chalets. A network of game-viewing roads allows visitors to explore the southern region of the park, which is the only area in the world to house the Big Seven: elephant, leopard, black rhino, Cape buffalo, lion and, in the marine section, great white shark and southern right whale.

Other animals inhabiting the dense thicket include kudu, eland, hartebeest and bushbuck. However, visitors tend to overlook one of the park's smallest and most fascinating creatures: the flightless dung beetle. Signs warn motorists not to drive over

Dung beetles are protected in Addo

them. Apart from self-drive, guided game drives can be booked at reception. On night drives, unusual species such as porcupine, spring hare and genet may be spotted.

⓭ Shamwari Game Reserve

Road map D5. 72 km (44 miles) N of Port Elizabeth. **Tel** 042 203 1111. **Open** to guests staying at the lodges only. ☑ **shamwari.com**

At 200 sq km (77 sq miles), Shamwari is the largest private reserve in the Eastern Cape. Day visitors are not permitted, but there are seven luxury lodges in the reserve. Overnight packages include all meals and game activities. The reserve consists of undulating bushveld country in the catchment area of the Bushmans River. The recipient of several international awards, Shamwari is the brainchild of entrepreneur Adrian Gardiner, who originally bought the ranch in the hills near Paterson as a retreat for his family. Over the years, several neighbouring farms were incorporated and wildlife reintroduced. The reserve is now home to the Big Five *(see pp76–7)*, as well as zebras, giraffes and antelope species including eland, kudu, impala, gemsbok, hartebeest, springbok and black wildebeest.

Shamwari was the first private reserve in the Eastern Cape to reintroduce large mammals to an area where they had become extinct, but there are now more than 20 private Big Five reserves

A rustic chalet in Addo Elephant National Park

in the vicinity of Addo Elephant National Park. They offer a safari experience similar to those at the private reserves adjoining Kruger, with accommodation in luxury lodges, guided game activities and fine dining and wines. Some also accept day visitors – check their websites for programmes. Reserves include Schotia Safaris Private Game Reserve (tel 042 235 1436; www. schotiasafaris.com), Amakhala Game Reserve (tel 041 581 0993; www.amakhala.co.za), Lalibela Game Reserve (tel 041 581 8170; www.lalibela.net) and Pumba Private Game Reserve (tel 046 603 2000; www. pumbagame reserve.co.za).

ⓔ Alexandria

Road map D5. R72, E of Port Elizabeth.

Alexandria was founded in 1856 around a Dutch Reformed Church. A dirt road, just west of town, crosses chicory fields before entering the enchanted Alexandria forest, which is home to 170 tree species including superb, towering specimens of yellowwood. The forest and the largest active dune system in South Africa lie within the **Woody Cape** section, which is part of the Addo Elephant National Park. The two-day, 35-km (22-mile) Alexandria Hiking Trail, one of the finest

White rhino, Shamwari Game Reserve

coastal walks in South Africa, passes through dense indigenous forest to reach sand dunes rising to 150 m (488 ft) above the sea, before returning via a circular route. Overnight huts are located at the start and at Woody Cape.

✉ Woody Cape
8 km (5 miles) off R72. **Tel** 041 468 0916. **Open** 7am–7pm daily. 🚶🏃 bookings on 041 468 0916.
w sanparks.org

ⓕ Port Alfred

Road map D5. R72, 150 km (93 miles) E of Port Elizabeth. 🏘 25,900.
ℹ Causeway Rd, 046 624 1235.
w sunshinecoasttourism.co.za

Port Alfred, a charming, upmarket seaside resort in the Eastern Cape, is well known for its superb

beaches. Those west of the river mouth are more developed; those to the east are unspoiled and excellent for long walks. Kelly's Beach offers safe bathing. The entire stretch of coast is perfect for surfing and is popular with rock and surf fishermen.

Environs
The **Kowie Nature Reserve** has an 8-km (5-mile) hiking trail with various exit and entry points for those wanting shorter walks. It passes through a thickly forested canyon, and there are picnic sites next to the river. A variety of birds and small animals can be seen.

✉ Kowie Nature Reserve
R67, 5 km (3 miles) N of Port Alfred.
Open 7am–7pm daily. 🚶 (hiking permits available at the gate).

Many luxury yachts, catamarans and fishing vessels are moored at Port Alfred's marina

⓰ Grahamstown

After the Fourth Frontier War of 1812, Colonel John Graham established a military post on an abandoned farm near the southeast coast. In an attempt to stabilize the region, the Cape government enticed 4,500 British families to the farmlands. Many of these "1820 Settlers" preferred an urban life, and Grahamstown became a thriving trading centre, home to the largest concentration of artisans outside Cape Town.

Drostdy Gateway, the entrance to Rhodes University

Exploring Grahamstown

Grahamstown is known for its 50 plus churches, university and superb schools. Its major attractions lie within a 500-m (1,625-ft) walk from the **City Hall** in High Street. Some 60 buildings have been declared national monuments, and a host of beautifully restored Georgian and Victorian residences line the streets.

🏛 Albany Museum Complex
Tel 046 603 8111. **W** ru.ac.za/albanymuseum

Owned by Rhodes University, this complex incorporates six separate venues. Two of them, the **History and Natural Sciences museums**, display fossils, settler artifacts and Xhosa dress. Another, the **Old Provost**, was built in 1838 as a military prison. **Drostdy Gateway**, which frames the university entrance, is all that remains of the 1842 magistrate's offices. **Fort Selwyn**, adjacent to the 1820 Settlers Monument, was built in 1836 and was formally used as an artillery barracks. It offers scenic views of the town.

🏛 History and Natural Sciences museums
Somerset Street. **Open** 9am–5pm Mon–Fri. **Closed** Public hols.

🏛 Old Provost
Lucas Avenue. **Open** by appt.

🏛 Fort Selwyn
Fort Selwyn Drive. **Open** by appt.

⛪ Cathedral of St Michael and St George
High St. **Tel** 046 622 2445. **Open** 9am–3pm Mon–Fri, 9am–noon Sat . **W** grahamstowncathedral.org

The town's most prominent landmark has a towering 51 m (166 ft) spire. The original St George's Church, built in 1824, is the oldest Anglican Church in South Africa, and the organ is one of the country's finest.

🌿 Makana Botanical Gardens
Lucas Ave. **Tel** 046 603 8240. **Open** 8am–4:30pm daily.
W bots.ru.ac.za

Reminiscent of an English park, these gardens adjoining the university, laid out in 1853, are a national monument. Indigenous plants including aloes, cycads and proteas attract more than 100 species of garden birds.

🏛 Observatory Museum
Bathurst Street. **Tel** 046 622 2312. **Open** 9am–1pm, 2–4:30pm Mon–Fri, 9am–1pm Sat. **Closed** Good Fri, 25 Dec. (except turret).

Also part of the Albany Museum Complex, but on a different site, is the historic home and work-shop of a mid-19th-century Grahamstown jeweller. It has a Victorian camera obscura in the turret, which projects images of the town onto a wall.

🏛 Rhodes University
Artillery Road. **Tel** 046 603 8111. multi-entry ticket. **W** ru.ac.za

This beautiful old university complex also houses the world-famous **South African Institute for Aquatic Biodiversity**, where the most interesting displays are two rare embalmed coelacanths. This prehistoric deep-water fish was presumed extinct until its "discovery" in East London in 1939. There is also a collection of other marine and freshwater fish. Visitors interested in traditional African music should visit the **International Library of African Music**, which is also on the campus.

🏛 South African Institute for Aquatic Biodiversity
Somerset Street. **Tel** 046 603 5800. **Open** 8am–4pm Mon–Fri. **Closed** Good Fri, 25 Dec. **W** saiab.ac.za

🏛 International Library of African Music
Rhodes University. **Tel** 046 603 8557. **Open** by appointment.
W ru.ac.za/ilam

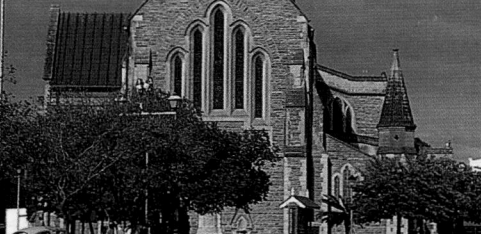

The Cathedral of St Michael and St George on High Street

🏛 National English Literary Museum

87 Beaufort St. **Tel** 046 622-7042. **Open** 8:30am–1pm, 2–4:30pm Mon–Fri. **Closed** Good Fri, 25 Dec. ♿ 🖥 **w** ru.ac.za/nelm

Preserved here are documents, early manuscripts and personal letters relating to South Africa's most important writers.

🏛 1820 Settlers Monument

Gunfire Hill.

Tel 046 603 1100. **Open** 8am–4:30pm Mon–Fri. ♿ 🖥

Reminiscent of an old fort, this monument on Gunfire Hill was built in 1974 in the shape of a ship, and commemorates the British families who arrived in the area in 1820. The modern Monument Theatre complex nearby is the main venue for the annual 11-day National Arts Festival *(see p43)*. Many paintings decorate the impressive foyer.

Camera obscura in the Observatory Museum

Environs

34 km (21 miles) north of Grahamstown lies the 445-sq-km (172-sq-mile) **Great Fish River Nature Reserve**. After the Fifth Frontier War of 1819, the land between the Keiskamma and Great Fish rivers was declared neutral territory, and British settlers were brought in to act as a buffer against the Xhosa incursions.

Today its semiarid bushveld vegetation sustains large populations of plains game, including blue wildebeest, waterbuck, kudu, zebra and giraffe, as well as some larger mammals such as buffalo, elephant and hippo. There are tracks suitable for cars along the two rivers, and the area is

The Old Provost was once a military prison

VISITORS' CHECKLIST

Practical Information
Road map D5. 🚗 67,300.
ℹ️ 63 High Street, 046 622 3241. **Open** 8:30am–5pm Mon–Fri, 9am–noon Sat. **Closed** Good Fri, 25 Dec, pub hols. 🎭 National Arts Festival (Jul). **w** grahamstown.co.za

Transport
✈️ Port Elizabeth, 127 km (79 miles) to NE. 🚌 Bathurst St.

also suitable for those wishing to hike.

🏞 Great Fish River Nature Reserve

R67 towards Fort Beaufort. **Tel** 087 2866 545. **Open** Sunrise–sunset daily. 📷 🥾 **w** visiteasterncape.co.za

Grahamstown City Centre

① South African Institute for Aquatic Biodiversity
② Drostdy Gateway
③ Albany Museum Complex
④ Rhodes University
⑤ Old Provost
⑥ Fort Selwyn
⑦ 1820 Settlers Monument
⑧ Makana Botanical Gardens
⑨ Cathedral of St Michael and St George
⑩ City Hall
⑪ Observatory Museum
⑫ National English Literary Museum

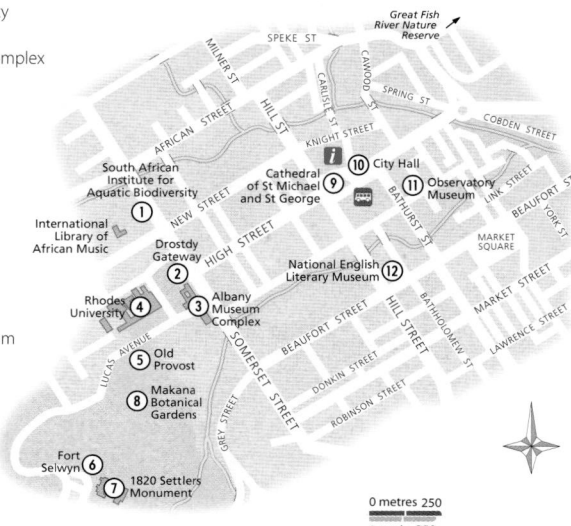

0 metres 250
0 yards 250

For keys to symbols *see back flap*

THE EAST COAST
AND INTERIOR

Introducing the East Coast and Interior

Crowned by southern Africa's highest mountains, a serrated spine that runs the length of this region, the Eastern Cape, Lesotho and KwaZulu-Natal offer rugged mountain scenery, undulating hills and superb beaches. The powerful currents of the warm Indian Ocean carve the wave-battered cliffs of the Wild Coast. Although an almost continuous chain of coastal resorts extends 160 km (100 miles) south of Durban, (Africa's largest port), much of the coastline remains unspoiled and accessible only along winding dirt roads. In the far north, subtropical forests and savannah provide a haven for an abundance of big game and birds, while coastal lakes and the ocean lure fishermen and holiday-makers.

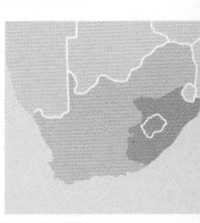

Locator Map

Golden Gate Highlands National Park in the northeastern Free State lies in the foothills of the Maluti mountains. Magnificent scenery, impressive sandstone formations such as Sentinel Rock, abundant wildlife and pleasant walks are the attractions in this park *(see p275)*.

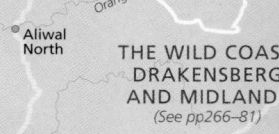

Kroonstad

Bethlehem

Maseru

Caledon

Orange

Aliwal North

THE WILD COAST DRAKENSBERG AND MIDLANDS *(See pp266–81)*

Cala

Mt

Queenstown

King William's Town

East London

The Hole in the Wall is situated just off the coast at the mouth of the Mpako River. It is one of the best-known sites on the romantic Wild Coast *(see p271)*.

◄ Marine life teeming on the coral reef at Sodwana Bay, along the Maputaland coast

Cape Vidal separates the Indian Ocean and Lake St Lucia. It forms part of the iSimangaliso Wetland Park *(see pp300–301)*, which borders the unspoiled Maputaland coast, the breeding ground of leatherback and loggerhead sea turtles.

Ermelo

Piet Retief

Volksrust

Phongolo

Newcastle   Vryheid

rrismith

DURBAN AND
ZULULAND
(See pp282–301)   St Lucia

Ladysmith

Empangeni

Estcourt   Tugela

KwaDukuza

Pietermaritzburg

Durban

Amanzimtoti   **Church Street Mall** in
Pietermaritzburg is
surrounded by a
number of historic
buildings such as the
beautiful City Hall,
which was built in
1893 *(see p281)*.

Kokstad

Port
Shepstone

Lusikisiki

ndian
)cean

Durban's Beachfront, a
6-km (4-mile) long stretch
of hotels, restaurants and
entertainment venues
along the Indian Ocean
shoreline, is also known
as the Golden Mile
(see p286).

Zulu Culture

The Zulu people's reputation for being a fierce warrior nation, fuelled by written accounts of the 1879 Anglo-Zulu War, has been enhanced by dramatic films such as *Zulu,* and the internationally acclaimed television series *Shaka Zulu.* Many sites associated with Zulu history can be visited in the Ulundi, Eshowe and Melmoth districts of KwaZulu-Natal. It is true that the Zulu fought determinedly to defend their land, but their culture also reflects other, gentler, aspects in beadwork, pottery, basketry and dancing. In the remote Tugela River Valley and the northern parts of the province, rural people uphold many old customs.

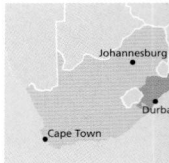

Locator Map
▮ KwaZulu-Natal

Oxhide is stretched on the ground and cured to make clothing and shields.

Fence made of poles and woven reeds.

Zulu Beehive Hut
A framework of saplings is covered with plaited grass or rushes. A hide screen affords additional privacy.

Zulu Crafts

The Zulu people are renowned as weavers and for their colourful beadwork. Baskets and mats made from *ilala* palm fronds and *imizi* grass are very decorative and especially popular. Most baskets display the traditional triangle or diamond shape, a symbol representing the male and female elements. Shiny glass beads introduced by the early 19th-century traders created a new custom. Today, artistic beadwork forms an important part of Zulu culture. Every pattern and colour has symbolic significance, as shown in the *incwadi*, or love letters, that are made by young women and presented to eligible men.

Zulu beadwork and spoon

Maize, the staple grain, is ground and boiled to form a stiff, lumpy porridge.

Basket weaver

Utshwala (beer) is prepared by the women, using sorghum. The fermented liquid is then strained through long grass sieves to separate the husks.

Traditional Dancing

In Zulu society, social gatherings almost always involve dancing. Most Zulu dances require a high level of fitness – and a lack of inhibition. While ceremonial dances can involve large crowds of gyrating, clapping and stamping performers, small groups of performers need only the encouragement of an accompanying drum and singing, whistling or wailing onlookers. Lore and clan traditions may be related through the dance; alternatively, the movements may serve as a means of social commentary.

Zulu dances require stamina and agility

Water is always carried on the head, sometimes over long distances.

Clay pots, for water, grain or sorghum beer, are smoothed and decorated before firing.

Grain Storage
To protect their grain from birds and rodents, the Zulu stored maize and sorghum in a hut on long stilts.

Cattle are a symbol of wealth and play an important part in Zulu society. They are kept in a kraal (securely fenced enclosure) at night.

The Zulu Kraal

Historically, the umuzi *(Zulu kraal) was a circular settlement that enclosed several* uhlongwa *(beehive-shaped grass huts) grouped around an enclosure in which the cattle were corralled at night. Although the principle of the kraal continues, traditional architectural styles are seldom seen nowadays. Cement, bricks, concrete blocks and corrugated iron sheeting are the modern choices.*

King's hut

Meeting area

Main entrance

Traditional weapons are an integral part of Zulu culture, even today, and men often carry wooden staffs and clubs. At political meetings and rallies, tempers tend to flare, and as a result the carrying of traditional weapons has been outlawed.

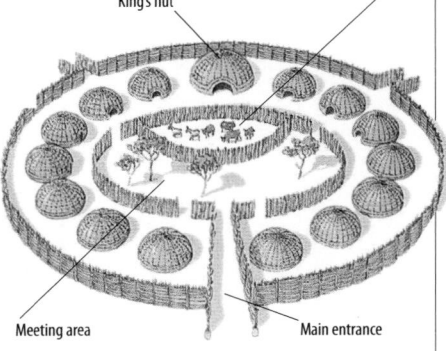

Durban's Surfing Scene

The invention of fibreglass surfboards in the 1960s caused a surge in devotees of the sport. Durban, with its warm currents, consistent waves and perfect beaches, quickly became the country's surfing capital. Popular and consistent sites capable of holding sizeable winter and summer swell are the Bay of Plenty, New Pier, North Beach, Wedge, Dairy and – for more experienced surfers – Cave Rock Bluff. In recent decades, Jeffreys Bay *(see p247)*, in the Eastern Cape, has emerged as a rival to Durban as South Africa's top 10 surfer hang-out, thanks to the 1 km- (half a mile-) long ride offered by the Supertubes break.

Jordy Smith, who began surfing in Durban aged six, competes professionally in the World Surf League (WSL). In 2014 he won the Hurley Pro in southern California.

"Bottom turn" is the term used to describe the manoeuvre at the base of a wave. It is often followed by a "floater", which is when the surfer floats across the top of the wave to generate speed.

The perfect wave provides an exhilarating ride. Durban is famous for its superb waves.

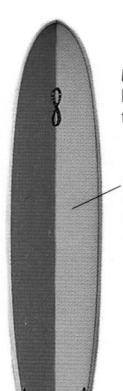

Modern boards are smaller, lighter and more manoeuvrable than the clumsy early models.

Competition long boards must exceed 2.8 m (9 ft) in length and weigh between 5.2 kg and 7 kg (11–15 lbs).

Short boards are lighter, more manoeuvrable, and are not allowed to exceed 3.2 kg (7 lbs) to qualify for contests.

Cave Rock

Cave Rock is Durban's premier big-wave surf spot. The presence of a deep ocean channel (see p29) and a reef near the shore produces powerful, big waves that compare with those that have made Hawaii world-famous.

Wax is rubbed on the top of the board to improve the surfer's grip.

Learning to Surf
With its sheltered beaches along the Golden Mile, protected from the big ocean swells, Durban is an excellent place to learn to surf. Surf schools offer tuition either in groups or one-to-one with a professional surfer, and the sandy beaches with small waves and tropical warm water are beginner-friendly.

The lip forms as the base of the wave encounters the reef.

Surf-wear fashion is a lucrative spin-off industry. Imaginative creations that reflect surfing's way of life are produced by brands such as Quiksilver and Billabong, and they retail at designer-wear prices.

The tube of the wave curls up and around behind the surfer.

Surfing heroes, such as American Kelly Slater, have a cult following. The world's biggest surf competitions, in Hawaii, California and Florida, USA, and Australia and South Africa, attract massive crowds.

The Ballito Pro Presented by Billabong is South Africa's premier professional surfing event. It takes place in Ballito, 45 km (28 miles) north of Durban over six days every June–July, and features top surfers such as Jack Freestone (pictured above).

Surfing Lingo

Tube – ride through the concave curve formed by the body of the wave.
Lip – the tip of the wave (its most powerful part).
Barrel – ride through the curve of a wave that ends in the wave breaking on the surfer.
Bomb – enormous wave.
Filthy – excellent surf.
Grommet – a beginner.
Shundies – thank you.
Tassie – a young woman.
Cactus – any person who surfers do not like.

THE WILD COAST, DRAKENSBERG AND MIDLANDS

The Zulus call the jagged peaks of the Drakensberg, southern Africa's highest mountains, *uKhahlamba*, "a barrier of spears". Where the lofty summits of the Drakensberg slope down towards the coastline, the unspoiled Wild Coast promises excellent fishing and hiking.

Some 1,000 years ago the lush, well-watered valleys of the Drakensberg were home to the hunter-gatherer San who stalked antelope with their bows and arrows. The colonizing vanguards of Zulu, Xhosa, Afrikaner and British soon drove them from the region, and, apart from the delicate paintings that survive under overhangs and in caves, the diminutive hunters left no evidence of their presence.

At the beginning of the 19th century, the Xhosa's heartland was part of the expanding Cape Colony, while the centre of the Zulu kingdom stretched north of the Tugela River. Facing attacks on several fronts, the Basotho tribe sought refuge in the high mountains that would eventually become the kingdom of Lesotho. By 1848, the Kei River had become the frontier line between the British and Xhosa, while to the north, the territory between the Mzimkhulu and Tugela rivers was declared the Colony of Natal. Over the centuries, countless territorial wars raged in this fertile region now known as the Midlands, and many of the old battle sites can be visited today.

In 1976, under apartheid, the Xhosa territory of Transkei was officially declared "independent", but was reincorporated into South Africa in 1994. This is an area of immense natural beauty and splendour. The enchanted coastline, too remote for modern development, has remained virtually unspoiled and offers secluded bays and beaches, rocky headlands and some of the best fishing to be found anywhere along the coast.

The sandstone buildings at the Rorke's Drift battle site

◀ Traditional round stone-and-thatch hut, or rondavel, in eastern Lesotho

Exploring the Wild Coast, Drakensberg and Midlands

The remote Lesotho highlands and the Drakensberg, southern Africa's highest mountain range, form the backbone of this region. Breathtaking views and streams flowing through secluded valleys attract nature lovers, hikers, bird-watchers and trout fishermen. A plateau dotted with traditional Xhosa huts lies between the mountains and the Wild Coast's sheltered coves and forested cliffs. North of here, in the KwaZulu-Natal Midlands, a pastoral landscape of green hills and forest patches serves as the perfect backdrop for charming country hotels, myriad arts and crafts enterprises and dairy farms.

The distant Champagne Castle, Monk's Cowl and Cathkin Peak in the Drakensberg Mountains

Key

- ▬▬ Motorway
- ▬▬ Major road
- ▭▭▭ Minor road
- ▪▪▪ Untarred road
- ▬▬ Scenic route
- ▬▬ Main railway
- ▬▬ Minor railway
- ▬▬ International border
- ▬▬ Provincial border
- ⤬ Pass

The memorial *laager* (encampment) on the site of the Battle of Blood River (1838), near Dundee

For hotels and restaurants in this region see pp388–9 and pp406–7

kilometres 50
miles 25

Mbabane

Ermelo

N11

Amsterdam

Scheepmoor

Vaal

N2

Amersfoort

Piet Retief

Johannesburg

Perdekop

Richards Bay

Dirkiesdorp

Vrede

Volksrust

Commondale

Laingsnek Pass

Balelesberg

Bivane

Ingogo

Bivane

Warden

Newcastle

Utrecht

R33

Vryheid

N3

BATTLEFIELDS TOUR 5

Blood River

Harrismith

Fort Mistake

Dundee

Nqutu

GATE
TIONAL PARK

N11

Glencoe

Van Reenens
Pass

K W A Z U L U -

Ladysmith

N A T A L

oyal Natal
tional Park

SPIOENKOP DAM 6
NATURE RESERVE

R33

Cathedral
Peak

Winterton

UKHAHLAMBA-DRAKENSBERG 3
PARK

Estcourt

Champagne Valley
Monk's Cowl

N3

Greytown

Mooi River

Giant's
Castle

Kamberg

MIDLANDS 7
MEANDER

Sani Pass

Midmar Dam

8

Durban

HO

PIETERMARITZBURG

Underberg

Donnybrook

R617

Port
Shepstone

Fort Donald

Rode

N2

Redoubt

Flagstaff

Tsitsa
Bridge

Palmerton

Mkambati Nature
Reserve

Port Grosvenor

Mthatha

Port St. Johns

PE

Tshani

Coffee Bay

1

WILD COAST

San rock art at Giant's Castle in
uKhahlamba-Drakensberg Park

Getting Around

The N2 links East London with KwaZulu-
Natal. Roads leading to the Wild Coast are
mostly untarred, and private transport is
necessary to reach the remote beaches.
Many Lesotho roads require a 4WD
vehicle, although the network is being
extended. There is no easy road access to
Lesotho from the east. The N3 highway in
KwaZulu-Natal, which carries one-tenth of
South Africa's traffic, provides access to the
Drakensberg resorts. Roads leading to the
hotels and resorts are mostly tarred. Large
bus companies offer regular services
between regional centres. There are
domestic airports in East London, Mthatha
and Pietermaritzburg, and international
airports at Durban and Maseru.

Sights at a Glance

❶ Wild Coast
❷ Lesotho pp272–3
❸ uKhahlamba-Drakensberg
   Park
❹ Golden Gate Highlands
   National Park
❻ Spioenkop Dam
   Nature Reserve
❼ Midlands Meander
❽ Pietermaritzburg

Tour

❺ Battlefields Tour p278

The City Hall of Pietermaritzburg

For keys to symbols see back flap

❶ The Wild Coast

The appropriately named Wild Coast is an outdoor paradise with rugged cliffs, sheltered bays and dense coastal forests. The region roughly stretches 280 km (175 miles) from East London to the Umtamvuna Nature Reserve next to Port Edward in KwaZulu-Natal. Much of the land is communally owned by the Xhosa, whose rural communities live off the land and adhere to age-old traditions. Spectacular beaches front a section of the Indian Ocean that is notorious for its shipwrecks.

East London's Orient Beach is popular with bathers and surfers

Exploring the Wild Coast

The resorts, reserves and villages are accessible from the N2, and most of the roads are tarred, though some are not in great condition, and potholes are a hazard. There is no public transport to speak of, but buses ply the N2 and some of the resorts arrange transfers.

East London

Road map E5. 720,000. R347, 12 km (7 miles) W of East London. Station Rd. Oxford St.

East London was originally founded as a military camp on the banks of the Buffalo River in 1847, and its strategic position as a river port was soon recognized. Today, the second-largest city in the Eastern Cape is predominantly an industrial centre, but it does have good swimming beaches, washed by the warm waters of the Indian Ocean.

Among several historic sites is the statue of Black Consciousness leader Steve Biko in front of the City Hall. Born in the Eastern Cape, he died under dubious circumstances while in police custody.

The statue was unveiled by Nelson Mandela in 1997 to mark the 20th anniversary of Biko's death.

The **East London Museum**, established in 1921, has an interesting collection of natural and cultural exhibits, including fossils found in the region. There are also displays on maritime history and on the Xhosa people.

🏛 **East London Museum**
319 Oxford St. **Tel** 043 743 0686.
Open 9:30am–4:30pm Mon–Fri (to 4pm Fri). 🅿 ♿ 📷
🌐 **elmuseum.za.org**

Morgan Bay and Kei Mouth

Road map E4. Off the N2, 85 km (53 miles) E of East London. 400.
ℹ Morgan Bay Hotel, Beach Rd, 043 841 1062. 🌐 **morganbayhotel.co.za**

These coastal villages lie on a stretch of coast renowned for its scenery. At Kei Mouth, a pont transports vehicles across the Great Kei River to the former Xhosa "homeland" known as Transkei. The Morgan Bay Hotel adjoins the beach, and the Ntshala Lagoon offers safe swimming. Walks along the cliffs afford superb views of the sea. Further south, at Double Mouth, a spur overlooking the ocean and estuary provides one of the finest views in the whole country.

Rock angling is a popular sport

Kei Mouth to Mbashe River

Road map E4. 95 km (59 miles) E of East London.

The Kei River marks the start of the Wild Coast. Twenty rivers enter this 80-km (50-mile) long stretch, along which is strung a succession of old-fashioned family hotels. Kei Mouth is only an hour's drive from East London, making it a popular weekend destination.

Further north, Dwesa Nature Reserve extends along the coast from the Nqabara River. The reserve is home to rare tree dassies and samango monkeys. The grassland, coastline and forest are all pristine. On the

---

Coelacanth

In 1938 a boat fishing off the Chalumna River mouth near East London netted an unusual fish. The captain sent it to the East London Museum, whose curator, Marjorie Courtenay-Latimer,

The coelacanth

contacted Professor JLB Smith, ichthyologist at Rhodes University. The fish belonged to a species believed to have become extinct with the dinosaurs. The reward offered for another *Latimeria chalumnae* was claimed only in 1952, when one was netted off the Comoros Islands. The coelacanth is steel-blue and covered in heavy scales; it is distinguished by its six primitive, limb-like fins.

Traditional Xhosa huts dot the hillsides of the Eastern Cape

eastern banks of the Mbashe River is the Cwebe Nature Reserve. The adjoining reserves conserve 60 sq km (23 sq miles) of dense forest, home to bushbuck and blue duiker, as well as coastal grasslands inhabited by eland, hartebeest, wildebeest and zebra. A hiking trail follows the entire Wild Coast, but the section from Mbashe to Coffee Bay is the most spectacular.

Coffee Bay

Road map E4. Off the N2. 🚗 500. 🛈 Ocean View Hotel, Main Rd, 047 575 2005/6. 🌐 **oceanview.co.za**

Allegedly named after a ship carrying coffee which was wrecked at the site in 1863, Coffee Bay is popular for fishing, swimming and beach walks.

There are a number of superbly sited hotels set above the sandy beaches. A prominent detached cliff, separated from the mainland by erosion, has been named Hole in the Wall; it is a conspicuous landmark located 6 km (4 miles) south along the coast. Many centuries of swirling wave action have carved an arch through the centre of the cliff.

Umngazi Mouth

Road map E4. 25 km (16 miles) S of Port St Johns. 🛈 Umngazi River Bungalows & Spa, 047 564 1115. 🌐 **umngazi.co.za**

An idyllic estuary framed by forested hills, the Umngazi offers superb snorkelling, canoeing and board-sailing. Umngazi River Bungalows & Spa *(see p388)*, on the northern bank, is one of the leading resorts on the Wild Coast, and is renowned for its food and service. There is a lovely sandy beach and the rugged coastline extends south to the cliffs that are known in isiXhosa as *Ndluzulu*, after the crashing sound of the surf.

Mkambati Nature Reserve

Road map E4. Off R61 N of Port St Johns. 🛈 Eastern Cape Parks, 079 496 7821. 🌐 **visiteasterncape.co.za**

Wedged between the Mzikaba and Mtentu rivers, Mkambati is the Wild Coast's largest nature reserve. Apart from conserving a 13-km (8-mile) long strip of grassland and unspoiled, rocky coastline, the reserve is known for its endemic plants such as the Mkambati palm, found only on the north banks of the rivers. Cape vultures breed in the Mzikaba Gorge. Large grazing herbivores such as eland, red hartebeest, blue wildebeest and blesbuck have been introduced into the grasslands. The Mkambati River flows through the reserve in a series of water-falls, of which Horseshoe Falls, near the sea, is the most striking.

Accommodation ranges from a stone lodge to cottages. An added attraction is that the reserve is near the Wild Coast Sun Resort *(see p292)*.

The Xhosa word for Hole in the Wall, *esiKhaleni*, means "the place of sound"

❷ Lesotho

Surrounded by South Africa, this mountain kingdom, or "Kingdom in the Sky" as it is sometimes referred to, achieved independence from Britain on 4 October 1966. The rugged highlands of Lesotho, formed by the Drakensberg, Maluti and Thaba-Putsoa mountains, are a popular destination for visitors who enjoy camping, hiking and climbing. Lesotho also boasts fertile river valleys, a rich variety of flora and fauna, and a strong cultural heritage that is very much kept alive by the Basotho people.

★ **Teyateyaneng**
This town, easily accessible from Maseru, is the "craft capital" of Lesotho. The colourful woven jerseys, carpets and wall hangings are a local speciality.

Maseru
Founded by the British in 1869, Maseru lies on the Caledon River. The main attraction is Makoanyane Square, a monument to the Basotho who died in the two World Wars.

KEY

① **The Maletsunyane Falls** plunge 192 m (629 ft) into a rugged gorge.

② **The Cave Houses** at Ha Kome, sculpted from mud, are good examples of indigenous architecture.

Snowfalls
In May and June the high country becomes a winter wonderland, attracting skiers and snowboarders.

★ **Katse Dam**
The first phase of this
impressive engineering feat
was completed in 1998. The
reservoir feeds water into
South Africa's Vaal Dam.

Key

▬ Major route
═ Main road (tarred)
═ Main road (untarred)
▬ Minor road (tarred)
═ Minor road (untarred)
▬ · International boundary
▬ ▬ District boundary

0 kilometres   25
0 miles   10

★ **Sani Pass**
The only access route
to Lesotho from
KwaZulu-Natal, this
pass ascends to a
height of 2,874 m
(9,429 ft) over
20 km (12 miles).

Rock Paintings and Dinosaur Tracks

Due to ts remoteness, Lesotho has remained relatively
uncommercialized. The high mountains, where stout Basotho
ponies are often the only form of transport, contain some of the finest
examples of rock art in southern Africa. Thaba Bosiu near Maseru and
the Sekubu Caves at Butha-Buthe in the north are just two of the more
than 400 worthwhile sites. Fossilized dinosaur tracks are found at
places such as Moyeni (Quthing) and the Tsikoane Mission at Hlotse.

An example of rock art in Lesotho

For keys to symbols see back flap

❸ uKhahlamba-Drakensberg Park

Extending over 2,350 sq km (907 sq miles), the uKhahlamba-Drakensberg Park, a UNESCO World Heritage Site, protects a dramatic and rugged escarpment that provides an awesome backdrop to the pastoral midlands of KwaZulu-Natal. A hiker's paradise, this scenic range of secluded valleys, green highland meadows and dense mist-shrouded forests incorporates all of South Africa's tallest peaks. Wildlife ranges from the massive eland antelope and vociferous Chacma baboon to majestically soaring raptors such as the jackal buzzard and bearded vulture. The rock overhangs of the Drakensberg shelter offer some of the world's most prolific and best-preserved prehistoric rock art.

Exploring uKhahlamba-Drakensberg

The provincial conservation authority, Ezemvelo KZN Wildlife, has subdivided uKhahlamba-Drakensberg into individually administered wilderness and conservation areas. Several government rest camps and private hotels have been set up in the foothills as a base for exploring the middle and upper slopes on foot. Shorter hikes range from hour-long rambles to ancient rock art sites (many of which can be visited only on guided tours, to protect them from vandalism), to a demanding full-day hike to Cathedral Peak. Within the park, unequipped caves and camp sites cater to more intrepid overnight hikers and mountaineers.

Kamberg

Road map E3. Estcourt. 🛈 033 267 7251. **Open** daily. 🅿️ 🏕️ 🚶 🍽️ ⛰️
🌐 **kznwildlife.com**

Nestling in the foothills of the uKhahlamba-Drakensberg

Park, Kamberg is known for its trout-fishing locations. There are several small dams near the trout hatchery, and fishing gear can be hired from the reserve shop. Walking trails cut through the valley or meander along the river.

Shelter Cave has some superb San rock paintings and can be visited with a guide –the return walk takes about three hours. There is also the San Rock Art Interpretation Centre to visit.

VISITORS' CHECKLIST

Road map E3. Winterton.
🛈 (and reservations) Ezemvelo KZN Wildlife, 033 845 1000.
🅿️ 🏕️ 🚶 🍽️ ⛰️
🌐 **kznwildlife.com**

Giant's Castle
Road map E3. Estcourt. 🛈 036 353 3718. **Open** daily. 🅿️ 🛶 🚶 🍽️ ⛰️
🌐 **kznwildlife.com**

In 1903 a sanctuary was established in this area to protect some of the last surviving eland in South Africa. They now number around 2,000 – one of the largest populations in the country.

A camouflaged hide allows visitors to view endangered bearded vultures (lammergeyer), an estimated 200 pairs of which are found here.

The main camp, with chalets, a camp site and the Izimbali Restaurant, overlooks the Bushman's River, with Giant's Castle (3,314 m/10,770 ft) dominating the skyline.

A short walk brings visitors to the Main Caves, where 500 San rock paintings, some of which are 800 years old, can be seen.

The high-lying Giant's Castle is covered with snow in winter

The Drakensberg Range

The Drakensberg, "dragon mountains", is South Africa's greatest mountain wilderness. It follows the border of Lesotho for 250 km (155 miles) – an escarpment that separates the high interior plateau from the subtropical coast of KwaZulu-Natal. The Drakensberg is divided into the rocky High Berg and the pastoral Little Berg. Both are superb hiking areas.

Giant's Castle

Giant's Castle Pass

Die Hoek

Hodgson's Peaks

Champagne Valley & Monk's Cowl

Road map E3. Winterton. ℹ️ 036 488 1103. **Open** daily. 🅿️ 🚲 🚶 ⛺ ⛰️

Champagne Castle, at 3,377 m (10,975 ft), is the second-highest peak in South Africa. It juts out from the surrounding escarpment and dominates the horizon in a delightful valley. This has been dubbed Champagne Valley, thanks to the 31-km (19-mile) road from Winterton to Monk's Cowl being lined with a cluster of luxury hotels and timeshare resorts. Monk's Cowl is the peak between Champagne Castle and Cathkin, where there is a camp site and a number of hiking trails.

Cathedral Peak

Road map E3. Winterton. ℹ️ 036 488 1800. **Open** daily. 🅿️ 🚲 🏠 🚶 ⛰️ ⛰️ 🌐 **kznwildlife.com**

Some of the Drakensberg's finest scenery is to be found in this region. The road from Winterton winds for 42 km (26 miles) through Zulu villages that are scattered across the gentle folds of the Mlambonja Valley. The towering peaks of the Drakensberg form a spectacular backdrop.

The hike to the top of Cathedral Peak (3,004 m/ 9,855 ft) is one of the most exciting and strenuous hikes in the Drakensberg, and the views from the top are unforgettable. There are also guided drives to the top of Mike's Pass, which gains 500 m (1,625 ft) in 5 km (3 miles), and the Rock Art Centre at Ezemvelo KZN Wildlife's Didima Resort explains the complicated meaning of many of the San paintings.

Royal Natal National Park

Road map E3. Bergville. ℹ️ 036 438 6411. **Open** daily. 🅿️ 🏠 🚶 ⛰️ ⛰️ 🌐 **kznwildlife.com**

The Royal Natal National Park comprises some of Africa's most spectacular scenery. One of its main features is an awe-inspiring natural Amphitheatre – a crescent-shaped basalt wall 6 km (4 miles) wide, and 1,500 m (4,875 ft) high. Here, the Tugela River plunges 948 m (3,080 ft) into the valley below on its journey to the Indian Ocean, making this the second-highest waterfall in the world. Chalets at the award-winning Thendele Resort, above the Tugela River, provide unrivalled views of the amphitheatre and countryside below.

In the valleys, the Mahai camp site provides easy access to an extensive network of hiking trails that can be used to explore the 88-sq-km (34-sq-mile) reserve.

❹ Golden Gate Highlands National Park

Road map E3. Clarens. **Tel** 058 255 1000. **Open** daily. 🅿️ 🚶 🏠 ⛰️ 🏠 🌐 **sanparks.co.za**

Situated in the foothills of the Maluti Mountains in the eastern Free State, this national park encompasses 48 sq km (18 sq miles) of grassland and sandstone formations. The park was proclaimed in 1963 to protect the sandstone cliffs above the Little Caledon valley. Black wildebeest, grey rhebok, blesbok, mountain reedbuck, eland and oribi can be seen, as well as endangered bearded vultures, black eagles, steppe buzzards and bald ibises. SANParks accommodation and camping is in Glen Reenen Rest Camp and the Highlands Mountain Retreat, while a more upmarket option is provided by the privately run Golden Gate Hotel.

Bearded vulture

Royal Natal National Park, an unspoiled wilderness

Grinding Corn Champagne Castle Cathedral Peak Mnweni Needles Eastern Buttress Mont-aux-Sources

thkin Pyramid South Peak Amphitheatre
eak Gatberg

San rock art at Kamberg in uKhahlamba-Drakensberg Park ▶

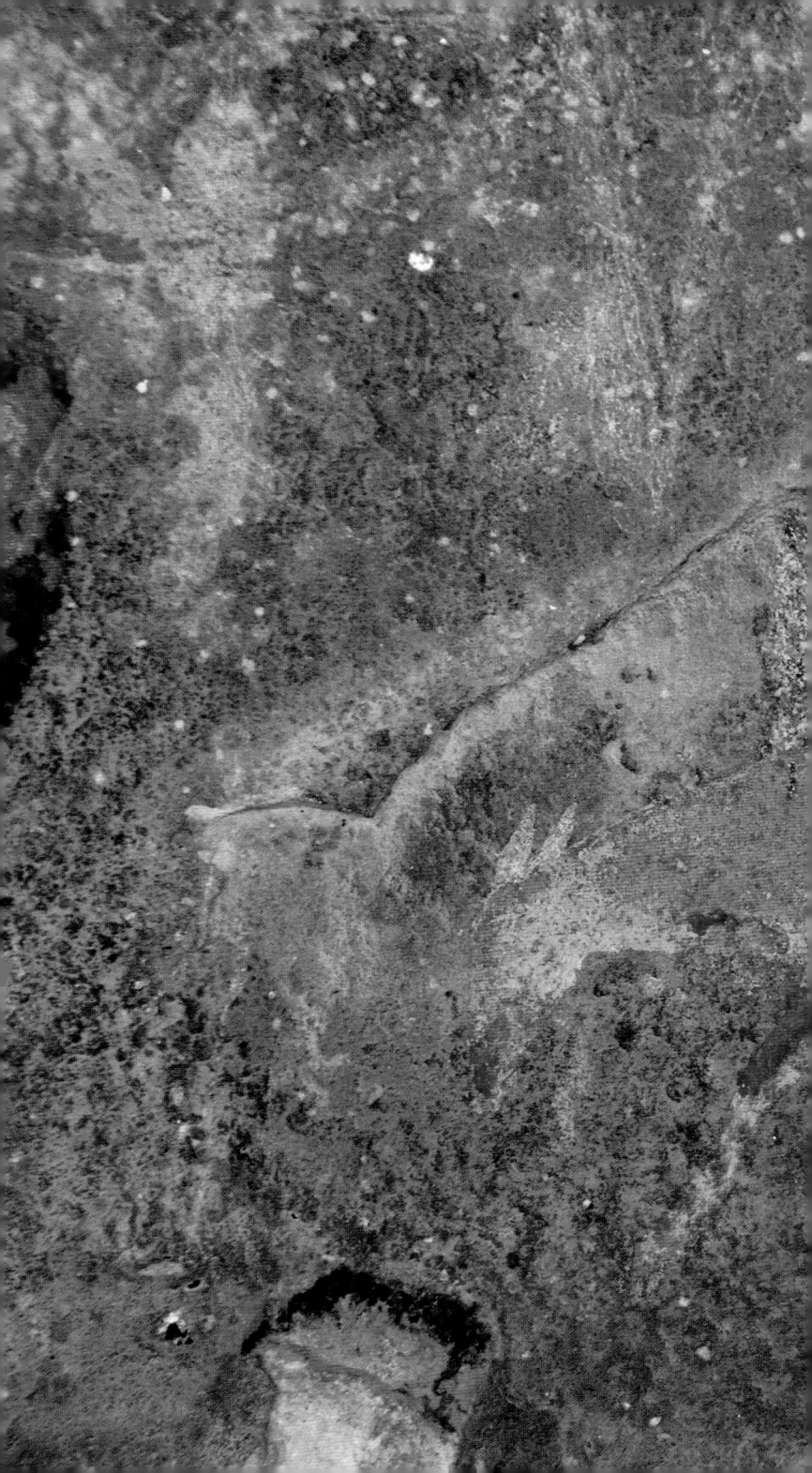

❺ Battlefields Tour

The peaceful, rolling grasslands and tree-covered hills of northwestern KwaZulu-Natal retain few reminders of the bloody battles that were waged in this corner of South Africa during the 19th century. In the 1820s, Zulu king Shaka's campaign to seize control of the scattered tribes plunged the entire region into turmoil. Over the following 80 years many wars were fought, pitting Zulu against Ndwandwe, Afrikaner against Zulu and British against Afrikaner and Zulu. A detailed guide to the battlefields lists more than 50 sites of interest and is available from the local publicity associations and the Talana Museum, where expert guides can also be hired.

② Elandslaagte
The Boer and British forces clashed here on 21 October 1899, during a severe storm. The British were forced to retreat to nearby Ladysmith.

③ Talana Museum
This museum commemorates the first battle of the South African War (29 October 1899), when 4,500 British soldiers arrived in Dundee to defend the town and its coal mines.

① Ladysmith
On 2 November 1899, Boer general Piet Joubert laid siege to Ladysmith and its 12,000 British troops for 118 days.

⑤ Rorke's Drift
This museum has displays depicting the battle during which some 100 British soldiers repelled 4,000 Zulus for 12 hours, earning them a total of 11 Victoria crosses.

Key

■ Motorway
■ Tour route
= Other roads

0 km ____ 25
0 miles __ 10

Tips for Drivers

Length: 380 km (236 miles).
Stopping-off points: The towns of Ladysmith and Dundee have restaurants and accommodation. Audio tapes can be bought from the Talana Museum in Dundee and at Fugitives Drift, which also offers guided tours and accommodation.

⑥ Isandlwana
Zulu *impis*, angered by an invasion of their territory, attacked a British force on 22 January 1879.

④ Blood River
For years seen as a symbol of the Afrikaners' victory over the Zulus, this battle gave rise to a public holiday – 16 December – now called Day of Reconciliation.

Map labels: Ermelo, R543, Majuba, Skuinshoogte, Volksrust, Laingsnek, N11, Fort Amiel Museum, R34, Utrecht, Newcastle, R33, Fort Mistake, Glencoe, Dundee, R68, Fort Pine, R602, R33, Harrismith, R103, N11, ② Ladysmith, ① Ladysmith, R103, Sundays, Colenso, Weenen, N3, Bloukrans, Estcourt, Fort Dunfort Museum, R74, R622, Durban, Buffalo

Midmar Dam, one of the tranquil places to stop at on the Midlands Meander

❻ Spioenkop Dam Nature Reserve

Road map E3. 35 km (22 miles) SW of Ladysmith on Winterton Rd. **Tel** 036 488 1578. **Open** Apr–Sep: 6am–6pm daily; Oct–Mar: 5am–7pm daily. 🐾 🏔 🎿 🛶
ⓦ kznwildlife.com

The picturesque dam nestles at the foot of the 1,466-m (4,810-ft) high Spioenkop (broadly meaning "lookout hill"), which in 1900 was the scene of a decisive battle between the British and Boer forces in the South African War *(see p57)*. The battlefield site is accessible from the road, and countless graves and memorials are scattered across the mountain's summit as a grim reminder of what was one of the worst defeats suffered by British forces during that conflict.

Today, Spioenkop is very popular with outdoor enthusiasts. The dam offers fishing and boating, while eland, hartebeest, zebra, giraffe, kudu and white rhino can be seen in the surrounding nature reserve, together with a wide variety of bird species. There is also a pleasant camp site here, as well as a small shop. Picnic sites are situated along the southern shoreline, and two short trails (in an area free of dangerous animals) encourage visitors to view game on foot.

Situated at the base of Spioenkop on the northern shore of the dam, Iphika Bush Camp offers rustic tented self-catering accommodation and is reached by walking along a private track.

Tapestry detail, Rorke's Drift

❼ Midlands Meander

Road map: E3. Mooi River.
ⓘ 033 330 8195.
ⓦ midlandsmeander.co.za

The undulating hills of the KwaZulu-Natal Midlands, with their green patches of forest and their dairy farms, have long been a retreat favoured by artists and craftspeople. In 1985, six studios established an arts and crafts route: the Midlands Meander. The route quickly gained popularity and now consists of around 400 members and studios.

There are four routes that meander between the small towns of Hilton, Nottingham Road, Howick and Mooi River. Goods on offer include herbs, cheese, wine, pottery, woven cloth, leather items, furniture, stained glass and antiques.

The symbol of the Midlands Meander seen on road signs marking the routes is the endangered Karkloof blue butterfly, which is indigenous to this region of KwaZulu-Natal.

Accommodation along the way ranges from idyllic country hotels, tranquil guest farms and picturesque lodges to comfortable bed and breakfast establishments. There are also many quaint country pubs.

The monument to the Battle of Spioenkop overlooks the dam

For hotels and restaurants in this region see pp388–9 and pp406–7

❽ Street-by-Street: Pietermaritzburg

From its humble beginnings as an irrigation settlement established by Afrikaner farmers in 1836, Pietermaritzburg (in the municipality of Msunduzi) has developed into the commercial, industrial and administrative centre of the KwaZulu-Natal Midlands. An intriguing blend of Victorian, Indian, African and modern architecture and culture combine to produce a distinctly South African city. Many historic buildings and monuments, as well as galleries and museums, are located around the city centre and in the western suburbs, which nestle at the foot of a range of densely wooded hills. Visitors can ramble through the surrounding forests and botanic gardens, and visit several nature reserves and recreation resorts located within the city or a few minutes' drive away.

Gandhi Statue
In Pietermaritzburg, in 1893, Gandhi had to leave a first-class train carriage because he wasn't white.

Church Street Mall is shaded by stinkwood trees and lined with well-preserved historic buildings.

Presbyterian Church

★ Tatham Art Gallery
Housed in the old Supreme Court, displays at this gallery include works by South African artists, as well as European masters such as Edgar Degas, Henri Matisse and Pablo Picasso.

Key

— Suggested route

Parliament Building
The seat of the colonial government prior to 1910, it now houses KwaZulu-Natal's provincial legislature.

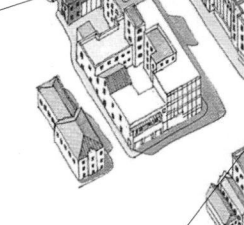

Colonial Houses
The Renaissance Revival J H Isaacs building and the Edwardian First National Bank are two examples of colonial architecture in Langalibalele Street.

VISITORS' CHECKLIST

Practical Information
Road map: E3. 223,500.
Publicity House, 177 Chief Albert Luthuli Rd, 033 345 1348. **Open** 8am–5pm Mon–Fri, 8am–1pm Sat. Royal Agricultural Show (May).
W pmbtourism.co.za

Transport
Durban, 80 km (49 miles) SE.
Pietermaritzburg Airport, S of the city. Top of Church Street.
Cnr Burger and Chief Albert Luthuli streets.

★ City Hall
This edifice, the largest brick building in the southern hemisphere, was completed in 1893. The clock tower, a later addition, rises 47 m (153 ft) above the street.

Publicity House

0 metres 50
0 yards 50

Msunduzi Museum Complex
The Church of the Vow, built by the Voortrekkers after the Battle of Blood River *(see p55)*, is the focus of this complex on the corner of Langalibalele and Boshoff streets.

★ KwaZulu-Natal Museum
Displays include African mammals, birds and dinosaurs, San rock art and a gallery focusing on Portuguese shipwrecks.

Exploring Pietermaritzburg

The town is a treasure trove of architecture and lends itself well to walking excursions. One of the oldest quarters, the Lanes – a labyrinth of alleys between Church and Langalibalele streets – gives visitors an idea of what Pietermaritzburg was like in days gone by.

Environs

Midmar Dam, a weekend and holiday venue for water sports enthusiasts and fishermen, lies 27 km (17 miles) north of Pietermaritzburg in the **Midmar Dam Nature Reserve**, which is home to red hartebeest, blesbok, reedbuck, black wildebeest, oribi and zebra, which can be seen from the gravel roads.

The origins of Howick, 18 km (11 miles) north of Pietermaritzburg, date back to 1850. In the town, a viewing platform and restaurant overlook the beautiful Howick Falls, equal in height to the Victoria Falls in Zimbabwe.

On the R103 just north of Howick, the **Nelson Mandela Capture Site** marks the spot where Nelson Mandela *(see p61)* was arrested by security police on 5 August 1962. The museum and its huge sculpture of Mandela's face, made up of 9 m (30 ft) steel columns, was opened in 2014.

Midmar Dam Nature Reserve
R617. **Tel** 033 330 2067. **Open** 24 hours daily.
W kznwildlife.com

Mandela Capture Site
R103. **Tel** 071 834 4349. **Open** daily.
W thecapturesite.co.za

The Howick Falls

TELL IT TO
THE
GENERATION
FOLLOWING

EXCEPT A CORN OF WHEAT
FALL INTO THE GROUND AND DIE
IT ABIDETH ALONE
BUT IF IT DIE
IT BRINGETH FORTH MUCH FRUIT

DURBAN AND ZULULAND

Caressed by the warm currents of the Indian Ocean, this picturesque region is one of the country's leading tourist destinations. Abundant rainfall and year-round sunshine sustain a prosperous sugar industry and a profusion of coastal holiday resorts. North of the Tugela River, an untamed tapestry of wildlife, wilderness, beaches and wetland evokes the essence of tropical African coastline.

Near the end of the 15th century, a sailing ship captained by the Portuguese mariner Vasco Da Gama passed the east coast of Africa on Christmas Day. The intrepid seafarer sighted a large bay, flanked by forested dunes, and named it "Rio de Natal", the Christmas River. Subsequently, on sailors' maps, the name "Natal" was given to the uncharted land that lay beyond the wide beaches and forested dunes along the coast.

In the 1820s, rumours of the Zulu chief and military genius Shaka *(see p53)* began to reach the Cape Colony. Shaka forged the scattered clans of the Natal region into a near-irrepressible force, and 60 years would pass before the British Empire succeeded in subduing the mighty Zulu army. The passage of time has brought many changes. "Rio de Natal"

has developed into Durban, today the largest port in Africa and third-largest city in the country. Where the coastal grasslands once tumbled down to the sea, a wide band of sugar cane plantations now separates luxury hotels overlooking sandy beaches and the warm currents of the Indian Ocean from the rolling hills of the interior. Many major rivers meander through the undulating hills, and the coastline is enhanced by tropical forests and tranquil estuaries and lagoons rich in birdlife.

In the northern corner of the region, some of the country's finest game reserves, with melodious Zulu names such as Hluhluwe-Imfolozi, uMkhuze, Ndumo and Tembe, preserve a timeless landscape that has remained unchanged since the reign of Shaka.

Traditional reed fishtrap, Kosi Bay

◀ Durban's City Hall and World War I memorial

Exploring Durban and Zululand

This region is renowned for its subtropical climate, sandy beaches, tepid ocean currents and unspoiled game reserves. Durban, with its high-rise hotels, beachfront and shopping centres, is perfectly situated for exploring a scenic and varied coastline, and the N2 coastal highway allows holiday-makers easy access to many attractions. As well as tourism, this coastal belt also sustains the vast plantations that produce most of South Africa's sugar. North of Richards Bay, three hours from Durban on excellent roads, beckons a wilderness of swamps, forests and savannah. The iSimangaliso Wetland Park is a paradise for bird-watchers and nature lovers. The wooded hills of the nearby Hluhluwe-Imfolozi Game Reserve are home to rhinos, zebras, elephants, buffaloes and lions.

Grazing Burchell's zebras in Hluhluwe-Imfolozi Game Reserve

Durban's attractive beachfront development, with uShaka Marine World in the foreground

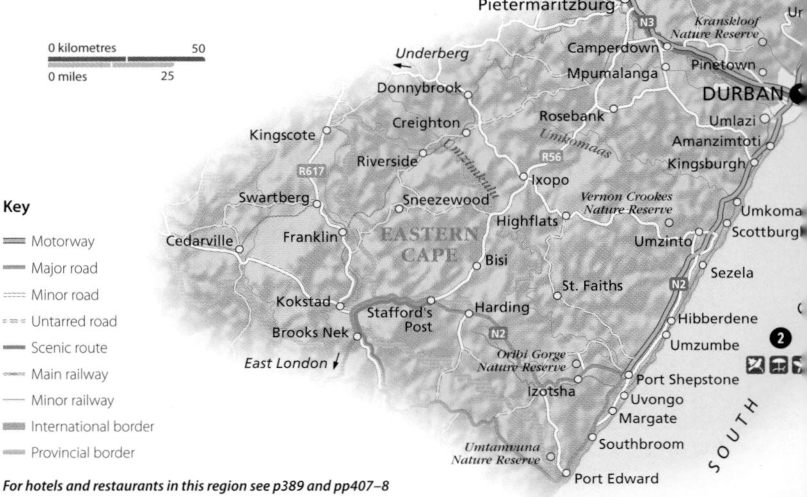

0 kilometres 50

0 miles 25

Key

━━━ Motorway

━━━ Major road

┅┅┅ Minor road

▪═▪═ Untarred road

━━━ Scenic route

━━━ Main railway

━━━ Minor railway

━━━ International border

━━━ Provincial border

For hotels and restaurants in this region see p389 and pp407–8

Glu

No

R68

Baba

Nk

Dlolwana

Tugela

KWAZU
NATAL

Greytown

R

Mapu

Sevenoaks

Umx

R33

Dalton

R6

Mpolweni

Estcourt

Ndwedwe

Pietermaritzburg

N3

Kranskloof
Nature Reserve

Ur

Underberg

Camperdown

Pinetown

Donnybrook

Mpumalanga

DURBAN

Rosebank

Umlazi

Kingscote

Creighton

Umkomaas

Amanzimtoti

R617

Riverside

R56

Kingsburgh

Swartberg

Sneezewood

Ixopo

Vernon Crookes
Nature Reserve

Umkoma

Cedarville

Franklin

EASTERN
CAPE

Highflats

Umzinto

Scottburg

Bisi

Sezela

St. Faiths

Kokstad

Stafford's
Post

Harding

Hibberdene

Brooks Nek

N2

Umzumbe

East London

Oribi Gorge
Nature Reserve

Port Shepstone

Izotsha

Uvongo

Margate

Umtamvuna
Nature Reserve

Southbroom

SOUTH

Port Edward

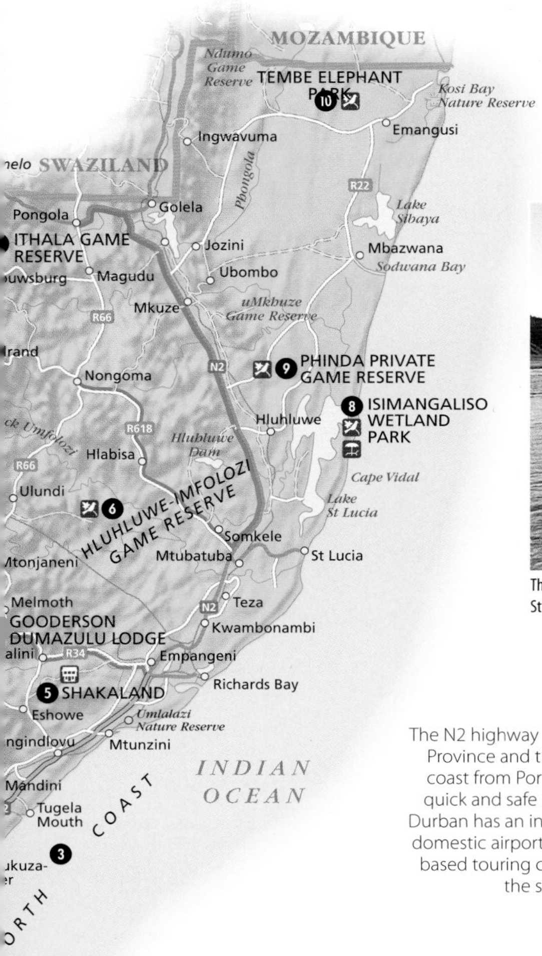

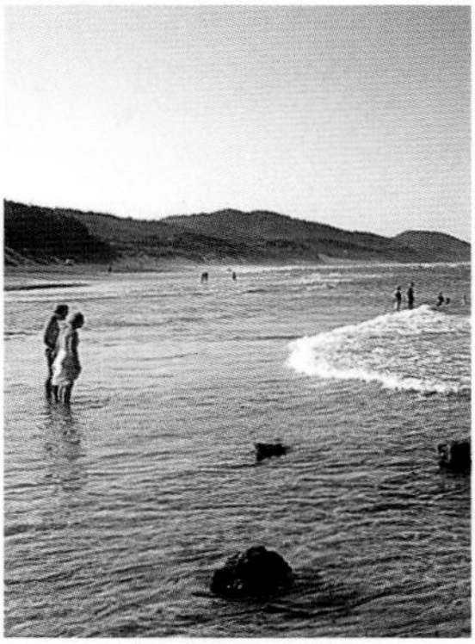

MOZAMBIQUE

Ndumo Game Reserve

TEMBE ELEPHANT PARK ❿ ✈

Kosi Bay *Nature Reserve*

Ingwavuma

Emangusi

SWAZILAND

R22

Lake Sibaya

Pongola

Golela

ITHALA GAME RESERVE

Jozini

Mbazwana

Sodwana Bay

uwsburg

Magudu

Ubombo

Mkuze

uMkhuze Game Reserve

R66

Irand

Nongoma

N2

✈ ❾ PHINDA PRIVATE GAME RESERVE

Hluhluwe

❽ ISIMANGALISO WETLAND PARK

R618

Hluhluwe Dam

ck Umfolozi

Hlabisa

✈

Cape Vidal

R66

Ulundi

✈ ❻

HLUHLUWE-IMFOLOZI GAME RESERVE

Lake St Lucia

Somkele

St Lucia

Mtonjaneni

Mtubatuba

Melmoth

Teza

GOODERSON DUMAZULU LODGE

Kwambonambi

alini

R34

Empangeni

❺ SHAKALAND

Richards Bay

Eshowe

Umlalazi Nature Reserve

ngindlovu

Mtunzini

INDIAN OCEAN

Mandini

Tugela Mouth

ukuza- er

❸

NORTH COAST

The unspoiled beach at Cape Vidal, near St Lucia, on the North Coast

Getting Around

The N2 highway that leads from the Eastern Cape Province and the Wild Coast runs parallel to the coast from Port Shepstone onwards. It provides quick and safe access to the region's attractions. Durban has an international airport, and there is a domestic airport at Richards Bay. Several Durban-based touring companies offer package tours to the splendid northern game reserves.

Sights at a Glance

Sugar cane is a major crop in subtropical Zululand

❶ Durban

Vasco Da Gama's Port Natal was renamed Durban in honour of Cape Governor Benjamin D'Urban, after Zulu chief Shaka gave the land to the British in 1824. Today, the former trading post is South Africa's principal harbour and the holiday capital of KwaZulu-Natal. Sunny days and warm waters attract visitors to a beachfront flanked by high-rise hotels. Most attractions are on the Golden Mile, but Durban also offers historic buildings, museums, theatres and exciting markets.

The Paddling Pools on Durban's Golden Mile

Exploring Durban

Most of the attractions located along the beachfront are within walking distance of the hotels. By far the most useful of Durban's bus services is the People Mover, which passes by every 15 minutes (5am–10pm). The three routes are the Beach Line between Suncoast Casino and Entertainment World in the north and uShaka Marine World in the south; The City Line that serves the city centre; and the Circle Line, a wider loop that takes in Victoria Embankment and the railway station.

The Golden Mile

OR Tambo Parade.
The land side of this 6-km (4-mile) long holiday precinct is lined with a continuous row of hotels, while the seaward edge consists of amusement parks, an aerial cableway, craft sellers, pubs, restaurants, ice-cream parlours, piers, sandy beaches and a promenade.

Along the Golden Mile visitors will find many brightly decorated rickshaws. Their colourful drivers are festooned in beads and tall, elaborate headdresses, which are a curious amalgamation of traditional African practices and Indian influences. At the southern end, the leading Golden Mile attraction is **uShaka Marine World**, a massive beachfront complex that offers numerous attractions. Sea World is an aquarium where the highlight is the phantom ship that visitors can walk through to see ragged-tooth sharks and game fish; Wet 'n' Wild has swimming pools, waterslides and rides;

Dangerous Creatures is a snake and reptile park; and the Village Walk is an attractive open-air shopping and restaurant mall.

At the northern end of the Golden Mile on Battery Beach, **Suncoast Casino and Entertainment World** is another entertainment complex built in an Art Deco Miami Beach style. As well as the casino, there is a cinema, restaurants, bars, a fast-food court and two hotels.

Behind Battery Beach, the **Moses Mabhiba Stadium** was built for the 2010 FIFA World Cup and named after an anti-apartheid activist. The "arc of triumph" over the top is now Durban's most striking landmark and is beautifully lit at night. As well as hosting soccer matches and concerts, the stadium also has the SkyCar, a funicular railway car that climbs the curve to the top of the arc, and other activities including the Adventure Walk up and down the 550 steps and the Big Rush Swing, a bungee-like 220-m (720 ft) swing beneath it.

Moses Mabhiba Stadium
Isaiah Ntshangase Rd. **Tel** 031 582 8242. **Open** 10am–5pm daily.
🎟 🚻 🅿 🆆 mmstadium.com

🎰 **Suncoast Casino and Entertainment World**
Suncoast Boulevard. **Tel** 031 328 3000. 🅿 🚻 🆆
🆆 suncoastcasino.co.za

🐠 **uShaka Marine World**
1 King Shaka Ave, Point. **Tel** 031 328 3000. **Open** 9am–5pm daily.
🎟 🚻 🅿 🚻 🆆
🆆 ushakamarineworld.co.za

Durban's impressive Moses Mabhiba Stadium

For hotels and restaurants in this region see p389 and pp407–8

The mock-Tudor façade of The Playhouse Company

Central Durban

Beautifully restored buildings and interesting museums can be found in the city centre, all within walking distance. The cafés and restaurants that line the streets offer respite from the heat and humidity.

Completed in 1910, Durban's **City Hall** was modelled after that of Belfast, in Northern Ireland. The central dome is 48 m (156 ft) high while statues symbolizing art, literature, music and commerce flank the four smaller domes.

The **Natural Science Museum** is situated on the ground floor of the City Hall. Exhibits vary from a display of South African wildlife to a mammal gallery, a bird hall, a dinosaur exhibit and an Egyptian mummy. Fascinating, if disturbing, are the oversized insects featured in the *KwaNunu* section. Upstairs, the **Durban Art Gallery** began

collecting black South African art in the 1970s, the first in the country to do so.

What was once Durban's Court now houses the **Old Court House Museum**. It contains relics of early colonial life in what was then Natal.

The **Playhouse Company** offers top-class entertainment, from opera to experimental theatre.

🏛 Natural Science Museum
City Hall, Anton Lembede St. **Tel** 031 311 2256. **Open** 8:30am–4pm daily (from 11am Sun). **Closed** Good Fri, 25 Dec. 🖼 📷

🏛 Durban Art Gallery
City Hall, Anton Lembede St. **Tel** 031 311 2265. **Open** 8:30am–4pm daily (from 11am Sun). **Closed** Good Fri, 25 Dec.

🏛 Old Court House Museum
77 Samora Machel St. **Tel** 031 311 2229. **Open** 8:30am–4pm Mon–Sat. **Closed** Good Fri, 25 Dec.

In the Natural Science Museum

Durban City Centre

① Victoria Street Market
② Tourist Junction
③ Old Court House Museum
④ City Hall
⑤ The Playhouse
⑥ Port Natal Maritime Museum
⑦ Victoria Embankment
⑧ uShaka Marine World
⑨ Suncoast Casino and Entertainment World

Exploring Durban

Away from the beachfront and central business district, beautiful mosques, richly-decorated temples and vibrant street markets await the visitor. Nature reserves and sanctuaries are situated on the outskirts of Durban, among them the Umgeni River Bird Park, north of the city, which houses exotic birds in walk-through aviaries, while the Hare Krishna Temple of Understanding, in the suburb of Chatsworth, never fails to impress with its grandiose opulence. Tour operators offer city tours to most of these sights.

Exotic curry and masala spice

Old Station Building

Durban's former railway station, a four-storey, red-brick building, was completed in 1894. In the entrance of the building stands a statue in memory of Mahatma Gandhi, who bought a train ticket to Johannesburg here in June 1893.

The building's most curious feature is the roof, which is designed to carry the weight of 5 m (16 ft) of snow. The London firm of architects accidentally switched the plans with those for Toronto in Canada and the roof of Toronto station caved in during the first heavy snowfalls.

The Tourist Junction has a wide range of maps and brochures; the staff can advise on all the sights in the city centre and beyond. There is also a booking office for accommodation at the national parks (the only other offices are in Cape Town and Pretoria), and a booking office for Durban Tourism's informative walking tours.

Victoria Embankment

Margaret Mncadi Avenue.
The Victoria Embankment was built in 1897 as an upmarket residential area. Today it is called Margaret Mncadi Avenue and is lined with modern skyscrapers. There are, however, still a few sights worth seeking out.

At the eastern end is the late-Victorian cast-iron **Da Gama Clock**, erected to commemorate the 400th anniversary of Vasco Da Gama's discovery of a sea route to India in 1847.

Photographs and memorabilia of Durban's seafaring past are displayed in the **Port Natal Maritime Museum**. The tugboats *Ulundi* and *J R More* and the minesweeper SAS *Durban* form part of the exhibits.

Just to the west of the museum is the Dick King statue, commemorating a British trader who embarked on an epic horse-ride to Grahamstown to request reinforcements during the Boer siege of Port Natal in 1842.

The fine Durban Club, built in 1904, on the opposite side of the road is one of the few original buildings remaining on the Victoria Embankment, while further to the west, the **Royal Natal Yacht Club** was founded in 1858 and is the oldest yacht club in Africa. Its restaurant is open to the public.

Ⅲ Port Natal Maritime Museum
Margaret Mncadi Avenue.
Tel 031 311 2231. **Open** 8:30am–3:30pm Mon–Sat, 11am–3:30pm Sun. &

Ⅲ Royal Natal Yacht Club
Yacht Mole, Margaret Mncadi Avenue. **Tel** 031 301 5425.
Open Restaurant: 8am–10pm daily. & W rnyc.org.za

▦ Victoria Street Market
Cnr Bertha Mkhize & Denis Hurley sts.
Tel 031 306 4021. **Open** 6am–6pm Mon–Sat, 10am–4pm Sun.

At the end of the N3 flyover, where the motorway meets the streets of central Durban, is the Victoria Street Market. The building is striking – each of its 11 domes was modelled on a notable building in India.

In this crowded bazaar, visitors can sample the tastes and aromas of the Orient as they browse through more than 170 stalls offering spices and incense, fabrics, leather goods, brassware and ceramics. Its street food stalls serve up delicious snacks such as samosas and Durban curry.

◪ Juma Masjid Mosque
Cnr Denis Hurley & Dr Yusuf Dadoo sts. **Tel** (031) 306-0026.
Open 9am–4pm Mon–Sat. book in advance.

The impressive Juma Masjid Mosque lies across the road from the Victoria Street Market. Completed in 1927, it is the largest mosque on the African continent. Visitors are allowed inside, except at prayer times.

Pleasure craft, large and small, moored at Durban's Royal Natal Yacht Club

A strict dress code is enforced, and shoes must be removed before entering the building.

🔵 Durban Botanic Gardens
John Zikhale Rd. **Tel** 031 322 4021. **Open** 7:30am–5:15pm Apr–Sep; 7:30am–5:45pm Sep–Apr. ♿ 🅿 Ⓦ durbanbotanic gardens.org.za

Located near the Greyville Racecourse, these attractive gardens were established in 1849 as an experimental station for tropical crops.

The spectacular cycad and palm collection on the 15-ha (38-acre) property is one of the largest of its kind in the world. It includes several rare species, such as a male *Encephalartos woodii* from the Ngoye forest, which was successfully transplanted in 1916. Among the garden's 480 tree species are the oldest jacarandas in South Africa, brought here from Argentina.

Durban's Botanic Gardens are the perfect setting for a picnic

The Hare Krishna Temple of Understanding in Chatsworth

Other attractions include a sensory garden, a Victorian sunken garden, an orchid house and an ornamental lake with ducks. Music by the Lake (www.musicatthelake.co.za) is a series of Sunday afternoon concerts (May–Aug), when Durbanites relax on the lawns with a picnic.

🔵 Umgeni River Bird Park
490 Riverside Rd, 16 km (10 miles) north of Durban off the M4. **Tel** 031 579 4600. **Open** 9am–5pm daily. **Closed** 25 Dec. 📷 🅿 ♿ Ⓦ urbp.co.za

Bordered on three sides by steep cliffs, and overlooking the north bank of the Umgeni River, 2 km (1 mile) from its mouth, the Umgeni River Bird Park enjoys a superb location. Four waterfalls cascade down the cliffs into ponds fringed by palms and lush vegetation. The four large walk-through aviaries allow visitors a face-to-

face encounter with some of the 700 birds. Among the 180 resident species are rare exotic parrots, toucans, cranes, macaws and hornbills.

Entertaining bird shows are held every day (except Mondays) at 11am and 2pm.

Hare Krishna Temple of Understanding
Bhaktiveedante Swami Rd, Chatsworth. **Tel** 031 403-3328. **Open** 10am–1pm, 2–8pm daily. 📷 🚫

This large, ornate temple of the International Society for Krishna Consciousness was designed by the Austrian architect Hannes Raudner. It is encircled by a moat and a garden laid out in the shape of a lotus flower.

The daily guided tours take in the awe-inspiring marble temple room and the inner sanctuary, and there is also a good vegetarian restaurant.

The Hindu Population of Durban

When the first sugar was produced from sugar cane in 1851, the Natal Colony experienced a major economic boom. Cheap labour was required to work in the plantations, and the colony entered into negotiations with the colonial government in India. Between 1860 and 1911, a total of 152,000 indentured labourers were shipped to Durban from Madras and Calcutta. Tamil and Hindi were the main languages spoken. At the end of their five-year contracts, the workers were offered a free passage back to India. More than half of them opted to remain in South Africa, and became active as retailers and vegetable farmers; in later years many entered commerce, industry and politics. Of the current population of 900,000 (the largest Indian community outside Asia), an estimated 50 per cent are Hindu. Diwali is their most important festival, and begins with the lighting of a lamp for the Goddess of Light, symbolizing the conquest of good over evil.

Statue of Bhaktivedanta Swami Prabhupada, a respected religious teacher

Durban's North and South Coasts

Durban is the central focus of South Africa's most popular holiday coastline. Blessed with a subtropical climate, this picturesque area is a delightful blend of sun, sand, surf and nature reserves. Extending 162 km (100 miles) south of Durban is a string of coastal towns and holiday resorts, such as Scottburgh. Uncrowded beaches at holiday villages including Ballito are hallmarks of the 154-km (96-mile) stretch of coast that lies north of Durban.

Crocworld
In a 60-ha (148-acre) indigenous botanic garden near Scottburgh, Crocworld has 12,000 Nile crocodiles and the largest eagle cage on the African continent.

Oribi Gorge
The Oribi Gorge, 21 km (13 miles) inland from Port Shepstone, is a scenic, thickly-forested area where cliffs rise from the deep chasms and open out to reveal the spectacular Samango Falls.

Port Edward
This village near the Umtamvuna Nature Reserve is the location of Caribbean Estates, a popular timeshare resort.

San Lameer
Two good golf courses, a private beach and a nature reserve make San Lameer a sought-after holiday resort.

For hotels and restaurants in this region see pp389 and pp407–8

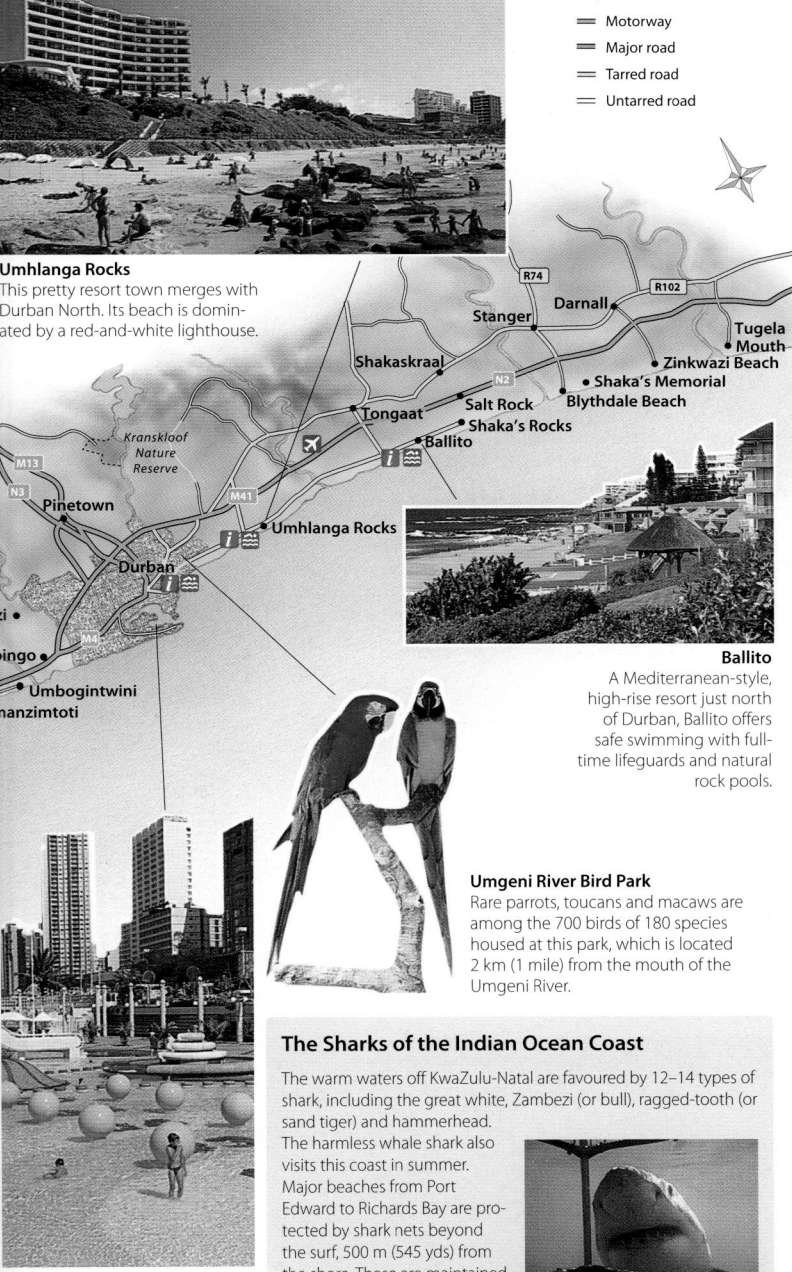

Key

— Motorway
— Major road
— Tarred road
— Untarred road

Umhlanga Rocks
This pretty resort town merges with Durban North. Its beach is dominated by a red-and-white lighthouse.

R74   R102

Darnall

Stanger   Tugela Mouth

Shakaskraal   Zinkwazi Beach

N2   Shaka's Memorial

Tongaat   Salt Rock   Blythdale Beach

Shaka's Rocks

Ballito

Kranskloof Nature Reserve

M13

N3

M41

Pinetown   Umhlanga Rocks

Durban

zi

ingo   M4

Umbogintwini

nanzimtoti

Ballito
A Mediterranean-style, high-rise resort just north of Durban, Ballito offers safe swimming with full-time lifeguards and natural rock pools.

Umgeni River Bird Park
Rare parrots, toucans and macaws are among the 700 birds of 180 species housed at this park, which is located 2 km (1 mile) from the mouth of the Umgeni River.

The Sharks of the Indian Ocean Coast

The warm waters off KwaZulu-Natal are favoured by 12–14 types of shark, including the great white, Zambezi (or bull), ragged-tooth (or sand tiger) and hammerhead. The harmless whale shark also visits this coast in summer. Major beaches from Port Edward to Richards Bay are protected by shark nets beyond the surf, 500 m (545 yds) from the shore. These are maintained by the KwaZulu-Natal Sharks Board, which finds about 1,200 sharks caught in the nets each year.

A "great white" encounter

Durban
This large city has the most developed beachfront in the country, with amusement parks, paddling pools, fun rides, a water park and a salt water pool.

For keys to symbols *see back flap*

➋ South Coast

A year-round combination of sunshine, sand, sea and surf has created an irresistible attraction for visitors coming from the cooler inland climates. Some 30 resort towns form a coastal playground that stretches for 162 km (100 miles) from Durban to the Eastern Cape border. Those towns closest to Durban are fairly built-up with holiday apartments, but the further south you go, the more the coastline opens up to reveal beautiful beaches, secluded lagoons and nature reserves.

Port Edward

Road map E4. N2, 20 km (12 miles) S of Margate. 🚗 4,500. 🚌 Margate. 🛈 Panorama Parade, Margate, 039 312 2322. 🌐 **gosouthcoast.co.za**

Port Edward on the Umtamvuna River is the southernmost beachside resort in KwaZulu-Natal. It is popular for swimming, fishing and boating, and the estuary is navigable far upstream, making it ideal for ski-boats. It was established in 1925 and named in honour of the Prince of Wales, later King Edward VIII of England.

Between 1976 and 1994 the land south of the Umtamvuna River bridge fell within the homeland known as Transkei. At that time, gambling was illegal under South African law, and a casino resort, the Wild Coast Sun, was built here to lure visitors from Durban and the South Coast. Today, it overlooks an unspoiled coastline covered in dense forest and grassland. A challenging 18-hole golf course stretches from the banks of the river to the shores of the lagoon.

The Mzamba Village Market opposite the resort's main entrance offers a range of locally-crafted curios, such as woven grass baskets, stone and woodcarvings and beadwork. The **Umtamvuna Nature Reserve**, some 8 km (5 miles) north of Port Edward, protects a 30-km (19-mile) section of the Umtamvuna River gorge. The trails that explore the dense, subtropical forest are excellent for bird-watching.

🌲 **Umtamvuna Nature Reserve**
Port Edward. Road to Izingolweni. **Tel** 039 313 2383. **Open** Apr–Sep: 7am–5pm; Oct–Mar: 6am–6pm. 🅿
🌐 **kznwildlife.com**

Margate

Road map E4. N2. 🚗 26,800. 🚌 Beachfront. 🛈 Panorama Parade, 039 312 2322.
🌐 **gosouthcoast.co.za**

Margate is the tourist capital of the South Coast. Its focal point is a broad expanse of golden sand lined by the tall, white towers of dozens of hotels and apartments.

The approach to the sandy beach leads across well-tended palm-shaded lawns that attract many sunbathers.

Along the main beachfront there is a variety of attractions for holiday-makers to enjoy. Among these are paddling pools, a fresh-water swimming pool, water slides, a mini-golf (putt-putt) course and ice-cream parlours.

Fishing is allowed off the pier and off Margate Rocks and there are plenty of tackle shops in town. Designated surfing and boogie-boarding areas are on Main Beach and at Lucien Point.

Margate's fishing area is one of the attractions of the town

Uvongo

Road map E4. N2, 12 km (7 miles) N of Margate.

Just before it empties into the sea, the iVungu River plunges down a 23-m (75-ft) waterfall into a lagoon. High cliffs, overgrown with wild bananas, protect the sheltered lagoon with its spit of sandy beach separating the river from the ocean. It is popular with families with young children for swimming, and pedal boats can be hired to explore the upper reaches of the river.

There are also walking trails in the Uvongo River Nature Reserve, which falls on both sides of the river. A two-hour circular walk winds through beautiful coastal forest full of a wide variety of indigenous trees, ferns, orchids and plentiful birdlife, including such rarities as the buff-spotted flufftail, purple-banded sunbird and the grey waxbill.

A luxurious hotel resort on the South Coast

For hotels and restaurants in this region see p389 and pp407–8

The Hibiscus Coast

Lying approximately 120 km (75 miles) south of Durban, the Hibiscus Coast extends from Hibberdene in the north to Port Edward in the south. As well as beaches and golf courses, this stretch of coastline is home to the famous "Sardine Run". Every June or July, millions of the tiny silver fish head north from their spawning grounds off the Eastern Cape to reach the waters of Port Edward. They are followed by predators such as dolphins, sharks and seals, while numerous seabirds rain down from above to take their fill. The Sardine Run lasts for several weeks, then lessens as the shoal continues its northbound migration.

Birds diving into a shoal of fish during the Sardine Run

Oribi Gorge Nature Reserve

Road map E4. 21 km (13 miles) inland of Port Shepstone. **Tel** 033 845 1000. **Open** 6:30am–7:30pm daily. ✷ 🏃 🏕 🌐 kznwildlife.com

In a region where population densities are high and where sugar cane plantations and coastal resort developments have replaced most of the natural vegetation, the ravine carved by the Umzimkulwana River is a delight for nature-lovers. The impressive gorge is 24 km (15 miles) long, up to 5 km (3 miles) wide and 300 m (975 ft) deep.

There is a scenic circular drive, as well as three walking trails and many beautiful picnic spots along the river, and at viewpoints overlooking the Samango, Hoopoe and Lehr's waterfalls in the gorge.

Small, forest-dwelling animals such as bushbuck, duiker and samango monkeys occur in the dense forest while the cliffs provide nesting sites for birds of prey.

Oribi Gorge was formed by the Umzimkulwana River

Scottburgh's beaches and lawns are popular with sunbathers

Scottburgh

Road map E4. N2, roughly 30 km (19 miles) S of Amanzimtoti. 🏠 11,500. 🚌 🅸 Scott St, 039 976 1364. 🌐 scottburgh.co.za

An almost continuous carpet of sugar cane plantations lines this stretch of South Coast, and the town of Scottburgh was once used as a harbour for exporting the crop. Today, the neat and compact little town has a distinct holiday atmosphere, and is a popular beach resort. It occupies the prominent headland overlooking the mouth of the Mpambanyoni River, and most of the hotels and holiday apartments offer superb sea views.

In the previous century, a spring used to cascade from the bank above the river, but today a large water slide occupies the site. A restaurant, small shops, a miniature railway and tidal pool are added attractions. Further south, a caravan park adjoins the beach and the town's popular golf course has a prime site overlooking the Indian Ocean surf.

Frangipani

Amanzimtoti

Road map F4. N2, 27 km (17 miles) S of Durban. 🏠 13,850. ✈ Durban. 🚌 🅸 95 Beach Rd, 031 903 7498.

It is claimed that Amanzimtoti derives its name from a remark made by Shaka Zulu *(see p53)*. In the 1820s, returning home from a campaign further down the South Coast, Shaka drank from a refreshing stream and is said to have exclaimed, *"amanzi umtoti"* (the water is sweet). Today, Amanzimtoti is a lively coastal resort. Its beaches are lined with hotels, holiday apartments, take-away outlets, restaurants and beachwear shops.

The most popular beach extends for 3 km (2 miles) north of the Manzimtoti River and offers safe bathing, picnic sites and a fine salt-water pool.

The N2 passes within 400 m (400 yrds) of the coast, providing easy access to the town's attractions, such as the small bird sanctuary, a nature reserve and two fine golf courses in the vicinity of the beach.

❸ North Coast

This subtropical region is renowned for attractive towns, sheltered bays, quiet beaches and forested dunes that give way to a green carpet of sugar cane and timber plantations. Northern KwaZulu-Natal has escaped the rampant development of the South Coast and offers unspoiled nature at its best.

Visitor canoeing in a lagoon on the Mlalazi River

Umhlanga

Road map F3. 20 km (12 miles) NE of Durban. 🏨 24,500. 🚌 Umhlanga Express. 🛈 Chartwell Drive, 031 561 4257. **Open** Mon–Sat.
🌐 umhlanga-rocks.com

Now a suburb of Durban, modern development lines the ridge above Umhlanga and includes shopping malls and business parks. But it retains its atmosphere as the premier holiday resort on the North Coast and has excellent beaches, timeshare resorts, hotels and restaurants. The promenade, which extends for 3 km (2 miles), provides stunning views of the golden sands that have made Umhlanga famous. A local landmark is the red-and-white Umhlanga Lighthouse, in front of the Oyster Box hotel.

Further north, at the mouth of the Ohlanga River, forested dunes form part of a nature reserve. A boardwalk crosses the river and the forest teems with blue duikers, birds and monkeys.

Hibiscus flower

Ballito

Road map F3. N2, 30 km (19 miles) N of Umhlanga. 🏨 19,200. 🚌 Baz Bus. 🛈 Ballito Drive, 032 946 1997. **Open** Mon–Sat. 🏄 Mr Price Pro (Jul).
🌐 thedolphincoast.co.za

Ballito and the neighbouring Salt Rock extend for 6 km (4 miles) along a coast known for its beaches, rocky headlands and sheltered tidal pools. Lining the main coastal road are many good restaurants. Accommodation ranges from luxury holiday apartments and timeshare resorts to family hotels and attractive caravan parks.

Mtunzini

Road map F3. N2, 29 km (19 miles) SW of Richards Bay.

The pretty village, whose name means "in the shade", is set on a hillside overlooking the sea. Its streets are lined with coral trees and in winter their red flowers add splashes of colour to the townscape. It is well-known for its grove of raffia palms, which has been designated a National Monument. The nearest known other group of these rare plants is on the Mozambique border, 260 km (163 miles) north. The rare palm-nut vulture is a fruit-eating raptor that may be spotted here, and the swamp forest and raffia palms can be seen from a raised boardwalk.

Mtunzini lies in a belt of unspoiled coastal forest that falls within the **Umlalazi Nature Reserve**. Comfortable log cabins tucked into the forest border a marsh, and along the banks of the Mlalazi River there is a circular walk through a mangrove swamp that is alive with crabs and mud-skimmers.

A second walk leads through the dune forest to a wide, sandy beach and reveals glimpses of fish eagles and kingfishers. Shy forest animals such as vervet monkeys, red duiker and bushbuck are often seen.

🏞 **Umlalazi Nature Reserve**
Entrance in Mtunzini village. **Tel** 035 340 1836. **Open** 5am–10pm. 🚗
🌐 kznwildlife.com

❹ Gooderson Dumazulu Lodge and Traditional Village

Road map F3. Bushlands Rd, Hluhluwe. **Tel** 035 562 2260. **Open** daily. 🚗 🚗 🚗 🚗
🌐 goodersonleisure.co.za

Situated in the heart of Zululand, this lodge is a thriving cultural village, where guides give

Holiday apartments and hotels line the beach at Ballito

◄ The dizzying suspension bridge across Oribi Gorge, which cuts through the sugar cane farmlands of KwaZulu-Natal

guests a rare insight into local customs. Visitors can particiapte in dancing, and taste Zulu beer while watching spears, shields, baskets and clay pots being made. The *isangoma* (diviner) is also available for a personal reading. The property includes a 3,000-sq-m (32,292-sq-ft) bird aviary with an elevated walkway, waterfall features and an extensive reptile park.

Guests can reside in self-contained or luxury rooms on an all-inclusive meal plan in ethnic huts arranged to resemble a traditional Zulu village.

Zulu warriors at the cultural village of Shakaland

❺ Shakaland

Road map F3. Eshowe. R68. **Tel** 035 460 0912. **Open** 6am–9pm daily. 🕐 Day visitors: 11am & noon daily (3-hour tours); overnight guests: 4pm culture tour, Zulu dancing after dinner & 9am morning tour. 🅿️ 🏕️ 🆆 aha.co.za/shakaland

For the 1984 TV series *Shaka Zulu*, several authentic 19th-century Zulu *kraals* were constructed. For the series' grand finale, the villages were set alight – only that of Shaka's father was spared and opened to the public as Shakaland.

The unique Zulu village is open for day visits, while visitors wishing to stay overnight are accommodated in large luxury beehive nets. A video explaining the origin of the Zulu people is shown, and

Zulu "love letter" pouch, Shakaland

guests enjoy traditional Zulu fare, followed by a traditional dancing display.

On a tour of the 40-hut village, visitors are introduced to a variety of traditional skills such as hut-building, spear-making, beer-brewing, artistic beadwork and pottery.

Framed by thorn trees and aloes, Goedertrou Dam in the valley below is an attractive body of water. The sunset river boat cruises are an added attraction. In the hills east of Shakaland, and commanding a superb view over the wide Mhlatuze Valley, is the site of Shaka's famed military stronghold, KwaBulawayo. Construction of this historic facility began in 1823, but today almost nothing remains of the citadel that once held so much of southern Africa in its grasp.

Traditional Muthi Healing

In traditional Zulu society, the *inyanga* (herbalist) was male and concentrated on medicinal cures, while the *isangoma* (diviner) was a woman who possessed psychic powers and the ability to communicate with the ancestral spirits.

Today, this strict division is no longer accurate. *Muthi* is an assortment of medicine and remedies made from indigenous bulbs, shrubs, leaves, tree bark and roots. Animal products such as fat, claws, teeth and skin are also often used.

Despite the advances of Western culture, the faith in traditional healing methods is still widespread in rural and urban settlements. In order to meet the demand for the plants and to ensure a regular supply, special "muthi" gardens" have been established in a number of nature reserves.

Shakaland offers unusual hotel accommodation

Zulu *inyanga* (herbalist)

For hotels and restaurants in this region see p389 and pp407–8

Southern bald ibis roosting site in Hluhluwe-Imfolozi Game Reserve

❻ Hluhluwe-Imfolozi Game Reserve

Road map F3. N2: Nyalazi Gate for the Imfolozi sector and Memorial Gate for the Hluhluwe sector.
ℹ️ Imfolozi office: 035 550 8476; Hluhluwe office: 035 562 0848; reservations: Ezemvelo KZN Wildlife, 033 845 1000. **Open** Apr–Sep: 6am–6pm daily; Oct–Mar: 5am–7pm daily. 🚗🛏️🍴📷
Ⓦ kznwildlife.com

An unspoiled wilderness of rolling hills, subtropical forest, acacia woodland and palm-fringed rivers, the 964-sq-km (372-sq-mile) park is world-renowned for its rhino conservation programme.

In 1895 two wildlife reserves, Hluhluwe and Imfolozi, were established to protect the last rhinos in South Africa. In the early 1950s a corridor of land between the two was added. The park was consolidated in 1989, and is now the fourth-largest in the country. One of Africa's leading wildlife sanctuaries, it is home to an astonishing diversity of wildlife. The varied vegetation supports large herds of nyala, impala, wildebeest, kudu, zebra and buffalo, as well as elephant, rhino, giraffe, lion, leopard, hyena and cheetah.

In 1958 a single male lion suddenly appeared – possibly from the Kruger National Park some 350 km (220 miles) to the north. Two lionesses were relocated from Kruger some time later, and their offspring have re-established prides throughout the park. What is unusual about the reserve is the hilly terrain, which provides great vantage points for viewing.

Nyalazi Gate, the park's main entrance, is reached from the N2 at Mtubatuba. It is a perfect starting point for exploring the park's 220-km (138-mile) road network. Heading south, the route traverses open woodland before fording the Black Imfolozi River. Then it ascends to Mpila Camp, which has magnificent views over the reserve.

A trio of exclusive reed-and-thatch rest camps on the banks of the Black Imfolozi, Sontuli, Gqoyeni and Nselweni rivers allow visitors to savour the most secluded corners of this wilderness. Game rangers conduct game-viewing walks.

From Nyalazi Gate north, the route follows a tarred road that curves across rolling hills teeming with wildlife. The journey to Hluhluwe climbs a range of hills, 400 m (1,300 ft) above the Hluhluwe River. These hills trap moisture-laden clouds, resulting in an average rainfall of 985 mm (38 inches) per year. In the dense woodland and forests live red duiker, bushbuck, nyala and samango monkeys. Buffalo, zebra, white rhino and elephant can be seen roaming the northeastern grasslands near Memorial Gate.

Hilltop Camp, at an altitude of 450 m (1,460 ft), offers panoramic views over the surrounding countryside and can accommodate up to 210 guests in its chalets. Facilities at the central complex include a restaurant, bar, shop, petrol station and swimming pool.

A short trail through the adjoining forest is excellent for bird-watching.

A female waterbuck at Hluhluwe-Imfolozi Game Reserve

❼ Ithala Game Reserve

Road map F3. Vryheid. R69 via Louwsburg, 50 km (31 miles) NE of Vryheid. **Tel** 034 983 2540; reservations: Ezemvelo KZN Wildlife, 033 845 1000. **Open** Oct–Mar: 5am–7pm daily; Apr–Sep: 6am–6pm daily. 🚗🍴
Ⓦ kznwildlife.com

From the unhurried village of Louwsburg on the R69, a tarred road descends a steep escarpment to the wilderness of Ithala, a 296-sq-km (114-sq-mile) tract of grassland with dramatic mountain scenery and densely wooded valleys.

The reserve was established in 1972 from previous farmland and since then it has been stocked with large species of

Hilltop Camp at Hluhluwe-Imfolozi Game Reserve

For hotels and restaurants in this region see p389 and pp407–8

Mhlangeni Bush Camp, Ithala Game Reserve

game and has reverted back to its natural state. The Pongolo River flows along the northern boundary for some 37 km (23 miles). Seven tributaries have carved the deep valleys that dissect this park and enhance its scenic splendour. The Ngoje escarpment rises dramatically to 1,446 m (4,700 ft), providing a striking backdrop.

A 7-km (4-mile) tarred road leads from the entrance to the prestigious Ntshondwe Camp. Its 67 chalets have been carefully tucked away between boulders and wild fig trees. The central complex contains a reception area, restaurant, store and coffee shop, and offers panoramic views over the entire reserve. In front of the building, an extensive wooden platform overlooks a reed-fringed waterhole and is perfect for birdwatching. As no fences surround the camp, animals such as warthogs often wander between the chalets. A path leads to a swimming pool tucked into a clearing at the base of the mountain. Ntshondwe Lodge is a lavish three-bedroomed cabin perched on a hill top. The far-reaching vista from its wooden deck and sunken swimming pool is arguably Ithala's finest.

Game-viewing at Ithala is excellent. Visitors will see white rhino, giraffe, hartebeest, kudu, eland, impala, wildebeest, warthog and zebra, as well as the only population in KwaZulu-Natal of the rare tsessebe antelope. Elephant, buffalo, leopard and black rhino are also present, but are more difficult to locate.

Ngubhu Loop, a 31-km (19-mile) circuit that crosses a broad basin, is the best drive in the park. Another route winds down the thickly wooded Dakaneni Valley to the Pongolo River. Although game is not as plentiful here as it is on the higher grasslands, the scenery is spectacular.

Game-viewing in Ithala Game Reserve

❽ iSimangaliso Wetland Park

See pp300–301.

❾ Phinda Private Game Reserve

Road map F3. 23 km (14 miles) northeast of Hluhluwe off the R22. **Tel** 011 809 4300. **Open** restricted access. 🚗 🚫 **W** andbeyond.com

Extending over 170 sq km (65 sq miles) of bushveld, wetland, savannah and sand forest, the privately owned Phinda is sandwiched between the iSimangaliso Wetland Park and uMkhuze Game Reserve. Wildlife likely to be seen is the same as

wildlife seen at uMkhuze. Activities on offer include sunset cruises on the Mzinene River and outdoor dining, as well as game-viewing drives, bush walks and fishing or diving expeditions. Wildlife includes nyala, kudu, wildebeest, giraffes, zebras, elephants, lions, white rhinos and cheetahs. There are six lodges, each with its own unique atmosphere and bush or wetland views. The reserve has its own air strip and arranges air transfers from Johannesburg, or road transfers from Richards Bay.

❿ Tembe Elephant Park

Road map F3. 65 km (40 miles) north of Mbazwana on the R22. **Tel** 035 592 0001 **Open** Apr–Sep: 6am–6pm daily; Oct–Mar: 5am–7pm daily. 🚗 🚫 **W** kznwildlife.com

This 290-sq-km (112-sq-mile) wilderness reserve bordering Mozambique protects the flood plain of the Pongolo River along the northern boundary of KwaZulu-Natal. The park was established in 1983 to protect the elephants that migrate between the two countries. Access is limited to 4WD vehicles, and only 10 groups of visitors per day. There is a tented camp near the entrance, and two hides overlook areas where elephants come to drink. The park has South Africa's largest population of suni antelopes and 430 species of birds.

Environs

West of Tembe and bordering Mozambique, the **Ndumo Game Reserve** is famous for its rich riverine life, particularly waterbirds – over 420 species have been recorded. Hides on the Nyamithi and Banzi pans offer excellent views. The pans also sustain hippos and crocodiles and white and black rhinos. Guided tours are available to book at the office.

🚗 Ndumo Game Reserve
98 km (61 miles) northeast of Mbazwana via the R22. **Tel** 035 591 0098. **Open** Apr–Sep: 6am–6pm daily; Oct–Mar: 5am–7pm daily. 🚗 🏕 🛶 ⚠ **W** kznwildlife.com

⑧ iSimangaliso Wetland Park

Chosen as South Africa's first UNESCO World Heritage Site in 1999, the 3,320-sq-km (1,282-sq-mile) iSimangaliso Wetland Park is the country's third-largest protected area and easily its most biodiverse. Nelson Mandela once described it as "the only place on the globe where the oldest land mammal (rhinoceros) and the world's biggest terrestrial mammal (elephant) share an ecosystem with the world's oldest fish (coelacanth) and the world's biggest marine mammal (whale)."

St Lucia Estuary offers excellent shore-based fishing

Exploring iSimangaliso Wetland Park

Comprising more than half-a-dozen separate reserves and sanctuaries, iSimangaliso – a Zulu phrase meaning "something wondrous"– encompasses a diverse range of habitats, from Africa's most southerly coral reefs to mountains, grassland and coastal forest. The park is particularly suited to self-drive exploration, ideally basing yourself in St Lucia village for a few nights, then striking out to some of the isolated rest camps and lodges at more northerly sites such as Sodwana, Sibaya and Kosi Bay. Even without your own vehicle, though, St Lucia makes an excellent base for organized day excursions, ranging from boat trips on the estuary and seasonal whale-watching on the open sea to turtle-tracking tours and guided safaris to various nearby game reserves.

St Lucia Village

Carved into a jungle-like peninsula that separates the Indian Ocean from the 368-sq-km (142-sq-mile) Lake St Lucia, this is perhaps the only South African urban centre patrolled nocturnally by hippopotamus, warthog, red duiker, bushbaby and other small predators. Walking trails starting from the village offer excellent birding – notably trumpeter hornbill and purple-crested turaco – while launch trips on the estuary provide good hippo and crocodile sightings. The village is flanked by a gorgeous sandy beach, while the Crocodile Farm to its north is one of the finest in the country.

Loggerhead turtles lay their eggs on sandy beaches

Cape Vidal and the Eastern Shores

Set below forested dunes on a beach 32 km (20 miles) north of St Lucia, Cape Vidal offers seasonal land-based whale- and dolphin-viewing. The sandy coastline here forms a vital nesting site for loggerhead and leatherback turtles, which mostly come ashore to lay eggs in December. Between St Lucia and Cape Vidal, the Eastern Shores sector has some of the world's tallest forest dunes, and resident wildlife includes several types of antelope. A game-viewing loop to Lake Bhangazi offers a chance of sighting buffalo, rhino, elephant and cheetah.

uMkhuze Game Reserve

Created in 1912, this 400 sq km (154 sq miles) inland spur of iSimangaliso offers excellent game viewing, with substantial numbers of rhino, elephant, giraffe and antelope. Wildlife photographers frequent the trio of well-sited hides overlooking shallow pans that attract a stream of nyala, kudu, zebra and other large mammals. The park is also known for its birdlife, with more than 420 species recorded. Nsumo Pan, encircled by yellow-fever trees and low hills, is an excellent spot for water birds, while sand forests harbour "iSimangaliso specials" such as yellow-spotted nicator, Neergard's sunbird and African broadbill. Geared mainly to self-drivers, uMkhuze offers activities such as a Fig Forest Walk near Nsumo Pan and a cultural village providing insights into traditional Zulu lifestyle and crafts.

Sodwana Bay

Located on an unspoiled stretch of coast 65 km (41 miles) north of St Lucia, Sodwana Bay is South Africa's premier scuba destination, operating all year round, though the best conditions for diving are from April through to September. The world's southern-most tropical coral reefs lie offshore and are, in most cases, named after their imperial distance from the main launch site. The closest and most popular is Two Mile Reef, which is a ten-minute boat ride away and offers dives from 9 m (30 ft) to below 30 m (100 ft) in depth. Nearby, Quarter Mile Reef is famed for the ragged-toothed sharks that congregate there in January and February, while the deeper Five Mile Reef comprises a stunning variety of branching, table and plate corals. Further

African fish eagle

out, Seven Mile Reef, with its overhangs, drop-offs and mushroom rocks, is considered one of the world's most beautiful dive sites. Aside from a swirl of colourful reef fish, larger marine creatures often seen include blue-spotted ray, sand shark, kingfish, dolphins and turtles.

For non-divers, there are several good snorkelling spots, while a wealth of birds, along with the pretty red duiker and animated samango and vervet monkeys, are likely to be seen along a 5 km (3 miles) trail starting at the reserve headquarters.

Lake Sibaya

It is a measure of South Africa's scarcity of water resources that Lake Sibaya, extending over a relatively modest 65 sq km (25 sq miles), is the country's largest natural freshwater body. The centre of a catchment area just ten times larger than its own surface, Sibaya is fed almost entirely by subterranean springs and drained only by

 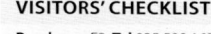
solar evaporation, despite lying 3 km (2 miles) inland of the Indian Ocean. Aquatic wildlife includes an endemic fish, the Sibaya goby, as well as around 150 hippos and plenty of crocodiles. Sibaya also hosts more than 20,000 water birds. Rarities regularly observed in the area include Stanley's bustard, pink-throated longclaw, pygmy goose and rufous-bellied heron.

Kosi Bay Nature Reserve

iSimangaliso's most northerly component, the 110-sq-km (42-sq-mile) Kosi Bay Nature Reserve, protects eight lakes and a labyrinth of streams and channels abutting the Mozambican border. The three lakes closest to the estuary mouth have a composition similar to seawater, and are separated by a series of less saline lakes from the freshwater expanse of Lake Amanzamnyama (literally "black water"). Culturally, Kosi Bay is notable for the local Thonga people's continued use of traditional woven grass fishing traps. This is an excellent example of sustainable, traditional management of natural resources, since the estuary's wide mouth ensures that its fish population is readily replenished from the open sea. A large rocky reef within the estuary offers some of the region's best snorkelling conditions, with high tide being the best time to take a dip in search of the likes of butterfly fish, moray eel, parrot-fish and devil's firefish. Kosi Bay is also home to South Africa's most diverse mangrove swamp and largest groundwater forest, as well as the world's most southerly stand of raffia palms. Canoe trips along the Sidhadla river into Lake Amanzamnyama often yield sightings of samango monkey, crocodile and hippo, along with birds such as the African finfoot, and Pel's fishing owl.

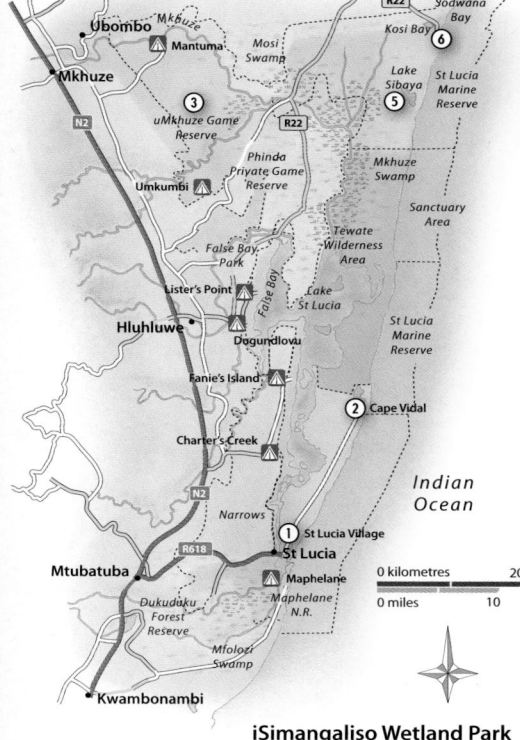

iSimangaliso Wetland Park

① St Lucia Village
② Cape Vidal
③ uMkhuze Game Reserve
④ Sodwana Bay
⑤ Lake Sibaya
⑥ Kosi Bay Nature Reserve

Key

━━ Major route
══ Road (tarred)
══ Road (untarred)

GAUTENG, LIMPOPO AND MPUMALANGA

Introducing Gauteng, Limpopo and Mpumalanga

From natural marvels to bustling modern cities – this region offers something for everyone. Built above one of the world's wealthiest gold seams, Johannesburg is Africa's most sophisticated city, though its sleek business districts and exclusive suburbs contrast strikingly with its modest "other half" Soweto. Further east, the Kruger National Park, set on the hot plains of the Lowveld, supports some of Africa's largest concentrations of wildlife. To the west lies the Magaliesberg range and grandeur of the Lost City. Further north, subtropical Limpopo Province is home to the Waterberg Mountains (South Africa's premier malaria-free, game-viewing region) and rigged landscapes of historic Mapungubwe National Park.

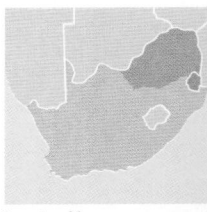

Locator Map

The Palace of the Lost City, a part of the opulent Sun City resort and casino complex, is a spectacular architectural indulgence of age-stressed concrete, beautifully crafted pillars and ornate domes set in a man-made tropical garden and surrounded by a variety of water features such as Roaring Lagoon.

Lephalale

Modimolle

GAUTENG AND
SUN CITY
(See pp310–29)

Sun City

Mmabatho   Rustenburg   Pretoria

Lichtenburg

Johannesburg
Soweto

Gern

Potchefstroom

Klerksdorp   Vereeninging

Johannesburg is the largest city in South Africa and has grown phenomenally from the simple mining camp of 1886 into one of Africa's most important commerical, industrial and financial centres.

◄ Seen here in the Kruger National Park, the elephant is one of the "Big Five" African animals

Lions *(Panthera leo)* can live in almost any habitat except desert and thick forest. They are nocturnal and diurnal and occur in prides of 3 to 40 individuals (although 6 to 12 is more usual). In the Kruger, which is accessible through several gates, they are often seen resting in the shade of a tree.

Musina

Louis Trichardt

Modjadiskloof

kwane

Tzaneen

BaPhalaborwa

kopane

LIMPOPO, MPUMALANGA AND KRUGER
(See pp330–47)

Pilgrim's Rest

Groblersdal

Mbombela
(Nelspruit)

Emalahleni

Mbabane

Ermelo

cunda

Big Bend

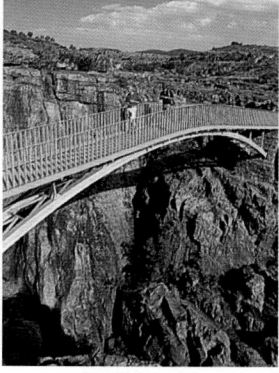

Bourke's Luck is a series of intriguing potholes, scoured into the yellow dolomite rock by the Treur and Blyde rivers. The potholes were named after gold miner Tom Bourke, who owned the land adjacent to the main gold-bearing reef.

```
0 kilometres        100
0 miles        50
```

Pilgrim's Rest is a beautifully restored old mining town which owes its existence to South Africa's first gold rush in 1873. By the end of that year, more than 1,500 diggers had converged on the area and Pilgrim's Rest had grown into a large mining camp.

Conservation in the Kruger National Park

The Kruger National Park stretches for 352 km (220 miles) along South Africa's northeastern border. The 19,633-sq-km (7,580-sq-mile) conservation area supports an astounding array of fauna and flora. There are no longer fences between Kruger and the private reserves on the park's western side, so game can roam freely between them. This enormous region is now generally referred to as Greater Kruger and it extends from the Crocodile River in the south to the Limpopo River in the north, and from the eastern Drakensberg escarpment to the Mozambique border.

Extent of the Kruger National Park

▨ Park boundaries

Dry hills provide a habitat for kudu and eland, animals that do not need to drink water regularly.

Zebra flourish when artificial water points are provided, but large zebra herds can have a negative impact on animals such as roan, sable and reedbuck, which feed on tall grass.

Zebra

Giraffe

The Olifants River is the largest of the park's seven major watercourses. Since water is scarce, artificial water points have allowed elephants to move into areas that were previously accessible only in the wet summer months.

Tall trees along the riverbed shelter animals such as baboons, grey duiker, bushbuck and giraffes.

Managing for Diversity

Scientists are only now beginning to understand the complicated African savannah. In an effort to manage the ecosystem in a way that maintains its diversity, artificial water points, which caused habitat-modifiers such as elephants to flourish (to the detriment of other species), are now being closed.

The giraffe is the tallest of the browsers and favours areas where acacias are abundant.

Kudu are large antelopes that do not need to drink frequently, and live in dense woodland.

Sable antelopes require tall grass of a high quality that grows on well-drained soils.

Radio tracking enables scientists to monitor the endangered predators. Only about 120 cheetahs and 120 wild dogs inhabit the park's vast expanse. Research has shown that competition from the more aggressive lion is a major limiting factor.

The Great Limpopo Transfrontier Park

This cross-border initiative links the Kruger National Park in South Africa, Limpopo National Park in Mozambique, and Gonarezhou National Park, Manjinji Pan Sanctuary and Malipati Safari Area in Zimbabwe, into one huge conservation area covering 37,700 sq km (14,556 sq miles) – roughly the same size as the Netherlands. By taking down the fences along the country borders, which also divided conservation areas, the habitat available to the wildlife has been greatly increased, and the natural migratory routes of the animals have been extended. The floodplains and tributaries of five major river systems water this vast area.

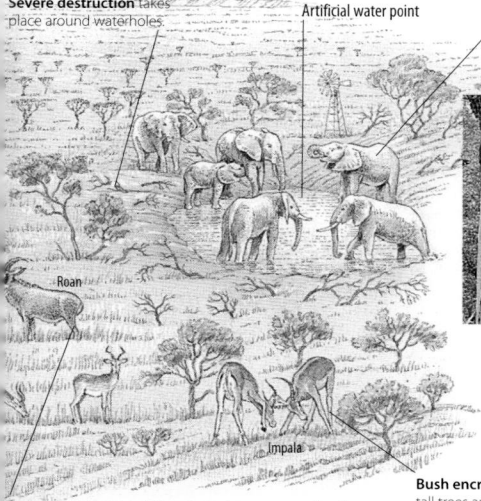

Severe destruction takes place around waterholes.

Artificial water point

Elephants are termed habitat-modifiers, because they destroy trees, which brings about significant changes in vegetation.

Roan

Impala

Destructive feeders, elephants strip bark off umbrella thorn acacias and fever trees. Kruger's 13,000 elephants each consume up to 250 kg (550 lb) of vegetation daily and comprise one-quarter of the park's total biomass.

Endangered roan antelopes require open woodland, with tall grass to hide their young. They are unable to adapt to the short-grass conditions caused by an increase in zebra herds around artificial water points.

Bush encroachment, resulting from elephants damaging tall trees and from concentrations of grazing animals near water, benefits browsers such as impala, kudu and giraffe.

Tourist Guidelines

To ensure the safety of visitors and maintain the park's essential attributes, a few regulations are necessary. It is important to observe speed limits, as the animals, too, use the roads as thoroughfares. Since camp closing times are strictly enforced, a good rule of thumb is to calculate an average travelling speed, including stops, of 20 kph (12 mph). Visitors are not permitted to leave their cars except at the designated picnic sites and facilities such as shops and takeaways at the larger rest camps – all of the animals are wild and unpredictable, and the predators are superbly camouflaged. Although baboons and vervet monkeys may beg for food, particularly around the camp sites, feeding them is a punishable offence. It disrupts natural behaviour, and often produces aggression, particularly in male baboons.

Baboons can be aggressive

Visitors blatantly ignoring the rules

Gold Mining

Vast natural resources make South Africa one of the richest countries on the continent. Ancient sediments in this geological treasure chest yield silver, platinum, chromite, uranium, diamonds – and gold. Over the years, small-scale miners have left behind evidence of their labour all around the country. The most poignant of these historic sites is Pilgrim's Rest *(see p336)*, a well-preserved mining town in Mpumalanga. Today, South Africa is the world's sixth-largest gold producer, and the industry is controlled by giant corporations.

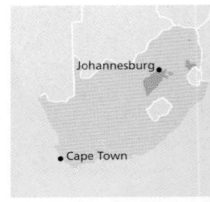

Extent of Gold Fields

▨ Main mining operations

The headgear, set up after the initial shaft has been sunk, carries the ropes, wheels and other mining equipment.

In 1889, Johannesburg was a sprawling tent settlement. Three years earlier, a prospector named George Harrison had discovered the greatest gold reef in history on a farm named Langlaagte, just west of today's Johannesburg.

South Deep Mine

The South Deep Mine in Mpumalanga, 45 km (28 miles) southwest of Johannesburg, forms a part of the Witwatersrand Basin, and deep-level mining commenced in 1961. Today it is the world's second-largest mine after the Grasberg Mine in Indonesia. With a depth of 2,995m (9,826ft), it is also the world's seventh-deepest mine.

The main shaft in a deep-level gold mine is encased in a concrete "collar" to support the headgear. South African gold-mine shafts are the deepest in the world because the reefs extend downwards underground. Currently Mponeng in the North West Province is the world's deepest shaft, at 4 km (2.5 miles).

Miners work underground in 8-hour shifts. Rock temperatures in the confined working place (stope) may reach up to 55°C (131°F).

Canteen staff have to cater for the different traditional diets of miners, as well as their exceptionally high calorie intake.

The processing plant produces gold bars of 90 per cent purity, ready for transport to the refinery.

The ore is crushed and pumped into a leach tank where cyanide is added to dissolve it. The product is then heated to remove impurities, and smelted into gold bars. A yield of one troy ounce (31.1 grams) of gold from a ton of ore is considered very rich indeed.

The Krugerrand, a collector's gold coin, was first produced by the South African Mint in 1967 to help to market South African gold. It was named after President Paul Kruger, whose face is on one side, while the other side depicts a springbok. A special edition bears Nelson Mandela's portrait.

The gold price is determined twice daily (except at weekends and on British bank holidays) by a group of London bullion dealers. It is quoted in US dollars per troy ounce.

A carat denotes the purity of gold (measured per part of gold in 24 parts other metal).

The Kruger Millions

Legend has it that when Paul Kruger, last president of the Zuid-Afrikaansche Republiek (1883–1900), left to go into exile in Europe in 1900, all the gold in the State Mint at Pretoria travelled with him to keep it out of the hands of the advancing British army. At the town of Nelspruit (Mpumalanga), the presidential train was delayed while mysterious wooden crates were unloaded and carried away into the bush. Kruger had little money (or any assets at all) in Europe, and it is surmised that the missing gold – in Kruger pounds, coin blanks and bars – still awaits discovery somewhere between Nelspruit and Barberton. The search continues to this day.

President Paul Kruger

GAUTENG AND SUN CITY

Johannesburg is an urban conglomerate that developed around the rich gold mines of the Witwatersrand in Gauteng. To the north lies sedate and elegant Pretoria, founded by the Voortrekkers before the discovery of gold and today South Africa's administrative capital. In the northwest, the glittering Sun City complex provides fast-paced entertainment, while the neighbouring Pilanesberg reserve offers Big Five game-viewing.

The rocky Witwatersrand ("ridge of white waters") escarpment lies about 1,600 m (5,250 ft) above sea level and stretches for 80 km (50 miles) from west to east. After the discovery of the main reef on the Witwatersrand in 1886, gold fast became the basis of the national economy and dictated the development of the then mostly rural Transvaal Boer republic. While Johannesburg was founded on gold and industry, Pretoria was founded as a capital during the Voortrekker period of South Africa's past, and is still today the home of government departments and diplomatic missions.

Those who wish to escape the cities do not have far to go. Northwest of Johannesburg and Pretoria is the Hartbeespoort Dam, where water sports enthusiasts flock at weekends, and where the shores are lined with resorts and holiday homes. The Magaliesberg mountain range is a nearby nature retreat whose lower slopes are popular for hiking. The ambitious Sun City development turned the most unpromising terrain in the former homeland of Bophuthatswana, now part of the North West Province, into an opulent leisure resort. Subsequent expansion produced the exotic fantasy called The Palace of the Lost City, where tropical jungle now covers what once was overgrazed farmland, and computer-generated waves wash onto pristine, man-made beaches. Even those who do not find the complex to their taste have to admire the effort and planning that went into its creation. Adjoining Sun City is the Pilanesberg Game Reserve, which was created out of an extinct volcanic crater in 1979, and is today home to all the large animals visitors expect to see on safari.

In October, the streets of Pretoria are ablaze with lilac jacaranda blossoms

◀ Doors of the Constitutional Court, Johannesburg, with carvings symbolizing the rights enshrined in the Constitution

Exploring Gauteng and Sun City

With an estimated population of around seven million, the greater Johannesburg metropolitan area is the most densely populated region of the country. Its choice of attractions is ever-expanding, and places of interest include museums dedicated to the city's gold-mining past as well as the apartheid struggle. Pretoria is just 56 km (35 miles) north of Johannesburg along the N1 motorway, and today the two cities are almost joined up by the burgeoning development that surrounds them on the Highveld. To the northwest, Sun City and Pilanesberg Game Reserve lie next to each other and are nearly always visited together.

History comes alive in Gold Reef City

Sights at a Glance

1. Johannesburg
2. Soweto
3. Gold Reef City
4. Sandton and Rosebank
6. Pretoria
7. Sun City
8. Pilanesberg Game Reserve
9. Madikwe Game Reserve

Tour

5. *Touring Gauteng pp322–3*

Key

- ▬▬ Motorway
- ▬▬ Main road
- ▭▭▭ Minor road
- ▪▪▪ Untarred road
- ▬▬ Scenic route
- ▭▭▭ Main railway
- ——— Minor railway
- ▬▬▬ International border
- ▬▬▬ Provincial border
- △ Summit

Spanwerk
Rooi
Sent
Maricosdraai
Thabaz
Derdepoort
Ramotswa
Ganskuil
Midde
9 **MADIKWE GAME RESERVE**
Nietverdiend
Silkaatskop
Northam
PILANESBERG GAME RESERVE 8
Blairbeth
Mabaalstad
7 **SUN**
Kromellenboog Dam
R565
Zeerust
Bospoort Dan
Groot-Marico
Millvale
N4
Mmabatho
Wondermere
Rustenburg
Mafikeng
Elandsputte
Koster
R53
Derby
Lichtenburg
Swartplaas
R30
NORTH WEST
Klerkskraal
Deelpan
Coligny
Madibogo
Biesiesvlei
N14
Ventersdorp
Carletonv
Sannieshof
Gerdau
Harts
Kuruman
R53
Brakspruit
Foc
Delareyville
N12
Hartbeesfontein
Potchefstroom
Ottosdal
Renosterspruit
Klerksdorp
Orkney
Pa
N12
Vaal
Vierfontein
Wolmaransstad
FRE
Leeudoringstad
Kimberley
Viljoenskroon
Makwassie
Bothaville
Roc
Bloemfontein

For hotels and restaurants in this region see pp389–90 and pp408–10

Monte Christo
Villa Nora
Marken
Lephalale
R33
Groesbeek
Mokolo
Dam
Mokamole
Tinmyne
Hermanusdorings
Sterk
Mokopane
LIMPOPO
Vaalwater
Polokwane
Hangliipberge
erberge
Vanalphensvlei
Haakdoring
R33
N1
Mookgophong
oiberg
Modimolle
Middelfontein
N11
R516
Bela-Bela
Holme Park
R33
euport
Nutfield
Radium
Settlers
Elands
on
m
Siyabuswa
Pienaarsrivier
Rust de Winter
Dennilton
Marokolong
Soutpan
pies
Kwamhlanga
Loskop Dam
Game Reserve
Mabopane
R25
Wilge
espoort
Lammerkop
am
6 PRETORIA
Bronkhorstspruit
Middelburg
GAUTENG
Emalahleni
N4
SANDTON &
NG ROSEBANK
N14
Nelspruit
4
Ogies
D
1 JOHANNESBURG
N12
Coalville
N11
TY
3
MPUMALANGA
2
Germiston
Kriel
Daleside
Nigel
Devon
N17
Kinross
Bethal
Heidelberg
Evander
Davel
Vereeniging
Balfour
Charl Cilliers
Ermelo
asolburg
R23
Dasville
Greylingstad
Bettiesdam
Morgenzon
Vaal
Vaal Dam
N3
Waterval
ranjeville
Vaal
ATE
Villiers
Heilbron
Cornelia
Frankfort
Wilge
Harrismith

0 kilometres   50

0 miles   25

The Valley of the Waves at Sun City

Getting Around

Major roads radiate in all directions from Johannesburg and Pretoria, but the most direct roads linking them are the N1 and R21. Heading west, the N4/R104 from Pretoria heads to the popular weekend retreat of Hartbeespoort Dam. Sun City and Pilanesberg are approximately 140 km (87 miles) west of Pretoria, and 170 km (105 miles) northwest of Johannesburg. There are a number of approaches but the most direct is to take the N4 to Rustenberg, from where it is 50 km (31 miles) northwest on the R565 to the entrance of Sun City.

The Union Buildings, the seat of parliament in Pretoria

For keys to symbols *see back flap*

❶ Johannesburg

The densely populated city of Johannesburg is the country's financial and commercial heartland. The city has many names, and most of them, including Egoli and Gauteng, mean "place of gold". Indeed, gold and glamour are close companions in this place, which grew from a primitive mining camp to a metropolis in little over a century. The city pulsates with entrepreneurial energy while, at the same time, retaining the spirit of a frontier town. It lies at an altitude of 1,763 m (5,784 ft) above sea level, but at the Western Deep gold mine, the shafts reach an astonishing 3,777 m (12,388 ft) below ground.

Traditional arts and crafts are sold at many markets in Johannesburg

Exploring Johannesburg

Johannesburg's attractions are widely spread so it is advisable to hire a car or make use of the Gautrain or bus services such as Rea Vaya or the hop-on-hop-off City Sight-seeing bus, or to take one of the many half-day tours on offer. While most of the sights in the city centre can be explored on foot, this is a busy place and caution is required.

City Centre

🚇 Origins Centre

Yale Rd, Braamfontein. **Tel** 011 717 4700. **Open** 10am–5pm daily. **Closed** public hols. 🖼 🖵 ✏ 📷
W origins.org.za

Part of the University of the Witwatersrand (Wits), this centre traces the origins of man from the Stone Age, and houses the country's most important Khoi and San rock art. A technical exhibit focuses on how genetic testing contributes to understanding our ancestry. Also here is the Wits Art Museum, with displays of traditional African art.

🎭 Market Theatre Complex

Crn Bree and Miriam Makeba. **Tel** 011 832 1641. ✏ 🖵 ♿
W markettheatre.co.za

The Market Theatre Complex is the centre of the Newtown Cultural Precinct, which includes the Market Theatre, SAB World of Beer, the Workers' Museum and Library and Museum Africa. A great effort has been made to make this a safe place to visit.

Originally an Indian fruit market, the complex now houses three theatres, two art galleries, cafés, restaurants and shops. Each Saturday morning, traders gather on Mary Fitzgerald Square outside to sell curios.

Opposite the Market Theatre, the Africana Museum (1935) was relaunched in 1994 as **Museum Africa**. The theme is Johannesburg and its people at various stages of socio-political transformation.

West of the theatre on Jeppe Street, the **Oriental Plaza** bazaar is permeated by the aroma of Eastern spices. Here, some 360 shops and stalls sell everything from carpets to clothing. Many traders are descendants of the Indians who came here in the 19th century after their contracts on the sugar plantations expired.

🏛 Museum Africa

121 Bree St, Newtown. **Tel** 011 833 5624. **Open** 8am–5pm daily.
🖼 ♿ 📷

🏰 Oriental Plaza

Bree and Margaret Mcingana sts, Fordsburg. **Tel** 011 838 6752. **Open** 8:30am–5pm Mon–Fri, 8:30am–3pm Sat. **Closed** noon–2pm Fri. ✏
📷 **W** orientalplaza.co.za

🏛 SAB World of Beer

15 Helen Joseph St (entrance in Gerard Sekoto St), Newtown. **Tel** 011 836 4900. **Open** 10am–6pm Tue–Sat, 10am–5pm Sun & Mon. 🖼 ✏ 📷
W worldofbeer.co.za

South African Breweries (SAB), established in 1895, is the largest brewer by volume in the world. In this modern museum there is an entertaining display of the company's long history. Other exhibits focus on the development of brewing in ancient

Museum Africa, part of the Market Theatre Complex in Newtown

Mesopotamia and illustrate how beer-brewing came to Africa and Europe, with excellent reconstructions of a "gold rush" pub, a traditional Soweto shebeen (see p320) and a full-scale brewhouse.

SAB World of Beer, a museum tour with beer (or a non-alcoholic cocktail) included

Diagonal Street

Between President and Jeppe sts.
This characterful street was first established in the mid-1880s by Indian and Chinese settlers who set up businesses to serve the original mining town. Today, the row of Victorian and Edwardian shops with their balconies and filigree work still sell fabrics, hardware and kitchen utensils. One of the more interesting modern buildings on the street is the 20-storey building at No. 11, which was built in the shape of a multi-faceted diamond for mining company Anglo American. Nearby at No. 17 is the Old Johannesburg Stock Exchange building.

At the end of Diagonal Street, at the junction of Albertina Sisulu Street, is a delightful statue of anti-apartheid activists Walter and Albertina Sisulu. The figures sit opposite each other holding hands, and the inscription reads: "Walter and Albertina Sisulu married in 1944. Through their enduring love and dedication they became parents to the nation."

At No. 14, **Kwa-Zulu Muti** is a working herbalist shop that represents a traditional side of Africa still very much a part of daily life for many South Africans. Not all the potions and remedies are herbal. Its fascinating stock includes animal skins, horns and claws, as well as dried bats, frogs and insects. Visitors can seek advice from a *sangoma*, a traditional African healer.

🏠 Kwa-Zulu Muti
14 Diagonal St. **Tel** 011 836 4470.
Open 8am–5pm Mon–Fri, 8am–1pm Sat. **Closed** Sun, public hols.

VISITORS' CHECKLIST

Practical Information
Road map E2. Gauteng Province.
7 million. Park City Transit Centre, Johannesburg Station, Crn Rissik and Wolmarans Str, 011 028 7743. **Open** 8am–5pm Mon–Fri. FNB Dance Umbrella (Feb); Standard Bank Joy of Jazz (Aug); Arts Alive (Sep).
joburgtourism.com

Transport
20 km (12 miles) E of the city. Park Station cnr Rissik and Wolmarans sts, Braamfontein. Park Station.

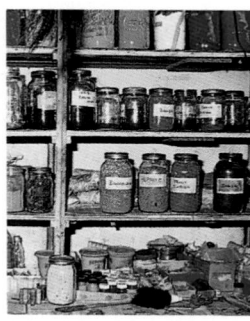

Traditional African herbal remedies

Johannesburg

1. Origins Centre
2. Market Theatre Complex
3. Museum Africa
4. Oriental Plaza
5. Diagonal Street
6. SAB World of Beer
7. Kwa-Zulu Muti
8. Standard Bank Art Gallery
9. Main Street Mall
10. Gandhi Square
11. Carlton Centre & Top of Africa
12. Johannesburg Art Gallery
13. Constitution Hill

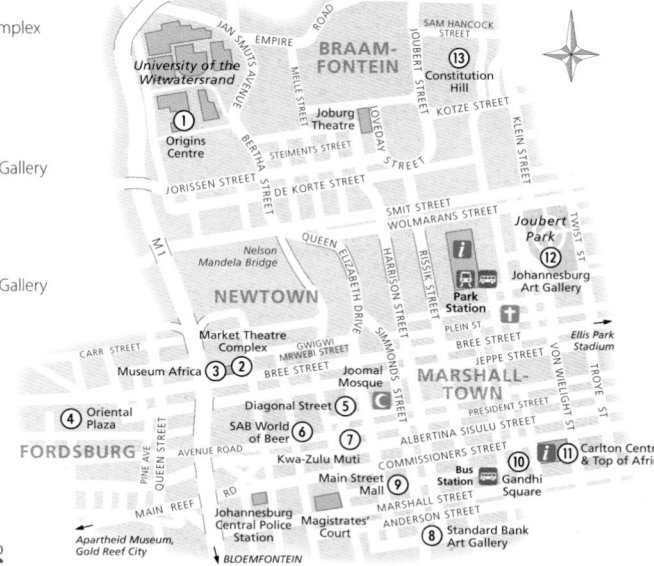

0 metres 750
0 yards 750

For keys to symbols *see back flap*

The impressive Carlton Centre, a landmark on the downtown Johannesburg skyline

🏛 Standard Bank Art Gallery
Cnr Simmonds and Fredericks sts.
Tel 011 631 4467. **Open** 8am–
4:30pm Mon–Fri, 9am–1pm Sat.
Closed Sun, public hols. 🚹
W sponsorships.standardbank.com

The unusual setting of a
working bank conceals a
sophisticated gallery that
provides a remarkable
showcase for talented local and
international artists. As well as
changing exhibitions, the
display features part of the
Standard Bank's own extensive
collection. The gallery has easy-
to-follow explanations of both
the collection and the African
fine art form. The building also
hosts recitals and concerts.

🚇 Main Street Mall
In the heart of the central
business district, this traffic-free
section of Main Street runs from
the Magistrates Court on Ntemi
Piliso Street in the west to
Gandhi Square in the east. It is
lined with office blocks that are
home to many corporate and
mining companies. Dubbed the
Mining District Walk, an outdoor
museum along the street

includes relics from the early
gold-rush days as well as
modern sculptures and water
features. On weekdays Main
Street is filled with office-
workers enjoying the street
cafés and with a high security
presence, it's a safe area to
explore. Look out for the
Leaping Impala sculpture
outside the Anglo American
building; a mine headgear
structure on the corner of Sauer
Street that was once at the
Langlaagte Mine; the Art Deco
bas relief on the side of the BHP
Billiton building, showing
scenes of early miners working
above and below ground; and
the stamp mill in front of the
Chamber of Mines building.

🚇 Gandhi Square
The former Government
Square, dating from 1893,
was completely refurbished as
a large piazza-style public
space in 2002 as part of a
wider redevelopment of the
surrounding district. The
square was also given a new
name, after the prominent
Indian politician Mahatma

Gandhi, who came to
Johannesburg in 1903 and
worked as a lawyer and civil
rights activist. Gandhi's
profession often brought him
to the Transvaal Law Courts
(now demolished), which were
located in the square.

In 2003, a larger-than-life-
sized statue of Gandhi in his
lawyer's robes by sculptor
Trinka Christopher was
unveiled here. Trendy shops,
restaurants and cafés line the
southern side of the square.

🚇 Carlton Centre & Top of Africa
150 Commissioner Street. **Tel** 011 308
1331. **Open** 9am–6pm Mon–Fri, 9am–
5pm Sat, 9am–2pm Sun. 🚹 🖥 🏛

A key downtown landmark, the
Carlton Centre is 50 storeys or
223 m (730 ft) tall, making it
the African continent's highest
building. For a small fee visitors
can take the lift up to the Top
of Africa observation deck on
the 50th floor, where amazing
panoramic views of the city
can be enjoyed. On very clear
days, the Voortrekker
Monument near Pretoria can
be seen. The building was
completed in 1973 as part of
a hotel complex, although the
hotel no longer operates.
Today there is a shopping mall
on the lower levels.

🏛 Johannesburg Art Gallery
King George St, Joubert Park. **Tel** 011
725 3130. **Open** 10am–5pm Tue–Sun.
Closed Good Fri, 25 Dec. 🖥 🏛

This gallery offers displays of
traditional, historical and
modern South African art, as

Gandhi Square, with a statue of the Indian pacifist

well as several works from European schools, including 17th-century Dutch and Flemish paintings and a collection of Pre-Raphaelite artwork. There are also interesting collections of ceramics, sculpture, furniture and textiles on view.

🏛 Constitution Hill
11 Kotze St, Braamfontein. **Tel** 011 381 3100. **Open** 9am–5pm daily. **Closed** Good Fri, 25 Dec. 🅿 ♿ 🎫 last tour: 4pm
🌐 **constitutionhill.org.za**

This remarkable development is a living museum documenting South Africa's turbulent past and its transition to democracy. The site incorporates the Old Fort Prison Complex, a notorious jail for more than a century where many, including Nelson Mandela, were imprisoned. South Africa's Constitutional Court, established in 1994 after the country's first democratic elections, now occupies the eastern side of the complex.

🦁 Johannesburg Zoo
Cnr Jan Smuts Ave and Upper Park Drive, Parkview. **Tel** 011 646 2000. **Open** 8:30am–5pm daily. 🅿 🎫 ♿ 🍴 🌐 **jhbzoo.org.za**

Established in 1904, today this is one of the best-regarded zoos in the world, with spacious, natural enclosures that are home to some 2,000 animals from more than 350 species,

Blackburn Buccaneer in the South African National Museum of Military History

including the only polar bears in Africa. It offers plenty of activities and occasionally opens in the evenings for night-time tours to see the nocturnal animals.

Across Jan Smuts Avenue, Zoo Lake is a large park with well-established lawns and mature trees. Rowing boats can be hired, and there's a large open-air swimming pool and a tea garden.

🏛 South African National Museum of Military History
20 Erlswold Way, Saxonwold. **Tel** 011 646 5513. **Open** 9am–4:30pm daily. **Closed** Good Fri, 25 Dec. 🅿 ♿ 🌐 **ditsong.org.za**

Initially opened by the then prime minister Field Marshal Jan Smuts in 1947 to commemorate South Africa's role in the two World Wars, this outstanding museum also covers the Anglo-Zulu War, the Anglo-Boer War and the

South African resistance movements. It displays more than 44,000 items, divided into 37 separate categories, including the nation's official war art and war photography collections. It also has some of the world's rarest military aircraft, including the only surviving night fighter version of the feared German Me 262 pioneer jet aircraft.

🏛 Apartheid Museum
Northern Parkway and Gold Reef Road, Ormonde. **Tel** 011 309 4700. **Open** 9am–5pm daily. **Closed** Good Fri, 25 Dec. 🅿 🎫 Tue–Sun. 🍴 🌐 **apartheidmuseum.org**

The darkest days of South Africa's turbulent past are chillingly evoked at this fascinating museum. To set the mood, there are separate entrances for whites and non-whites. Documenting the triumph of the human spirit over adversity, the displays recall the National Party's apartheid policy, which came into force in 1948 and turned 20 million non-whites into legally defined second-class citizens. Particularly powerful exhibits include a room with 131 nooses representing the number of political prisoners hanged during apartheid, BBC footage taken in 1961 of Nelson Mandela when he was in hiding from the authorities, and a series of evocative photographs taken by Ernest Cole before he was sent into exile during the late 1960s.

Allow at least two hours to visit the museum, but note that it is not suitable for children under 11 because of the harrowing nature of the material on display.

The entrance to the Apartheid Museum, with its separate doorways

❷ Soweto

Soweto is the oldest, largest and best-known of the so-called "townships" in Gauteng. Its oldest quarter, Pimville (originally Klipspruit), was established in 1904; the suburb of Orlando sprung up in the 1930s; another settlement of 20,000 squatters took root in the 1940s; and Meadowlands was created to accommodate people evicted from Sophiatown in 1959. This cluster of settlements was formally amalgamated as "Soweto" in 1963. Several pivotal events associated with the anti-apartheid struggle took place in Soweto, most notably the drawing up of the Freedom Charter in 1955 and the student uprising of 1976. It has also been home to some of the country's most revered figures, including Nelson Mandela and Archbishop Desmond Tutu, who once lived a few houses apart on Vilakazi Street.

Mandela House Family Museum, former home of Nelson Mandela

Exploring Soweto

Although it is no longer unsafe to visit, Soweto is still best explored on a guided tour and a half- or full-day here ranks among Johannesburg's most popular tourist activities. Tours are usually guided by Soweto residents and take in key landmarks associated with the anti-apartheid move-ment, along with a visit to a local *shebeen* (bar) or restaurant, while avoiding potential trouble spots.

🏛 Hector Pieterson Memorial and Museum

Khumalo Street, Orlando West. **Tel** 011 536 0611/2. **Open** 10am–5pm Mon–Sat, 10am–4pm Sun. 🎫 museum only.

On 16 July 1976, 13-year-old Hector Pieterson became the first victim of police action in the Soweto Uprising, a landmark wave of anti-apartheid clashes triggered by student protests against the proposed introduction of Afrikaans in local schools. More than 20,000 people took part in the protests, and a subsequent commission attributed 451 student deaths and 2,389 injuries to the police. The poignant Hector Pieterson Memorial, erected in the early 1990s two blocks from where its namesake was shot by police, is dominated by Sam Nzima's iconic photograph of the dying Pieterson being carried by another student, accompanied by his elder sister Antoinette. Next to the memorial, the Hector Pieterson Museum houses photographs, oral testimonies and historical documents that

illuminate and contextualise the Soweto Uprising – an event whose broader significance can be gauged by the fact that 16 June, the anniversary of the first protest, is now commemorated as a public holiday.

🏛 Mandela House Family Museum

Vilakazi Street. **Tel** 011 936 7754. **Open** 9am–5pm daily. 🎫 **W** mandelahouse.com

This small museum preserves 8115 Orlando West, the modest house where Nelson Mandela lived from 1948, until he was imprisoned in 1963, initially with his first wife Evelyn Ntoko Mase, then from 1958 with his second wife Winnie Madikizela-Mandela. It was restored in 2009 and now functions as a museum dedicated to the Mandela family.

🚩 Regina Mundi Church

Khumalo Street. **Tel** 011 986 2546. **Open** 9am–5pm daily. 🎫 **W** reginamundichurch.co.za

Built in 1964, Regina Mundi is South Africa's largest Catholic church. Up to 5,000 people can

fit into the structure, an unusual A-frame with low side walls only a quarter as high as the pinnacle of the tall sloping roof. The church served as a clandestine rendezvous for activists during the apartheid era, when overt political meetings were outlawed. It also provided refuge to demonstrators fleeing the police in the 1976 Soweto Uprising, and scars of gunfire associated with that event can still be seen on the interior and outside walls. US president Bill Clinton and his wife Hillary took communion at Regina Mundi in 1998, and former First Lady Michelle Obama made an address here in the company of Nelson Mandela's wife Graca Machel in 2013.

Walter Sisulu Square

Cnr Klipspruit Valley & Union Rd. **Tel** 011 945 2200. **Open** 9am–5pm Mon–Fri, 9am–4pm Sat & Sun. **W** walter-sisulusquare.co.za

Describing itself as "South Africa's first township entertainment explosion centre", Walter Sisulu

The interior of the Regina Mundi Church

For hotels and restaurants in this region see pp389–90 and pp408–10

Square is a modern shopping mall named after the deeply respected late ANC Deputy President who served 26 years in prison alongside Nelson Mandela. Its centrepiece is an open-air museum that celebrates the Freedom Charter – the document that forms the very cornerstone of the present-day South African constitution – drawn up on the site (then an empty field) by 3,000 representatives of various resistance organizations in June 1955.

Orlando Towers

Dynamo St. **Tel** 071 674 4343.
Open noon–5pm Thu, 10am–6pm Fri–Sun & public holidays (bungee jumps & other activities operate on a first-come, first-served basis).
W **orlandotowers.co.za**

One of Soweto's most distinctive landmarks, the 100-m (330-ft) tall twin towers were constructed as cooling towers for the coal-fired Orlando Power Station, which was established in 1935 and decommissioned in 1998. Their once-bleak concrete façade received a facelift in 2002, when they became the canvas for a colourful mural featuring local icons such as the Soweto String Quartet and Nelson Mandela. The disused towers now also double as a commercial vertical adventure facility offering activities such as bungee jumping, abseiling and zip-lining.

FNB Stadium

Soccer City Avenue. **Tel** 011 247 5300.
9am, 10:30am, noon & 3pm, except when the stadium is in use.
W **stadiummanagement.co.za**

One of the world's ten largest stadiums, the 95,000-seater Calabash-shaped arena known as "Soccer City" has hosted several legendary football matches, notably the 2010 FIFA World Cup between Spain and the Netherlands, South Africa's 2–0 championship victory over Tunisia in the 1996 Africa

VISITORS' CHECKLIST

Road map E2. 1.3 million.
OR Tambo 55km (33 miles).
N Walter Sisulu Square (cnr Klipspruit Valley & Union Rd)
Tel 011 342 4316.
Open 8am–5pm Mon–Fri.
W joburgtourism.com

Nations Cup, and the 2013 Africa Cup of Nations final between Nigeria and Burkina Faso. It has also hosted several other important national events, including the official memorial service to Nelson Mandela in December 2013. It debuted as a music venue when U2 performed there in 2011, and has since hosted concerts by Lady Gaga, Rihanna and Bruce Springsteen, among others. The stadium is best visited when an international or major domestic football or rugby fixture is underway, but guided tours operate four times daily at other times.

The FNB Stadium, also known as "Soccer City"

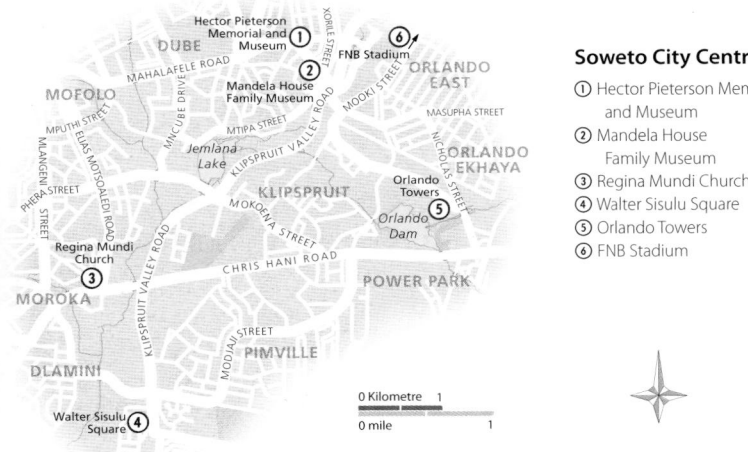

Soweto City Centre

① Hector Pieterson Memorial and Museum
② Mandela House Family Museum
③ Regina Mundi Church
④ Walter Sisulu Square
⑤ Orlando Towers
⑥ FNB Stadium

The Spirit of Sophiatown

Sophiatown – 10 km (6 miles) from Johannesburg's city centre in the 1950s – was a rather seedy shanty town, yet it was also the cradle of urban black culture and became part of South Africa's mythology. Much of the creative black African talent of Johannesburg lived in this overcrowded slum. Artists, journalists from *Drum* (the first "black" magazine in the country) and musicians would meet in the vibrant dance halls and debate politics in the shebeens (illegal bars). In the 1950s, the government ordered the forcible removal of the community to Meadowlands (now Soweto) – a characterless settlement on the far edge of the city – and the white suburb of Triomf replaced Sophiatown. The old name Sophiatown was reinstated for the suburb in 1997.

Shebeens
The Casbah Gang Den was the most notorious shebeen. At these illegal drinking spots, workers and teachers, both white and black, would meet.

Washing was done without access to tap water.

Sophiatown Gangs
Gangsters looked to the USA for role models. The most admired gang in Sophiatown was a snappily dressed, limousine-driving group known as "The Americans".

Essence of Sophiatown

Despite the poverty, squalor, petty crime and violence, Sophiatown's stimulating vibe differed from that of other townships in the country. People of all races could (and did) buy and own properties here.

Skokiaan was a potent, backyard-brewed alcoholic cocktail.

Building materials were bits of wood, cardboard boxes, tin and old sacks.

The Sounds of Music
The sounds of the penny whistle, saxophone, harmonica, piano, trumpet and clarinet filled the streets and halls.

Leaving Sophiatown
It took four years to remove all of the inhabitants to Meadowlands. By 1959, Sophiatown had been demolished.

Visitors at the family-friendly theme park in Gold Reef City

🟢 Gold Reef City

Road map E2. ℹ️ Northern Parkway, Ormonde, Johannesburg, 011 248 6800. **Open** 9:30am–5pm Wed–Sun (daily during school hols). **Closed** 25 Dec. 📷 incl. all rides & shows. 🎭 9am, 10am, 11am, 2pm & 3pm; multilingual. ♿📠📷 **W** goldreefcity.co.za

Situated next to the Apartheid Museum 8 km (5 miles) south of the centre, Gold Reef City reconstructs the Johannesburg of the early 1890s. It aims to recapture that transient time during which the town evolved from a mining camp to a modern city. An interactive tour includes a visit to the underground mine it is built around, the chance to see gold panning, and a demonstration of the heavy-footed Isicathulo "gumboot" dance (probably conceived by migrant miners as an alternative to traditional drumming, which was restricted by the authorities).

This theme park also incorporates thrilling rides such as the roller-coaster-like Anaconda, and a plethora of curio shops and eateries.

🟠 Sandton and Rosebank

Road map E2.

North of Johannesburg, the metropolitan sprawl blends into expensively laid-out residential areas with high walls, spacious gardens, swimming pools and tennis courts.

Affluent Sandton is a fashionable shoppers' paradise, with **Sandton City** reputedly the most sophisticated retail centre in the southern hemisphere. It is especially noted for its speciality shops, trendy boutiques, jewellers and dealers in African art, curios and leatherwork. The centre also has cinemas and dozens of excellent restaurants and bistros. A number of five-star graded hotels adjoin the Sandton City complex and Nelson Mandela Square, where an Italianate fountain is the focal point in a little piazza, lined with coffee shops and restaurants.

The residential suburb of Rivonia, north of Sandton, is home to **Liliesleaf Farm**, once

Posing for a photograph with the 6 m (50 ft) statue of Nelson Mandela

a rural farmhouse and now a museum dedicated to the apartheid era. It was on this farm that, on 11 July 1963, the South African security forces carried out a raid that ended with the arrest of most of the leaders of the African National Congress. The ANC representatives, including Walter Sisulu and Govan Mbeki, were imprisoned after the Rivonia Trials later that year. Although Nelson Mandela had been arrested six months earlier, he was also part of the Rivonia Trials, which marked the beginning of his 27-year incarceration.

South of Sandton is Rosebank, where the **Rosebank Mall** offers a mix of chain stores, upmarket boutiques, restaurants and entertainment, including a ten-pin bowling alley and cinemas.

🏛️ **Sandton City**
Cnr Sandton Dr & Rivonia rds. **Tel** 011 217 6000. **Open** 9am–7pm Mon–Thu, 9am–8pm Fri, 9am–6pm Sat & Sun. ♿📠📷🏛️ **W** sandton-city.co.za

🏛️ **Liliesleaf Farm**
George Ave, Rivonia. **Tel** 011 803 7882. **Open** 8:30am–5pm Mon–Fri, 9am–4pm Sat & Sun. 📷♿📷📠 **W** liliesleaf.co.za

🏛️ **Rosebank Mall**
Cradock St, Rosebank. **Tel** 011 788 5530. **Open** 9am–6pm Mon–Sat, 10am–5pm Sun. ♿📠📷🏛️ **W** rosebankmall.co.za

Playing in the fountain at Nelson Mandela Square, Sandton

For hotels and restaurants in this region see pp389–90 and pp408–10

❺ Touring Gauteng

Much of Gauteng consists of the industrial areas that have helped to generate the nation's wealth, but the vibrant metropolitan centres of Johannesburg and Pretoria are surrounded by a green belt that offers various facilities for outdoor recreation. Popular destinations such as the Ann van Dyk Cheetah Centre, Hartbeespoort Dam and the hiking trails of the Magaliesberg mountain range are accessible via an excellent network of motorways.

② **The Magaliesberg Range**
This chain of low hills between Pretoria and Rustenburg is popular with hikers. The area has many hotels, guest farms, caravan parks and camp sites.

① **Maropeng Visitor Centre**
Housed in the Tumulus Building, this is the official visitor centre of the Cradle of Humankind, a paleoanthropological site which was declared a World Heritage Site in 1999 *(see pp48–9)*.

⑪ **Sterkfontein Caves**
This extensive cavern network – part of the Cradle of Humankind Heritage site – is one of the world's most important archaeological locations. Guided tours leave every 30 minutes.

Tips for Drivers

Length: 200 km (124 miles). Hartbeespoort Dam is an hour's drive from Pretoria and Johannesburg.
Stopping-off points: Past Hartebeesport at the Damdoryn crossroads, the Welwitschia Country Market has shops and restaurants.

⑩ **Walter Sisulu National Botanical Garden**
The Witpoortje Falls form the focus of the garden, where indigenous highveld flora such as aloes and proteas attract many bird species.

Map labels:
Rustenburg
Mooinooi
Buffelspoort Dam
Magalie
Nooitgedacht Battlesite
Block
R560
R563
①
Rhino Nature R
Upington
Krug

③ **Hartbeespoort Dam**
A 17-sq-km (7-sq-mile) water surface makes this a prime weekend destination for those living in Johannesburg and Pretoria.

0 kilometres   10
0 miles   5

De Wildt

R566

nbi

R511   R13   ④

Cableway ●   R514

amtloryn ●
Kosmos ●   ③   ● **Hartbeespoort**

Hartbeespoort Dam   *Pretoria*

N4

ersberg   ⑤

⑥   R511

R512

⑦

⑧   R511

⑨

R512

⑩

R24

N1

Johannesburg

oort

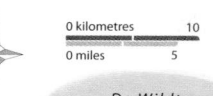

④ **Ann van Dyk Cheetah Centre**
This sanctuary near Brits initiated a breeding programme for captive king cheetahs in 1971. The project is a great success. Booking is essential.

⑤ **Lesedi Cultural Village**
This mock-up of four typical African villages – Xhosa, Zulu, Pedi and Sotho – illustrates all aspects of tribal life, including traditional singing and dancing. The three-hour tour includes a meal.

Key

■ Motorway
▬ Tour route
═ Other roads

⑥ **Crocodile Ramble**
Visitors driving along this arts and crafts route can stop off at a variety of workshops to watch the craftspeople in action and to buy fine art, furniture and metalware.

⑦ **Heia Safari Ranch**
Impala, blesbok and zebra wander freely through the grounds. A restaurant and bungalows sit on the banks of the Crocodile River.

⑨ **Lion Park**
A one-way road passes through a 200-ha (493-acre) lion enclosure and a separate park stocked with blesbok, black wildebeest, impala, gemsbok and zebra. There is also a picnic site and a restaurant.

⑧ **Aloe Ridge Nature Game Reserve**
Here visitors can see giraffes, buffalo, hippos and many antelope and bird species. There is also a Zulu crafts centre.

❻ Pretoria

The monuments and grandiose official buildings, some dating back to the 1800s, are softened by Pretoria's many parks and gardens. Each spring, the flowers of the jacaranda trees add splashes of lilac to the streets of South Africa's administrative capital, which is also one of the country's foremost academic centres. The South African government has changed the name of the larger municipality to Tshwane, the Setswana name of the Apies River, but the city centre itself has retained the name Pretoria.

Paul Kruger Monument, Church Square, Pretoria

Exploring Pretoria

Historic buildings, gracious parks, theatres and restaurants can be found throughout this elegant, compact city, which centres on the attractive, pedestrianized Church Square.

🦓 National Zoological Gardens

232 Boom St. **Tel** 012 339 2700.
Open 8:30am–5:30pm daily. 🚼
♿ 🚻 📷 **w** nzg.ac.za

Better-known as Pretoria Zoo, this parkland lies in the heart of the city on the bank of the Apies River. One of the top ten zoos in the world, it is very conservation conscious. Much time and effort is spent on breeding programmes of rare or endangered species such as the Cape mountain zebra and the stately Arabian oryx.

🏛 Church Square

Cnr WF Nkomo and Paul Kruger sts.
Among the buildings on the square are the **Raadsaal** (1890), one-time parliament of the former Boer Republic, and the **Palace of Justice** (1899), used as a military hospital until 1902 by the British. Anton van Wouw's statue of Paul Kruger was cast in Italy in 1899, the year the Transvaal Republic went to war against the British Empire.

🎭 South African State Theatre

Pretorius St. **Tel** 012 392 4000.
w statetheatre.co.za
This Japanese-style complex has five theatres where ballets, dramas, operas, musicals and classical concerts are performed regularly.

🏛 City Hall

Paul Kruger St.
The imposing City Hall was built in 1931 in Neo-Classical style. In front of it stand two statues depicting Marthinus Pretorius, founder of the city, and his father, Andries. A statue of the mythical chief Tshwane stands nearby.

🏛 National Museum of Natural History

432 Paul Kruger St. **Tel** 012 322 7632.
Open 8am–4pm daily. **Closed** Good Fri, 25 Dec. 📷 ♿ **w** ditsong.org.za
This natural history museum has a remarkable collection of stuffed animals, as well as permanent archaeological and geological exhibitions.

Many of South Africa's indigenous birds are displayed in the Austin Roberts Bird Hall.

🏛 Melrose House

275 Jeff Masemola St. **Tel** 012 322 2805. **Open** 10am–5pm Tue–Sun.
Closed public hols. 📷 🖥
w melrosehouse.co.za

In the 1880s, British architect William Vale designed this home for transport contractor George Heys. The house, featuring nearly all forms of precast embellishment available, was inspired by Cape Dutch architecture, English country houses and Indian pavilions. Today, the museum still has many of its original contents.

During the South African War, Melrose House was the residence of Lord Kitchener, British commander-in-chief. It was here that the Treaty of Vereeniging was signed on 31 May 1902, ending the war.

Ndebele Arts and Crafts

The Ndebele are noted for their colourful dress and their art, which includes sculpted figurines, pottery, beadwork, woven mats, and their celebrated wall painting (see p413). An outstanding example is the beaded *nguba*, a "marriage blanket" which the bride-to-be, inspired by her ancestors, makes under the supervision and instruction of the older women in her tribe. Traditionally, the women work the land and are the principal decorators and artists, while the men fashion metal ornaments such as the heavy bracelets, anklets and neck rings that are worn by women.

Typical Ndebele art

⊞ Union Buildings

Government Ave, Meintjies Kop.
Open daily (grounds only).

Designed by the renowned
architect Sir Herbert Baker,
the Union Buildings were built
to house the administrative
offices of the Union of South
Africa in 1910. Baker himself
chose the imposing hill site
from where the two large office
wings overlook landscaped
gardens and an impressive
amphitheatre.

Although it is not open to the
public for reasons of security,
the impressive Renaissance-
style building with its Cape
Dutch and Italian influences
may be admired from the
peaceful gardens.

Environs

Visible on the left as visitors
approach Pretoria on the
N1 from Johannesburg, the
Voortrekker Monument and
museum commemorate the
Afrikaner pioneers who trekked
from the Cape in the 1830s to
escape British domination.

Begun in 1938, the centenary
of the Battle of Blood River *(see
p55)*, it became a focus of
Afrikaner unity. The structure
features a cenotaph in the
Hall of Heroes which is lit by a

The Voortrekker Monument

beam of sunlight at noon on
16 December, the date of the
Battle of Blood River.

East of Pretoria on the R104
lies **Sammy Marks Museum**,
once the elegant residence of
industrial pioneer Sammy Marks
(1843–1920), the founder of the
South African Breweries. The
house has been beautifully
furnished in a Victorian style.

⊞ Sammy Marks Museum
Route 104, Bronkhorstspruit Rd.
Tel 012 755 9541. 🕐 9:30am–4pm
Tue–Sun (tours every 2 hours). 🅿 ♿
📷 🆆 ditsong.org.za

⊞ Voortrekker Monument
Eeufees Rd. **Tel** 012 326-6770.
Open 8am–6pm daily (to 5pm May–
Aug). **Closed** 25 Dec. 🅿 📷
🆆 vtm.org.za

Historic Melrose House is set in a splendid garden

Pretoria City Centre
① National Zoological Gardens
② Church Square
③ Raadsaal
④ South African State Theatre
⑤ City Hall
⑥ National Museum of Natural History
⑦ Melrose House
⑧ Union Buildings

For keys to symbols *see back flap*

The Cascades Hotel at Sun City

❼ Sun City

Road map D2. Rustenburg. N4, take R565 turn-off. ℹ️ Welcome Centre, 014 557 1580. ✈️ Pilanesberg, 014 552 1261; Johannesburg and Cape Town. 🚌 Sun International Central Reservations, 011 780 7855; tour buses from Johannesburg and Pretoria. **Open** day visitors: 8am–9pm daily. 🛝 ♿ 📷 🖥️ 🏠 🛍️ 🎭

Set in a fairly bleak part of the North West Province, two hours by road from Johannesburg and Pretoria, Sun City was the brain-child of hotelier Sol Kerzner. In the 1970s, when the complex was built, the land formed part of the quasi-independent "republic" of Bophuthatswana, where gambling, officially banned in South Africa at the time, was legal. The casino was a key part of the initial success of the resort, which then included only one luxury hotel, a man-made lake and a challenging 18-hole golf course

designed by the former South African golfing champion Gary Player.

It soon became apparent that the complex could not cope with the influx of visitors, and a further two hotels were added in 1980 and 1984 respectively – the Cabanas and the attractive Cascades. Then in 1992, the Palace of the Lost City *(see pp328–9)* opened, and today it is still Sun City's five-star flagship hotel. In the same year, the Valley of the Waves was constructed below the hotel and a second golf course added to the complex. The Valley of the Waves is one of Sun City's favourite attractions – a huge waterpark with a man-made beach with palm trees, a "roaring lagoon" with

Casino entrance

a wave machine, and a number of thrilling waterslides, including the 70-m (230-ft) Temple of Courage. To enter this, visitors cross the Bridge of Time, an ingenious mock-volcano that erupts every hour in a theatrical display of rumbling volcanic sounds and smoke.

Although changes in gambling law introduced in 1996 mean that casinos have sprung up around the country, Sun City continues to attract visitors with its many other entertainment options. Not only does it offer a chance of winning a fortune at the spin of a wheel, there are also elaborate stage shows and music concerts at the Superbowl, a man-made lake for parasailing, water-skiing and jet-skiing, horse-riding stables and a 10-pin bowling alley. The complex also houses restaurants and coffee shops, boutiques, a cinema, a spa and swimming pools. At the entrance to the resort is **Kwena Gardens**, home to more than 7,000 Nile crocodiles that can be seen from elevated walkways.

🐊 **Kwena Gardens**
Tel 014 552 1262. **Open** 10am–6pm daily. Feeding: 4:30pm daily. 🛝 🖥️ 🏠
🌐 **kwenachalets.co.za**

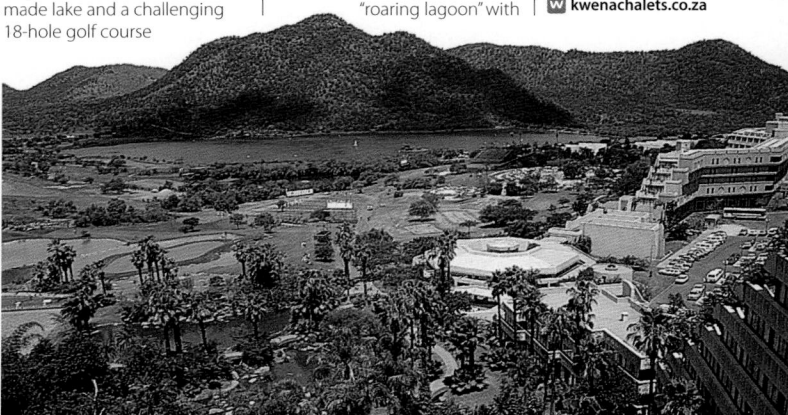

Sun City is a completely man-made oasis in the North West Province

For hotels and restaurants in this region see pp389–90 and pp408–10

The man-made rainforest at Sun City

Hot-Air Ballooning in the Pilanesberg

Hot-air balloon trips over Pilanesberg Game Reserve are a popular safari option. Drifting in total silence over the herds of wildlife that peacefully graze within the rim of the extinct volcano is a remarkable experience. The trips are operated by Air Trackers (tel 014 552 5020, www.hotairballoonsafarisa.co.za), and can be booked either through the Pilanesberg accommodation or at the Welcome Centre in Sun City. Rates include a one-hour balloon ride from the centre of the reserve and a game drive before breakfast at one of the lodges.

A hot-air balloon glides over the bushveld

❽ Pilanesberg Game Reserve

Road map D2. Follow signs from Sun City on R565, or take the Mogwase turnoff from R510. **Tel** 014 555 1600. **Open** 6am–6pm daily (times may vary). 🐾 🧭 🏕 🛒 🌐 parksnorthwest.co.za/pilanesberg

The circular layout of this park can be traced to prehistoric times, when this area was the crater of a volcano. Around the central Mankwe Dam lie three rings of little hills – mounds of cooled lava – and the whole area is raised above the plain.

The decision to establish a reserve here was economic: to benefit the local people, and to complement the nearby resort of Sun City. Re-stocking the overgrazed farmland turned into one of the most ambitious game relocation ventures ever attempted in South Africa. Appropriately called Operation Genesis, it involved the release of 6,000 mammals of 19 species into the new reserve. To ensure the success of the challenging venture, alien plants were removed and replaced with indigenous ones, telephone lines were diverted, farming structures demolished and the ravages of erosion repaired.

Elephant, black rhino and leopard head an impressive list of wildlife that can be seen at Pilanesberg today. More than 200 km (125 miles) of good gravel roads traverse the park, and there are a number of walk-in viewing hides. For visitors staying overnight, there is also the excitement of night drives.

The Pilanesberg is also home to a number of birds, notably a variety of raptors. Cape vultures nest on the steep cliffs of the mountains and a number of feeding stations have been established to encourage the survival of this endangered bird.

Pilanesberg Game Reserve offers a choice of accommodation, from the luxurious Kwa Maritane Resort, Tshukudu Bush Lodge and Bakubung Lodge, which overlooks a hippo pool, to bungalows and pleasant camp sites.

Young elephants in Pilanesberg Game Reserve

❾ Madikwe Game Reserve

Road map D2. **Tel** 018 350 9931, 071 687 2782. **Open** Access to overnight visitors only. 🌐 madikwe-game-reserve.co.za

South Africa's premier malaria-free safari destination, the 750-sq-km (290-sq-mile)

Madikwe Game Reserve abuts the Botswana border three-hours' drive northwest of Gauteng and two hours from Sun City. The reserve was established in 1991 following a government study that indicated what was then an unproductive tract of former ranchland could be utilized more profitably, with greater benefits to local communities, for conservation. Over the subsequent decade, around 8,000 head of game were introduced, including an elephant herd from drought-stricken southeast Zimbabwe.

Today, giraffe, plains zebra, greater kudu, springbok, red hartebeest and tsessebe are conspicuous among the reserve's 65 mammal species. Of the Big Five, lion, elephant and white rhino are seen by most visitors, while buffalo and leopard are uncommon. Madikwe is possibly South Africa's most reliable reserve for sightings of the endangered African wild dog.

The 250 species of birds found here include many Kalahari woodland specials, among them crimson-breasted shrike and pied babbler. Madikwe caters primarily for the middle and upper end of the safari market, studded as it is with around 15 exclusive bush camps offering all-inclusive guided safari packages, comparable to the private reserves bordering Kruger.

The Palace of the Lost City at Sun City

In an ancient volcanic crater, some 180 km (112 miles) northwest of Johannesburg, lies the mythical "lost city" of a vanished people, where time seems to have stood still. Here, innovative design and fanciful architecture in a lush, man-made jungle have created a complex that promises an unforgettable holiday: luxurious hotels, world-class golf courses, the glamorous Superbowl entertainment centre, glittering casinos and blue waves lapping palm-fringed beaches.

The Desert Suite
Oak panelling, a private library, bar and panoramic views make this one of the Palace hotel's most opulent suites.

Lost City Golf Course
This 18-hole championship course offers a choice of tees. A crocodile pool at the 13th hole is a unique water hazard.

Cheetah Fountain
This superb bronze sculpture shows impalas, frozen in flight from the feared predator.

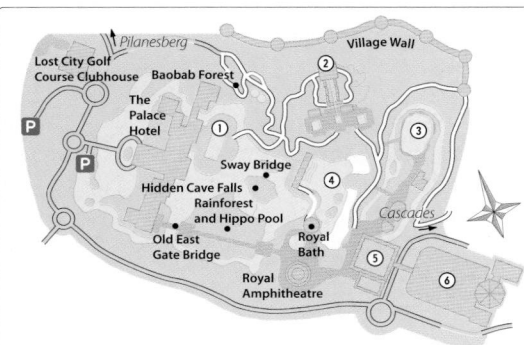

Sun City Complex

① Grand Pool
② Temple of Courage
③ Adventure Mountain
④ Valley of the Waves
⑤ Bridge of Time
⑥ Entertainment Centre

Key

— Road (tarred)

▢ Building

★ Elephant Atrium and Shawu Statue
This sculpture honours an elephant bull that roamed the Kruger National Park until his death in 1982, aged 80. It graces a large chamber at the end of the vaulted Elephant Atrium.

VISITORS' CHECKLIST

Practical Information
Road map D2. N4 to Rustenberg, then R565. **Tel** 014 557 4307; Sun International Central Reservations 011 780 7855. ♿ ✏ 🖥 🏠
Ⓦ **suninternational.co.za**

★ Central Fresco
The fresco that adorns the dome of the reception area measures 16 m (52 ft) in diameter and took 5,000 hours to complete.

0 metres 20
0 yards 25

KEY

① **Buffalo Wing**

② **King's Tower**

③ **Desert Suite and Presidential Suites**

④ **Queen's Tower**

⑤ **Elephant Atrium**

⑥ **Some 1,600,000 trees, shrubs, plants and groundcovers** were planted at the Lost City

⑦ **The porte-cochère** leads to the domed lobby.

The Valley of the Waves

For hotels and restaurants in this region see pp389–90 and pp408–10

LIMPOPO, MPUMALANGA AND KRUGER

The attractions in the northeastern part of the country include a deeply carved canyon and the nature reserves that surround it, panoramic views, trout-fishing dams, and the charming gold-mining town of Pilgrim's Rest, preserved as a living museum.

South Africa's topography is at its most dramatic where the Drakensberg's northern reaches drop sheer to the hot bushveld plains below. From here, visitors can look out over the Eastern Escarpment to where the savannah merges with the distant coastal plains of Mozambique, and hike through the ravines of the Blyde River Canyon.

High rainfall on the steep mountain slopes contributes to the growth of dense forests, as well as the country's greatest concentration of waterfalls. More timber is produced here than anywhere else in South Africa, and there are vast pine and eucalyptus tree plantations. Scenic drives include the Panorama Route, with its unobstructed view sites, which is accessible from the busy little town of Graskop.

Much of the Lowveld plains is occupied by the Kruger National Park, one of the world's oldest and largest wildlife reserves. The southern part, south of the Letaba River and closer to the metropolitan area of Gauteng, is very popular and the most frequently visited. Tourist numbers are considerably lower in the east and the remote north, which is renowned for its long-tusked elephants. Strict management policies prevent the Kruger National Park from becoming a victim of its own success, while some of the tourist pressure is relieved by the privately-run luxury reserves along its western border.

Lowveld farming produces a variety of citrus fruit from a number of large estates. Tobacco, nuts, mangoes and avocados are also successfully grown.

The graceful impala, a common sight in the Kruger National Park

◀ The MacMac Falls in the Drakensberg, named for the Scottish miners who came here in search of gold

Exploring Limpopo, Mpumalanga and Kruger

Early prospectors flocked to the eastern part of the country in search of gold, and found it in the rivers and streams. Today, visitors are attracted by the natural beauty and the superb nature reserves. Here, the Blyde River has cut a mighty canyon, and close by, the edge of the Drakensberg range rises from the grassy plains a kilometre below. This is wildlife conservation country, home of the renowned Kruger National Park and a cluster of exclusive private reserves. There are airstrips and excellent accommodation – just a few hours' drive away from the cities in Gauteng.

Sights at a Glance

1 Dullstroom
2 Lydenburg
3 Mbombela
5 Pilgrim's Rest
6 Blyde River Canyon
7 Waterberg
8 Polokwane
9 Tzaneen
10 Mapungubwe National Park
11 *Kruger National Park pp340–45*
12 Private Reserves
13 *Swaziland pp346–7*

Tour

4 *Waterfalls Tour p335*

Key

- Motorway
- Major road
- Minor road
- Untarred road
- Scenic route
- Main railway
- Minor railway
- International border
- Provincial border
- ▲ Summit
- ✕ Pass

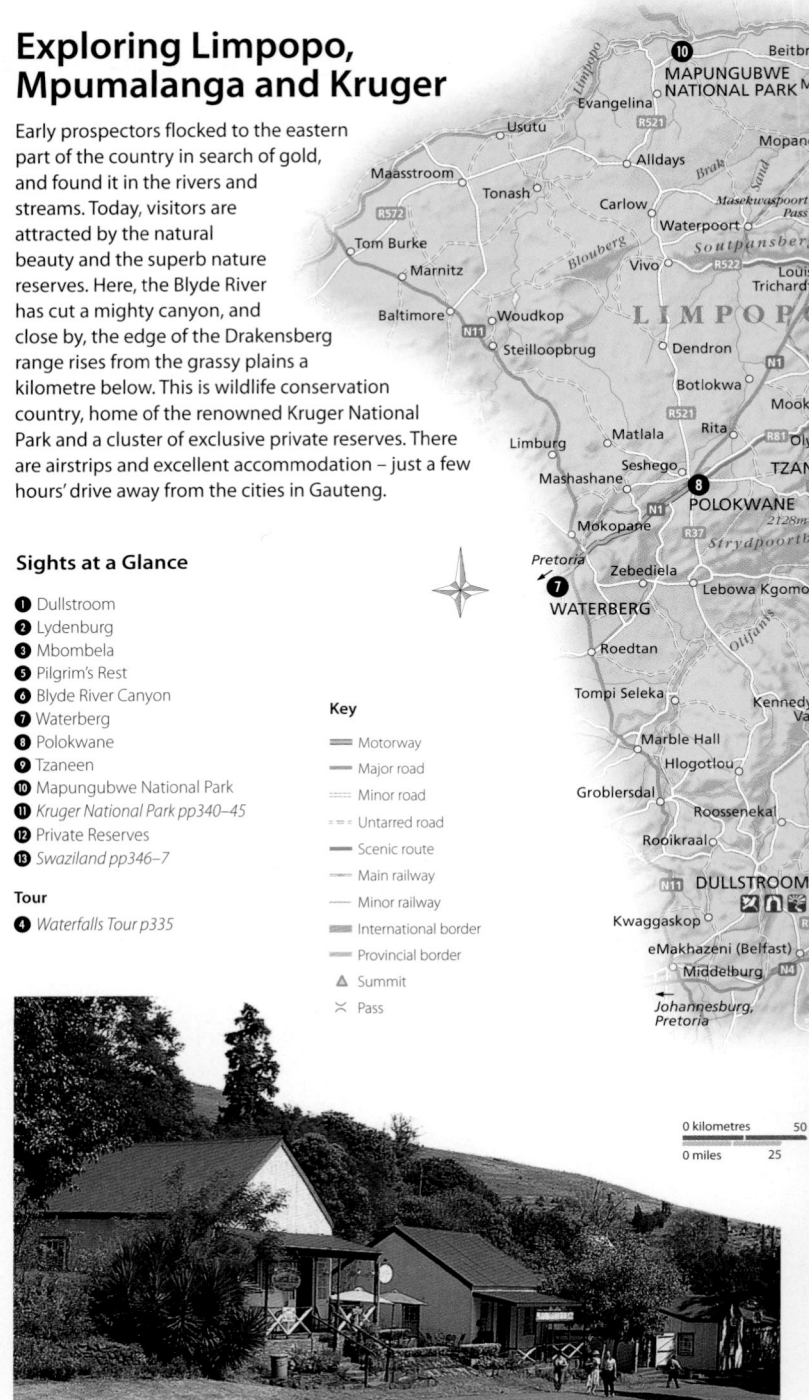

Quaint corrugated iron houses in the old mining village of Pilgrim's Rest

For hotels and restaurants in this region see pp390–91 and pp410–11

The mighty canyon carved by the Blyde River

Getting Around

The N4 national road, running east from Johannesburg and Pretoria, is the smoothest and most direct route to the border of Mozambique. Leave Johannesburg on the N12, which joins the N4 near Witbank. For destinations in the Kruger Park or at Blyde River, turn north onto other good, tarred roads – a few of the escarpment passes may seem narrow and steep. The Panorama Route, one of the highest and most scenic roads in South Africa, includes the picturesque old mining village of Pilgrim's Rest *(see pp336–7)*. Slow down and use the car's headlamps and fog lights in misty conditions (usually during late winter and early summer).

Wildlife gathers at a waterhole in the Kruger National Park

For keys to symbols *see back flap*

❶ Dullstroom

Road map E2. Middelburg. ⚇ 500.
Ⓦ **dullstroom.co.za**

Chilly Dullstroom, set at an
altitude of 2,076 m (6,811 ft), is
the site of the country's highest
railway station, and experiences
winter temperatures that drop
to -13°C (9°F). It is best-known as
South Africa's top destination for
fly-fishing, an activity focused
on **Dullstroom Dam Nature
Reserve**, which is set amidst
luxuriant sub-alpine vegetation
as well as various privately-
owned reservoirs. The **Mavungana Flyfishing Centre** has
some excellent trout-stocked
waters.

🐾 **Dullstroom Dam
Nature Reserve**
Tel 061 762 3209. **Open** daily. 🈯

Mavungana Flyfishing Centre
Tel 013 254 0270 Ⓦ **flyfishing.co.za**

Tranquil dam near Dullstroom

❷ Lydenburg

Road map F2. 58 km (36 miles) N of
Dullstroom. ⚇ 37,000.

Lydenburg (literally "Town of
Suffering") was founded in 1849
by the bereaved survivors of a
malaria epidemic at Ohrigstad,
a lower-lying Voortrekker
settlement established four years
earlier only 50 km (31 miles)
to the north. The **Lydenburg
Museum** houses replicas of the
Lydenburg Heads *(see p49)*, seven
large, unique terracotta masks
believed to have been used in
ceremonial rituals circa AD 700.

🏛 **Lydenburg Museum**
Long Tom Pass Rd. **Tel** 013 235 2213.
Open 8am–4pm Mon–Fri, 8am–5pm
Sat & Sun. **Closed** 25 Dec. 🈯

The serpentine curves of Long Tom Pass near Lydenburg

Environs
Some 53 km (33 miles) east of
Lydenburg, Sabie is reached via
the scenic Long Tom Pass, an
old wagon road whose rocks
still bear the marks of metal-
rimmed wheel ruts. Sabie is
surrounded by plantations
of fast-growing exotic trees,
established in the 19th century
to provide timber for use in
the local gold mines, and its
Forestry Museum is dedicated
to wood and its many uses.

🏛 **Forestry Museum**
Ford St, Sabie. **Tel** 013 764 1058.
Open 8am–4:30pm Mon–Sat (to noon
Sat). 🈯 Ⓦ **komatiecotourism.co.za**

❸ Mbombela

Road map F2. KLCBT House, cnr N4
and R40. ⚇ 600,000. **Tel** 013 755
1988. Ⓦ **krugerlowveld.com**

The low-lying provincial capital
of Mpumalanga, rapidly-growing
Mbombela (a siSwati word
meaning "Crowded Place") is
an important agricultural centre
for oranges, mangoes, bananas,
avocados and macadamia nuts.
Formerly called Nelspruit, it has
experienced a high level of
industrialization since the
1990s, and has also grown in
significance as a trade funnel
on the main road and rail route
between Gauteng and the
Mozambican capital, Maputo.

Environs
The beautifully landscaped
**Lowveld National Botanical
Garden**, on the confluence
of the Nels and Crocodile rivers,
protects prehistoric cycads and
other plants associated with the
subtropical lowveld. Hippo and

vervet monkey
are present,
along with
250 bird
species. **Chimp
Eden**, 15 km
(9 miles) along
the R40, is the
setting
of South
Africa's only
chimpanzee
sanctuary.
Operated
by the Jane Goodall Institute,
it houses 30 chimps rescued
from elsewhere in Africa in
three large wooded enclosures
overlooked by viewing platforms.
Alongside the N4, about
30 km (19 miles) east of
Mbombela, guided tours into
the impressive **Sudwala Caves**
lead through cool subterranean
passages past beautiful limestone formations to a natural
dolomite chamber that can
seat 500.
South of Nelspruit, **Barberton
Museum** was established in
1883 to service a short-lived
gold rush that led to it becoming
the first stock exchange in the
former Transvaal Republic. It
is set below the Makhonjwa
Mountains, whose 3.5-billion-
year-old rocks comprise the
planet's oldest exposed strata.
It has an excellent history and
geological museum, and several
architectural relics of its
Victorian heyday survive.

🌿 **Lowveld National
Botanical Garden**
Madiba Drive. **Tel** 013 752 5531.
Open 8am–5pm daily.
Ⓦ **sanbi.org**

🐾 **Chimp Eden**
Tel 079 777 1514. 📷 75-minute
tours at 10am, noon & 2pm.
Ⓦ **chimpeden.com**

🐾 **Sudwala Caves**
Tel 083 446 0228. **Open** 8:30am–
4:30pm daily. 📷 Hourly tours
every 15 minutes.
Ⓦ **sudwalacaves.co.za**

🏛 **Barberton Museum**
Crown St. **Tel** 013 712 4208.
Open 8am–5pm daily.
Ⓦ **barberton.co.za**

❹ Waterfalls Tour

High-lying ground, generous rainfall and heavy run-off have created spectacular waterfalls in this old gold-mining area along the eastern Drakensberg escarpment. There are, in fact, more waterfalls here than anywhere else in southern Africa. Several of them can be seen on an easy round trip of less than 100 km (60 miles) between the towns of Sabie and Graskop. Most are well signposted and easy to reach by car. Enchanting as they are, waterfalls can be slippery and dangerous, and visitors are urged to heed the warning notices.

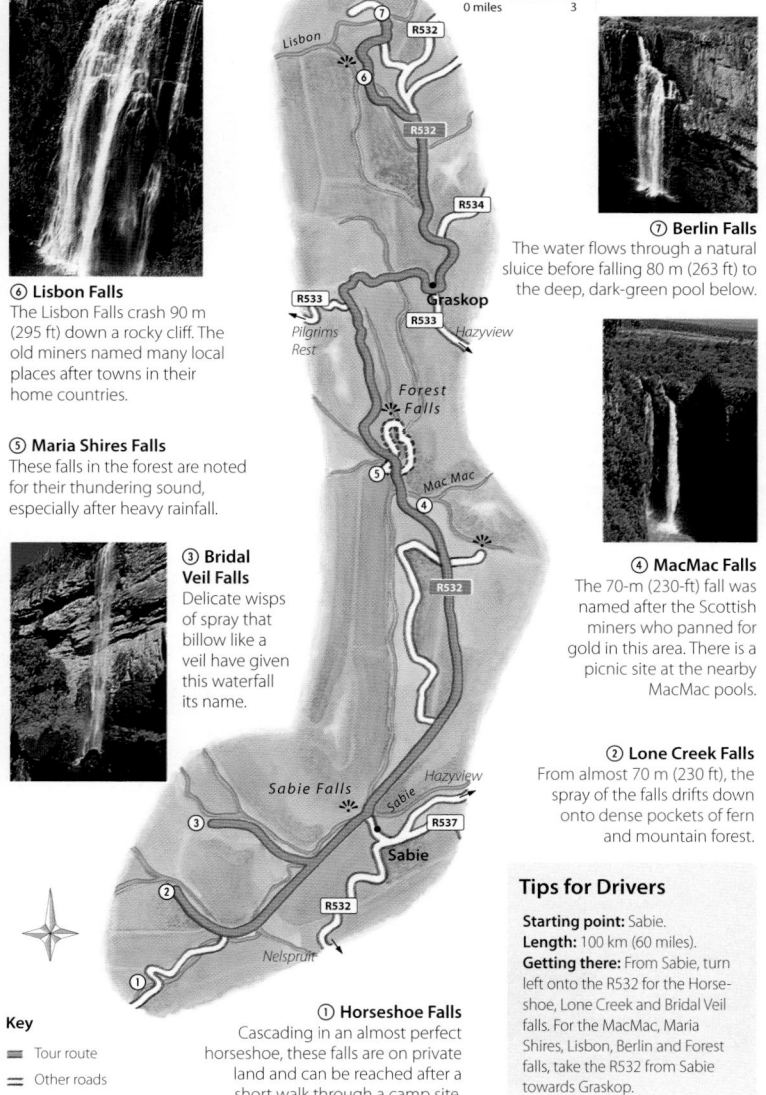

⑥ Lisbon Falls
The Lisbon Falls crash 90 m (295 ft) down a rocky cliff. The old miners named many local places after towns in their home countries.

⑤ Maria Shires Falls
These falls in the forest are noted for their thundering sound, especially after heavy rainfall.

③ Bridal Veil Falls
Delicate wisps of spray that billow like a veil have given this waterfall its name.

⑦ Berlin Falls
The water flows through a natural sluice before falling 80 m (263 ft) to the deep, dark-green pool below.

④ MacMac Falls
The 70-m (230-ft) fall was named after the Scottish miners who panned for gold in this area. There is a picnic site at the nearby MacMac pools.

② Lone Creek Falls
From almost 70 m (230 ft), the spray of the falls drifts down onto dense pockets of fern and mountain forest.

Tips for Drivers

Starting point: Sabie.
Length: 100 km (60 miles).
Getting there: From Sabie, turn left onto the R532 for the Horseshoe, Lone Creek and Bridal Veil falls. For the MacMac, Maria Shires, Lisbon, Berlin and Forest falls, take the R532 from Sabie towards Graskop.

① Horseshoe Falls
Cascading in an almost perfect horseshoe, these falls are on private land and can be reached after a short walk through a camp site.

Key

▬ Tour route
═ Other roads
═ Trail

For keys to symbols *see back flap*

❺ Pilgrim's Rest

Prospectors struck it rich in 1873, ending their search for gold in a picturesque valley of the Eastern Escarpment. Their original village, today restored to its modest glory, is unique: the diggers built in "tin and timber", thinking that, once the gold was exhausted, they would move on. But the gold lasted almost 100 years, and Pilgrim's Rest, 15 km (9 miles) west of the eastern Drakensberg escarpment, is a living part of history.

VISITORS' CHECKLIST

Practical Information
Road map F2. 35 km (21 miles) N of Sabie. 🛈 Main St, Uptown; 013 768 1060. 🅿 multi-entry. Alanglade House: 3 km (2 miles) NE at R533 fork. **Tel** 013 768 1060. 🎟 11am, 2pm daily. 🅿 book in advance. 🅦 **pilgrims-rest.co.za**

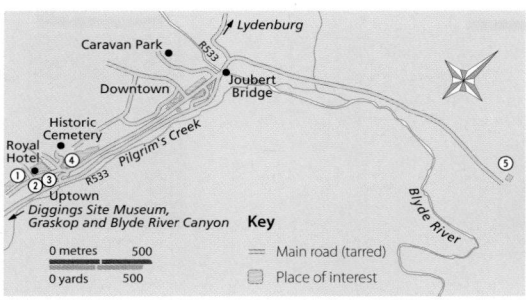

Key

| 0 metres | 500 |
| 0 yards | 500 |

=== Main road (tarred)
▢ Place of interest

Scenic view from God's Window, Panorama Route

Key to Town Plan

① Pilgrim's & Sabie News Museum
② Information Centre
③ Victorian House Museum
④ Dredzen Shop & House Museum
⑤ Alanglade House

Exploring Pilgrim's Rest

The entire village is a National Heritage Site. Historical displays and exhibits on gold-panning techniques can be found at the Pilgrim's Rest Information Centre and Museum, and several small museums are housed in old miners' cottages within walking distance.

At the Diggings Site Museum, on Pilgrim's Creek, visitors can try panning for alluvial gold. The Pilgrim's & Sabie News Museum displays hand-printing equipment from the 1900s, when news of the expanding goldfields was distributed to interested stockbrokers, prospectors and the Boer government.

The Victorian House Museum, a typical building of corrugated iron sheets on a timber frame, shows that the prospectors led a simple life, despite being surrounded by gold. The Dredzen Shop & House is a typical 1930s–50s general store, with the owner's house at the back. The most interesting tombstone in the village cemetery is the enigmatic Robber's Grave.

Stately Alanglade, a mine manager's residence built for Alan and Gladys Barry in 1916, is a large

The famed Robber's Grave tombstone at Pilgrim's Rest

Edwardian mansion located in a wooded glen, well away from the dust and noise of the village, and now restored and furnished as a period museum, complete with enclosed verandas and a rose garden.

Environs

Timber and tourism are the economic mainstays of the dramatic escarpment formed by the eastern Drakensberg Mountains. From the village, the R533 winds across Bonnet Pass to Graskop, a convenient centre for exploring the escarpment, and only 70 km (43 miles) from Skukuza, the main camp in the Kruger National Park.

The R534, or Panorama Route, starts 3 km (2 miles) north of Graskop and passes cliff-top sites and lovely waterfalls (see p335).

The escarpment drops almost 1,000 m (3,281 ft) to the Lowveld. The scenery in this area – among the most beautiful parts of South Africa – includes spectacular vistas extending 100 km (60 miles) east to Mozambique.

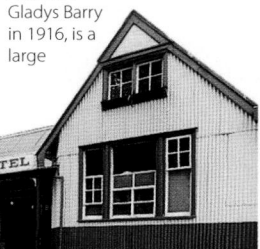

The bar of the Royal Hotel was once a chapel

The Three Rondavels in Blyde River Canyon

❻ Blyde River Canyon

Road map F2. On R534.

The fast-flowing Blyde River has, over the centuries, carved its way through 700 m (2,300 ft) of shale and quartzite to create a scenic jumble of cliffs, islands, plateaus and bush-covered slopes that form a 20-km (12-mile) canyon. At the heart of this canyon lies the Blydepoort Dam.

Blyde means "river of joy", and the river was named after Voortrekker Hendrik Potgieter and his party returned safely from an expedition to Delagoa Bay (Mozambique) in 1844. The abundant flora in the canyon ranges from lichens and mosses to montane forest, orchids and other flowering plants.

Exploring the Blyde River Canyon Nature Reserve

A 300-km (186-mile) circular drive from Graskop via Bosbokrand, Klaserie, Swadini and Bourke's Luck affords panoramic vistas of the escarpment rising above the plains, the Blydepoort Dam and the breathtaking view deep into the canyon itself. There are several overnight trails and short walks, and accommodation is available at the resorts of Swadini and Blyde Canyon.

Kowyn's Pass

The tarred R533 between Graskop and the Lowveld provides views of the escarpment and its soaring cliffs. It also passes the scenic Panorama Gorge, with its feathery waterfall.

Forever Resorts Swadini

On R531. **Tel** 015 795 5141. **Open** daily. **W** foreverswadini.co.za

This resort, set deep in the canyon on the shores of Blydepoort, offers accommodation, a restaurant and a base for boating trips on the dam. The visitors centre and low-level view site have information on the dam and the Kadishi Falls, the world's largest active tufa (calcium carbonate) formation.

Three Rondavels

Resembling the traditional cylindrical huts of the Xhosa or Zulu, these three hills were shaped by the erosion of soft rock beneath a harder rock "cap" that eroded more slowly. The capping of Black Reef quartzite supports a growth of evergreen bush. The Three Rondavels is one of three sites that can be

Bourke's Luck Potholes, formed by unusual patterns of erosion

viewed from the road that overlooks the canyon – the other two are World's End and Lowveld View.

Bourke's Luck Potholes

Open 7am–5pm daily.

Grit and stones carried by the swirling waters at the confluence of the Blyde ("joyful") and Treur ("sad") rivers have carved these extraordinary holes. The name "Bourke's Luck" comes from Tom Bourke, a prospector who worked a claim here in the vain hope that he would find gold. The visitor centre includes an exhibition outlining the geological history of the area.

The Pinnacle, seen from one of the viewpoints on the Panorama Route

Panorama Route

The 18-km (11-mile) stretch of the R534 that loops along the top of the cliff, right at the very edge of the escarpment, is a scenic marvel. Wonderview and God's Window may sound like purely fanciful names until one explores the sites and stands in silent awe at the breathtaking scenery.

The Pinnacle

This impressive column of rock, also on the Panorama Route, appears to rise sheer from a base of evergreen foliage. An optical illusion seems to place it almost within reach. Exposed layers of sandstone show the rock's sedimentary origins. It becomes clear that, even at this lofty height above present sea level, the top of the escarpment was once covered by a primordial sea.

An orange-breasted bush shrike and its chicks at Nylsvley Nature Reserve

❼ Waterberg

Road map E2. **Tel** 014 736 4328.
W golimpopo.com

The 14,500-sq-km (5,598-sq-mile) Waterberg massif is a UNESCO biosphere reserve that rises to around 1,830 m (6,004 ft) some 200 km (120 miles) north of Gauteng. An attractive but rather unfocused region, it supports a mosaic of farms and private nature reserves, as well as the provincial Mokolo Dam, a popular site for water sports. A focal point is the 670-sq-km (259-sq-mile) **Marakele National Park**, which protects 90 mammal species including elephant, lion, leopard, black rhino, white rhino, giraffe and a wide variety of antelope. The proximity to Gauteng and the absence of malaria make Marakele a popular choice with families.

Environs
A worthwhile stop en route between Gauteng and Water-berg is the **Nylsvley Nature Reserve**, which protects the Nyl Floodplain, one of South Africa's most important water-bird sites. More than 375 bird species have been recorded in this small reserve, including the rare slaty egret and rufous-bellied heron. Walking trails also offer a chance to get close to non-dangerous large mammals such as giraffe, wildebeest and warthog.

☒ Marakele National Park
Tel 014 777 6928.
W sanparks.org

☒ Nylsvley Nature Reserve
Tel 014 743 6925. **Open** May–Aug: 6:30am–5:30pm daily; Sep–Apr: 6am–6pm daily. **W** nylsvley.co.za

❽ Polokwane

Road map E1. **⚠** 135,000.
🛈 Cnr Thabo Mbeki & Church.
Tel 015 290 2010. **W** golimpopo.com

Polokwane, a Sepedi name meaning "Place of Safety", is the capital of Limpopo, South Africa's most northerly province. Established by the Voortrekker leader Andries Potgieter in 1886, it was named Pietersburg, (after Commandant-General Piet Joubert of the Transvaal Republic), until 2005. The **Hugh Exton Photographic Museum**, set in a late 19th-century Dutch Reformed Church, offers revealing insights into the town's early history (particularly the Anglo-Boer War, when a British concentration camp housed 4,000 prisoners) through the thousands of images captured by its namesake between 1892 and 1945.

Environs
A good network of game-viewing roads and walking trails through the 32-sq-km (12-sq-mile) **Polokwane Game Reserve** on the southern outskirts of town provides an opportunity for close encounters with white rhino, giraffe, sable antelope and several other reintroduced large mammals.

Bordering the reserve, the **Bakone Malapa Open-Air Museum** offers informative guided tours through a faithful reconstruction of a traditional Pedi (North Sotho) homestead as it would have been in the 18th-century.

🏛 Hugh Exton Photographic Museum
Church St. **Tel** 015 290 2186. **Open** 9am–3pm Mon–Fri.

☒ Polokwane Game Reserve
Main entrance on Silicon Rd about 2 km (1 mile) south of town. **Tel** 015 290 2331. **Open** May–Sep: 7am–5:30pm; Oct–Apr: 7am–6:30pm (last entrance 2 hours before closing time).

🏛 Bakone Malapa Open-Air Museum
R37, 8 km (5 miles) out of town. **Tel** 073 216 9912. **Open** 8am–4pm Mon–Fri.

A male and female giraffe at Polokwane Game Reserve

Scenic view of the Tzaneen in Limpopo

❾ Tzaneen

Road map E1. ⚑ 25,000. ℹ R71.
Tel 015 307 3582. 🅦 tzaneeninfo.
co.za

Tzaneen is a small and pleasant mid-altitude town set within an agricultural region associated with tea, tomato, mango and avocado production. It stands alongside the pretty Tzaneen Dam and is surrounded by lush forests.

The small **Tzaneen Museum** houses an interesting collection of ethnographic items from all around Africa, these include a 19th-century drum and other items associated with the Modjadji Rain Queen – a revered local monarch whose matrilineal line reputedly dates back to the 16th century but ended in 2005 with the untimely death of Makobo Constance Modjadji VI.

Environs

Some 30 km (19 miles) north of Tzaneen, tiny Modjadjiskloof – also sometimes referred to by its former Afrikaans name Duiwelskloof ("Devil's Gorge") – has two main claims to fame. The misty forests of **Modjadji Cycad Reserve**, 17 km (11 miles) to the east, support one of two extant populations of the eponymous cycad, a peculiar prehistoric palm-like tree that grows up to 12 m (39 ft) tall and was protected for generations by the Modjadji

Rain Queen. The thousand-year-old **Sunland Baobab**, 5 km (3 miles) northwest of town, is reputedly the world's tubbiest specimen of this magnificent species, with a circumference of 47 m (155 ft) and a bar set within its central cavity.

🏛 Tzaneen Museum
Agatha Rd. **Tel** 083 280 4966.
Open 9am–4pm Mon–Fri, 9am–noon Sat.

🌿 Modjadji Cycad Reserve
Off the Mohlakamosoma Rd.
Open 7am–4:30pm daily.

Sunland Baobab
Leeudraai Rd. **Tel** 082 413 2228.
🅦 bigbaobab.co.za

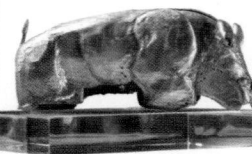

The golden rhinoceros of Mapungubwe

❿ Mapungubwe National Park

Road map E1. **Tel** 015 534 2014.
Open Apr–Aug: 6:30am–6pm;
Sep–Mar: 6am–6:30pm.
🅦 sanparks.org

Overlooking Rudyard Kipling's "great grey-green, greasy Limpopo" as it flows past the three-way border with

Botswana and Zimbabwe, Mapungubwe Hill was the capital of an indigenous trade empire that supplied copious amounts of gold, copper and ivory to the Swahili Coast of East Africa in its medieval prime. The city of 5,000 was abandoned in the 13th century, when its inhabitants migrated 300 km (180 miles) north to establish the stone city of Great Zimbabwe, but the hilltop citadel can still be visited on daily guided tours, following a rickety flight of 147 wooden steps, through a breach used by its former inhabitants.

Inscribed as a UNESCO World Heritage Site in 2003, Mapungubwe today is the centrepiece of South Africa's most northerly national park, a 280-sq-km (108-sq-mile) boulderscape of wild baobab-studded granitic hills inhabited by elephant, greater kudu, klipspringer and small populations of lion, leopard and cheetah.

A highlight of the park is the Mapungubwe Interpretation Centre, which provides an overview of its history, alongside artifacts such as an iconic 12cm-long gold-plated rhino sculpture unearthed there in 1933. The park houses more than 100 prehistoric rock art sites.

⓫ Kruger National Park

South Africa's largest national park, Kruger, ranks among the most rewarding wildlife sanctuaries anywhere in the world. Equivalent in size to Israel, this vast wilderness covers an area of 19,633 sq km (7,580 sq miles), extending for 352 km (220 miles) from the Limpopo River in the north to Crocodile River in the south, and averaging 60 km (38 miles) from east to west. It comprises 16 distinct vegetation zones, ranging from open grassland to dense forest, and supports an astonishing species count: 148 mammals, 505 birds, 118 reptiles, 35 amphibians and 50 fish. Kruger is readily accessible to tourists thanks to an excellent network of rest camps, picnic sites, and surfaced and unsurfaced roads.

Key

Kruger National Park

0 km   20
0 miles   10

Game-watching
Elevated viewing platforms are found at many of the Kruger National Park's rest camps.

The Big Five
Kruger supports around 35,000 buffaloes, 14,000 elephants, 1,600 lions and 1,000 leopards. It is also the world's most important rhinoceros preserve, with estimated populations of 6–8,000 white and 500-plus black rhinos.

KEY

① **Berg-en-Dal** is studded with magnificent ancient granite outcrops including Khandzalive, the park's highest point at 839 m (2,752 ft).

② **Lower Sabie** This small, relaxed camp stands at the pivot of two productive game-viewing roads.

③ **Central savanna**, the park's most open habitat, attracts herds of wildebeest and zebra, and is the best place to look for cheetahs.

④ **Olifants Camp** stands on a wooded cliff overlooking the river after which it is named.

Avian wonders
Dedicated twitchers can easily notch up 100 species in a day, especially during the southern summer. Even casual visitors should prepare to be wowed by Kruger's colourful array of rollers, bee-eaters, kingfishers and hornbills, as well as the outsized ostrich and Kori bustard, and raptors such as African fish-eagle and lappet-faced vulture.

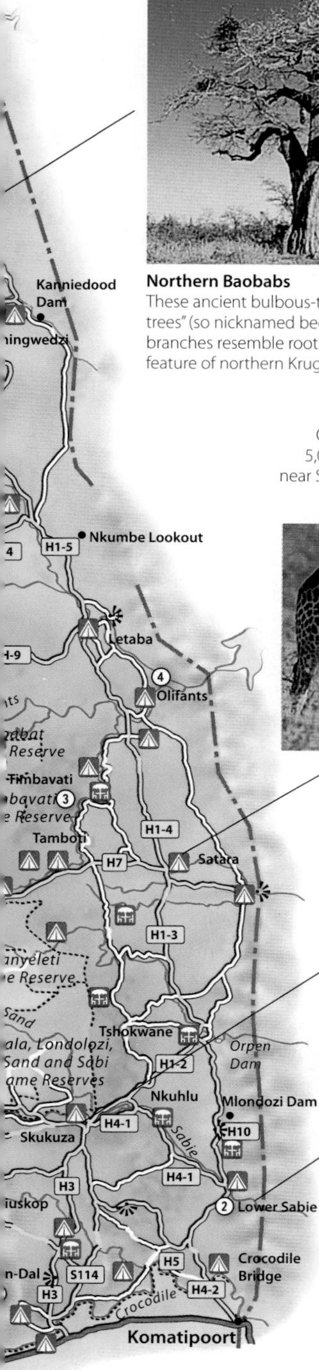

Northern Baobabs
These ancient bulbous-trunked "upside-down trees" (so nicknamed because the bare branches resemble roots) are a striking feature of northern Kruger.

VISITORS' CHECKLIST

Practical Information
Road map F1–2. Tel 012 428 9111 or 082 233 9111 (SANParks, central reservations). **Open** 5:30am–6:30pm Sep–Mar, 6am–6pm Apr–Aug. 🅿️ ♿ 📷 ✏️ 📷 🆆 sanparks.org

Transport
✈ Nelspruit, Hoedspruit, Mpumalanga, Phalaborwa, Skukuza.

Key
----- International boundary
━━ Major route
═══ Road (tarred)
═══ Road (untarred)
▪▪ Park Border

Giraffe
One of the park's 5,000-plus giraffes, near Satara rest camp.

Impala
Particularly abundant around Skukuza, the graceful impala is the most common of the park's 22 antelope species, with a population estimated at around 150,000.

Sabie River
One of six rivers flowing through the park, the Sabie is home to many of the Kruger's 3,000-plus hippos, while the fringing woodland supports a small population of leopards.

For hotels and restaurants in this region see pp390–91 and pp410–11

Map labels: Kanniedood Dam, Shingwedzi, H1-5, Nkumbe Lookout, Letaba, H1-9, Olifants, Reserve, Timbavati, bavati Reserve, Tamboti, H1-4, H7, Satara, H1-3, anyeleti Reserve, Sand, Tshokwane, Orpen Dam, H1-2, Nkuhlu, Mlondozi Dam, H4-1, Sabie, H10, Skukuza, H3, H4-1, iuskop, Lower Sabie, n-Dal, S114, H5, Crocodile Bridge, H3, H4-2, Komatipoort

Exploring Southern Kruger

Tourism in Kruger is focused on the park's southern half, which offers superior game-viewing compared with the wilder, drier north, has better tourist amenities, and is more accessible. Southern Kruger is divided into two sectors by the Sabie River – the busier of these runs south to Crocodile River and supports a cover of dense acacia woodland. The second, a swathe of lightly-wooded savannah, runs to the Olifants River. With a good road network and well-equipped, affordable rest camps, both are ideal for a self-drive safari. Alternatively, privately-managed lodges offer a guided safari experience similar to the private reserves along the western border *(see p345)*.

One of the many rest camps in Southern Kruger

Crocodiles basking in the sun on the banks of Crocodile River

Crocodile River

Flowing eastward along the park border for 60 km (37 miles), the Crocodile River forms a natural barrier between the untamed wilderness of Kruger and the lush farmland to its south. It is overlooked by Crocodile Bridge, the park's most easterly rest camp –situated 115 km (71 miles) from the provincial capital Mbombela – and one of its smallest, set in an area renowned for its dense population of white rhino.

On the Crocodile River, a short drive east of camp, stands a hippo pool and a fascinating prehistoric rock painting site. Set between Crocodile Bridge and the Lebombo Mountains on the Mozambique border, the 150-sq-km (58-sq-mile) Mpana-mana Concession, reserved exclusively for the private Shishangani Lodge and two satellite camps, is good for spotting white rhino, lion and elephant.

Berg-en-Dal

Situated 13 km (8 miles) north-west of Malalane Gate, this modern rest camp is well-positioned for a first night in the bush after travelling from Gauteng. The accommodation is perhaps the most comfortable of any public rest camp, and the hilly setting, overlooking a tree-lined dam, is lovely. One night here is sufficient before pushing on deeper into the park.

Pretoriuskop

Accessed via Numbi Gate – which opened 8 km (5 miles) to its west in 1926, to be used by a total of three cars during its first year of operation – Pretorius-kop, the park's oldest rest camp, seems more attuned to the sensibilities of local holiday-makers than to international tourists. Game-viewing in the surrounding acacia woodland is erratic, but the Voortrekker Road (connecting it to Afsaal picnic site) is a good place to look for the shy black rhino, stately eland and sable antelope.

The yellow billed hornbill can be spotted in Kruger

Skukuza

Overlooking the Sabie River 13 km (8 miles) east of Paul Kruger Gate, Skukuza is the park's second-oldest rest camp, and by far the largest, comprising 230 accommodation units and 80 camp sites, with a total capacity of 1,000-plus visitors. Originally known as Sabie Bridge (after a railway bridge still standing today), the camp was renamed in 1936 after the pioneering warden James Stevenson-Hamilton, whose Tsonga nickname Skukuza means "he who sweeps clean". Skukuza today doubles as the park's research and administrative headquarters, and its excellent range of facilities include an airport, car-hire service, bank, ATM, petrol station, post office, museum, restaurant and shop. Naysayers complain Skukuza is too large and impersonal, but these flaws are more than compensated by its strategic location at the junction of three superb game-viewing roads: the H3 to Malalane, H4–1 to Lower Sabie and H1–2/3 to Satara. Also in Skukuza's favour are the sprawling green grounds teeming with birds and small mammals, and the river below that attracts plenty of thirsty wildlife.

Lower Sabie

Favoured by many old Kruger hands, Lower Sabie, like Skukuza 43 km (27 miles) upstream, stands at the junction of three excellent game-viewing roads, but the camp is far smaller and more intimate. The chalets survey an expanse of the Sabie River regularly visited by elephants and buffaloes, while Sunset Dam, 2 km (1 mile) outside the camp, is exceptional for hippos, storks, kingfishers and other aquatic birds. The roads running south towards Crocodile Bridge are as reliable for rhinos as anywhere in the park.

The H4-1 and Nkuhlu Picnic Site

Dubbed Piccadilly Circus, the surfaced H4-1 between Skukuza and Lower Sabie is probably the park's most reliably rewarding game-viewing road, but – as its nickname suggests – it also carries a high volume of tourist traffic. Following the south bank of the Sabie River for 43 km (27 miles), you might spot lion, elephant, rhino, buffalo, giraffe and greater kudu, and it's the best place in Kruger to look for leopards. Be sure to stop at Nkuhlu Picnic Site, set on the shady riverbanks of the Sabie River, where crocodiles float past, monkeys play in the canopy, and African fish-eagle and half-collared kingfisher hawk above the water. To complete a round trip between Skukuza to Lower Sabie, return via the dirt Salitje Road north of the Sabie River.

The H10 from Lower Sabie to Tshokwane

This quiet road running north from Lower Sabie offers access to several superb vantage points overlooking reservoirs. Mlondozi Dam has picnic facilities and a shady terrace overlooking the valley. Nkumbe Lookout offers unparalleled views over the plains below. Orpen Dam, at the foot of the N'wamuriwa hills, often attracts greater kudu, elephant and giraffe. The H10 connects with the main H1-2 to Satara at Tshokwane Picnic Site, which lies along an old wagon trail cut in the 1880s, and is named after a Shangaan chief who lived there until his death in 1915. Tshokwane is shaded by a giant Kigelia africana (known as the sausage tree due to its large elongated fruit) and the kiosk underneath is a pleasant place to stop for breakfast or lunch.

Satara and the Central Plains

North of Tshokwane, the countryside transforms into

A group of Giraffes gathered in a clearing in Kruger National Park

an open savannah of grassland and scattered trees. Situated in the thick of these central plains 90 km (56 miles) from Skukuza, Kruger's second-largest rest camp, Satara is rather characterless but well positioned for game drives. Although no major rivers flow across this flat part of the Kruger, large herds of zebra, wildebeest and other grazers forage on the open grassland here and its scattering of artificial waterholes attract plenty of predators. The open terrain is particularly suited to cheetahs, which are often seen crossing the roads around Satara, and it also makes it relatively easy to see lion kills.

About 50 km (31 miles) west of Satara, near Orpen Gate, the self-catering Tamboti Camp offers a fabulous budget bush experience in standing tents carved into the riparian forest along the seasonal Timbavati River. At the other end of the price range, the ultra-exclusive Singita Lebombo and Sweni Lodges combine safari chic with superb game-viewing in a ruggedly mountainous 150 km sq (58 sq mile) concession on the Mozambique border, 25 km (15 miles) east of Satara.

Olifants Camp

The most northerly camp on the main tourist circuit situated 55 km (34 miles) past Satara, Olifants has a stunning location on a tall cliff overlooking the broad flood-plain of the river after which it is named. Lookout platforms allow one to see the river below as an eagle would survey it. It offers arguably the best in-house game-viewing of any public rest camp, thanks to the large numbers of elephant that come to drink at the river below. Game-viewing roads around Olifants are often crossed by large thousand-strong herds of buffalo, and the area is also a stronghold for two antelope species: the handsome greater kudu and the smaller cliff-loving klipspringer.

The Olifants rest camp bungalows in Kruger National Park

Exploring Northern Kruger

An immense wilderness of semi-arid Mopani woodland bisected by a few sandy seasonal rivers, northern Kruger sees very few tourists compared with the south. The long drive from Gauteng is one reason for the north's obscurity, but there are also far fewer tourist amenities north of the Olifants River, and game-viewing tends to be more challenging. Despite this, many experienced safari-goers are besotted with northern Kruger, returning time and time again to absorb its untrammelled bush atmosphere. Few organized safaris head to northern Kruger, but a good network of surfaced roads means it is easily explored as an extension of a self-drive safari to the southern.

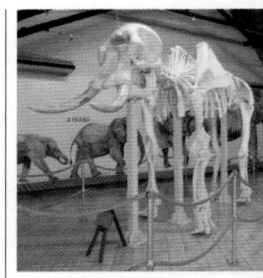

An elephant skeleton inside the Letaba Elephant Hall at Letaba Camp

Letaba Camp

Enjoying a commanding position overlooking the seasonal Letaba river 30 km (19 miles) north of Olifants, this camp has chalets arranged in semi-circles overlooking the river, where tame bushbucks stroll past and fig trees attract colourful birds. Game drives along the river often yield elephant sightings, while the mopani-swathed plains running west towards Phalaborwa are the main stronghold of the rare sable antelope. Set within the camp, Letaba Elephant Hall, a museum dedicated to the evolution and ecology of elephants, displays the tusks of six of the so-called "Magnificent Seven", a generation of massive tuskers that thrived in the 1970s.

Mopani and Shingwedzi Camps

Mopani, 50 km (30 miles) north of Letaba, is a modern hillside camp overlooking an artificial reservoir that attracts thirsty wildlife out of the surrounding

dry woodland. Elephants are plentiful, and the area supports several localised antelope species, but game viewing tends to be erratic. Far better to drive 63 km (38 miles) north to Shingwedzi, whose location alongside the Shingwedzi River makes it a contender for Kruger's best-kept game-viewing secret. The dirt road south to Kanniedood Dam runs through the territory of some of the Kruger's biggest elephants. It is also good for buffalo and greater kudu, and the birdlife is spectacular.

Punda Maria

Set at the base of Dimbo Hill 72km (43 miles) northwest of Shingwedzi, Punda Maria is an intimate camp with a remote wilderness feel and white-washed thatched huts whose

A colourful Narina trogon one of the many bird species

exteriors are little changed since their construction in 1933. The surrounding bush is a good place to look for the rare Lichtenstein's hartebeest and African wild dog. Punda Maria is the closest public rest camp to Pafuri and the base for guided tours to the 16th-century stone ruins at the Thulamela Heritage Site.

Pafuri and Makuleke

The shady woodland that verges the Luvuvhu River 60 km (37 miles) north of Punda Maria offers some of the best bird-watching in Kruger. The exquisite Narina trogon is the star of the public Pafuri Picnic Site on the south bank, and while wildlife viewing is erratic, the nyala antelope is abundant. North of the Luvuvhu, a triangle of land bounded by the Limpopo rivers to the north was appended to Kruger in 1969 when its Makuleke inhabitants were forcibly ejected by the apartheid regime. Traditional ownership was restored in the 1990s and the triangle now forms Makuleke Contractual Park, which is managed as part of Kruger but hosts two exclusive private lodges – intimate Pafuri Camp on the north bank of the Luvuvhu and The Outpost on a hill offering stunning views over its floodplain – leased from the community. Both now operate similarly to the private reserves.

The Shingwedzi Rest Camp in Kruger National Park

For hotels and restaurants in this region see pp390–91 and pp410–11

⑫ Private Reserves

Along the western boundary of the national park, and bordered by the Sabie and Olifants rivers, a mosaic of private reserves provides a vital buffer between the densely populated areas of Lebowa and Gazankulu and the Kruger. A fence erected along the park's boundary in the 1960s to prevent the spread of diseased animals also blocked migration routes. An agreement between all parties made possible its removal, and by 1994 herds were free once again to trek along their ancient paths.

Hippos in the natural pool at Sabi Sands Game Reserve

Exploring the Private Reserves

Luxury lodges, often recipients of international awards for service excellence, offer exclusive "bush experiences" to small groups of visitors. Emphasis is placed on personal attention; experienced rangers guide visitors on night drives and interesting bush walks.

Sabi Sands Game Reserve

Shaws and Newington gates off the R536; Gowrie Gate off the R40. **Tel** 013 735 5102. **Open** restricted access. 🐾 🏊 fully incl.
W sabi-sands.com

This famous reserve is made up of a block of contiguous reserves north of the Sabie River, which include the Lion Sands, Londolozi, Mala Mala, Singita and Ulusaba private game reserves, and shares a 50-km (31-mile) boundary with Kruger National Park. There are no fewer than 30 all-inclusive luxury lodges and camps in Sabi Sands and entry is only to overnight visitors. Thanks to the Sand and Sabie rivers, the area has a rich water supply, which results in a lush environment that animals enjoy all year round. Sightings of the Big Five are virtually guaranteed, and hyenas, cheetahs and wild dogs may also be seen.

Manyeleti Game Reserve

Gate close to Kruger's Orpen Gate off the R40. **Tel** 011 341 0282. **Open** restricted access. 🐾 fully incl.
W manyeleti.co.za

This reserve adjoins the Orpen area of the Kruger National Park, known for its varied wildlife. Visitors can stay in the comfortable tented Honeyguide Camp, the luxurious Khoka Moya chalets and other lodges.

Timbavati Game Reserve

South of Hoedspruit off the R40. **Tel** 015 793 2436. **Open** restricted access. 🐾 fully incl. W timbavati.co.za

This 550-sq-km (210-sq-mile) reserve, adjoining Kruger's central region, extends from Orpen to the region just south of the Olifants River. it lies entirely in Limpopo province. There are a dozen lodges, each with access to a different part of the reserve, and they all offer drives and guided walks.

Of these, Umlani Bush Camp is situated in the north, while the luxurious Ngala and Tanda Tula lodges lie in the central region. Also renowned is the Gomo Gomo Game Lodge.

Klaserie Private Nature Reserve

South of Hoedspruit off the R40. **Tel** 015 793 3051. **Open** restricted access. 🐾 fully incl.
W klaseriereserve.co.za

Klaserie encompasses many private reserves, extends over 620 sq km (235 sq miles) and borders on the Kruger National Park, as well as on the Olifants River. The Klaserie River meanders across the semiarid bushveld and is the reserve's central focus as many animals and birds gather on its banks to drink.

Tourists on a game drive

Klaserie as yet has only three bush camps. They are not in the top end of the luxury category, so will appeal to those who want a more rustic experience.

A luxurious lounge at Mala Mala Lodge, within Sabi Sands Game Reserve

⑬ Swaziland

The kingdom of Swaziland achieved its independence from Britain on 6 September 1968. King Mswati III has ruled the almost one million Swazis since 1986. In the west of the country, the highlands offer many opportunities for hikers. The middleveld has the perfect growing conditions for tropical fruit and is known for its arts and crafts. In the east, lush sugar cane plantations contrast with the dense brown bushveld of game reserves and ranches.

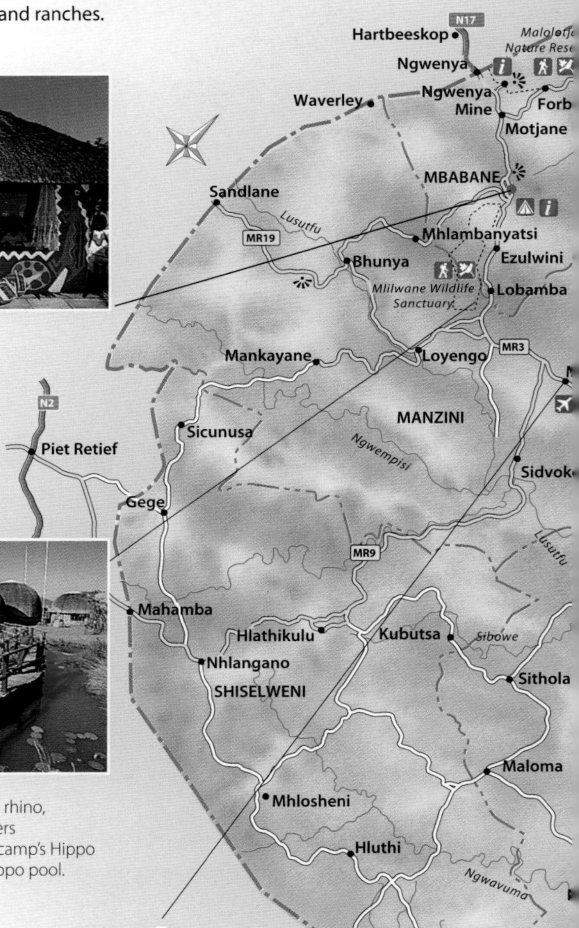

Mbabane
Swaziland's capital city developed around the site where Michael Wells opened a pub and trading post at a river crossing in 1888. Today, trade is brisk at the Swazi Market.

Mlilwane Wildlife Sanctuary
Mlilwane, which supports white rhino, giraffe, zebra and antelope, covers 45 sq km (17 sq miles). The rest camp's Hippo Haunt restaurant overlooks a hippo pool.

KEY

① **Phopanyane Lodge and Nature Reserve** is privately owned. The subtropical vegetation attracts many birds.

② **At Big Bend**, near the Lugumbo Mountains, sugar cane thrives along the Lusutfu River.

Manzini
Swaziland's biggest town is close to the airport. An industrial centre, it also has colourful markets that sell fresh produce, crafts and fabric.

★ **Peak Craft Centre, Piggs Peak**
Local artists display their crafts on the road leading to a casino hotel further north.

Malolotja Nature Reserve
Ngwenya, in the reserve, is the oldest mine in the world. Specularite haematite, used for cosmetics, was excavated here 43,000 years ago. From here there are spectacular views over the countryside.

0 kilometres   20
0 miles   10

Key

-·- International boundary

-- Provincial boundary

▬ Major route

═ Road (tarred)

═ Road (untarred)

★ **Hlane Royal National Park**
Hlane and the adjacent Mlawula Reserve protect 370 sq km (143 sq miles) of dense woodland and the Lubombo Mountains. Elephant, lion, white rhino, various antelopes, hippo and giraffe can be seen, and it is also home to abundant bird life. Guided walking safaris can be arranged.

For additional keys to symbols *see back flap*

THE ARID
INTERIOR

Introducing the Arid Interior

The semiarid, sparsely populated Karoo extends across the
Northern Cape and parts of the Free State, Eastern and
Western Cape provinces. Sleepy country towns and
villages, often treasure chests of Cape Dutch and Victorian
architecture, serve as supply centres for surrounding farms.
North of the Orange River lie the red dunes of the Kalahari
Desert, one of South Africa's finest wilderness areas. A rich
assortment of wildlife inhabits this remote territory. In the
Northern Cape, the most famous diamond mines
in the world extract shining riches from the earth.

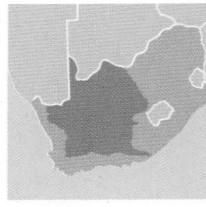

Locator Map

The IAi-IAis/Richtersveld Transfrontier Park is a bleak
moonscape with curious flora such as the *kokerboom*
(quiver tree), from which Khoi hunters made arrows.

Upington

Orange

Pofadder

Kenhardt

Prieska

Verneuk Pan

**SOUTH OF
THE ORANGE**
(See pp356–67)

Calvinia

Fish

Beaufort
West

Sutherland

The Camel Rider Statue in Upington
honours the memory of the policemen
and their tireless mounts who patrolled
the Kalahari in the early 20th century.

◀ Road through the red dunes of the Kalahari Desert, Kgalagadi Transfrontier Park

Kimberley's diamond mines, once owned by De Beers Mining Company, are nowadays controlled by the Anglo American global mining company. Impressive headgear dominates the skyline on the outskirts, while in the city itself lie many beautiful historic buildings such as the City Hall.

Bloemfontein's Civic Centre, a tall modern structure of glass and concrete, represents a bold departure from the traditional, stately sandstone buildings in the town.

Vryburg

an

ORTH OF
E ORANGE
e pp368–77)

Bloemhof

Vaal

ampbell

Kimberley

Bloemfontein

Orange

The Gariep Dam is the largest water storage reservoir in South Africa and has become a popular weekend resort.

town

De Aar

Colesberg

Middelburg

u Bethesda

aff-Reinet

Cradock

Sundays

Somerset
East

King William's
Town

Nieu-Bethesda's quaint Dutch Reformed Church was completed in 1905. The main attraction of this little Karoo town, however, is the bizarre Owl House.

| 0 kilometres | 100 |
| 0 miles | 50 |

Life in the Desert

The Kalahari Desert forms part of a vast inland steppe that stretches from the Orange River to the equator. It extends across portions of the Northern Cape and Namibia, and also covers much of Botswana. Rainfall in this region varies from 150mm to 400 mm (6–16 inches) per year and is soon soaked up or simply evaporates. There is little surface water and the flora consists mainly of grass, shrubs and the hardy camel-thorn acacias that line the dry beds of ancient rivers. Although the landscape may appear to be lifeless, it supports an astonishing variety of wildlife that is superbly adapted to survive in this harsh environment.

Seasonal river beds, such as that of the Auob, carry water only every few years, usually after exceptionally heavy downpours.

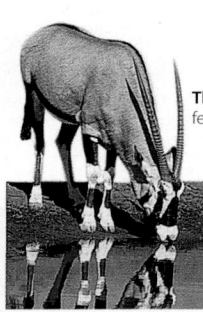

The quiver contains arrows poisoned with the juice of beetle larvae.

The gemsbok *(oryx)* feeds on grass, leaves and roots, and can do without water for many days. The animal's temperature fluctuates in response to climatic changes: during the day it may soar to above 45°C (113°F).

Bat-eared foxes' large ears allow them to detect underground prey, such as harvester termites and beetle larvae, in the barren areas.

Kalahari lions are unique to the Kgalagadi Transfrontier Park, and have learned to depend on smaller prey, taking porcupines and bat-eared foxes when antelopes migrate.

The brown hyena is primarily a scavenger, but it also eats wild fruit, beetles, termites, birds' eggs and small animals. Restricted to the drier desert regions of southern Africa, it can survive without fresh water for extended periods of time.

The Tsamma melon's bitter-tasting flesh is eaten by the San and by animals, as it is a vital source of vitamin C and moisture.

Steppe buzzards are one of the many raptor species that can be seen in the Kalahari. As migrant visitors, they arrive in southern Africa during October and depart in March.

Namaqua sandgrouse males fly distances of up to 60 km (37 miles) every three to five days to drink and to soak their specially adapted chest feathers. The water retained in these feathers sustains the chicks.

Digging sticks are used to unearth a variety of edible and water-bearing roots and tubers.

Ostrich eggs are a source of moisture and protein.

The puff adder is highly venomous and bites readily when threatened. The snake propels itself forwards leaving deep, straight tracks which can sometimes be seen on the Kalahari sand dunes.

The San

These nomads, once known as Bushmen, have all but vanished from the subcontinent. A small community lives on land south of the Kgalagadi Transfrontier Park allocated to them in 1997. The modern age has severely affected their culture. Even in the remote reaches of Botswana, clans now live in settlements around waterholes – the nomadic lifestyle replaced by a sedentary existence. Before these camps were established, water and food were obtained from the bush: the San knew of 20 edible insects and 180 plants, roots and tubers.

Barking geckos herald sunset in the desert by emitting a series of sharp clicking sounds. When threatened, they tend to freeze, camouflaged against the red sand.

The *Sparrmannia flava* scarab has a furry coat which enables it to remain active at night when temperatures can drop drastically.

Windmills pump precious water from below the surface into metal reservoirs. Farming activities in the Kalahari region include Karakul sheep, goat and wildlife rearing, while hardy Afrikaner cattle survive only where a water supply is assured.

The Orange River

South Africa is predominantly a dry country, with precipitation decreasing from east to west and only 8 per cent of rainfall reaching the few major rivers. Also known in parts of South Africa as the Gariep River, the mighty Orange and its tributaries drain 47 per cent of the country. For much of the 2,450-km (1,530-mile) long journey from its source in northeast Lesotho to the Atlantic Ocean, the Orange meanders across the arid plains of the Northern Cape. Here, wooden wheels draw the precious water from canals to sustain a narrow, fertile corridor of vineyards, date palms, lucerne and cotton fields, tightly wedged between the river and the unrelenting desert.

The IAi-IAis/Richtersveld Transfrontier Park is located in a jagged, mountainous landscape where water is scarce. The hardy vegetation relies on the early morning fog that rolls in from the Atlantic.

Alexander Bay is the site of large-scale diamond dredging operations. The nearby Orange River estuary is a wetland renowned for its splendid birdlife.

The Fish River Canyon lies across the Namibian border.

Vioolsdrif, a small settlement and the border post with Namibia, serves as a departure point for canoe trips down the Orange River.

| 0 kilometres | | 50 |
| 0 miles | 25 | |

Orange River canoe trips *(see p418)* are very popular and several Cape Town-based adventure companies offer exciting multi-day tours that include camping along the river banks.

Augrabies Falls, christened *Aukoerebis* ("place of great noise") by the early Khoi inhabitants of this region, is where the Orange River plunges 56 m (182 ft) into a constricted granite gorge. The falls and surrounding area were declared a national park in 1966.

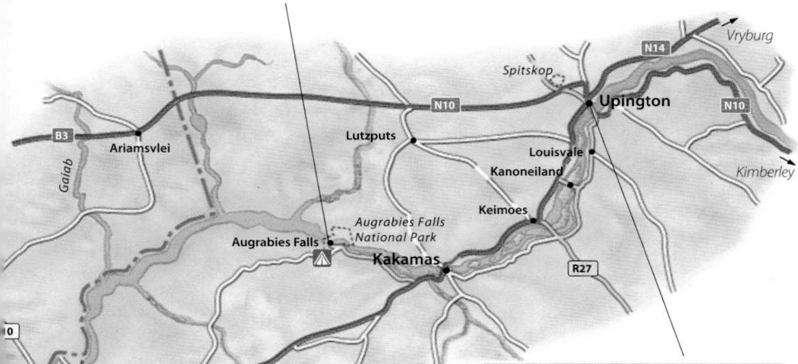

Pella Mission, with its rows of date palms and the tall spire of its Catholic church, exudes a distinctly Mexican ambience. The church was built by two missionaries whose only building manual was an encyclopedia.

Upington is the largest town on the Orange River. As it is an important centre for the dried fruit industry, sultanas drying in the sun are a common sight along the road. The pleasant riverside guesthouses are a popular stopover on the way to the Kgalagadi Transfrontier Park.

Key

━━ Major route

═══ Road (tarred)

═══ Road (untarred)

━━▸ International boundary

SOUTH OF THE ORANGE

Vast and unrelenting, the great Karoo is a uniquely South African landscape of dolerite outcrops, buttes and endless plains. In restful towns and villages the harshness of the terrain is softened by the large, low, sandstone homesteads, typical of Karoo architecture. Several nature reserves and national parks have been established to conserve the territory's fascinating environment and wildlife.

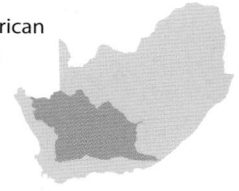

The indigenous Khoi called the region *Karoo* ("land of great thirst") and the Dutch colonists of the 17th century were hesitant to venture into this forbidding terrain. Ensign Schrijver was the first European to explore the eastern reaches of the Karoo in 1689, and by 1795 the Cape Colony had expanded to include the southern and eastern Karoo regions. The vast plains were partitioned into sheep ranches, and large migrating herds of springbok, hartebeest, black wildebeest, eland and quagga were decimated through uncontrolled hunting. Some 80 years later, the quagga was extinct, and the large herds of Cape mountain zebra and black wildebeest had been reduced to tiny remnant populations.

With the expanding frontier, several new towns were established. Graaff-Reinet, founded in 1786, prospered quickly as it became an important centre for the surrounding community of sheep farmers. Today, it has the highest number of national monuments in South Africa and is renowned for its Cape Dutch architecture. Elsewhere, the typical Karoo vernacular includes steep-roofed sandstone farmhouses surrounded by broad verandahs and delicate latticework.

The Camdeboo National Park surrounds Graaff-Reinet on three sides, while the Karoo National Park lies just north of Beaufort West. The Mountain Zebra National Park, near Cradock, is credited with saving the Cape mountain zebra from extinction. In the eastern Karoo, South Africa's largest storage reservoir, the Gariep Dam on the Orange River, provides water to the drought-prone Eastern Cape, and has developed into a relaxing and remote lakeside resort.

A fiery show of low-growing *vygies,* drought-resistant plants that flower only after it has rained

◀ The spectacular Swartberg Pass, a UNESCO World Heritage Site

Exploring South of the Orange

The Karoo is a region of endless vistas and clear blue skies, where the road runs straight as an arrow to the distant horizon. Large sheep farms produce much of South Africa's mutton and wool. Steel windmills, standing in the blazing sun, supply the area's lifeblood: water. Only 70 small towns and villages, of which Beaufort West is the largest, cling tenaciously to the drought-prone land. Many of them, for example Graaff-Reinet, are architectural treasure chests. At Beaufort West, Graaff-Reinet and Cradock, nature parks conserve the characteristic landscape, fauna and flora of the region.

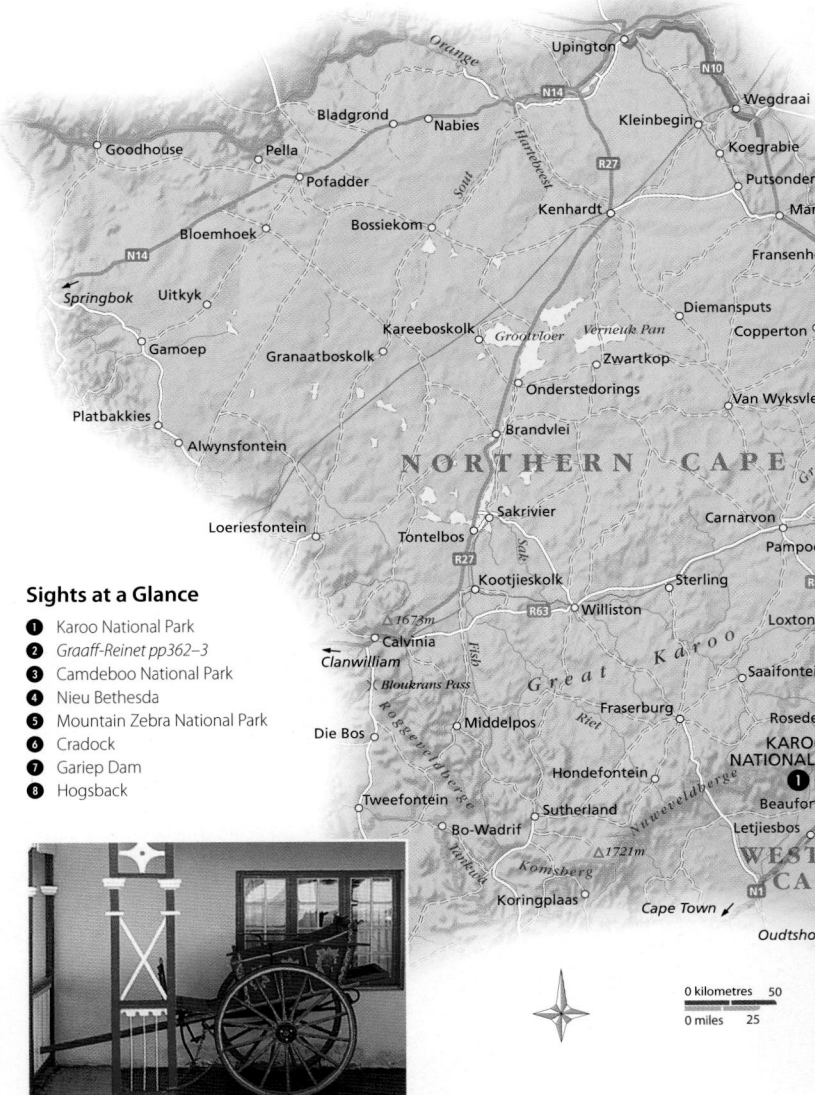

Sights at a Glance

1. Karoo National Park
2. *Graaff-Reinet pp362–3*
3. Camdeboo National Park
4. Nieu Bethesda
5. Mountain Zebra National Park
6. Cradock
7. Gariep Dam
8. Hogsback

A painted horse cart on a verandah in Cradock

Getting Around

The N1 national route that links Cape Town and Johannesburg passes right through Beaufort West. The N9, which connects Graaff-Reinet to the Southern Cape coast, branches off the N1 at Colesberg. Cradock and the nearby Mountain Zebra National Park to the west of the town are located on the N10. Tarred provincial roads connect most of the smaller villages, allowing visitors to explore the more remote parts of the region. Although distances are great, the volume of traffic is moderate and many of the Karoo towns have comfortable bed and breakfast establishments and restaurants. The long-distance bus companies stop in Beaufort West, Graaff-Reinet and Cradock.

Ostrich in the Mountain Zebra National Park

The Drostdy in Graaff-Reinet, a typical example of a Cape Dutch-style magistrate's office, now a hotel

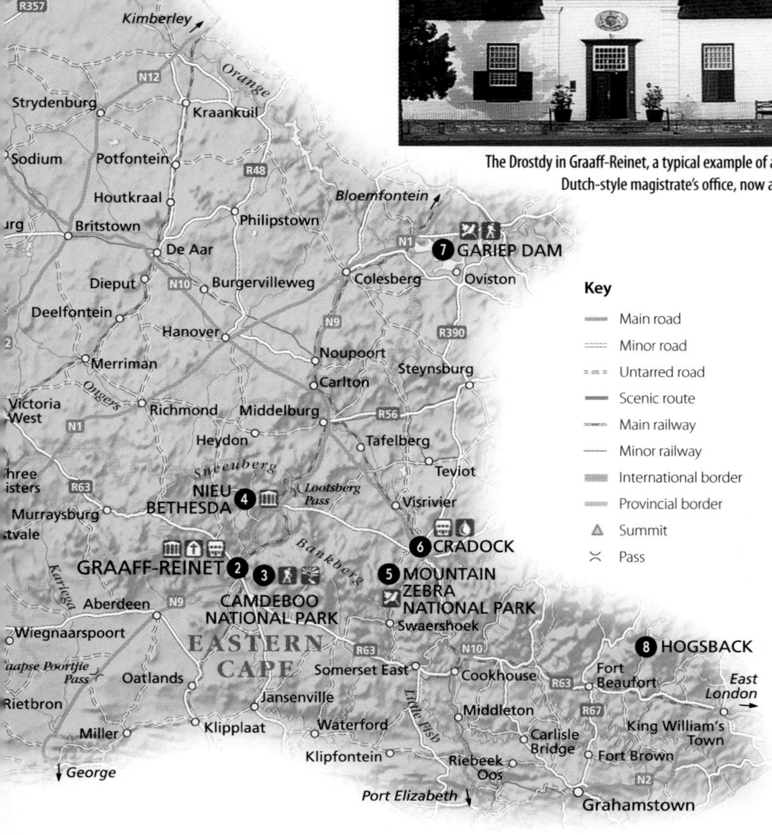

Key

— Main road

===== Minor road

==== Untarred road

— Scenic route

-·-·- Main railway

—— Minor railway

▬ International border

▬ Provincial border

△ Summit

⋈ Pass

For keys to symbols see back flap

❶ Karoo National Park

Road map C4. N1, 7 km (4 miles) S of Beaufort West. ℹ️ 023 415 2828. **Tel** Reservations: 012 428 9111. **Open** 5am–10pm daily. 🚗 🎒 ♿ 🍴 🚶 ⛺ 🌐 sanparks.org

The Karoo National Park was established on the outskirts of Beaufort West in 1979, to conserve a representative sample of the region's unique heritage. It has been enlarged over the years and now encompasses vast, flat plains as well as the rugged Nuweveld Mountains. Animals such as mountain reedbuck, grey rhebok, kudu, steenbok, jackal and aardwolf occur naturally, while reintroduced species include lion, black rhino, springbok, hartebeest, gemsboks (oryx), black wildebeest, Cape mountain zebra and the endangered briverine rabbit. Some 196 bird species have been recorded, and the park also sustains more than 20 black eagle pairs.

A comfortable rest camp is set at the base of the Nuweveld Mountains. Its spacious Cape Dutch chalets provide a convenient overnight stop that is easily accessible from the N1. The camp has good facilities, including a shop, swimming pool, restaurant and caravan park. Nearby, the historic Ou Skuur Farmhouse contains the park's information centre. A

Springbok once roamed the Karoo plains in their thousands

4WD trail has been laid out in the rugged western region of the park, and night drives provide the very best chances of seeing many of the region's shy nocturnal animals, such as the aardwolf.

The short Fossil and Bossie trails are accessible from the rest camp and allow visitors to learn about the Karoo's fascinating 250-million-year-old geological history and its unique vegetation.

The Fossil Trail is designed to accommodate wheelchairs and incorporates Braille boards. An easy circular day hike of 11 km (7 miles) is also accessible from the rest camp.

❷ Graaff-Reinet

See pp362–3.

❸ Camdeboo National Park

Road map C4. R63, 8 km (5 miles) NW of Graaff-Reinet. ℹ️ 049 892 3453. **Tel** Reservations: 012 428 9111. **Open** 6am–6pm (Oct–Mar: to 7pm). 🚗 🍴 🚶 🌐 sanparks.org

In a bid to conserve typical Karoo landforms and wildlife, an area of 145 sq km (56 sq miles) around Graaff-Reinet (*see pp362–3*) was set aside. West of the town is the Valley of Desolation, where spectacular columns of weathered dolerite tower 120 m (390 ft) over the valley floor.

A 14-km (9-mile) road leads to a view site and a short walk, while the circular day hike is reached from the Berg-en-dal gate on the western edge of town. A two- to three-day hike explores the scenic mountainous terrain in the southeast.

The eastern region of the nature reserve includes the Driekoppe peaks, which rise 600 m (1,950 ft) above the plains. This section sustains more than 220 species of bird. The populations of Cape mountain zebra, buffalo, hartebeest, springbok, kudu and blesbok are expanding, and many of them may be seen.

There are game-viewing roads and picnic sites situated around the Nqweba Dam in the centre of the reserve, and both boating and fishing are permitted.

The Valley of Desolation in Camdeboo National Park

The backyard of the Owl House is populated with many strange figures

❻ Nieu Bethesda

Road map C4. 50 km (31 miles) N of Graaff-Reinet. 1,550. Martin St, 049 841 1642. **nieu-bethesda.com**

The turn-off to this village lies on the N9, 27 km (17 miles) north of Graaff-Reinet. From there, a good dirt road traverses the Voor Sneeuberg ("in front of snow mountain") and leads to Nieu Bethesda.

The Kompasberg (Compass Peak), at 2,502 m (8,131 ft), is the highest point in the Sneeuberg range. It received its name in 1778 when Cape Governor Baron van Plettenberg, accompanied by Colonel Jacob Gordon, visited the mountain and noted that the surrounding countryside could be surveyed from its summit.

Nieu Bethesda was founded by Reverend Charles Murray, minister of the Dutch Reformed Church in Graaff-Reinet. The fertile valley in the arid terrain reminded him of the Pool of Bethesda (*John 5:2*), and so he named the town after it.

In 1875 he acquired a farm in the valley and by 1905 the church (now in Parsonage Street) was completed. It cost £5,600 to build, but at the time of its consecration two-thirds of the amount was still outstanding. To raise funds, arable church land was divided into plots and sold at a public auction. The debt was finally settled in 1929.

Today, Martin Street, the quaint main road, is lined with pear trees, and many of the bordering properties are framed by quince hedges. Irrigated fields and golden poplar trees complement and soften the rugged Karoo mountains, which create a bold contrast. Pienaar Street crosses over the Gat River to its western bank, and passes an old water mill that was built in 1860 by the owner of the original farm, Uitkyk. The first water wheel was made of wood, but was later replaced with the existing steel wheel.

The peaceful village has attracted much artistic talent, including one of South Africa's leading playwrights, Athol Fugard, who achieved world acclaim for his thought-provoking plays such as *Master Harold and the Boys* (see p252).

🏛 The Owl House

River St. **Open** 9am–5pm daily. **Tel** 049 841 1603. **theowlhouse.co.za**

Owl statue

The Owl House is considered one of South Africa's top 50 heritage sites. Its garden is cluttered with an intriguing assembly of concrete statues: owls, sheep, camels, people, sphinxes and religious symbols, created over more than 30 years by Helen Martins and her assistant, Koos Malgas. The walls, doors and ceilings of the house are decorated with finely ground coloured glass. Mirrors reflect the light from candles and lamps. Her work, unusual in its quantity and range of subject, has been classified as "Outsider Art" (art that falls outside the artistic mainstream as a result of isolation or insanity) and "Naive" (an expression of innocence and fantasy).

Helen Martins (1897–1976)

Born in Nieu Bethesda on 23 December 1897, Helen left home to study at a teachers' training college in Graaff-Reinet, and later married a young diplomat. The relationship did not last. Neither did a second marriage, and Helen returned home to nurse her irascible, elderly father. After his death, the naturally retiring woman retreated increasingly into her own fantasy world, and began to populate her garden with bizarre figures, an expression of her personal, mythical universe. In later years her eyesight began to fail due to having worked with ground glass over a long period of time. In August 1976, aged 78, she committed suicide by drinking a lethal dose of caustic soda. As an artist she remains an enigma.

The bedroom with its "wallpaper" of ground glass

❷ Street-by-Street: Graaff-Reinet

In 1786, a *landdrost* (magistrate) was appointed by the Dutch East India Company to enforce Dutch law and administration along the remote eastern Karoo frontier. The settlement that grew up around the magistrate's court was named after Governor Cornelis Jacob van de Graaff and his wife, Hester Cornelia Reinet. Nine years later, the citizens of Graaff-Reinet expelled the *landdrost* and declared the first Boer Republic in South Africa. Within a matter of a few months, however, colonial control was re-established.

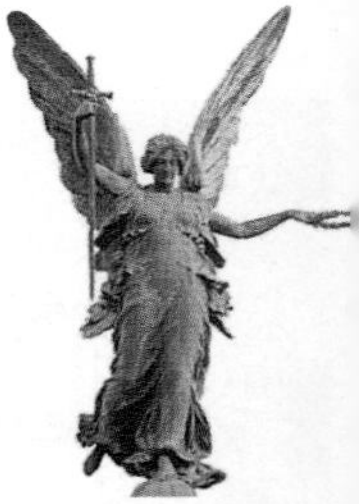

The War Memorial
The memorial honours t fallen of both World Wa

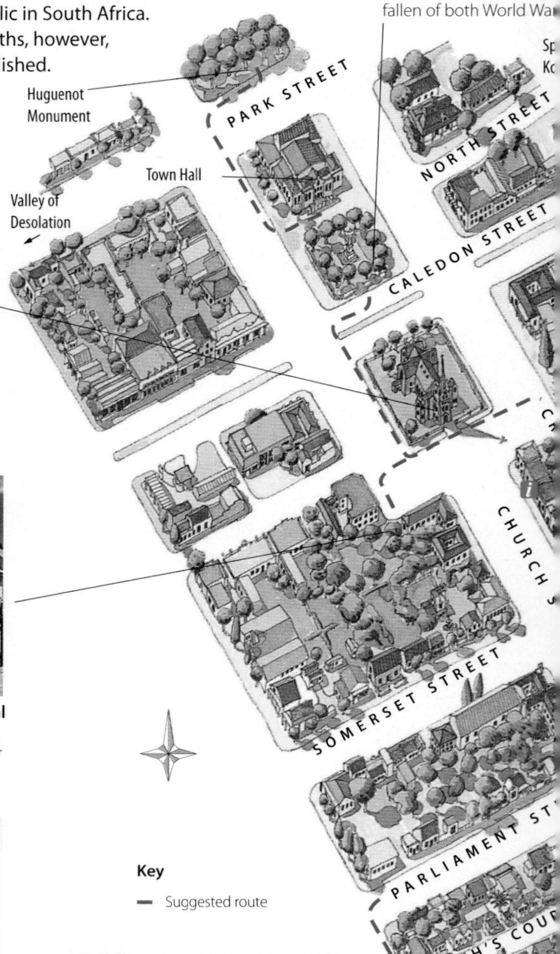

Huguenot Monument
Town Hall
Valley of Desolation
PARK STREET
NORTH STREET
CALEDON STREET
CHURCH S
SOMERSET STREET
PARLIAMENT ST
STRETCH'S COU
STRETCH'S

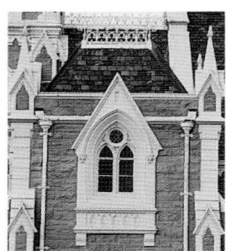

Dutch Reformed Church
The beautiful *Groot Kerk* (great church), completed in 1887, was constructed using two different types of local stone.

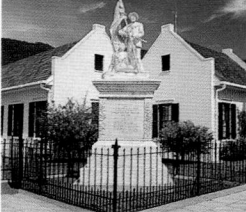

The South African War Memorial
This monument, unveiled in 1908, commemorates the efforts of Boer soldiers against the British troops.

Key

— Suggested route

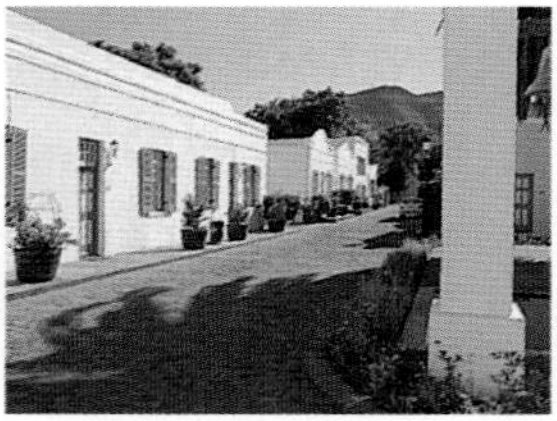

★ Stretch's Court
These cottages were built in the 1850s to house labourers and freed slaves.

VISITORS' CHECKLIST

Practical Information
Road map C4. 35,000
Church St, 049 892 4248.
graaffreinet.co.za
Reinet House: **Tel** 049 892 3801.
Open 8am–5pm Mon–Fri, 9am–noon Sat & Sun.
graaffreinetmuseums.co.za

Transport
Port Elizabeth, 236 km (147 miles) SE. Engen petrol station, Church St.

For hotels and restaurants in this region see p391 and p411

Spandau Kop looms over the town

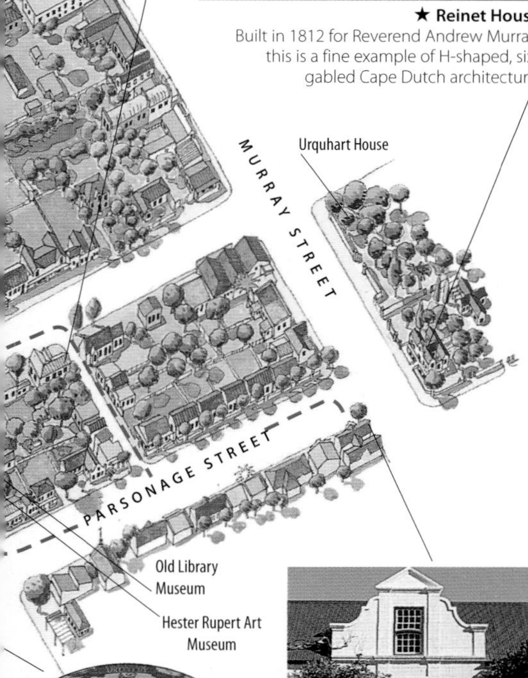

| 0 metres | 100 |
| 0 yards | 100 |

St James's
Church

★ **Reinet House**
Built in 1812 for Reverend Andrew Murray,
this is a fine example of H-shaped, six-
gabled Cape Dutch architecture.

Urquhart House

M U R R A Y   S T R E E T

P A R S O N A G E   S T R E E T

Old Library
Museum

Hester Rupert Art
Museum

The Drostdy
Heraldic detail on a plaque at
the Drostdy (magistrate's court),
a building designed by French
architect Louis Michel Thibault
in 1804.

★ **The Old Residency**
This imposing Cape Dutch
manor was completed in the
1820s, and the original fanlight
can still be seen above the front
door. Today, the gabled manor
is an annexe of Reinet House.

Exploring Graaff-Reinet

Graaff-Reinet lies in a valley
eroded by the Sundays River.
The gardens and tree-lined
avenues form a striking contrast
to the bleak expanse of the surrounding Karoo. Many of the
town's historic buildings have
been painstakingly restored, and
over 200 are national monuments. The main architectural
attractions lie between Bourke
and Murray streets.

🏛 Dutch Reformed Church

This beautiful church is
considered to be the finest
example of Gothic architecture
in the country. Completed in
1887, it was modelled on
Salisbury Cathedral.

🏛 Stretch's Court

In 1855 Captain Charles Stretch
bought land near the Drostdy to
build cottages for his labourers.
Restored in 1977, these are now
an annexe of the Drostdy Hotel.

🏛 Old Library Museum

Church St. **Tel** 049 892 3801.
Open 8am–1pm, 1:45–4:30pm
Mon–Fri, 9am–1pm Sat & Sun. 🖼
W graaffreinetmuseums.co.za

This 1847 building displays Karoo
fossils, old photographs and
reproductions of rock art.

🏛 Hester Rupert Art Museum

Church St. **Tel** 049 892 2121.
Open 9am–12:30pm, 2–5pm
Mon–Fri, 9am–noon Sat & Sun. 🖼
W rupertartmuseum.co.za

This former Dutch Reformed
Mission Church displays works
by contemporary South African
artists, among them Irma Stern
and Cecil Skotnes *(see p376)*.

The Dutch Reformed Church

A Cape mountain zebra in Mountain Zebra National Park

❺ Mountain Zebra National Park

Road map D4. 26 km (16 miles) W of Cradock. **Tel** Park: 048 881 2427; reservations: 012 428 9111. **Open** 7am–6pm May–Sep; 7am–7pm Oct–Apr. 🚻🍴🏃⚠️ 📝🏕️ **W** sanparks.org

While the national park west of Cradock is the second-smallest in the country, its modest acreage in no way detracts from the visitor's enjoyment. It was originally conceived as a sanctuary that was intended to rescue the Cape mountain zebra from imminent extinction. When the park was proclaimed in 1937, there were six zebras; by 1949 only two remained. Conservation efforts were successful, however, and the park now protects about 300 zebras.

The plains and mountains of this Karoo landscape also support a wide variety of other mammals, including cheetah, black wildebeest, kudu, eland, red hartebeest, springbok, buffalo, black rhino and caracal. More than 200 species of bird have been recorded here, including many raptors and the endangered blue crane.

The rest camp, which overlooks a valley, consists of chalets, a camp site, a restaurant, shop and information centre. A short walk leads past the chalets to the swimming pool set at the base of a granite ridge.

For convenience, the park can be divided into two sections. From the camp, a circular drive of 28 km (18 miles) explores the wooded Wilgeboom Valley, noted for its rugged granite land forms. The road passes the Doornhoek Cottage where the screen adaptation of Olive Schreiner's *The Story of an African Farm* was filmed, and leads to a shady picnic site at the base of the mountains. The northern loop, which starts just before Wilgeboom, climbs steeply to the Rooiplaat Plateau, and offers splendid views across the vast Karoo, where most of the park's wildlife congregates. The early mornings and late afternoons are the best times to visit the area.

❻ Cradock

Road map D4. 🚗 36,000. 🚉 Church St. 🚌 Struwig Motors, Main St. 🛈 JA Calata St, 074 188 7087. **Open** daily. **W** cradock-info.co.za

In 1812, towards the end of the Fourth Frontier War, Sir John Cradock established two military outposts to secure the eastern border. One was at Grahamstown, the other at Cradock. Merino sheep flourished in this region, and Cradock soon developed into a sheep-farming centre. The Dutch Reformed Church was inspired by London's St Martin-in-the-Fields. Completed in 1867, it dominates the town's central square. The **Great Fish River Museum**

The Dutch Reformed Church in Cradock

behind the town hall preserves the history of the early pioneers. In Market Street, **Die Tuishuise** *(see p391)* is the result of an innovative project to restore a series of 30 mid-19th-century Karoo cottages and to create comfortable bed and breakfast accommodation. Each is furnished simply and charmingly in the style of the period, with meals taken in the adjoining Victoria Manor hotel.

🏛 **Great Fish River Museum** Commissioner St. **Tel** (048) 881 4509. **Open** 8am–4:15pm Mon–Fri. 🚷

Olive Emilie Schreiner (1855–1920)

The Story of an African Farm is widely regarded as the first South African novel of note. Olive Schreiner began writing it while she worked as a governess on farms in the Cradock district. The manuscript was released in 1883 under the male pseudonym Ralph Iron, and was an immediate success. Schreiner, an active campaigner for women's equality and a supporter of "Native" rights, wrote extensively on politics. She died in Wynberg (Cape Town) in 1920. Her husband, Samuel Cronwright-Schreiner, buried her on Buffelskop, 24 km (15 miles) south of Cradock, beside their daughter, who had died 25 years earlier just 18 hours after her birth, and Olive's dog.

Olive Schreiner

Cottages with striped awnings and painted *stoeps* (verandahs) line the streets of Cradock

❼ Gariep Dam

Road map D4. NE of Colesberg on R701.

In 1779, when Colonel Robert Gordon reached the banks of a watercourse that was known to the Khoina as *Gariep,* he renamed it the Orange River, in honour of the Dutch Prince of Orange. Little did he know that a dam would be constructed at this point nearly 200 years later.

In 1928, Dr A D Lewis advanced the idea of building a tunnel linking the Orange River to the Eastern Cape. Although a report was presented to the government in 1948, it was only in 1962 that the prime minister Hendrik Verwoerd gave the ambitious project the go-ahead. Work began in 1966, and in September 1970 the last gap in the wall was closed.

The Orange River is South Africa's largest and longest river, and the Gariep forms the country's largest body of water. The dam wall rises 90 m (297 ft) above its foundations and has a crest length of 948 m (3,110 ft). At full supply level it covers an area of 374 sq km (144 sq miles).

A corridor of bushveld surrounds the Gariep Dam, and is home to a few springbok, blesbok and black wildebeest. The **Forever Resorts Gariep**, at the dam wall, offers comfortable chalets, a camp site and a range of activities such as fishing and boating. There are also tours of the dam wall.

🦌 Forever Resorts Gariep
Gariep Dam. **Tel** (051) 754-0045.
Open daily (day visitors must call ahead). 🏊 🚣 🏃 🎣 🛶 ⛱ ⚠ 🏕
W forevergariep.co.za

❽ Hogsback

Road map D4. 🏔 1,030.
ℹ Main Rd, 045 962 1245.
Open 10am–4pm Mon–Sat, 9am–3pm Sun. **W** hogsback.com

The quiet village of Hogsback lies at an altitude of 1,200 metres (4,000 ft) in the beautiful forested surroundings of the Amatola Mountains. Its name derives from one mountain peak that resembles the back of a hog when viewed from a particular angle.

The earliest known written reference to "Hogsback" was found in the journal of the painter Thomas Baines, who passed the "Hogs Back" while on his travels deeper inside South Africa in 1848. The Amatola Forest is often claimed as J R R Tolkien's inspiration for *The Lord of the Rings*, in particular for his fictional forest of Mirkwood. Tolkien was born in South Africa.

The village is made up of a string of cottages, guesthouses, tea gardens and crafts shops. It is well-known for its lovely English-style gardens of flowering plants such as rhododendrons and azaleas and its orchards of soft fruits such as blackcurrants, blackberries and gooseberries. There are delicious jams for sale in Hogsback's shops. Local hikes from 30 minutes to two hours lead up to some pretty waterfalls in the forests.

Chalets built on the water's edge at the Gariep Dam

Spandau Kop Mount in the Karoo plateau near Graaff-Reinet ▶

NORTH OF THE ORANGE

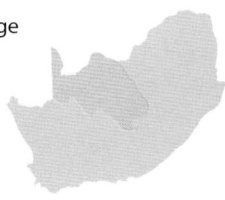

The red dunes of the Kalahari Desert stretch north of the Orange River like the waves of an inland sea. Three mountain ranges break the monotony until the dunes give way, at last, to the grasslands of the Highveld plateau. In this remote wilderness, oasis-like towns such as Upington welcome the traveller, and in a narrow band along the river, vineyards produce sultana grapes and fine wines.

At the beginning of the 19th century, the uncharted Northern Cape was home to the last nomadic hunter-gatherers, the San. In 1820, Robert and Mary Moffat built a mission and school in Kuruman, 263 km (163 miles) northeast of Upington, and devoted 50 years to translating and printing the Bible in the Setswana language. The journeys of exploration undertaken by their son-in-law, David Livingstone, focused European attention on Africa.

In the Cape Colony, Afrikaner farmers became increasingly discontented with the British administration. Many trekked north in search of new land. In 1836, a group of Voortrekkers (see pp54–5) crossed the Orange River and settled near Thaba Nchu, east of present-day Bloemfontein, where they established an independent republic, the Orange Free State, in 1854.

The discovery of diamonds in 1866 transformed South Africa's economy. At the town of Kimberley, countless fortune-seekers carved out the Big Hole, an enormous crater that had yielded a total of 2,722 kg (5,988 lb) of diamonds by the time work stopped in 1914.

Further west along the Orange River, a local Griqua leader invited early missionary Reverend Christiaan Schröder to establish a mission station on the banks of the river, and the town of Upington was founded. Irrigation canals soon transformed the desert into a fertile crescent of vineyards, orchards, wheat and lucerne fields.

Although mining is still the main contributor to the region's economy, today visitors are enticed by the area's history, desert scenery and diverse wildlife, such as various raptor species and the unique Kalahari lion.

Suricates, or slender-tailed meerkats, live in close-knit family groups

◄ The stark outline of a quiver tree, perfectly adapted to arid conditions, in Augrabies Falls National Park

Exploring North of the Orange

Upington is the perfect base for exploring South Africa's last frontier: the red-dune wilderness bordering the Kalahari Desert. Although no permanent rivers have flowed across this ancient landscape for thousands of years, and grass-covered dunes seem to stretch to infinity, wildlife is abundant. Kimberley was once the scene of the world's greatest diamond rush and retains many reminders of its frenetic heyday. Driving eastwards, annual rainfall increases. The grasslands of the Free State support cattle and sheep, as well as fields of sunflowers and maize. Historic Bloemfontein, once the capital of a Boer republic named Orange Free State, has many superb old buildings.

Devil's claw plant, Kgalagadi Transfrontier Park

For hotels and restaurants in this region see p391 and p411

Sights at a Glance

1. Upington
2. Augrabies Falls National Park
3. Kgalagadi Transfrontier Park
4. Tswalu Kalahari Reserve
5. Kimberley
6. Bloemfontein

Key

— Major road

---- Minor road

=== Untarred road

— Scenic route

--- Main railway

--- Minor railway

▬ International border

— Provincial border

▲ Summit

The Big Hole in Kimberley, begun in the 1870s

Getting Around

Most of the towns north of the Orange River lie more than 200 km (125 miles) apart, and there are few petrol stations or refreshment stops along the way. But as the volume of traffic is low and all the main roads are tarred, travel in this region need not be arduous. The R360 runs north from Upington to the Kgalagadi Transfrontier Park. Although the roads in the park are sandy, 4WD vehicles are not required. National roads link the major regional centres to Johannesburg and to the Western and Eastern capes. The east-west N8 connects Upington, Kimberley and Bloemfontein. There are regional airports in all three centres, and long-distance coaches provide links to other towns.

0 kilometres   50

0 miles   25

Sunflowers constitute one of the Free State's major crops

For keys to symbols *see back flap*

The Reverend Christiaan Schröder's cottage in Upington

❶ Upington

Road map B3. 🏘 75,000. ✈ 7 km
(4 miles) NE of town. 🚌 Lutz St.
ℹ Public Library Building, Mutual St,
054 338 7152. 🅦 **kharahais.gov.za**

Upington lies in a vast plain
dotted with low shrubs. Only
where the road reaches the
Orange River does the landscape
change abruptly, as the
river paints a green
stripe across the
barren territory.

As the Northern
Cape's second-largest
settlement after
Kimberley, Upington
serves a district of
lucerne, cotton, fruit
and wine farms lining a fertile
river corridor along the river.

In the late 19th century the
Northern Cape was a wild
frontier. The nomadic bands
of Khoi hunter-gatherers
resented the intrusion of
the white settlers into this region
and frequently stole
livestock from them. In
1871, however, at the
request of Korana chief
Klaas Lukas, the Reverend
Christiaan Schröder
established a mission
station in the wilderness
and the first irrigation
canals were dug. His
original church is part
of the **Kalahari-Oranje
Museum** in Schröder
Street. Here too, is the
statue of a camel and
rider, which honours the
policemen and their

The "stone" plant

tireless mounts who once
patrolled this desert region.

Occupying an island in the
Orange River, just outside town,
Die Eiland is a municipal resort
which has an avenue of more
than 200 palm trees that were
planted in 1935.

The five wine cellars in this arid
region all belong to the **Orange
River Cellars**, which offers
tastings. On the south-
ern bank of the river,
the South African
Dried Fruit Co-
op on Louisvale Road
is capable of proces-
sing up to 250 tonnes
of dried fruit daily.

🏛 **Kalahari–Oranje Museum**
4 Schröder St. **Open** 9am–12:30pm,
2–5pm Mon–Fri; 9am–noon Sat. 🚻

🍷 **Orange River Cellars**
Industria St. **Tel** 054 337 8800.
Open tastings: 10am–6pm
Mon–Fri, 10am–3pm Sat. 🅿
🅦 **orangeriverwines.com**

❷ Augrabies Falls National Park

Road map B3. 100 km (62 miles) W
of Upington. **Tel** 054 452 9200;
reservations: 012 428 9111.
Open 7am–6:30pm daily. 🚻 🏕
🚶 🚌 🏔 🅿 🅦 **sanparks.org**

The Augrabies Falls National
Park was established in 1966
to protect the Augrabies Falls,
which rush through the largest
granite gorge in the world.
During periods of normal
flow, the main waterfall
plunges 56 m (182 ft) into the
gorge. The lesser Bridal Veil
Waterfall, located along the
northern wall of the gorge,
cascades 75 m (244 ft) into
the river below.

At the main complex near the
entrance to the park are a shop,
restaurant and bar. Paths lead
from here down to the falls.
There are safety fences to
prevent visitors from falling into
the chasm, but you should take
care near the waterfall, as the
rocks are very slippery.

Apart from the waterfall
itself and the attractive rest
camp, which consists of
59 chalets, three swimming
pools and an extensive camp
site, Augrabies has much to
offer. The 39-km (24-mile) long
Klipspringer Trail explores
the southern section of the
park and affords superb views
of the gorge and surrounding
desert. Wildlife to look out for
includes klipspringer, kudu,
gemsbok and springbok, which
are often seen standing in the
shade of camel thorn and olive
trees to escape the heat.

The Augrabies Falls in the national park of the same name

❸ Kgalagadi Trans-frontier Park

Road map B2. 280 km (174 miles) N of Upington. ℹ️ 054 561 2000. **Tel** Reservations: 012 428 9111. **Open** daily; hours vary. 🏞️ 🥾 🧗 🏕️ 📷 **w** sanparks.org

An immense wilderness of grass-covered dunes traversed by two dry, ancient riverbeds, this national park is Africa's largest and extends 34,390 sq km (13,278 sq miles) across territory almost twice the size of the Kruger National Park. Jointly managed by South Africa and Botswana, the border within the park is unfenced and the wildlife is free to migrate.

From Upington the tarred R360 cuts a course across a landscape that seems devoid of human habitation. The tar road ends near Andriesvale and a sandy track hugs the border fence for 58 km (36 miles) before reaching the southern entrance. A dusty camp site is situated near the gate, while the nearby camp of Twee Rivieren offers chalets, a restaurant and a swimming pool. From Twee Rivieren, two roads follow the dry courses of the Auob and Nossob rivers on their way to the camps of Mata Mata and Nossob. There are four lovely picnic spots along the Nossob. To cross over to Namibia at Mata Mata, visitors must stay in the park for at least two nights.

Although Twee Rivieren is situated in the most arid region of the park, wildlife is surprisingly plentiful, with an astonishing 19 species of carnivore present, including the black-maned Kalahari lion, cheetah, brown hyena, wild cat and honey badger. Several species of raptor – including martial, tawny and bateleur eagles, as well as the pale chanting goshawk – are also commonly sighted.

A total of 40 windmills have been erected in the riverbeds, providing water for wildlife.

Springbok *(Antidorcas marsupialis)*, Kgalagadi Transfrontier Park

❹ Tswalu Kalahari Reserve

Road map C2. 115 km (71 miles) NW of Kuruman. ℹ️ 053 781 9311. 📷 **w** tswalu.com

An ambitious project without equal, Tswalu is South Africa's largest private reserve. It protects around 750 sq km (285 sq miles) of red Kalahari dunes and the picturesque Korannaberg mountains. The reserve came into existence through the tireless efforts of British businessman Stephen Boler. First, he bought and amalgamated 26 cattle farms. Work teams then removed some 800 km (500 miles) of fencing, as well as 2,300 km (1,440 miles) of electric lines, 38 concrete dams and the

Buffalo bull

farmsteads. Approximately 7,000 cattle were sold off and the reserve was fenced.

Boler invested over R54 million to develop the reserve. A total of 4,700 animals, representing 22 species, have been reintroduced, including lion, cheetah, buffalo, three types of zebra, red hartebeest, blue and black wildebeest, giraffe, gemsbok, kudu, impala and wild dog. But the jewels in Tswalu's crown are, without doubt, the small number of desert black rhino (subspecies *Diceros bicornis bicornis*) relocated with the permission of the Namibian government. The reserve is now owned by the Oppenheimer family (of gold and diamond mining fame).

Tswalu's two luxury, all-inclusive lodges have their own airstrip, and most visitors arrive by charter plane.

Sir Laurens van der Post (1906–96)

Soldier, writer, philosopher, dreamer and explorer, Laurens van der Post was the son of an Afrikaner mother and a Dutch father. During World War II he obtained the rank of colonel and was a prisoner of the Japanese in Java until 1945. Upon his return to South Africa, he began his journeys into the wilderness. A fascinating account of his expedition in search of the San people of the Kalahari was published in 1958. *The Lost World of the Kalahari* was one of the first books to detail this intriguing and highly spiritual culture. A personal friend of the British Royal Family, van der Post is remembered for his insightful, philosophical writings, most of which deal with the moral and social issues of his time.

Sir Laurens van der Post

❺ Kimberley

The first Diamond Rush in the Kimberley district took place in 1869 when diamonds were found in the walls of a house on the Bultfontein farm. In July 1871, prospectors camped at the base of a small hill, 4.5 km (3 miles) to the northwest. The party's cook was sent to the summit as punishment for a minor offence and returned with a diamond. Within two years, New Rush tent town, renamed Kimberley in 1873, had become home to 50,000 miners. By the time Cecil John Rhodes *(see p56)* arrived, 3,600 claims were being worked.

A re-created street scene at The Big Hole: Kimberley Mine Museum

Exploring Kimberley

The angular street pattern of Kimberley is in contrast with the neat grid pattern characteristic of other South African cities, a legacy of its formative, tent-town years. Although reminders of the past are not always apparent, Kimberley has several interesting historic landmarks that are well worth visiting.

🔲 The Big Hole: Kimberley Mine Museum

West Circular Rd. **Tel** 053 839 4600. **Open** 8am–5pm daily. 🎨 ♿ 🗹 🖉 📷 📶 thebighole.co.za

Centred around the Big Hole, this museum tells South Africa's diamond-mining history through several elements. The Old Mining Village consists of cobbled streets lined with buildings dating to the late 19th century, including a watchmaker's shop, a pawnbroker's and an old bar with original fittings. The 90-m (295-ft) viewing platform over the Big Hole allows visitors to look into the murky lake below, and there is a mock-up of a mine shaft, too. The Real Diamond Display holds replicas of uncut stones.

🔲 Kimberley Club

70–72 Du Toitspan Rd. **Tel** 053 832 4224. **Open** daily. ♿ 📶 kimberleyclub.co.za

Dating from 1896, this luxurious club was the meeting place of the mining magnates and saw much wheeling and dealing. The club also has a boutique hotel and conference facilities.

🔲 Oppenheimer Memorial Gardens

Jan Smuts Blvd.
In the gardens, five bronze miners surround the Digger's Fountain. A marble colonnade contains a bust of Sir Ernest Oppenheimer, the German-born diamond buyer who in 1917 founded the giant Anglo American Corporation.

🔲 William Humphreys Art Gallery

Cullinan Crescent, Civic Centre. **Tel** 053 831 1724. **Open** 8am–4:45pm Mon–Fri, 10am–4:45pm Sat, 9am–11:45pm Sun. ♿ 🎨 🗹 📶 whag.co.za

This gallery houses a superb collection of paintings by European masters and South African artists.

🔲 McGregor Museum

S Atlas Rd, Belgravia. **Tel** 053 839 2717. **Open** 9am–5pm Mon–Sat, 2–5pm Sun. 🎨 ♿ 🗹 📷 📷 📶 museumsnc.co.za

Cecil John Rhodes stayed in this building during the South African War. It now houses a museum of natural and cultural history, with ethnological and archaeological displays, as well as rock paintings.

🔲 Duggan-Cronin Gallery

Egerton Rd. **Tel** 053 839 2700. **Open** 9am–4pm Mon–Fri.
The gallery contains 8,000 photographs of anthropological interest taken over 20 years by Alfred Duggan-Cronin, who, arriving in Kimberley in 1897, became deeply interested in the indigenous people of the Northern Cape.

VISITORS' CHECKLIST

Practical Information
Road map D3. 🗺 225,500.
ℹ Jan Smuts Blvd, 053 830 6911.
📶 solplaatje.org.za

Transport
✈ 7 km (4 miles) S of town.
🚉 Old de Beers Rd. 🚌 Shell Ultra City.

The McGregor Museum, Kimberley

For hotels and restaurants in this region see p391 and p411

The Kimberley Diamond Rush

Kimberley Mine, or the Big Hole, as it is known, is the only one of four diamond mines in the Kimberley area that is still open. Within two years of the discovery of diamond-bearing kimberlite pipes in 1871, the claims were being worked by up to 30,000 miners at a time. Early photographs reveal a spider's web of cables radiating upwards from the edge of the excavation. With little more than picks and shovels to aid them, the miners dug deep into the earth, and by 1889, the hole had reached an astounding depth of 150 m (488 ft). The deeper the miners delved, the more difficult it became to extract the diamond-bearing soil, and the chaotic arrangement of cables, precipitous paths and claims lying at varying heights encouraged the diggers to form syndicates. These groupings were absorbed into various companies that were later acquired by Cecil John Rhodes.

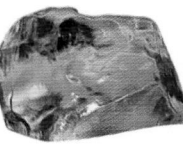

The Cullinan Diamond is the largest diamond ever found. A replica is displayed at the Kimberley Mine Museum.

Cecil John Rhodes, depicted as a victorious empire builder in this 19th-century *Punch* cartoon, was one of the most influential people in Kimberley.

The Big Hole

Covering an area of 17 ha (43 acres), the hole has a perimeter of 1.6 km (1 mile). It eventually reached a depth of 800 m (2,600 ft), the first 240 m (780 ft) of which was laboriously dug by hand. An underground shaft increased the depth to 1,098 m (3,569 ft). By 1914, some 22.6 million tonnes of rock had been excavated, yielding a total of 14.5 million carats of diamonds.

Diamond miners' lives were exhausting during the 1870s: they worked six days a week, surrounded by heat, dust and flies.

Cocopans (wheelbarrows on narrow-gauge tracks) were used to transport diamond-bearing rock out of the hole.

De Beers Consolidated Mines, owned by Cecil John Rhodes, bought Barney Barnato's diamond mines for the sum of £5,338,650 in 1889.

The Big Hole was closed as a working mine in 1914. It is the largest man-made hole in the world, and the focus of the Big Hole: Kimberley Mine Museum.

❻ Bloemfontein

Situated in the heartland of South Africa, Bloemfontein, capital of the Free State and seat of the province's parliament, is also the country's judicial capital. Part of the municipality of Mangaung, it lies at the hub of five major national road routes. An altitude of 1,400 m (4,593 ft) means that summers are moderate and winters mild to cool. The city was named after a fountain where early travellers used to stop on their treks through the interior. The city's history – and that of many of its stately old sandstone buildings – is firmly connected with the Afrikaners' struggle for independence. In 1854, when Major Henry Warden, the region's official British representative, was recalled to the Cape, the Afrikaners established a republic, with Bloemfontein as its capital.

The Appeal Court building, Bloemfontein

Exploring Bloemfontein

Although Major Warden's fort has long disappeared, a portion of Queen's Fort, dating back to 1848, can still be seen south of the city centre.

President Brand Street is lined with many fine old sandstone buildings, such as the **Appeal Court**, built in 1929, opposite the **Fourth Raadsaal**, which now houses the Free State's provincial legislature. This brick-and-sandstone building was constructed around 1893, during the presidency of Frederick Reitz.

🏛 The National Museum

36 Aliwal St. **Tel** 051 447 9609.
Open 8am–5pm Mon–Fri, 10am–5pm Sat, noon–5:30pm Sun & pub hols. ♿ 🅿 🖥 📷 🌐 **nasmus.co.za**

This museum contains a good collection of dinosaur fossils, and a reconstruction of a typical 19th-century Bloemfontein

street, complete with a cluttered general dealer's store.

🏛 National Museum for Afrikaans Literature

Cnr President Brand & Maitland sts. **Tel** 051 405 4711.
Open 8am–4pm Mon–Fri, 9am–noon Sat.

Near the Appeal Court, this museum is devoted to leading Afrikaans writers, even those who, like André Brink (see p33), opposed apartheid.

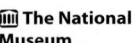

Detail of the National Women's Memorial

🏛 Old Presidency

President Brand St. **Tel** 051 448 0949.
Open 8am–3:30pm Mon–Fri. 🖥

Three blocks south from the Literature Museum, on the site once occupied by the homestead of Major Warden's farm, stands the Old Presidency, an attractive building completed in 1861. It was the home of the republic's Afrikaner presidents

before the British invasion in 1900, and now houses a small museum depicting this time. There is a pleasant café in the stables.

🏛 First Raadsaal Museum

95 St George St. **Tel** 051 447 9609.
Open 10am–1pm Mon–Fri, 2–5pm Sat & Sun. ♿ 🌐 **nasmus.co.za**

This, the oldest building in the city, is a white, unpretentious structure near the National Museum. Built by Warden in 1849, it was used as a school. After Warden was withdrawn in 1854, it became the meeting place of the republic's *Volksraad* (people's council).

🏛 Tweetoringkerk

Charles St. **Tel** 051 430 4274.
Dedicated in 1881, the Dutch Reformed Tweetoringkerk (twin-spired church) is unique in the country. It was inspired by Europe's Gothic cathedrals and designed by Richard Wocke. The interior, too, is Gothic. Especially noteworthy is the woodwork around the pulpit and organ.

🏛 National Women's Memorial and Anglo-Boer War Museum

Monument Rd. **Tel** 051 447 3447.
Open 8am–4:30pm Mon–Fri, 10am–5pm Sat, 11am–5pm Sun. 📷 ♿ 🌐 **wmbr.org.za**

South of the city, this site commemorates the countless Boer and black African women and children who died in British concentration camps during the South African War.

Emily Hobhouse, a British woman who campaigned for better treatment of the prisoners, is buried at the foot of the monument.

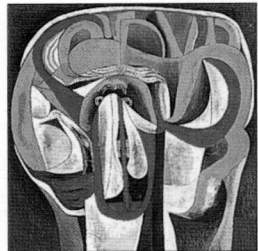

Abstract painting by Cecil Skotnes, Oliewenhuis Art Museum

Exterior of the Oliewenhuis Art Museum, Bloemfontein

Environs

North of the city centre, the **Franklin Nature Reserve** occupies Naval Hill. The name originated during the South African War when a cannon was mounted here by the British Naval Brigade. In 1928, the University of Michigan (USA) built an observatory on the summit. Over 7,000 star systems were discovered before it closed in 1972. It now houses a theatre.

Further north of the city, the **Oliewenhuis Art Museum** is set in a spacious garden. This gallery is renowned for its superb collection of South African art.

Several excellent wildlife reserves can be found north of Bloemfontein. The **Soetdoring Dam Nature Reserve** borders on the expansive Krugerdrif Dam whose wall, at 5 km (3 miles), is one of the longest in South Africa.

The river and shoreline of this reserve provide excellent picnic spots and are popular for carp fishing. This area is home to gemsbok, eland, black wildebeest, springbok and zebra, and 290 bird species within three distinct ecosystems – wetland, thornveld and grassland.

The turn-off to the **Willem Pretorius Game Reserve** lies some 150 km (93 miles) north of Bloemfontein on the N1. It was established by a farmer as a sanctuary to protect black wildebeest, and today is home to several hundred of these gregarious animals. It is also a good place to see eland, blesbok, springbok and giraffe on the grasslands around Allemanskraal Dam. Birds such as korhaans and double-banded coursers are also commonly seen.

⚐ Franklin Nature Reserve
Union Ave, Naval Hill. **Open** daily.

🏛 Oliewenhuis Art Museum
Harry Smith St. **Tel** 051 447 9609.
Open 8am–5pm Mon–Fri, 10am–5pm Sat, 1–5pm Sun. **Closed** Good Fri, 25 Dec. ♿ Ⓦ **nasmus.co.za**

VISITORS' CHECKLIST

Practical Information
Road map D3. 🚂 747,500.
ℹ️ Bloemfontein Tourist Centre, 60 Park Rd. 051 405 8489.
Open 8am–4pm Mon–Fri, 8am–noon Sat. 🎭 Bloem Show (Apr–May); Rose Festival (Oct).
Ⓦ **mangaung.co.za**

Transport
✈️ N8, 10 km (6 miles) E of city.
🚉 Harvey Rd. 🚌 Tourist Centre.

⚐ Soetdoring Dam Nature Reserve
R64 (Kimberley Rd). **Tel** 051 433 9002.
Open 6:30am–6pm daily. 🚗 ⚲ 🚶

⚐ Willem Pretorius Game Reserve
N1 to Kroonstad. **Tel** 057 651 4168.
Open 7am–6:30pm daily. 🚗 ⚠️

Giraffe, Franklin Nature Reserve on Naval Hill, Bloemfontein

Bloemfontein City Centre

① Appeal Court
② National Museum for Afrikaans Literature
③ Old Presidency
④ First Raadsaal Museum
⑤ Fourth Raadsaal
⑥ National Museum
⑦ Tweetoringkerk

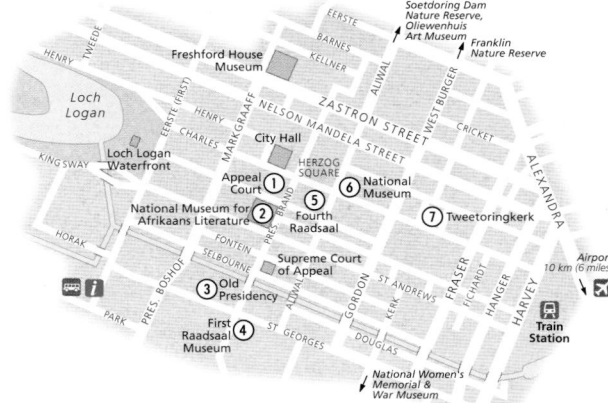

0 metres 500
0 yards 500

For keys to symbols *see back flap*

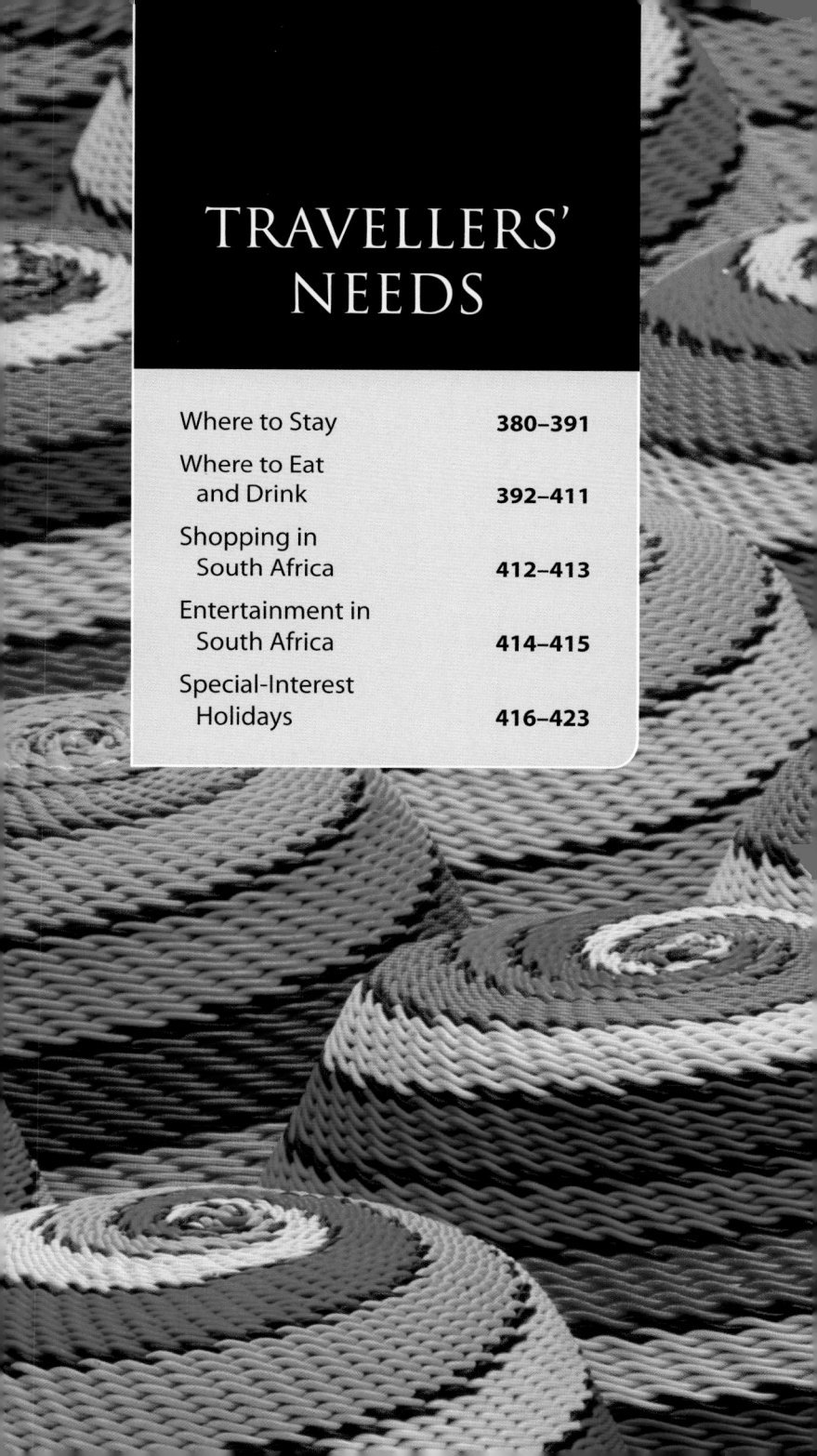

TRAVELLERS' NEEDS

WHERE TO STAY

The slow journeys of earlier centuries, when the vast distances between settlements had to be covered on horseback or by ox wagon, led to a proud local tradition of hospitality. In South Africa, "hospitality" is more than a catchword, and establishments, from the largest hotel chain to the smallest bed and breakfast, do their utmost to make the modern traveller feel welcome. The wide range of accommodation available is a reflection of the diversity of the country itself. A fantasy resort hotel such as the Palace of

the Lost City at Sun City *(see pp328–9)* and the elegant colonial hotel, Mount Nelson in Cape Town *(see p384)*, offer every conceivable luxury, and bear comparison with the best in the world. Charming alternatives are the guesthouses found in small towns, where tranquillity and hearty, home-cooked fare are valued far more than modern convenience. Safari lodges provide an idyllic and expensive Africa experience, while camp sites and backpacker hostels offer basic amenities and cater for younger visitors on limited budgets.

Where to Look

Visitors touring South Africa by car may be worried by the distances that separate cities and towns. Fortunately, hotels, bed and breakfasts, and self-catering cottages are found in even the remotest towns.

South Africa's cities offer a great variety of places to stay, whether you want family, luxury or business accommodation. Well-visited country and resort areas also offer accommodation to suit every taste and budget: many game parks, for example, have luxurious lodges as well as basic self-catering chalets and camp sites, while most coastal resorts offer hotels, camp sites, holiday apartments and guesthouses. If you are seeking quiet surroundings, try the smaller, simpler hostelries found inland, or hotels on the coast that are set away from obvious attractions. Enquire at the local tourist information office (usually well

signposted) or contact one of the many umbrella associations such as the **Tourism Grading Council of South Africa**, or country-wide agencies such as **AA Travel Accommodation** *(see p383)*.

Hotel Prices

Prices quoted tend to be per person sharing, though the larger chains quote prices per room. There might be a single supplement for solo travellers. Taxes are included in the rates.

Where rates are stated as including "dinner, bed and breakfast" or "bed and breakfast", you are likely, unless you come to some agreement when booking, to be charged for these meals whether or not you take them. Notify the hosts in advance, too, if you have any special dietary requirements.

Prices vary slightly outside high season (Nov–Feb, Easter weekend and the mid-year

school holidays), but do ask your travel agent about any special offers made by hotel groups, or contact the hotel directly.

Hotel Grading

South African hotels are classified by organizations such as Satour, the national tourism authority, and the Tourism Grading Council of South Africa. Satour divides hotels into 5 categories, indicated by a plaque carrying from 1 to 5 stars. A typical 5-star hotel is luxurious, offering suites as well as rooms, and a wide range of services such as hairdressing, dry-cleaning and room service. In a country town, a 1-star hotel may prove comfortable and entirely satisfactory, while in a city it may be little more than a noisy local rendezvous spot. Many charming hotels have low ratings, and some hotels with higher ratings – although they boast more than the required minimum of facilities and service – turn out to be impersonal business warrens.

Facilities

Facilities vary according to location and grading. Parking is usually available, but not always under cover or supervised by a guard. Some hotels offer a car-wash, and may have chauffeur-driven vehicles for local transfers. Most hotels provide telephone and TV (with satellite channels) in rooms; there is almost always a TV in the guests' lounge, too.

Luxury bush accommodation at Singita Boulders Lodge, Sabi Sands Reserve *(p391)*

◄ Colourful baskets woven from plastic-coated wire on a market stall

Ellerman House in Cape Town, ranked among the world's finest boutique hotels *(p384)*

Internet access is available at almost all accommodation, unless it is especially remote. At the very least, a computer is provided, on which guests can check emails, but most establishments have Wi-Fi, either complimentary or available with a voucher bought from reception.

Air-conditioning or at least a fan is fairly standard, but central heating in winter is not the norm, although most places do provide portable heaters and extra blankets. Many self-catering cottages, especially on farms, have indoor fireplaces.

As well as restaurants, large hotels and safari lodges have full bars. At smaller guesthouses and B&Bs there may be an unstaffed "honesty bar" with cold beers, wine, soft drinks and mineral water. Hotels usually have a locked, secure safe where guests can deposit valuables.

In country towns, the hotel frontage may be on the main street making the noise level uncomfortable. Before asking to be moved to a room at the back, however, check that there are no large hidden cooling units, as those are likely to disturb your sleep even more.

Hotel Groups

Many of the better-class hotels are controlled by one of the national hotel chains such as **City Lodge**, **Sun International**, **Tsogo Sun** or **Protea** *(see p383)*. These maintain good standards across their properties and may offer incentives or package deals that include lower family rates or out-of-season tariffs.

Children

Many venues are very family-friendly, while some upmarket hotels, guesthouses and safari lodges do not accept children under the age of 10. Where children are accepted, families may be able to share a room at little extra cost, if tariffs are per room not per person, and some hotels have adjoining rooms.

Booking

If possible, confirm a reservation online or by email. It is normal for establishments to ask for debit or credit card details in advance; in the event that you cancel your booking at short notice or are a no-show, an amount agreed in the booking terms will be deducted. The hotel is legally obliged to inform you if there has been a tariff increase since you made your booking.

Even if you have reserved a specific room, ask to see it before you sign the register. And if you require special

Mountain views at the Cape Town Hollow hotel, in the city's Gardens district *(p384)*

arrangements, first ensure that these are satisfactory. Unless otherwise stated, check-in is usually at 2pm and check-out is at 10am.

During the popular domestic tourism seasons and the longer school holidays, reservations should be made well in advance, especially for the national parks and game reserves and along the coast.

Self-Catering

The choice in style and price of self-catering accommodation in South Africa is vast. Cottages may be referred to as chalets, bungalows or rondavels (if they are round and grass-thatched). Many of the game parks have luxurious, East African-style safari tents with private outdoor kitchens, while farm-style cottages in the vast Karoo *(see pp360–61)* feature large indoor hearths to fend off the bitter cold on winter nights. Municipal chalets in caravan parks may offer only the mere basics, while cottages on Cape wine estates *(see pp196–209)*, for example, may even have satellite TV and Wi-Fi. The larger resorts and game reserves will usually have a selection of chalets. These may be self-contained units or have shared kitchen, laundry and bathroom facilities. They are usually well-equipped, comfortably furnished and include towels and bedding, although it is always advisable to check this beforehand.

Upon arrival, a member of staff may check to ensure that all the items on the inventory are supplied and intact. You could also be asked to pay a small deposit (refundable at the end of your stay) to cover potential loss or breakage.

It is advisable to approach individual tourist information offices of towns or regions for the addresses and contact numbers of self-catering cottages. **Self-Catering Accommodation of South Africa** is the national association of self-catering establishments, which also operates a grading system like hotels.

Guesthouses and B&Bs

Accommodation in small guesthouses and B&Bs, which are often private homes, has become very popular, especially along the Garden Route and in bigger cities such as Cape Town, Port Elizabeth and Johannesburg. Some are simple, practical overnight rooms, while at the more luxurious end, rooms may be in historic buildings or particularly scenic locations. The hosts, who concentrate on a small number of guests staying only a night or two, take pride in being able to provide personal attention. Breakfast is almost always included and, in some places, evening meals can be prepared if you make prior arrangements.

For listings look at the websites of the national association of guesthouses, **Guest House Accommodation of South Africa** (GHASA), or the **Portfolio Collection**.

City Hotels

There is an excellent choice of hotels in South Africa's cities. While B&Bs and guesthouses often offer a personal experience, larger city hotels tend to provide a more anonymous environment but more facilities, such as a restaurant and bar on site and often a swimming pool and spa, and long reception hours.

Budget Accommodation

There are many private backpackers hostels, especially

African art and artifacts in a contemporary settting at Derwent House, Cape Town (p384)

in the cities and along the coast. For more details, it is worth acquiring a copy of the accommodation guidebook published by **Coast to Coast**. This is available for free from hostels and the listings are on the website. No age limit is imposed on guests, but a laid-back attitude is required. Most hostels offer dorm beds in communal rooms, as well as private accommodation with either shared or private bathrooms, and some have space to pitch a tent in their garden. Other facilities usually include a self-catering kitchen, TV lounge, Internet access and swimming pool.

Safari Lodges

The safari lodges in most private reserves (see pp66–71) cater for affluent visitors. They typically offer excellent cuisine, luxurious pseudo-rustic accommodation, highly skilled staff and game rangers who ensure that guests see as much of the African wildlife as possible. Rates are typically high, but they are inclusive of all meals, most drinks and

game-viewing activities such as drives or walks. Guests tend to stay at least two nights to appreciate the experience.

National Park and Game Reserve Accommodation

Rest camps are the less expensive alternative to luxurious safari lodges and are found in national parks and provincial game reserves (see pp66–71). Most of them offer a variety of facilities such as swimming pools and shops selling basic provisions and firewood, and some may have an additional restaurant and petrol pump.

Accommodation is nearly always self-catering and options range from small rondavels sleeping two people, to chalets and bungalows sleeping six or more. At reception in the larger rest camps, like those in the Kruger National Park, it is also possible to arrange guided game drives and walks.

Accommodation in national parks across the country is booked through South African National Parks (**SANParks**), while in the Western Cape the smaller nature and game reserves are managed by **Cape Nature** and those in KwaZulu-Natal by **Ezemvelo KZN Wildlife**.

Under Canvas

Camp sites can be found throughout South Africa, and camping equipment can be bought or hired locally. Many sites are run as part of a local caravan park, or a beachside or mountain resort, and all the national parks, game and nature reserves have them. Communal

Villa Lobengula, a luxury safari lodge in the Shamwari Game Reserve, Port Elizabeth (p388)

bathroom blocks are provided, and at some sites, each pitch has a water tap and an electrical power socket. Most campers do their own cooking – the method of choice is the South African *braai* or barbecue. Cooking places or "*braai* sites" are provided – one per pitch – and firewood is usually available. Camp sites can be noisy at night, so choose a spot well away from the entrance gate and reception office.

Verandah of a chalet at the Rocktail Beach Camp, Kosi Bay, on the KwaZulu-Natal coast *(p389)*

Price Bands

All accommodation options listed in this book have been given a price band indicating the approximate rate for a standard double room in high season. All options fall within three price bands. The lowest R category (up to R1,000) would be called inexpensive in South African terms. Most backpackers hostels and some guesthouses and self-catering cottages fall into this category. The RR category (R1,000–R2,000) covers mid-range accommodation. Many guesthouses and B&Bs and some smaller hotels fall in this category. RRR options (over R,2,000) are considered expensive in South Africa, including all upmarket hotels

and luxury safari lodges. Prices are affected by location. Cape Town, for example, is relatively expensive, and a guesthouse that in the countryside would be a budget option may, in Cape Town, fall in the RR or even RRR category.

Recommended Hotels

The places to stay listed on pages 384–91 have been carefully selected, taking into account the facilities offered, atmosphere, location and value for money. A wide variety of accommodation types has been included, ranging from basic rest camps, B&Bs and self-catering options to luxurious lodges, historic buildings and smart boutique hotels.

Establishments that are outstanding in some way have been designated as DK Choices. These have been singled out for exceptional features that make them stand out from the crowd. They may be set in especially magnificent or interesting natural surroundings or in a historically important building. They may offer exceptional service in their category, whether it be the opulent comforts of a 5-star hotel or lodge, the multi-ranging facilities of a large resort or the warm welcome offered by a family farmstead. They may have an especially romantic ambience, a terrific restaurant or a great spa. Whatever the reason, it is a guarantee of a memorable stay.

DIRECTORY

Hotel Groups Booking Offices

City Lodge
Tel 011 557 2600 or 0800 113 790.
W clhg.com

Protea Hotels
Tel 021 430 5300 or 0861 119 000.
W protea.mariott.com

Sun International
Tel 011 780 7855.
W suninternational.com

Tsogo Sun Hotels
Tel 011 461 9744 or 0861 447 744.
W tsogosunhotels.com

Self-Catering Accommodation

Self-Catering Accommodation of South Africa
Tel 021 762 0880.
W selfcateringsouthafrica.com

National Parks and Game Reserves

Cape Nature
Tel 072 446 9977 or 082 869 0433.
W capenature.co.za

Ezemvelo KZN Wildlife
Tel 033 845 1000.
W kznwildlife.com

SANParks
Tel 012 428 9111.
W sanparks.org

Guesthouses and B&Bs

Guest House Accommodation of South Africa
Tel 021 762 0880.
W ghasa.co.za

Portfolio Collection
Tel 021 250 0015.
W portfoliocollection.com

General

AA Travel Accommodation
Tel 011 799 1400.
W aatravel.co.za

Coast to Coast
W coasttocoast.co.za

Tourism Grading Council of South Africa
Tel 011 895 3013.
W tourismgrading.co.za

Where to Stay

Cape Town

City Bowl

Ashanti Backpackers Gardens R
Hostel **Map** 5 A3
11 Hof St, Gardens, 8001
Tel *021 423 8721*
w ashanti.co.za
Set in a converted mansion with
gardens, this is a friendly and
secure hostel.

Acorn House RR
Guesthouse **Map** 5 A4
1 Montrose Ave, Oranjezich, 8001
Tel *021 461 1782*
w acornhouse.co.za
This homely B&B is in a National
Monument building.

Cape Town Hollow RR
Boutique **Map** 5 B2
88 Queen Victoria St, 8001
Tel *021 423 1260*
w seasonsinafrica.com
Overlooking the historic
Company's Garden, this hotel is
ideally located for the museums.

Daddy Long Legs RR
Boutique **Map** 5 A2
134 Long St, 8001
Tel *021 422 3074*
w daddylonglegs.co.za
Each room is decorated by a
different local artist at this trendy
hotel in Cape Town's nightlife hub.

DK Choice

Derwent House RR
Boutique **Map** 4 F3
14 Derwent Rd, 8001
Tel *021 422 2763*
w derwenthouse.co.za
Excellent service and African-
chic decor feature at this owner-
managed hotel with 10 rooms in
the hip Tamboerskloof area. The
central courtyard has a pool.

Mount Nelson Hotel RRR
Historic **Map** 5 A3
76 Orange St, Gardens, 8001
Tel *021 483 1000*
w belmond.com
A lovely colonial hotel at the base
of Table Mountain, with old-world
charm and all mod cons.

The Westin Cape Town RRR
Modern **Map** 5 A2
Lower Long St, 8001
Tel *021 412 9999*
w westincapetown.com
Slick, state-of-the-art luxury, well-
appointed rooms and rooftop pool.

V&A Waterfront

Breakwater Lodge RR
City hotel **Map** 2 D4
Portswood Rd, 8001
Tel *021 430 5300*
w protea.mariott.com
Right on the waterfront, this
former 19th-century prison has
plenty of character.

DK Choice

Cape Grace RRR
Luxury **Map** 2 E4
West Quay Rd, 8001
Tel *021 410 7100*
w capegrace.com
The most luxurious hotel in this
area, Cape Grace has impeccable
service and stylish decor. Afternoon tea is served in the library;
the restaurant is excellent.

Radisson Blu Waterfront RRR
Modern **Map** 2 D3
Beach Rd, Granger Bay, 8002
Tel *021 441 3000*
w radissonblu.com
This well-established hotel has
excellent facilities, an indoor pool
and a choice of restaurants.

Atlantic Seaboard

The Villa Rosa RR
Guesthouse **Map** 1 A5
277 High Level Rd, Sea Point, 8005
Tel *021 434 2768*
w villa-rosa.com
A charming guesthouse with
friendly staff. Breakfast is home-
made muesli and free-range eggs.

Ellerman House RRR
Boutique **Map** 3 B2
180 Kloof Rd, Bantry Bay, 8005
Tel *021 430 3200*
w ellerman.com
An Edwardian mansion with
stylish rooms and superb service.

Ellerman House, a luxury boutique hotel in
Cape Town overlooking the ocean

Hout Bay Manor RRR
Historic
Baviaanskloof, Hout Bay, 7872
Tel *021 790 0116*
w houtbaymanor.com
Built in 1871, this hotel offers
old-world charm with modern
facilities. Rooms are luxurious.
Excellent restaurant and spa.

O on Kloof RRR
Boutique **Map** 3 B2
92 Kloof Rd, Bantry Bay, 8005
Tel *021 439 2081*
w oonkloof.co.za
Beautifully decorated, this villa
has plush rooms. Outside dining
with sea and mountain views.

DK Choice

The Twelve Apostles RRR
Luxury **Map** 3 B5
Victoria Rd, Camps Bay, 8005
Tel *021 437 9000*
w 12apostleshotel.com
This secluded 5-star retreat has
views over the coastline. The
award-winning restaurant
serves excellent Cape fusion
cuisine. Beautiful spa and gym.

Green Point

Avatara Guesthouse RR
Guesthouse
25 Leinster Rd, Green Point, 8051
Tel *021 433 0341*
w avatara.co.za
A restored Victorian homestead
houses this guesthouse. Breakfast
is served in a courtyard.

Jambo Guesthouse RR
Guesthouse
1 Grove Rd, Green Point, 8051
Tel *021 439 4219*
w jambo.co.za
Very friendly, personal service, the
owners are on hand to help with
all your needs. Lovely garden.

**Cape Royale Luxury Hotel
& Spa** RRR
Luxury **Map** 1A4
47 Main Rd, Green Point, 8051
Tel *021 430 0500*
w caperoyale.co.za
An ultra-modern hotel with a
roof-top pool, Sky Bar and a
superb restaurant.

South Peninsula

Kopanong Bed & Breakfast R
B&B
C329 Velani Crescent, Khayelitsha Township, 7784
Tel *021 361 2084*
W kopanong-township.co.za
A friendly, family-owned B&B in the heart of the township.

Lord Nelson Inn R
Historic
58 St Georges St, Simon's Town, 7975
Tel *021 786 1386*
W lordnelsoninn.co.za
In a historic building, the homely Lord Nelson is a short walk from Boulders Beach and its penguins.

Afton Grove Country Retreat RR
B&B
Chapman's Peak Rd, Noordhoek, 7979
Tel *021 785 2992*
W afton.co.za
This classy B&B also offers self-catering accommodation, poolside dinners and picnic baskets.

Quayside Hotel RR
Modern
Jubilee Square, Simon's Town, 7995
Tel *021 786 3838*
W quaysidehotel.co.za
Sunny rooms have balconies and views over the harbour at this hotel with nautical decor.

The Last Word, Long Beach RRR
Boutique
1 Kirsten Ave, Kommetjie, 7976
Tel *021 783 4735*
W thelastword.co.za
Rooms have private patios and sea views at this luxurious hotel on the beach in a pretty village.

Stillness Manor and Spa RRR
Boutique
16 Debaren Close, Tokai, 7945
Tel *021 713 8800*
W stillnessmanor.co.za
The spacious suites have all mod cons at this Cape Dutch manor.

Southern Suburbs

Off the Wall Backpackers R
Hostel
117 Roscommon St, Claremont, 7708
Tel *021 671 6958*
W offthewallbackpackers.com
Newly built double-storey building with great facilities at good prices.

Dongola Guest House RR
Guesthouse
30 Airlie Place, Constantia, 7806
Tel *021 794 8283*
W dongolahouse.co.za
Set in gardens full of birdlife, this guesthouse has a solar-heated swimming pool and deck.

The pool at Ashanti Backpackers Gardens, Cape Town, one of the first hostels in South Africa

Houtkapperspoort Mountain Retreat Cottages RR
Self-Catering
Hout Bay Main Rd, Constantia Nek, 7806
Tel *021 794 5216*
W houtkapperspoortresort.co.za
These nicely-furnished cottages have barbecues. There's a pool, tennis court and kids' play area.

White Lodge Guest House Constantia RR
Guesthouse
28 Evergreen Lane, Constantia, 7806
Tel *021 794 2951*
W whitelodge.com
The house is set in park-like grounds with mountain views. Rooms have private entrances, and guests have access to a lounge and pool.

Alphen Boutique Hotel RRR
Boutique
Alphen Drive, Constantia, 7806
Tel *021 795 6300*
W alphen.co.za
Rooms are luxurious and bathrooms opulent at this converted manor house and National Monument building dating to 1753.

The Cellars-Hohenort RRR
Boutique
93 Brommersvlei Rd, Constantia, 7800
Tel *021 794 2137*
W collectionmcgrath.com
In large, landscaped gardens, this 5-star hotel has a golf course, pool and a wellness spa.

DK Choice

Steenberg Hotel RRR
Luxury
Steenberg Rd, Tokai, 7945
Tel *021 713 2222*
W steenbergfarm.com
Set on a wine estate, this 5-star hotel offers understated luxury, personalized service and spectacular farm views, as well as an award-winning restaurant.

Cape Winelands

FRANSCHHOEK: Otter's Bend Lodge R
Hostel
Dassenberg Road, Franschhoek, 7690
Tel *021 876 3200*
W ottersbendlodge.co.za
Unique travellers' lodge located on the banks of Franschhoek River.

FRANSCHHOEK: La Fontaine RR
Guesthouse Road Map B5
21 Dirkie Uys St, 7690
Tel *021 876 2112*
W lafontainefranschhoek.co.za
Two heritage buildings house large, comfy rooms. There's a swimming pool and free Wi-Fi.

FRANSCHHOEK: Franschhoek Manor RRR
Luxury Road Map B5
Dassenberg Rd, 7690
Tel *021 876 4455*
W franschhoekmanor.co.za
Facing the river, this hotel is set in stunning gardens with two pools.

DK Choice

FRANSCHHOEK: Le Quartier Francais RRR
Boutique Road Map B5
Cnr Berg and Wilhelmina sts, 7690
Tel *021 492 2222*
W www.lqf.co.za
Rooms and suites are stylish, some with luxuries like under-floor heating and iPod docking stations, at this plush hotel with an award-winning restaurant.

HERMON: Bartholomeus Klip RRR
Lodge Road Map B5
PO Box 36, Hermon, 7308
Tel *022 448 1087*
W www.bartholomeusklip.com
Set on a working farm and game reserve, this lodge has lovely rooms and a self-catering house.

For more information on types of hotels *see pp380–83*

MONTAGU: Airlies Guest House R
Guesthouse　　　　**Road Map** B5
36 Bath St, 7560
Tel *023 614 2943*
W airlies.co.za
This owner-run, atmospheric 1912 house has lovely grounds, a pool and log fires in winter.

MONTAGU: Montagu Country Hotel　　　　　**RR**
Historic　　　　**Road Map** B5
27 Bath St, 7560
Tel *023 614 3125*
W montagucountryhotel.co.za
A charming hotel with mountain views and a wellness centre.

PAARL: Picardie Guest Farm R
B&B　　　　**Road Map** B5
Laborie St, 7646
Tel *021 863 3357*
W picardie.co.za
Both B&B and self-catering rooms are offered at this working farm.

PAARL: Lemoenkloof Guest House　　　　　**RR**
Guesthouse　　　　**Road Map**
Cnr Malan and Main rds, 7646
Tel *021 872 3782*
W lemoenkloof.co.za
A well-appointed 19th-century Victorian homestead with a pool.

PAARL: Grande Roche Hotel RRR
Luxury　　　　**Road Map** B5
Plantasie St, 7646
Tel *021 863 5100*
W granderoche.com
Historic manor house with award-winning restaurant, tennis courts, pools, gym, spa and hair salon.

ROBERTSON: Rosendal Winery & Wellness Retreat　　**RR**
Guesthouse　　　　**Road Map** B5
Klaas Voogds West, 6705
Tel *023 626 1570*
W rosendalwinery.co.za
Rooms have breathtaking views at this hotel with a French-inspired restaurant and a luxurious spa.

SOMERSET WEST: Penny Lane Lodge
B&B　　　　**Road Map** B5
5 North Ave, Westridge, 7130
Tel *021 852 9976*
W pennylanelodge.co.za
Comfortable B&B with some self-catering rooms, as well as a pool and barbecue areas.

STELLENBOSCH: Stumble Inn Backpackers Lodge　　R
Hostel　　　　**Road Map** B5
12 Market St, 7600
Tel *021 887 4049*
W stumbleinnstellenbosch.
hostel.com
A lively, central hostel with pool, barbecue area and satellite TV.

STELLENBOSCH: Devon Valley　　　　　**RR**
Country hotel　　　　**Road Map** B5
Devon Valley Rd, Devon Valley, 7600
Tel *021 865 2012*
W devonvalleyhotel.com
There are views of the mountains, vineyards and olive groves at this hotel with a colonial feel. Most rooms have wheelchair access.

DK Choice

STELLENBOSCH: Lanzerac Hotel & Spa　　　**RRR**
Luxury　　　　**Road Map** B5
1 Lanzerac Rd, 7600
Tel *021 887 1132*
W lanzerac.co.za
This is one of South Africa's most outstanding examples of Cape Dutch architecture, set in stately gardens on a 300-year-old working wine estate. It offers fine dining, comfortable lounges, several swimming pools, a tasting room and a spa.

STELLENBOSCH: Oude Werf Hotel　　　　　**RRR**
Historic　　　　**Road Map** B5
30 Church St, 7600
Tel *021 887 4608*
W oudewerfhotel.co.za
Established in 1802, this is South Africa's oldest hotel. The restaurant is noted for fine dining.

TULBAGH: De Oude Herberg RR
Guesthouse　　　　**Road Map** B5
Church St, 6820
Tel *023 230 0260*
W deoudeherberg.co.za
A National Monument building with two beautiful rooms and a cottage. The small restaurant specializes in wine-pairing menus.

West Coast and Southern Cape

BETTY'S BAY: Buçaco Sud R
Guesthouse　　　　**Road Map** B5
2609 Clarence Drive, 7141
Tel *028 272 9750*
W bucacosud.co.za
A pool in the garden and cosy fireplaces providing warmth in winter are the highlights.

CEDERBERG: Kagga Kamma　　　　　**RRR**
Safari lodge　　　　**Road Map** B4
Kagga Kamma Nature Reserve, between Ctrusdal and Ceres
Tel *021 872 4343*
W kaggakamma.co.za
Accommodation is in luxury chalets and unique cave rooms

Inyathi Guest Lodge, Knysna, set in a lush forest garden

built in the sand formations at this private reserve in the southern Cederberk, known for its rock art and resident San village.

DK Choice

CLANWILLIAM: Bushmans Kloof　　　　　**RRR**
Safari lodge　　　　**Road Map** B4
Clanwilliam, 8135
Tel *021 437 9278*
W bushmanskloof.co.za
This lodge is in a private game reserve with the densest concentration of San rock art in South Africa. It offers outstanding dining, a superb wine cellar and luxurious rooms and suites, all inclusive of meals and activities, plus a wellness centre.

HERMANUS: Harbour Vue RR
Guesthouse　　　　**Road Map** B5
84 Westcliff Rd, 7200
Tel *028 312 4860*
W harbourvue.co.za
Next to the famous Hermanus cliff paths, this venue has tasteful suites. Whales are often spotted from the dining room.

HERMANUS: The Marine RRR
Luxury　　　　**Road Map** B5
Marine Drive, 7200
Tel *028 313 1000*
W collectionmcgrath.com
Individually decorated rooms and suites, a heated salt-water swimming pool and an excellent beauty spa feature at this hotel.

OUDTSHOORN: Protea Hotel Riempie Estate　　　R
Country hotel　　　　**Road Map** C5
Baron van Rheede St, 6620
Tel *044 272 6161*
W protea.mariott.com
Rooms are in thatched rondavels at this cosy retreat in a tranquil setting. The restaurant serves hearty Karoo fare.

OUDTSHOORN: Queens Hotel RR
Historic   Road Map C5
Baron van Rheede St, 6625
Tel *044 272 2101*
W queenshotel.co.za
Lovely, renovated colonial-style
accommodation (dating from
1880) offering great service and
a welcoming restaurant.

**OUDTSHOORN: Rosenhof
Country House   RRR**
Historic   Road Map C5
264 Baron van Rheede St, 6625
Tel *044 272 2232*
W rosenhof.co.za
Set in a pretty rose garden with a
swimming pool, this carefully
renovated homestead (c.1852) is
furnished with antiques.

**SALDANHA: Saldanha Bay
Protea Hotel   RR**
Resort   Road Map A5
51B Main Rd, 7395
Tel *022 714 1264*
W protea.mariott.com
This comfortable, well-equipped
harbourfront hotel is a good base
for the West Coast National Park.

**ST HELENA BAY:
The Oystercatcher Lodge RR**
Guesthouse   Road Map A4
1st Ave, Shelley Point, 7282
Tel *022 742 1202*
W oystercatcherlodge.co.za
Right at the water's edge, all
rooms have private balconies
with good sea views. Golf course
and spa within walking distance.

SWELLENDAM: The Hideaway RR
B&B   Road Map B5
10 Hermanus Steyn St, 6740
Tel *028 514 3316*
W hideawaybb.co.za
There are just four elegant rooms,
along with an indoor pool, in this
National Monument building.
The breakfasts are legendary.

**SWELLENDAM: De Kloof Luxury
Estate   RRR**
Boutique   Road Map B5
8 Weltevrede St, 6740
Tel *028 514 1303*
W dekloof.co.za
A pool, gym, a cigar lounge and
free wine tasting can be enjoyed
at this hotel in park-like gardens.

**VELDDRIF: Kersefontein
Guest Farm   RR**
Guesthouse   Road Map A3
Between Hopefield and Velddrif, 7355
Tel *083 454 1025*
W kersefontein.co.za
At this homely working farm, the
beautiful rooms feature antiques
taken from the farm's attics.
Dinner is served in the 19th-
century dining room.

Garden Route to Grahamstown

ADDO: Addo Rest Camp RR
Rest camp   Road Map D5
Addo Elephant National Park, 6105
Tel *042 233 8600*
W sanparks.org
A range of accommodation units.
The lookout platform provides
views over a waterhole.

**THE CRAGS: Hog Hollow
Country Lodge   RRR**
Lodge   Road Map C5
Askop Rd, 6600
Tel *044 534 8879*
W hog-hollow.com
Beautifully decorated log cabins
have forest views. The freshest
food is served in the restaurant.

GEORGE: Fancourt Hotel RRR
Modern   Road Map C5
Montague St, Blanco, 6529
Tel *044 804 0000*
W fancourt.com
In an elegant setting, this
comfortable hotel has several
restaurants and pools, walking
trails, a tennis court and a gym.

**GRAHAMSTOWN: The Cock
House   RR**
Historic   Road Map D5
10 Market St, 6140
Tel *046 636 1287*
W cockhouse.co.za
A Grahamstown landmark, this
guesthouse offers country home
comfort and elegant dining. It is
furnished with period antiques.

**GRAHAMSTOWN: Makana
Resort   RR**
Cottages   Road Map D5
Grey St, 6139
Tel *046 622 2159*
W makanaresort.co.za
Simple chalets and cottages set in
a large garden with a pool. Each
has its own barbecue area.

KNYSNA: Eden's Touch R
Self-catering   Road Map C5
Off the N2, east of Knysna
Tel *083 2536366*
W edenstouch.co.za
In a private indigenous forest,
Eden's Touch offers fully
equipped, self-catering cottages.

KNYSNA: Inyathi Guest Lodge R
Self-catering   Road Map C5
38 Trotter Street, 6571
Tel *044 382 7768*
W inyathiguestlodge.co.za
Self-contained chalets dotted
around a thriving garden.

KNYSNA: St James RRR
Boutique   Road Map C5
The Point, 6570
Tel *044 382 6750*
W stjames.co.za
This owner-run, 5-star country
hotel is set in a landscaped estate
on the shore of the lagoon.

**MATJIESFONTEIN: The Lord
Milner Hotel   RR**
Historic   Road Map C5
1 Logan St, 6901
Tel *023 561 3011*
W matjiesfontein.com
A splendid, well-preserved
colonial vestige of what was once
a glamorous Victorian spa town.

**MOSSEL BAY: Protea Hotel
Mossel Bay   RR**
Historic   Road Map
Cnr Church St & Market St, 6500
Tel *044 691 3738*
W protea.mariott.com
The main building of this hotel is
one of the oldest in Mossel Bay.
Lovely sea and harbour views.

**MOSSEL BAY:
The Point Hotel   RRR**
Resort   Road Map C5
Point Rd, The Point, 6500
Tel *044 691 3512*
W pointhotel.co.za
All rooms have balconies facing
the sea at this hotel built on rocks.

Lanzerac Hotel & Spa in Stellenbosch, nestled among ancient oak trees

For more information on types of hotels *see pp380–83*

**PLETTENBERG BAY: Albergo for
Backpackers** R
Hostel **Road Map** C5
8 Church St, 6600
Tel *044 533 4434*
W albergo.co.za
Facilities include dorms, individual
rooms, a bar, kitchen and TV room.

**PLETTENBERG BAY: Bitou River
Lodge** RR
B&B **Road Map** C5
*10 km (6 miles) from Plettenberg Bay
on the R340*
Tel *044 535 9577*
W bitou.co.za
Every room has direct access to
the well-tended garden at this
farmhouse-style B&B on the
banks of the Bitou River.

**PORT ALFRED: Halyards Hotel
and Spa** RR
Modern **Road Map** D5
Albany Rd, 6170
Tel *046 604 3300*
W riverhotels.co.za
This 3-star hotel at the Royal Alfred
Marina is popular with families.
Activities on offer include river
cruises and deep-sea fishing.

**PORT ELIZABETH: Brighton
Lodge** RR
Guesthouse **Road Map** D5
*21 Brighton Drive, Summerstrand,
6001*
Tel *041 583 4576*
W brightonlodge.co.za
Luxury suites here have a small
kitchen and a separate entrance.
There's also a pool and an airport
shuttle service on request

**PORT ELIZABETH: Shamwari
Game Reserve** RRR
Safari lodge **Road Map** D5
*Off N2, between Port Elizabeth and
Grahamstown, 6139*
Tel *042 203 1111*
W shamwari.com
Six luxury lodges feature in this
reserve. Rates are all-inclusive of
meals and activities such as
game drives and walking safaris.

DK Choice

**TSITSIKAMMA: Storms River
Mouth Rest Camp** RR
Rest camp **Road Map** C5
Off N2 at Storms River Mouth, 6308
Tel *042 281 1607*
W sanparks.org
Located on one of the most
beautiful stretches of coastline
in South Africa, this retreat offers
camping, basic forest huts and
self-contained chalets. The
restaurant has a great position,
with the waves crashing below
and 180-degree ocean views.

**WILDERNESS: The Old Trading
Post** RR
Guesthouse **Road Map** C5
Off N2, 6560
Tel *044 882 1207*
W oldtradingpost.co.za
Plenty of birdlife can be seen
in the garden of this friendly
guesthouse on a country road.

**WILDERNESS: The Wilderness
Hotel** RR
Country hotel **Road Map** C5
George Rd, 6560
Tel *044 877 1110*
W thewildernesshotel.co.za
A short walk from the village, this
large hotel has two pools, a
beauty spa and tennis courts.

Wild Coast, Drakensberg and Midlands

**BUTHA BUTHE, LESOTHO:
Oxbow Lodge** RR
Lodge **Road Map** E3
*Moteng Pass, 50 km (31 m) E of
Butha Buthe*
Tel *051 933 2247*
W oxbow.co.za
These rondavels are ideal bases
for hiking in the Maluti Mountains.

**CHAMPAGNE VALLEY:
Inkosana Lodge** R
Hostel **Road Map** E3
Winterton, 3340
Tel *036 468 1202*
W inkosana.co.za
Use the kitchen or order home-
cooked meals at this hostel set in
gardens with mountain views.

**CHAMPAGNE VALLEY:
Drakensberg Sun Resort** RRR
Resort **Road Map** E3
R600 Central Drakensberg, 3340
Tel *036 468 1000*
W tsogosunhotels.com
Smart rooms have all mod cons at
this upmarket mountain resort
that offers outdoor activities.

Essenwood House in Durban, located high
up in the fashionable Berea district

DUNDEE: Royal Country Inn R
Historic **Road Map** E3
61 Victoria St, 3000
Tel *034 212 2147*
W royalcountryinn.com
This inn on the battlefields route
has ensuite bedrooms and back-
packer lodging. Cosy dining room.

**EAST LONDON: Premier Hotel
King David** RR
City hotel **Road Map** E5
27 Inverleith Terrace, 5211
Tel *043 722 3174*
W premierhotels.co.za
Rooms and suites are well-
appointed at this central hotel
near the beaches.

DK Choice

**MOOI RIVER:
Hartford House** RRR
Boutique **Road Map** E3
Hlatikulu Rd, 3300
Tel *033 263 2713*
W hartford.co.za
Set in beautiful gardens, this
small and luxurious hotel has
a wellness centre and helipad.
The restaurant is top-notch and
at weekends a local dance
troupe entertains.

**PIETERMARITZBURG: Imperial
Hotel** RR
Historic **Road Map** E3
224 JabuNdlovu St, 3200
Tel *033 342 6551*
W imperialhotel.co.za
This centrally-located, century-
old hotel has modern finishes.

**PORT ST JOHNS: Umngazi River
Bungalows & Spa** RR
Resort **Road Map** E4
Mgazi, Port St Johns, 5120
Tel *047 564 1115*
W umngazi.co.za
There are 69 bungalows and the
restaurant serves local food.
Fishing and tennis are offered.

**QOLORA MOUTH:
Trennerys Hotel** RR
Resort **Road Map** E4
Kentani, 4980
Tel *047 498 0025*
W trennerys.co.za
These thatched rondavels and
bungalows are in tropical gardens.

**RORKE'S DRIFT: Fugitives'
Drift Lodge** RRR
Lodge **Road Map** E3
Rorke's Drift, 3016
Tel *034 642 1843*
W fugitivesdrift.com
Spacious cottages each have
a verandah at this reserve
overlooking battlefield sites.
There are two swimming pools.

The Eagles Crag central lodge at the Shamwari Game Reserve, Port Elizabeth

WINTERTON: Cathedral Peak Hotel RRR
Resort **Road Map** E3
1 Cathedral Peak Rd, 3340
Tel *036 488 1888*
W cathedralpeak.co.za
In an amazing setting, these cottages include a wedding chapel and helipad. Flights over the mountains are offered.

Durban and Zululand

BALLITO: Fairmont Zimbali Lodge RRR
Resort **Road Map** F3
Zimbali Estate, 4390
W fairmont.com
Set in a coastal forest reserve, the rooms here have a classical feel. A golf course and a spa are on site.

DURBAN: Tekweni Backpackers Hostel R
Hostel **Road Map** F3
169 9th Ave, Morningside, 4000
Tel *031 303 1433*
W tekwenibackpackers.co.za
Dorms and private rooms make up this budget accommodation. The poolside sports bar is lively.

DURBAN: City Lodge Hotel RR
City hotel **Road Map** F3
Cnr Silvester Ntuli and K.E. Masing, 4001
Tel *031 332 1447*
W clhg.com
The rooms are simple, but the lush grounds and pool are a bonus at this conveniently located venue with all mod cons.

DURBAN: Essenwood House RR
Guesthouse **Road Map** F3
630 Stephen Dlamini Rd, 4000
Tel *031 207 4547*
W essenwoodhouse.co.za
The six rooms at this hotel offer views over the city and the sea, and have great bathrooms.

DURBAN: Southern Sun Elangeni & Maharani RRR
Modern **Road Map** F3
63 Snell Parade, 4001
Tel *031 362 1300*
W tsogosunhotels.com
This large beachfront hotel has a full range of facilities: pools, free Wi-Fi, business centre and spa.

HLUHLUWE: Hilltop Camp RR
Rest camp **Road Map** F3
Hluhluwe Game Reserve, 3960
Tel *035 562 0848*
W kznwildlife.com
Budget rondavels and chalets have great views over the reserve.

HLUHLUWE: Zululand Tree Lodge RR
Safari lodge **Road Map** F3
1020 Main Rd, 3960
Tel *035 562 1020*
W ubizane.co.za
These stilted, thatched houses are in a fevertree forest. Meals and activities are all included.

DK Choice

KOSI BAY: Rocktail Camp RRR
Lodge **Road Map** F2
kwaNgwanase, 3886
Tel *011 807 1800*
W wilderness-safaris.com
These luxurious thatched tree-house chalets in iSimangaliso Wetland Park are just a dune away from an unspoiled beach. There is a homely atmosphere and communal dining.

PONGOLA: White Elephant Safari Lodge RRR
Safari lodge **Road Map** F3
Farm Leeuwspoor, Pongola Reserve S
Tel *034 413 2489*
W whiteelephant.co.za
Eight luxurious safari tents, with each having a luxurious bathroom, private verandah and personal bar.

PORT EDWARD: The Estuary Hotel & Spa RR
Historic **Road Map** E4
Main Rd (R61), 4295
Tel *039 311 2675*
W estuaryhotel.co.za
Set in a manor house, this hotel is within a short walk of the beach.

UMHLANGA ROCKS: Beverly Hills Hotel RRR
Modern **Road Map** F3
Lighthouse Rd, 4320
Tel *031 561 2211*
W tsogosunhotels.com
An award-winning, luxurious hotel on the seafront looking onto miles of unspoiled beaches.

UMHLANGA ROCKS: The Oyster Box RRR
Boutique **Road Map** F3
2 Lighthouse Rd, 4319
Tel *031 514 5000*
W oysterboxhotel.com
This elegantly renovated 1930s Art Deco building is right on the beach with its own lighthouse. It is famous for high tea and oysters.

Gauteng and Sun City

JOHANNESBURG: Die Agterplaas B&B R
B&B **Road Map** E2
66 Sixth Ave, Melville, 2092
Tel *011 726 8452*
W agterplaas.co.za
The homely Agterplaas B&B is a short walk to the trendy shops and restaurants of Melville.

JOHANNESBURG: The Backpackers' Ritz R
Hostel **Road Map** E2
1A North Rd, Dunkeld West, 2196
Tel *011 325 7125*
W backpackers-ritz.co.za
Enjoy friendly service and tourist tips at the city's oldest hostel. Swimming pool and lively bar.

JOHANNESBURG: African Pride Melrose Arch Hotel RR
Modern **Road Map** E2
1 Melrose Square, Melrose Arch, 2196
Tel *011 214 6666*
W protea.mariott.com
Hip 5-star hotel offering designer decor and a fusion restaurant.

JOHANNESBURG: Garden Place Guest Houses RR
Guesthouse **Road Map** E2
53 Garden Rd, Orchards, 2192
Tel *011 485 3800*
W gardenplace.co.za
Set in lovely gardens, this is near the hip Norwood suburb. It has a shuttle service to nearby areas.

For more information on types of hotels *see pp380–83*

JOHANNESBURG:
The Michelangelo Hotel RRR
Modern **Road Map** E2
135 West St, Nelson Mandela Square,
Sandton, 2146
Tel 011 282 7000
W legacyhotels.co.za
This prestigious, lavish 5-star
hotel is surrounded by upmarket
shops and restaurants.

DK Choice

JOHANNESBURG: Saxon
Hotel, Villas & Spa RRR
Boutique **Road Map** E2
36 Saxon Rd, Sandhurst, 2196
Tel 011 292 6000
W saxon.co.za
Close to the upmarket malls of
Sandton City, this luxurious
hotel in landscaped gardens
has contemporary African-style
decor and a world-class spa.

MAGALIESBERG: African
Pride Mount Grace Country
House & Spa
Country hotel RR
Road Map D2
Old Rustenburg Rd, 1791
Tel 014 577 5600
W protea.mariott.com
A countryside hideaway with
stone-and-thatch cottages and
great outdoor spa treatments.

MAGALIESBERG: Protea Hotel
Rustenburg Hunters Rest RR
Resort **Road Map** D2
R24, Rustenburg-Krugersdorp Rd, 0300
Tel 014 537 8300
W protea.mariott.com
An extensive resort with
excellent recreational facilities,
children's activities and a crèche.

PILANESBERG GAME RESERVE:
Kwa Maritane Bush Lodge RRR
Safari lodge **Road Map** D2
Rustenburg, 0300
Tel 014 552 5100
W legacyhotels.co.za
A luxurious resort with family-
friendly suites and chalets.

PILANESBERG GAME RESERVE:
Tshukudu Bush Lodge RRR
Safari lodge **Road Map** D2
Rustenburg, 0300
Tel 014 552 6255
W legacyhotels.co.za
Perfect for a romantic getaway,
these chalets have open-plan
rooms, a fireplace and a balcony.

PRETORIA: Protea Hotel
Hatfield R
City hotel **Road Map** E2
1141 Burnett St, Hatfield, 0083
Tel 012 364 0300
W protea.mariott.com
Located in an classy suburb close

to shops and restaurants. Rooms
have air-con and Wi-Fi.

PRETORIA: The Farm Inn RR
Country hotel **Road Map** E2
Silverlakes Rd, Silverlakes, 0021
Tel 012 809 0266
W farminn.co.za
This 4-star accommodation in
an African stone-and-thatch
palace is set in a private game
sanctuary, complete with hiking
trails and a pool.

PRETORIA: La Maison RR
Luxury **Road Map** E2
235 Hilda St, Hatfield, 0083
Tel 012 430 4341
W lamaison.co.za
This guesthouse in an old French-
style castle has a rooftop patio.

Limpopo,
Mpumalanga and
Kruger

DULLSTROOM: Walkersons
Hotel & Spa RRR
Country hotel **Road Map** E2
Walkersons Private Estate, 1110
Tel 013 253 7000
W walkersons.co.za
Each room has a private patio, a
fireplace and lake views at this
plush lodge in fly-fishing country.

GRASKOP: Graskop Hotel RR
Boutique **Road Map** F2
3 Main St, 1270
Tel 013 767 1244
W graskophotel.co.za
Rooms in this country hotel each
feature the work of a contem-
porary South African artist.

DK Choice

HAZYVIEW: Rissington Inn RR
Country hotel **Road Map** F2
R40, 1242
Tel 013 737 7700
W rissington.co.za
Each room at this comfortable,
simple hotel in a bush setting
very near the Kruger has its
own entrance and verandah.
The à la carte restaurant offers
good fare, and there's a lovely
pool, and a guest library with TV.

HAZYVIEW: The Windmill Wine
Shop & Cottages RR
Self-catering **Road Map** F2
R536, between Hazyview and Sabie
Tel 013 737 8175
W thewindmill.co.za
Set in bushveld alive with game
and birds, the cottages and farm-
houses here have self-catering
facilities, and are ideal for families.

Luxury accommodation at a safari lodge in
Camp Jabulani, Hoedspruit

HAZYVIEW:
Highgrove House RRR
Boutique **Road Map** F2
R40, Kieperol, 1241
Tel 083 675 1500
W highgrove.co.za
This award-winning colonial-
style lodge offers rooms with
spectacular views, gourmet food
and fine wines in a farm setting.

HOEDSPRUIT:
Camp Jabulani RRR
Safari lodge **Road Map** F2
Kapama Private Game Reserve,
Hoedspruit, 1380
Tel 015 793 1265
W campjabulani.com
Every modern luxury is offered at
this upmarket, all-inclusive lodge.
Each suite has an indoor and
outdoor plunge pool.

DK Choice

THE KRUGER NATIONAL
PARK: Camps (various) RR
Rest camps **Road Map** F2
Box 787, Pretoria, 0001
Tel 012 428 9111
W sanparks.org
A wide variety of good-value
accommodation is dotted
around the Kruger. Main camps
have most facilities (swimming
pools, petrol stations and shops);
small camps offer a quieter
bush experience and visitors
need to be self-sufficient.

THE KRUGER NATIONAL PARK:
Singita Lebombo Lodge RRR
Safari lodge **Road Map** F2
Tel 013 735 5500
W singita.com
This dramatic lodge is home to
15 loft-style suites with a stylishly
contemporary feel. Service and
food are impeccable and the
bush spa is highly rated.

PILGRIM'S REST: Crystal Springs Mountain Lodge RR
Self-catering   Road Map F2
Robber's Pass, 1290
Tel *013 768 5000*
W crystalsprings.co.za
These cottages high up in a game reserve have tennis courts, mini-golf, a gym, indoor heated pool and Jacuzzi.

PILGRIM'S REST: Royal Hotel RR
Historic   Road Map F2
Main St, 1290
Tel *013 768 1100*
W pilgrimsrest.org.za
Rooms are furnished with antique brass beds and other period furniture at this hotel from the late-Victorian gold-mining days.

SABI SANDS RESERVE: Earth Lodge RRR
Safari lodge   Road Map F2
Sabi Sabi Private Reserve
Tel *013 735 5260*
W sabisabi.com
This lodge is sculpted into a slope of the ground, almost invisible in the landscape. Each luxury suite has a private plunge pool.

SABI SANDS RESERVE: Singita Boulders Lodge RRR
Safari lodge   Road Map F2
Singita Sabi Sands, Sabi Sands Reserve
Tel *013 735 9800*
W singita.com
Gourmet cuisine, a large wine cellar, day and night drives and walking safaris are all included in the rates at this luxurious lodge.

SWAZILAND: Milwane Rest Camp R
Rest camp   Road Map F2
Milwane Wildlife Sanctuary
Tel *268 2528 3943*
W biggameparks.org
Accommodation options include camping, traditional beehive huts, basic rest camp huts, self-catering cottages and a backpacker's hostel.

SWAZILAND: Royal Swazi Spa Valley RRR
Resort   Road Map F2
Main Rd between Mbabane and Manzini, Ezulwini Valley, H100
Tel *268 2416 5000*
W suninternational.com
Renowned for its golf course and casino, rooms here are comfortable with all mod cons.

TIMBAVATI NATURE RESERVE: Kings Camp RRR
Safari lodge   Road Map F2
Tel *013 751 1621*
W kingscamp.com
A luxury colonial-style camp situated in prime game-viewing

territory. Rates are fully inclusive of game drives, wildlife walks and all meals.

TZANEEN: Coach House Hotel & Spa RRR
Country hotel   Road Map E1
Old Coach Rd, Agatha, 0850
Tel *015 306 8000*
W www.coachhousehotel.co.za
Built in 1892 in the days of the gold rush, these individual cottages have private verandahs in beautiful manicured gardens.

WHITE RIVER: Belgrace Boutique Hotel RRR
Boutique   Road Map F2
R538, White River, 1240
Tel *076 539 0409*
W belgrace.co.za
This romantic luxury hotel has an opulent European decor, Jacuzzis and dedicated service.

North and South of the Orange

BEAUFORT WEST: Matoppo Inn R
Guesthouse   Road Map C4
7 Bird St, 6970
Tel *023 415 1055*
W matoppoinn.co.za
Housed in a beautifully restored 17th-century Drostdy building, this hotel has period furniture. Dinner is a three-course set menu served in the stylish dining room.

BLOEMFONTEIN: Liedjiesbos B&B RR
B&B   Road Map D3
13 Frans Kleynhans Rd, Groenvlei, 9301
Tel *083 282 5701*
W bloemfonteinaccommodation.biz
This innovative guesthouse combines airy contemporary architecture with African and Eastern-influenced decor.

DK Choice

CRADOCK: Die Tuishuise & Victoria Manor RR
Historic   Road Map D4
36 Market St, 5880
Tel *048 881 1322*
W tuishuise.co.za
Traditional iron-roofed Karoo cottages have been restored and furnished with antiques in the 1800s style of English and Dutch settlers. A delicious Karoo dinner is served. There's also a pool and wellness centre.

GRAAFF REINET: Buiten Verwagten Guest House RR
Guesthouse   Road Map C4
58 Bourke St, 6280
Tel *049 892 4504*
W buitenverwagten.co.za
Set in a handsome 1840 mansion, and easily the most appealing option in town, this characterful, friendly hotel has a heated and unheated pool and a health spa.

KIMBERLEY: The Kimberley Club and Boutique Hotel RR
Historic   Road Map D3
72 Du Toitspan Rd, Kimberley, 8310
Tel *053 832 4224*
W kimberleyclub.co.za
Founded by a group of diamond magnates, this is now a 4-star boutique hotel in colonial style.

DK Choice

UPINGTON: Le Must River Manor RR
Guesthouse   Road Map B3
12 Murray Ave, 8000
Tel *054 332 3971*
W lemustupington.com
This beautiful Georgian-style house is in a manicured garden on the banks of the Orange River. The comfortable rooms have contemporary furniture.

Inviting waterside loungers at the Saxon Hotel, Villas & Spa, Johannesberg

For more information on types of hotels *see pp380–83*

WHERE TO EAT AND DRINK

South Africa has a wide variety of restaurants and eateries, from franchise steakhouses and sizzling street-corner *boerewors* (farmer's sausage) stands to upmarket business venues and seafood, Asian, French and Mediterranean-style cuisines. Whenever the weather is fine, South Africans eat outside, and coffee shops do a roaring trade. African menus, often tailored to the Western palate,

are found in the cities, while some township tours *(see p420)* include authentic, traditional meals. South Africa's multicultural heritage is also evident in the proliferation of Indian restaurants and stalls serving spicy eastern and KwaZulu-Natal-style curries. In the Western Cape, fragrant, sweet Malay curries are popular quick lunches; in the Winelands, more formal fare and elegant dining prevails.

Atmospheric cellar vaulting at the Haute Cabrière estate in the Winelands *(see p402)*

Tipping should always reflect your experience of the service. If simply average, leave 10 per cent; if excellent, 15 per cent. Tips are sometimes placed in a communal jar near the cashier.

Eating Patterns

In South Africa it is common to find restaurants closed on Sundays or Mondays. Coffee shops are open during the day, usually from 8am to 5pm, and serve breakfasts, light lunches and teas. Dinner is the main meal of the day, served from 6:30pm to 10pm. In urban areas, bars, popular restaurants and fast-food outlets stay open until midnight, or even later.

Places to Eat

You can always eat well in South African cities and in the well-visited outlying areas. The annual *Eat Out* magazine, which is available at news-agents, recommends restaurants nationwide and has a useful website with user reviews (www.eatout.co.za). Another good website when choosing where to eat is www.dining-out.co.za.

It is best to telephone ahead and reserve a table in order to avoid disappointment. If you cannot keep a reservation, call the restaurant and cancel.

Prices and Tipping

Eating out in South Africa is usually inexpensive. The average price of a three-course meal for one (excluding wine and a tip) at a good restaurant is about R170–220. But certain items, such as seafood, can increase the total substantially. A freshly-made deli sandwich with tasty fillings will seldom cost more than R45, while a large, hearty breakfast costs around R60.

What to Eat

In the cities, try some of the African, Indian (in KwaZulu-Natal) or Malay (in Cape Town) restaurants. If you are on the coast, do not miss the delicious seafood – calamari, mussels, tuna, crayfish, yellowtail and local kingklip. On the West Coast there are scenic open-air seafood barbecues. The cities and larger towns offer excellent international cuisine: Thai, Portuguese, Indonesian, Italian, Greek, French and Chinese. There are also typical South African restaurants, where traditional fare and drinks such as *witblits*, strong spirit distilled from peaches, are served.

South Africa is a meat-loving nation. Beefsteaks are a good

Smart dining at Seafood at The Marine, Hermanus *(see p403)*

bet, and franchise steakhouses offer great value for money – the selection of substantial salads and vegetable dishes will satisfy vegetarians, too. *Boerewors* (sausage) on a breadroll can be bought from informal street vendors. At someone's home, you might join in a South African meat *braai*, or barbecue *(see p25)*. Pizza chains are very popular and offer good value.

For breakfasts, try the traditional cooked dish of eggs, bacon and sausages. Various muffins (also available at supermarkets, delis and even petrol-station stores) such as bran, banana and date are popular.

Salads, open sandwiches and quiches are popular offerings for lunch, while cakes (carrot, chocolate and cheese) or local *melktart* (custard tart) are often served at afternoon tea.

Wine Choices

South African wines offer something for everybody, and most restaurants stock a mainstream selection of local labels – usually with a significant price mark-up. Many serve a great variety, from easy-drinking wines to vintage bottlings. Most restaurants offer a choice of bottled wines by the glass, although house wines in bars are, more usually, from an inexpensive 5-litre box. Fine-dining venues will have an international wine list, and the better eateries offering the cuisine of a specific country will have wines from that country. Some restaurants (mainly in the Cape) allow you to bring your own bottle and charge corkage (from R30).

Delivery Services

In the cities and larger towns, food-delivery services are popular. The company known as "Mr Delivery" is contracted to a variety of eateries and restaurants (not only fast-food outlets) and will deliver hot food, for a reasonable fee, during lunch time, and from early to late evening. The local telephone directory will provide details.

Smoking

Strict anti-tobacco laws are enforced in South Africa. Smoking inside restaurants is not allowed. Some restaurants have an outside smoking section, and patrons should specify their requirements when booking.

Children

Apart from some top fine-dining establishments, most restaurants and eateries are child-friendly, but it does no harm to check when making a booking.

Outdoor, informal and day-time venues (and their menus) are all child-friendly; expect to pay three-quarters of the price for a child-sized meal. High-chairs and children's menus are sometimes available, as are gardens to play in. Franchises such as the Spur Steak Ranches are a good family standby: they all have an appetizing children's menu, crayons and colouring-in books; some have jungle gyms.

Dress Code

Many upmarket restaurants require patrons to wear smart-casual attire. While you will not be able to wear shorts and sports shoes at such venues, you may comfortably do so just about anywhere else.

Wheelchair Access

A growing awareness for the special needs of the physically disabled visitor has led to the construction of ramps and

Melt-in-the-mouth beef and venison fillet at The Girls restaurant, Wilderness *(see p405)*

wider toilet doors at many restaurants in the major cities. Restaurants in more rural areas however, may not have these facilities and it is advisable to check in advance.

Recommended Restaurants

The restaurant options on pages 398–411 have been selected based on their popularity, quality and value for money. For each area, a range of establishments catering for different tastes, from traditional, home-cooked recipes to award-winning gourmet fare, has been included.

The restaurants highlighted as DK Choices have been chosen for one or more exceptional feature: a star chef and/or impeccable service, a wonderful setting or simply a warm welcome and great, tasty food. These special places are highly recommended.

Family-friendly Café Ruby, among the Klein Roosboom vineyards, Cape Town *(see p400)*

The Flavours of South Africa

In 1652, the Dutch East India Company established a refreshment station in the Cape to provide its ships with fresh supplies. These early settlers learned much from the local people who were hunter-gatherers, and a multi-ethnic cuisine began to emerge. The spice traders brought exotic flavours to the country, and the diversity of ingredients increased with the arrival of British, Indian and German settlers. Finally, the French Huguenots contributed culinary finesse. This range of influences is evident today in both traditional and modern dishes.

Rooibos tea

Preparing for a *braai* at a restaurant on the West Coast

Cape Malay Cooking

The Malay slaves, who were brought from Java to the Cape Colony in the late 1600s, carried with them an intimate knowledge of spices that had a profound influence on Cape cooking. Authentic specialities can still be found in Cape Town's historic Bo-Kaap district. Although spiced with traditional curry ingredients such as turmeric, ginger, cinnamon, cardamom, cloves and chilies, Cape Malay cuisine is never fiery. Meat is often cooked with fruit, marrying sweet and savoury flavours, while fish, especially snoek and seafood, is also important. Malay cooks were much sought after by the settlers and these cooks soon learned how to prepare traditional Dutch fare such as *melktert* (custard tart), adding cinnamon and grated nutmeg to suit their own tastes. Other South African baked puddings and tarts show a strong Dutch influence, while the delicious fruit preserves are mainly French Huguenot in origin.

Sea bass
Oysters
Prawns
Squid
Orange roughy
Mussels

Selection of fresh South African seafood

South African Dishes and Specialities

Biltong

From the Malay kitchen comes *bobotie*, served with *geelrys* (rice with raisins and spices) and *blatjang* (spicy fruit chutney). Durban's most popular dish is bunny chow (food of the Indians), a hollowed-out loaf filled with curry and garnished with pickles. The dish dates from apartheid when black South Africans were not allowed in restaurants, so were served this portable meal through the back door. Larded saddle of venison is the signature dish of the Karoo, and venison is also dried, salted and spiced to create a type of jerky called *biltong*. The Cedarberg region has its own speciality, Rooibos tea, which has a light and fruity taste. The warm Benguela and cold Atlantic currents ensure a plentiful supply of fresh fish, and snoek is a traditional favourite.

Smoorsnoek mixes flaked snoek (a barracuda-like fish) with potato slices and tomato in a tasty braise.

A vast array of South African fruit laid out at a Cape Town market

KwaZulu-Natal Cuisine

In the mid-1800s, indentured labour was brought from India to work in Natal's sugar cane fields. Many workers stayed on after their contracts expired, and Gujarati traders soon began supplying traditional spices to the growing community, who blended them with local foodstuffs to create distinctly South African flavours. Today, spice stores specialize in all manner of blends, some unique to South Africa, which create delicious dishes. The early Indian settlers later gained a strong foothold in the regional fruit and vegetable trade, introducing tropical Asian fruit to KwaZulu-Natal cuisine. Mangoes, lychees, banana, paw paw (papaya) and watermelon are enjoyed fresh, or as ingredients and accompaniments to curries.

Fresh fish is also very popular in this region, and the annual sardine runs on the coast are awaited with great anticipation. As soon as the fish are spotted, locals rush to the sea, collecting them by the dozen. The sardines are immediately sprinkled with salt, dipped into a South African spice mixture and fried.

South African bream caught by a local KwaZulu-Natal fisherman

Braai

The South African *braai* (barbecue) is much more than a meal cooked over an open fire. It is a social tradition cherished throughout the land. Lamb chops, steak, chicken, *sosaties* (kebabs) and *boerewors* (farmer's sausage) are the most common items. The Western Cape is famous for grilling whole snoek, basted with a mixture of apricot jam, white wine and fruit chutney. Grilled crayfish is another favourite *braai* dish.

ON THE MENU

Erwtensoep Dutch pea soup, slow cooked then liberally laced with diced, salted pork.

Groenmielies Corn on the cob, grilled over an open fire and thoroughly basted with butter. A favourite for a summer *braai*.

Koeksisters "Cake sisters" is a sweet Malay snack, best described as a doughnut infused with sugary syrup.

Perlemoen Tenderized and soaked in milk, abalone is lightly pan fried, which brings out the fresh sea taste.

Sosaties Skewers of meat, onions and dried fruit are marinated in a curry sauce and then grilled over an open fire.

Waterblommetjiebredie A Cape stew made of lamb and *waterblommetjies*, a water plant which resembles an artichoke.

Bobotie is minced beef, spiced with bay and turmeric, topped with an egg custard and baked.

Roast springbok or venison remains succulent when basted continuously with a sour cream marinade.

Melktert dates back to early Cape Malay-Dutch cooking. This sweet custard tart is sprinkled with cinnamon.

What to Drink in South Africa

South African wine may be classified as "New World", but the country actually has a long history in wine-making. The first vines were planted in the Cape of Good Hope by Commander Jan van Riebeeck in 1655. The most important figure in the industry, however, was Simon van der Stel, who founded both the Stellenbosch and Constantia vineyards, the latter's dessert wine gaining an international reputation by the end of the 17th century. In 1885, the vineyards were devastated by an infestation of the phylloxera insect. The subsequent recovery led to over-production and this, along with the establishment of trade sanctions as a result of apartheid, led to a decline in quality. Recent years have seen major changes in the industry, with a move towards smaller, independent vineyards producing some world-class wines. South Africa is now the world's ninth-largest producer.

Grape picker in the scenic Dieu Donné vineyard, on the slopes of the Franschhoek

Meerlust Estate wine

White Wine

With its Mediterranean-style climate, the country's southwestern tip is the best area for wine production. The growing conditions are perfect for the once-ubiquitous Chenin Blanc grape, used in high-volume, low-cost wines, and for brandy-making. Since the quota system ended in 1992, a greater variety of grapes has been planted. Sauvignon Blanc, Chardonnay and even some German, Spanish and Portuguese vines are now well established, and have taken on their own distinctive style. Stellenbosch, Constantia and the cool-climate Walker Bay all produce some of the finest white wines.

Cellars of Avondale, on Klein Drakenstein slopes, near Paarl

Red Wine

The dominant red grape variety is Merlot but it now has strong competition from the homegrown Pinotage cultivar (see pp188–9). South Africa still produces plenty of basic drinking reds but producers such as Bouchard Finlayson with its Pinot Noir and Boekenhoutskloof with its Cabernet Sauvignon have dramatically expanded the country's portfolio of excellent reds.

Morgenhof Estate-bottled red, from vineyards near Stellenbosch

Sparkling and Other Wines

Méthode Cap Classique is the nomenclature devised for the Champagne-style sparkling wines produced in all of the country's major wine districts (see p194). The delightfully honeyed Constantia dessert wine has been produced since 1685, but the wine industry has not stood still, and a wide range of increasingly popular rosé wines are being produced from grapes such as Gamay and Shiraz. Additionally, South Africa offers a number of port-style fortified wines, with Calitzdorp, in the Klein Karoo region, the main area of production, although Paarl and Stellenbosch also offer some good examples. Axe Hill, J P Boplaas and De Krans are among the best on offer.

Graham Beck Brut non-vintage

Beer

South African Breweries (SAB) was founded as Castle Brewery in 1895 to cater for the miners of Johannesburg. Since the 1990s it has been swallowing up rival breweries across the globe – in 2002 it purchased The Miller Brewing Company in North America and is now known as SABMiller. The company now brews beer in 75 countries. Castle, Black Label and Hansa are its ubiquitous South African labels. At the company's SAB World of Beer Museum in Johannesburg *(see pp314–15)*, the guided tour has guaranteed refreshment at the end in the form of a couple of cool "frosties".

Black Label   Castle   Hansa

Brandy

The word brandy is derived from the Dutch *brandewijn* ("brandywine") meaning burned or distilled wine. The Dutch used the method for preserving wine aboard ships, and South Africa's first brandy was distilled aboard the Dutch ship *Pijl*, anchored in Table Bay harbour in 1672. Today it's a favourite tipple of South Africans and an important export. Chenin Blanc and Colombard are mainly used for the base wine. The Western Cape's Brandy Route was established in 1997 and stretches from Stellenbosch through Paarl and Franschhoek to the Breede River Valley. The Van Ryn's Brandy Cellar *(see p199)*, Louisenhof, Tokara, Uitkyk, Avontuur and Kaapzicht are some of the estates on the route that offer brandy tastings.

A 10-year-old KWV   Boplaas Potstill Brandy

Spectacular vineyard setting in the Franschhoek Mountains

Variety	Regions	Producers
White		
Chenin Blanc	Breede River Valley, Stellenbosch, Cederberg, Swartland	De Trafford, Kleine Zalze, Nederburg, Beaumont Hope
Sauvignon Blanc	Darling District, Elim Ward Overberg, Cape Point, Stellenbosch	Groote Post, Paul Cluver, Steenberg Vineyards, Hamilton Russell
Chardonnay	Breede River Valley, Overberg, Paarl, Swartland, Cederberg	Springfield Estate, Neil Ellis, Glen Carlou, Jordan Wines
Red		
Cabernet Sauvignon	Cederberg, Paarl, Stellenbosch, Swartland, Tygerberg	Thelema Mountain Cederberg Cellars, Neil Ellis, Rupert & Rothschild
Shiraz	Franshhoek, Paarl, Stellenbosch	Fairview, Neil Ellis, Boekenhoutskloof
Pinotage	Overberg, Tulbagh, Breede River Valley, Stellenbosch	Rijk's Private Cellar, Fairview Primo, Graham Beck
Merlot	Constantia, Tygerberg, Paarl	Le Riche, Veenwouden, Glen Carlou
Pinot Noir	Overberg, Elgin, Constantia, Walker Bay, Darling District	Newton Johnson, Bouchard Finlayson, Paul Cluver, Groote Post
Sparkling		
Cape Classic	Cape Peninsula	J C Le Roux, Villiera Wines, Graham Beck Wines
Fortified		
(Port style)	Klein Karoo	Axe Hill, De Krans, J P Bredell

Reading the Label

South Africa operates strict wine labelling laws as a guarantee of quality. According to the WO (Wine of Origin) system, information provided on the grape variety and the vintage must apply to at least 85 per cent of what has gone into the bottle. However, 100 per cent of the grapes must have come from the stated place of origin. This can be the region (for example, Olifants River, Breede Valley River or Hex River Valley), the precise district therein (such as Paarl, Stellenbosch and Swartland) or, narrowing it down even more, the ward (Elgin, Waterberg, Cederberg). Top-end wines can be labelled as estate wines provided that the product is grown, vinified and bottled on one parcel of land that is farmed as a single unit and registered as such.

Where to Eat and Drink

Cape Town

City Bowl

Arnolds　　　　　　　**R**
African　　　　　**Map** 4 B3
60 Kloof St, Gardens, 8001
Tel *021 424 4344*
Popular with both locals and tourists, Arnolds offers good food, a pleasant location, attentive service and magnificent views of Table Mountain. On the menu are game dishes such as crocodile and warthog ribs.

Baran's　　　　　　　**R**
Mediterranean　　　**Map** 5 B1
36 Burgh St, Greenmarket Square, 8001
Tel *021 426 4466*
This Kurdish terrace restaurant serves excellent Turkish food. The meze platters are recommended and the cocktails are particularly good value. The setting has the vibe of an authentic Kurdish establishment, with hookah pipes included.

Biesmiellah　　　　　**R**
Cape Malay　　　　**Map** 5 B1
Wale Street, Bo-Kaap, 8000
Tel *021 423 0850*　**Closed** *Sun*
In the atmospheric Bo-Kaap area, this no-frills café serves local specialities such as *bobotie* (a sweet minced beef bake – *see p395*) and tomato breedie (tomato and lamb).

Carlyles on Derry　　**R**
Italian　　　　　　**Map** 5 C4
17 Derry St, Vredehoek, 8001
Tel *021 461 8787*　**Closed** *Mon*
This informal restaurant offers filling meals on the slopes of the mountain in Vredeshoek. Pizza and pasta are the main menu choices, but there are also some salads and meat dishes.

Deer Park Café　　　**R**
Bistro　　　　　　**Map** 5 B5
2 Deer Park Drive, Vredehoek, 8000
Tel *021 462 6311*
A popular venue for families, the outside tables here are next to a safe play area. The café serves a variety of breakfasts and light lunches, and all can be ordered in children's portions.

Mama Africa　　　　**R**
African　　　　　　**Map** 5 A2
178 Long St, 8001
Tel *021 424 8634*　**Closed** *Sun*
A Long Street institution, Mama Africa provides a full African experience, and not just a meal –

there is often live music. Menu specials include mixed game grill and *bobotie (see p395)*.

Oasis　　　　　　　**R**
Bistro　　　　　　**Map** 5 A2
Mount Nelson Hotel, 76 Orange St, 8001
Tel *021 483 1000*
The sun-splashed terrace of this restaurant in the famous Mount Nelson hotel overlooks the gardens and is perfect for a hearty breakfast, a lavish lunch, a decadent dessert or a cocktail.

Royale Eatery　　　　**R**
Hamburger restaurant　**Map** 5 A2
273 Long St, 8000
Tel *021 422 4536*　**Closed** *Sun*
Gourmet burgers: beef, lamb, ostrich, chicken and vegetarian are all on offer, all served with regular or sweet potato fries. There is a trendy bar upstairs for after-dinner drinks.

Table Mountain Café　**R**
International
Upper Cableway Station, 8000
Tel *021 424 0015*
The café on top of Table Mountain has self-service meals and snacks, including options for kids, as well as pastries and desserts. Closing time is half an hour before the last cable car down.

Vida e Caffe Kloof Street　**R**
Café　　　　　　　**Map** 4 F3
34 Kloof St, Gardens, 8001
Tel *021 426 0627*
This busy, trendy coffee shop is popular with locals and tourists alike. There is a delicious selection of muffins and pastries to choose from, and the latte is considered the best in town.

The Groove Bar at Café Caprice, a landmark on the Camps Bay Promenade in Cape Town

> **Price Guide**
> Prices are based on a three-course meal for one, including a half-bottle of house wine, cover charge, tax and service.
>
> | R | up to R180 |
> |---|---|
> | RR | R180 to R400 |
> | RRR | over R400 |

Addis in Cape　　　　**RR**
Ethiopian　　　　　**Map** 5 B1
41 Church St, 8001
Tel *021 424 5722*　**Closed** *Sun*
The ideal place to try Ethiopia's delicious cuisine. Vegetarians are well catered for, but there is a good selection of meat dishes too.

Bistrot Bizerca　　　**RR**
French　　　　　　**Map** 5 B1
98 Shortmarket Street, Heritage Square, 8001
Tel *021 423 8888*
Bistrot Bizerca offers fine dining in true bistro style. With few permanent dishes on the menu, the emphasis is on fresh produce. Fish dishes are recommended.

> **DK Choice**
>
> **Gold Restaurant**　　**RR**
> African　　　　　　**Map** 2 D5
> *15 Bennett St, 8005*
> **Tel** *021 421 4653*
> Housed in the Gold of Africa Museum, this stylish restaurant offers a complete African experience, including live entertainment and an optional drumming workshop before dinner. There is a set 14-course menu covering dishes from Cape Town to Timbuktu. Beautifully dressed waiters explain each dish and its origins.

Manna Epicure Restaurant　**RR**
French–African fusion　**Map** 4 F3
151 Kloof St, Gardens, 8001
Tel *021 426 2413*
A dynamic coupling of chic French flair and a rustic South African approach is offered at this trendsetting restaurant. A speciality is the South African *braai* or barbecue, and every meat lover should try the expertly aged Chalmer beef.

Miller's Thumb　　　**RR**
Seafood　　　　　**Map** 4 F3
10B Kloofnek Rd, Tamboerskloof, 8001
Tel *021 424 3838*
Solly and Jane's eatery specializes in seafood, but there are some tasty meat dishes as well. The ever-changing specials board features ingredients that are fresh from the ocean.

95 Keerom
Italian   **RRR**
95 Keerom St, 8000   **Map** 5 B2
Tel *021 422 0765*   **Closed** *Sun*
The roots of the dishes at this
elegant modern restaurant lie in
authentic Milanese cuisine. The
food is simple, unpretentious
and very fresh.

Aubergine Restaurant
International   **RRR**
39 Barnet St, Gardens, 8001   **Map** 5 B3
Tel *021 465 0000*   **Closed** *Sun*
Situated in a restored 19th-
century mansion, this classy
restaurant has received accolades
for its innovative cuisine, which
fuses elements of South African,
French and Asian cooking to
sublime effect.

Bukhara
Indian   **RRR**
33 Church St, 8001   **Map** 5 B1
Tel *021 4240 000*
Considered one of the best
Indian restaurants in the city, the
dishes here are cooked in an
authentic tandoori oven. The
view of the chefs in the glass-
encased open-plan kitchen
adds to the ambience.

Café Paradiso
Mediterranean   **RRR**
110 Kloof St, 8001   **Map** 4 F3
Tel *021 423 8653*
Hearty meals and an extensive
wine list are offered at this down-
to-earth, well-established
restaurant with an innovative
menu. The home-made pasta
dishes are recommended.

Haiku Restaurant
Asian   **RRR**
58 Burg St, 8001   **Map** 5 B1
Tel *021 424 7000*
The wide menu at this trendy
Asian tapas venue includes
translucent steamed dumplings,
five-spice calamari and the
restaurant's famous Peking duck.
Pricey, but worth it.

DK Choice

Savoy Cabbage
International   **RRR**
101 Hout St, 8001   **Map** 5 B1
Tel *021 424 2626*   **Closed** *Sun*
Modern, warehouse-style decor
fuses with the historic setting of
one of the oldest fine-dining
venues in Cape Town. The
emphasis is on fresh local
ingredients – the menu
changes daily accordingly.
There is a carefully selected
wine list, including a good
selection available by the glass.

Baia Seafood Restaurant, offering views over Victoria Wharf, Cape Town

V&A Waterfront

Quay Four
Seafood   **R**
West Quay Rd, 8001   **Map** 2 E3
Tel *021 419 2008*
One of the oldest, most popular
restaurants at the Waterfront,
Quay Four has outside seating on
a large wooden deck overlooking
the harbour. Especially tasty
are the linefish and calamari.

Den Anker
Belgian   **RR**
Pierhead, 8001   **Map** 2 E3
Tel *021 419 0249*
In an excellent spot to watch the
comings and goings of fishing
boats and yachts, Den Anker
offers authentic dishes including
generous pots of mussels and
frites, and imported beers.

Baia Seafood Restaurant
Seafood   **RRR**
Upstairs at Victoria Wharf, 8001   **Map** 2 E3
Tel *021 4210935*
The menu combines fine
continental cuisine with
Portuguese colonial traditions at
this restaurant with views of the
ocean and Table Mountain. Try
the bouillabaisse, a feast of
prawns, langoustines, mussels,
calamari and linefish.

Balducci's
International   **RRR**
Shop 6162, Victoria Wharf, 8001   **Map** 2 E3
Tel *021 421 6002*
The main menu features Italian
food but there is a Japanese
section offering sushi and other
delicacies as well. The mood is
sophisticated, the service slick.

Belthazar Restaurant & Wine Bar
International   **RRR**
Shop 153, Victoria Wharf, 8001   **Map** 2 E3
Tel *021 421 3753*
The speciality here is steak, with
an immensely varied and
impeccable wine list to match.
An impressive selection of wines
are available by the glass.

City Grill
Steakhouse   **RRR**
Shop 155, Victoria Wharf, 8001   **Map** 2 E3
Tel *021 421 9820*
The portions are generous and
the atmosphere is lively and
unpretentious at this traditional
steakhouse. Aside from matured
beef dishes, specialities include
South African specials such as
bobotie, ostrich fillet steak and
venison options.

Sevruga
International   **RRR**
Shop 4, Quay 5, 8001   **Map** 2 E3
Tel *021 421 5134*
The decor is showy at this
sophisticated restaurant. The
menu has interesting dishes
such as tomato tarte tatin and
springbok carpaccio. There is also
a good selection of sushi and
dim sum dishes.

Atlantic Seaboard

Café Caprice
Café   **R**
37 Victoria Rd, Camps Bay, 8001   **Map** 3 B5
Tel *021 438 8315*
This is a popular haunt on the
Camps Bay promenade which is
always buzzing, particularly in
the summer months. Breakfast is
particularly recommended and
in the evening a resident DJ
plays in the bar.

La Cucina
International   **R**
Victoria Mall, Victoria Rd, 7806   **Map** 3 B5
Tel *021 7908008*
Focusing on food that is freshly
made, free of preservatives and
mostly organic, this restaurant
and deli has a breakfast and
lunch buffet and a limited à la
carte menu.

The Codfather   RRR
Seafood
37 The Drive, Camps Bay, 8001
Tel *021 438 0782*
This was one of the first sushi
venues in Cape Town. Sushi and
other seafood dishes are still the
main focus. There are no written
menus, but the waiters help you
put together your meal.

Green Point and Mouille Point

Caffé Neo   R
Café   **Map** 1 B3
129 Beach Rd, Mouille Point, 8005
Tel *021 433 0849*
This café is well positioned to
enjoy great views. The decor is
unpretentious and the service
friendly. The menu offers
sumptuous and healthy breakfast
options as well as sandwiches
and salads for lunch.

Anatoli   RR
Turkish   **Map** 2 D5
24 Napier St, Green Point, 8001
Tel *021 419 2501*   **Closed** *Sun*
Serving up Cape Town's best
Turkish cuisine since 1984.
The vibrancy of the culture is
reflected in the decor and the
food, with an ever-changing list
of specials. Flat bread and meze
are great appetizers.

Il Leone Mastrantonio   RR
Italian
*22 Cobern Street, Green Point,
Cape Town*
Tel *021 421 0071*   **Closed** *Mon*
The restaurant offers traditional
Italian fare in a sophisticated
setting. The menu boasts a great
selection of fish dishes and
seafood, and there is also a
walk-in wine cellar and a bar.

Pigalle Cape Town   RR
International   **Map** 2 D5
57A Somerset Rd, Green Point, 8001
Tel *021 421 4343*   **Closed** *Sun*
Renowned for its fresh fish, prime
cut 28-day-aged steaks, local
seafood, shellfish and Portuguese
classics, Pigalle is a great dinner
and live jazz venue, with the
resident band playing nightly.

Sotano   RR
Mediterranean   **Map** 1 B3
121 Beach Rd, Mouille Point, 8005
Tel *021 433 1757*
Breakfasts, tapas, sushi and
delicious desserts are offered
at this family-run restaurant
located by the seaside. Every
Wednesday from 5pm, it serves
its popular two-for-one Lamb
Burger Special.

Beluga   RRR
International   **Map** 2 D5
*The Foundry, Prestwich St, Green
Point, 8001*
Tel *021 418 2948*
The varied menu at this fine-
dining restaurant includes sushi,
dim sum and à la carte specials
such as fresh Atlantic oysters and
springbok. There is a great
cocktail menu as well.

Northern Suburbs

Café Ruby   R
Café
*Klein Roosboom Boutique Winery,
Tyger Valley Rd, Durbanville, 7551*
Tel *021 975 7965*   **Closed** *Mon*
Surrounded by the lush Klein
Roosboom vineyards, this eatery
offers a relaxed atmosphere and
a safe playground for children. The
changing chalkboard menu
displays dishes prepared with
fresh seasonal ingredients.

Col'Cacchio   R
Pizzeria
*Shop 7 & 8, Spiro's Corner, cnr Main St
& Vrede St, Durbanville, 7550*
Tel *021 976 7750*
The traditionally inspired Italian
food at this family-friendly
restaurant includes crispy, thin-
crust pizzas, salads and pasta
dishes. Childrens are given
dough to play with, which is
then cooked for them.

Die Boer   RR
African
6 Chenoweth St, Durbanville, 7551
Tel *021 979 1911*
At this dinner and live entertainment venue, there are six theatre
shows a week. Dinner is usually
served from 6:30pm to 8:30pm,
before the show. The limited
menu has some South African
specials such as *boereburger*
(beef burger) and *bobotie*.

South Peninsula

Cape to Cuba   R
Cuban
165 Main Rd, Kalk Bay, 7975
Tel *021 788 1566*
An impressive mix of chandeliers,
vases, and references to Ernest
Hemingway and Che Guevara
adorn this shack on the beach.
It is a great place for cocktails
and light snacks.

Kalky's   R
Seafood
Kalk Bay Harbour, Kalk Bay, 7975
Tel *021 788 1726*
Right in the middle of a working
harbour, this beloved fish and
chips mecca serves good hake

Fine dining at the popular Beluga
restaurant, Cape Town

and calamari. The combo platter
prices compare with fancier joints,
but if you keep things simple it
remains good value.

The Lighthouse Café   R
Bistro
90 St Georges St, Simon's Town, 7975
Tel *021 786 9000*
This well-ventilated bistro has a
French and coastal feel. Special
attention is given to all the
guests. The owner, who is also
the chef, prepares everything
using fresh produce.

**Octopus' Garden Restaurant &
Wine Bar**   R
Mediterranean
*The Old Post Office Building, Main Rd,
St James, 7945*
Tel *061 005 1694*
Set in a former post office, this
funky, laid-back venue serves
breakfast, lunch and dinner.
The crispy, thin-crust pizzas are
considered the best in the area
and the desserts are divine.

Olympia Café and Deli   R
Bistro
134 Main Rd, Kalk Bay, 7945
Tel *021 7886396*
This bustling restaurant serves
simple rustic food including fish
and seafood. The bread is freshly
baked in the bakery next door.
No reservations are taken, so
arrive early.

Bertha's Restaurant   RR
Seafood
1 Wharf Rd, Simon's Town, 7995
Tel *021 786 2138*
Catch of the day, oysters,
prawns and the renowned
Bertha's seafood platters are
some of the signature dishes
here. There is a nautical feel
and great views over Simon's
Town harbour.

Black Marlin Seafood
Restaurant RR
Seafood
Miller's Point Rd, Simon's Town, 7995
Tel *021 786 1621*
The varied menu at Cape Town's oldest seafood resaurant includes platters, fish and chips and calamari, and more adventurous choices such as prawn curry and bacon-wrapped seafood skewers. This is also a great spot for whale-watching.

The Brass Bell RR
International
Kalk Bay Station, Main Rd, Kalk Bay, 7975
Tel *021 788 5455*
This casual seaside restaurant offers everything from pub fare to seafood platters and pizzas from the wood-fired oven. There is a substantial cocktail menu.

Carla's Restaurant RR
Portuguese
9 York Rd, Muizenberg, 7945
Tel *021 788 6860* **Closed** *Sun*
This restaurant is run by its owner, Carla, a Mozambican expat who creates a friendly, cosy atmosphere. The signature dish is LM prawns (Mozambique prawns) served with rice or chips, and home-made peri-peri sauce.

Polana RR
International
Kalk Bay Harbour, Kalk Bay, 7945
Tel *021 788 7162*
In a great location with a cocktail lounge on the rocks just metres away from crashing waves, Polana focuses on meat dishes. The menu includes free-range beef fillet, ginger pork ribs, lamb cutlets and gourmet burgers.

Harbour House RRR
Seafood
Kalk Bay Harbour, Kalk Bay, 7945
Tel *021 788 4133*
The cuisine here is international with Mediterranean elements underpinned by classic French methods. The restaurant has its own boat to supply all its fish – a simple fresh linefish is the signature dish.

The Roundhouse RRR
South African **Map** 3 C5
Round House Rd (off Kloof Rd), The Glen, Camps Bay, 8040
Tel *021 438 4347* **Closed** *Mon*
At this restaurant in a historic guardhouse with views over the coast, the chef combines classic European cuisine with South African produce to create a seasonal four-course menu with optional wine-pairing.

Southern Suburbs

Rhodes Memorial Restaurant
and Tea Garden R
Bistro
Rhodes Memorial, Rondebosch, 7740
Tel *021 687 0000*
A family-friendly restaurant offering fantastic views across the City Bowl and the Cape Flats to the ocean. The on-site home-style bakery is renowned for delicious cakes and desserts.

Barrister Restaurant RR
Steakhouse
Cardiff Castle, cnr Kildare Rd & Main St, Newlands, 7700
Tel *021 671 7907*
The extensive menu here includes the great steak dishes for which this popular restaurant is famous. The wine list is inspiring too, with a good selection available by the glass.

DK Choice

Jonkershuis RR
Bistro
Groot Constantia Wine Estate, 7800
Tel *021 794 6255*
Dine alfresco under ancient oak trees overlooking False Bay or in the courtyard under the vines in this beautiful vineyard. The food has distinct Malay flavours, with dishes such as *bobotie* and karoo lamb, chicken breast and vegetable and lentil curry as favourites.

Peddlars & Co RR
Italian
13 Spaanschemat River Rd, Constantia, 7800
Tel *021 794 7747*
Casual dining with versatile seating in the restaurant, pub and beer garden. Volaré restaurant offers authentic Italian dishes, while gourmet bar food is offered in the bar area. The Oak Terrace is great for children.

Wijnhuis Wine Bar & Grill RR
Italian
Cnr Kildare St and Main St, Newlands, 7700
Tel *021 671 9705* **Closed** *Sun*
Good modern dishes, matched by an extensive wine list are served in a relaxed atmosphere with comfortable sofas for post-dinner lounging. Cold meat and cheese platters are a favourite.

Buitenverwachting RRR
International
Klein Constantia Rd, Constantia
Tel *021 7943522* **Closed** *Mon, Sun*
Set on a historic wine farm, this restaurant offers a warm atmosphere and great service. Highlights include grilled loin and cutlet of springbok, roasted pork belly and Caesar salad.

Catharina's at Steenberg RRR
International
Steenberg Estate, Steenberg Rd, Tokai, 7945
Tel *021 7137178*
The glass walls look out on a vista of sun-drenched vineyards at this airy restaurant. Menu highlights include duck livers with cream, mushrooms and muscadel on toast and warm *koeksisters* (syrup doughnuts) with cinnamon ice cream.

DK Choice

La Colombe RRR
French–African fusion
Silvermist Wine Estate, Main Rd, Constantia Neck, 8001
Tel *021 795 0125*
Located on the Silvermist organic wine estate, La Colombe consistently features among the world's top 50 restaurants. Flavours are French in origin, but with a distinctive Cape accent. It is ideal for special occasions that require simple elegance, with à la carte and gourmet tasting menus.

The leafy lawns in front of Jonkershuis in the Groot Constantia Wine Estate

For more information on types of restaurants *see pp392–3*

Cape Winelands

FRANSCHHOEK: Café des Arts R
International
7 Reservoir Street West, 7690
Tel *021 876 2952*
Simple food served in a relaxed ambience, with a menu that changes regularly. All ingredients are fresh and a selection of local wines is available.

FRANSCHHOEK: Essence R
Café **Road Map** B5
7 Huguenot Square, 7690
Tel *021 876 4135*
With comfortable sofas and outdoor tables, this relaxed eatery offers generous breakfasts, filled paninis and bagels, local favourites such as *bobotie* and lamb curry, and scones with jam and cream.

FRANSCHHOEK: Bread & Wine Vineyard Restaurant RR
Mediterranean **Road Map** B5
Moreson Farm, Happy Valley Rd, 7690
Tel *021 876 3692*
The speciality of the chef at this characterful rustic restaurant is home-made charcuterie. There are tables under the lemon trees for alfresco dining.

DK Choice

FRANSCHHOEK:
Picnics RR
Vineyard **Road Map** B5
Boschendal Wine Estate, Pniel Rd, Groot Drakenstein, 7680
Tel *021 870 4272*
In summer, Boschendal gardens with its dramatic mountain views is perfect for a picnic. Collect your basket, filled with terrines, roulades, bread, cold meats, salads, cheese and a dessert, grab a bottle from the wine list and you're all set.

DK Choice

FRANSCHHOEK:
Haute Cabrière RRR
French **Road Map** B5
Lambrechts Rd, 7690
Tel *021 876 8500* **Closed** *Mon*
This supremely elegant cellar restaurant is regularly placed among South Africa's top 10. Many dishes use ingredients found in the valley, including fresh salmon and trout. Stand-outs are spiced sweet potato soup with coconut foam and rye croutons, garlic-crusted lamb loin and assiette of aubergine.

The Tasting Room in Franschhoek, elegant sister restaurant to Bread & Wine

FRANSCHHOEK:
La Petite Ferme RRR
International **Road Map** B5
Franschhoek Pass Rd, 7690
Tel *021 876 3016*
The setting is spectacular and the menu simple at this grand, family-run institution that has stood the test of time. Eat a beautifully cooked trout caught in the restaurant's dam while looking over vineyards to the mountains.

FRANSCHHOEK:
The Tasting Room RRR
South African **Road Map** B5
Le Quartier Francais Hotel, 9 Wilhelmina St, 7690
Tel *021 876 2151* **Closed** *Sun, Mon*
This is regularly featured in *Restaurant* magazine's top 50. Guests have a choice of four-, six- or eight-course dining experiences from a menu that uses only local ingredients.

FRANSCHHOEK: The Werf Restaurant RRR
French–African **Road Map** B5
Boschendal Wine Estate, Pniel Rd, Groot Drakenstein, 7680
Tel *021 870 4206*
Situated in the original cellar of Boschendal Manor House, the emphasis here is on using local, seasonal ingredients. Lunch is buffet-style with chefs making the final preparations at an interactive food station.

PAARL: Eat@Simonsvlei R
Bistro **Road Map** B5
Simonsvlei Winery, Old Paarl Rd, 7624
Tel *021 863 3845* **Closed** *Mon*
Dine alfresco on the verandah or inside the dining room with air conditioning in summer or a fireplace for the winter months at this relaxed restaurant. The menu has fresh, slow-cooked food. Open only for breakfast and lunch.

PAARL: Kikka R
Café **Road Map** B5
217 Main Rd, 7646
Tel *021 872 0685* **Closed** *Sun*
The standard breakfast and coffee shop favourites feature here, plus a few quirkier dishes. The "cake platter" allows you to sample four of the decadent confections on offer, from towering red velvet cake to rich baked cheesecake.

PAARL: Harvest at Laborie RR
South African **Road Map** B5
Laborie Estate, Taillefer St, 7646
Tel *021 807 3095* **Closed** *Mon*
Simple, fresh ingredients are used in the bistro-style classics at this restaurant that has shady tables beneath the trees. Dishes are paired with Laborie's own wine. The adjacent playground is great for children.

PAARL: Bosman's RRR
International **Road Map** B5
The Grande Roche Hotel, Plantasie St, 7646
Tel *021 863 5100*
Providing a classic fine-dining experience, Bosman's has an international team of chefs who maintain its position as one of the world's great eateries. There is a private dining room that can be booked for special occasions.

SOMERSET WEST:
96 Winery Road RR
International **Road Map** B5
Zandberg Farm, Winery Rd, 7599
Tel *021 842 2020*
Delicious, home-style food with a South African flavour is served with good, friendly service. This is an ideal spot for a lazy, long lunch. Stand-out dishes include crispy pork belly and duck and cherry pie.

SOMERSET WEST: The Avontuur Restaurant RR
Mediterranean **Road Map** B5
Avontuur Estate, 7129
Tel *021 855 4296*
Fresh country ingredients with a Mediterranean flavour form the delicious dishes here. Outdoor tables have sweeping views over the vineyard to Table Mountain.

SOMERSET WEST:
Steffanie's Place RR
Italian **Road Map** B5
113 Irene Avenue, 7130
Tel *021 852 7584*
In a great location overlooking the mountains and the sea, this is a popular family-run restaurant. Menu highlights include grilled kingklip with salsa, queen prawns and chocolate torte.

SOMERSET WEST: La Vigna   RR
International   **Road Map** B5
The Lord Charles Hotel, cnr Main Rd
(M9) and Broadway Blvd (R44), 7130
Tel *021 855 1040*
The stylish restaurant in this hotel
has a modern interior, a garden
terrace and an adjacent wine
cellar. There is a varied menu to
choose from and traditional tea is
served in the afternoon.

STELLENBOSCH: The Bistro at
Blaauwklippen   R
Bistro   **Road Map** B5
Blaauwklippen Vineyards, 7599
Tel *021 880 8221*
This wine estate provides the
setting for elegant yet informal
dining, with outdoor tables under
the canopies of ancient trees.
Recommended is the home-made
charcuterie, which gives a modern
twist to traditional specialities.

STELLENBOSCH: Oude Werf
Restaurant   RR
International   **Road Map** B5
Oude Werf Hotel, 30 Church St, 7600
Tel *021 887 4608*
Cape classics with a contemporary
gourmet twist from chef Albert
van der Loo are offered at this
"modern-meets-vintage" bistro.
For dinner there is an à la carte or
three-course set menu served al-
fresco or inside around a fireplace.

STELLENBOSCH: Wijnhuis   RR
Wine bar   **Road Map** B5
Cnr Church St and Andringa St, 7600
Tel *021 887 5844*
While this bar and grill is mainly
about the wines (there are more
than 300 on offer), it offers light
meals too, such as carpaccio,
game, tapas, cheese platters and
great pasta.

STELLENBOSCH: Terroir   RRR
Mediterranean   **Road Map** B5
Kleine Zalze, Strand Rd (R44), 7600
Tel *021 880 8167*
The chalkboard menu at Terroir
lists simple dishes influenced by
what is in season. Where possible,
local ingredients are used. It overlooks a lake and there is outside
seating under shady oak trees.

West Coast and
Southern Cape

BLOUBERG: Blue Peter
Lighthouse Restaurant   RR
International   **Road Map** B5
8 Popham Rd, Bloubergstrand, 7441
Tel *021 554 1956*
There is fine dining on the upper
level and a casual bistro on the
lower deck of this establishment.

It is popular for Sunday lunches,
and the pizzas are highly
recommended. The view of Table
Mountain is a big attraction.

BLOUBERG: On the Rocks   RRR
International   **Road Map** B5
45 Stadler Rd, Bloubergstrand, 7441
Tel *021 554 1988*
Located right at the water's edge,
this upmarket establishment
offers great seafood, but also
has some good meat and
vegetarian options. Try the
game fish or the delicious "death
by chocolate" dessert.

CLANWILLIAM: Reinhold's
Restaurant   RR
Steakhouse   **Road Map** B4
Main St, 8135
Tel *027 4822163*   **Closed** *Sun*
The menu revolves around
the grill at this old-school
steakhouse. Apart from a few
token pasta and poultry options,
expect hefty steaks and racks of
juicy lamb chops.

DARLING: Evita se Perron   RRR
International   **Road Map** B5
Old Darling Railway Station,
8 Arcadia St, 7345
Tel *022 492 2851*   **Closed** *Mon*
The food is good, but this is
more about the show than the
dinner. Evita Bezuidenhout,
alter ego of satirist Pieter-Dirk
Uys, is a national treasure.
Expect a hilarious stand-up
routine that ruthlessly satirizes
the Rainbow Nation.

HERMANUS: Savannah Café   R
International   B5
25 High St, 7200
Tel *028 312 4259*
The ambience is casual here,
with a choice of indoor or
alfresco space in the French-style
courtyard. The menu offers fresh
and healthy options. Cakes,
bread and pastries are baked
on the premises.

DK Choice

HERMANUS:
Bientang's Cave   RR
Seafood   **Road Map** B5
Marine Drive, 7200
Tel *028 312 3454*
This award-winning restaurant
is carved into the depths of a
cave that extends over the
rocks to the water's edge.
Seafood dominates the menu –
the signature dish is Bientang's
Bouillabaisse Soup.

HERMANUS: Seafood at The
Marine   RRR
Seafood   **Road Map** B5
Marine Drive, 7200
Tel *028 313 1000*
The seafood is fresh from the
ocean and the menu blends local
produce with European and Asian
influences. The must-try dish is
the Rich Man's fish and chips.

L'AGULHAS: Agulhas Country
Lodge   RR
South African   **Road Map** B5
Main Rd, 7287
Tel *028 435 7650*
Country-style gourmet dishes vary
daily and focus on traditional
South African cuisine with a
modern twist. Organic venison
and seafood feature regularly.

DK Choice

LAMBERT'S BAY:
Muisbosskerm   R
Seafood   **Road Map** A4
47 Church St, 8130
Tel *027 4321017*
Meals are eaten right on the
beach and stretch over 3 or 4
hours – an endless open-air
buffet of seafood indulgence,
with baked, smoked and grilled
fish, crayfish and a variety of
potjiekos (stews) on offer. It is
essential to book.

Seafood at The Marine, perched above the sea in Hermanus's prestigious Marine hotel

For more information on types of restaurants *see pp392–3*

LAMBERT'S BAY:
Bosduifklip RR
Seafood **Road Map** A4
R364, 4 km (2 miles) outside Lambert's Bay, 8130
Tel *027 432 2735*
On a West Coast farm surrounded by ancient rock formations, Bosduifklip offers a buffet-style spread that includes crayfish, mussels, snoek and sweet potato, lamb cooked on a spit, salads, bread, jams and sweet dumplings.

LANGEBAAN: Pearly's on the Beach
International **Road Map** A5
46 Beach Rd, 7357
Tel *022 7722734*
At this Langebaan favourite, on the main beach overlooking the lagoon, the menu includes seafood, grilled meat, pizza and pasta. This is the perfect spot to watch the sunset with a cocktail.

LANGEBAAN: Boesmanland Plaaskombuis
RR
South African **Road Map** A5
Club Mykonos, 7357
Tel *022 772 1564* **Closed** *Mon, Tue*
All the dishes are prepared on open fires in big black pots at this informal outdoor venue on the beach. The eat-as-much-as-you-like menu includes seafood, African dishes and Afrikaans *boerekos* sausage.

LANGEBAAN:
Die Strandloper RR
Seafood **Road Map** A5
On the beach, 7357
Tel *022 772 2490*
There are great views at this beach restaurant. Buffet meals include grilled sardines, yellowtail, salty snoek, smoked angelfish and garlicky crayfish straight from the ocean onto the barbecue.

OUDTSHOORN: Nostalgie
International **Road Map** C5
74 Baron van Rheede St, 6625
Tel *044 272 4085*
Ranging from classic to eclectic, the menu includes ostrich and Karoo dishes. The extensive breakfast options feature free-range eggs and home-baked breads warm from the oven.

OUDTSHOORN: Jemima's
RR
African **Road Map** C5
94 Baron van Rheede St, 6620
Tel *044 272 0808*
Ostrich is popular here, whether it comes as a burger, piled high with toppings and with crispy potato skins on the side, or in the creamy stroganoff. Other classic hits include Karoo lamb pie and home-made *bobotie*.

STANFORD: Mariana's at Owls Barn
R
South African **Road Map** B5
12 Du Toit St, 7210
Tel *028 341 0272* **Closed** *Mon–Wed*
Overlooking vegetable gardens, Mariana's offers an unpretentious taste of Cape cuisine, with French and Italian influences. Everything is made from scratch, from pasta to pickles. The decor is cosy, with mismatched vintage furniture.

SWELLENDAM: The Old Gaol
R
South African **Road Map** B5
8A Voortrek St, Church Square, 6740
Tel *028 514 3847*
Traditional local dishes rule at this rustic eatery. You can see *melktert (see p395)* being cooked in copper pans in the outdoor oven. *Roosterkoek* (grilled bread) filled with everything from salmon to springbok, is baked daily.

SWELLENDAM: Roosje van de Kaap
RRR
International **Road Map** B5
5 Drosty St, 6740
Tel *028 514 3001* **Closed** *Mon*
This restaurant serves distinctive country cuisine in a historic stable overlooking the Drostdy building. The menu includes seafood cooked in a wood-fired oven, pan-seared fillet of beef, and chicken with a classic French sauce.

SWELLENDAM: La Sosta
RRR
Italian **Road Map** B5
145 Voortrek St, 6740
Tel *028 514 1470* **Closed** *Sun, Mon*
This is sophisticated dining. The innovative wine list includes Italian wines, as well as plenty of wines from across the Cape. On cooler evenings a lit fireplace adds to the cosy atmosphere.

YZERFONTEIN: Strandkombuis
R
Seafood **Road Map** A5
16 Mile Beach, Dolphin Way, 7351
Tel *022 451 2360*
Help yourself to the large buffet and bread fresh from the coal fires. Right on the beach, this venue is perfect for children to run around while parents unwind.

Garden Route to Grahamstown

GEORGE: Bayleaf Café
R
Café **Road Map** C5
24 Cathedral St, 6529
Tel *044 873 4422* **Closed** *Sun*
Excellent coffee and fresh, high-quality light meals are served at this quirky café with outside seating in a European-style courtyard.

East Head Café in Knysna, a great choice for a relaxed weekend brunch

GEORGE: La Locanda
RR
Italian **Road Map** C5
124A York St, 6529
Tel *044 874 7803* **Closed** *Sun*
Probably best-loved for its thin-crust pizza, the menu at La Locanda extends to traditional *primi* (pasta), *secondi* (meats) and fresh local fish. The excellent charcuterie and creamy mozzarella are uncompromisingly authentic.

GRAHAMSTOWN: The Cock House
R
International **Road Map** D5
10 Market St, 2014
Tel *046 636 1287*
This established guesthouse and restaurant in a listed building offers home-baked breads, fresh-cut herbs, an innovative menu and a lovingly compiled wine list. The menu changes regularly.

GRAHAMSTOWN: The Rat & Parrot
R
Pub **Road Map** D5
59 New St, 2014
Tel *046 622 5002*
A landmark eatery, especially popular with students, this venue has a varied menu. Dishes include sandwiches, pizzas, burgers, snack baskets, great signature *biltong* and avocado and sourcream beef rump. There is regular live entertainment.

KNYSNA: East Head Café
R
Seafood **Road Map** C5
25 George Rex Drive, 6570
Tel *044 384 0933*
This is considered by some as the spot with the best view of Knysna lagoon, and is a neighbourhood favourite for breakfast over the weekend. Stand-out dishes are fresh fish and chips and the Spring Tide breakfast, which is served with a burger pattie.

KNYSNA: Ile de Pain R
Café **Road Map** C5
The Boatshed, Thesen's Island, 6570
Tel *044 302 5707* **Closed** *Mon*
Using a wood-fired oven and locally-grown ingredients, chef Liezie Mulder creates delicious breads and much more. Sicilian bruschetta or Cambodian curry are recommended lunch options.

KNYSNA: 34 South RR
Seafood **Road Map** C5
Quay 19, Knysna Quays, Waterfront Drive, 6571
Tel *044 382 7331*
Situated right in the harbour, this deli-cum-bar is always buzzing. The extensive wine list features some of the best wines in the Western Cape.

KNYSNA: Drydock Food Co. RR
International **Road Map** C5
Waterfront Shop 1, Knysna Quays, 6570
Tel *044 382 7310*
Overlooking the yacht basin, this lovely wood and glass restaurant offers great seafood, as well as meat dishes, salads and sinful desserts. This is a great place for drinks at sundown.

KNYSNA: Pembreys Bistro RR
Mediterranean **Road Map** C5
Brenton Rd, Belvidere, 6571
Tel *044 386 0005*
Relax and enjoy the old farmhouse setting, warmed by a roaring fire in winter. The chalkboard menu changes daily but home-made ravioli, slow roasts and fresh seafood is always available.

MOSSEL BAY: Punjabi Kitchen R
Indian **Road Map** C5
Eden Plaza, 8 Grave St, 6500
Tel *044 690 5020*
The friendly, informal Punjabi Kitchen is committed to serving unpretentious, wholesome dishes, including curries, roti rolls, bunny chows and other favourites. Vegetarians are well-catered for.

MOSSEL BAY: Café Gannet RR
Seafood **Road Map** C5
Bartholomeu Dias Museum Complex, cnr Church St and Market St, 6500
Tel *044 691 3738*
The speciality here is seafood. Fresh linefish, calamari and prawns are cooked to perfection. There are top-quality grilled meats too.

PLETTENBERG BAY: Le Fournil de Plett R
Café **Road Map** C5
Lookout Centre, cnr Church St and Main St, 6600
Tel *044 533 1390*
Slow-rise artisan breads are baked daily using organic stone-ground flour, as well as pastries, desserts and croissants. Breakfast and lunch can be enjoyed in the relaxing courtyard.

PLETTENBERG BAY: Cornuti al Mare RR
Italian **Road Map** C5
1 Perestrella St, 6600
Tel *044 533 1277*
The thin, crispy pizzas are highly recommended, as is the seafood meze. The bar is where the action is, with a good selection of cocktails and wines by the glass.

DK Choice

PLETTENBERG BAY: Seafood at The Plettenberg RRR
South African **Road Map** C5
Lookout Rocks, 40 Church St, 6600
Tel *044 533 2030*
A sophisticated dining experience not to be missed. The modern local fare is seasonally influenced. Seafood is what it's all about, and the platter featuring crayfish from Hermanus is a must. The award-winning wine list showcases cool climate wines, especially chosen to pair with seafood.

PORT ELIZABETH: Royal Delhi R
Indian **Road Map** D5
10 Burgess St, 6001
Tel *041 373 8216* **Closed** *Sun*
This is an unpretentious, good-value family-run restaurant. Recommended dishes include the deboned lamb curry, closely followed by the curried oxtail.

PORT ELIZABETH: Ginger RR
International **Road Map** D5
The Beach Hotel, Marine Drive, Summerstrand, 6000
Tel *041 583 1229*
With a friendly atmosphere, this chic restaurant has an eclectic menu boasting some innovative cuisine. Try salt and pepper squid on a Thai-inspired salad, harissa fish soup and cinnamon, fennel and ginger ice cream.

PORT ELIZABETH: Natti's Thai Kitchen RR
Thai **Road Map** D5
Park Lane, 6000
Tel *041 373 2763* **Closed** *Sun, Mon*
Natti's Thai Kitchen has earned a respected reputation due to its authentic cuisine. The menu includes fragrant green curry, very hot red curry, searingly hot "angry duck", stir-fries and dishes featuring tamarind.

WILDERNESS: Pomodoro R
Italian **Road Map** C5
George Rd, 6560
Tel *044 877 1403*
The outside terrace of Pomodoro is the locals' meeting place and is always alive with activity. A wide range of pizzas and pasta dishes makes this restaurant popular with families.

WILDERNESS: The Girls RRR
African **Road Map** C5
Caltex Centre, 1 George Rd, 6560
Tel *044 877 1648* **Closed** *Mon*
The African-inspired atmosphere here is highlighted by artwork from local artist Peter Pharoah. Popular menu items include fresh linefish, succulent prawns, tender steaks and curries, all cooked in an open kitchen.

WILDERNESS: Serendipity RRR
South African **Road Map** C5
Serendipity, Freesia Avenue, 6560
Tel *044 877 0433* **Closed** *Sun*
Husband and wife team Rudolf and Lizelle Stolze focus on fine dining with a tangible personal touch. Dinner is a five-course South African-inspired *table d'hôte* menu to be experienced at a leisurely pace in a refined atmosphere.

Fresh, modern decor at the Punjabi Kitchen, Mossel Bay

For more information on types of restaurants *see pp392–3*

Wild Coast, Drakensberg and Midlands

BERGVILLE: Bingelela R
International **Road Map** E3
Needwood Farm, on the R74, 3360
Tel *026 448 1336*
Owner-managed restaurant in a rustic farm setting. Children can swim in the pool and dogs roam around freely. The varied menu includes a good selection of steaks, pasta dishes and pizzas.

EAST LONDON: Irana R
Indian–Mauritian **Road Map** E5
Chamberlain Rd, Berea, 5214
Tel *043 721 2652*
This popular restaurant offers a mix of classic Indian and Mauritian cuisine. Snacks include roti rolls and bunny chows. There are great curry dishes using mutton, chicken and prawns cooked in different ways.

EAST LONDON: Ocean Basket R
Seafood **Road Map** E5
Shop 10B, Vincent Park Centre, Devereux Avenue, Vincent, 5214
Tel *043 726 8809*
Good-quality mains at this popular chain include grilled salmon and linefish. Calamari and prawns can be ordered as starters or mains, and there's a children's menu.

EAST LONDON: Grazia RRR
Italian **Road Map** E5
Upper Esplanade, Beach Front Rd, 5214
Tel *043 722 2009*
There are views of the ocean and an award-winning wine cellar at Grazia. The pasta and pizza are popular, but the varied menu also offers dishes such as beef on the bone, and white chocolate and banana cigars.

HIMEVILLE: Moorcroft Manor RR
International **Road Map** E3
Sani Rd, Himeville, 3256
Tel *033 702 1967*
The menu offers local trout, meats, salads and cheeses. The elegant dining room has an open wine cellar and there are amazing views of the Drakensberg Mountains from the terrace.

HOWICK: Corner Post RR
International **Road Map** E3
124 Main St, Howick, 3290
Tel *033 330 7636*
Charming pub-cum-restaurant overlooking Howick Falls. Quality menu choices are grass-fed steaks and renowned Midlands cheeses. There is a kids' area and, often, local art on show.

HOWICK: Yellowwood RR
International **Road Map** E3
1 Shafton Rd, 3290
Tel *033 330 2461* **Closed** *Mon*
There are both fine-dining and bar menus at this restaurant on a country farm with superb views from the verandah tables. Children will enjoy the play-ground and farm animals.

MOOI RIVER: Hartford House RRR
International **Road Map** E3
Hlatikulu Rd, 3300
Tel *033 263 2713*
A sumptuous menu has earned this fine-dining restaurant, stud farm and luxury hotel many accolades. Reservations are recommended for non-residents.

NOTTINGHAM ROAD: The Bierfassl R
Austrian **Road Map** E3
Nottingham Rd, 3280
Tel *033 266 6320*
Great pub food and a good selection of beers are served, including favourites such as eisbein, pork kassler chops with sauerkraut and hamburgers. Also has a children's play area.

DK Choice

NOTTINGHAM ROAD: Blueberry Café RR
Café **Road Map** 3
Netherwood Farm, R103, 3280
Tel *033 266 7132*
This classy, barn-like venue has great views of the Natal Midlands through large sliding windows. The menu changes regularly, but some favourites are constant, such as the blueberry cheese-cake and blueberry lemonade. Portions are quite small, with a focus on quality over quantity.

NOTTINGHAM ROAD: Linga Lapa RR
Steakhouse
Nottingham Road Exit 132, 3280
Tel *033 266 7001*
Linga Lapa is famous for its quality mature steaks, relaxed atmosphere and warm fires. The monthly barbecue is highly recommended.

PIETERMARITZBURG: The Fat Aubergine R
Bistro **Road Map** E3
155 Boom St, 3201
Tel *033 342 3046* **Closed** *Sat, Sun*
Everything is fresh: smoked salmon, locally-grown herbs and vegetables, Cape cheeses, Dargle Valley trout and pork from the Drakensberg – all used to make delicious tarts, salads and wraps.

PIETERMARITZBURG: Saki Pacific Grill R
Asian **Road Map** E3
137 Victoria Rd, 3201
Tel *033 342 6999*
Saki Pacific Grill offers a sushi bar and fabulous Pacific Rim cuisine, incorporating Thai, Indonesian and Japanese dishes, in relaxed but contemporary surroundings.

PIETERMARITZBURG: Traffords RR
European **Road Map** E3
43 Miller St, 3201
Tel *033 394 4364* **Closed** *Sun, Mon*
The à la carte menu in this eatery in an elegant Victorian house follows the seasons and the wine list changes with it. Three dining rooms perfect for small groups.

PORT ST JOHNS: Delicious Monster R
Seafood **Road Map** E4
Second Beach, 5120
Tel *083 997 9856* **Closed** *Sun*
Delicious, fresh linefish and mussels, prawns and crayfish, when in season, are served at this New-age restaurant. Vegetarians are well catered for with the meze platter and falafel shwarmas.

DK Choice

TWEEDIE: Snooty Fox RR
French **Road Map** E3
Fern Hill Hotel, 3255
Tel *033 330 5071*
Hearty breakfasts, filling pub lunches and romantic candle-lit dinners are available at this 5-star country hotel, built in Tudor style. The legendary Sunday carveries are highly recommended, to be enjoyed next to a log fire on a chilly day, or on the outside thatched deck on fine, warm days.

Ocean views at Grazia in East London, serving sophisticated Italian fare

UNDERBERG: Lemon Tree   R
Bistro   **Road Map** E3
Clock Tower Centre, Main Rd, 3257
Tel *031 701 1589*
The menu at this homely venue includes venison pie, deboned rainbow trout and kudu. Croissants are baked daily; the toasted sandwiches are excellent.

UNDERBERG:
The Old Hatchery   R
Portuguese   **Road Map** E3
Drakensberg Gardens Rd, 3257
Tel *081 011 6311*
Popular restaurant-cum-bar with a cosy fireplace and a big-screen TV for sports events. Barbecue on the deck is a Saturday special, with prawns, espetada and peri-peri chicken. The à la carte menu has vegetarian options.

WINTERTON: The Pig and
Plough   R
Bistro   **Road Map** E3
R74, Winterton, 3340
Tel *036 488 1542*
Great coffee, light meals and wood-oven pizzas are offered at this family-oriented farm shop and deli. There is a fenced-in play area and children can pet the farm animals. Freshly baked goods are available daily.

WINTERTON: The Waffle Hut   R
Café   **Road Map** E3
KwaZulu Weavers, R600, Champagne Valley, 3340
Tel *036 448 1500*
Connected to the KwaZulu Weavers Co-op, The Waffle Hut specializes in sweet and savoury waffles and pancakes. It serves breakfasts, light lunches and a special children's menu. Food can be taken away.

Durban and Zululand

BALLITO: Al Pescatore   RR
Italian   **Road Map** F3
14 Edward Place, 4420
Tel *032 946 3574*
Quality and consistency have kept this restaurant on the map since 1989. The seafood is some of the best around and the Fisherman pizza is amazing. Finish with Rose's cheesecake.

BALLITO: MO-ZAM-BIK   RR
Portuguese   **Road Map** F3
4 Boulevard Centre, Compensation Rd, 4420
Tel *032 946 0979*
The quirky menu here includes delectable fish topped with a variety of different sauces, grilled

Moyo uShaka, offering an authentic African experience

prawns, succulent marinated chicken and the traditional espatada, trinchado and prego rolls.

DURBAN: The Hops   R
International   **Road Map** F3
Riverside Hotel & Spa, 10 Kenneth Kaunda Rd, 4065
Tel *031 573 1657*
Featuring splendid views of the ocean, The Hops offers an affordable menu with burgers, seafood and steaks as well as interesting salads and wraps. Pub baskets with finger food for sharing are available as well.

DURBAN: Circus Circus
Beach Café   RR
Café
Snell Parade, Bay of Plenty, 4001
Tel *031 337 7700*
Circus Circus is ideally located on the promenade with great sea views. Salads, Lebanese flatbreads and gourmet burgers are popular menu items and there are some good vegetarian options as well.

DURBAN: 9th Avenue Bistro RRR
International   **Road Map** F3
2 Avonmore Centre, 9th Avenue, Morningside, 4001
Tel *031 312 9134*   **Closed** *Sun*
This unpretentious venue offers a warm welcome and innovative cosmopolitan cuisine. The emphasis is on quality seasonal produce and dishes are exquisitely presented. The six-course tasting menu is a treat.

DURBAN: Cargo Hold   RRR
Seafood   **Road Map** F3
1 King Shaka Avenue, Point, 4001
Tel *031 328 8065*
Nestling at the stern of the Phantom Ship at uShaka Marine World, with direct views into a shark tank, Cargo Hold specializes in delicious seafood.

DK Choice

DURBAN: Moyo uShaka   RRR
African   **Road Map** F3
1 Bell St, uShaka Marine World, Point, 4001
Tel *031 332 0606*
African flavours rule here. You can build your own starter platters with anything from *biltong* to molasses-grilled calamari, kofte to prawn samosas, snoek pâté to springbok carpaccio. Prawn and mussel feasts are popular, as are tagines, curries and grilled Karoo lamb.

DURBAN: Roma Revolving
Restaurant   RRR
Italian   **Road Map** F3
32nd Floor, John Ross House, Margret Mncadi Avenue, 4001
Tel *031 337 6707*   **Closed** *Sun*
Situated 105 m (350 ft) above sea level, Roma gently revolves for 360-degree views of the city. The cuisine is based on Italian fare, with a good mix of seafood and game dishes.

ESHOWE: Shakaland   RR
African   **Road Map** F3
Normanhurst Farm, Nkwalini, 3816
Tel *035 460 0912*
This buffet restaurant is made up of two giant beehive domes. The buffet is prepared in three-legged pots on an open fire. Dishes include wild spinach, stews and barbecued meat.

PORT EDWARD: Clearwater Café
and Trails   R
Café   **Road Map** E4
Clearwater Farm, D595, 4295
Tel *083 549 6710*
A range of breakfasts and light lunches, as well as freshly baked cakes, are offered at this alfresco café. Milkshakes and soda floats come in many flavours, topped with a scoop of vanilla ice cream.

For more information on types of restaurants *see pp392–3*

RAMSGATE: Burlesque Café R
European   **Road Map** E4
957 Marine Drive, 4285
Tel *039 314 9886*
This is one of the most quirky places to dine on the South Coast, with vintage French café-style interiors. Expect seasonal, organic, Mediterranean food with a strong vegetarian slant, including meze, tapas, pasta and seafood.

RAMSGATE: The Waffle House R
Café   **Road Map** E4
839 Marine Drive, 4285
Tel *039 314 9424*
Located at the edge of Ramsgate lagoon, this café offers savoury and sweet waffles with a wide range of toppings. Favourites include ham, cheese and tomato, hummus and chocolate chip. Salads are available, too.

RAMSGATE: Flavours RR
International   **Road Map** E4
The Bistro Village, 1303 Marine Drive, 4285
Tel *039 314 4370*
This low-key, award-winning restaurant serves a varied range of classic dishes from around the world. Try the maple syrup-glazed duck breast or the herbed kingklip with prawns. There is outside seating in a lush garden.

SCOTTBURGH: Enzo Pizzeria R
Italian   **Road Map** E4
Shop 5, Marine Drive, 4180
Tel *039 978 3674*
A family-run trattoria, Enzo Pizzeria offers value-for-money pasta, salads, grilled fish and meat dishes, as well as delicious pizzas. The varied desserts include tiramisu, chocolate mouse and crème brûlée. The home-made sangria is recommended.

ST LUCIA: Alfredo's Restaurant R
Italian   **Road Map** F3
54 McKenzie St, 3936
Tel *035 590 1150*   **Closed** *Sun*
Specializing in Italian cuisine, this family-run restaurant offers a variety of pasta dishes, veal, fresh fish, excellent steaks, chicken, pizzas and desserts

ST LUCIA: Reef and Dune R
International   **Road Map** F3
51 McKenzie St, 3936
Tel *035 590 1048*
Pasta, grilled meat dishes, fish and wood-fired oven pizzas are offered at this lively restaurant and sports bar. There is a big-screen TV for sporting events and outside seating under thatch.

UMHLANGA ROCKS: Lord Prawn RR
Seafood   **Road Map** F3
Umhlanga Plaza, 2 Lagoon Drive, 4319
Tel *031 561 1133*
Combine grilled prawns with linefish, oysters, poussin or crayfish to create generous platters. There are also pasta dishes, curries and steak. The decor is modelled on rustic thatched beach huts.

UMHLANGA ROCKS: The Grill Room RRR
Seafood   **Road Map** F3
The Oyster Box, 2 Lighthouse Rd, 4319
Tel *031 514 5000*
A true fine-dining restaurant, the menu here boasts a wide selection of freshly caught seafood, and the exceptional wine cellar offers a superb choice of national and international vintages.

UMHLANGA ROCKS: Ile Maurice RRR
French–Mauritian   **Road Map** F3
9 McCausland Crescent, 4319
Tel *031 561 7606*   **Closed** *Mon*
Established in 1976, this old-school, fine-dining restaurant serves great, authentic dishes, including linefish in a tomato and coconut sauce and quail stuffed with rice and fruit. There is a fine wine list and the service is excellent.

UMHLANGA ROCKS: The Sugar Club RRR
International   **Road Map** F3
Beverly Hills Hotel, Lighthouse Rd, 4319
Tel *031 561 2211*
This stylish restaurant offers a romantic setting with superb views of the Indian Ocean. The gourmet fusion cuisine makes use of quality local produce, and the Sunday lunches are sumptuous.

Gauteng and Sun City

JOHANNESBURG: Da Vicenzo R
Italian   **Road Map** E2
29 Montrose Rd, Barbeque Downs, Kyalami, 1684
Tel *011 466 2618*   **Closed** *Mon*
Enjoy authentic food in a country setting at Da Vicenzo. Everything is prepared fresh each day, and special dietary requirements can be accommodated. Among the most popular dishes are the oysters, crab, rabbit, and lamb on the bone.

Gourmet dining at The Grill Room, situated in the Oyster Box hotel, Umhlanga Rocks

DK Choice

JOHANNESBURG: Fisherman's Plate R
Taiwanese   **Road Map** E2
18 Derrick Avenue, Cyrildene, 2198
Tel *011 622 0480*
On a busy, intoxicating strip in Chinatown lined with supermarkets and little eateries, Fisherman's Plate is a legendary spot. It offers authentic cuisine, with particularly good seafood such as curried prawns. The kitchen closes by 9pm.

JOHANNESBURG: Fruits 'n' Roots R
Vegetarian   **Road Map** E2
Hobart Corner Shopping Centre, Bryanston, 2191
Tel *011 463 2928*   **Closed** *Sun*
This is a health-food store and vegetarian restaurant. Enjoy the daily buffet or pop in for an organic coffee with a freshly baked treat, such as gluten-free carrot cake.

JOHANNESBURG: Leafy Greens Café R
Vegan   **Road Map** E2
Rocky Ridge Rd, Muldersdrift, 1739
Tel *010 595 4563*   **Closed** *Mon, Tue*
Johannesburg's first raw vegan café offers an à la carte menu and a buffet lunch at weekends. Even the desserts are raw and are free of refined sugar and dairy.

JOHANNESBURG: Parea R
Greek   **Road Map** E2
Shop 3D, Corlett Drive, Illovo, 2196
Tel *010 595 4563*
Good-value, delicious fare includes kleftiko (slow-baked lamb), souvlaki, lamb chops in lemon and rosemary, and a good meze selection. There is traditional entertainment on Friday and Saturday nights.

JOHANNESBURG: Tashas Café R
Café   **Road Map** E2
Oxford Road, Rosebank, 2196
Tel *011 447 7972*
This trendy restaurant's decor is inspired by New York, and attention to detail is key. There are two menus, one that offers café classics and the other 'Inspired by' menu features New York favourites.

JOHANNESBURG: Topo Gigio R
Italian   **Road Map** E2
12 Gleneagles Rd, Greenside, 2193
Tel *011 646 9573*
At this casual spot on the Greenside strip tables spill out onto the pavement. Perennial favourites include pizzas and pasta dishes, but there are also Mediterranean meat, chicken and fish specialities.

JOHANNESBURG: 33 High Street RR
Portuguese   **Road Map** E2
33 High St, Modderfontein, 1609
Tel *011 608 0733*   **Closed** *Mon*
Some of the best Mozambique-influenced Portuguese food in South Africa is served at this old colonial-style venue with lush gardens, that are great for alfresco dining. Good bread, exquisite salads and tasty grills.

JOHANNESBURG: Werner's Bistro RR
European   **Road Map** E2
25 Boeing Rd West, Bedfordview, 2008
Tel *011 615 0460*
This very popular restaurant offers European fare as well as South African dishes. Private rooms are available for special occasions or groups, and the garden is a great spot for drinks.

JOHANNESBURG: Browns of Rivonia RRR
International   **Road Map** E2
21 Wessel Rd, Rivonia, 2128
Tel *011 803 7533*   **Closed** *Sun*
This old farmhouse has a sunny garden for summer and an open fire inside for cooler evenings. The exquisite wine and cheese selection, seafood and venison options have won the restaurant several awards.

JOHANNESBURG: Bukhara RRR
Indian   **Road Map** E2
Nelson Mandela Square, cnr of West St and Naude St, Sandton, 2196
Tel *011 883 5555*
Enjoy succulent meats cooked in the charcoal tandoor and aromatic curries at this superb gourmet North Indian restaurant. Diners can watch the chefs at work in the glass-fronted kitchen.

JOHANNESBURG: The Butcher Shop & Grill RRR
Steakhouse   **Road Map** E2
Nelson Mandela Square, Corner of West St and Naude St, Sandton, 219
Tel *011 784 8676*
An atmospheric setting for one of South Africa's top steakhouses. Rump, fillet, ribeye and T-bones are hand-cut to suit the diner, and come with delicious sauces.

JOHANNESBURG: Cube Tasting Kitchen RRR
International
24 Albrecht St, 2043
Tel *082 422 8158*   **Closed** *Sun, Mon*
The 12-course tasting menu here changes every couple of months, and the open-plan kitchen encourages interaction with the chefs as each course is explained.

DK Choice

JOHANNESBURG: Les Delices de France RRR
French   **Road Map** E2
2 Keith Avenue, Roodepoort, 1709
Tel *011 027 8668*   **Closed** *Mon*
This cosy restaurant serves authentic food in a modern style. The high-quality produce is sourced personally by the French owners. The menu is small but carefully put together and there is a daily changing selection of cheeses. The wine list features champagne and other French wines, along with Cape classics.

JOHANNESBURG: Moyo Melrose Arch RRR
African   **Road Map** E2
Shop 5, High St, Melrose Arch, 2196
Tel *011 684 1477*
Set over four levels in a spectacular building with mosaics and African art, this restaurant's extensive menu includes dishes from around the continent.

PRETORIA: Burger Bistro R
American   **Road Map** E2
Corner of 24th and Pierneef St, 0186
Tel *012 756 5286*   **Closed** *Mon*
This hamburger joint with 1950s decor and a cool vibe has perfected the pattie, from simple and vegetarian to exotic and gourmet. Try the Marilyn Monroe with melted Brie, strawberry-balsamic and black pepper jam.

PRETORIA: Café Riche R
Café   **Road Map** E2
2 Church Square, 0002
Tel *012 328 3173*
A charming Art Nouveau-style building houses the oldest café in Pretoria serving salads and filled baguettes. The pub lunch is great value for money.

DK Choice

PRETORIA: La Madeleine RR
French–Belgian   **Road Map** E2
122 Priory Rd, Lynnwood Ridge, 0081
Tel *012 361 3667*   **Closed** *Mon*
Portions are generous and the atmosphere is relaxed at this award-winning restaurant that offers classic cuisine at affordable prices. There is no written menu and the chef visits each table to describe the ever-changing dishes of the day. The three-course Sunday lunch is very popular.

PRETORIA: Mosaic at the Orient RRR
European   **Road Map** E2
The Orient Boutique Hotel, Crocodile River Valley, Elandsfontein
Tel *012 371 2902*   **Closed** *Mon, Tue*
Fine dining in a unique Art Nouveau setting. Award-winning chef Chantel Dartnall always meets the diners to explain the menu. The wine cellar contains more than 40,000 bottles.

Beautiful stained glass in the Tiffany dining room, Mosaic at the Orient, Pretoria

For more information on types of restaurants *see pp392–3*

Sakhumzi, serving up typical local fare in a historic Soweto setting

PRETORIA: Prue Leith **RRR**
International **Road Map** E2
262 Rhino St, Centurion, 0157
Tel *012 654 5203* **Closed** *Sun–Tue*
Housed in the Prue Leith College
of Food & Wine, this is a training
academy for aspiring chefs and
catering staff. Daily lessons
dictate what's on the menu,
which consists of delicious,
high-quality fare prepared to
a superb standard.

SOWETO: Sakhumzi **R**
South African **Road Map** E2
6980 Vilakazi St, Orlando West, 1804
Tel *011 536 1379*
Located on historic Vilakazi
Street, where the first homes
of Nelson Mandela and Bishop
Tutu are found, Sakhumzi
restaurant and cocktail bar
offers typical township
streetfood and ambience.

SOWETO: Wandie's Place **R**
South African **Road Map** E2
618 Makhalemele St,
Dube Village, 1800
Tel *011 982 2796*
Meals are buffet style at this cosy
eatery in Soweto township.
They feature grilled and roasted
meats, and specialities such as
dumplings, *ting* (soft porridge)
and *umqushu* (grits and beans).
There is a large selection of
salads, making this a popular
venue for vegetarians.

STERKFONTEIN: Greensleeves
Medieval Kingdom **RRR**
English **Road Map** E2
Hekpoort Rd, R563, 1739
Tel *082 602 2958*
A medieval-themed banqueting
experience, with spit-roast beef
and whole chickens served on
platters. Live entertainment by the
Baron and his Troubadours adds to
the fun. Open Friday and Saturday
evenings and for Sunday lunch.

SUN CITY: The Sun Terrace **R**
International **Road Map** D2
Sun City Hotel, 0316
Tel *014 557 1211*
The vast lunch buffet at this
eatery and lounge features
specialities from across the
globe, including meat, poultry,
seafood and vegetarian options.
It is an ideal place in which to
unwind over a relaxed meal.
Booking is essential.

SUN CITY: The Grill Room **RR**
Steakhouse **Road Map** D2
Sun City Hotel, 0316
Tel *014 557 4307*
A classic New York steakhouse
menu is served in this traditional
setting overlooking the Palace
lakes. The Grill Room is famous
for serving the best steaks at
Sun City, with an excellent wine
list to match.

SUN CITY: Bocado **RRR**
Mediterranean **Road Map** D2
Cascades Hotel, 0316
Tel *014 5575850*
This restaurant on the Cascades
Hotel's pool deck offers a
wide selection of delicious
Mediterranean dishes such
as kleftiko (slow-baked lamb),
meze platters with fresh oysters
and other seafood specialities.
There is also a special menu
for children.

SUN CITY: Crystal Court **RRR**
International **Road Map** D2
The Palace of the Lost City, 0316
Tel *014 557 4307*
Superbly prepared and varied
cuisine with African influences
is offered in this sophisticated
and elegant setting with tall
ceilings and long windows. The
breakfast buffet is fabulous and
the lavish High Tea spread has
become a delightful attraction
in its own right.

Limpopo, Mpumalanga and Kruger

GRASKOP: Harrie's Pancakes **R**
Café **Road Map** F2
Cnr Louis Trichardt and Church sts,
1270
Tel *013 767 1273*
This popular lunch spot serves
meal-sized pancakes stuffed with
a variety of sweet and savoury
fillings – try the *bobotie* or the
banana with caramel.

GRASKOP: Canimambo
Restaurante **RR**
Portuguese **Road Map** F2
Cnr Louis Trichardt and Hoof sts, 1270
Tel *013 767 1868*
Try bean stew, espetada and piri-
piri prawns at this family-run
venue serving Mozambican
Portuguese food. The wine list
includes Portuguese wines.

HAZYVIEW: Kuka **RR**
African **Road Map** F2
Perry's Bridge Trading Post, R40, 1242
Tel *013 7376 957*
All-day breakfasts, wraps, seafood
combos and curries, and
delicious cocktails can be
enjoyed at this modern, bright
Afro-chic restaurant.

DK Choice

HAZYVIEW: Pioneer's Butcher
& Grill **RR**
Steakhouse **Road Map** F2
Rendezvous Tourism Centre, 1242
Tel *013 737 7397*
At this modern restaurant the
speciality is in-house aged roasts,
steaks and other grills but there
are fish and vegetarian dishes,
too. There is also a lounge and
bar with large-screen TV for
sports events. Children are well
catered for with their own
menu and a playroom.

HAZYVIEW: Tides Seafood
Diner **RR**
Seafood **Road Map** F2
Rendezvous Tourism Centre, 1242
Tel *013 737 8087* **Closed** *Sun*
Pancakes, wraps, salads, seafood
combos and popular seafood
platters, along with ice-cold beer
on tap, are offered here. There is
also a children's menu.

NELSPRUIT: Saffron **RR**
Mediterranean **Road Map**
Chez Vincent Guesthouse, 56 Ferreira
St, 1201
Tel *013 744 1146* **Closed** *Sun*
This guesthouse restaurant
specializes in tapas dishes from

all around the Mediterranean, matched with wines from an interesting, well-priced list.

SWAZILAND: eDladleni Swazi Restaurant R
Swazi **Road Map** F2
Off the MR3, Ezulwini Valley
Tel 268 404 5743
In a wooden log building set among the trees, this restaurant serves traditional fare. There is an outside deck and on cool evenings a log fire is lit inside.

SWAZILAND: Ramblas Restaurant RR
International **Road Map** F2
Mantsholo Road, Mbabane
Tel 268 2404 4147 **Closed** *Sun*
Specializing in seafood, Ramblas also serves pizzas, salads and home-baked cakes. There are also combo platters for sharing.

WHITE RIVER: Magnolia RR
International **Road Map** F2
Casterbridge Lifestyle Centre, cnr Hazyview Rd (R40) and Numbi Rd (R538), 2809
Tel 013 751 1947
Set in lovely manicured gardens, this upmarket bistro draws on a range of global cuisines, while still retaining a local flavour.

WHITE RIVER: Oliver's RR
Mediterranean **Road Map** F2
Pine Lake Drive, White River Country Estate, 1240
Tel 013 750 0479
Mediterranean cuisine with an Austrian touch. Try the venison platter of kudu, eland and gemsbok, or the prawn risotto.

North and South of the Orange

BLOEMFONTEIN: Seven on Kellner R
International **Road Map** D3
7 Kellner St, Westdene, 9332
Tel 051 447 7928 **Closed** *Sun*
Fine dining coupled with friendly service are the hallmarks of this venue set in a beautiful Victorian mansion with eclectic decor.

BLOEMFONTEIN: De Oude Kraal Country Estate & Spa RRR
International **Road Map** D3
35 km (22 miles) S of Bloemfontein, exit 153 on the N1 to Cape Town, 9301
Tel 051 564 0733
The dinner buffet, six-course set menu and excellent wine list provide adventures in gastronomy at this farmhouse that has high ceilings and wooden floors, open fires and antique furniture.

GRAAFF-REINET: Blue Magnolia Coffee Shop R
Café **Road Map** C4
3 Muller St, 6280
Tel 049 891 0792 **Closed** *Sun*
Breakfasts and light lunches, as well as freshly baked cakes and Illy coffee, are served here. There is alfresco seating on a bright patio.

GRAAFF-REINET: The Coldstream Restaurant R
International **Road Map** C4
3 Church St, 6280
Tel 049 891 1181 **Closed** *Sun*
This restaurant is housed in the building of the second-oldest men's club in the country (1875). The varied menu includes seafood, steak and vegetarian dishes.

GRAAFF-REINET: Pioneers Restaurant RR
South African **Road Map** C4
3 Parsonage St, 6280
Tel 049 8926059
Housed in a National Monument building, guests can choose to sit in any one of the four dining rooms or outside in the garden. There is traditional food on offer and a few adventurous dishes.

DK Choice

GRAAFF-REINET: Gordon's Restaurant RRR
Karoo **Road Map** C4
Andries Stockenström Guest House, 100 Cradock St, 6280
Tel 049 892 4575
Owner and chef Gordon Wright attracts national and international clients with his fine four-course dinners. Slow Karoo food is a passion here and the dinners are legendary. The menu is never the same, but one starter on offer is whiskey-and-honey-infused baked guinea fowl samosa with mango chilli salsa and rocket.

DK Choice

KIMBERLEY: Copper Oryx RR
South African **Road Map** D3
Kimberley Anne Hotel, 60 Mac Douglass St, 8301
Tel 053 492 0004
The Swiss trained chef at this establishment combines international cuisine with South African flavours, which offers a true fine-dining experience. The menu is limited but everything is freshly prepared. The Wild Coast fish pot is recommended and the baked aubergine stuffed with Cape Malay curry is a good vegetarian option.

KIMBERLEY: Rhodes Grill Restaurant RRR
International **Road Map** D3
The Kimberley Club, 72 Du Toitspan Rd, 9320
Tel 053 832 4224
Fine food is served in the elegant dining room of this renovated gentleman's club. Traditional and modern dishes include T-bone steaks, Karoo lamb and eisbein.

NIEU BETHESDA: The Ibis Lounge RR
International **Road Map** C4
Martin St, 6286
Tel 082 442 3174
A standard menu of burgers, pitas, steaks, pasta and curry is supplemented by tasty, fresh-baked bread, muffins and cakes and a range of speciality coffees.

UPINGTON: BI-LO R
Bistro **Road Map** A3
9 Green Point Rd, 8801
Tel 054 3380616
A casual, good-value eatery and pub. The ostrich steak is excellent and the lamb chops are recommended. Outdoor seating offers views of wildlife roaming in the neighbouring ranch.

Elegant decor at Ramblas in Swaziland

For more information on types of restaurants *see pp392–3*

SHOPPING IN SOUTH AFRICA

South Africa's principal shopping attraction is, undoubtedly, its superb range of handcrafted goods, as well as jewellery made from locally-mined gold, inlaid with precious or semi-precious stones. Intricate beadwork, woven rugs and carpets, decorative baskets, stone and woodcarvings, wood-and-bone spoons and traditional, flowing African garments with geometric motifs are sold at curio shops and markets countrywide. Crafters from the rest of Africa, attracted by South Africa's thriving tourism industry, frequent markets in the larger centres, selling, for example, ceremonial wooden masks and malachite bracelets. All manner of other handiwork can be found in crafts markets, too, from windchimes, wooden beach chairs and painted duvet covers to African chili sauces and leather goods.

Eye-catching works in malachite

Shopping Hours

City shopping malls have extended hours, staying open until around 9pm for the convenience of their patrons, while most small-town shops observe the nine-to-five rule. Village shops may even close at noon; siestas are still very much a part of rural South Africa. Outdoor flea markets usually begin trading around 10am and end at sunset.

How to Pay

Credit cards such as Visa and MasterCard are readily accepted in malls and city shops. Small shops and informal traders prefer cash. In remote areas and rural villages, it is advisable to carry cash in a concealed wallet or pouch. After hours, most banks (and many petrol stations and shopping malls) have automatic teller machines (ATMs) that allow you to make withdrawals with your credit card or international ATM card.

Bargaining

African traders are prepared to bargain hard, mostly because they would rather make a sale than lose one. Indian salespeople also enjoy haggling over prices and seem to expect a little resistance from their customers.

VAT

Most goods (except basic foodstuffs) are subject to 14 per cent Value Added Tax (VAT), included in the price. Any shop (though not informal markets) can issue a VAT receipt. Departing tourists can reclaim the 14 per cent on their purchases (very worthwhile for expensive items such as jewellery) at VAT reclaim desks at the international airports (Johannesburg, Cape Town and Durban), or at border posts. The procedure is explained on the government's **Tax Refunds for Tourists** website.

Victoria Wharf Shopping Centre, Cape Town

Refunds

If the merchandise you have bought is defective in any way, you are entitled to a refund. If you decide that you don't like an item, you may have to settle for a credit note or an exchange. In general, the larger the store, the more protected you are. If you are unhappy with the service, talk to the customer services department or the manager.

Where to Shop

Large shopping malls are found in all cities and towns, and feature everything from giant chain stores to small speciality boutiques. These have not, however, forced out the smaller high street shops, where specialist book, fashion and wine stores jostle with delis

Street vendors display their goods outside The Workshop Mall in Durban *(see pp286–9)*

and art studios. When shop-keepers don't have shops, they take to the streets: large flea markets are found in all major centres, and hawkers and craftspeople ply their wares on pavements along major thoroughfares, selling everything from sweets and fruit to souvenirs and home furnishings. South Africa's rural areas are dotted with arts and crafts markets and farm stalls selling local produce.

Shipping Packages

The post office *(see pp434–5)* will send parcels of up to 30 kg (66 lb) to the UK, Australia and New Zealand, and up to 20 kg (44 lb) to the United States. They may not be larger than 2.5 sq metres (8 sq feet). Surface mail will take 6–8 weeks; airmail one week. The post office offers additional insurance and "track and trace" options and also operates its own local and international courier service known as EMS (Expedited Mail Service).

Many upmarket stores will arrange all packaging and shipping. To organize your own exports, contact one of the courier companies, such as **DHL**, or a shipper such as **Trans Global Cargo Pty Ltd**. They will arrange customs and packaging, and will deliver to your home or the office of their local agent. There is no maximum or minimum size or weight, and prices are competitive.

A bottle of wine to suit any taste

Swaziland is a treasure trove of woven baskets and mats

Strictly South African

In Johannesburg and other large cities, you can buy almost anything. Johannesburg in particular attracts consumers from all over the subcontinent. It is the queen of mall culture, and the best place to find indigenous arts and crafts. However, much of the wood and stone carving is from West and Central Africa and Zimbabwe.

The crafts in Durban *(see pp286–9)* and KwaZulu-Natal *(see pp262–3)*, on the other hand, are more likely to be local. Zulu baskets are usually of outstanding quality, as are the woven beer strainers, grass brooms, pots, shields and drums. Sometimes brightly coloured baskets are made from telephone wire.

These wares, as well as many charming and often brightly painted wooden animal and bird figures, can be bought on the side of the N2 highway from Durban to the game parks: Hluhluwe-Imfolozi and uMkhuze. Gazankulu and Venda also have a reputation for crafts.

Clay pots with distinctive angular designs in gleaming silver and ochre are popular, as are the woodcarvings, tapestries, fabrics and batiks.

Ndebele bead blankets, belts, aprons and dolls are also worth looking out for *(see p324)*. They can be found at most of the crafts markets, especially in the northern parts of the country. Knysna *(see pp244–5)* is yet another craftwork "capital". A major timber centre, this is the place to buy stinkwood

and yellowwood chairs and tables, door knobs and other unusual decor accessories. Colourful woven mohair blankets, shawls, cushion covers and jackets are also found in this region.

The label "Scarab Paper" represents a truly unique South African craft: handmade paper, notelets and cards in nation-wide crafts and curio stores are produced from (now fragrance-free) elephant dung!

Swazi candles are also sold countrywide: look out for the distinctive "stained-glass" effect of these slow-burning bright candles in animal, bird and more traditional candle shapes.

Throughout the country, gift stores and jewellers offer an unusual array of necklaces, rings, earrings and bracelets, using local diamonds and semi-precious stones, often combined with South African gold and platinum.

DIRECTORY

VAT

Tax Refunds for Tourists
Tel 011 979 0055.
w taxrefunds.co.za

Shipping Packages

DHL
Tel 011 921 3666.
w dhl.co.za

Trans Global Cargo Pty Ltd
Tel 011 230 1620.
w trans-global.co.za

ENTERTAINMENT IN SOUTH AFRICA

In the three main cities – Johannesburg, Cape Town and Durban – people party as hard as they work. There is always something happening and the choices of entertainment vary from nightclubs and stadium concerts to community theatre and gallery openings. This does not mean, however, that other South African cities and towns are dull. Even rural places have music, restaurant and clubbing venues. The demand for cinemas and casinos is high, and exciting new venues are opened regularly. The dramatic arts are innovative and of a very high standard, with theatre companies committed to the development of a local arts culture. The vibrant music scene spans classical, jazz and African genres.

The Oude Libertas amphitheatre, Stellenbosch *(see p41)*

Information

For details of entertainment in the cities, check the local daily press and the weekly papers, such as the *Mail & Guardian*, available nationwide. They review and list theatre productions, current film festivals, art exhibitions, music performances and other interesting events.

Reviews and listings also appear on a number of websites – that of *Cape Town Magazine* in Cape Town (www.capetown magazine.com); JHBLive in Johannesburg (www.jhblive.com); and Durban Live in Durban (www.durban live.com) are good places to start. However, the best source of information is Computicket *(see below)*.

Booking Tickets

Computicket is South Africa's nationwide booking agency for all concerts, plays and live performances, plus cinema, events and sports fixtures. It has a comprehensive website for booking online or you can phone its call centre. In addition, tickets can be purchased via mobile phone using the Computicket mobisite, or by visiting one of its branches in major shopping malls or at any Shoprite or Checkers super-market. Tickets can be collected from these outlets or printed at home.

A credit or debit card is required, which also means you can book tickets before arriving in South Africa. However, cash is also accepted at the outlets, and tickets can be purchased directly at the venues.

Cinema

Mainstream Hollywood film productions are the main fare – South Africa's film industry is still in the fledgling stage, and there is relatively little demand for foreign-language films with subtitles. The cities host regular film festivals whose themes range from French, Italian and Dutch to natural health, the environment and gay and lesbian. Multi-screen **Ster-Kinekor** and **Nu Metro** cinema complexes are found in larger shopping malls.

Theatre, Opera and Dance

Comedy, satire, cabaret and musicals are particularly

Dancers at the National Arts Festival in Grahamstown *(see p43)*

"Cross Roads", Rupert Museum, Stellenbosch

popular in South Africa, as are modernized and "localized" adaptations of Shakespeare.

Arts Alive, a Johannesburg festival held in September, is a major celebration of the performing arts. The FNB Dance Umbrella, held in Johannesburg in February and March, is an important platform for new choreographers. The National Arts Festival *(see p43)*, held in Grahamstown in July, is the best place to go for an overview of innovative, exciting South African theatre, dance, artistic and musical talent.

Opera, too, is well supported, especially in Cape Town, where the Cape Town Opera *(see p174)* performs at the Artscape Theatre Centre from May to September. Artscape is also the main venue for the Cape Town City Ballet *(see p174)*.

Music

Symphony and classical orchestras are well supported in the cities: concerts are held in venues such as the Durban City Hall *(see p287)*, Cape Town's City Hall and the Johannesburg College of Music in Parktown.

Outdoor, twilight performances, for example at Durban's Botanic Gardens *(see p289)* and Kirstenbosch National Botanical Garden in Cape Town *(see pp164–5)*, are popular. Look out for the carols by candlelight events in the cities every December.

Nowadays, international bands, pop and opera singers regularly include South Africa on their world tours. Local bands offer a wide range of

sounds: rock, jazz, gospel, reggae, rap and Afro-fusion. The members of the popular Soweto String Quartet charm audiences with their unique compositions and African-flavoured interpretations of classical pieces.

Local rock bands such as Springbok Nude Girls and Parlotones enjoy a loyal following, and appear at clubs countrywide. Check the listings guides and local radio stations for details of gigs and venues.

Music from the rest of Africa is filtering down to South Africa, and clubs are rocking to sounds from Ghana, Mali and Benin.

Art

Johannesburg, Durban, Cape Town, Port Elizabeth and Bloemfontein, as well as some of the larger towns such as Knysna, have excellent art galleries. These showcase local and international works, from the traditional to the

Merry-go-round at the Carousel Casino, close to Gauteng

somewhat more bizarre, from ceramics and photography to multimedia works and installations. Exhibitions change regularly, and openings are popular social events, with high-profile speakers as well as a buffet and drinks.

Gaming

South Africa has more than 40 casinos in large entertainment complexes on the fringes of most major centres. They are typically designed around a lavish theme and include hotels, restaurants and bars and a range of activities for the whole family. Among the most popular is the famed Sun City in the North West province *(see p326)* and Gold Reef City, Montecasino and Emperor's Palace in Johannesburg. In Durban, the Sun Coast Casino has its own private beach in addition to the gaming offerings. More than a dozen of these casino complexes are operated by **Sun International**.

Gaming tables include black-jack, roulette, poker and punto banco. Larger casinos usually have a *salon privé*, in addition to a hall of slot machines.

DIRECTORY

Booking Tickets

Computicket
Tel 0861 915 8000.
W online.computicket.com

Cinemas

Nu Metro
W numetro.co.za

Ster-Kinekor
W sterkinekor.com

Gaming

Sun International
Tel 011 780 7855.
W suninternational.com

SPECIAL-INTEREST HOLIDAYS

South Africa, with its moderate climate, long hours of sunshine, endless coastline and varied landscape, is a country that can provide a wide range of outdoor pursuits almost all year round. South Africans, in general, enjoy the great outdoors: during summer, visitors to Cape Town may well believe that the entire city is in training for forthcoming running and cycling marathons, as locals take to the streets to get fit. Activities go beyond competitive sports,

however. Whether it is canoeing on the Orange River, taking plant-hunting trips in the coastal forests of KwaZulu-Natal, mountaineering in the Drakensberg, bungee jumping along the Garden Route, board-sailing in the Western Cape or visiting historic battlefields and museums, there is something to interest everyone. Moreover, South Africa's fascinating multicultural past and present can be experienced at regional festivals *(see pp40–43)* and on special tours.

Hiking

Even the smallest farms in the most remote regions have laid-out trails, with distance-marked paths and maps provided upon booking and payment. Most overnight hikes are situated on private land or state reserves, with accommodation in rustic huts, with firewood, mattresses and cold-water washing facilities usually included. Favourite trails such as the four-night Otter Trail and four-night Tsitsikamma Trail *(see pp238–9)* need to be booked more than a year in advance. Most outdoor equipment stores are able to advise on day and longer hikes, and they also sell guide books, maps and trail provisions. **Green Flag Trails**, an arm of the Hiking Organization of Southern Africa (HOSA), lists and grades more than 100 accredited hiking trails

Kloofing, or madcap jumping, into pools, a new dimension of hiking

around the country, including descriptions, facilities available and reservation details.

Most private reserves and some of the provincial reserves and national parks offer guided game- and bird-watching rambles, as well as overnight bushveld and wilderness trails. The real attraction of these hikes, is the unrivalled experience of walking through the African bush, surrounded by the sounds and smells of its diverse fauna and flora.

The Kruger National Park *(see pp340–5)* offers at least seven such trails: the Bushman Trail includes finding rock paintings in the hill shelters. Due to the popularity of these walks, bookings should be made months in advance. Contact **South Africa National Parks (SANParks)** for details.

Rock Climbing and Kloofing

Rock climbing (whether traditional, sport or bouldering) has a large following in South Africa. Climbing equipment stores can provide enthusiasts with gear, information and route ideas. Some of the best traditional climbing is found in KwaZulu-Natal's Drakensberg *(see pp274–5)*, while Cape Town's Table Mountain *(see pp136–7)* offers interesting challenges for experienced climbers. Coming back down from the climb can take the form of a fast and thrilling abseil descent, or the Australian SAS-created counterpart, known as a rapp jump. This involves descending at high speed while facing forward with the rope attached to your back and your feet pounding down the rock face.

Hiking in KwaZulu-Natal

Kloofing (or canyoning) is an extreme adventure sport involving boulder hopping and wading while following the course of a river. It requires a good level of fitness and daring, since it includes long jumps into mountain pools, which can be dangerous. The **Mountain Club of South Africa** provides information for anyone tempted to try this activity.

Fishing

More than a million anglers enjoy the local waters, which are subject to strict regulations – enquire at the nearest police station. More than 250 species of fish can be caught through fly, line, game, surf or reef fishing. The merging of the cool Atlantic and the warm Indian oceans off the Southern Cape coast creates the conditions for a high concentration of game fish, including marlin and tuna. Mpumalanga and KwaZulu-Natal offer excellent trout fishing. Kalk Bay in Cape Town has one of the few line-fishing harbours in the world.

Almost all harbours and marinas offer the opportunity to join commercial or semi-commercial boats on short trips. In addition, many tour groups, including **Big Blue Fishing Charters** in Cape Town and **Lynski Fishing Charters** in Durban, offer fishing charters and expeditions.

Hot-air ballooning, for a fabulous view of the game

Air Sports

Throughout the country there are opportunities for ballooning, hang-gliding, microlighting and parachuting. With a good head for heights, there is no finer way to see the land than from the basket of a hot-air balloon. Flights are available at many locations, but some of the most popular are the trips over the Winelands or game parks. Early morning or late evening, when the thermals guarantee plenty of lift, are the best times to book. It is important to note that flights are sometimes cancelled due to too much or too little wind. Given the relative silence of the hot-air balloon, it's a wonderful way of getting a close view of big game animals. Contact **Airtrackers** for game-viewing trips in Pilanesberg Game Reserve (see p327) and **Bill Harrop's Original Balloon Safaris** for flights over the Magaliesberg Mountains (see p322) north of Johannesburg.

Helicopter rides are widely available and are an exciting way to take in the panorama of Cape Town and Table Mountain (see pp136–7). It is even possible to arrange a ride in a Huey ex-military helicopter.

Paragliding and hang-gliding courses (contact the **South African Hang Gliding and Paragliding Association**) and tandem flights are also popular. Bridge jumping and bungee jumping can be found on the Garden Route, including the spectacular 216-m (709-ft) Bloukrans Bungee Jump, which claims to be the highest

commercial challenge of its kind in the world. This is operated by **Face Adrenalin**, which also offers a bridge arch walk of Bloukrans Bridge.

Mountain biking in Knysna

Cycling

In South Africa even the cities offer spectacular cycling routes: at least 35,000 cyclists take part in the annual Cape Town Cycle Tour (the world's largest timed cycle race) around the Cape Peninsula (see pp122–3). Cycling organizations such as the **Pedal Power Association** and **Cycling South Africa** organize weekend rides, which often include off-road routes on otherwise out-of-bounds farmlands. Bikes can be rented in South Africa from numerous outlets in holiday regions such as Cape Town and along the coast. Tour operators can organize a variety of cycling tours – both off-road and on smooth tar – along the Garden Route, for example, and in the Karoo.

Sport fishing at Cape Vidal, in the iSimangaliso Wetland Park

A close encounter with a great white shark, while cage diving

Water Sports

South Africa has 2,500 km (1,553 miles) of coastline and many rivers. The coast is defined by a series of points and bays, and the country has some of the world's greatest surfing, which is a hugely popular pastime. Some of the best spots are at Jeffrey's Bay in the Eastern Cape, Muizenberg in Cape Town, the Golden Mile in Durban and up the West Coast. **Wavescape** is the leading authority on the sport and publishes daily surf reports, lists locations and even runs an annual surfing film festival.

Windsurfing and sailing are also popular, and many resorts rent out equipment. The beaches are also ideal for sand boarding, the land-based version of surfing, which takes advantage of the country's abundance of massive sand dunes.

Scuba diving is widely available – instructors should be accredited to the **National Association of Underwater Instructors** (NAUI) or **Professional Association of Diving Instructors** (PADI). South Africa's best diving site is Sodwana Bay in the iSimangaliso Wetland Park *(see pp300–301)* on KwaZulu-Natal's northern coast. This has the most southerly coral reef in the world, teeming with tropical fish, turtles, sharks and game fish. In Cape Town, wreck-diving and exploring kelp forests are popular activities.

Canoeing on the Orange River in the Northern Cape has a growing number of fans. Cape Town-based **Amanzi Trails** and **Umkulu** provide transport and both also have base camps on the river where you can park and leave luggage. Two-person inflatable canoes are used and nights are spent camping under the stars on the riverbanks, making for a gentle and relaxing trip.

One of the most popular sea-kayaking trips in South Africa is with **Kaskazi Kayaks** in Cape Town, who offer guided tours along the Atlantic Seaboard with the opportunity of spotting dolphins and sea birds. More exhilarating white-water rafting is offered by a number of tour operators around the country, and some of the best rivers for foamy rapids are the Vaal River (in Gauteng and the Free State), Blyde River (Mpumalanga), and the Umkomaas and Bushman's rivers (both in KwaZulu-Natal).

For the ultimate thrill, cage diving takes participants as close to a great white shark as they would ever wish to be. A popular venue is Shark Alley, near the village of Gansbaai *(see p228)*. Several guests at a time are lowered from a catamaran in a steel cage fitted with viewing ports. **White Shark Ventures** offer one- to 10-day tours that include accommodation and equipment hire. **Apex Shark Expeditions'** trips depart from Simon's Town, near Cape Town. They offer the smallest groups in the industry (6 to 12 people) and the longest trips.

Visitors enjoy pony-trekking in Lesotho *(see pp272–3)*

Horse Riding and Pony-Trekking

Equestrian options range from spending an hour or two ambling through vineyards to multi-day wilderness treks. Many private game reserves offer horseback safaris. For families, **Cape Nature** runs horse trails in the Goukamma, Anysberg and Marloth reserves in the Western Cape, as does **Ezemvelo KZN Wildlife** in the uKhahlamba-Drakensberg Park in KwaZulu-Natal.

Malealea Lodge & Pony-Trekking in Lesotho offers a real African experience. Guides accompany riders through unfenced landscapes to see

Canoeing on the Orange River *(see pp354–5)*

Nectar-feeding Malachite sunbird, with emerald plumage

dinosaur tracks or San rock art. Accommodation is in Basotho huts, with traditional food and dancing provided by the local people.

Bird-Watching, Flora and Fauna Trails

Blessed with a prodigious variety of indigenous birds, along with vast flocks of migratory birds that pass through during the colder European winters, South Africa is a bird-watchers' paradise. **BirdLife South Africa** provides checklists of the more than 800 species recorded in the country. It also recommends the best birding spots.

There is also a wide range of fauna to be seen. Seal or whale-watching *(see pp190–91)* are very popular along the coast, either from a boat or dry land with binoculars. Safaris or wilderness trails both offer an amazing opportunity to view wild animals and flora in their natural habitat, and are an essential part of any trip to South Africa, but it is essential to book well in advance *(see pp66–71)*.

Spectator Sports

For those who prefer watching to participating, world-class rugby and cricket can be enjoyed at modern stadiums, such as the Newlands sports grounds in Cape Town

(see p162), and the Wanderers cricket grounds in Johannesburg.

The country's favourite sport is football, but the game has only recently started to attract serious financial investment. The legacy of the 2010 FIFA World Cup, which was hosted by South Africa, includes 10 major stadiums, which today are used by teams in the **South African Premier Soccer League** (PSL). This is made up of 15 clubs with the Chiefs, Sundowns, Wits, Pirates and Ajax being consistently the highest-ranking teams. As with rugby, match day is always a great event, attracting enthusiastic supporters in their tens of thousands.

Beautiful view from the green of Leopard Creek golf course

Golf

The game of golf was introduced to South Africa by British – and notably Scottish – colonialists during the early 19th century, and has a long

and proud tradition here. The game has produced such great golfers as Gary Player, winner of a record 163 international competitions, and more recently Ernie Els, who upholds Springbok pride in the world's major tournaments.

Since the 1980s and the start of the global golf boom, South Africa has seen an extensive programme of course upgrades and new builds. These include Jack Nicklaus' signature course at **Pearl Valley Golf and Country Estate** and **Fancourt Golf Club Estate**, which is picturesquely set on the Garden Route and widely acknowledged as one of the world's best and most scenic challenges.

The most famous course of all is the **Gary Player Country Club** at Sun City, whose immaculate greens host the Nedbank Golf Challenge. Other top courses to have featured on the European PGA Tour, the local Sunshine Tour and the South African Open include Durban's **Erinvale Golf Club**, **Leopard Creek Country Club** and **Glendower Golf Club**.

The country's terrain and balmy climate, especially in and around the Winelands *(see pp192–209)* and the Garden Route *(see pp236–45)*, are perfect for the best enjoyment of the game, and the facilities are usually just as outstanding. This has led to an increase in the popularity of golf package holidays, and South Africa now claims to be the most successful golfing nation per capita in the world.

Watching cricket at Newlands grounds, with Table Mountain as a backdrop

Robben Island, an important historical and ecological heritage site

Townships and Cultural Tours

Soweto *(see pp318–20)* holds an important place in the heart of modern South Africa for its role in the rise of the people's voices that contributed to the demise of apartheid. Soweto tours are hugely popular with visitors – often a highlight of their exploration of Johannesburg. Visitors are accompanied by experienced guides to jazz clubs, clinics, schools, shebeens (bars) and thought-provoking museums.

Other fascinating tours in and around Johannesburg include a visit to the Lesedi Cultural Village to encounter Zulu, Xhosa and Sotho culture. Contact one of the dozens of tour operators in Johannesburg such as **Vhupo Tours**; they all offer a range of half- and full-day guided tours and pick visitors up from hotels.

In Cape Town, tours visit Bo-Kaap *(see p133)* and include traditional meals and hospitality. District Six, crafts and education centres, mosques, as well as the former townships on the Cape Flats, are also included on the itinerary. Tour operators such as **Andulela Experience**, **Cape Capers** and **Cape Rainbow Tours** offer half-day tours looking at historical and cultural aspects of Cape Town, from slave history to today's social and environmental projects.

For those with an interest in what life was like under the apartheid regime, a trip to the infamous Robben Island *(see pp146–7)* is a must when in Cape Town. Tours in and around Durban offer insights into the Indian community, the former townships and the city's traditional Zulu heritage. Again, there are many tour operators and **Durban Tourism** offers its own insightful half-day tours, either on foot or on an open-top double-decker bus known as the Ricksha Bus. A trip to Shakaland *(see p297)* also reveals traditional Zulu society, crafts and medicine, and is a popular outing for families.

Battlefield Tours

As a frontier land, South Africa's soil has been fought over by succeeding waves of settlers. Battlefield tours *(see p278)* around the historic sites are a fascinating way to explore this aspect of South Africa's history, and many of the local museums and lodges organize guided tours. The storytelling skills of many of the guides, such as those at **Fugitives' Drift Lodge** *(see p388)* and **Isandlwana Lodge**, are remarkable. These trips take in some of the poignant war memorials dedicated to various conflicts, including South Africa's active role in both World Wars, that are scattered across the land.

In the 1820s, the ruthless King Shaka created the Zulu nation from nothing – building one of history's most fearsome fighting forces. Rorke's Drift *(see p278)* is the site of the battle in which 150 British soldiers defended a supply station against 4,000 Zulus, thereby earning 11 Victoria Crosses in 12 hours. The battle was immortalized in the 1964 film *Zulu,* which has helped to turn the area into a popular visitor attraction.

Other major stops on the Boer War tour include Ladysmith *(see p278)*, Mafeking, where Robert Baden-Powell later conceived and started the Boy Scout movement, and lofty Spioenkop *(see p279)*, strategically sited on a 1,466-m (4,764-ft) peak, which saw the fiercest of all fighting. Also on the battlefield trail is Blood River *(see p278)* near Dundee, where Afrikaner forces defeated a huge Zulu army on 16 December 1838.

Site of the Battle of Isandhlwana, KwaZulu-Natal, the first engagement of the Anglo-Zulu War

DIRECTORY

Hiking

South Africa National Parks (SANParks)
Tel 012 428 9111.
W sanparks.org

Trail Guide
W trailguide.co.za

Rock Climbing and Kloofing

Mountain Club of South Africa
Tel 021 465 3412.
W mcsa.org.za

Fishing

Big Blue Fishing Charters
Wharf St,
Simon's Town,
Cape Town.
Tel 021 786 5667.

Lynski Fishing Charters
Tel 031 539 3338.
W lynski.com

Air Sports

Airtrackers
Tel 014 552 5020.
hotairballoonsafarisa.
co.za

Bill Harrop's Original Balloon Safaris
Tel 011 705 3201.
W balloon.co.za

Face Adrenalin
Bloukrans Bridge,
Garden Route.
Tel 042 281 1458.
W faceadrenalin.com

South African Hang Gliding and Paragliding Association
Tel 012 668 3186.
W sahpa.co.za

Cycling

Cycling South Africa
Tel 021 917 1736.
W cyclingsa.com

Pedal Power Association
Tel 021 671 6340.
W pedalpower.org.za

Water Sports

Amanzi Trails
Tel 021 559 1573.
W amanzitrails.co.za

Apex Shark Expeditions
Quayside Building,
Main Rd, Simon's Town,
Cape Town.
Tel 021 786 5717.
W apexpredators.com

Kaskazi Kayaks
179 Beach Rd, Three
Anchor Bay, Cape Town.
Tel 083 346 1146.
W kayak.co.za

National Association of Underwater Instructors (NAUI)
70 Van Gorkom St,
Elarduspark, Pretoria.
Tel 079 718 7604.
W naui.org

Professional Association of Diving Instructors
Tel (+44) 0117 300 7234.
W padi.com

Umkulu
Tel 021 853 7952.
W orangeriver
rafting.com
W umkuluadventures.
com

Wavescape
W wavescape.co.za

White Shark Ventures
Tel 021 532 0470.
W white-shark-
diving.com

Horse Riding and Pony-Trekking

Cape Nature
Tel 072 446 9977.
W capenature.co.za

Ezemvelo KZN Wildlife
Tel 033 845 1000.
W kznwildlife.com

Malealea Lodge & Pony-Trekking
Malealea, Lesotho.
Tel 082 552 4215.
W malealea.com

Bird-Watching, Flora and Fauna Trails

BirdLife South Africa
Tel 011 789 1122.
W birdlife.org.za

Spectator Sports

South African Premier Soccer League (PSL)
Tel 011 715 2500.
W psl.co.za

Golf

Erinvale Golf Club
Lourensford Road,
Somerset West.
Tel 021 847 1906.
W erinvalegolf
club.com

Fancourt Golf Club Estate
1 Montagu Rd, George.
Tel 044 804 0000.
W fancourt.co.za

Gary Player Country Club
Sun City Resort,
North West Province.
Tel 014 557-1245/6.
W suninternational.
com

Glendower Golf Club
20 Marias Rd,
Edenvale, Johannesburg.
Tel 011 453 1013.
W glendower.co.za

Leopard Creek Country Club
Malelane, bordering
Kruger National Park,
Mpumalanga.
Tel 013 791 2000.
W leopardcreek.co.za

Pearl Valley Golf and Country Estate
Wemmershoek Rd, Paarl.
Tel 021 867 8000.
W pearlvalley.co.za

Township and Cultural Tours

Andulela Experience
Tel 021 418 3020.
W andulela.com

Cape Capers
Tel 021 448 3117.
W tourcapers.co.za

Cape Rainbow Tours
Tel 021 551 5465.
W caperainbow.com

Durban Tourism
90 Florida Rd, Durban.
Tel 031 322 4164.
W durbanexperience.
co.za

Vhupo Tours
Tel 011 936 0411.
W vhupo-tours.com

Battlefield Tours

Fugitives' Drift Lodge
On the R33 south of
Dundee.
Tel 034 642-1843.
W fugitivesdrift.com

Isandlwana Lodge
Off the R68 southeast of
Dundee.
Tel 034 271-8301.
W isandlwana.co.za

Scenic Rail Travel

Taking a holiday, or part of a holiday, in the form of a rail tour aboard a well-equipped sleeper train is an increasingly popular choice. Once perceived as the domain of elderly travellers, scenic train travel now attracts adults of all ages, although it is not aimed at families with young children. This is a year-round activity, but prices will be higher in the busy holiday periods. The advantages of such a tour are many: the "hotel" travels with its guests, it is possible to reach remote destinations while remaining in comfortable surroundings, and then, of course, there is the pleasure of rail travel. The lazy pace of a steam locomotive is perfect for enjoying South Africa's wonderful sights.

A Rovos Rail steam train winding through the Eastern Transvaal

Choosing an Itinerary

South Africa, with its year-long pleasant climate and beautiful scenery, is the ideal destination for luxury train travel. However, it is not a cheap holiday and it can be sensible to avoid certain times of the year. In general the cheapest fares are available in May and August, while the period from September to December can be markedly more expensive.

South Africa's rail holiday itineraries are carefully chosen to reveal some truly stunning views, and reach many destinations that are difficult to access by road. It is a good idea to study the itineraries carefully. The Blue Train, for example, is best taken from south to north as this route passes through the loveliest stretches of scenery by day rather than at night. Other trips include safari expeditions and stops in neighbouring countries. Rovos Rail offers routes to Victoria Falls in Zimbabwe and a magnificent tour to Dar es Salaam in Tanzania.

Which Train to Choose

There are several different companies arranging a variety of tours, from short day-trips to more lengthy affairs.

Rovos Rail, which calls itself "the most luxurious train in the world", lives up to its reputation, with traditional furnishings and exquisite decor. Two beautifully rebuilt trains carry a maximum of 72 passengers each. All suites

Border-crossing itineraries may take in sights such as Victoria Falls in Zimbabwe

are of a five-star hotel standard, with air-conditioning and shower or bath facilities. The most expensive suites, occupying half-a-coach each, have a full-size Victorian roll-top bath. The trains provides 24-hour room service and there are two dining cars, which allow the entire complement of passengers to enjoy dinner at a single sitting.

The **Shongololo Express** specializes in adventure and excitement, and is therefore a big hit with the younger crowd. As a result, the style of the trains is more casual, and the cabins are fairly basic but comfortable. There are two en suite options, but the cheaper twin or single cabins entail a walk to use shower and toilet facilities. All trains carry a fleet of air-conditioned touring cars and include a safari expedition.

Crisp linens, marble-clad bathrooms and faultless service set the tone for the magnificent **Blue Train**, one of the world's most famous scheduled services. Beautiful wood veneers and fine detail add a 1950s ambience to the train. The suites offer a choice of shower or bath and a selection of film and radio channels. The lounge cars are the perfect place to observe the panoramic views as the train winds its way through the Winelands, the Karoo Desert and other impressive scenery.

Routes and Sights

The scheduled route for the Blue Train links Cape Town and Pretoria, and is a 2,600-km (994-mile) journey taking 27 hours through some of South Africa's most spectacular scenery. Rovos Rail has a variety of itineraries. Its three-day Cape Town to Pretoria route, which can be taken in either direction, includes visits to Kimberley's famous Big Hole and diamond museum, as well as the historic town of Matjiesfontein. The three-day route linking Pretoria and Durban visits the Battlefields and Zululand. A game safari in the Nambiti Private Game Reserve is also included on the itinerary. Possibly the most intriguing trip is the 14-day African Adventure, which links Cape Town with Dar Es Salaam in Tanzania, passing Zimbabwe, Zambia, Victoria Falls and Selous Game Reserve – the continent's largest – on the way.

The Shongololo Express has itineraries that criss-cross South Africa, dipping into neighbouring countries such as Namibia, Mozambique, Botswana, Zambia and Tanzania. There are two popular "limited edition" trips; one which focuses on wildlife and another which follows in the footsteps of Dr Livingstone.

On-Board Cuisine and Service

The standard of catering and service on board will be that of a five-star hotel. These trains have a very high ratio of staff to guests, especially in the restaurant car. Meals are of gourmet standard prepared by executive chefs and usually an added extra is afternoon tea.

What to Take

It pays to pack light because there are limits to the size and number of cases that can be stowed away (check with the train company). However, guests should bring formal wear for evenings as they tend to be rather grand occasions, with ladies dressing in traditional evening wear and gentlemen either

Matjiesfontein

The Lord Milner Hotel, Matjiesfontein

A short off-train excursion on both the Blue Train and Rovos Rail journey between Pretoria and Cape Town is the village of Matjiesfontein in the Karoo. Established in 1884 it is today a national monument because of its well-preserved Victorian houses. A young Scot, Jimmy Logan, an official on the Cape Government Railways in the 1890s, originally came here hoping that the dry Karoo air would cure a chest complaint, which it did. He quickly saw the opportunity to supply water to steam trains from his farm, and while the engines took on water, he served the passengers drinks and meals. So successful was his business that he built the Lord Milner Hotel, where today's rail passengers still stop for refreshments and to enjoy the historical village.

The Blue Train travels past an impressive Table Mountain view

in a smart lounge suit or a tuxedo. The daytime dress code is more relaxed, smart casual clothes.

What is Included

Rates include food, drink and off-train excursions by coach. In addition, each suite has an inclusive mini-bar fully stocked to the passengers' choice, although some companies may charge extra for champagne. There are comfortable lounges with

large windows offering panoramic views.

Health and Safety

All trains have a member of staff trained in first aid. It is also important to find out if the train is passing through malaria risk areas, as suitable preventative medication will need to be taken. There is little need to worry about personal security, but, as always, keep valuables locked in an on-board safe.

DIRECTORY

Blue Train

Tel 012 334 8459.

W bluetrain.co.za

Rovos Rail

Tel 012 315 8242.

W rovos.co.za

Shongololo Express

Tel 021 421 4020.

W shongololo.com

Dining car on a Rovos Rail train with original teak pillars

SURVIVAL GUIDE

PRACTICAL INFORMATION

South Africa hosts around 10 million foreign visitors a year. Throughout the country, the peak seasons coincide with the South African school holidays – the busiest times are from early December to late February, especially along the south and east coasts. The Easter weekend is also busy at both inland and seaside resorts, as are the four-week winter school holidays during June and July. Although the number of tourists increases every year, the country nevertheless offers a sense of the "undiscovered". Local people still have wide, sandy beaches largely to themselves, and in the interior, visitors cannot fail to be captivated by the peace and solitude in the natural splendour offered by the game parks and nature reserves.

When to Go

Many parts of South Africa are at their best in September and October, when the spring season's growth is fresh and the temperature comfortably warm. Game-watchers may prefer June to August, when many trees are bare and large numbers of animals converge on the diminishing number of drinking places. Winter days are usually sunny and warm, but temperatures drop as the sun sets.

Temperatures from December to February may be close to unbearable in high-lying areas such as the Northern Cape and along the East Coast, but relief is delivered through thunderstorms almost every afternoon. The moderating influence of the sea is welcome at the coast, although some people find the increased humidity difficult to deal with. The southwestern areas have winter rainfall and hot summers. Much of the southern coast receives rain throughout the year. Almost all attractions stay open all year round.

What to Take

Do not underestimate South African winters, or the windchill factor in summer; central heating is uncommon so pack warm clothes. Sunblock and specialized provisions can be bought locally, but do carry a supply of medication if you suffer from a chronic condition.

Visas and Passports

Most nationalities, including citizens of the United States, Canada, Australia, New Zealand and most European Union nationals, need only a valid passport to stay in South Africa for 90 days. All visitors are granted a temporary visitor's permit at the point of entry, and may also be asked to prove that they can support themselves financially while in the country and that they own a return ticket or have the means to buy one. A passport must be valid for at least 6 months after the date of departure from South Africa and have at least one completely empty page to receive a permit.

Inspiring new ways

Logo and slogan of South Africa

Visas to enter Swaziland are issued free of charge at the border. Visa requirements for Lesotho depend on your nationality. The South African consulate or embassy in your country will be able to advise. A full list of these can be found on the website of South Africa's **Department of International Relations and Cooperation**.

Visitors should be up-to-date with routine vaccinations. However, if you arrive from a country where yellow fever is endemic, you will need a vaccination certificate. Malaria is still prevalent in parts of Kwa-Zulu-Natal and Mpumalanga, and caution is advised.

Travel Safety Advice

Visitors can get up-to-date travel safety information from the **Foreign and Commonwealth Office** in the UK, the **Department of State** in the US and the **Department of Foreign Affairs and Trade** in Australia.

Tourist Information

Tourist offices, identified by the letter "i" on a green background, offer advice about what to see and where to go. They may also carry the name of an umbrella organization or a local publicity association. The offices are usually sited on the main road in the

Summer game-viewing at Addo Elephant National Park, Port Elizabeth *(see p254)*

◀ A beautifully rebuilt classic train, part of the luxurious Rovos Rail fleet, at Capital Park station in Pretoria

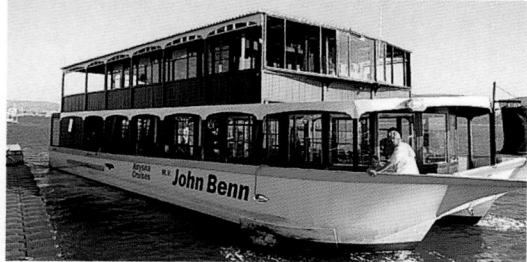

The *John Benn* takes sightseers around the Knysna Lagoon *(see p244)*

smaller towns, sometimes adjoining (or inside) the offices of the local authority, or forming part of the local museum or library. Each of South Africa's nine provinces has a tourist board, and planning and advance information can be found on their websites, as well as from **South African Tourism**.

Disabled parking

Opening Times

Business hours are usually from 8:30am to 5pm Monday–Friday, while banks and post offices are open 8:30am–3:30pm Monday–Friday and 8:30am–11:30am on Saturday. Shops generally close at 5:30pm (often at 1pm on weekends), but larger super-markets open until late in the evening and usually on Sunday,

too. Shopping malls in the cities are open daily, some until 9pm. Most museums and galleries open 9am–5pm daily. Outdoor attractions, such as parks and reserves, are usually open from sunrise to sunset.

Etiquette

Dress code in South African cities is casual, except for a few top restaurants and formal events. On the beach, it is illegal for women to swim or sunbathe topless. The consumption of alcohol on beaches and in public places is illegal, as is smoking in buses, trains, taxis and most public buildings. It is vital to observe religious customs when visiting mosques, temples and other places of worship.

Disabled Travellers

The rights of disabled people are enshrined in South Africa's constitution, and legislation requires that wherever possible public buildings can accommodate visitors with disabilities. All modern shopping malls, museums and tourist attractions have ramps, lifts and reserved parking. Local airlines provide assistance for disabled passengers. The newer transport systems found in the cities, such as Cape Town's MyCiTi Bus and Johannesburg's Gautrain, can accommodate wheelchairs. South Africa also has a growing number of hotels that cater for the disabled, and most SANParks national parks have specially adapted chalets.

Visitors must remove their shoes before entering a Hindu temple

DIRECTORY

Visas and Passports

Dept of International Relations and Cooperation
Tel 012 351 1000.
w dirco.gov.za

Travel Safety Advice

Australia
Department of Foreign Affairs and Trade
w dfat.gov.au
w smartraveller.gov.au

UK
Foreign and Commonwealth Office
w gov.uk/foreign-travel-advice

US

US Department of State
w travel.state.gov

Embassies and Consulates

Australian High Commission
Pretoria. **Tel** 012 423 6000.
w southafrica.embassy.gov.au

British High Commission
Cape Town: **Tel** 021 405 2400.
Pretoria: **Tel** 012 421 7500.
w gov.uk

Canadian High Commission
Pretoria. **Tel** 012 422 3000.
w canadainternational.gc.ca

Embassy of Ireland
Pretoria. **Tel** 012 342 5062.
w dfa.ie

New Zealand High Commission
Pretoria. **Tel** 012 435 9000.
w nzembassy.com

US Consulate General
Cape Town: **Tel** 021 702 7300.
Durban: **Tel** 031 305 7600.

US Embassy
Pretoria. **Tel** 012 431 4000.
w za.usembassy.gov

Tourist Offices

Eastern Cape Tourism
w visiteasterncape.co.za

Free State Tourism
w freestatetourism.org

Gauteng Tourism
w gauteng.net

Limpopo Tourism
w golimpopo.com

Mpumalanga Tourism
w mpumalanga.com

Northen Cape Tourism
w experience northerncape.com

South African Tourism
w southafrica.net

Tourism KwaZulu Natal
w zulu.org.za

Western Cape
w thewesterncape.co.za

Discovery tour at Oudtshoorn's Cango Wildlife Farm *(see p232)*

Tour operators specializing in tours for people with disabilities, including sight- and hearing-impaired visitors, include **Epic Enabled** and **Flamingo Tours**.

Travelling with Children

South Africa is an ideal destination for a family holiday and the sunny weather allows for a variety of outdoor activities. There is plenty of family accommodation, many restaurants have kid's menus, and children receive significant discounts on entry fees to tourist attractions and game parks.

However, make sure that they drink plenty of water, wear a high-protection sun screen, and are fully aware of the potential dangers of wild animals, snakes and insects in the bush. Consult your doctor if travelling with children in a malaria zone.

There is plenty of children's entertainment – especially during local school holidays – from aquarium tours and petting farmyards, to theatre and craft workshops.

The local press, entertainment and listings websites *(see p414)* and the **SA Kids on the Go** website are all good sources of ideas.

Women Travellers

Women should never walk alone after dark, even on the beach. While the incidence of rape in South Africa is not high in popular tourist areas, it is still a risk for the unwary. There are **Rape Crisis** centres in major towns and cities. Women are, however, ready targets for mugging, so keep to well-lit public areas and don't exhibit any valuables *(see also Personal Safety, p430)*. Always look as if you know where you are going and do not offer a lift to, or accept a lift from, anyone. Sexual harassment is not too common, although many South African males do hold rather chauvinistic attitudes, so be careful not to come across as too friendly, as your interest may be perceived as sexual.

Gay and Lesbian Pride Parade

Gay and Lesbian Travellers

Enshrined in the constitution is a clause protecting the rights of gays and lesbians. But while Cape Town is certainly the "gay capital of Africa", smaller towns still retain conservative attitudes.

The cities have a host of gay bars and theatre venues; the **Pink South Africa** website is a good resource for gay and lesbian event listings. **Purple Roofs** lists gay- and lesbian-friendly venues all over the country, including accommodation options. **Out 2 Africa** is a Cape Town-based travel agency that can organize tours and safaris all over South Africa, specifically for the gay and lesbian market. There are also gay-friendly tour operators, such as **Friends of Dorothy** in Cape Town who offer day trips with gay guides to places such as the Winelands and Hermanus for whale-watching.

Jo'burg Pride in September, **Cape Town Pride** in February, and the **Pink Loerie Mardi Gras** in Knysna on the Garden Route in May are all major party events on the gay and lesbian calendar. But by far the biggest is **Mother City Queer Project** (MCQP) in December in Cape Town. This changes venue and theme each

Backpackers' accommodation in the centre of Cape Town

year, but the massive costume party attracts more than 10,000 revellers, many overseas visitors.

Student Travel

Students with a valid **International Student Identity Card (ISIC)** benefit from good airline travel discounts, but reduced admission to venues and events has not taken off in South Africa. **STA Travel**, an agency that specializes in student travel, has branches worldwide. Backpacking is gaining in popularity.

Time

South African Standard Time (there is only one time zone) is two hours ahead of Greenwich Mean Time (GMT) all year round, seven hours ahead of the United States' Eastern Standard Winter Time and seven hours behind Australian Central Time.

Public Toilets

There are public toilets everywhere and they are generally of a high standard. There are public toilets in shopping malls and in many public buildings such as civic centres, libraries and town halls. Most large urban vehicle service stations have toilets, but these are intended for the use of clients. On major tourist routes, most garages that have refreshment centres also usually have well-kept toilets. Public toilets can be found at railway and bus stations, although these toilets are often not very clean. Many have no soap or hand-drying facilities. An alternative is to use the toilets in a restaurant where you are a customer. Large shopping centres and tourist attractions usually have well-maintained facilities and customized toilets for wheelchair-users. Baby-changing facilities are also available.

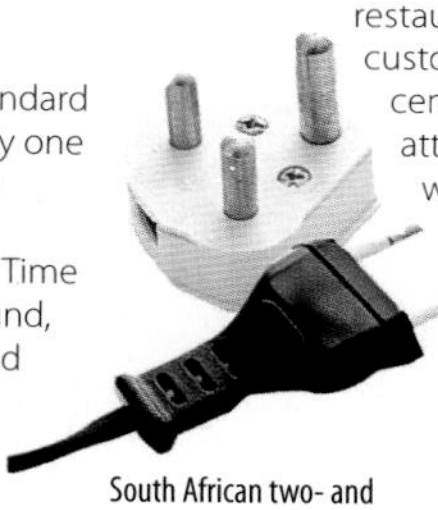

South African two- and three-pin plugs

Electrical Supply

Electricity (alternating current) is supplied by the state-owned utility company Eskom. Mains voltage is 220/230 volts (220V) at 50 cycles (50Hz). Most local power plugs are 5A (amperes) with two pins, or 15A with three rounded pins. Most appliances such as razors and chargers for phones, cameras etc. will fit the two-pin sockets, but an adaptor is needed for the rounded three-pin sockets. International travel adaptors are sold in many shops in South Africa, as well as at all the international airports.

Weights and Measures

South Africa uses the metric system. Normal body temperature of 98.4° F is equal to 37° C. If the weather chart shows 30° C, you are in for a hot day. A pressure of 30 pounds per square inch is equal to two bars.

Conversion Chart

Imperial to Metric

1 inch = 2.54 cm
1 foot = 30 cm
1 mile = 1.6 km
1 ounce = 28 g
1 pound = 454 g
1 pint = 0.57 litres
1 gallon = 4.6 litres

Metric to Imperial

1 mm = 0.04 inches
1 cm = 0.4 inches
1 m = 3 feet 3 inches
1 km = 0.6 miles
1 g = 0.04 ounces
1 kg = 2.2 pounds
1 litre = 1.8 pints

DIRECTORY

Disabled Travellers

Epic Enabled
Tel 021 785 7440 or 073 22 82 825.
W epic-enabled.com

Flamingo Tours
Tel 082 450 2031.
W flamingotours.co.za

Travelling with Children

SA Kids on the Go
W sakidsonthego.com

Women Travellers

Rape Crisis
Tel 021 447 9762.
W rapecrisis.org.za

Gay and Lesbian Travellers

Cape Town Pride
W capetownpride.org

Friends of Dorothy
Tel 083 555 6611.
W friendsofdorothytours.co.za

Jo'Burg Pride
W joburgpride.org

Mother City Queer Project
W mcqp.co.za

Out2Africa
99 Hope St, Cape Town.
Tel 021 469 2600.
W out2africa.com

Pink Loerie Mardi Gras
W pinkloerie.co.za

Pink South Africa
W pinksa.co.za

Purple Roofs
W purpleroofs.com

Student Travel

International Student Identity Card (ISIC)
W isic.org

STA Travel
14 Main Road, Rondebosch, Cape Town.
Tel 021 686 6800.
The Mall of Rosebank, 50 Bath Avenue, Johannesburg.
Tel 011 447 5414.

Student Travel Head Office
Tel 0861 781 781.
W statravel.co.za

Personal Security and Health

Security in South Africa is good in the places that tourists are likely to visit, where the risk of serious crime is very low. Although in some areas the incidence of violent crime can be high, visitors are more likely to be targets of petty crime such as bag-snatching and theft from vehicles, so it is important to stay vigilant. Common-sense precautions usually ensure a safe and crime-free stay. South Africa generally has no unusual or serious health risks, but malaria needs to be considered in certain areas. On safari, wildlife should be taken seriously and treated with respect. For your own safety, stay in your vehicle at all times, except in designated places such as a picnic site or hide.

Personal Safety

Bag-snatching, mugging and pickpocketing can occur in South Africa, but most are opportunist crimes. The golden rule is not to flash expensive items such as jewellery and mobile phones and other devices, and to leave anything of monetary or sentimental value at home. It is best to take out only what you need for the day or excursion, and to carry bags in front of you with the strap across the body if possible. A slim money belt concealed beneath clothes is a good idea. Don't put your possessions down when you need your hands (for example, when you are examining an intended purchase).

Avoid going out on your own, especially after dark; if you do, stick to busy and well-lit tourist areas. Women should never walk alone anywhere after dark. Follow local advice about which areas to avoid – such as townships or certain inner-city suburbs – and be vigilant about the people around you.

Visitors can use hotel safes to deposit passports and costly items. Hotel doors should be locked as noisy fans or air conditioning can provide cover for thieves. If travelling by public transport, especially on crowded suburban trains and minibus taxis, be vigilant and guard possessions fiercely.

If you are mugged, do not challenge the thief – simply hand over your phone or your money. Report the incident immediately. To make an insurance claim you will need to obtain a case reference number from a police station.

On the Road

When travelling by car, always keep the doors locked and the windows only slightly open. When you do leave the car, lock it, even if you're getting out for just a few moments (see also p440). Make sure that nothing of value is visible inside – leave the glove compartment open to show that there's nothing in there either. Use undercover or supervised parking wherever possible. Do not stop for hitch-hikers or to offer any help, even to an accident victim. If a hijacker or other criminal points a firearm at you, obey his or her orders.

In the event of a breakdown emergency in a remote area, stay in your locked vehicle if at all possible, and phone the AA Emergency Road Service from a mobile phone.

Pharmacies offer valuable medical advice and services

Medical Facilities

State and provincial hospitals do offer adequate facilities, but they tend to be under-funded and under-staffed. Patients who are members of medical insurance schemes are usually admitted to a private hospital, such as **Mediclinic** or **Netcare** – these are found in all South African cities and most of the larger towns. All visitors should take out travel insurance to cover everything, including emergencies. If you suffer from any pre-existing medical condition, or are on any long-term medication, make sure those who try to help you are aware of it.

Food and Water

Tap water is safe to drink, although chlorinated. There is a wide range of bottled waters available. Be careful of river or mountain water in heavily populated areas. The preparation of food in most restaurants and hotels meets international standards, but do

Police officers standing guard at Rustenburg Stadium

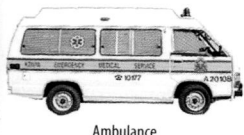

Ambulance

Police vehicle

Fire engine

exercise common sense. In the informal markets, avoid meat or dairy products that may have been lying in the sun, and wash all fruit and vegetables carefully.

Travellers to South Africa do not generally suffer the same stomach upsets as they may in the rest of the continent.

Outdoor Hazards

In many parts of South Africa, forest and bush fires are a major hazard, especially during the dry winter months. Never discard burning matches and cigarette ends and always ensure a *braai* fire is put out.

Always protect yourself from the harsh sun with a wide-brimmed hat, a high-factor sunblock and sunglasses. Before you climb or hike at high altitude, ask about the expected weather conditions. Be aware that these can change very quickly. If you are

caught in fog, keep warm and wait for the weather to lift. Be sure to tell a responsible person at your hotel which route you intend to take and the time you expect to return. Ensure you are familiar with your route before setting off.

Poisonous Bites and Stings

Few travellers are likely to find themselves in danger of being bitten or stung by any one of the venomous creatures of South Africa. People on safari or on hiking trails should nevertheless watch where they place their hands and feet.

Few snakes in South Africa are deadly, and most are not poisonous at all. They strike only when attacked or threatened. The most dangerous spider is the seldom-encountered button spider (*Latrodectus* species). Most of the species of scorpion are only slightly venomous. In general, those with thick tails and small pincers tend to be more poisonous. Because of their lower body weight, children are more susceptible to the toxins than adults.

Malaria

South Africa has a low seasonal risk of malaria in the extreme east of the country along the Mozambique border. This includes parts of the Kruger National Park in Mpumalanga and Limpopo provinces and in the extreme north of KwaZulu-Natal. The risk period is usually

between September and April but it is essential to obtain local advice about conditions. If you are travelling to these places during the risk period, consult your doctor or travel clinic about taking anti-malarials and ensure that you finish the course. If already in South Africa, **Netcare Travel Clinics** can be found in Johannesburg, Cape Town, Durban, Pretoria and Port Elizabeth. Experts here can advise on malaria and also vaccinations and other health requirements for travel beyond South Africa's borders.

DIRECTORY

Emergency Numbers

Ambulance
Tel 10177 all areas.

Fire
Tel 10111 all areas.

Police
Tel 10111 all areas.
W saps.gov.za

AA Emergency Road Service
Free call **Tel** 0861 000 234.
24-hours, all areas.
W aa.co.za

Netcare 911
Private medical rescue service
Tel 082911 all areas.
W netcare911.co.za

Medical Facilities

Cape Town Medi-Clinic
21 Hof St, Oranjezicht.
Tel 021 464 5500.
W mediclinic.co.za

Netcare Christiaan Barnard Memorial Hospital
181 Longmarket St, Cape Town.
Tel 021 480 6111.
W netcare.co.za

Netcare St Augustine's Hospital
107 Chelmsford Rd, Glenwood,
Durban. **Tel** 031 268 5000.
W netcare.co.za

Sandton Mediclinic
Peter Place, Bryanston, Jo'burg.
Tel 011 709 2000.
W mediclinic.co.za

Malaria

Netcare Travel Clinic
W travelclinic.co.za

The police station in Pietermaritzburg

Banking and Currency

Banks and bureau de change are plentiful in South Africa. Cash can be obtained upon arrival, as facilities at international airports stay open to meet all arriving flights. Even small towns have at least one bank that will make foreign transactions. ATMs are everywhere and generally offer the best rate of exchange when drawing cash from home bank accounts. There are no restrictions on the amount of foreign currency that may be brought into the country, but there are limits to the amount of any currency that may be taken out of South Africa.

A row of Standard Bank ATMs

Banks and Bureau de Change

South Africa's main banks are **ABSA**, **First National Bank (FNB)**, **Nedbank** and **Standard Bank**. They are found even in the smallest towns and all have foreign exchange services. Passports must always be presented when changing money. Branch addresses can be found on the websites. Banking hours are from 9am to 3:30pm on weekdays, and from 9am to 11:30am on Saturdays. Banks are closed on public holidays. You can also change cash in bureau de change such as those run by **Master Currency**, **Travelex** and **Bidvest Bank**, which have branches at the main airports and large shopping malls in the cities. Commission is charged for exchanging cash, but as branches are usually clustered together it is easy to compare the rates offered. In the larger shopping malls such

as the V&A Waterfront in Cape Town and Sandton City in Johannesburg, bureau de change have the same opening hours as the shops; often until 9pm and also open on Sundays and public holidays. At the international airports they have extended hours to serve all arrivals. Again, branch locations can be found on the websites.

ATMs

Automatic teller machines (ATMs) are widely distributed in the cities and towns. Cash withdrawals, up to a set limit per day per card, can be made with debit, credit and currency cards. The cards most widely used in South Africa are Visa and MasterCard. ATMs may run out of notes at the weekend, especially if there is a public holiday on the Monday, so make sure you draw money early. If you find the daily limit inadequate, you can always draw more from a bank (remembering to take your passport along), but it's best to avoid carrying too much cash with you.

Avoid drawing money while on your own, or at deserted ATMs after-hours, and decline all unsolicited offers of "help". ATM fraud is common: a fraudster may, for example, jam the

machine slot so you can't retrieve your card. While you alert the bank officials inside, the fraudster un-jams the slot and withdraws money from your account. It is better to wait outside at the ATM while a companion goes for help. All ATMs display a 24-hour emergency telephone number to call in the event of any problems with your card.

Credit Cards

Most businesses accept all major credit cards. Keep your card in sight when making a payment, especially in restaurants, to reduce the risk of it being "cloned". Informal traders do not usually accept credit cards. Not all petrol stations take credit cards, but most of the larger ones have ATMs – it is advisable to check before filling up. Find out what charges your bank will levy for use of your credit card in South Africa.

Currency Cards

Most currency or travel money cards are Visa or MasterCard linked. They can be pre-loaded (and topped up) with a number of currencies, and used in South Africa just like a debit card to pay

DIRECTORY

Banks and Bureau de Change

ABSA
W absa.co.za.

Bidvest Bank
W bidvestbank.co.za

First National Bank (FNB)
W fnb.co.za

Master Currency
W mastercurrency.co.za

Nedbank
W nedbank.co.za.

Standard Bank
W standardbank.co.za

Travelex
Tel 011 486 2145.
W travelex.co.za

Bureau de change at OR Tambo international airport, Johannesburg

for things and to withdraw cash from an ATM. As they are not linked to bank accounts, there is no risk of defrauding main home accounts. This also reduces the risk of identity theft in the event of a card being lost or stolen.

Currency

The South African unit of currency is the rand, indicated by the letter "R" before the amount. "Rand" is short for "Witwatersrand", Gauteng's gold-bearing reef).

The rand is divided into 100 cents (c). South African currency circulates – usually at face value – in neighbouring Lesotho, Namibia, Swaziland and Mozambique.

Banknotes

Banknotes, on which the "Big Five" wildlife animals are represented on one side and Nelson Mandela on the reverse, are issued in R10, R20, R50, R100 and R200 denominations.

R200 note

R100 note

R50 note

R20 note

R10 note

Coins (actual size)

The 10-cent, 20-cent and 50-cent coins are a brassy yellow and have milled edges. The R1, R2 and R5 coins are milled in a bright, silver colour. The only older copper-coloured, smooth-edged coin in circulation is the 5 cent.

5-cent piece

10-cent piece

20-cent piece

50-cent piece

R1

R2

R5

Communications and Media

South African telecommunications systems are among the most advanced in the world. The partly state-owned company Telkom provides home and public phone (payphone) services, while the mobile companies offer competitive mobile phone and Internet data access. A variety of postal options, from insured or signature on delivery mail to courier services, is offered by post offices and PostNet countrywide. Wi-Fi is available almost everywhere, and hotels and guesthouses provide their guests with access. Increasingly, some towns – especially where there are universities – offer free Wi-Fi in public places.

Telephones

It is possible to dial direct internationally from South Africa as long as you use the correct dialling code. The full 3-digit regional code must be dialled for every number in South Africa, even when you are calling from within the same area.

There are public telephone boxes in post offices, train stations and shopping malls, but many are being taken out of service given that almost everyone carries a mobile phone. Payphones take a range of South African coins, and phone cards can be bought from most post offices and convenience shops.

Mobile Phones

Mobile (or cell) phone coverage is excellent almost everywhere except for in the remotest wilderness areas. Mobile phones can be obtained in South Africa from private service providers on contract or on a pay-as-you-go tariff with pre-paid airtime.

Mobile phone rental facilities are found at the major airports. **Vodacom Rentals** has shops at OR Tambo International, Cape Town International, King Shaka International and Port Elizabeth airports. You can book online and collect and drop your rental at any of these shops or at those in major shopping malls in Johannesburg, Cape Town and Durban. Mobiles are often offered as part of a car-hire contract. It is always a good idea to carry a mobile phone when driving, in the event of an accident or emergency.

To avoid high roaming fees on an international mobile, buy a local SIM card to use in your own phone. Note that you can do this only if your handset is unlocked. SIM cards can be bought inexpensively at any **MTN**, **Cell C** or **Vodacom** shop. These shops also offer Internet packages for use on your mobile phone, as long as you are using a local SIM card; just ask them to set your phone up for Internet access.

Coin- and card-operated public telephones

Internet

Wi-Fi access is available almost everywhere. Like mobile phone coverage, only at remote lodges in the national parks and reserves will the Internet not be available.

With widespread modern technology, many internet cafés have closed, but there are still some in urban centres; to find the nearest one, consult the Yellow Pages. Most coffee shops offer Wi-Fi access free of charge; it is not unusual to see people on their laptops in cafés. Many restaurants also have this facility during the day, as do the more upmarket hotels and guesthouses and most of the airports and shopping malls.

Visitors at a coffee shop working on a laptop

Postal Services

Post offices are open from 8am to 4:30pm on weekdays and from 8am to noon on Saturdays. Smaller centres usually close for a lunch hour. The **South African Post Office** (SAPO) provides several ways of sending letters and goods: registered, cash-on-delivery (COD), insured, express delivery, and Speed Services for guaranteed delivery within 24 hours in South Africa. However, the delivery rate of letters and parcels is somewhat erratic, and coverage, although gradually improving, is still patchy, particularly in remote regions of the country. As a result **PostNet**, a private post and business service that also acts as an agent for DHL, is very popular. There are more than 230 stores in shopping malls across the country, and a branch locator

Post office in Matjiesfontein, Western Cape

can be found on the website. Opening hours depend on those of the mall, and as such many are open at weekends.

Courier Services

It is advisable to use a courier service to send valuable items home. Companies such as **DHL International** and **FedEx** have branches in larger South African centres and many small towns as well. They will collect from anywhere in South Africa, and deliver parcels, priced per kilo, nationally and internationally.

Newspapers and Magazines

Regional daily newspapers are found in all major cities. Most produce both morning and afternoon papers as well as Saturday and Sunday editions. There are also several national weekly and bi-weekly tabloids. The main English-language

Post office sign in Swellendam, on the Garden Route

dailies are **The Star** in Gauteng, the **Cape Argus** in the Cape and **The Mercury** in KwaZulu-Natal. Arguably, the best weekly newspaper is the **Mail & Guardian**, known for its hard-hitting reports.

Other weeklies are **The Sunday Independent** and the more populist **Sunday Times**. A variety of local and international magazines is widely available. Topics include travel, sport, wildlife and outdoor life.

South Africa receives editions of some overseas newspapers (mainly British), as well as a number of foreign magazines. All of these are distributed through selected newsagents, such as the CNA and Exclusive Books chains, or are placed in upmarket hotels.

Television and Radio

The South African Broadcasting Corporation (SABC) has four television channels and a number of national and regional radio stations. The main TV language is English, but local programming – including news – is produced in several languages including Afrikaans and isiZulu – some shows even combine different languages. British and US programmes tend to dominate, but there are also good home-grown productions. Local radio stations target specific audiences and language-groups. Many hotels and bars subscribe to multi-channel satellite TV, provided by DSTV (Digital Satellite TV).

TRAVEL INFORMATION

South Africa, historically a welcome stopover for seafarers, is well served by air links with most parts of the globe and by road to the rest of Africa. The national carrier is South African Airways (SAA), but most international airlines operate regular flights to and from here. Domestic destinations are served by SAA and other airlines. The road system in

South Africa is in good condition, though the accident rate is high. Intercity bus services operate along the main highways, and the rail network, though slow, covers the country. Public transport within the cities is fairly comprehensive and efficient, but in the smaller towns it is seldom satisfactory, and self-drive is often the better option.

South African Airways and Star Alliance carriers on the runway

Arriving by Air

The three international airports in South Africa are OR Tambo International Airport in Johannesburg, Cape Town International Airport in Cape Town and King Shaka International Airport in Durban. Most European carriers and almost all the Asian, African and Middle Eastern airlines fly to Johannesburg's OR Tambo (named after the late anti-apartheid activist Oliver Tambo). From there onward flights go to the other cities, and regardless of

your eventual destination, immigration is at Johannesburg. A few of the international airlines serve Cape Town and Durban directly, but there is a far greater choice of flights if you go via Johannesburg first. Domestic destinations served by the national carrier **South African Airways (SAA)** and by domestic low-cost, no-frills airlines include Johannesburg, Durban, Cape Town, Port Elizabeth, Bloemfontein, East London, Nelspruit, George and Upington. With a huge choice

of routes and flights, you need to book well in advance for the best fares, especially over the Christmas and New Year period, which is the peak summer holiday season in South Africa.

For flight information, contact the **Airports Company South Africa** (ACSA) call centre or check its website.

Public transport to and from the major airports includes privately operated shuttle buses to the nearest city centre *(see Directory)*. These can be pre-booked, in which case a representative meets you at the arrivals terminal and drops you at your hotel, or they have kiosks at the airports. To get to the airport, you need to book in advance. In Cape Town, there are also regular MyCiTi buses *(see p439)* to the city, while in Durban, the **King Shaka Airport Shuttle Bus** goes to Umhlanga, the city centre and beachfront. Visitors travelling from OR Tambo International Airport to Johannesburg and Pretoria can take the Gautrain *(see p438)*.

Approved ACSA metered taxis can be found outside the main terminal buildings but they cost

Airport	Information	Distance from City	Taxi Fare to City	Driving Time to City
✈ Johannesburg	**Tel** (086) 727-7888	**24 km (15 miles)**	**R400**	**40-60 mins**
✈ Cape Town	**Tel** (086) 727-7888	**20 km (12 miles)**	**R350**	**35–50 mins**
✈ Durban	**Tel** (086) 727-7888	**20 km (12 miles)**	**R450**	**30-40 mins**
✈ Port Elizabeth	**Tel** (086) 727-7888	**3 km (2 miles)**	**R60**	**7–10 mins**
✈ Bloemfontein	**Tel** (086) 727-7888	**10 km (6 miles)**	**R170**	**15-25 mins**
✈ East London	**Tel** (086) 727-7888	**15 km (9 miles)**	**R200**	**20-30 mins**
✈ George	**Tel** (086) 727-7888	**10 km (6 miles)**	**R170**	**10-15mins**

more than the shuttles. Most hotels, guesthouses and some backpackers' lodges in the larger cities will be able to provide transport on request.

Customs

Current customs legislation allows visitors to bring duty-free goods to the value of R5,000 into the country. Visitors may also bring in 50 ml of perfume, 2 litres (3½ pints) of wine, 1 litre (1¾ pints) of spirits, 250 g of tobacco, 200 cigarettes and 20 cigars.

Lesotho, Swaziland and South Africa are members of the Southern African Development Community, a common customs union, so there are no internal customs duties. For more information, visit the South Africa Revenue Services website (www.sars.gov.za). International departing passengers are able to claim back the 14% VAT on goods bought in South Africa at the airports; see page 412 for details.

International Flights

Johannesburg's OR Tambo International Airport is a major hub in the southern hemisphere and almost all large airlines fly there. A few also fly directly to Cape Town. Options from Europe include British Airways, Virgin and SAA from London, Air France from Paris, KLM from Amsterdam and Lufthansa from Frankfurt. Indirect flights from Europe include Egypt Air via Cairo, Kenya Airways via Nairobi, Qatar Airways via Doha and Emirates via Dubai. The only direct flights from the USA are with SAA from New York and Delta from Atlanta. Otherwise those flying from North America

go via Europe or the Middle East. From Australia, New Zealand and Asia to Johannesburg the options include SAA, Qantas, Singapore Airlines, Malaysia Airlines and Cathay Pacific.

Domestic and Regional Airlines

There are regular daily flights connecting the major cities, none of which are more than two hours' flying time of each other. Airlines that serve the domestic routes are **SAA**, **Kulula** (a low-cost subsidiary of British Airways), **Mango** (SAA's low-cost airline) and **Safair**. Between them, these airlines also offer regional flights between Johannesburg and Harare, Maputo, Windhoek, Livingstone and Victoria Falls, among other cities in neighbouring countries.

The current price structures are competitive, with return-fare and other attractive specials regularly on offer. In general, the earlier one books, the cheaper the fare. Pre-booking is essential, either directly or through Computicket (see p415).

Package Holidays

Package holidays and escorted tours will appeal to those who do not want to search for and book their own flights, and those who are on a restricted time frame and want to see as much as possible. Many begin with an international flight into Johannesburg or Cape Town and domestic flights then connect destinations on the tour such as Kruger, Sun City, Durban, Port Elizabeth and George.

Fly-Drive Deals

Many travel agents and car-rental firms organize fly-drive packages. This is usually cheaper (and involves fewer formalities) than renting a car on arrival. Most major car-rental firms including Avis, Hertz, Budget and Europcar have offices at the airports (see p441).

DIRECTORY

Arriving by Air

Airports Company South Africa (ACSA)
Tel 011 723 1400.
W airports.co.za

Airport Shuttles

Citi Hopper
Arrivals Hall, Cape Town International Airport.
Tel 021 936 3460.
W citihopper.co.za

King Shaka Airport Bus Transport
Tel 031 465 1660.
W airportbustransport.co.za

King Shaka Airport Shuttle Services
Arrivals Hall, King Shaka International Airport.
Tel 031 822 7783.
W kingshakashuttles.co.za

Magic Transfers
Tel 021 505 6300, Cape Town.
Tel 031 263 2647, Durban.
Tel 011 548 0800, Johannesburg.
W magictransfers.co.za

Sport Shuttle
Arrivals Hall, Cape Town International Airport.
Tel 021 447 4444.
W sportshuttle.co.za

Domestic and Regional Airlines

Kulula
Tel 011 921 0500.
W kulula.com

Mango
Tel 011 086 6100.
W flymango.com

Safair
Tel 087 135 1351.

South African Airways (SAA)
Tel 011 978 1111.
W flysaa.com

The interior of Cape Town International Airport

Travelling by Train and Bus

Train travel in South Africa is quite comfortable and economical, but seldom very fast. Intercity buses, on the other hand, are fast, far-reaching and affordable, though it is wise to compare long-distance fares with those of the cheaper airlines. City transport is a little more limited. Suburban trains and minibus taxis are used largely by commuters and can be crowded, meaning that personal safety cannot be guaranteed. However, modern buses and high-speed trains with good security have been introduced on many routes, including to and from the major airports. In addition, some forms of transport are specifically designed for visitors, such as luxury trains and sightseeing city buses.

The Braamfontein Railway Yards under the Nelson Mandela Bridge

Long-Distance Trains

Shosholoza Meyl operates trains from Johannesburg to Cape Town (27 hours), Port Elizabeth (21 hours), East London (15 hours) and Durban (13 hours). The services are affordable but much slower than long-distance buses – in addition, trains run overnight, so they may arrive at or leave some stations at inconvenient times. Full timetables can be found on the website.

There are two types of class: tourist and economy. Tourist class offers sleeping compartments with two or four bunks, a wash basin and a table. Bedding can be hired on the train for a fee. Communal toilets and showers are at the end of each coach. Solo travellers share a four-berth compartment with fellow travellers of the same gender. Economy class has reclining seats with headrests and a reasonable amount of leg room, and toilets can be found at the end of each coach. Simple meals are available from a restaurant coach. Snacks can also be purchased from a service trolley, and passengers can bring their own food and refreshments.

A tourist-class ticket costs about twice as much as an economy-class ticket. Children under nine travel at half price. Note that booking in advance is necessary during the school holidays.

Luxury Trains

Enormously popular, especially with foreign visitors, are the luxurious train safaris offered by the Blue Train, Rovos Rail and Shongololo Express *(see pp422–3)*.

Premier Classe is **Shosholoza Meyl**'s upmarket service between Johannesburg and Cape Town and Johannesburg and Durban – cars can be transported on these trains. More comfortable than regular trains, but not as opulent as the luxury rail services, Premier Classe trains have single, two- and four-berth coupés with air conditioning, toiletries and room service. There are shared bathrooms and a dining car and bar. Fares include breakfast, lunch, high tea and dinner.

Suburban Trains

Suburban train services run in most South African cities and are operated by **Metrorail**. These trains are used mainly by commuters and can be overcrowded. Theft may also be an issue. Timetables and tickets are available at the stations and on the website. A first-class ticket costs about twice as much as a third-class ticket but offers better seating and security. Children under 11 years of age travel at half price.

It is advisable to use suburban trains only in daylight hours, and preferably at peak times (early in the morning and mid- to late-afternoon). It is not recommended to travel alone on suburban trains at any time. Among the Cape Town trains that are popular with visitors is the Southern Line Tourism Route, which runs from the city centre through the Southern Suburbs and along the False Bay coast to Simon's Town. One- or two-day tickets offer unlimited travel on a hop-on/hop-off basis. Many of the attractions in this part of the Cape Peninsula are within walking distance of the stations.

The **Gautrain** is a rapid-rail network linking Johannesburg and Pretoria (a journey of about 40 minutes). There is also a branch line between Sandton and OR Tambo International Airport, a journey of around 15 minutes. At peak hours, trains run every 12 minutes, and off-peak about every 20–30 minutes. Fares are paid for by a Gautrain Gold Card, which can be purchased and topped up at ticket offices and vending machines. Children under the age of three travel free.

Long-Distance Buses

Citiliner, **Greyhound**, **Intercape** and **Translux** coaches travel to most towns, and the journeys are safe, comfortable and affordable. Greyhound, Intercape and Translux also run services to the capital cities in neighbouring countries: Maputo (Mozambique), Windhoek (Namibia), Livingstone (Zambia), Harare (Zimbabwe) and Gaborone (Botswana). The coaches are modern and air-conditioned, with on-board toilets and reclining seats, and they stop for refreshments. There are, however, long distances to cover, and some coaches depart or arrive at inconvenient times. Trips can be booked via Computicket (*see p415*), either online or at any branch in the country.

The **Baz Bus** hop-on/hop-off system, aimed at budget travellers, runs between Cape Town and Durban, and Durban and Johannesburg, picking up and dropping off passengers at backpackers' hostels. Tickets are priced in segments – Cape Town to Port Elizabeth, for example – and allow unlimited hop-on/hop-offs (but no backtracking) within that segment. This makes the Baz Bus convenient for shorter journeys, especially since buses travel only during the day. However, for longer journeys, conventional bus services offer better value.

Minibus taxis transport workers on some long-distance

Travelling by train, a lovely way to view South Africa's landscapes

routes. Services have a poor safety record and vehicles are overcrowded, so they are not recommended.

City Buses

All South African cities have a system of public buses. These are inexpensive and easy to use. They can accommodate wheelchairs and prams and are monitored by security cameras. In Cape Town, bus services are run by **MyCiTi**, which also operates a service to and from the airport. In Durban, the **People Mover** runs up and down the beachfront and in a loop around the city centre, while in Johannesburg **Metrobus** and **Rea Vaya** cover all the metropolitan areas.

Minibus taxis follow the same routes as regular buses but are driven erratically and are not recommended.

The hop-on/hop-off Baz Bus, a favourite among budget travellers

Travelling by Car

Although bus services in South Africa are fast, affordable and comprehensive, a car provides the greatest flexibility and is the only way to visit the more remote areas. Overall, South Africa's road network is very good, especially those routes that are part of the N-prefixed national road system. In rural areas, only main arteries may be tarred, but dirt roads are usually levelled and in good condition. Unfortunately, long distances and other road users constitute the major hazards. Along the major routes there are many service and petrol stations, and the main attractions are well signposted.

Busy interchange of the New Road Bridge and N1 motorway in Gauteng province

Car Rental

Drivers usually need to be over 23 years of age and have a driving licence printed in English with a photograph. Your licence must be carried in the vehicle at all times. A credit or debit card is essential to hire a car. Rates are set per day and per kilometre after the daily limit, usually 100 km (60 miles). Alternatively, drivers can choose an unlimited mileage option for long-distance trips. Check the small print for insurance cover. Most of the international companies are represented, including **Avis**, **Budget**, **Europcar** and **Hertz**, and some equally good local companies include **First Car Rental** and **Tempest Car Hire**. All have offices at the airports as well as locations in the cities. Cars can also be arranged through fly-drive packages *(see p437)*. **Around About Cars** is a national agency that is able to look for competitive rates across all the companies and has its own fleet of cars in Cape Town. Depending on the planned itinerary, car hire companies can advise on whether a four-wheel-drive vehicle is needed. With prior arrangement, and for an extra fee required to organize the paperwork, hire cars can be taken into South Africa's neighbouring countries.

Animal and rockfall warning signs

Rules of the Road

Traffic in South Africa drives on the left side of the road. Except where granted right of way by a sign or by an official on duty, yield to traffic approaching from your right. It is common courtesy to pull over onto the hard shoulder to let faster traffic pass on the right. When driving through villages in rural areas, be alert for pedestrians and straying livestock. Seat belts are compulsory in the front and in the back. Children must be properly restrained.

Speed limits are 120 km per hour (75 mph) on motorways and major roads and 40–80 km per hour (25–50 mph) in towns and cities. In parks and reserves, the speed limit is not more than 40 km per hour (25 mph).

South Africa has strict drink-driving laws. The legal blood alcohol level is 0.05 per cent maximum, which is the equivalent of one glass of beer or wine. Anyone caught driving above this limit is liable for a hefty fine, or up to six years' imprisonment.

Fuel

Motor vehicles run on 97 Octane petrol, unleaded petrol or diesel fuel, and the unit of liquid measurement is the litre (0.22 UK gallons or 0.264 US gallons). Service station attendants see to refuelling and other checks such as tyre pressure, oil, water, and cleaning the front and rear windows.

Due to the vast distances between towns, especially in the arid interior, it is advisable to refuel in good time, and to plan regular rest stops.

Parking

Most South African towns and cities have street parking, with numbered bays painted on the tarmac or at the kerb; check for signs posted on a nearby pole. A fee may be paid to a parking marshal with a handheld meter. There are also numerous multi-storey car parks and almost all visitor attractions and shopping malls have parking. In unofficial parking areas such as side streets, informal parking attendants expect a tip for guarding your car when you leave it.

Breakdown Services

In the event of a vehicle break-down, pull over onto the extreme left if possible and activate your hazard lights. The **AA Emergency Road Service** is available to its members. Contact your car hire company immediately and it will tell you what to do. It is highly recommended that you carry a mobile phone when driving.

In the event of an accident, notify the police immediately and do not move the vehicles until the police arrive.

Taxis

Taxis in South Africa cannot be hailed in the street, but there are taxi ranks outside all airports, bus and railway stations, shopping malls and at the major sightseeing attractions. Additionally, any hotel or restaurant can call for a cab. All taxis are metered. By law they must display a sticker on the side of the vehicle showing the price per kilometre.

Great Drives

South Africa's natural beauty, spectacular coastline and game parks make it an ideal destination for leisurely self-driving. Cape Town offers numerous day trips by road. The most popular is around the Cape Peninsula *(see p154)*, a round trip of about 160 km (100 miles) from the city centre, with plenty of distractions along the way, including seal and penguin colonies and the stunning ocean scenery at Cape Point. The 137-km (85-mile) coast road to Hermanus *(see pp226–7)* is a great vantage point for whale-watching from July until November, while the

Car hire facilities at Cape Town International Airport

roads skirting the West Coast are lined with wild flowers between August and September *(see pp220–21)*.

With its verdant forests, ocean-facing mountains and great swathes of beaches, the Garden Route *(see pp238–9)* offers one of the most scenic drives from Cape Town. Officially it runs for 200 km (124 miles), from Heidelberg in the west to the Tsitsikamma forests in the east, but the full drive from Cape Town to Port Elizabeth, in the Eastern Cape, where there are more parks and reserves to explore, is 748 km (465 miles). Route 62, which runs on inland roads via dramatic mountain passes and quaint farming settlements, provides an alternative route back to Cape Town.

The Panorama Route *(see p337)* follows the escarpments adjoining Kruger, and a day's drive takes in waterfalls, historic towns and views of the Blyde River Canyon. Kruger itself is very car-friendly due to the

numerous entrance gates along the entire length of the park, the excellent tarred roads and efficient rest camps.

In the southeast, history buffs will enjoy touring the evocative battlefield sites of KwaZulu-Natal *(see p278)*. The pretty country resorts in the foothills of the mighty Drakensberg Mountains make for great tours, too.

DIRECTORY

Breakdown Services

AA Emergency Road Service
Tel 0861 000 234 (24 hrs, all areas).
W aa.co.za

Car Rental

Around About Cars
Tel 021 422 4022.
W aroundaboutcars.com

Avis
Tel 0861 021 111.
W avis.co.za

Budget
Tel 011 387 8432.
W budget.co.za

Europcar
Tel 0861 131-000.
W europcar.co.za

First Car Rental
Tel 0861 178 227.
W firstcarrental.co.za

Hertz
Tel 021 935 4800.
W hertz.co.za

Tempest Car Hire
Tel 0861 836 737.
W tempestcarhire.co.za

Driving a jeep through South Africa's countryside

General Index

Acknowledgments

Dorling Kindersley would like to thank the following people whose contributions and assistance have made the preparation of this book possible.

Main Contributors

Michael Brett has visited many African countries, including Kenya, Malawi, Zimbabwe, Namibia and Mozambique, and has an extensive knowledge of South Africa. His first book, a detailed guide to the Pilanesberg National Park in North West Province, South Africa, was published in 1989. In 1996, he co-authored the *Touring Atlas of South Africa*. He has written *Great Game Parks of Africa: Masai Mara* and *Kenya the Beautiful*. Articles by Michael Brett have been published in several travel magazines, as well as in *Reader's Digest*.

Philip Briggs is a travel writer specializing in Africa. In 1991, his *Bradt Guide to South Africa* was the first such guidebook to be published internationally after the release of Nelson Mandela. Over the rest of the 1990s, he wrote a series of pioneering Bradt Guides including the first dedicated guidebooks to Tanzania, Uganda, Ethiopia, Malawi, Mozambique, Ghana and Rwanda. He also contributes to specialist travel and wildlife magazines including *Africa Birds & Birding*, *Africa Geographic*, *BBC Wildlife*, *Travel Africa* and *Wanderlust*.

Brian Johnson-Barker was born and educated in Cape Town, South Africa. After graduating from the University of Cape Town and running a clinical pathology laboratory for some 15 years, he turned to writing. His considerable involvement in this field has also extended to television scripts and magazine articles. Among his nearly 50 book titles are *Off the Beaten Track* (1996) and *Illustrated Guide to Game Parks and Nature Reserves of Southern Africa* (1997), both published by Reader's Digest.

Mariëlle Renssen wrote for South African general-interest magazine *Fair Lady* before spending two years in New York with *Young & Modern*, a teenage publication owned by the Bertelsmann publishing group. After returning to South Africa, several of her articles were published in magazines such as *Food and Home SA* and *Woman's Value*. Since 1995 she has been the publishing manager of Struik Publishers' International Division, during which time she also contributed to *Traveller's Guide to Tanzania*.

Additional Contributors

Duncan Cruickshank, Claudia Dos Santos, Luke Hardiman, Gail Jennings, Peter Joyce, Loren Minsky, Roger St Pierre, Anne Taylor, Ariadne Van Zendbergen.

Additional Photography

Greg & Yvonne Dean, Louise Dean, Charley van Dugteren, Hanne and Jens Erikesen, Christopher & Sally Gable, Nigel Hicks, Josef Hlasek, Anthony Johnson, Mathew Kurien, Cyril Laubscher, Ian O'Leary, Gary Ombler, John Reeks, Tony Souter, Linda Whitwam, Jerry Young.

Additional Illustrations Anton Krugel.

Additional Cartography Genené Hart, Eloïse Moss.
Research Assistance Susan Alexander, Sandy Vahl.
Additional Picture Research Rachel Barber, Phoebe Lowndes, Ellen Root.
Factcheckers Ariadne Van Zandbergen, Lizzie Williams.
Proofreader Debra Wolter.
Indexer Helen Peters.

Revisions Team

Louise Abbott, Beverley Ager, Hansa Babra, Claire Baranowski, Chris Barstow/Coppermill Books, Uma Bhattacharya, Hilary Bird, Subhadeep Biswas, Arwen Burnett, Caroline Elliker, Alice Fewery, Emer Fitzgerald, Sean Fraser, Anna Freiberger, Camilla Gersh, Thea Grobbelaar, Freddy Hamilton, Vinod Harish, Mohammad Hassan, Lesley Hay-Whitton, Victoria Heyworth-Dunne, Jacky Jackson, Cincy Jose, Vasneet Kaur, Juliet Kenny, Sumita Khatwani, Vincent Kurien, Maite Lantaron, Alfred Lemaitre, Carly Madden, Alison McGill, Glynne Newlands, Catherine Palmi, Marianne Petrou, Rada Radojicic, John Reeks, Marisa Renzullo, Gerhardt van Rooyen, Sands Publishing Solutions, Mitzi Scheepers, Ankita Sharma, Azeem Siddiqui, Susana Smith, Conrad Van Dyk, Laura Walker, Lizzie Williams.

Special Assistance

Joan Armstrong, The Howick Publicity Bureau; Coen Bessinger, Die Kaapse Tafel; Tim Bowdell, Port Elizabeth City Council; Dr Joyce Brain, Durban; Katherine Brooks, MuseuMAfrikA (Johannesburg); Michael Coke, Durban; Coleen de Villiers and Gail Linnow, South African Weather Bureau; Dr Trevor Dearlove, South African Parks Board; Louis Eksteen, Voortrekker Museum (Pietermaritzburg); Lindsay Hooper, South African Museum (Cape Town); Brian Jackson, The National Monuments Commission; Linda Labuschagne, Bartolomeu Dias Museum Complex (Mossel Bay); Darden Lotz, Cape Town; Tim Maggs, Cape Town; Hector Mbau, The Africa Café; Annette Miller, Bredasdorp Tourism; Gayla Naicker and Gerhart Richter, Perima's; Professor John Parkington, University of Cape Town; Anton Pauw, Cape Town; David Philips Publisher (Pty) Ltd, Cape Town; Bev Prinsloo, Palace of the Lost City; Professor Bruce Rubidge, University of the Witwatersrand; Jeremy Saville, ZigZag Magazine; Mark Shaw, Barrister's; Dr Dan Sleigh, Cape Town; Anthony Sterne, Simply Salmon; David Swane-poel, Voortrekker Museum; Johan Taljaard, West Coast National Park; Pietermaritzburg Publicity Association; Beyers Truter, Beyerskloof wine farm, Stellenbosch; Dr Lita Webley, Albany Museum, Grahamstown; Lloyd Wingate and Stephanie Pienaar, Kaffrarian Museum (King William's Town); and all provincial tourist authorities and national and provincial park services.

Photographic and Artwork Reference

Vida Allen and Bridget Carlstein, McGregor Museum (Kimberley); Marlain Botha, Anglo American Library; The Cape Archives; Captain Emilio de Souza; Petrus Dhlamini, Anglo American Corporation (Johannesburg); Gawie

Fagan and Tertius Kruger, Revel Fox Architects (Cape Town); Jeremy Fourie, Cape Land Data; Graham Goddard, Mayibuye Centre, The University of the Western Cape; Margaret Harradene, Public Library (Port Elizabeth); Maryke Jooste, Library of Parliament (Cape Town); Llewellyn Kriel, Chamber of Mines; Professor André Meyer, Pretoria University; Julia Moore, Boschendal Manor House; Marguerite Robinson, Standard Bank National Arts Festival; Christine Roe and Judith Swanepoel, Pilgrim's Rest Museum; Dr F Thackeray, Transvaal Museum (Pretoria); Marena van Hemert, Drostdy Museum (Swellendam); Kees van Ryksdyk, South African Astronomical Observatory; Cobri Vermeulen, The Knysna Forestry Department; Nasmi Wally, The Argus (Cape Town); Pam Warner, Old Slave Lodge (Cape Town).

Photography Permissions

Dorling Kindersley would like to thank the following for their assistance and kind permission to photograph at their establishments:

African Herbalist's Shop, Johannesburg; Alanglade, Pilgrim's Rest; Albany Museum Complex, Grahamstown; Bartolomeu Dias Museum Complex, Mossel Bay; BAT (Bartel Arts Trust) Centre, Durban; Bertram House, Cape Town; BMW Pavilion, Victoria & Alfred Waterfront; Bo-Kaap Museum, Cape Town; Cango Caves, Oudtshoorn; The Castle of Good Hope; Department of Public Works, Cape Town; Drum Magazine/Bailey's Archives; Dutch Reformed Church, Nieu Bethesda; The Edward Hotel, Port Elizabeth; Gold Reef City, Johannesburg; Groot Constantia, Heia Safari Ranch; Highgate Ostrich Farm, Oudtshoorn; Hindu (Hare Krishna) Temple of Understanding; Huguenot Museum, Franschhoek; Johannesburg International Airport; Kimberley Open-Air Mine Museum; Kirstenbosch National Botanical Garden; Kleinplasie Open-Air Museum; Koopmans-De Wet House, Cape Town; Mal a Mala Private Reserve; MuseuMAfricA, Johannesburg; Natural Science Museum, Durban; Old Slave Lodge, Cape Town; Oliewenhuis Art Gallery, Bloemfontein; Oom Samie se Winkel, Stellenbosch; Owl House, Nieu Bethesda; Paarl Museum; Pilgrim's Rest; Rhebokskloof Wine Estate; Robben Island Museum Service; Sandton Village Walk; Shakaland; Shipwreck Museum, Bredasdorp; Simunye; South African Library; South African Museum, Cape Town; Tatham Art Gallery, Pietermaritzburg; Two Oceans Aquarium, V&A Waterfront; Victoria & Alfred Waterfront; The Village Museum Stellenbosch; Sue Williamson, Cape Town; The Workshop, Durban.

Picture Credits

a = above; b = below/bottom; c = centre; f = far; l = left; r = right; t = top.

Works of art have been reproduced with the permission of the following copyright holders:
6-metre statue Nelson Mandela, Sandeton Square, © Mr. Kobus Hattingh, Proferro cc, website www.kobushattingh. co.za 321tr; *Lead Ox*, 1995–6, © Cecil Skotnes, Incised, painted wood panel 376br; *Portrait of a Lady*, Frans Hals (1580–1666), Oil on canvas, Old Town House (Cape Town), © Michaelis Collection 128bl; *Rocco Catoggio and Rocco Cartozia de Villiers*, artist unknown, c.1842, Oil on canvas, © Huguenot Museum (Franschhoek) 203bc.

The publisher would like to thank the following individuals, companies and picture libraries for permission to reproduce their photographs:
123RF.com: skywalker01 319tl. **4Corners**: Justin Foulkes 190; Leimer/Huber 165tl; SIME/Giovanni Simeone 366-7.
ACSA (Airports Company of South Africa): 437bl; **Shaen Adey**: 1t, 77tr, 34tr, 133bl, 142cla, 150br,165cl, 346cla, 346cl, 346bc, 347tc, 347cr; **Africa Image Library**: 72br, 72cla, 81br; Ariadne Van Zandbergen 83br, 87br, 88bl, 89tl, 96tl, 97cr, 99clb, 101tl, 102clb, 102cra, 103br, 103clb, 106bc, 108–9t, 115br; **Alamy Images**: Ace Stock Limited 80bc; Africa Image Library 73bl; Africa Media Online 245br; AfriPics.com 81bl, 95clb, 103cra, 105bc, 344tr; Anka Agency International 342cla; Arco Images / Nienhaus, H. 84br; Arco Images GmbH/ H. Nienhaus 87cla, /WHJ Sator 116tc; Arterra Picture Library/Clément Philippe 101br; Peter Barritt 83clb, 117tr; David Bartlett 281tc; blickwinkel 84clb; blickwinkel/Layer 87ca, 116tl; blickwinkel/McPHOTO/HPU 111br; blickwinkel/McPHOTO/PUM 106br; blickwinkel/Poelking 93bl; blickwinkel/ Tuengler 79tl; Bon Appetit/Hendrik Holler 13t; James de Bounevialle 93br; Penny Boyd 90cla; Michele Burgess 233br; David Buzzard 321bl; Cephas Picture Library/Juan Espi 397cr; Cephas Picture Library/Alain Proust 396clb; Cephas Picture Library/Mick Rock 396cla; David Noton Photography 15bc; Dennis Cox 420br; Danita Delimont/Amos Nachoum 228tl; Tim Davies 104tr; Reinhard Dirscherl 94cla; Ulrich Doering 24t; EcoPic 110cr; Greg Balfour Evans 126bl; Mark Eveleigh 91br; Alissa Everett 85tl; F1online digitale Bildagentur GmbH/Harald Trinkner 99tl; FLPA 111clb; Friedrichsmeier 164bl, 182-3; Jason Gallier 115tr; Gallo Images/Martin Harvey 16br; Simon de Glanville 106bl; Dacorum Gold 110br; Greatstock Photographic Library/SATourism 72clb; Jeff Greenberg 322clb; Andrew Haliburton 378-9; Hemis 302-3; Friedrich von Hörsten 73cr, 105bl, 114tr; Andre van Huizen 115tc; imageBROKER 121crb, 348-9, 400tr; Images & Stories 107cla; Images of Africa Photobank/David Keith Jones 86br, 90clb, 91bl, 98clb, 104tc; Images of Africa Photobank/Ivor Migdoll 117bc; Images of Africa Photobank/Lanz von Horsten 81cra; ImageState/Jonathan & Angie Scott 110clb; Interfoto 197cr; Mike Lane 116br; Frans Lemmens 73br; LH Images 126clb; Zute Lightfoot 16tr; LMR Media 114br; Paul Mayall 343br; Angus McComiskey 14tr; Eric Nathan 41cl, 144-5; Naturfoto-Online 422bc; Paul Thompson Images/Chris Ballentine 95cr, 238br, Photodisc/Anup Shah 83bl; Pictorial Press Ltd 85cr; Vic Pigula 106cla; Peter Pinnock 109bl; Stu Porter 109cr; Prisma Bildagentur AG 276-7; Juergen Ritterbach 229t; Robert Harding Picture Library Ltd 265tr; Jaco Le Roux 148; Willie Sator 97tl; Malcolm Schuyl 87tr, 110cla, 112br, 114tc; Kumar Sriskandan 432bl; Steve Bloom Images 93bc; Stockbyte /Tom Brakefield 105tr; Stock Connection Blue 282; Martin Strmiska 258-9; Sylvia Cordaiy Photo Library Ltd/Kjell Sandved 102tl; tbkmedia.de 103tl; tim gartside travel south africa 15tr; Peter Titmuss 98cla, 217cra, 394cla, 395c, 396tr, 434bl, 435bl, 441tr; Ann and Steve Toon 85br; travelstock44 396cr; Genevieve Vallee 344bl, 344cl; Vicki Wagner 294-5; Ross Warner 84cr; Sandy Watt 116bc; Terry Whittaker 85clb; Wildlife Gmbh 286br; Wildviews/Charles Tomalin 82bc, 83bc; WorldFoto 107bc; Ariadne Van Zandbergen 117tl, 159cl; Danita Delimont 228tl; Greatstock Photographic Library/Michael Meyersfeld 316tc; ImageState/

Pictor International 13bl; Jon Arnold Images 12bl; Geof Kirby 420tl; Suzanne Long 70tr; Eric Nathan 12tr; PCL 12c; Stu Porter 242c; Ben Queenborough 70c; Malcolm Schuyl 293tl; Travelstock 410cr; **Anita Akal:** 43c; **Anglo American Corporation of South Africa Limited:** 308br, 309tl, 309tr, 309cb, 309crb, 375bl; **Apartheid Museum:** 317bl; **The Argus:** 59clb, 61ca; **Ardea:** Thomas Dressler 109cr; Clem Haagner 86bc; **Ashanti Backpackers Gardens:** 385tr; **ASP Covered Images:** 264tr, 265cb; **AWL Images:** Niels van Gijn 266; Mark Hannaford 22; Hemis 412cr; Nigel Pavitt 100clb; Ian Trower 310. **Baia Seafood Restaurant:** 399tr; **Daryl Balfour:** 347br; **Ballito Pro Presented by Billabong:** Kelly Cestari 265bl; **Barnett Collection:** © The Star 56cla; **Bayworld:** 253bc; Port Elizabeth Museum Library 185cl; **Baz Bus:** 439bl; **Bible Society of South Africa:** 59bl; **The Blue Train:** 423ca; **Boom-shaka/Polygram:** 61tl; **Boplass Family Vineyards:** 397cl; **Michael Brett:** 33tl, 306cl, 307bl, 307br, 326b, 327tl, 373c, 415bc. **Cafe Caprice:** 398bc; **Café Ruby:** 393br; **Camp Jabulani:** 390tr; **The Campbell Collection of The University of Natal, Durban:** 58clb, 203cr; **Cango Wildlife Ranch:** 234tl; **Cape Archives:** 4tr, 32tr, 50bc, 51bl, 51c, 52cla, 57crb, 57br; **Cape Legends:** 187br; **Cape Photo Library:** © Alain Proust 25tr; 25c, 37cr, 147tl, 186cla, 186ca, 186cra, 187tr, 200cl, 201cra, 201br; **www.capespirit.com:** 169tr; **Cape Town City Ballet:** Pat Bromilow Downing 170br; **Cape Town Diamond Museum:** 142crb; **Cape Town Hollow Boutique Hotel:** 381bc; **Cape Town Philharmonic Orchestra:** 170tl; **Cape Quarter:** 164cr; **Carrol Boyes Functional Art:** 166bl, 166c; Zia Bird/Daniel Boshof 166bl, 166c; **Cloudbase Paragliding:** Khobi Bowden 243t; **Corbis:** James L. Amos 309cra; Yann Arthus-Bertrand 95br; Ralph A. Clevenger 112tl; John Conrad 80–1; Flame/DLILLC 80cla, 81cb, 92clb; Gallo Images/Anthony Bannister 99cra; Gallo Images/Hein von Horsten 116bl; Gallo Images/Martin Harvey 79bl; Gallo Images/Nigel J. Dennis 86bl; Gallo Images/Roger De La Harpe 81tc; epa/Kim Ludbrook 321cr; Martin Harvey 440cla; imageBROKER/Günter Lenz 151b; Peter Johnson 75b; Barbra Leigh 82br; Joe McDonald 80br, 92cla; Mary Ann McDonald 79clb; Momatiuk - Eastcott 81bc; Eric Reisinger 85c; Kevin Schafer 93tc; Gabriela Staebler 80crb; Sygma/ Hervé Collart 73tl; Jonathan Blair 17tr; Gallo Images/Luc Hosten 230br; Gallo Images/Shaen Adey 230tl; Martin Harvey 323br; Jon Hicks 316bl; Ian Trower 288bl; Xinhua Press/Liang Quan 414br; **The Cory Library of Rhodes University, Grahamstown:** 55cb; **Ruphin Coudyzer:** 32bc; **Gerald Cubitt:** 79cra, 104bc, 114bc, 117br. **De Beers:** 56bl; **Roger de la Harpe:** 5tr, 36cl, 37bc, 41tr, 271b, 273tl, 273crb, 274cb, 279bl, 416bl, 417tl, 417bl; **Nigel Dennis:** 28cr, 76–7c, 353clb, 353crb; **Department of Transport:** 427c; **Derwent House Boutique Hotel:** 382tr; **Dreamstime.com:** Patrick Allen 304bl, 438cl; Steve Allen 12tc; Bennymarty 158t; Neil Bradfield 133cra; Tyrone Cass 308clb; Patrice Correia 341br; Delstudio 158bc; Demerzel21 8-9; Denys Denysevych 289tr; Domossa 244b; Inna Felker 13clb; Ilko Iliev 330; Helen Jobson 322cl; Karelgallas 340bc; Holger Karius 2-3, Ian Kitney 28ca; Wesley Klue 43bl; Lcswart 261br; Ken Moore 28tr, 222; Natalyreinch 321tl; Nialldunne24 29tr; Photosky 28br, 210; Protea 338br; Andre Robberts 342crb; Luca Roggero 246c; Juergen Schonnop 10tl; Slew11 340cl; Socrates 120cl; David Steele 17tr, 341bb; Peter Titmuss 245t; Joshua Wanyama 138; Brad White 323bl; Andrea Willmore 14br, 237b; Hongqi

Zhang 12br, 236; Zhukovsky 297tr; Znm 23b. **Gerhard Dreyer:** 217cl, 220bl. **East Head Cafe:** 404tr; **Ellerman House:** 381tl, 384bc; **Essenwood House:** 388bc. **The Featherbed Company:** 244tr; **FLPA:** Neil Bowman 116tr; Minden Pictures/Vincent Grafhorst 117bl; David Hosking 91tl; Imagebroker 90bc; Frans Lanting 91bc; Minden Pictures/Tim Fitzharris 90br; Malcolm Schuyl 91cb; Martin B Withers 115bc; **Foto Holler,** © **Schirmer, Hermanus:** 188cl, 188–9c, 188bl. **Gallo Images:** © Anthony Bannister 28cl, 323cra, 352–3c; © David Gikey 42tr; © Kevin Carter Collection 37tr; G'echo Design: 42bl; **Getty Images:** Shaen Adey 142cb ; AFP/Jung Yeon-Je 430bl; De Agostini/G. Roli 90–1c; Beanstock Images 159cb; Heinrich van den Berg 339br; Deji Fisher 118-9; Flickr/ Luca Deravignone 441bl; Gallo Images/Heinrich van den Berg 103cra, 395tl; Gallo Images/Peter Chadwick 29cl; Gallo Images/Shem Compion 112clb; Gallo Images/Nigel Dennis 65b; Gallo Images/Roger de la Harpe 238 tr; Gallo Images/ Martin Harvey 106tc; Gallo Images/Eric Nathan 435tl; Gallo Images/Neil Overy 17bc; Gallo Images/Tier Images 78; GO! / Lawrette McFarlane 339t; Martin Harvey 424-5, 434crb; Marc Hoberman 318br; Homebrew Films Company 261tr; Richard I'Anson 261crb; Klaus Lang 318c; Robert C Nunnington 368; Photodisc/Anup Shah 94br, 95bc; Photographer's Choice/ James Warwick 84cla; Juergen Ritterbach 299c; Robert Harding World Imagery/James Hager 97tl; Robert Harding World Imagery/Steve & Ann Toon 221cb; Peter Scoones 270bc; Stone/Peter/Stef Lamberti 94bc; Nadine Swart 418crb; Warwick Tarboton 338tl; Ami Vitale 95tl; Workbook Stock/Tier Und Naturfotografie J & C Sohns 92–3c; Ernst Wrba 159tr; Ariadne Van Zandbergen 296tr, 336crb. **The Girls Restaurant:** 393bc; **Gleanings in Africa:** (1806) 189br; **Gold Fields Limited/South Deep:** 308-9; **Benny Gool/Trace:** 27c, 60–1c; Bob Gosani 320cla; **Grazia Fine Food and Wine:** 406bc; **Great Stock:** © Jürgen Schadeberg 320cra, 320cr, 320clb, 320br; **Graham Beck Wines:** Alain Proust 396br; **The Grill Room at The Oyster Box:** 408tr; **Guardian Newspapers Limited:** 59tc. **Rod Haestier:** 189cr, 248crb; **George Hallett:** 59crb, 61tl; **Haute Cabrière:** 392cla; **Lex Hes:** 31cr, 76bc, 77bl, 77bc; **Hermanus Tourism:** 227crb; **Hulton Picture Company:** 375cra. **i-Africa:** © Nic Bothma ,265cx; © Sasa Kralj 33br, 48cl; © Eric Muller 25b; **Inyathi Guest Lodge:** 386tr; **iStockphoto. com:** A-Shropshire-Lad 246br; ChandraDhas 121tl; Mlenny 356; RapidEye 4br, 126cl; THEGIFT777 412bl; wildacad 260bl. **Iziko Museums, Cape Town:** Cecil Kortjie 128c. **J&B Photographers:** 76clb; **Jacobsdal Wine Estate:** 186bl.; **Jonkershuis:** 401br. **King George VI Art Gallery, Port Elizabeth:** 55cb; **Klein Constantia:** 161cl; **Walter Knirr:** 59cr, 133clb, 278ca, 290cla, 311b, 318tr, 319br, 324bc, 325tc, 327tr, 327br, 337bc, 412cla; **KWV:** 397fcl. **Stefania Lamberti:** 143cl, 291br; **Lanzerac Hotel & Spa:** 387br; **Grant Leversha:** 419c; **Levi's:** 61cb; **Library Of Parliament, Cape Town:** © Mendelssohn Collection of watercolour paintings by Francois Vaillant 77tl; **Local History Museum, Durban:** 57bc; **Lonely Planet Images:** Craig Pershouse 229c; **Lord Milner Hotel Matjiesfontein:** 423tl; **Lutheran Church Cape Town:** Martin O'Carrol 132bl. **Mayibuye Centre, University of the Western Cape:** 58–9c, 60c; **Meerendal Wine Estate:** 186bc; **Michaelis Collection (Old Town House):** 128b; **Michelle Baxter:** 342tr. **Military Museum, Johannesburg:** 317tr; **Mosaic at the Orient:** 409br; **Moyo uShaka:** 407tr;

Museumafrica: 48ca, 54cla, 54cl, 55tl. **Naartjie:** Steve Eales 166tl; **The National Archives, Pretoria:** 309br; **National Geographic Stock:** 87cra; **naturepl.com:** Peter Blackwell 98br, 107ca; Bernard Castelein 98cr; Bruce Davidson 113cra; Tony Heald 92bc, 92br, 104br; Tony Phelps 107cra, 107tr; Premaphotos 106cra; Mike Read 117tc; Keith Scholey 83tl; Anup Shah 82crb, 95bl, 105tc; Lynn M. Stone 82cla; **Nelson Mandela Bay Tourism:** 250bl; **NHPA/Photoshot:** Anthony Bannister 86ca, 86cla, 89br, 94clb, 107bl; Nigel J Dennis 86cra, 104bl; Nick Garbutt 87bl; Martin Harvey 93cb; John Shaw 88cr; Ann & Steve Toon 105br; James Warwick 105tl, 111cr; **War Museum, London:** 56–7. **PA Photos:** AP/Francois Mori 26br; **Colin Paterson-Jones:** 30cra; **Anton Pauw:** 136bc, 219cr; **David Philips Publisher (Pty) Ltd:** 26tl, 26tc, 33cr; **Photo Access:** © Getaway/D Rogers 322tr; © Clarke Gittens 52br; © Photo Royal 272bc; © Mark Skinner 124; © David Steele 40c, 272cla, 272clb; © Patrick Wagner 273bl; © Alan Wilson 42c, 147cla; **Herman Potgieter:** 2–3; **Photolibrary:** Animals Animals /GERALD HINDE/ABPL - 94–5c; Animals Animals/Roderick Edward Edwards 113br; Hoberman Collection UK/Gerald Hoberman 62–3; imagebroker.net / jspix jspix 64; Monsoon Images Nabil Ezz 99br; Elliott Neep 82–3; Robert Harding Travel/Paul Allen 74; Gerard Soury 418tl; **Prince Albert Tourism Association:** Reinwald Dedekind 231bl, 231t; **Punjabi Kitchen:** 405br. **Ramblas Restaurant:** 411br; **Ratanga Junction Theme Park:** 161cra; **Reuters:** Howard Burditt 419br; Mike Hutchings 171tl, **Rex Features:** 146br; **Rhebokskloof Cellar:** 193br; **Robert Harding Picture Library:** Allstar 247br; Yadid Levy 171br; Ian Trower 247tr. **Rocktail Beach Camp:** Wilderness Safaris/Dana Allen 383tr; **Rovos Rail:** 422cla, 423bl; **Professor Bruce Rubidge:** 48clb. **WSA City Life:** © Sean Laurénz 427b; **Sakhumzi:** 410tc; **Saxon Hotel, Villas & Spa:** Mango PR 391br; **Seafood at the Marine:** 392br, 403br; **Shamwari Game Reserve:** 382bl, 389tl; **SIL (© Struik Image Library):** Shaen Adey 35crb, 41br, 122cl, 122clb, 122bl, 123tr, 123br, 130clb, 137bl, 137br, 146cla, 146bl, 147cra, 147br, 155tl, 160clb, 160br, 163cra, 186cr, 186br, 192cl, 192–3t, 196ca, 212cla, 301br, 351br; Daryl Balfour 216br; CLB (Colour Library): 29br, 30cla, 161tl, 251br, 301tl, 315cr, 345cla, 374cla; Credo Mutwa 32c; Roger de la Harpe 29ca, 31crb, 36br, 150tl, 165br, 263cr, 274tr, 280bl, 281c, 284cl, 297br, 298tc, 298cr; Nigel Dennis 31br, 31ca, 76tr, 76br, 77clb, 216cra, 216cl, 275ca, 284tr, 290cra, 291cra, 300tl, 305tr, 306bl, 306bc, 306br, 307tl, 340cr, 341t, 342bl, 352tr, 352cl, 352clb, 352crb, 352bl, 352br, 353tl, 353tr, 353cra, 355tl, 369b, 370bl; Gerhard Dreyer 30crb, 30bl, 30br, 31cl, 213tr, 216crb, 221cla, 233br, 248tr, 248cla, 248bl, 428tl; Jean du Plessis 157cr; Leonard Hoffman 30tr, 31tl, 31tc, 31tr, 31cra, 31clb, 263tl, 263bl, 283b, 413t; Anthony

Johnson 129tl, 143bl; Walter Knirr157bl, 223b, 268cl, 291bl, 313tr, 326c, 334tl, 371br; Mark Lewis 34bl; Jackie Murray 27br; Annelene Oberholzer 156c; Peter Pickford 216tr, 216clb, 298bl, 299tl, 352cla, 361tl; Mark Skinner 219c, 246cl; Erhardt Thiel 35tr, 39cr, 40br, 123cr, 123ca, 127cra, 134clb, 135bc, 156t, 160tr, 160bl, 160tl, 161cr, 191b, 220crb, 414cl; Hein von Hörsten 46, 130cla, 147crb, 153tl, 162cla, 195bl, 197br, 221tr, 235cr, 249tl, 255tr, 270cla, 270cb, 323tr, 358bl, 439tr; Lanz von Hörsten 26c, 27t, 30clb, 43tr, 131tl, 136clb, 152bl, 184cla, 219cla, 219bl, 220cl, 221cr, 275crb, 285br, 307cr, 345br, 353br, 354cra, Keith Young 271tl, 286cla, 293cla, 351cra, 357b, 362clb; **Singita www.singita.com :** 380bl; **Mark Skinner:** 251cr; **South African Airways:** 436cla; **South African Library:** 50cl, 50–1c, 52clb, 52-3 c, 53clb, 53crb, 54br, 56c, 56clb, 58b, 59c, 136tr, 373bl; **The South African Breweries Limited:** Brett May 315tl, 397tr (all 3); **South African Cultural History Museum:** 50clb, 51tc, 55bc; **South African Museum:** 49c, 49br; **South African National Defence Force Archives:** 58cla; **The South African National Gallery:** 51crb, 60clb; **South African National Parks Board:** 66br, 69tl, 70b, 71tr, 419tl; **Addo Elephant National Park** 67tl; Piet Heymans 66cla, 67cr; **Geoff Spiby:** 28bl, 29bl, 143br; **South African Tourism:** 426cra; **Standard Bank:** 432cla; **The Star:** 57tc; **State Archives:** 77tr, 308cla, 364bc, 375cl; **Sun International:** 252br, 328cl, 328tr, 329crb, 329br.

The Tasting Room: 402tc; **Tokara:** 199tr; **Topstones (PTY) Ltd:** 140cla; **Touchline:** © Duif du Toit 38cla; © Thomas Turck 38br; **Transvaal Museum:** © Dr Gerald Newlands 49ca; **The Truth And Reconcilliation Committee:** 61clb; **Two Oceans Aquarium:** 140cl. University Of Pretoria: © Professor André Meyer 49tl; **Pieter-Dirk Uys:** 61cr. **Chris Van Lennep:** 264cl, 264–5c; **Chris Van Rooyen:** 76cla; **V&A Waterfront:** 141crb, 169bl; **Hein Von Hörsten:** 354cla, 355bl; **André Vorster:** 428cr. **Wartburger Hof Country Hotel:** 36cr; **Wayne Photography:** Wayne Holtzhausen 242bl; **Ian Webb:** 416cr; **William Fehr Collection, Castle of Good Hope, Cape Town:** 47b, 160br; W. Daniel 155bl; **Peter Wilson Agencies:** 264br; **Keith Young:** 160c.

Front Endpapers: 4Corners: Justin Foulkes Lcl; **Alamy Images:** Stock Connection Blue Rcr; **AWL Images:** Niels van Gijn Rbr, Ian Trower Rtl; **Dreamstime.com:** Ilko Iliev Rtr, Ken Moore Ltc, Photosky Ltl, Anke Van Wyk Rbl, Hongqi Zhang Rbc.; **Getty Images:** Deji Fisher Lbl, Robert C Nunnington Ltr.

Cover Front and Spine: Getty Images: Richard du Toit. Back: **Dreamstime.com:** Kierran Allen All other images @ Dorling Kindersley. For further information see: www.dkimages.com

Special Editions of DK Travel Guides

DK Travel Guides can be purchased in bulk quantities at discounted prices for use in promotions or as premiums. We are also able to offer special editions and personalized jackets, corporate imprints, and excerpts from all of our books, tailored specifically to meet your own needs.

To find out more, please contact:

in the US **specialsales@dk.com**
in the UK **travelguides@uk.dk.com**
in Canada **specialmarkets@dk.com**
in Australia **penguincorporatesales@ penguinrandomhouse.com.au**

Cape Town and Environs

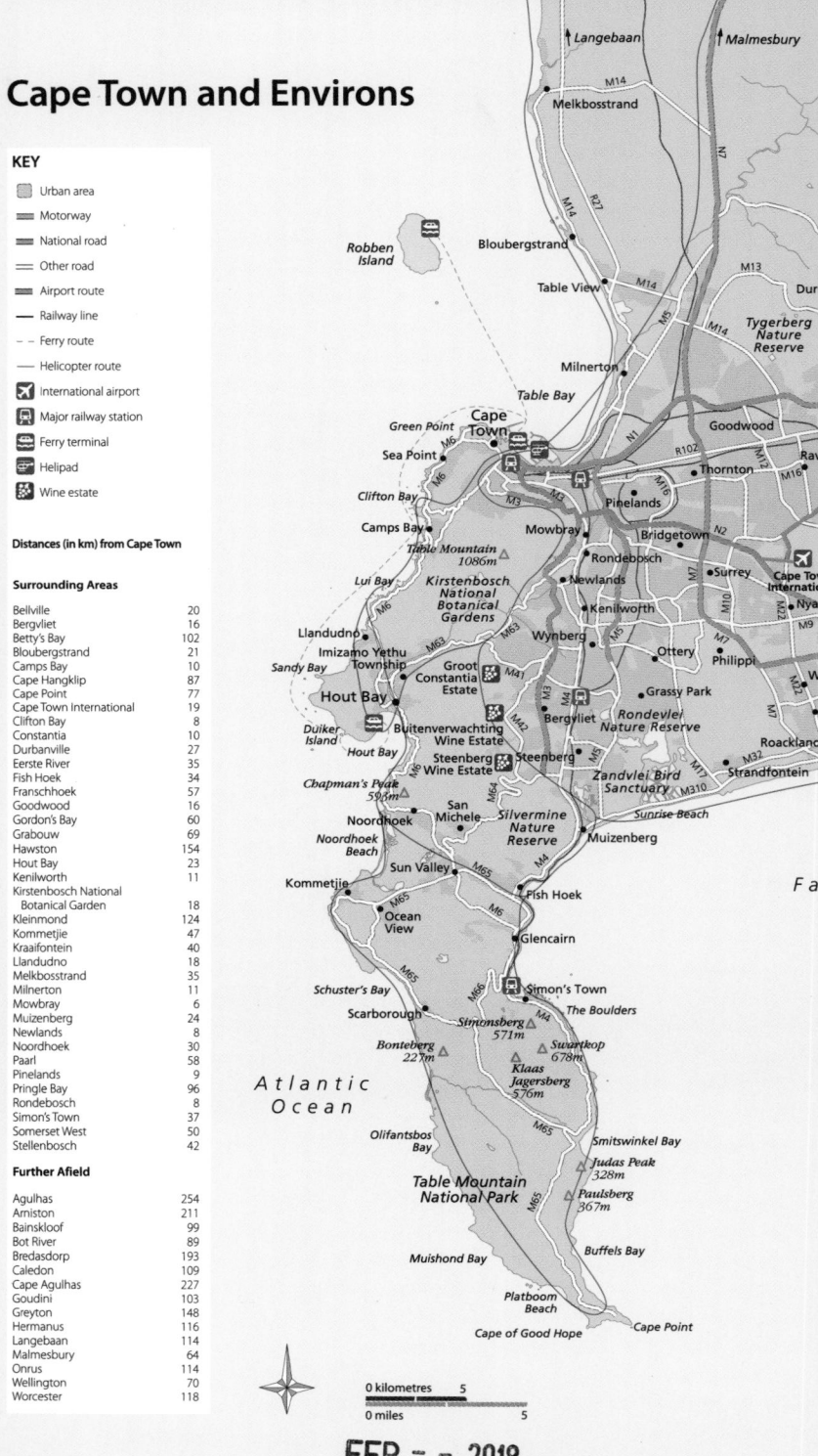

KEY

- ▢ Urban area
- ▭ Motorway
- ▭ National road
- ▭ Other road
- ▬ Airport route
- — Railway line
- – – Ferry route
- — Helicopter route
- ✈ International airport
- 🚆 Major railway station
- ⛴ Ferry terminal
- 🚁 Helipad
- 🍇 Wine estate

Distances (in km) from Cape Town

Surrounding Areas

Bellville	20
Bergvliet	16
Betty's Bay	102
Bloubergstrand	21
Camps Bay	10
Cape Hangklip	87
Cape Point	77
Cape Town International	19
Clifton Bay	8
Constantia	10
Durbanville	27
Eerste River	35
Fish Hoek	34
Franschhoek	57
Goodwood	16
Gordon's Bay	60
Grabouw	69
Hawston	154
Hout Bay	23
Kenilworth	11
Kirstenbosch National Botanical Garden	18
Kleinmond	124
Kommetjie	47
Kraaifontein	40
Llandudno	18
Melkbosstrand	35
Milnerton	11
Mowbray	6
Muizenberg	24
Newlands	8
Noordhoek	30
Paarl	58
Pinelands	9
Pringle Bay	96
Rondebosch	8
Simon's Town	37
Somerset West	50
Stellenbosch	42

Further Afield

Agulhas	254
Arniston	211
Bainskloof	99
Bot River	89
Bredasdorp	193
Caledon	109
Cape Agulhas	227
Goudini	103
Greyton	148
Hermanus	116
Langebaan	114
Malmesbury	64
Onrus	114
Wellington	70
Worcester	118

0 kilometres 5

0 miles 5

FEB – – 2018